Advance Praise for this Edition

"*Linguistics: An Introduction to Linguistic Theory* is a very impressive achieve-
ment, lucidly and engagingly presenting the major areas of Chomskian
theoretical linguistics. Readers who work their way through the comprehensive presentation and the abundant well-chosen exercises will attain a deep
understanding of what Chomskian generative grammar is all about, and,
even more, a feel for what it is to actually participate in the enterprise."
Howard Lasnik, University of Connecticut

"This is by far the best introductory book and the one that I will use. It
gives a real working knowledge of each area of linguistics and maintains
a consistent level of intellectual challenge throughout. The exercises are
excellent."
Edwin Williams, Princeton University

"This excellent and detailed introduction to the field of linguistics draws
on an impressive range of languages. Any student that wants to find out
about the scientific study of human language will profit immensely from
this book."
Richard Kayne, New York University

"This textbook fills in all the gaps that are characteristic of other introductory texts in linguistics. Each section is written by a leading figure in
a particular area of linguistic theory: morphology and syntax, semantics,
and phonetics and phonology. It is impressive both in breadth and depth.
Each section ends by considering how the particular principles that were
described in that section emerge in the course of language development,
thereby reinforcing the importance of linguistic theory for understanding
young children's universal mastery of natural language."
Stephen Crain, University of Maryland at College Park

"This is an outstanding new introduction to contemporary linguistics,
written by a team of the foremost scholars in the field. The orientation
throughout is towards real, usually current, research questions. A very
nice feature is the inclusion of chapters on language acquisition in connection with each subdiscipline of linguistics. I am sure this book will be
the standard introductory textbook for some time to come."
Ian Roberts, Universität Stuttgart

"This introductory textbook is unique in the extent and depth of the cover-
age it provides. Teachers and beginning students of linguistics and cognitive
science should find it both helpful and inspiring."
Maria Luisa Zubizarreta, University of Southern California

Linguistics

An Introduction to Linguistic Theory

Written by Victoria A. Fromkin (editor)

Susan Curtiss Bruce P. Hayes Nina Hyams Patricia A. Keating

Hilda Koopman Pamela Munro Dominique Sportiche

Edward P. Stabler Donca Steriade Tim Stowell Anna Szabolcsi

First published 2000

2 4 6 8 10 9 7 5 3 1

Blackwell Publishers Inc.
350 Main Street
Malden, Massachusetts 02148
USA

Blackwell Publishers Ltd
108 Cowley Road
Oxford OX4 1JF
UK

Library of Congress Cataloging-in-Publication Data has been applied for.

ISBN 0–631–19709–5 (hardback)
ISBN 0–631–19711–7 (paperback)

British Library Cataloguing in Publication Data
A CIP catalogue record for this book is available from the British Library.

Typeset in 10.5 on 13 pt Palatino
by Graphicraft Limited, Hong Kong
Printed in Great Britain by TJ International, Padstow, Cornwall

This book is printed on acid-free paper.

Contents

Preface

This textbook is intended for introductory courses in linguistic theory for undergraduate linguistics majors or first-year graduate students. Its aim is to provide the students who have no previous knowledge of linguistics with the background necessary to continue with courses in the core areas of the field – phonetics, phonology, syntax, morphology, semantics. In each part the book is concerned with discussing the underlying principles of Universal Grammar common to all languages, showing how these are revealed in language acquisition and in the specific grammars of the world's languages. Theoretical concepts are introduced through the analysis of a wide set of linguistic data from Arabic to Zulu. By working through real linguistic data, students will learn how to do linguistics. The interplay between theory and data is highlighted in all the chapters. In addition to the basic components of the grammar, the book includes discussion on child language acquisition of the core components of the mental grammar. This reflects the recognition that an understanding of the child's ability to acquire language is central to the theory of Universal Grammar.

The text is divided into four parts. Part I introduces the student to the science of linguistics and presents a bird's-eye view of the history of the field and how we got to where we are today. Part II covers morphology (chapter 2) and syntax (chapters 3–5) and the acquisition of morphology and syntax (chapter 6). Part III covers semantics and the acquisition of meaning (chapters 7–10), Part IV includes phonetics (chapter 11) and phonology (chapters 12–14) and the acquisition of the sounds and sound patterns of language (chapter 15).

Extensive problems are presented as exercises in each core chapter. As students work through these exercises while reading the text, the basic concepts and the empirical basis for the principles proposed are revealed. Additional exercises follow each of the core chapters in each part. References for further reading follow each chapter, and an extensive glossary and a general bibliography are also included.

The textbook can be used for either a quarter or a semester course. In a shorter course, of say, 10 weeks, the instructor may decide not to assign chapters 5, 9, and 14, chapters that contain enriched and ground-breaking material which may be postponed for more advanced study. The chapters on acquisition can be used independently in courses on language acquisition, as can other sections, as readings for graduate-level courses in the specific sub-areas.

This textbook is a collective effort by the authors, all of whom were faculty members in the UCLA Department of Linguistics at the time of writing, a department that has a reputation for both excellent teaching and research. All of us teach both undergraduate and graduate courses including the course for which this textbook was written.

We would like to express our deep appreciation to all the students who have read through our handouts and worked through our problems and who should in many ways be considered co-authors of this textbook. We are grateful to Philip Carpenter and Steve Smith of Blackwell Publishers for the confidence they showed in the UCLA *gang of twelve*.

Finally, we acknowledge the huge debt that we believe linguistics owes to Noam Chomsky. His pioneering research in transformational generative grammar, in both syntax and phonology, and his vision of linguistics as a central player in the new field of cognitive science, ushered in what has come to be called the Cognitive Revolution. The questions that he raised regarding the nature of language, the structure of the mental grammar, and the problem of explaining how this system of knowledge is acquired by children remain the central focus of our field and of this book.

Notes on Authors

Victoria A. Fromkin, editor and contributor to this textbook, is a professor of linguistics at the University of California, Los Angeles (UCLA), where she also served as department chair, and Graduate Dean and Vice Chancellor of Graduate Programs. She is the recipient of the UCLA Distinguished Teaching Award and is a past president of the Linguistic Society of America, a member of the National Academy of Sciences, and a Fellow of the American Academy of Arts and Sciences, the American Association for the Advancement of Science, the Acoustical Society of America, the American Psychological Society, and the New York Academy of Science. She is the author (with Robert Rodman) of *An Introduction to Language* (6th edition) and over 100 monographs and papers. Her primary research lies in the interface between the mental grammar and linguistic processing, and issues related to brain, mind, and language.

Susan Curtiss received her Ph.D. at UCLA, where she is now a professor. She is best known for her work on the critical period for language acquisition and modularity. Her book *Genie: A Psycholinguistic Study of a Modern-Day "Wild Child"* has become a classic in the field. She has also published widely on dissociations of language and cognition in development and breakdown and on language acquisition in atypical circumstances. She has authored numerous language tests, including the internationally used *CYCLE*, co-authored with Jeni Yamada.

Bruce P. Hayes received his Ph.D. from MIT in 1980 and is now a professor of linguistics at UCLA, with a primary interest in phonology. His publications in this area include *Metrical Stress Theory: Principles and Case Studies* (University of Chicago Press, 1995), and various papers on stress, the phonetics/phonology interface, metrics, and segment structure.

Nina Hyams is a professor of linguistics at UCLA. She is author of the book *Language Acquisition and the Theory of Parameters* (D. Reidel, 1986) and has published numerous papers on grammatical development in children acquiring English and other languages. She has been a visiting scholar at the University of Utrecht and the University of Leiden in the Netherlands, and has given numerous lectures throughout Europe and Japan.

Patricia A. Keating is professor of linguistics and director of the Phonetics Laboratory at UCLA. She completed her Ph.D. in 1979 at Brown University, and then held an NIH postdoctoral fellowship in the Speech Communications Group at MIT before coming to UCLA in 1981. In 1986 she won a UCLA Distinguished Teaching Award. Her main areas of research and publication are experimental and theoretical phonetics, and the phonology–phonetics interface. She is the author of "The Phonology-Phonetics Interface" in the 1988 *Linguistics: The Cambridge Survey*, and the contributor of the lead article on "Phonetics" to the MIT *Encyclopedia of the Cognitive Sciences*, as well as numerous articles in linguistics and phonetics journals.

Hilda Koopman was born in Nijmegen, the Netherlands, and studied General Linguistics at the University of Amsterdam. She received her Ph.D. from the University of Tilburg in 1984 and held a research position at the University of Québec for several years before joining the faculty at UCLA in 1985, where she currently is professor of linguistics. She is the author of numerous articles on syntactic theory, many of which are based on original fieldwork on African languages. Her books include *The Syntax of Verbs: From Kru Languages to Universal Grammar* (Foris Publications, 1984), *The Syntax of Specifiers and Heads* (Routledge, 1999), and *Verbal Complexes* (with Anna Szabolcsi; MIT Press, forthcoming).

Pamela Munro, a professor of linguistics at UCLA, received her Ph.D. from the University of California, San Diego. She has conducted fieldwork on over twenty indigenous languages of the Americas and is an author of ninety books and articles, descriptive and theoretical studies of the morphology, phonology, syntax, and historical development of languages of the Uto-Aztecan, Yuman, and Muskogean families of American Indian languages. Among her publications are dictionaries or grammars of Cahuilla, Chickasaw, Kawaiisu, and Mojave, as well as dictionaries of the Wolof language of Senegal and Gambia and of UCLA undergraduate slang.

Dominique Sportiche, after studying mathematics and physics in Paris, France, studied linguistics at the Massachusetts Institute of Technology, where he received a Ph.D. in 1984, supervised by Noam Chomsky. He was at the University of Québec in Montreal, Canada, before coming to UCLA where he is now a professor of linguistics and romance linguistics. His research and publications focus primarily on syntactic analysis and syntactic theory of natural languages. His most recent book is *Partitions and Atoms of Clause Structure* (London: Routledge, 1998).

Edward P. Stabler studied philosophy and linguistics at MIT, receiving a Ph.D. in philosophy in 1981. After holding several industrial and academic positions, he moved to the University of California, Los Angeles, in 1989, where he is currently a professor of linguistics. He is an active member of the European Association for Logic, Language and Information (FoLLI) and the Association for Computational Linguistics (ACL). He is the author of *The Logical Approach to Syntax* (MIT Press, 1992) and other books and papers on formal and computational models of syntax and semantics.

Donca Steriade was born in Bucharest, Romania, and trained as a classicist before becoming a linguist. She obtained her Ph.D. in 1982 from MIT and taught at the University of California, Berkeley, and at MIT before joining the Department of Linguistics at UCLA where she is now a professor of linguistics. Her research focuses particularly on phonology, the phonology/phonetics interface, and optimality theory. She is the author of numerous studies of segmental, syllabic and metrical structure.

Tim Stowell received his Ph.D. in linguistics from MIT in 1981. He is now a professor of linguistics at UCLA, having served as Chair of that department from 1994 to 1998; he has also held visiting positions at the University of Massachusetts (Amherst) and the University of Vienna, and has been a fellow of the Netherlands Institute for Advanced Study. His research has been primarily in syntactic theory; his early work on the theory of phrase structure played an influential role in arguing against the existence of phrase structure rules, and in favor of deriving properties of phrase structures from general principles. His recent research has focused on the interface between syntax and semantics, investigating the phrase structure and interpretation of tense and quantifier scope.

Anna Szabolcsi was born in Budapest and received her Ph.D. from the Hungarian Academy of Sciences. She held a research position in the Institute of Linguistics in Budapest before coming to UCLA as a professor of linguistics, and is currently a professor of linguistics at

New York University. Her research interests include formal semantics, the syntax/semantics interface, Hungarian syntax, and categorial grammar. Her recent books are *Ways of Scope Taking* (editor and contributor, Kluwer, 1997) and *Verbal Complexes* (with Hilda Koopman; forthcoming, with MIT Press).

Part I

Introduction

1

Linguistics:
The Scientific Study of Human Language

1.0 Introduction

Human language, that unique characteristic of our species, has been of interest throughout history. The scientific study of human language is called **linguistics**. A **linguist**, then, is not someone who speaks many languages (although many linguists do); such individuals are **polyglots**. A linguist is a scientist who investigates human language in all its facets, its structure, its use, its history, its place in society.

The form and structure of the kinds of linguistic knowledge speakers possess is the concern of theoretical linguistics. This theory of **grammar** – the mental representation of linguistic knowledge – is what this textbook is about. But the field of linguistics is not limited to grammatical theory; it includes a large number of subfields, which is true of most sciences concerned with phenomena as complex as human language.

SIDEBAR
1.1

A bird's-eye view of the field

Theoretical Linguistics (the concern of this textbook), often referred to as **generative linguistics,** has its basis in views first put forth by Chomsky's 1955 *The Logical Structure of Linguistic Theory.* In this and the subsequent books and articles by Chomsky and those that embraced these views, a major aim was to characterize the nature of human linguistic knowledge or **competence** (represented in the mind as a mental **grammar**); that is, to explain or account for what speakers know which permits them to speak and comprehend speech or sign (the languages of the deaf). The production and comprehension of speech is referred to as **performance,** distinct from competence but dependent on it.

Descriptive linguistics provides analyses of the grammars of languages such as Choctaw, Arabic, Zulu. 'Indo-European-linguistics,' 'Romance linguistics,' 'African linguistics,' refer to the studies of particular languages and language families, from both historical and synchronic points of view.

Historical linguistics is concerned with a theory of language change – why and how languages develop. The **comparative method,** developed in the nineteenth century by such philologists as the brothers Grimm and Hermann Paul, is a method used to compare languages in the attempt to determine which languages are related and to establish families of languages and their roots.

Anthropological or **ethno-linguistics** and **sociolinguistics** focus on languages as part of culture and society, including language and culture, social class, ethnicity, and gender.

Dialectology investigates how these factors fragment one language into many. In addition, **sociolinguistics** and **applied linguistics** are interested in language planning, literacy, bilingualism, and second language acquisition. Applied linguistics also covers such areas as discourse and conversational analysis, language assessment, language pedagogy.

Computational linguistics is concerned with natural language computer applications, e.g. automatic parsing, machine processing and understanding, computer simulation of grammatical models for the generation and parsing of sentences. If viewed as a branch of Artificial Intelligence (AI), computational linguistics has the goal of modeling human language as a cognitive system.

Mathematical linguistics studies the formal and mathematical properties of language.

Pragmatics studies language in context and the influence of situation on meaning.

Neurolinguistics is concerned with the biological basis of language acquisition and development and the brain/mind/language interface. It brings linguistic theory to bear on research on aphasia (language disorders following brain injury) and research involving the latest technologies in the study of brain imaging and processing (CT, PET, fMRI, MEG, ERP).

Psycholinguistics is the branch of linguistics concerned with linguistic performance – the production and comprehension of speech (or sign). An area of psycholinguistics, which in some ways is a field in its own, is child **language acquisition** – how children acquire the complex grammar which underlies language use. This is a subject of major concern, particularly because of the interest in the biology of language. (This topic will be covered in the text because of its relevance to theories of grammar.)

There are textbooks which deal with each of these subfields, among others. Basic to all of them is the nature of language itself, the subject of this textbook.

1.1 Panini to Chomsky and After

The interest in the nature of human language appears to have arisen when the human species evolved in the history of time. There is no culture that has left records that do not reveal either philosophical or practical concerns for this unique human characteristic. Different historical periods reveal different emphases and different goals although both interests have existed in parallel.

Egyptian surgeons were concerned with clinical questions; an Egyptian papyrus, dated ca. 1700 BCE, includes medical descriptions of language disorders following brain injury. The philosophers of ancient Greece, on the other hand, argued and debated questions dealing with the origin and the nature of language. Plato, writing between 427 and 348 BCE, devoted his *Cratylus Dialogue* to linguistic issues of his day and Aristotle was concerned with language from both rhetorical and philosophical points of view.

The Greeks and the Romans also wrote grammars, and discussed the sounds of language and the structures of words and sentences. This interest continued through the medieval period and the renaissance in an unbroken thread to the present period.

Linguistic scholarship, however, was not confined to Europe; in India the Sanskrit language was the subject of detailed analysis as early as the twelfth century BCE. Panini's Sanskrit grammar dated ca. 500 BCE is still considered to be one of the greatest scholarly linguistic achievements. In addition, Chinese and Arabic scholars have all contributed to our understanding of human language.

The major efforts of the linguists of the nineteenth century were devoted to historical and comparative studies. Ferdinand de Saussure (1857–1913), a Swiss linguist in this tradition, turned his attention instead to the structural principles of language rather than to the ways in which languages change and develop, and in so doing, became a major influence on twentieth-century linguistics.

In Europe and America, linguists turned to descriptive synchronic studies of languages and to the development of empirical methods for their analysis. Scholars from different disciplines and with different interests turned their attention to the many aspects of language and language use. American linguists in the first half of the century included the anthropologist Edward **Sapir** (1884–1939), interested in the languages of the Americas, language and culture, and language in society, and Leonard **Bloomfield** (1887–1949), himself an historical and comparative linguist, as well as a major descriptive linguist who emerged as the most influential linguist in this period. Both Sapir and Bloomfield were also concerned with developing a general theory of language. Sapir was a 'mentalist' in that he believed that any viable linguistic theory must account for the mental representation of linguistic knowledge, its 'psychological reality'; Bloomfield in his later years was a follower of behaviorism, which was the mainstream of psychological thought at the time, a view that precluded any concern for mental representation of language and, in fact, for the mind itself.

In Europe, Roman Jakobson (1896–1982), one of the founders of the Prague School of Linguistics, came to America in 1941 and contributed substantially to new developments in the field. His collaboration with Morris Halle and Gunnar Fant led to a theory of **Distinctive Features** in phonology, and Halle has remained one of the leading phonologists of the last decades. In England, phoneticians like Daniel Jones (1881–1967) and Henry Sweet (1845–1912) (the prototype for G. B. Shaw's Henry Higgins) have had a lasting influence on the study of the sound systems of language.

In 1957 with the publication of *Syntactic Structures*, Noam Chomsky ushered in the era of generative grammar, a theory which has been referred to as creating a scientific revolution. This theory of grammar has developed in depth and breadth. It is concerned with the biological basis for the acquisition, representation and use of human language and the universal principles which constrain the class of all languages. It seeks to construct a scientific theory that is explicit and explanatory.

The chapters that follow are based to a great extent on the developments in linguistic theory that have occurred since the publication of *Syntactic Structures* in 1957 and *Aspects of the Theory of Syntax* in 1965. In subsequent years, Chomsky has continued to develop his theory in such major works as *Remarks on Nominalization* (1970), *Conditions on Transformations* (1973), *Lectures on Government and Binding* (1981), *Barriers* (1986), *Principles and Parameters in Syntactic Theory* (1981), and *The Minimalist Program* (1995).

In the following chapters, basic notions in these publications as well as many others in areas other than syntax are presented at an introductory and basic level.

1.2 Aims of Linguistic Theory

Three key questions were posed by Chomsky in 1986 which remain pivotal in linguistics today:

What constitutes knowledge of language? (Competence)
How is knowledge of language acquired? (Acquisition)
How is knowledge of language put to use? (Performance/language processing)

As stated above, this text will be primarily concerned with the first question viewed in relation to the second. The development of language from infancy provides insights into the nature and structure of language itself and therefore is discussed in each part. An understanding of language use (performance), the main tenet of psycholinguistic research, depends on our understanding of what is being put to use. We will discuss the distinction between linguistic knowledge (**competence**) and use (**performance**) below.

1.3 What Constitutes Knowledge of Language? Grammar as the Representation of Linguistic Competence

Knowledge of a language permits one to connect sounds (or gestures in sign languages) with meanings, that is, to understand a spoken or signed utterance, and to express our thoughts through speech or signs. Note that the **sign languages** of the deaf are basically the same as spoken languages, using a gestural/visual modality instead of the sound/aural perceptual modality of speech. Except where specifically referring to speech sounds, discussion of the nature and characteristics of language should be interpreted as referring to both spoken and signed languages.

Linguistic knowledge as represented in the speaker's mind is called a **grammar**. Linguistic theory is concerned with revealing the nature of the mental grammar which represents speakers' knowledge of their language.

If one defines grammar as the mental representation of one's linguistic knowledge, then a general theory of language is a theory of grammar. A grammar includes everything one knows about the structure of one's language – its **lexicon** (the words or vocabulary in the mental dictionary), its **morphology** (the structure of words), its **syntax** (the structure of phrases and sentences and the constraints on well-formedness of sentences), its **semantics** (the meaning of words and sentences) and its **phonetics** and **phonology** (the sounds and the sound system or patterns). A theory of grammar specifies the nature of each of these components and the universal aspects of all grammars.

Each of these different kinds of linguistic knowledge constitutes a component of the mental grammar. But what kind of knowledge is this? What do speakers know? First it must be noted that we are not speaking of conscious knowledge. Most of us (before taking a course in linguistics) are totally unaware of the extent of our tacit unconscious knowledge of our language. We have no idea of the complexity of this knowledge. Some of this complex knowledge will be revealed in the chapters to come. As a way of introduction, however, we can illustrate the nature of this linguistic competence as represented in the components of our mental grammars.

1.3.1 The lexicon

Every speaker of language has a dictionary or **lexicon** in their head, with all the words which they know, words like *cat, witch, cauldron, Macbeth, jester, vocabulary, slay, betray, love, hate*. It has been estimated that the average person knows from 45,000 to 60,000 words; these must be stored in the mental lexicon (see chapter 2).

1.3.2 Morphology

A speaker of a language also knows how words are structured, that, for example, in English, words are composed of bare **roots** like *witch*, or roots with **suffixes** like *witch-es* or words with **prefixes** like *dis-en-chant* or words with prefixes and suffixes like *dis-en-chant-ment*, and furthermore they know that these parts of words must occur in a certain order. That is, to put a suffix like *ment* at the beginning of a word – **mentenchant* – would make it **unacceptable** or **ungrammatical**. (Throughout the book, linguistically ill-formed – unacceptable, or ungrammatical – words or phrases or sentences will be preceded by an **asterisk ***.) Since speakers can distinguish between acceptable and unacceptable forms, that is, they accept *lover* but reject **erlove*, for example, then this is part of our grammatical knowledge, represented in our mental grammars.

1.3.3 Syntax

Part of our linguistic knowledge tells us what constitutes a well-formed string of words, how to put words together to form phrases and sentences. We know when such strings of words are grammatical (**well-formed**) or ungrammatical (**ill-formed**), as in the difference between (1) and (2):

(1)   Lear had three daughters.

(2)   *Had three Lear daughters.

Note that grammaticality does not depend on our having heard the sentence before or whether it is true, since (3)

(3)   Lear had only two daughters.

is a grammatical sentence but according to the Shakespeare tragedy it is not a true sentence. And since Lear is a character in a play and does not nor did not exist as a King with three daughters, the acceptability of (1) does not depend on whether there is a referent in the real world for the information being conveyed.

Our knowledge of syntax (and semantics) also accounts for the fact that we know that (4) is an ambiguous sentence (a sentence with more than one meaning).

(4)   Cordelia loved Lear more than Regan.

Although one meaning may come to mind first upon our hearing such a sentence, perhaps

(4)   a.   Cordelia loved Lear more than Regan loved Lear.

speakers of English also know that (4b) may be the meaning of (4):

(4)   b.   Cordelia loved Lear more than Cordelia loved Regan.

The nature of syntax also accounts for the fact that there is an unlimited – infinite – set of sentences in any language. One cannot put a limit on the length of a sentence and thus cannot put a limit on the number of sentences.

(5)   Lear loved Cordelia.

(6)   Lear loved Cordelia and Cordelia loved Lear.

(7)   Lear, who had three daughters, loved Cordelia the most.

(8)   Lear, who loved Cordelia, became very angry with her when she would not tell him in words how much she loved him and that made him cut her off without any lands or riches, which pleased Regan and Goneril but was very unfair because Cordelia really loved him the most and was unselfish and kind and all of this led to the terrible tragedy of King Lear.

We are able to embed sentences within sentences as shown in (9a–c):

(9)   a.   Cordelia was Lear's youngest daughter.
     b.   She loved him.
     c.   Cordelia, who was Lear's youngest daughter, loved him.

We are also able to conjoin sentences as in (10):

(10)   Cordelia was Lear's youngest daughter and she loved him.

We know how to negate sentences and form questions.

(11)   Cordelia was not Lear's youngest daughter.

(12)   Was Cordelia Lear's youngest daughter?

We also know that in (13) *him* cannot refer to Lear, but in (14) *him* can refer to Lear or to someone else:

(13)   Lear loved him.

(14)   Regan told Lear she loved him.

   Chapters 3, 4, and 5 will deal with some of these questions and many more that have to do with our tacit knowledge of syntactic structure, knowledge which also must be represented in the mental grammar to account for our ability to make such judgments.

1.3.4   Semantics

Speakers also know quite a lot about what the expressions in their language mean or signify, and it is this knowledge which makes the patterns of sounds or gestures 'symbolic'. A sentence is like a sort of acoustic or gestural picture – it represents something – though the way they manage to be representational is different from pictures. For example, we know that the spoken or written word *Shakespeare* can be used to name a person; and we know that the spoken or written phrase *wrote plays* signifies a property that some people but not others have, and we can put these two ideas together to recognize the meaning of a sentence like:

(15)   Shakespeare wrote plays.

The simple idea that the subject names something and the rest of the sentence tells us about that thing is not quite right, though. For example, this does not work for sentences like

(16)   No witches wrote plays.

since sentence (16) is perfectly meaningful even though *no witches* does not refer to any particular person. In chapters 7, 8, and 9 we will provide an account of the meanings of sentences which handles both (15) and (16) equally well.

Furthermore, we can understand sentences that are built up in all the ways that the syntax allows: we understand sentences that are embedded and coordinated; we understand negated sentences and questions. Our ability to recognize syntactic structures comes with this parallel ability to understand what the infinite range of structures signifies.

When we consider the meanings of expressions, we also notice that similar meanings can sometimes be conveyed in very different ways. For example, the following two sentences have very similar meanings:

(17)   Usually, a witch does not write plays.

(18)   Most witches do not write plays.

This kind of knowledge represents semantic knowledge in our mental grammars and will be discussed in chapters 7, 8, and 9.

1.3.5 Phonetics and phonology

Speakers' knowledge of their language also includes knowledge of the sounds and sound patterns which occur. We know what sounds are in the language and what sounds are not. Speakers of English know, unconsciously for the most part, that there are more than five vowel SOUNDS in the language, as shown by the vowel sounds which differentiate the following words from each other: *bit, beat, bet, bait, bat, boot, but, boat, bought, put, pot.* We use five LETTERS – *a, e, i, o, u* – to represent these different vowel sounds in our writing system. We see that there is no one-to-one mapping between alphabetic symbols and the sounds they represent.

Speakers of English also know what strings of sounds are words, are possible words, and are impossible words in their language. Thus, *clasp* occurs in most speakers' mental dictionaries, while *clisp* or *klisp* does not (since no meaning is 'attached' to these sounds), but this nonsense form could become a word since it does not violate any constraints on sequences of sounds that are permitted in English. But **lkisp* is not a possible word in English nor is **ngisp* since in the first case, the sequence of the sounds *lk* cannot begin a word, and in the second case, *ng*, the sound which ends the word *king*, cannot begin a word. These are not 'rules' or 'laws' established by writers of textbooks but are constraints on the sound patterns of language which children learn when they acquire their language. Such constraints and additional information about speech sounds and sound patterns, discussed in chapters 11 through 14, are part of our phonological knowledge represented in the mental grammar of English.

1.4   Mental Grammar, Universal Grammar, Descriptive Grammars, Teaching Grammars, and Prescriptive Grammars

Grammar as viewed here is different from the usual notion of grammar. When viewed as the representation of a speaker's linguistic competence, a grammar is a mental system, a cognitive part of the brain/mind, which, if it is one's first native language, is acquired as a child without any specific instruction. The word *grammar* is often used solely in reference to syntax. But we use it to refer to all aspects of linguistic competence. In addition to its use as referring to the mental system, when linguists describe this knowledge shared by a language community, the description is also called the grammar of the language. Of course no two speakers of a language have identical grammars; some may know words that others do not, some may have some idiosyncratic rules or pronunciations. But since they can speak to each other and understand each other there is a shared body of knowledge, which is what we are calling their mental grammars. **Descriptive grammars** are thus idealized forms of the mental grammars of all the speakers of a language community.

The grammars of all languages are constrained by universal 'laws' or 'principles,' a view which differs from that of many linguists in the pre-Chomsky period some of whom held that languages could differ in innumerable ways. The more we look at the languages of the world, the more support there is for the position taken by Roger Bacon, a thirteenth-century philosopher, who wrote:

> He that understands grammar in one language, understands it in another as far as the essential properties of grammar are concerned. The fact that he can't speak, nor comprehend, another language is due to the diversity of words and their various forms, but these are the accidental properties of grammar.

There is much evidence to support this view, which today is based on the recognition that there is a biological basis for the human ability to acquire language. The child enters the world with an innate predisposition to acquire languages which adhere to these universal principles, that is, a genetically determined mental system which is referred to as **Universal Grammar** or **UG**. This will be discussed further below.

While UG constrains the form of the grammars of all human languages, there are the 'accidental differences' which constitute cross-linguistic variability. Using the theory of grammar which specifies UG, linguists investigate and analyze specific languages and construct the descriptive grammars, mentioned above. Thus, while UG may specify that the sound represented by *th* beginning the word *thane* (as in 'Macbeth, the *thane* of Cawdor') or *thigh* is a possible speech sound, the descriptive grammar of English will include this sound in its grammar but the grammar of French will not. Some languages permit the dropping of a pronominal subject, others do not. In some languages one complex word may be equivalent to a whole sentence in another language. These differences will be revealed in the descriptive grammars of these languages. Descriptive grammars also may serve as the basis for **teaching** or **pedagogical** grammars which are used to teach someone a second language or a variation (dialect) of one's native language.

Descriptive grammars aim at revealing the mental grammar which represents the knowledge a speaker of the language has. They do not attempt to prescribe what speakers' grammars should be. While certain forms (or dialects) of a language may be preferred for social or political or economic reasons, no specific dialect is linguistically superior to any other. The science of linguistics therefore has little interest in **prescriptive grammars**.

It should also be noted, as discussed in chapter 2, that the majority of languages of the world have no written form. They are, however, as complex and rational as languages with a written **orthography** or alphabet. Speech (or sign) is primary, part of the natural endowment of the human species; writing systems are derived from spoken languages, which is why every normal human anywhere in the world who receives linguistic input as a child will learn the language of the environment but will not necessarily learn to read or write unless being specifically taught. Even deaf children deprived of linguistic input 'invent' their own gestural language, which develops and changes to conform to the constraints of UG. But such children do not construct written languages on their own.

1.5　How is Knowledge of Language Acquired? The Logical Problem of Child Language Acquisition

Young children, limited in so many respects, accomplish with apparent ease a remarkable cognitive feat. In just a few short years, without benefit of any direct instruction or correction, they develop a very complex and uniform cognitive system of linguistic knowledge, a grammar of the language being acquired. Just how children do this is a central question that linguistic theory tries to answer. What makes the acquisition problem particularly intriguing is that we come to know vastly more about our language than we are provided evidence for in our linguistic environment. Consider, for example, the sentences in (19) and (20):

(19)   Polonius is eager to please.

(20)   Polonius is easy to please.

Superficially, these sentences are very similar. Only the adjective is different, *easy* in (20) and *eager* in (19). Yet, upon reflection an English speaker will know that they differ in a way that goes beyond the choice of adjective. In (19) the subject *Polonius* is the pleaser, while in (20) Polonius is the one being pleased and someone else, unspecified in the sentence, is the pleaser. The sentence in (20) might be paraphrased as 'It is easy to please Polonius,' while the sentence in (19) has no such paraphrase. *It is eager to please John* is not a good sentence in English. What we as speakers know about such sentences goes beyond what is exemplified in the superficial form.

Similarly, the sentence in (21) has two meanings associated with it:

(21)   Visiting witches can be dangerous.

Speakers of English know that this sentence can mean (a) that it is dangerous to visit witches, or (b) witches who are visiting are dangerous. The ambiguity of such a sentence is not given in the superficial form of the sentence. Yet, it is something we know. Just as we know that the sentence in (22) is a grammatical question in English while the sentence in (23) is not, though (22) and (23) mean essentially the same thing.

(22)   What did Caesar drink nectar with?

(23)   *What did Caesar drink nectar and?

Other examples of what constitutes our linguistic knowledge were mentioned above. The point is that we know more about our language than meets the eye – or ear. How did we come to know so much about the structure and meaning of sentences in our language when what we hear are simply sequences of sounds? This problem of explaining the ease, rapidity and uniformity of language development in the face of impoverished data is called **the logical problem of language acquisition**, and was first posed in this form by Noam Chomsky (1955).

The logical problem of language acquisition (LPLA)

The LPLA is one instance of a more general question concerning the acquisition of human knowledge, which the British philosopher Bertrand Russell summed up as follows:

> How comes it that human beings, whose contacts with the world are brief and personal and limited, are nevertheless able to know as much as we do know? Is the belief in our knowledge partly illusory? And if not, what must we know otherwise than through the senses?

What Russell alludes to in the last line, is the possibility that much of our knowledge is not learned, does not come to us through our experiences with the world, our senses, but is innate, biologically determined.

In the course of acquiring a language, children are exposed to only a finite set of utterances. Yet they come to use and understand an **infinite** set of sentences, as discussed above. This has been referred to as the **creative** aspect of language use. This 'creativity' does not refer to the ability to write poetry or novels but rather the ability to produce and understand an unlimited set of new sentences never spoken or heard previously. The precise linguistic input children receive differs from child to child; no two children are exposed to exactly the same set of utterances. Yet, they all arrive at pretty much the same grammar. The input that children get is haphazard in the sense that caretakers do not talk to their children to illustrate a particular point of grammar. Yet, all children develop systematic knowledge of a language. Thus, despite the severe limitations and variation in the input children receive, and also in their personal circumstances, they all develop a rich and uniform system of linguistic knowledge. The knowledge attained goes beyond the input in various ways. How do we come to know as much as we do about our language if not from the linguistic environment?

In answer to the question of the logical problem of language acquisition, it has been proposed that much of what we know about our language is not in fact learned from the input, but is rather part of an innate endowment, which we referred to above as Universal Grammar (UG). UG specifies the form and functioning of human language in general, hence principles which hold in all languages. On this view, the child's mind does not approach language as a *tabula rasa* (a blank slate) to be written on by experience alone, or armed only with general problem-solving skills such as imitation, memorization, analogy, or general induction. Rather, children are equipped with a set of specific expectations about linguistic structure and the principles which govern language. UG helps them overcome the limitations of the input and guides their grammatical development in

SIDEBAR
1.3

The problem of no negative evidence

Ungrammatical sentences such as (23) (repeated here)

(23)   *What did Caesar drink nectar and?

illustrate a particularly thorny aspect of the acquisition problem – the 'no negative evidence problem'. In (23) the questioned element is part of a coordination, as in *Caesar drank nectar and wine*. It seems that there is a restriction against questioning out of a coordinate structure and this restriction holds not just in English, but in all languages. But how can the child learn such a constraint since the relevant evidence is an ungrammatical sentence which he will never hear. The asterisk is a useful linguistic convention, but it is not part of the input to the child. In general, children do not have access to **negative evidence**, that is direct information that certain sentences are ungrammatical – yet another important respect in which the input to the child is deficient.

particular ways. So children develop language rapidly and efficiently, that is, with relatively few errors, and despite the **poverty of the stimulus** (for example, the lack of negative evidence), because the basic form of language is given to them by human biology. Our commonsense understanding of language acquisition is that children just 'pick up' language. This seems to be close to the truth. In fact it may be more appropriate to think in terms of language 'growth' rather than learning. This is not to say that there is no learning. Children must, of course, learn the lexicon of the particular language they are exposed to and other language-specific properties. As we will see throughout this book, languages such as English, French, Japanese, Swahili and so on share many essential properties – those that derive from UG – but they also differ from each other in various respects, and these differences must be learned by the child on the basis of experience. The best way to think about UG is as a kind of template with gaps that must be filled in through experience with a particular language.

There is an intimate connection between linguistic theory and language acquisition. By analyzing the structure of individual languages, linguists try to determine which aspects of our linguistic knowledge are universal and hence, arguably, available to the child as part of UG, and which aspects are language-particular and hence to be learned on the basis of linguistic input that the child receives. Thus, the study of particular grammars tells us something important about language development. At the same time, an understanding of the development of language in children can offer us further insight into the organization of human language. In chapters 6, 10, and 15 we will look more closely at the developmental stages that children go through on their way to adult linguistic competence.

1.6 How is Knowledge of Language Put to Use? Linguistic Performance

If the grammar is the mental representation of linguistic competence, how does this differ from how we use this knowledge when we speak and when we comprehend what is said to us? The distinction between the representation of what we know in our minds and how we put this knowledge to use is not specific to language. In performing music, for example, we may 'know by heart' how to play the *Moonlight Sonata* and we may play it perfectly from time to time. But we may also at some performances, produce a few clinkers, make a number of mistakes, even forget a specific passage. The fact that the next time we try to play it we may make no such mistakes shows that the knowledge was there but we just couldn't get to it in our performance. That is, we know the sonata but our performance reflects this knowledge in a non-perfect way.

This is also true of language. Although in principle we can understand and produce an infinite set of sentences, obviously in our mortal lives no speaker can actually do so. Although on hearing a sentence like (23) above, we know that there is something wrong with it, that it is ungrammatical, thus reflecting our linguistic competence, we may not be able to state what part of our grammar is violated, showing that this is unconscious knowledge.

Differences between linguistic knowledge (competence) and linguistic performance are revealed, for example, through slips of the tongue. When the Reverend Spooner, whose errors gave birth to the term *spoonerism*, referred to Queen Victoria as *that queer old dean* instead of the intended *that dear old queen* he knew that she wasn't a dean and wasn't strange. Everyone makes errors, and often we catch ourselves doing it and correct the errors, showing that we know what is the correct form of the word, phrase, or sentence which is involved in the error.

Memory lapses sometimes prevent us from remembering the beginning of a sentence, producing errors like (24) in which a singular *he* is mistakenly produced instead of the plural *they* to agree with the plural subject Macbeth and Banquo.

(24) Macbeth and Banquo, two generals of the King, rode to the castle which he saw in the distance.

The relationship between the grammar and linguistic performance is a complex one and is the major area of psycholinguistic research. This text will not discuss linguistic performance but rather the mental system which is accessed in speech and comprehension. However, given this distinction between competence and performance, how can linguists investigate competence, the nature of the mental grammar?

1.7 'Doing' Linguistics

There are a number of methods linguists use in 'doing' linguistics, in analyzing languages, in constructing grammars, and in developing a theory of grammar.

Linguists use both **naturalistic** data and **experimental** data. Naturalistic data consist of actual speech written down or recorded and are often a useful source of **positive evidence**, that is, evidence that a particular type of sentence is (probably) grammatical.

For example, suppose that in listening to recorded conversations or studying pages and pages of transcribed texts, one finds that the pronouns *him* and *her* always refer to someone other than the subject, in sentences like

(25)   Othello hates him.

(26)   Titania loved her.

while in sentences such as (27) and (28),

(27)   Othello hates himself.

(28)   Titania loved herself.

himself and *herself* always refer to the subject; one can infer which forms of the pronouns are grammatical in the different cases. But note the caveat above concerning the difference between competence and performance (specifically between **sentences**, generated by the mental grammar, and **utterances**, what speakers actually say, which, as shown above, may contain 'slips of the tongue,' false starts, the *ers* and *uhs* and *you know's* of filled pauses, etcetera).

In addition, naturalistic data are not a reliable source of negative evidence, that is, evidence that a particular sentence is ungrammatical. This is because it is impossible to infer that a sentence is ungrammatical just because we never hear it. As noted above, the number of possible grammatical sentences in any natural human language is infinite, but people only utter a finite number of sentences in their lives; therefore, many grammatical sentences have never been uttered (much less observed by a linguist). In order to gather negative evidence that a sentence is ungrammatical, linguists generally rely on experimental data, to determine whether native speakers can understand it and to determine whether they find it intuitively natural or acceptable.

In one kind of experiment, native speakers are presented with sentences and asked whether each 'sounds OK,' or whether they think it is an acceptable sentence. Similar kinds of experiments are conducted in morphology, with native speakers of the language under investigation asked to accept or reject conjoined morphemes, or in phonology, where speakers are asked whether some string of sounds is a possible word in the language. The study of speech sounds – their production, perception, and their acoustic characteristics – is also carried on in the phonetics laboratory with a wide variety of computerized and other technologies.

It is important to bear in mind that the notions of **acceptability** and **grammaticality** are not exactly the same, since factors not directly related to the grammar itself can also affect acceptability. For example, a native speaker might consider a sentence unacceptable because it contains a word that the speaker finds obscene or offensive, or because the sentence is so long they forget how it began, or because the sentence is ambiguous in a way that might be confusing. In such cases, the speaker's judgments about acceptability may not be a fully reliable indicator of grammaticality. Thus, native speakers' intuitions provide only indirect evidence about whether a sentence is grammatical. Since there is no more direct way of finding out whether a sentence is grammatical, linguists generally rely on speakers' intuitions about acceptability, despite these limitations.

To account for judgments such as those in the examples above, we postulate the existence of some form of syntactic rules in the unconscious mental grammar. The hypotheses about particular rules may turn out to be mistaken. If, on further investigation, this proves to be so, new hypotheses embodying the existence of other syntactic rules will have to be formulated to explain speakers' linguistic behavior in both naturalistic and experimental situations.

There will be further discussion on experimental evidence, and on grammaticality judgments and acceptability, in chapter 3. Throughout the book the methods used by linguists in 'doing' linguistics are discussed and you will be 'doing' your own analyses through the many exercises in the chapters that follow.

1.8 Summary

Linguistics is the scientific study of human language. There are many subfields of linguistics. This textbook will be primarily concerned with contemporary linguistic theory, or theoretical linguistics, which aims at an explanation of the nature and structure of all human languages. The interest in human language goes back as far as recorded history. The publication of Chomsky's *Syntactic Structures* in 1957 ushered in the current period of generative linguistics, the aims of which concern answers to three key questions: what constitutes knowledge of language (linguistic **competence**), how is the knowledge acquired, and how is this knowledge put to use in linguistic **performance**? Speakers' knowledge of their language is represented in their mind as a mental **grammar** which includes everything they know about the language, including its **lexicon** (the words in their vocabulary), the **morphology** (the structure of these words), the **syntax** (the structure of phrases and sentences), the **semantics** (the meanings of linguistic structures), and the **phonetics** and **phonology** (the sounds and sound patterns of the language). Thus a speaker's grammar is the mental representation of linguistic competence. Grammars of individual languages written by linguists, which mirror the mental grammars, are called **descriptive grammars**, which often are used as the basis for **teaching** or **pedagogic grammars** used by those wishing to learn a second (or third) language. Neither mental grammars nor descriptive grammars aim at prescribing what a speaker should say, but rather have as their goal to mirror what speakers know about their language.

Children acquire the complex grammars of their language quickly and with incredible ease without any instruction. How they do this is referred to as the logical problem of child language acquisition. To understand how they do this is a problem since children receive an impoverished set of finite data with no negative evidence (telling them what strings of sounds or words are incorrect) and yet are able to form the rules to produce and comprehend an infinite set of sentences and to distinguish between well-formed (**grammatical**) and ill-formed (**ungrammatical**) utterances. This has led to the suggestion that the human animal is endowed with an innate capacity for language, a **Universal Grammar – UG**.

In trying to understand the nature of language one must distinguish between linguistic **competence** (the representation of linguistic knowledge) and linguistic **performance** (the use of this knowledge in **speech processing** – speaking and comprehending). In performance, our knowledge of language interacts with non-linguistic knowledge and is influenced by many factors including short-term memory, other psychological processes, and pragmatic knowledge, among other things.

Linguists use both **naturalistic** data – actual speech, conversations, recorded texts – and **experimental** data. The chapters that follow will illustrate the methods used by linguists in developing a theory of language and in describing the languages of the world.

Further Reading

Chomsky, Noam. 1957. *Syntactic Structures*. The Hague: Mouton.

——. 1968. *Language and Mind*. New York: Harcourt Brace Jovanovich. Extended edition, 1972.

——. 1986. *Knowledge of Language: Its Nature, Origin and Use*. New York: Praeger.

Fromkin, Victoria A. and Robert Rodman. 1998. *An Introduction to Language*. Fort Worth, TX: Harcourt Brace.

Klima, Edward S. and Ursula Bellugi. 1979. *The Signs of Language*. Cambridge, MA: Harvard University Press.

Newmeyer, Frederick J. 1983. *Grammatical Theory: Its Limits and Its Possibilities*. Chicago and London: University of Chicago Press.

Pinker, Steven. 1994. *The Language Instinct: How the Mind Creates Languages*. New York: William Morrow and Co.

Part II

Morphology and Syntax

2

Morphology:
The Structure of Words

CHAPTER CONTENTS

2.0 Introduction

Morphology is the study of words and their structure. What is a **word**? Words are meaningful linguistic units that can be combined to form phrases and sentences. When a speaker hears a word in his language, he has an immediate association with a particular meaning.

2.1 The Structure of Words

Consider the words in the following English sentence:

(1) The friends promised to inquire carefully about a schoolmaster for the fair Bianca.

Each of the thirteen words in this sentence (twelve different ones, since *the* is repeated) can be used in many contexts (in an infinite number of sentences, in fact), or can be uttered alone. (The written forms of some languages such as English use a typographic convention of placing spaces between words. But the use of spaces between words is arbitrary. For example, some words in English are **compounds** composed of more than one word, and these words within a word may be separated by a hyphen, as in *jack-in-the-box*, or a space, as in *looking glass*, or nothing at all, as in *girlfriend*. Even speakers of unwritten languages have a feeling for which sequences of sounds are words and which sequences are not.)

Words are not the smallest units of meaning. They may be simple or complex. The word *promised* has two parts, *promise* and *-ed*; *friends* is composed of *friend* plus *-s*; and *carefully* may be divided into *careful* (itself composed of *care* plus *-ful*) and *-ly*. The word *schoolmaster* includes two words, *school* and *master*, which form a compound. Each of the words in this compound and the other smaller word parts which cannot be divided into even smaller parts, as mentioned above, is called a **morpheme**. We can rewrite the sentence above, using a hyphen to indicate the **boundary** between morphemes within words (a + is often used instead of a hyphen to indicate a morpheme boundary):

(2) The friend-s promis-ed to inquire care-ful-ly about a school-master for the fair Bianca.

Thus, the sentence contains eighteen different morphemes, one of which (*the*) occurs twice, for a total of seventeen separate units. (Even finer divisions are possible. Some scholars might argue that *promise* contains *pro-* plus *-mise*, that *inquire* contains *in-* plus *-quire*, and that *about* contains *a-* plus *-bout*.)

There is a difference between morphemes like *Bianca, promise, friend, inquire, fair,* and *about* and morphemes like *-ly, -ful, -ed,* and *-s*. The morphemes in the first group are all words, and can stand alone, while those in the second group are not. Morphemes like *-ly* and *-s* must be combined with other morphemes; they are **bound**. In contrast, words like *Bianca* and *friend* are **free** morphemes.

Words like *Bianca, promise, friend,* and *fair* are **lexical** morphemes, representing categories of words, such as **nouns** (*friend*), **verbs** (*promise*), and **adjectives** (*fair*). Names, like *Bianca*, are a special class of nouns. Lexical morphemes refer to items, actions, attributes, and concepts that can be described with words or illustrated with pictures. Morphemes like *-ed*, *-ly*, and *-s* are **grammatical** morphemes, which the speaker uses to signal the relationship between a word and the context in which it is used. For example, the **past** element *-ed* in *promised* shows that the event of promising occurred at some time before the sentence was uttered, and the **plural** element *-s* in *friends* shows that more than one friend is referred to. All the lexical and grammatical morphemes a speaker knows constitute his **lexicon** or mental dictionary, which the speaker uses along with a system of **rules** in producing and understanding sentences.

It is not the case that all lexical morphemes are free or that all grammatical morphemes are bound. Grammatical morphemes such as the **determiners** or **articles** *the* and *a* are **independent** words, for example. (*Article* is a term from traditional grammar, referring to English words like *a* or *an* – known as indefinite articles – and *the* – known as definite articles. In current linguistic theory these words are analyzed as determiners, a class that also includes words like *this* and *that*.) *To*, *about*, and *for* are **prepositions**. These words are sometimes identified as grammatical rather than lexical morphemes, in part because there are only a small number of such words – a closed class – and because they express a limited range of concepts. Although *school* and *master* are fused together in the compound *schoolmaster*, these are free morphemes, since either may occur on its own as well.

Analyze the following English sentences and phrases by **segmenting** them – putting hyphens between all morphemes you can identify. Identify each morpheme as bound or free, lexical or grammatical. For the first occurrence of each bound morpheme, give another word that contains that same bound morpheme. Some words are hard to divide into morphemes – discuss any problems you encounter. For example, *day* is certainly a separate word (morpheme); should the *yester* of *yesterday* be considered a morpheme? If so, what does it mean? Similarly, how many morphemes are there in the verb *told*, which refers to the past?

EXERCISE 2.1

1. Yesterday Ophelia picked wildflowers in the churchyard.
2. He told me that Desdemona had married a Moor.
3. Aren't you going to show me your newest quiver?
4. Portia argued her case long and well.
5. My horse! My horse! My kingdom for a horse! (*Richard III*, V, iv, 7)
6. All the perfumes of Arabia will not sweeten this little hand. (*Macbeth*, V, i, 56)
7. I'll put a girdle round about the earth in forty minutes. (*A Midsummer Night's Dream*, II, i, 163)
8. Merrily, merrily shall I live now, under the blossom that hangs on the bough. (*The Tempest*, V, i, 88)

We have considered several types of English words, **uninflected base forms** with no added grammatical morphemes (such as *Bianca*, *fair*, *promise*, *schoolmaster* and *inquire*) and **inflected** words (base forms with grammatical morphemes added, such as *promised* and *friends*). *Carefully* is a **derived** word, in which one base form is made from another: the **adverb** *carefully* is formed or derived by adding *-ly* to the adjective *careful*, which in turn is formed by the addition of *-ful* to the noun *care*. Morphemes like *-ly* and *-ful* are called **derivational morphemes**. (Derivational morphology is discussed further below.)

Words that contain more than one morpheme, such as *friends*, *promised*, *carefully*, and *schoolmaster*, are **complex**. In contrast, non-complex words containing only one morpheme are **simple** even if they are long words, such as *Massachusetts*, *Bianca*, *perestroika*, or *kangaroo*. Non-complex words longer than a few **syllables** are often either names or words borrowed from other languages. Such words may be complex (**analyzable**, or capable of being divided into several morphemes) in their languages of origin, but this structure is not relevant for English morphology, since English speakers are not familiar with the morphemes of these other languages, except as they occur in their borrowed forms in English.

Many speakers of English have heard the following complex word:

(3)   antidisestablishmentarianism

Even those who have no clear idea of the meaning of this word have no trouble breaking it up into seven or more morphemes used in other words: *anti-dis-establish-ment-ari-an-ism*. There are actually more than seven morphemes. For example, the suffix *-ism* is composed of the suffix *-ize* (see table 2.1) plus an additional suffix *-m* (as in *baptize/baptism*). The single free lexical morpheme, here the **root** of the word, is *establish*. A root morpheme is a lexical morpheme (usually free, in English) which is the base to which grammatical or **derivational** morphemes are added to form a complex word.

Anti- and *dis-* are **prefixes**, bound morphemes added before the root; bound morphemes added after the root, such as *-ment*, are **suffixes**, like *-er*, *-ed*, *-est*, and *-s*, discussed above. Prefixes and suffixes are included in the class of **affixes**.

EXERCISE 2.2

Consider the following list of actual and possible words in English. Segment them into their component morphemes. Comment on each word: is it a 'real' word (does it occur in your mental dictionary)? Is it a possible word (an item that you don't know but which you think could be a word)? Is it an impossible word (one that could not be in any English speaker's lexicon)? (You might want to discuss the contexts in which words whose existence might be debatable could be used, and any other difficult cases.)

anti-Trotskyite, beautifully, boys, children, children's, childrens, disenchanting, girled, hims, hors-d'œuvres, lovelily, morphologist, nounize, overs, post-positional, stealize, sweetie, unman, unwoman, verballiest

2.2 Word and Morpheme Classes

2.2.1 Word classes

Affixes may be described in terms of the **class** or **category** of the word (noun, verb, adjective, adverb) they combine with, and the category of word formed by the root+affix combination. Table 2.1 presents a few examples.

Table 2.1 Some English affixes and word classes

AFFIX	ATTACHES TO	FORMING	EXAMPLES
anti-	nouns	nouns	*anti-matter, anti-aircraft*
	adjectives	adjectives	*anti-democratic*
un-	adjectives	adjectives	*un-happy, un-lucky*
	verbs	verbs	*un-bridle, un-lock*
re-	verbs	verbs	*re-establish, re-assure*
dis-	verbs	verbs	*dis-enfranchise, dis-own*
	adjectives	adjectives	*dis-ingenuous, dis-honest*
-ment	verbs	nouns	*establish-ment, amaze-ment*
-ize	nouns	verbs	*burglar-ize, Miranda-ize*
	adjectives	verbs	*steril-ize, Islamic-ize*
-ism	nouns	nouns	*Ito-ism, gangster-ism*
	adjectives	nouns	*real-ism, American-ism*
-ful	nouns	adjectives	*care-ful, soul-ful, master-ful*
-ly	adjectives	adverbs	*careful-ly, nice-ly, angri-ly*
-er	adjectives	**comparative** adjectives	*fair-er, nic-er, angri-er*
-s	nouns	plural nouns	*friend-s, girl-s, cat-s*

Note: Some affixes listed above have additional less common uses that are not exemplified.

Just as there are **homophones**, pairs of words that sound alike but mean different things (*fair* is both the adjective used in (1) and a noun referring to a festival), there may be several different affixes with the same **form**. For example, in addition to the comparative *-er* suffix on adjectives, there is an *-er* suffix that attaches to verbs, forming nouns (*rider, teacher, runner*); in addition to the plural *-s* suffix on nouns, there is a **singular** *-s* suffix on verbs (*promises, inquires, establishes*).

As the examples in table 2.1 show, sometimes the word class of a word changes when an affix is added, and sometimes it does not.

EXERCISE 2.3

Consider each of the following groups of words, and answer questions (a–d) below about each group. Looking the words up in a dictionary is not necessary, but may be helpful.

(i)   badness, fairness, goodness, insurmountableness, wellness
(ii)   incorrigible, incongruous, indefinite, inflexible, insurmountable
(iii)   cowardly, daily, fatherly, lonely, lovely, womanly
(iv)   fifth, fourteenth, sixth, thirtieth, seventieth, seventy-seventh
(v)   dependent, descendant, defiant, prudent, reverent, servant
(vi)   democracy, idiocy, jealousy, monarchy, photography, victory

(a)   Is there any morpheme that occurs in all the words in the group? If so, what is it?
(b)   If your answer to (a) was yes, give three additional words containing that morpheme.
(c)   If your answer to (a) was yes, tell the meaning of that morpheme.
(d)   If you can, tell what class of words the morpheme you found in (a) is added to, and what the class of the words formed by its addition is. Discuss any problems you have arriving at these answers.

Spelling is often a clue to morpheme relatedness, but it may be misleading. Don't assume that two morphemes are necessarily different because they are spelled differently. For example the *-ly* in *lonely* and the *-li-* in *loneliness* represent the same morpheme.
The words in (vii) are a special case:

(vii)   glare, gleam, glimmer, glisten, glitter, glow

These words beginning with *gl* seem to have something in common semantically (what is it?). However, *gl* does not seem to be a morpheme like *-ness*, *-er*, *-ly*, or any of the others you found above. Explain why. (Hint: look at what is left of each word in (vii) when you eliminate the *gl*.)

In the same way that affixes can be classified in terms of what word class they attach to (table 2.1), we can identify members of many word classes in terms of what affixes may be used with them: for example, most nouns form plurals with *-s* (singular *friend*, plural *friend-s*) and most adjectives and some adverbs form a **comparative** with *-er* and a **superlative** with *-est* (*pretty, pretti-er, pretti-est*). Verbs are more complicated: most verbs form a singular **present** with *-s*, a **past** with *-ed*, and a **present participle** with *-ing*. A fourth verb form, the **past participle**, used in sentences like *I have promised to do it*, is the same as the past for many verbs, but different for others – compare *I wrote the letter* (*wrote* is the past form) with *I have written the letter* (*written* is the past participle form).

The set of related words made from a single root is called a **paradigm**. Thus, the paradigm of *friend* includes *friend* and *friends*, and the paradigm of *promise* includes *promise*, *promised*, and *promising*. (Both *-ed* and *-ing* forms of English verbs are often used as adjectives, as in *the promised visit, a promising theory*. We are concerned here with the verbal forms in *The friends promised to do it* and *The friends were promising to do it*.)

English verbs vary considerably in terms of how different their paradigms are, as table 2.2 shows. Verbs in the first group, including *chew, kiss*, and *promise*, are **regular** verbs, with four different forms made by adding *-s, -ed, -ing*, or *-ed* to the verb root (for these verbs, the past and past participle are identical). Verbs like *hit* have only three different forms, since the past and past participle are identical with the verb root. Verbs like *find, sit*, and *teach* have four distinct forms, like the regular verbs, but the past and past participle are formed differently (usually with a change in the root's vowel sound). Verbs like *know, sing*, and *write* have five different forms, since their pasts and past participles are different.

Table 2.2 Some English verb paradigms

VERB	PRESENT	PAST	PRESENT PARTICIPLE	PAST PARTICIPLE
chew	chews	chewed	chewing	chewed
kiss	kisses	kissed	kissing	kissed
promise	promises	promised	promising	promised
hit	hits	hit	hitting	hit
find	finds	found	finding	found
sit	sits	sat	sitting	sat
teach	teaches	taught	teaching	taught
know	knows	knew	knowing	known
sing	sings	sang	singing	sung
write	writes	wrote	writing	written

The most **irregular** verb in English is the verb *be*, which does not follow the regular patterns of other verbs, but has eight forms: the root, three present forms (*am, is*, and *are*), two past forms (*was* and *were*), a present participle (*being*), and a past participle (*been*).

2.2.2 The distribution of words

The types of sentences and **phrases** a word can occur in – its **distribution** – may also indicate its word class. For example, a morpheme added to the sentence **frame** in (4) will be a singular noun:

(4) A _____ promised to inquire about a schoolmaster.

Singular nouns like *girl*, *friend*, or *stegosaurus* can occur in this frame, but *girls*, *friends*, and *stegosauruses* cannot follow the word *a*. Similarly, the frame in (5) must be filled by an adjective:

(5)   A friend made a promise to the _____ Bianca.

(Adjectives such as *fair*, *idiotic*, or *virtuous* can occur in this frame, but other types of words cannot.)

Identification of word class by frame tests is helpful with words like *about*, *under*, and *for*, **prepositions** that specify the relationship of nouns like *schoolmaster* or *Bianca* to the event of a sentence like (1). Unlike nouns, verbs, and adjectives, affixes are not attached to English prepositions. A preposition like *to* or *about* occurs in a sentence frame such as (6):

(6)   The schoolmaster made a promise _____ Bianca.

Diagnostic frames like these can be rewritten in simpler ways to indicate that only the word class, not the specific word chosen, is relevant. For example, the partial frames in (7) are sufficient to identify singular nouns and adjectives:

(7)   Singular noun frame: . . . a _____ VERB . . .
      Adjective frame: . . . the _____ NOUN . . .

In addition, there are many subgroups of the word classes mentioned here that can be identified through their occurrence with particular morphemes and in particular types of phrases. (See Sidebar 2.1.) Sentence and phrase structure, **syntax**, will be discussed in following chapters.

2.2.3   Inflectional morphology

The use of certain types of grammatical morphemes can also be illustrated with sentence frames. For example, the blank in affix frame (8) must be filled with the plural suffix *-s*:

(8)   The friend- ____ inquire about Bianca.

The friends inquire about Bianca is an acceptable sentence (grammatical, in the sense discussed in chapter 1), but in standard English **The friend inquire about Bianca* is not. (The asterisk precedes an ungrammatical sentence, phrase, or word, as explained in chapter 1.) Similarly, past *-ed* must be used in affix frame (9):

(9)   The friends inquire- ____ yesterday.

SIDEBAR
2.1

Proper nouns, common nouns, and morphology

The name *Bianca* in a sentence like *Bianca saw the schoolmaster* is generally called a **proper noun**. This word is used to refer to a specific, clearly identifiable, unique individual named *Bianca*; it is thus different from a **common noun** like *girl*, which has a more general meaning, since it can refer to any young female human being. A proper noun is normally not used with plural *-s* or in a frame following the indefinite articles *a* or *an*.

However, the following sentences sound fine:

Two Biancas go to my brother's school.
I know a Bianca.

Does this mean that proper nouns aren't any different from common nouns? Not really. In the last two sentences, *Bianca* is not used to mean 'the individual named Bianca', but rather (any) 'girl named Bianca'.

Proper nouns may be used with the definite article *the*, as in *the fair Bianca.* Can you explain why this makes sense? This additional evidence suggests another reason why defining the meaning of the proper noun *Bianca* as 'the individual named Bianca' may be too restrictive. Explain why.

The friends inquired yesterday is acceptable, but **The friends inquire yesterday* is not. The necessity of using *-s* in one frame and *-ed* in the other has nothing to do with the particular words in the sentence. You can substitute other nouns for *friend* or other verbs for *inquire* in (8–9) and get the same results. These affixes are required by the rules that govern how sentences and phrases are formed – the **syntactic rules** in a speaker's mental grammar.

These examples show that grammatical morphemes like *-s* and *-ed* must be used to construct certain sentences of English. Morphemes like these whose presence is mandated by specific sentence structure are called **inflectional** morphemes.

2.2.4 Derivational morphology

New words enter the language in two main ways – through the addition of words unrelated to any existing words (for example, words borrowed from other languages) and through word-building or derivational morphology, the creation of new open-class words by the addition of morphemes to existing roots.

Morphemes like *anti-, dis-, un-, -ment, -ful,* and *-ly* are derivational morphemes. Derivational morphemes are not required by the grammar in the

Bound lexical morphemes

Consider the word *cranberry*. We know that *berry* is an independent word, so *cran-* must be a separate morpheme. *Cran-* is not a grammatical morpheme, but it cannot be used alone. New words like *cranapple* show that *cran-* can attach to other free morphemes. It's not easy to define *cran-* (it refers to whatever makes a cranberry a cranberry!), but this bound root morpheme clearly has a lexical, rather than a grammatical meaning.

The morpheme *re-* in verbs like *replay* or *rebuild* is another example of a derivational morpheme with a lexical meaning (usually roughly equivalent to that of the adverb *again*). (See table 2.1.)

In words like *remit* or *receive*, the prefix *re-* is attached to an element that is itself bound. *-Mit* and *-ceive* must be morphemes (they occur in other combinations in words like *submit* and *deceive*). But unless you took a course in vocabulary building or have studied Latin, you probably can't give precise definitions for these morphemes. (If you consult a dictionary, you'll see how the original meaning of these morphemes in Latin contributes to their modern English use.) *-Mit* and *-ceive* are bound root morphemes that must combine with derivational prefixes to create complex verbs.

As these examples show, derivational morphemes and bound lexical morphemes are often **irregular** in the way they combine (they do not always follow set rules), and speakers may not have a clear idea of their meaning or function. English words may contain a great number of derivational morphemes, but they usually contain only one or two inflectional morphemes. Derivational morphemes and bound lexical morphemes are also more likely than inflectional morphemes to attach only to certain roots. For instance, the derivational 'again' prefix *re-* and the derivational 'not' prefix *un-* sound good with some verbs (*refasten*, *unfasten*), but not with others (*refind, *unfind). Can you think of more examples?

same way that inflectional morphemes are; they increase the vocabulary and may allow speakers to convey their thoughts in a more interesting manner, but their occurrence is not related to sentence structure. Thus, for example, while *establish-ment* is a useful word, it's simply a noun; there's no sentence frame that demands a *-ment* noun. (See Sidebar 2.2.)

2.2.5   Open and closed classes

The classes of nouns, verbs, adjectives, and adverbs are **open classes** of words, since new words can freely be added to these classes, as shown in the discussion of derivational morphology above. They are also referred to as **lexical content words**.

Not all classes of words are open classes. The classes of prepositions and determiners, for example, are **closed classes**. New items cannot be added to closed classes of words, and these classes are generally more grammatical than lexical. These closed-class words are sometimes called **function words**.

As stated earlier, formation of new words with derivational morphemes may involve a change in word class (*establish* is a verb, *establishment* a noun). On the other hand, adding an inflectional morpheme keeps the word class constant, but allows that word to be used in a specific type of phrase or sentence.

(a)   Decide whether each of the bound morphemes you discussed in Exercise 2.3 is inflectional or derivational. Explain your answers.
(b)   English has fewer inflectional morphemes than many other languages. List as many of them as you can. (You'll be reminded of a lot of them by going through the previous part of this chapter.)

EXERCISE 2.4

2.3   Analyzing Morphological Structure

2.3.1   Complex verbs in Swahili

All the data discussed so far were from English, but the general principles of word formation, closed and open classes and inflection and derivation pertain to all languages. Completely unfamiliar linguistic data can be segmented and analyzed in a similar way. Consider seven sentences from Swahili, a Bantu language of East Africa, in (10):

(10)   a.   Ninasoma.   'I am reading.'
      b.   Anasoma.   'He is reading,' 'She is reading.'
      c.   Tunasoma.   'We are reading.'
      d.   Nilisoma.   'I read.' [past]
      e.   Alisoma.   'He read,' 'She read.'
      f.   Nitasoma.   'I will read.'
      g.   Tutasoma.   'We will read.'

Notice that two alternative translations are given for (10b) and (10e). An important difference between English and Swahili is that in Swahili there is no grammatical **gender** indicating the sex of a human referred to by a word like *he* or *she*. These Swahili sentences can be used about either a male or a female. (Semantic oppositions – such as English masculine vs. feminine – differ from language to language. In Swahili, although all humans are referred to with the same kinds of sentences, the translation of 'it' varies from noun to noun.)

You may not know Swahili, but you can develop the analytical skills necessary to segment each sentence into morphemes and figure out their meanings.

First, notice that each sentence in (10) ends with *-soma*. Since the only morpheme that recurs in each English translation is 'read' (English translations are given in single quotation marks), you can deduce that *-soma* means 'read'. (In Swahili, this verb is a bound morpheme. In many languages verb roots need affixes in order to be used as words.)

The prefix *ni-* occurs in (10a), (10d), and (10f). Looking again at the English translations, you can deduce that *ni-* means 'I'. By the same procedure, you can discover that *a-* means 'he' or 'she' and *tu-* means 'we'. The Swahili sentences vary in form according to who the **subject** of the sentence is (who is performing the action or accomplishing the verb idea – here, what person is doing the reading).

Finally, look at the remaining three morphemes, a set of prefixes that follow *ni-*, *a-*, and *tu-*. The first of these, *na-*, occurs in the first three sentences, all of which have translations in the present, so we can determine that *na-* is a present **marker**. Similarly, *li-* indicates the past and *ta-* the **future**. Swahili verbs thus provide information both about their subjects and about their **tense** or time.

Now that we've observed these patterns, we can rewrite the sentences above with hyphens between the morphemes, as follows:

(10′)   Ni-na-soma.   'I am reading.'
    A-na-soma.   'He is reading,' 'She is reading.'
    Tu-na-soma.   'We are reading.'
    Ni-li-soma.   'I read.' [past]
    A-li-soma.   'He read,' 'She read.'
    Ni-ta-soma.   'I will read.'
    Tu-ta-soma.   'We will read.'

You should now be ready to try to construct and interpret some additional words. How would one say 'He will read' in Swahili? Can you translate the Swahili sentence *Tulisoma*?

EXERCISE 2.5

(a)   The following Swahili sentences use many of the same morphemes you encountered above.

Ninasema.   'I am speaking.'
Tulisema.   'We spoke.'
Atasema.   'He will speak.'
Watasema.   'They will speak.'

Rewrite the sentences with hyphens separating the morphemes, as in the text. These sentences contain two new morphemes. What are they, and what do they mean?

(b)   Translate the following sentences into Swahili:

'They read' [past]; 'I will speak'; 'He is speaking'

(c)   The verbs of Swahili sentences can include an additional morpheme to indicate the **object** of the sentence, as with

Nilikisoma. 'I read it' (where 'it' refers to an item like a book).

How many morphemes does a verb like *Nilikisoma* contain? What order do they come in?

(d)   Here are some new Swahili sentences. (They contain two additional morphemes you have not seen before.) Analyze them (separate them into morphemes), explaining what each morpheme means.

Anamfukuza.	'He is chasing him.'
Ananifukuza.	'He is chasing me.'
Tulimfukuza.	'We chased him.'
Walitufukuza.	'They chased us.'

(e)   Translate the following sentences into English:

Ninamfukuza; Nitamfukuza; Anatufukuza.

(f)   You've seen that Swahili verbs change to indicate present, past, and future tense, and that certain English verbs have different forms for present and past tense. Can a single English verb change to show the future?

2.3.2   Complex verbs in Tolkapaya Yavapai

Perhaps the most striking difference between Swahili and English revealed by these examples is the fact that complete sentences may be expressed in Swahili with just one word (like *Tu-na-soma*), while English sentences need more words to express the same ideas (as in *We are reading*).

Languages vary considerably in terms of whether they express grammatical concepts with bound morphemes or independent words. Languages that can convey complicated sentences with a single word, like Swahili, are sometimes called **polysynthetic**. In fact, however, despite the fact that English and Swahili use different morphemes (*read* versus *-soma*, *will* versus *ta-*) and arrange these morphemes differently, there is a striking parallelism in the way the two languages express different types of subjects.

SIDEBAR 2.3

Orthography

Writing systems or orthographies are systems of rules or conventions for how spoken language should be represented – there is no single rule for how a writing system will work, and what is accepted by the speakers of one language might seem inappropriate to speakers of another. Such systems follow several different organizational principles.

The majority of the world's languages are unwritten. A language's lack of a writing system is not related to the complexity or sophistication of that language or its grammar or to its speakers' ability to think clearly or to communicate orally, but this lack makes it far less likely that the language will be used for commerce or education. Any language can have a writing system, however – new systems are being developed every day (often by linguists). Relatively new orthographies like those used for Swahili and Tolkapaya Yavapai usually follow the principle that each letter (or letter combination) represents only one sound (and that each sound is represented by only one letter or letter combination) better than do writing systems with a long history (you probably can think of many English spelling irregularities, for example!).

No orthography indicates everything about pronunciation. For example, Swahili speakers know that every word in their language is stressed on the next-to-last syllable. Because Swahili stress is **predictable** (if one knows the rule), it is not marked in the orthography. Similarly, Tolkapaya speakers know to insert extra short vowels between the *ch* and *th* of *chthúli* and between the *m* and *'* of *m'úu* when they pronounce these words. This vowel insertion rule must be part of any description of Tolkapaya orthography. Language learners must learn these rules to be able to pronounce words properly.

In contrast, consider the following sentences from Tolkapaya Yavapai, a language of the Yuman family of American Indian languages spoken in Arizona:

(11) Chthúl-ma.   'He washes,' 'She washes.'
       '-chthúl-ma.   'I wash.'
       M-chthúl-ma.   'You wash.'

(12) 'úu-ma.   'He sees,' 'She sees.'
       '-'úu-ma.   'I see.'
       M-'úu-ma.   'You see.'

The morphemes in these examples have been segmented. Most examples in this chapter are presented in **orthography**, the written form of the spoken language (see Sidebar 2.3). The apostrophe in these examples represents a sound called the **glottal stop**, a sound (or cessation of sound) like that in the middle of the English word *uh-uh* 'no' (see chapter 11).

Like Swahili, Tolkapaya often expresses whole sentences with just a single verb word. In the Tolkapaya examples above, *chthúl-ma* can be identified as 'wash' and *'úu-ma* as 'see'. As in Swahili, Tolkapaya verbs change according to what their subject is. The prefix *'-* is used with sentences with an 'I' subject, and the prefix *m-* in sentences with a 'you' subject.

Some additional Tolkapaya sentences are given in (13–14):

(13) a. Chthúl-ch-ma.   'They wash.'
      b. '-chthúl-ch-ma.   'We wash.'
      c. M-chthúl-ch-ma.   'You guys wash,' 'You [plural] wash.'

(Square brackets in the translation enclose explanatory material; no one says *you plural* to address several people. In English, we have only one word for *you*, regardless of how many people are being addressed, but phrases like *you guys*, *you all* (especially in Southern American English), and *you lot* (in British English) are often used to clarify a plural reference. In this chapter we will often use the expression *you guys* as a translation for the plural *you*.)

(14) a. 'úu-ch-ma.   'They see.'
      b. '-'úu-ch-ma.   'We see.'
      c. M-'úu-ch-ma.   'You guys see,' 'You [plural] see.'

Comparing these with the first six Tolkapaya sentences, we see only one additional morpheme, a *-ch* suffix that goes before the *-ma* suffix at the end of these verbs.

2.3.3 Analyzing the structure of words

This example illustrates a second way to divide words into morphemes. One way to identify a morpheme is to see if it alternates with another morpheme (the way the Swahili tense markers *na-*, *li-*, and *ta-* or the Tolkapaya subject markers *m-* and *'-* alternate). You can also tell that there should be a boundary between two morphemes if another morpheme can intervene in that position. Both *chthúl-ma* and *'úu-ma* end in *-ma*, but we can't tell for sure what *-ma* means from these examples, since it does not alternate with anything. However, because we see both *chthúl-ma* and *chthúl-ch-ma*, we can tell that *-ma* is a separate element from *chthúl-* and *'úu-*.

Organizing the morphemes you have segmented in a chart or table can be a great help in figuring out their meanings. Table 2.3 shows how the English translations are related to the way the Tolkapaya morphemes are used on verbs:

Table 2.3   Tolkapaya morphemes and linguistic analysis

	USED WITHOUT -*CH*	USED WITH -*CH*
'- prefix on verb	'I'	'we'
m- prefix on verb	'you'	'you [plural]'
no prefix on verb	'he', 'she'	'they'

The arrangement of the six categories that appear in the table is probably familiar to you if you've studied a foreign language. The 'used without -*ch*' column contains singular subjects, while the 'used with -*ch*' column contains plural subjects – thus, we can identify -*ch* as a plural marker.

The first, second, and third rows of the chart are typically referred to as **first person** (including the speaker), **second person** (including the hearer), and **third person** (everyone else), respectively, terminology that reflects the notion that speakers are the most important (first) persons in their own conversations.

When the form of the verb changes in keeping with the number, person, or gender of a subject, this is referred to as **subject–verb agreement**. In English this occurs only in regard to number, with the present tense of a regular verb, as in *The boy runs* for the singular and *The boys run* for the plural, but Swahili and Tolkapaya verbs change to indicate both person and number.

Different languages may thus divide the same semantic concept into morphemes in different ways. In English, the words *I* and *we* do not look (or sound) similar; similarly, there is no apparent connection between Swahili *ni-* and *tu-*. The same '- prefix is used in Tolkapaya for 'I' and 'we', though: in Tolkapaya, then, 'we' looks like 'I' plus plural. But actually the Tolkapaya '- prefix means first person, not 'I'.

EXERCISE 2.6

(a) Here are some additional sentences that help demonstrate that Tolkapaya is a polysynthetic language. State what two additional morphemes these sentences contain, and explain how they change the meanings of the words to which they are added:

'ich-'-chthúl-ma.	'I wash something.'
'ich-'úu-ch-ma.	'They see something.'
M-'úu-v-ch-ma.	'You guys are visible.'
Chthúl-v-ma.	'He is washable.' (or more sensibly 'It is washable')

(b) Now translate the following sentences into Tolkapaya: 'I am visible'; 'You guys wash something'; 'You are washable'; 'He sees something'.

(c) *Tpóqma* means 'He pours it'.
Divide the following Tolkapaya sentences into morphemes, and tell what they mean: *'tpóqchma*; *'ichmtpóqma*; *Tpóqvchma*.

Look at the Tolkapaya sentences in (11–14) again, and see if you can tell what morpheme indicates the present tense. All the verbs end in *-ma*, but these sentences provide no evidence about the meaning of this morpheme. Recall that we were able to identify the tense morphemes in Swahili because we had sentences showing a **contrast** between present, past, and future. All the Tolkapaya sentences above are translated in the present tense, so they do not exhibit any contrast. In fact, each of these sentences could be used by a speaker to refer to either a present or a past event:

(15) Chthúl-ma. 'He washes,' 'She washes,' 'He washed,'
'She washed.'

(16) '-'úu-ma. 'I see,' 'I saw.'

Without any further data, however, we can only speculate about the meaning of *-ma*. Sentences like those in (15–16) are needed to demonstrate conclusively that verbs ending in *-ma* refer to **non-future** events, in contrast to verbs ending in the *-ha* future suffix, like those in (17–18):

(17) Chthúl-ha. 'He will wash,' 'She will wash.'

(18) '-'úu-ha. 'I will see.'
'-'úu-ch-ha. 'We will see.'

Linguists often present segmented data with an abbreviated **gloss** underneath each morpheme, as in

(13c') M-chthúl-ma.
2-wash-nonfut
'You wash.'

where '2' means 'second person' and 'nonfut' identifies the 'non-future' suffix *-ma*. (See Sidebar 2.4.)

Glossing linguistic data

When linguists cite examples like the Swahili and Tolkapaya verbs discussed in the text, they often present them with the morphemes separated by hyphens (or plus signs), with a **gloss** under each morpheme, as in (10c′) and (13c′):

(10c′)   Tu-na-soma.
         first.person.plural-present-read
         'We are reading.'

(13c′)   M-chthúl-ma.
         second.person-wash-non.future
         'You wash.'

The gloss helps a reader unfamiliar with the language to see how the parts of a word containing several morphemes are arranged to present the meaning specified in the translation (which is usually given in single quotation marks, either beside the data or underneath the gloss). The number of analyzed morphemes in the gloss must be the same as the number of segmented morphemes in the data, so that by matching them up, the reader can identify each morpheme precisely. This means that the number of hyphens in the data and in the gloss must be identical. If you give the gloss of (a) as 'first-person-plural-present-read,' the reader might assume that *tu-* meant 'first', *na-* meant 'person', and *soma* meant 'plural' – but then there would be no morphemes in the data left to identify with 'present' and 'read'. If you used 'non-future,' with a hyphen, in the gloss for (b), it might appear that the gloss contained an extra morpheme not present in the data. When a gloss contains more than one word, you should either run the words together (as in 'firstpersonplural') or separate the component parts in some way other than by using a hyphen or space (as in 'first.person.plural'). If you put extra hyphens in one line or another, a reader unfamiliar with the data may have a lot of trouble understanding your analysis, even if it seems clear to you.

Similarly, with longer examples, containing more than one word, the number of spaces in the data and gloss should match up too. Even for a one-word sentence like (a), you may confuse the reader if you use spaces in one line and not in the other.

In presenting glosses, linguists commonly use abbreviated forms of technical terminology to save space. Thus, the examples above would usually be presented as in (10c″):

(10c″)   Tu-na-soma.
         1pl-pres-read
         'We are reading.'

(13c″)   M-chthúl-ma.
2-wash-nonfut
'You wash.'

Probably '1pl' for 'first person plural' and 'pres' for 'present' would be clear to everyone, but some linguistic abbreviations are harder for the reader to figure out. If you're writing a paper with unfamiliar glosses for morphemes, you should give a list of the abbreviations you use. Below is a list of all the abbreviations used in glosses in this chapter:

1 = first person, 2 = second person, nom = nominative, nonfut = non-future, perf = perfective, pl = plural, pres = present, R = reduplicated part of the word.

**EXERCISE
2.7**

You already saw the prefix 'ich-', which indicates the object 'something' in a Tolkapaya verb. As in Swahili, Tolkapaya verbs can indicate other objects as well as subjects, all in the same word. First of all, 'úuvma, 'He sees', could also be translated into English as 'He sees him' (or 'He sees her' – in other words, a third-person subject sees a third-person object), and *Mchthúlma*, 'You wash', also means 'You wash him' (or 'You wash her'). Thus, just as there is no Tolkapaya prefix to indicate a third-person subject, there is no prefix to indicate a third-person object. Other objects are indicated with prefixes. Here are some examples with 'me' objects:

Nychthúlma.   'He washes me.'
Nym'úuvma.   'You see me.'

You've seen that a *-ch* suffix can make a Tolkapaya subject plural. Plurality of an object is indicated somewhat similarly in Tolkapaya:

Paa'úuvma.   'He sees them.'
Paamchthúlma.   'You wash them.'
Paanychthúlma.   'He washes us.'
Paa"úuvchma.   'We see them.'

(a)   Translate the following English sentences into Tolkapaya: 'I wash them'; 'They see me'; 'We wash him'; 'You guys wash them'. Present each new Tolkapaya sentence with hyphens separating the morphemes and a gloss underneath the word showing what each morpheme means, as explained in Sidebar 2.4.

(b)   It is claimed above that Tolkapaya has no prefix to indicate a third-person object. On the other hand, someone might say that *paa-* was such a prefix. Explain why this is not so (you might want to compare *paa-* with *-ch*).

We've seen that prefixes are added before a word's root, while suffixes follow the root. But this isn't the whole story. *Vyám-*, 'run', is a new Tolkapaya verb root (the hyphen indicates that this is not an independent word, but must have one or more other morphemes added). How would a Tolkapaya speaker say 'You guys ran', when talking to more than one person?

In Tolkapaya, 'You [plural] ran' is

(19)   M - vyám - ch - ma.

(Note that the morphemes must come in the right order: first the second person prefix *m-*, next the verb stem, next the plural suffix *-ch*, and finally the non-future ending *-ma*.) In the examples we've already seen, the Tolkapaya plural suffix *-ch* always immediately follows the verb root, before either the non-future suffix *-ma* or the future suffix *-ha*. The morphological structure of Tolkapaya verbs like these follows the **template** in (20):

(20)   (PERSON) - VERB - (PLURAL) - TENSE

A linguistic template is a schematic representation like a mathematical formula, using terms or symbols to indicate categories that can be filled by specific morphemes.

The template in (20) has four **slots**, since sentence words like *Mvyámchma* contain four morphemes.

The category of PERSON in the template includes the prefixes '- and *m-*. In verbs with third-person subjects ('he', 'she', 'they'), there is no prefix, so the category PERSON is enclosed in parentheses in the template, indicating that it is not a required part of the verb; that is, in some verbs this slot will be filled, while in others it will not. Every verb has the VERB slot filled. The PLURAL slot can be filled only by the *-ch* suffix, which appears only in verbs with plural subjects (so it too is enclosed in parentheses). The TENSE slot may be filled by the non-future suffix *-ma* or the future suffix *-ha*. Like VERB, TENSE is a required part of the template for the words we have seen.

EXERCISE 2.8

(a)   Make a template for Swahili verbs, incorporating the material introduced in the text and in Exercise 2.5.

(b)   The template in (20) reflects the fact that a Tolkapaya verb like those introduced in the text must contain two morphemes, VERB and TENSE, and may contain either one or two additional ones. The Tolkapaya verbs in Exercises 2.6 and 2.7 are more complex, however. Make a more complete template than (20) for Tolkapaya verbs, incorporating every morpheme introduced in Exercises 2.6 and 2.7. You have not been given enough information to be sure of the relative ordering of every Tolkapaya morpheme, but you may be able to deduce that certain morphemes are incompatible (they would not make sense if used together). Discuss the template you come up with.

2.3.4 Morpheme order

There may be several ways to arrange the words in a sentence and still express the same meaning, but normally the order of morphemes within a word is completely **fixed** – it is not something a speaker has the option of varying. The template above illustrates this fact, that words have **internal structure**. That is, one cannot string morphemes together in any order; there is an order to the sequences of morphemes in a word. This is true in English as well as Tolkapaya (and all other languages). What do you think of the words **employsment*, **lonerly*, **radicaledize*? Each of these contains a root plus two suffixes, which have been added in the wrong order (instead of the correct orders in *employments*, *lonelier*, and *radicalized*). As English speakers, we know that singular *-s*, comparative *-er*, and past *-ed* must be the last suffixes in any words in which they occur. (An important generalization is that inflectional suffixes follow derivational suffixes.) The Tolkapaya tense suffixes are similarly always final.

2.4 Variation in Morphology

2.4.1 Analyzing types of variation

Morphemes often look different in different contexts. Tolkapaya has another tense suffix, in addition to the non-future *ma* and the future *ha* – the **absolutive** suffix *-i*, which is often very similar in meaning to the suffix *-ma* in (11–16) above. In simple sentences, verbs containing *-ma* and *-i* are normally translated the same, but there are some differences – for example, a second person *-i* sentence can be translated as an **imperative** or command (thus, *M-chthúl-i* not only means 'You wash', but also 'Wash!'), but this is not true of a *-ma* sentence. (21) presents pairs of verbs containing the suffixes *-ma* and *-i*, each of which can be translated in either the present or the past:

(21)	'-chthúl-ma.	'-chthúl-i.	'I wash,' 'I washed.'
	M-chthúl-ch-ma.	M-chthúl-ch-i.	'You guys wash,' 'You guys washed.'
	Vyám-ma.	Vyám-i.	'He runs,' 'He ran.'
	'úu-ch-ma.	'úu-ch-i.	'They see,' 'They saw.'
	'thíi-ch-ma.	'thíi-ch-i.	'We drink,' 'We drank.'

Non-future (*-ma*) and absolutive (*-i*) Tolkapaya verbs don't always work the same, however, as the examples in (22) illustrate:

| (22) | M-'úu-ma. | M-'úu. | 'You see,' 'You saw.' |
| | Thíi-ma. | Thíi. | 'He drinks,' 'He drank.' |

Verbs like *M'úu* and *Thíi* (in the second column of (22)), which have no added suffix, are equivalent to the verbs with suffixed -*i* in the second column of (21): the relationship between the -*ma* and -*i* verbs in (21) is identical to the relationship between the -*ma* and unsuffixed verbs in (22). However, -*ma* can appear on any present/past verb, but -*i* appears in only one **environment** (one arrangement of sounds or classes of sounds), but not in another – -*i* appears after a consonant, as in (21), but not after a vowel, as in (22).

Several ways to analyze this situation are suggested below:

- we might simply say that the absolute form of the verb is made by adding -*i* after consonants, but not adding anything after vowels. (In other words, according to this analysis the absolute morpheme has two different forms, or **allomorphs**, which are used in different phonological contexts.)
- alternatively, we might assume that there is a single absolute suffix, -*i*, which is added to all absolute forms, but later deleted from words in which its appearance would result in a vowel–vowel sequence. (In fact, **m'úui* and **thíi-i* are ungrammatical Tolkapaya words, an observation that supports the idea that Tolkapaya does not allow sequences of two vowels.)
- still another approach might be to assume that absolute forms basically have no ending, but that -*i* is added to prevent the occurrence of verbs ending in a consonant. (In fact, **'chthúl*, **mchthúlch*, **vyám*, **'úuch*, and **thíich* are not good Tolkapaya words either.)

Which of these grammatical descriptions a linguist selects would depend on other facts about Tolkapaya and on the particular grammatical theory assumed. In each case, though, the analysis describes the variation with a rule. Speakers do not need to memorize the absolute form of each Tolkapaya verb; each absolute verb is regular, according to the rule.

EXERCISE 2.9

Consider the three analyses of Tolkapaya -*i* presented in the text. Rewrite each one to include a specific rule expressed as an *if . . . then* statement. Then consider the template describing Tolkapaya verb structure in (20) (and modified in Exercise 2.8), in which VERB and TENSE were presented as required categories. Is this template compatible with each of the suggested analyses? Discuss your answers.

2.4.2 Conditioned variation

The distribution of the Tolkapaya absolute morpheme -*i* (where it appears, in other words) illustrates **conditioned variation**: in one environment (under one condition), the morpheme appears, in another, it doesn't. Conditioned variation is the most common form of morphological variation. It may take the form of appearance or non-appearance, as in the case of Tolkapaya absolutive forms, or may involve a difference in pronunciation.

For example, the English plural morpheme -*s* changes its pronunciation in different environments – consider the sound of the -*s*'s in (23) and (24) below:

(23)   tap —— taps, cat —— cats, Reebok —— Reeboks

(24)   tab —— tabs, cad —— cads, bog —— bogs

The regular English plural morpheme is always spelled -*s* (or -*es*), and it has the sound [s] in the plurals in (23). (Linguists write **phonetic** forms – representing actual sounds – in square brackets.) However, the plural -*s*'s in (24) have a different sound. If you were going to write these words as they sound, they would be spelled more like *tabz*, *cadz*, and *bogz*. The English plural morpheme is regularly pronounced as [z] rather than [s], whenever it follows *b*, *d*, *g*, and certain other consonants (you'll learn more about this in later chapters). This too is conditioned variation.

There will be many other examples from English and other languages of conditioned variation in later chapters.

2.4.3 Free variation

Reverential verb forms in the Zapotec language spoken in San Lucas Quiaviní (SLQ), Oaxaca, Mexico, illustrate a different kind of variation. SLQ Zapotec speakers differentiate many levels of respect in their verb forms. Compare some SLQ Zapotec **formal** verbs (whose subject might be a parent, priest, or teacher), in (25) below, with comparable reverential verbs (whose subject is God or another holy entity), in (26):

(25)   R-a'ihsy-ëb.   'He (formal) sleeps.'
       R-zhihby-ëb.   'He (formal) gets scared.'
       R-àa'izy-ëb.   'He (formal) hits.'
       R-e'ihpy-ëb.   'He (formal) tells.'

(26)   R-a'ihsy-iny. / R-a'ihsy-ni'.   'He (reverential) sleeps.'
       R-zhihby-iny. / R-zhihby-ni'.   'He (reverential) gets scared.'
       R-àa'izy-iny. / R-àa'izy-ni'.   'He (reverential) hits.'
       R-e'ihpy-iny. / R-e'ihpy-ni'.   'He (reverential) tells.'

As these examples show, the formal ending is -*ëb*, while the reverential ending is either -*iny* or -*ni'*. Speakers of SLQ Zapotec report that there is no difference in meaning between the two reverential forms (presented here separated by a slash, /), and that both sound equally good in all contexts. This is an example of **free variation**, morphological variation in which no conditioning environment can be stated. Free variation is generally less common in language than conditioned variation, and when supposed cases of free variation are examined carefully, it often turns out that there is some slight difference in meaning or usage. (Note that free variation also occurs in the pronunciation of certain words in a language. This will be discussed in later chapters.)

EXERCISE 2.10

Consider the following verbs from Chickasaw, a Muskogean language spoken in Oklahoma, and their corresponding first-person plural ('we') subject forms (in Chickasaw orthography, underlining a vowel indicates that it is **nasalized**, or pronounced with the air released through the nose rather than the mouth):

afama 'meet'	ilafama / kilafama 'we meet him'
bashli 'cut'	iibashli / kiibashli 'we cut it'
hilha 'dance'	iihilha / kiihilha 'we dance'
impa 'eat'	ilimpa / kilimpa 'we eat'
loshka 'tell a lie'	iiloshka / kiiloshka 'we tell a lie'
oochi 'kindle'	iloochi / kiloochi 'we kindle it'
o̱loshka 'tell a lie about'	ilo̱loshka / kilo̱loshka 'we tell a lie about him'
paska 'make bread'	iipaska / kiipaska 'we make bread'

Analyze the sentences into morphemes; then answer the following questions:

(a) What do these sentences suggest about the way a third-person singular object is indicated in Chickasaw?

(b) What are the allomorphs (the different forms) of the first-person plural prefix in Chickasaw?

(c) The allomorphs of the first-person plural prefix illustrate both free and conditioned variation. Explain which allomorphs are in free variation. Then tell which allomorphs illustrate conditioned variation, and explain the conditioning factor.

We have thus seen a number of cases where a single morpheme may have several different allomorphs. There are two allomorphs of the SLQ Zapotec reverential morpheme, *-iny* and *-ni'*, and [s] and [z] are two allomorphs of the English plural morpheme (even though both are written *s*). The case of the Tolkapaya absolutive morpheme is trickier – are its allomorphs *-i* and nothing? Some linguists would say that the absolutive suffix *-i* has a **zero allomorph**. (The idea of zero morphemes is discussed further below.)

2.4.4 Portmanteau morphology and suppletion

Sometimes dividing words into morphemes is more difficult than illustrated with the examples presented so far. Compare example (1) of this chapter with a similar one, (27):

(1)   The friends promised to inquire carefully about a schoolmaster for the fair Bianca.

(27)   The friends swore to inquire carefully about a schoolmaster for the fair Bianca.

(27) looks a lot like (1) – but morphological analysis reveals that (27) contains only seventeen morphemes rather than the eighteen in (1):

(27')   The friend-s swore to inquire care-ful-ly about a school-master for the fair Bianca.

We can segment or divide *promised* into two morphemes, *promise* plus past *-ed* – but although *swore* is the past tense form of *swear*, it is difficult to separate out its past morpheme. *Swore* is a complex word that includes a grammatical morpheme we might represent with a **feature**, [+past], but this feature cannot be segmented – its presence in the word *swore* is shown only by the change in the vowel of *swear*.

In some cases it is not possible to identify any particular parts of a word that are associated with its component morphemes, yet the word is still complex. Consider the following additional sentences based on example (1):

(28)   I promised to inquire carefully about a schoolmaster for the fair Bianca. (*The Taming of the Shrew*, I, ii, 162–3)

(29)   The fair Bianca promised to inquire carefully about a schoolmaster for me.

A comparison of (28) and (29) shows that the **grammatical roles** of the first-person speaker (*I, me*) and the noun phrase *the fair Bianca* are reversed in these two sentences. In (28), *I* is the subject of the sentence, the one who did the promising, while in (29) *Bianca* fills this role. In (28), the inquiring is done for the benefit of *Bianca*, while in (29), it is for *me* – these are non-subjects. (More technically, the subject forms may be called **nominative** and the non-subject forms **accusative**.) However, although the form of the word *Bianca* is the same in both sentences, the speaker is represented by *I* when a subject, *me* when a non-subject.

EXERCISE 2.11	Substitute a blank into sentences (28) and (29) to create subject and non-subject frames, similar to those in (4–9) above. Most English noun phrases work like *Bianca* in these frames: they look the same whether they are subjects or non-subjects. What other English words can you find that work like *I* and *me*?

The alternation between *I* and *me* suggests that these should be analyzed as complex words: *I* contains a first-person singular element plus a subject element, and *me* contains a first-person singular element plus a non-subject element. But there is no way to tell which part of *me* means first-person singular, and which means non-subject. A morpheme which contains more than one non-segmentable meaningful element is called a **portmanteau** morpheme (from the name of an old type of trunk, in which much could be packed).

EXERCISE 2.12	Consider the following verbs from Lakhota, a Siouan language spoken in South Dakota:

Pajája.   'He washed him.'
Wapájaja.   'I washed him.'
Yapájaja.   'You washed him.'
Mapájaja.   'He washed me.'
Nipájaja.   'He washed you.'

(a) Find one lexical and four grammatical morphemes in the Lakhota sentences above. What are they, and what do they mean?

(b) How are third-person singular subjects and objects marked in Lakhota? Consider these additional Lakhota sentences:

Mayápajaja.   'You washed me.'
Chipájaja.   'I washed you.'

(c) The first sentence contains three morphemes, as expected according to the analysis you developed in (a) above (discuss the analysis of this sentence). The other, however, contains a portmanteau morpheme. Identify the portmanteau morpheme, explain its meaning, and tell what sentence you would have expected instead of the one containing the portmenteau.

(d) Can you tell what the rule is for where the accent mark is placed in Lakhota, according to these examples?

The variation within a paradigm can be dramatic: *be, is, am, was, were,* and *are* are all members of the paradigm for the English verb we call *be*. Though these words have a few similarities, they don't follow any regular rules of English morphology, as was noted in the discussion of table 2.2. Other related words look even more different from each other: why is *went* the past of *go*, rather than **goed*? Why is *well* the adverb derived from *good*, rather than **goodly*? (Unlike **goed*, which is not a word of standard English, *goodly* is a word, so you may wonder why it is starred here. *Goodly* is a real English word meaning 'large' or 'considerable', but it is ungrammatical as an adverb meaning 'in a good manner' – *goodly* does not mean *well*. Thus, sometimes * is used to mean 'ungrammatical in this particular context' rather than 'completely unacceptable in any context'.)

Irregular related forms like *be* and *were*, *good* and *well*, and *I* and *me* are called **suppletive**; the occurrence of such forms in a paradigm is called **suppletion**. These examples are **fully suppletive** (neither *be* nor past *-ed* appears in *were*, and *well* does not contain either *good* or *-ly*). Other irregular forms, such as *buy* and its past, *bought* (which is pronounced somewhat like the expected regular past **buyed*), are **partially suppletive**. In cases of full suppletion, the expected base form of the paradigm is usually missing: there is no trace of *be* in *were* or of *good* in *well*. In partial suppletion, we can generally see some trace of the root, but either it or its affixes do not have the expected form.

EXERCISE 2.13

Irregular forms can often be analyzed as portmanteau morphemes. Consider the underlined words in the following English sentences, each of which might be considered a portmanteau. Describe the different morphemes that contribute to the meaning of each word, and the form you would expect the word to take if it was regular.

Take Antony Octavia to his wife, whose beauty claims no <u>worse</u> a husband than the <u>best</u> of men. (*Antony and Cleopatra*, II, ii, 136–7)

In Aleppo once, where a Turk <u>beat</u> a Venetian, I smote him thus. (shortened from *Othello*, V, ii, 354ff)

The fault, dear Brutus, is not in <u>our</u> stars. (*Julius Caesar*, I, ii, 134)

Mice and rats and such small <u>deer</u> have been Tom's food. (*King Lear*, III, iv, 142)

There are often recurrent patterns of partial suppletion in a language with a complex morphology, such as English. Present–past verb patterns like those in (30), for example, illustrate **sub-regularity**: patterns that do not follow the regular rule, but about which generalizations could still be made.

(30) sing —— sang   ring —— rang
      tell —— told   sell —— sold
      swear —— swore   wear —— wore

Similarly, there are sub-regularities in English plural formation, some of which are illustrated in (31):

(31)   mouse —— mice   louse —— lice
       alumnus —— alumni   locus —— loci
       sheep —— sheep   fish —— fish

Just as we might say that the Tolkapaya absolute suffix -*i* has a zero allomorph in words like *M-'úu*, 'You see', (22), we could say that the English plural -*s* has a zero allomorph in the plurals *sheep* and *fish*.

Sidebar 2.3 presents the basics of glossing linguistic data, but glossing suppletive and irregular forms can be challenging. Data from familiar languages like English are not usually glossed, but of course can be. Regular English plural nouns can be glossed as in (32):

(32)   ring-s
       ring-pl

Suppletive plural nouns like *mice* present a problem, because the plural morpheme (which is clearly part of the meaning of the word) cannot be segmented with hyphens. It would be incorrect to present a gloss like that in (33):

(33)   mice
       mouse-pl

because the number of hyphens in the gloss does not match the number of hyphens in the data. (In a simple example, there's little possibility of confusion, but in a complicated one the reader might not be able to identify the morphemes correctly.) One approach is to use a symbol like '+' to separate the different morphemes in the gloss of a portmanteau or hard to segment word:

(33') mice
       mouse+pl

In this case, + represents a special kind of morpheme boundary, one that is present in the speaker's mental analysis of a word, but that does not correspond to a division between actual subparts of that word.

EXERCISE 2.14	(a) If you can, show that the irregular forms in (30–31) illustrate sub-regularities by finding an additional verb or noun that works similarly (or relatively similarly) to each of these cases if you can. You may have trouble with some of them.
	(b) Find a list of fifty or more English verbs with irregular past tenses (like all but the first group of verbs in table 2.2 above) – one good place to look for such a list is in a bilingual dictionary, which may list them for

the convenience of non-native speakers of English. Organize the verbs you find into groups of words that work similarly, and formulate a description of how their past tenses are derived. You may include verbs that have been discussed so far in the chapter. (In organizing your results, it is probably best to focus on similarities of pronunciation rather than spelling.)

Other languages have suppletive forms too – for example, consider the SLQ Zapotec habitual and imperative verb forms in the first and second columns of (34):

(34)   r-zhihby 'gets scared'   b-zhihby! 'get scared!'
       r-àa'izy 'hits'   gw-àa'izy! 'hit!'
       r-a'ihsy 'sleeps'   b-ta'ihsy! 'sleep!'
       r-e'ihpy 'tells'   gw-u'ahts! 'tell!'

We can identify a habitual prefix (*r-*) and two forms of an imperative prefix (*b-* or *gw-*) in these examples. Verb roots like *-zhihby* and *-a:a'izy* look the same with both prefixes. Roots like *-a'ihisy / -ta'ihisy* are related irregularly: they are partially suppletive. Roots like *-e'ihpy* and *-u'ahts* show no regular relationship – they are fully suppletive.

Although some of the SLQ Zapotec verb forms in (34) illustrate partial and full suppletion in their roots, the distribution of habitual and imperative prefixes follows rules. Consider the examples in (34) and the additional examples below:

ràann 'looks'	gwàann 'look!'
ra'uh 'eats'	bda'uh 'eat!'
rcwààa'ah 'throws'	bcwààa'ah 'throw!'
rde's 'lifts'	bde's 'lift!'
rgùùu'b 'sucks'	bdùùu'b 'suck!'
rgùunny 'scratches'	blùunny 'scratch!'
rihah 'goes'	gweheh 'go!'
rzah 'walks'	bzah 'walk!'

Given only a habitual verb (from the first column) or an imperative verb (from the second column), it is not possible to predict if the other will have a suppletive root or not. However, the allomorph of the imperative prefix (*b-* or *gw-*) which will be used for a given verb is predictable from another part of the data. Segment the prefixes from the habitual and imperative forms above, look at the roots of these verbs (minus the *r-*, *b-*, and *gw-* prefixes), and find the generalization that explains which roots use the imperative allomorph *b-* and which use the imperative allomorph *gw-*.

EXERCISE 2.15

2.5   The Hierarchical Structure of Words

2.5.1   Hierarchy in morphological structure

We've seen how complex words can be analyzed as roots with attached affixes. The way affixes are attached to words usually reflects **hierarchical structure**, in that certain affixes must be attached before others. Consider (35):

(35)   happi-ness-es

The derivational suffix *-ness*, a **nominalizer** that forms a noun from an adjective, is attached to the root *happy* before the plural suffix *-es*. There is a reason why the morphemes occur in this order. The plural suffix attaches to nouns, not to adjectives (there is no word **happies*). Thus *-ness* must be attached to *happy* to derive a noun before *-es* can be added.

Arguments about hierarchical structure can be made even when affixes are attached on different sides of a root. Take a simple example:

(36)   un-fasten-ed

The derivational morpheme *un-* is used to make a verb whose meaning is opposite to that of the root verb, forming a new verb in the speaker's lexicon, while the inflectional past morpheme *-ed* forms a word used in a particular type of sentence, such as *He unfastened his belt*.

We have already noted that derivational morphemes are added to roots before inflectional morphemes, so we can assume that *un-* is added to *fasten* before *-ed* is. In fact, *fasten* is itself a complex word, since *fast* is an old word for 'secure' (as in *to make fast the sails*) and *-en* is a derivational suffix meaning 'make' (as in *darken*). So this example also provides further illustration that *-ed*, a verb suffix, cannot be added to the adjective *fast* until *-en* is added to make a verb.

2.5.2   Tree diagrams

Linguists often use **trees** to represent hierarchical structure graphically. The fact that adjectives like *happy* combine with *-ness* to form nouns can be represented as follows:

(37)

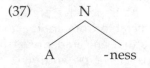

This tree shows that an A(djective) combines with a following suffix *-ness* to form a N(oun). (Labels for the other word classes discussed above include

V(erb), Adv(erb), P(reposition), and D(eterminer).) The positions N, A, and *-ness* in the tree above are **nodes**; *-ness* is a **terminal node**, because it is an actual morpheme (not just a class node). The node N **dominates** the nodes A and *-ness* in (37); it is above them in the tree, and they descend immediately from it.

The A may be specified with a terminal node too. In (38), A is *happy*:

(38)

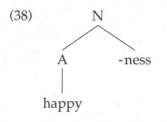

Here, A and *-ness* are **sister** nodes, **daughters** of the **mother** node N (this terminology makes an analogy with a human family tree).

We can represent the addition of the plural morpheme *-s* to a noun like *girl* in a similar way, as follows:

(39)

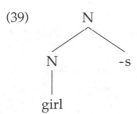

Here, the class of the word does not change with the addition of the suffix – both *girl* and *girls* are nouns. Because plural *-s* is an inflectional morpheme, it does not change the category of the word to which it is attached.

We know that the plural morpheme *-(e)s* is attached after *-ness* in *happiness*. We can represent this later attachment as follows:

(40)

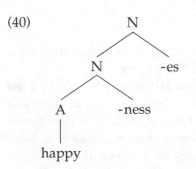

In (40), the complex structure in (38) substitutes for *girl* in (39), illustrating how tree structures express hierarchical structure. The noun *happiness* (the lower N node in the tree) must be formed before the plural suffix *-es* can be added.

What about the word *unhappinesses*? Where should the extra morpheme *un-* be attached? To answer this question, think about how *un-* is used. *Un-* attaches to adjectives and verbs, not to nouns. So even though *un-* appears at the beginning of the noun *unhappinesses*, it must have first attached to the adjective *happy* (forming *unhappy*):

(41)

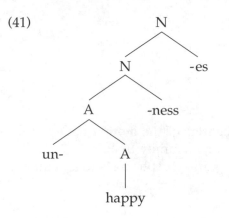

(41) is the correct tree structure for *unhappinesses*, rather than, for example,

(41′)

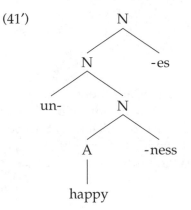

because (41′) shows *un-* attaching to a noun, and this is not consistent with what we know about the distribution of this morpheme.

Tree structures represent **constituency**. A **constituent** consists of all the elements dominated by a single node of a tree. Thus, *un-*, *happy*, *-ness*, and *-es* compose a constituent in (41), because all these elements are dominated by the highest (top) N in the tree. In (41), *un-happy* is a constituent, because *un-* and *happy* are both dominated by the highest A. Even though *happiness* is a word, it is not a constituent in (41), because there is no single node that dominates both *happy* and *-ness* and no other element. (The prefix *un-* is also part of the constituent dominated by the lower N in (41).)

> Draw trees to illustrate the structure of the following English words, labeling as many nodes in the trees as you can. If there are two possible ways to draw a tree, show the alternative trees and present an argument in favor of the one you choose, explaining why the constituency within the tree must be as you have represented it.
>
> *greener, kissed, driver, buildings, cowardly, unkindness, replays, anti-Trotskyite.*

EXERCISE 2.16

2.5.3 Labeled bracketing

Another way that the structure of a word like *un-happi-ness-es* can be represented is with **labeled bracketing**:

(42) $[_N [_N [_A un- [_A happy]] -ness] -es]$

Each class node or constituent has its own bracket (surrounded by [...]), labeled with the appropriate class node abbreviation. Labeled bracketing is convenient because it takes less space than a tree, but it may be more difficult to understand at a quick glance.

> Give labeled bracketings equivalent to the correct trees you drew for Exercise 2.16.

EXERCISE 2.17

2.6 Beyond Prefixes and Suffixes

Words can be derived in other ways than by the simple addition of prefixes or suffixes to the beginning or end of a stem. **Infixes** can be added within a stem, and other new words can be derived without any **affixation** (addition of prefixes, suffixes, or infixes) at all. For example, two words may be put together to form a new word as in **compounding** or **incorporation**, or the pronunciation of a word may be modified without the addition of any extra morphemes, as in **reduplication** or **ablaut**.

2.6.1 Infixation

Prefixes and suffixes are familiar to all of us, since they occur in English, but other types of affixes are less common. Consider the following examples of two types of derived verbs in the Austronesian language Tagalog. The verb stem is listed in the first column (between ‖'s). The next two columns list verbs derived with the verb-forming affixes *mag* and *um*. Look

An English infix

Infixes are relatively rare in the languages of the world, and English does not have any ordinary grammatical morphemes that are infixed. However, there is a common English infix whose use is shown in the examples below:

absofuckinglutely
Massafuckingchusetts
morphofuckinglogical
antidisestablishmentfuckingtarianism

The English expletive *fucking* (or as it is often pronounced in casual speech *fuckin'*), along with several other similar words, can be infixed into many words. (This infix *fucking* is an **affective** morpheme – it doesn't add lexical meaning, but its use reveals something about the speaker's attitude.) As examples like *Massafuckingchusetts* show, even non-complex words consisting of only one morpheme can have *fucking* inserted – neither *massa* nor *chusetts* is meaningful on its own. Since *fucking* breaks up a single morpheme, then, it is a true infix, just like Tagalog *um*. (Thus, we could analyze words like those above using commas, as explained in the text (p. 59): *abso,fucking,lutely*!)

So how is *fucking* placed in the word? Its position is not random, as shown by ungrammatical examples like **Massfuckingachusetts* or **Massachufucking-setts*. As the grammatical examples above illustrate, the numbers of vowels, consonants, and syllables both before and after the infix can vary, so the rule for infixing *fucking* is different from the rule for infixing Tagalog *um*. *Fucking* is not positioned relative to the **segmental structure** of the word (the arrangement of its sounds), but relative to the **prosodic structure**: it is always infixed immediately before the word's main stressed syllable. This is why words stressed on the first syllable have *fucking* added before the whole word.

fucking Caesar

The same option is available for words with non-first-syllable stress, too:

fucking Massachusetts
Massafuckingchusetts

With a longer phrase, there are also two possibilities:

fucking Julius Caesar
Julius fucking Caesar

Both *Julius* and *Caesar* are stressed on the first syllable. But the phrase *Julius Caesar*, like most proper names or noun phrases has its primary stress on the first syllable of *Caesar*, the last word of the phrase. So *fucking* may be placed either before the whole phrase or before the main stress of the phrase, on the first syllable of *Caesar*.

at the examples, and try to figure out where you would put the morpheme boundaries in them. We have added ' to indicate the glottal stop in these words. This sound is normally not represented in standard written Tagalog; its presence in a word like *mag'alis* is indicated by a hyphen in conventional spelling, as 'mag-alis').

(43) |labas| maglabas 'bring out' lumabas 'come out'
  |pasok| magpasok 'bring in' pumasok 'enter'
  |'alis| mag'alis 'remove' 'umalis 'leave'
  |hiwalay| maghiwalay 'separate humiwalay 'separate
    from each other' from'
  |bili| magbili 'sell' bumili 'buy'
  |'abot| mag'abot 'hand to' 'umabot 'reach for'

Clearly, *mag-* is a prefix added to the stems in the first column. *Um*, however, is neither a prefix nor a suffix, since it is inserted within the stem (after the stem's first consonant). Affixes like *um* are called **infixes**.

Infixes are often written with both preceding and following hyphens, to indicate that they do not occur at the beginning or end of a word. But the tradition of writing infixes like -*um*- in this way suggests a misleading conclusion. If a morpheme boundary both precedes and follows -*um*-, then we should be able to segment *lumabas* as *l-um-abas*. We know that *um* is an affix that occurs in other verbs. But what is the meaning of the morpheme *l*-, or the morpheme -*abas*? These elements are simply part of the stem *labas*. For this reason, some linguists separate infixes from the morphemes in which they are infixed with commas rather than the traditional morpheme-boundary symbols – and +, representing our example as *l,um,abas*. (Sidebar 2.5 provides another example of how the elements before and after an infix may not be meaningful on their own.)

EXERCISE 2.18

Consider the following Tagalog verbs, which may occur in three forms, depending on which sentence role is 'focused' or emphasized, and answer the questions that follow. Each verb can be used in sentences with three nouns, such as 'The man brings rice to a woman'. AF (actor focus) verb forms are used when the actor (roughly, the subject) is focused; OF (object focus) verb forms have a focused object; and in DF (directional focus) verb forms the third noun is focused. In the example above, 'the man' is the actor, 'rice' is the object, and 'a woman' is the directional.

	AF	OF	DF
'accuse of'	*magbintang*	*ibintang*	*pagbintangan*
'base on'	*magbatay*	*ibatay*	*pagbatayan*

	AF	OF	DF
'borrow from'	*humiram*	*hiramin*	*hiraman*
'bring out of'	*mag'alis*	*'alisin*	*'alisan*
'bring to'	*mag'akyat*	*i'akyat*	*'akyatan*
'entrust with'	*magbilin*	*ibilin*	*pagbilinan*
'give to'	*magbigay*	*ibigay*	*bigayan*
'hand to'	*mag'abot*	*i'abot*	*'abutan*
'offer to'	*mag'alok*	*i'alok*	*'alukin*
'scrape from'	*magkuskos*	*kuskusin*	*kuskusan*
'sing to'	*umawit*	*awitin*	*awitan*
'throw at'	*magbalibag*	*ibalibag*	*balibagin*
'throw at'	*magpukol*	*ipukol*	*pukulin*
'write to'	*sumulat*	*isulat*	*sulatan*

(a)   What morphemes may indicate AF, OF, and DF? (Don't try to find a semantic (meaning) explanation of why one verb uses one, and another another.) Classify each as a prefix, suffix, or infix. (You may also be able to use the term **circumfix**, meaning an affix that surrounds a root.) One of the morphemes appears to be used in two different ways with different verbs.

(b)   What is the root of each verb? (For four verbs, the root has two alternating forms. List both of these.)

(c)   The variation in these alternating roots is conditioned, based on the overall distribution of sounds in these Tagalog verbs. Propose an explanation which accounts for the variation you observe. (There are several possible explanations based on the data presented above.)

(d)   What is the explanation for the two different uses of the affix *um* that you discovered in (a)?

2.6.2   Compounding

A more familiar **morphological process** that builds new words is **compounding**, the formation of words like the earlier example *schoolmaster*. Compare the compounds in the first column in (44) with the phrases in the second column:

(44)   blackbird   black bird
       redwood   red wood
       hotdog   hot dog
       whitecap   white cap
       Deadhead   dead head

The first column contains single words, while the second contains phrases consisting of an adjective and a noun. The phrases in the second column have **literal** meanings derived **compositionally**, by putting together the meanings of the adjective and the noun, while the words in the first column have special **lexicalized** meanings that speakers must learn individually – a blackbird is a particular species of black bird (and, as the phrase *albino blackbird* shows, may not even be black) and redwood is a particular species of wood (which might be painted another color); a hotdog is not a type of dog and a whitecap is not a type of cap; Deadhead fans of the Grateful Dead are not dead. Another difference concerns stress – in American English, phrases consisting of an adjective plus a noun like those in the second column are regularly pronounced with the heaviest stress on the noun, but compounds like those in the first column regularly have stress on the first element, the adjective.

Many English compounds with lexicalized meanings and first-syllable stress are not written as single words. Sometimes *hotdog* is written as *hot dog*; below are some more examples (the stressed word is written with an accent):

(45) cóld cream (face cream)   cold créam (chilled cream)
      Néw Year's (Jan. 1)   new yéar's (referring to another year)

Phrases like *cóld cream* and *Néw Year's* are exactly parallel to *blackbird*, *redwood*, and the like. As these examples show, English compounds are unpredictable – if *Bigfoot* is a compound, why isn't *bighand*? If we have *blackbird*, why not *brownbird*? Some other languages, however, use compounding or the related process **incorporation** as a regular part of the grammar (see Sidebar 2.6).

2.6.3 Reduplication

Another type of morphological change that does not involve affixation is **reduplication**, a process by which all or part of a word is copied or duplicated to indicate a change in meaning or usage. For example, (46) presents some verbs referring to color from Lakhota. (Do not be confused by the fact that in some languages (such as English) these color words would be adjectives rather than verbs. This is just one way languages can differ.) The words in the first column are used with singular subjects, while those in the second column are used with plural subjects:

(46) gí   gigí   'to be rusty brown'
      ská   skaská   'to be white'
      shá   shashá   'to be red'
      thó   thothó   'to be blue or green'
      zí   zizí   'to be yellow'

SIDEBAR 2.6

Object incorporation

Incorporation usually refers to a special type of compounding in which one sentence element can regularly be compounded with another – most commonly, this refers to the compounding of an object with a verb, to make a single word. Object incorporation does not occur as a regular process in English. English compounds like *truckdriver* appear to contain an object and a verb, but occur only as nouns – there is no English verb **truckdrive*. Some people have suggested that the English word *babysit* illustrates object incorporation. If so, however, the meaning is odd. Does *babysit* really refer to sitting a baby? What do you think?

In Southern Paiute, a Uto-Aztecan language spoken in Utah and Arizona, object nouns are very often incorporated into verbs. Here are some examples of how this works:

paa 'water'	tu'uma 'to take'	paa-ru'uma 'to take water'
	pïni 'to see'	paa-vïni 'to see water'
qwo'a-ppï 'tobacco'	tïqa 'to eat'	qwo'a-ttïqa 'to eat tobacco (to smoke)'
pagïu 'fish'	tïqa 'to eat'	pagïu-rïqa 'to eat fish'
achï 'bow'	pïga 'to keep'	achï-ppïga 'to put away one's bow'
quqqwa-ppi 'wood'	maga 'to give'	quqqwa-mmaga 'to give wood'
	pïga 'to keep'	quqqwa-ppïga 'to gather wood'
	pïni 'to see'	quqqwa-ppïni 'to see wood'

The first column gives nouns, the second verbs, and the third shows verbs with incorporated objects. There is much evidence that the verbs in the third column are, in fact, single words.

First, these verbs change their form in regular ways following the nouns. Some Southern Paiute noun roots cause the first consonant of a following morpheme to double, while other noun roots cause the first consonant of a following morpheme to be pronounced differently: in such cases, *t* is pronounced as *r*, and *p* is pronounced as *v*. Doubled consonants, *r*, and *v* only occur following vowels in Southern Paiute; they may not occur at the beginning of a word – so the occurrence of these sounds at the beginning of the verbs with incorporated objects is an indication that the object–verb combinations are single words.

Second, the form of the object noun is different when it occurs alone and when it is incorporated. For example, certain suffixes that occur on nouns used as separate words, such as the *-ppi* in 'tobacco' and 'wood', drop when those nouns are incorporated. Finally, although Southern Paiute sentences allow some freedom of word order, verbs with incorporated objects must always occur in the fixed object–verb order shown above. The specific changes that occur in the Southern Paiute verbs with incorporated objects are not important, but these separate pieces of evidence demonstrate that the object words actually become part of the verb words.

The words in the second column are derived by **complete reduplication**, copying the entire singular form, whether it consists of a single consonant and vowel (like *gí*, *zí*, or *shá* – *sh* is pronounced as in English) or two consonants plus a vowel (as with *ská* or *thó*, which starts with *t* followed by the separate sound *h*).

Other types of reduplication are less regular. Consider the following examples of singular and plural nouns from Pima, a Uto-Aztecan language spoken in central Arizona:

(47) gogs 'dog'   gogogs 'dogs'
     'uvi 'woman'   'u'uvi 'women'
     jiosh 'god'   jijiosh 'gods'
     kun 'husband'   kuukun 'husbands'
     piigo 'pickaxe'   pipgo 'pickaxes'
     toobi 'cottontail rabbit'   totobi 'cottontail rabbits'

As you can see, Pima plural formation involves only **partial reduplication** (copying only part of the singular form) and is also irregular. In some cases, the first consonant and vowel of the word are copied, while in others it is only the consonant. Some vowels are shortened during the reduplication process, while others are lengthened. Despite these lexical irregularities (a Pima speaker must memorize the form of each plural noun), the process is pervasive – almost all Pima nouns have reduplicated plurals, even words borrowed into Pima from other languages (*piigo* and *jiosh* are borrowed from the Spanish words *pico* and *dios*).

Linguists have different ways of glossing reduplicated words or other words that have morphological elements for which it is hard to give a meaning. Here is one way that the Pima words *pipgo*, 'pickaxes', and *totobi*, 'cottontail rabbits', might be glossed:

(48) a. pi-pgo 'pickaxes'
         R-pickaxe
     b. to-tobi 'cottontail rabbits'
         R-rabbit

Here, the reduplicated syllables in each word are glossed simply with 'R'. (Even glosses for content words can be abbreviated. The two-word phrase *cottontail rabbit* (a particular type of rabbit), which corresponds to a single

Pima morpheme, is given simply as 'rabbit' in the gloss above. Alternatively, the word might have been abbreviated as something like 'cottrabb'.)

Since reduplication involves repeating all or part of a word, it is almost certainly not a coincidence that in many languages reduplication refers to some type of plurality: of a verb's subject (as in Lakhota), of a noun (as in Pima), or even of the number of times a verb's action occurs, or of the intensity of that action.

EXERCISE 2.19

Below are some more Tagalog verbs. The verbs in the first column have derived reduplicated intensive verbs (translated with 'repeatedly' or 'thoroughly') in the second column.

	BASIC VERBS	INTENSIVE VERBS
'become kind'	buma'it	magpakaba'itba'it
'become rich'	yumaman	magpakayamanyaman
'cook'	magluto	magluluto
'cry'	'umiyak	mag'i'iyak
'get hungry'	maggutom	magpakagutumgutom
'get quiet'	magtahimik	magpakatahitahimik
'open'	buksan	pagbubuksan
'throw'	'itapon	'ipagtatapon
'travel'	maglakbay	maglalakbay
'walk'	lumakad	maglalakad

(a) Segment the verbs above. (Many of the morphemes they contain are familiar from the text and Exercise 2.18. You also may observe the conditioned variation you identified in Exercise 2.18.) Identify each morpheme as a root, prefix, infix, suffix, or as a reduplicated element.

(b) What part of the basic verb gets reduplicated? Illustrate the different possibilities with examples.

(c) Two different types of reduplication are used in the derived verbs. Explain how these differ morphologically (in terms of how the reduplication processes operate). What differences, if any, can you see between the verbs in the two groups?

(d) Now, go back to the grammatical morphemes you segmented in (a). Which of these elements are associated with basic verbs, and which with derived intensive verbs? Is the presence of any affix associated with the difference in reduplication type? What signals the intensive meaning in the derived verbs – reduplication or some other element? Explain your answer.

2.6.4 Ablaut

Another type of morphological change that does not involve the addition of affixes is **ablaut**, the change from one sound to a related one to express a change in meaning. The term ablaut is usually used to refer to changes in vowels. The pairs of related English words in (49) and (50) contain examples of vowel ablaut:

(49)   swear —— swore, see —— saw, run —— ran,
       fight —— fought

(50)   mouse —— mice, tooth —— teeth, man —— men

Ablaut is used in (49) to form the past tense of a verb (the past tense verbs have a different vowel sound from the present ones), and in (50) to form the plural form of a noun (the plural nouns have different vowels from the singulars). Most instances of vowel ablaut in English reflect an earlier historical process known as **umlaut** that is common in the Germanic languages.

Other languages use ablaut in similar ways. For instance, consider the following absolutive forms of Tolkapaya verbs:

(51)   Pí.   'He dies.'   Púuyi.   'They die.'
       Qé.   'It's sticky.'   Qáayi.   'They are sticky.'
       Náli.   'He goes down.'   Náali.   'They go down.'

The plural verbs in the second column are not formed by the regular suffixation of -*ch* that we saw in table 2.1, but rather by ablaut of (change in) the stressed vowel of the root. The root vowel of the verbs in the first column either changes to a completely different vowel or **diphthong** (a combination like *uuy* or *aay*) or changes its **length**, from a short (single) vowel to a long (double) one.

Vowel ablaut is often irregular. The irregular English singular–plural pairs in (50) above can be compared with the pairs in (52):

(52)   spouse —— spouses, booth —— booths, can —— cans

The examples in (52) form their plurals regularly, by adding the usual plural morpheme -*s*. (Some people pronounce the *th* sounds in *booth* and *booths* differently, but the plural ending is regular.) The three singular words in (50) are remarkably similar to the three singular words in (52), but the plurals are formed differently – we do not use ablaut to form the plurals of the nouns in (52) (so **spice*, **beeth*, and **cen* are not acceptable plurals), and most speakers do not use -*s* to form the plurals of the nouns in (50) (so **mouses*, **tooths*, and **mans* are not acceptable either). (You may have heard unexpected plurals like *spice* and *mouses* used as a joke. See Sidebar 2.7.)

SIDEBAR
2.7

More about irregular English plurals

Spouse, unlike *mouse*, does not have an irregular plural derived by vowel ablaut; the plural of *spouse* is formed regularly, by the addition of the plural suffix -*s*. Speakers sometimes use the plural *spice* jocularly, pretending that *spouse* has an irregular plural. Because these speakers are aware of the relationship between words like *mouse* and *mice*, they extend this irregular pattern to the regular word *spouse*, making use of an **analogy** of the form

mouse is to *mice* as *spouse* is to *spice*.

But probably no speaker actually believes that *spice* is a grammatical plural form. The same sort of analogical reasoning is behind a change from an irregular to a regular plural, whereby, for example,

spouse is to *spouses* as *mouse* is to *mouses*.

Adult speakers are aware that *mouses* is not a grammatical plural of the noun referring to a small gray or white rodent (though children and cartoon characters might not be). English once had many more noun plurals formed by vowel ablaut than there are today; most of them have disappeared by becoming **regularized**. Regularization is a change that makes the lexicon less complex, since fewer irregular forms must be memorized.

Some adult speakers who would say *mice* to refer to household rodents say *mouses* to refer to parts of their computers. Similarly, although the plural of *leaf* for most speakers is *leaves*, the Toronto team is the *Maple Leafs*, not the *Maple Leaves*. Frequently when a noun acquires a new meaning or is used in a new phrase, it loses its irregular plural, and forms its plural in the regular way, by adding -*s*.

**EXERCISE
2.20**

(49) presents four different types of English ablauted past tense verb forms – words in which the only morphological indication of the meaning change is a change in the stressed vowel of the word. Find at least five additional different types of past tense ablaut, classified according to the change in the verb's vowel. (You may have already identified these in your answer to Exercise 2.14.) Then try to find several more examples of each type of change you've identified. (This may not be possible for every example.) For each type of change that you discover, try to find a verb that sounds similar but forms its past form regularly (comparable to the noun plurals in (52), versus those in (50)).

English speakers know the regular rules for forming plurals of nouns and pasts of verbs. Any noun or verb that does not follow these rules, like the ablauting nouns and verbs in (49) and (50), must be marked as an **exception** in the lexicon, and the speaker must memorize its irregular plural or past tense form. Just as English speakers have to memorize irregularly related pairs like *ran* and *run*, Tolkapaya speakers must memorize pairs like *pí* and *púuyi*.

Consonants may also undergo morphological ablaut. (See Sidebar 2.8.)

SIDEBAR 2.8

Consonantal ablaut

Here are some examples of consonantal ablaut from Luiseño, a language of the Uto-Aztecan family spoken in Southern California:

chóri 'to saw'	*chódi* 'to saw (something small)'
kúuri 'to skin'	*kúudi* 'to skin (a small animal)'
ngári 'to fasten'	*ngádi* 'to fasten (something small)'

In Luiseño, changing an *r* to a *d* (the sound of *th* in English *that*) regularly forms a word referring to a smaller than expected object. (This type of change can be called sound symbolism.)

Now, here are some English examples that could be seen as illustrating consonant ablaut:

(nouns)	(verbs)
house	*house*
life	*live*
teeth	*teethe*
bath	*bathe*

The first column contains nouns, while the second contains verbs whose meaning is something like 'have (a) ____' or 'get (a) ____ for'. The nouns in the first two pairs have as their last consonant *s* and *f*. The corresponding verbs in the second column end in the sound [z] (spelled *s* here, as in the plurals discussed earlier) and *v*. The verbs in the second column are formed by consonantal ablaut, a systematic change in the pronunciation of a consonant correlated with a morphological change.

A similar process relates the members of the last two pairs. When you say them aloud, you'll see that the *th* sounds they contain are not the same: the nouns contain the *th* sound used in *thin*, while the verbs contain the *th* sound of *then*. (Did you know that English *th* represents two different sounds? This is one case in which the English spelling system is inconsistent, as discussed in Sidebar 2.3. The relation between sounds and letters will be discussed in the chapter on phonetics.)

2.7 Heads and Hierarchy

Some types of morphological structure are hard to represent with trees of the type used above – for instance, infixes and ablaut are **non-linear** in their placement (they're not simply added at the right or left **edge** of a word). Although reduplication might be seen as adding something to the edge of the word, it too is hard to specify in a tree-like structure, since what is added is not a single identifiable morpheme, but rather varies according to the shape of the non-reduplicated word.

English compounds (section 2.6), however, may be represented easily with tree structures. Consider the following:

(53)

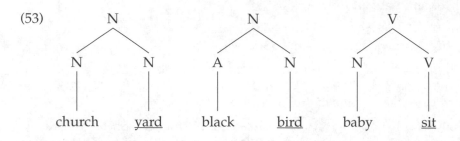

Churchyard, a noun, is a noun–noun compound: it names a kind of yard, analogous to *schoolyard* or *jailyard*. As noted earlier, *blackbird*, also a noun, is an adjective–noun compound referring to a kind of bird. *Babysit*, a verb, is a noun–verb compound that might be thought of as describing a kind of sitting. The second word in each of these compounds (underlined in (53)), which determines the compound's broad meaning and word class, is known as the **head** of the compound. In English, the head always comes at the end of a compound word, and the class of the head is the same as the class of the whole compound word.

This **head-final principle** helps a speaker determine the meaning of unfamiliar compounds composed of familiar words. If you heard someone refer to a *bed house*, you could not be sure if this was a house that looked like a bed, or a house with a lot of beds, or a house with one particular important bed – but you'd know that the item in question was in fact a house, because you would identify the second element of the compound, *house*, as its head. According to the rules of English compound formation, a *bed house* cannot be a type of bed shaped like a house, for instance – that would be a *house bed*.

Compounds can be more complicated. Consider the following example:

(54)   California history teacher

This phrase can refer to a teacher of California history, or to a history teacher who happens to be from (or simply associated with) California. (A restatement of the meaning of a word or phrase, like 'teacher of California history' for *California history teacher*, is called a **paraphrase**.) In both cases, though, the compound refers to a type of teacher. We can draw tree diagrams for the two interpretations of the compound in the following way:

(55) a. 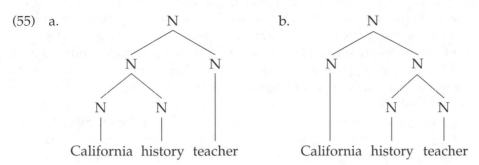 b.

In (55a), a compound *California history* (with its own head, *history*) modifies the main head *teacher*. In (55b), *teacher* is the head of a compound *history teacher*, which is itself the head of a larger compound modified by *California*. Both of the hierarchical diagrams illustrate structures like those discussed in section 2.5; either could also be represented with labeled bracketing. For instance, (56) is a labeled-bracketing representation of one of the two trees in (55) – make sure you can tell which one:

(56) [[[California]$_N$ [history]$_N$]$_N$ [teacher]$_N$]$_N$

Consider the following English N–N–N compounds and compound phrases. Some of them would typically receive only one of their logically possible interpretations, while others could be interpreted in more than one way. For all those with more than one plausible interpretation, give all these structures, and explain (with a paraphrase) what each means. For those which have only one sensible interpretation, give that structure, and then explain what any interpretation or interpretations that you did not represent would mean. Describe any difficulties you encounter.

apartment plumbing contractor, art appreciation course, baby buggy bumper, ballpoint pen, hair care product, Korean English dictionary, linguistics department secretary, metal filing cabinet, mother seagull, rubber ducky lover, Shakespeare sonnet meter, World Trade Center.

EXERCISE 2.21

2.8 The Status of Words

2.8.1 Word boundaries and clitics

Up till now, we have assumed that it is easy to divide an utterance into words. As English speakers, we often rely on spelling (which puts a space between what speakers agree are separate words) to tell what a word is, so our notion of 'word' is partly governed by our exposure to written language. However, sometimes spelling can lead to wrong analyses – as we saw, even though *cóld cream* and *blackbird* are written differently (one with a space, one without), they are similarly pronounced and are analyzable compounds. Expressions like *cóld cream* function as single **phonological words**. The space between *cold* and *cream* in this expression does not represent the same sort of **word boundary** as the spaces between most other words in written English. The adjective contained within the compound *cóld cream* (face cream) cannot undergo comparison, for example, as can the first word of the noun-plus-adjective phrase *cold créam* (chilled top milk): the phrase *colder cream* is a form of the phrase *cold créam*, not of the compound *cóld cream*.

Frequently, small grammatical morphemes traditionally written (and thought of) as separate words are pronounced as part of a single phonological word together with a lexical morpheme in the same phrase. Differences in pronunciation often follow from this phonological word formation, as the English articles illustrate. Consider the definite article *the*. When this word is pronounced **in isolation** (not as a part of a phrase), it may rhyme with *he*. When it is used before a word starting with a consonant, in a phrase like *the fire engine*, its vowel is **reduced** (sounding shorter, more like the last vowel in *sofa*). Before a vowel, as in *the engine*, this change in pronunciation usually does not take place, but in very rapid speech, the vowel of *the* may be dropped entirely, producing something like *th'engine*. It makes sense to think of at least the reduced pronunciations of *the* as forming phonological words with the words that follow them, since these pronunciations are not used in isolation – yet in terms of spelling, except in some songs and poetry, *the* is always written as a separate word. (The English article *a/an* provides a similar case. See Sidebar 2.9.)

The phonological attachment of a morpheme like *the* to another word or morpheme is called **cliticization**. Cliticization is a process that differs from ordinary affixation because **clitics** like *the* attach at a fixed position in a phrase, rather than attaching to members of a given word class. *The* and *a* appear at the beginning of a **noun phrase**, but they do not precede only nouns – the word that follows these articles may be a noun (*the dagger*), an adjective (*the big dagger*), an adverb (*the very big dagger*), or a **genitive** (possessor) noun (*the king's dagger* – see Sidebar 2.10).

Both word-like elements like *the* and *a* and bound morphemes like *'s* can cliticize. These English morphemes are attached at the edge of a noun phrase. Another type of cliticization occurs in English with **contractions** like *'s*, the reduced form of *is* in sentences like *He's going*.

SIDEBAR
2.9

Change in speakers' perception of word boundaries: reanalysis and *an*

What's her name?
Nell, sir, but her name and three quarters, that's an ell [an old measurement,
about 45 inches] and three quarters, will not measure her from hip to hip.
(The Comedy of Errors, III, ii, 107–11)

One of the major changes that may occur as a language evolves is **reanalysis**,
a change in speakers' perception of the location of a word or morpheme
boundary. Reanalysis has frequently occurred in words used with the English
indefinite article.

The indefinite article is *a* before a consonant, *an* before a vowel. When the
following word starts with *n*, the resulting sequence of sounds can present
perception problems for the hearer. Suppose you ask someone what something is, and hear, '*It's anell*.' You can't be sure if the person is saying '*It's
a nell*' or '*It's an ell*.' Shakespeare and other writers have played on such
confusion, punning on the similarity of words like *Nell* and *an ell*.

Reanalysis of the indefinite article has led to change in the form of certain
English words beginning with vowels and *n*. King Lear's Fool used *nuncle* for
uncle (*King Lear*, 3, iv, 109), and the same pronunciation is still used in some
dialects of British English, showing that speakers misperceived – reanalyzed –
an uncle as *a nuncle*. On the other hand, our word *apron* arose from speakers'
misperception of *a napron* as *an apron*. (Related words like *napkin* illustrate
how the *n* of *an apron* is analyzed as part of the noun, rather than part of
the article.) As these examples show, reanalysis can go in either direction.

Many other languages have clitics attached relative to the structure of
another phrase, or a sentence. For instance, in San Lucas Quiaviní Zapotec,
the clitic *-zhyi'* attaches to the first element (first word or phrase) in a sentence, adding the idea of English 'must' (expressing a conclusion by the
speaker):

(57) Banguual-zhyi' nàa Gyeeihlly.   'Michael must be old.'
      old-must   be   Michael

This example illustrates how linguistic examples containing more than one
word are often glossed. As noted in Sidebar 2.3, the number of words (and
spaces), like the number of morphemes (and hyphens), in the gloss and the
data must match exactly. The gloss is thus different from an ordinary
translation, like '*Michael must be old*': a translation expresses the meaning,
but may not reflect the order or number of words and morphemes in the
data.

SLQ Zapotec allows some freedom of word order in sentences like (57),
so that any of the three words in the sentence may appear initially. In each

SIDEBAR 2.10

English -'s

> This is a guy that I had a very pleasant time working with's form of grief about me not working with him any more.
> Val Kilmer, *Los Angeles Times*, Calendar, p. 6, April 3, 1997

Most English possessed noun phrases include the morpheme -s attached to the possessor or **genitive** word or phrase, more than one of which may occur in a series:

Bianca's schoolmaster
my father's dagger
Love's Labour's Lost
your friend's mother's dog's collar . . .

In these examples, -s (which in English is written with a preceding apostrophe) always follows the actual noun that names the possessor. Thus, it seems parallel to the homophonous English plural suffix -s (which is written without an apostrophe):

schoolmasters
fathers
dogs

But in more complicated genitive expressions, when the possessor is followed by a modifying phrase, 's may follow a word that is not the possessor. In the following example, the possessor is the *King*, but 's follows the whole phrase

King of England:
the King of England's subjects (*King John*, II, i, 267)

When the modifying phrase after a noun is a **relative clause**, the morpheme 's may follow a word of almost any class – a verb, an adverb, a pronoun, or an adjective (or a preposition, as in the Kilmer quote above, which could also be stated as 'this is the form of grief about me not working with him any more of a guy that I had a very pleasant time working with')!:

the girl I saw's flowers
the girl I saw yesterday's flowers
the girl who helped me's flowers
the girl who was helpful's flowers

Such genitive phrases are often regarded as 'awkward' in written English, but they are extremely common in speech (listen for them!).

These examples show that genitive -'s is used differently from plural -s. The plural of *King of England* is not **King of Englands*, but *Kings of England*. To make phrases like *girl I saw, girl we were talking about*, or *girl who helped me* plural, you add -s to *girl* (*girls I saw, girls who helped me*). The plural -s does not go at the end of the whole phrase, so no one would say, for example,

*But there were two girl I saw yesterdays!

Despite their similarity, plural -s is a suffix (attaching only to words of a single lexical class, nouns), while genitive -'s is a clitic, since it attaches to whatever word is at the end of a possessive noun phrase. However, both -s morphemes are bound, since they must attach to a preceding word, and cannot be pronounced by themselves.

As noted in the text, English contractions like 's (for *is* or *has*) are clitics, just as genitive 's is. How many other English contractions can you think of? Choose one of them and construct examples like those in Sidebar 2.10 to show that it may follow words of different lexical classes.

EXERCISE 2.22

---

case, the clitic -*zhyi'* follows the first element:

(58)   Gyeeihlly-zhyi' nàa banguual.
        Nàa-zhyi' Gyeeihlly banguual.

We can identify -*zhyi'* as a clitic rather than a suffix because of where it is attached in the sentence. In these examples, -*zhyi'* follows either an adjective (*banguual*), a noun (the proper-noun subject *Gyeeihlly*), or a verb (*nàa*). Its position is determined not by the class of the preceding word, but by the word order of the sentence as a whole.

Although words with clitics attached can be seen as complete phonological words, they must be distinguished from lexical words of the type considered earlier in this chapter. Words like English *king's* or SQL Zapotec *banguualzhyi'* would not be listed in a dictionary of either language, for example.

2.8.2   The lexicon

Speakers of any language have the knowledge to produce an infinite number of sentences, as was discussed in the first chapter, and will be further discussed in the following chapters on syntax. We've seen many examples in this chapter of how words are built up by adding morphemes to roots. However, no language contains an infinite number of words. Unlike sentence structure, word structure is restricted: each language has a limited (though sometimes quite large!) number of grammatical morphemes, and a given grammatical morpheme usually occurs only once per word.

Each speaker's lexicon includes all the root words he or she knows – nouns, verbs, adjectives, and so on – plus the **productive** inflectional and derivational grammatical morphemes that the speaker knows how to add to these root words. For a language like English, it would be feasible to list all the separate lexical words in a given speaker's lexicon: the number of root words each speaker knows is quite large – about 60,000 for the average person – but each word has only a limited number of inflected forms, as we saw in Part I. (However, see Sidebar 2.10.)

Unlike English, many languages have such a large number of productively formed words (particularly verbs) that it would not be reasonable to expect all of them to be listed in the dictionary. For instance, we have already seen that verbs in SLQ Zapotec are extremely complicated. Examples (25) and (26) above illustrated SLQ Zapotec formal versus reverential subject verb forms: in fact, there are six different third-person singular verb forms in SLQ Zapotec, varying according to formality and distance. A Zapotec speaker selects the form that is most appropriate in a given context. There are two second-person singular forms (formal versus informal, as in many European languages) and one first-person singular form, making a total of nine singular subject forms of any given verb, with a corresponding number of plural forms. A nineteenth **unmarked** form is used when a verb's subject is a question word like 'who' or a noun like 'the man'. Here is a complete paradigm of the habitual verb *r-guèe'ez*, 'hugs':

(59) r-guèe'ez   'hugs . . .' (unmarked)
      r-guèe'ez-a'   'I hug . . .'
      r-guèe'ez-yuu'   'you (singular formal) hug . . .'
      r-guèe'ez-ùu'   'you (singular informal) hug . . .'
      r-guèe'ez-iny   'he (reverential) hugs . . .'
      r-rguè'ez-ëb   'he (formal) hugs . . .'
      r-guèe'ez-ahzh: 'he (respectful) hugs . . .'
      r-guèe'ez-ëng   'he (proximate) hugs . . .'
      r-guèe'ez-ih   'he (distal) hugs . . .'
      r-guèe'ez-ëmm   'he (animal) hugs . . .'
      r-guèe'ez-ënn   'we hug . . .'
      r-guèe'ez-yud   'you (plural formal) hug . . .'
      r-guèe'ez-ad   'you (plural informal) hug . . .'
      r-guèe'ez-riny   'they (reverential) hug . . .'
      r-guèe'ez-rëb   'they (formal) hug . . .'
      r-guèe'ez-rahzh: 'they (respectful) hug . . .'
      r-guèe'ez-rëng   'they (proximate) hug . . .'
      r-guèe'ez-rih   'they (distal) hug . . .'
      r-guèe'ez-rëmm   'they (animal) hug . . .'

In comparison with the 19 different forms in (59), English present tense verbs have only two different forms (*hug* and *hugs*, for instance); the most irregular English verb has only three (*am*, *is*, *are*). Although some European languages logically distinguish as many as ten forms, these are never fully differentiated from each other. But the complexity of SLQ Zapotec verbs does not end with the differentiation of subjects shown in (59). Zapotec verbs also have separate forms for six different verb aspects (somewhat like tenses) such as the habitual (shown by the *r-* prefixes on the verbs in (59)). In addition, there are a large number of adverbial and other suffixes that may appear following a verb stem, before any subject suffix, such as *-ag*, 'still', in (60):

(60)   R-guèe'ez-ag-a'   'I still hug . . .'

If we assume that there are 20 of these suffixes, we can calculate that a given SLQ Zapotec verb has at least 19 (subject forms) × 6 (aspects) × 21 (1 unsuffixed and 20 adverbially suffixed forms), giving a total of 2394 separate words derived from any single verb. There are at least three reasons why this is not an accurate figure: there are probably considerably more adverbial suffixes, not all adverbial suffixes may make sense when combined with each verb, and combinations of two or more adverbial suffixes are often possible. Many standard desk dictionaries of English list 80,000 words. This number could be easily reached in SLQ Zapotec simply by listing the derivatives of no more than 40 verbs! This example shows clearly that it is not feasible to list all the words in certain languages in a dictionary (see Sidebar 2.11).

2.9 Problems in Morphological Analysis

2.9.1 Zero morphemes and unmarked forms

Consider the following Tolkapaya and Chickasaw sentences, which have similar translations and somewhat similar morphology:

(60)

	Tolkapaya	Chickasaw
'I am tall.'	'-kyúl-ma.	Sa-chaaha.
'You are tall.'	M-kyúl-ma.	Chi-chaaha.
'He is tall,' 'She is tall.'	Kyúl-ma.	Chaaha.

These Tolkapaya and Chickasaw sentences use morphemes that have been exemplified earlier in this chapter. The Chickasaw 'I' and 'you' subject prefixes *sa-* and *chi-* seem comparable to the Tolkapaya prefixes '- (the glottal stop sound) and *m-*. In each case, the 'he'/'she' subject form has no prefix.

SIDEBAR 2.11

What words appear in the dictionary?

It is claimed in the text that it would be feasible to list all the separate lexical words in an English speaker's lexicon. In fact, if you look at a good dictionary, you'll see that even regularly formed derived words, such as noun plurals, adjectival comparative and superlative forms, and verb past, present participle, and past participle forms, are listed along with their roots, and even a small dictionary will list irregular or suppletive forms such as *children*, *better*, or *were*. So English dictionaries do a good job of listing a very large percentage of the vocabulary used by speakers.

Printed dictionaries are not the same as speakers' mental lexicons, however. A dictionary is unlikely to reflect a particular speaker's lexical knowledge, since few speakers are familiar with every word listed in the dictionary, and all speakers know many words that do not appear in the dictionary – technical vocabulary or **jargon**, slang expressions, personal names, and so on.

There are several large classes of derived words that do not appear in an English dictionary. For example, genitive -*'s* can appear following many English words that are not nouns, like those in the possessive phrases in Sidebar 2.10. But words containing this clitic, like *Bianca's*, *saw's*, *about's*, *yesterday's*, *me's*, and *helpful's* do not appear in the dictionary. Contracted forms like *he's* do not appear in the dictionary, either (though irregular contracted forms like *ain't* are listed). Finally, plurals of words other than nouns, such as *if*, *were*, *but*, or *proud*, are not listed, even though all speakers say things like the following on occasion:

He uses too many ifs.
There are too many weres in this sentence.
But me no buts.
Proud me no prouds.   (*Romeo and Juliet*, III, v, 152)

Neither the dictionaries we buy in bookstores nor our mental lexicons need to list such words since our mental grammars, as discussed in chapter 1, include the rules for word formation. No dictionary of English accurately reflects any speaker's lexicon. And English is a language with relatively little morphological complexity, compared with Tolkapaya Yavapai, Swahili, or SLQ Zapotec – dictionaries of languages like those can only list a tiny proportion of the words a speaker knows and uses, since in those languages words are often comparable to English sentences.

The mental lexicon is more complex than a simple listing of words with their pronunciations and meanings. Through the work of psycholinguists, who study speech production and comprehension, and neurolinguists who have studied language deficits after brain damage (aphasia), we have learned a great deal about the ways in which lexical and grammatical morphemes and words are represented.

As suggested earlier, the unprefixed 'he'/'she' forms in languages like Tolkapaya and Chickasaw could be analyzed in two different ways:

- On one hand, we could say that there is a 'he'/'she' zero morpheme: a prefix *0-* (zero) corresponds to the **overt** (physically present) prefixes '-, *m-*, *sa-*, and *chi-* to indicate a third-person singular subject on these verbs; in Tolkapaya and Chickasaw these zero prefixes mean third-person singular in just the same way that '- and *sa-* respectively mean first-person singular.
- On the other hand, we could say that verbs like the 'he'/'she' subject forms in (53) are simply **unmarked**; they contain no marking relative to subject at all. We could claim further that in contexts like the sentences above an unmarked Tolkapaya or Chickasaw verb (in the absence of other subject marking) is interpreted as having a third-person singular subject.

When we considered three different possible analyses of Tolkapaya absolutive verb forms above (section 2.4), we concluded that choosing among them depended more on the theoretical assumptions of the analyst than the empirical facts of the language. It might seem that there is not too much difference between the two approaches to the Tolkapaya and Chickasaw zero morpheme question either, but this is not the case. Often other aspects of the language provide evidence as to which of two analyses is superior.

For example, let's consider 'want to' sentences in these two languages. Here are some 'want to be tall' sentences in Tolkapaya:

(61) '-kyúl-a '-'í-ma.   'I want to be tall.'
      M-kyúl-a m-í-ma.   'You want to be tall.'
      Kyúl-a 'í-ma.   'He wants to be tall,' 'She wants to be tall.'

The Tolkapaya verb meaning 'want' here is '*í*, which in the sentences above is used with the same *-ma* ending used on other verbs in examples in section 2.3. (This verb is irregular: 'you want' is *m-í-ma*, not **m-'í-ma* as you would expect on the basis of earlier Tolkapaya data.) The 'to be tall' parts of these sentences use the same *kyúl-* 'be tall' verb you saw in (60), with an ending *-a*. What may seem unusual about these sentences is that the first verb in each of the sentences in (61) is marked for the same subject as the verb 'want', almost as though in English we said something like 'I want for me to be tall'.

Now let's look at comparable sentences in Chickasaw:

(63)   Chaaha sa-banna.   'I want to be tall.'
      Chaaha chi-banna.   'You want to be tall.'
      Chaaha banna.   'He wants to be tall,' 'She wants to be tall.'

Just as in Tolkapaya, these sentences contain a 'be tall' verb followed by a 'want' verb, and the 'want' verb has the expected subject markings. But in Chickasaw the 'be tall' verb is unmarked each time – it contains no subject prefix, even when it refers to a first- or second-person subject doing the wanting. This is comparable to English (since in English each of the sentences contains the same phrase, 'to be tall', regardless of who the hearer will interpret this phrase as referring to), but different from Tolkapaya, in which each 'to be tall' is marked for subject in the regular way.

   This simple example shows that third-person subject forms like those in (61) have a different analysis in the two languages:

- In Tolkapaya, every time a verb has no other subject prefix, in every sentence type, it is interpreted as having a third-person subject. Thus, the lack of a prefix is entirely comparable with the presence of a subject prefix like '- and *m-*, so it would certainly make sense to analyze this prefix as a true zero morpheme marking third person.
- In Chickasaw, different sentence types work differently. In a **simple sentence** with only one verb, like those in (61), an unmarked verb (one with no other subject prefix) is interpreted as having a third-person subject. In many types of **complex sentence** (with more than one verb), such as the 'want' sentences in (63), however, an unmarked Chickasaw verb may not be interpreted as having a 'he' or 'she' subject. Thus, unmarked Chickasaw verbs are interpreted differently according to the sentences they are used in, and do not contain a third-person zero subject prefix.

EXERCISE 2.23

Consider the following Tolkapaya and Chickasaw imperative sentences, using verbs you have seen earlier in this chapter.

Tolkapaya	*Mchthúli!*	'Wash it!'
	Mvyámi!	'Run!'
	Mthíi!	'Drink it!'
Chickasaw	*Isso!*	'Hit it!'
	Afama!	'Meet him!'
	Hilha!	'Dance!'

First, analyze these sentences into morphemes, with a complete gloss for each sentence (if necessary, review the Tolkapaya and Chickasaw data presented earlier).

(a)   See if you can construct an additional argument concerning the question of whether these languages have third-person zero subject prefixes, based on this data.

(b)   Given the 'want' sentences and the imperatives that you have seen, which language, Tolkapaya or Chickasaw, is more like English? Explain why.

2.9.2   Discontinuous morphemes

Another difficult problem in morphological analysis concerns **discontinuous morphemes** – morphemes that appear to represent a single meaning, but which occur separated from each other by other elements of a word. Discontinuous lexical morphemes occur whenever single lexical morphemes have affixes infixed into them, as we saw with the Tagalog infix *um* in (43) above. Lexical morphemes like *hiwalay* and *bili* can be separated by the infix *um* in words like those in the third column of (64). (Commas are used to separate the infix from the morpheme into which it is infixed.)

(64) |hiwalay| *mag-hiwalay*   'separate from   *h,um,iwalay*   'separate
                                                              each other'   from'
          |bili| *mag-bili*   'sell'   *b,um,ili*   'buy'

There is no evidence for segmenting *h-* and *-iwalay* or *b-* and *-ili* as separate morphemes. The lexical roots of words like *h,um,iwalay* and *b,um,ili,* are discontinuous.

Another example of morphemes that are sometimes discontinuous comes from La Huerta Diegueño (a Yuman language related to Tolkapaya Yavapai, spoken in Baja California, Mexico; as with Tolkapaya, speakers of La Huerta add extra vowels when pronouncing words like those written here):

(65)   *Miny.*   'You give it to   *Mshmay.*   'You look for him.'
                           him.'
          Kiny!   'Give it to him!'   *Kshmay!*   'Look for him!'
          Nym'iny.   'You give it   *Nymsh'may.*   'You look for me.'
                           to me.'
          Nyk'iny!   'Give it to me!'   *Nyksh'may!*   'Look for me!'
          Ny'iny.   'He gives it   *Nysh'may.*   'He looks for me.'
                           to me.'

The recurrent element in each sentence in the first column is *iny*; we can tentatively identify this as meaning 'give it to'. The second column contains a discontinuous recurrent element, *sh . . . may* – in the first three

SIDEBAR 2.12

Discontinuous morphemes in Semitic languages

The languages of the Semitic family of the Middle East are famous for having a unique type of morphological structure in which verb and noun roots appear discontinuous in most words. Here are some examples of selected verb forms from Egyptian Arabic (the symbol ʕ represents a sound called a voiced pharyngeal fricative).

katab 'he wrote'	daras 'he studied'	ʕamal 'he did'	naʔal 'he copied'
baktib 'I write'	badris 'I study'	baʕmil 'I do'	banʔil 'I copied'
iktib 'write!'	idris 'study!'	iʕmil 'do!'	inʔil 'copy!'
kaatib 'writer'	daaris 'studier'	ʕaamil 'doer'	naaʔil 'copier'
maktuub 'written'	madruus 'studied'	maʕmuul 'done'	manʔuul 'copied'

Study the forms above and see if you can see what determines the meaning in each case, before you read on.

Semitic languages have what are called **triliteral roots**: verb and noun roots consisting of three consonants. We might write the Egyptian Arabic root for 'write' as *k-t-b* or *ktb* or, since it clearly sometimes involves discontinuous elements, as *k . . . t . . . b*. As you can see, the root for 'study' is *d-r-s* and the root for 'do' is *ʕ-m-l*. What is the root for 'copy'?

Grammatical morphemes in Egyptian Arabic (and other Semitic languages) are often discontinuous as well. Sometimes they are analyzed as patterns of vowels and occasionally other consonants which are infixed into the root. For example, the perfective third-person masculine singular pattern (seen in the first line above) is *— a — a —* (where the dashes indicate the position of the consonants of the root), the imperfective first-person singular pattern (in the second line) is *ba — — i —*, and the imperative pattern (in the third line) is *i — — i —*. See if you can isolate the active participle and passive participle patterns in the fourth and fifth lines.

---

sentences, we see *shmay*, while the second has *sh'may*, with an infixed glottal stop. We can identify *sh . . . may* as meaning 'look for'. (Discontinuous morphemes are often written with an ellipsis, . . . , between the parts.)

Making a chart is a good way to analyze the remaining morphemes. Organizing the data this way helps identify meanings with sounds. Each sentence with a 'you' subject (the first and third in each column) contains a prefix *m-*, so we can identify the prefix *m-* as meaning 'you' (subject). Each imperative (command, the second and fourth in each column) contains a prefix *k-*, so we can identify *k-* as an imperative prefix. Each 'me' object sentence contains *ny* and *'*, in that order. It thus makes sense to identify *ny . . . '-* as a usually discontinuous morpheme meaning 'me' (object). If the verb following this morpheme is longer than a single consonant–vowel–consonant syllable, the *'* of this prefix is infixed after the

Table 2.4 Analyzing La Huerta Diegueño verb prefixes

RECURRENT MEANING	FORMS WITH THIS MEANING	RECURRENT ELEMENT
first-person subject	*miny, nym'iny; mshmay, nymsh'may*	*m*
imperative	*kiny, nyk'iny; kshmay, nyksh'may*	*k*
first-person object	*nym'iny, nyk'iny, ny'iny; nymsh'may,* *nyksh'may, nysh'may*	*ny . . . '*

first consonant of that verb. If the verb is shorter, the ' is infixed after the first following prefix, if there is one; if there is no prefix, the ' follows the *ny*. Thus, the combination

(66) ny . . . ' + k + shmay

(with a relatively long verb, *shmay*) becomes

(67) nyksh'may

(the glottal stop is infixed following the first consonant, *sh*, of the verb stem – the letter combination *sh* is considered one consonant because it represents a single sound), while the combination

(68) ny . . . ' + k + iny

(with a very short verb, iny) becomes

(69) nyk'iny

(the glottal stop is infixed following the imperative prefix). When this infixation occurs in a word like *nyk'iny*, the two parts of the prefix *ny . . . '* are separated by the prefix *k*, and when the infixation occurs in a word like *nyksh'may*, both the prefix and the verb are discontinuous.

The Semitic family of languages is famous because each verb can be analyzed as a discontinuous morpheme (see Sidebar 2.12).

2.10 Morphology and Typology

The morphological structure of words often mimics that of sentences. We've seen that in polysynthetic languages a single word can express the idea of a whole sentence. Often the order of morphemes in a word is parallel to that used in a sentence.

In English, the basic order of the major sentence elements or consti-tuents, **subject**, **verb**, and **object**, is just that – for example, in a sentence like

(70)   Othello married Desdemona.

the subject is *Othello*, the verb is *married*, and the object is *Desdemona*. Even in a longer or more complicated sentence the same basic order is used. In the first sentence of (71), the object is the phrase *no debts*; in the second, the subject is *the very rats* and the verb is the phrase *instinctively have quit*:

(71)   Words pay no debts. (*Troilus and Cressida*, III, ii, 56)
       The very rats instinctively have quit it. (*The Tempest*, I, ii, 147)

Linguists refer to this subject, verb, object order as **SVO**. The order of these elements in a language is generally called that language's **word order** or **basic word order** – but it could more properly be called 'phrase order' or 'constituent order.' The study of the relationships between basic word order and other linguistic phenomena is a major concern of the branch of linguistics known as **typology**.

Languages use a variety of basic word orders. The English order, SVO, is one of the most common; the other two common orders are **SOV** and **VSO**. We've seen a number of one-word sentences from the Muskogean language Chickasaw in this chapter. In Chickasaw, the basic word order is SOV, as in

(72)   Hattakat   chipota shoo-tok.   'The person hugged the child.'
       person-subj child   hug-past

Here, the subject *hattak* (*hattak-at* includes a suffix specifying that that word is a subject) comes before the object, *chipota*, which in turn precedes the verb, *shoo-tok*.

In San Lucas Quiaviní Zapotec, the basic word order is VSO:

(73)   B-guèe'ez bùunny mnìi'iny.   'The person hugged the child.'
       perf-hug   person child

Here, the perfective verb *b-guèe'ez* comes first, followed by the subject *bùunny* and the object *mnìi'iny*.

Both Chickasaw and SLQ Zapotec are polysynthetic, in that they can express many full sentences in a single verb word. Look at the order of the morphemes in these single-word sentences:

(74) Is-sa-shoo-tok.   'You hugged me.'
      you-me-hug-perf

(75) B-guèe'ez-ùu'-ng.   'You hugged him.'
      perf-hug-you-him

In the one-word Chickasaw sentence (74), the morpheme indicating the subject comes first, next the morpheme indicating the subject, and finally the morpheme indicating the verb – exactly paralleling the word order in the full SOV sentence (72). In SLQ Zapotec there is a similar parallelism: following the VSO order in the full sentence (73), in the one-word sentence (74), the verb morpheme comes first, followed by the subject morpheme, with the object morpheme last.

The same types of hierarchical structure that you have seen in words are reflected in sentence structure, as you will see in the next chapters.

The parallelism between the order of subject, object, and verb morphemes in a complex word and the order of these elements in a sentence is not always as complete as in Chickasaw and SLQ Zapotec. For example, Tolkapaya has SOV word order, and Swahili has SVO word order. What order do the subject, object, and verb elements of polysynthetic words in these languages come in? (Look back at the templates you devised in Exercise 2.8.) Are these cases parallel?	**EXERCISE 2.24**

2.11 Summary

Morphology is the study – and analysis – of words and their structure. As this chapter has demonstrated, some words have a very simple structure, consisting only of a single morpheme or unit of meaning, while others have a complex structure, containing more morphemes and sometimes reflecting complicated formation processes. The formation of words follows regular rules, which speakers learn as part of their acquisition of language. The structure of words is hierarchical.

Words themselves are arranged into larger phrases and sentences (as exemplified in the last section). The study of these larger units of language is syntax.

Further reading

Anderson, Stephen R. 1992. *A-Morphous Morphology*. Cambridge: Cambridge University Press.

Aronoff, Mark. 1976. *Word Formation in Generative Grammar*. Cambridge, MA: MIT Press.

—— 1993. *Morphology by Itself: Stems and Inflectional Classes. Linguistic Inquiry Monograph, no. 22*. Cambridge, MA: MIT Press.

Bauer, Laurie. 1983. *English Word-Formation*. Cambridge: Cambridge University Press.

Di Sciullo, A.-M. and Williams, E. 1987. *On the Definition of Word*. Cambridge, MA: MIT Press.

Hammond, Michael and Noonan, Michael, eds. 1988. *Theoretical Morphology: Approaches in Modern Linguistics*. San Diego: Academic Press, Inc.

Jensen, John T. 1990. *Morphology: Word Structure in Generative Grammar*. Amsterdam/Philadelphia: John Benjamins Publishing.

Marchand, Hans. 1969. *The Categories and Types of Present-Day English Word-Formation*, 2nd edn. Munich: C. H. Beck'sche Verlagsbuchhandlung.

Matthews, P. H. 1991. *Morphology: An Introduction to the Theory of Word Structure*. Cambridge: Cambridge University Press.

Scalise, Sergio. 1984. *Generative Morphology*. Dordrecht, Holland/Cinnaminson, USA: Foris Publications.

Selkirk, E. 1982. *The Syntax of Words*. Cambridge, MA: MIT Press.

Spencer, Andrew. 1991. *Morphological Theory*. Oxford: Blackwell.

References on languages cited

Chickasaw

Munro, Pamela and Catherine Willmond. 1994. *Chickasaw: An Analytical Dictionary*. Norman, OK, and London: University of Oklahoma Press.

Egyptian Arabic

Abdel-Massih, Ernest T. 1975. *An Introduction to Egyptian Arabic*. Ann Arbor, MI: Center for Near Eastern and North African Studies, University of Michigan.

Ineseño Chumash

Applegate, Richard Brian. 1972. *Ineseño Chumash Grammar*. Ph.D. dissertation, University of California, Berkeley.

La Huerta Diegueño

Hinton, Leanne and Margaret Langdon. 1976. Object-Subject Pronominal Prefixes in La Huerta Diegueño. In Margaret Langdon and Shirley Silver, eds., *Hokan Studies* (Janua Linguarum, Series Practica, 181), pp. 113–28. The Hague–Paris: Mouton.

San Lucas Quiaviní Zapotec

Munro, Pamela and Lopez, Felipe H., et al. 1999. *Di'csyonaary X:tèe'n Dìi'zh Sah Sann Lu'uc (San Lucas Quiaviní Zapotec Dictionary/ Diccionario Zapoteco de San Lucas Quiaviní)*. Los Angeles: UCLA Chicano Studies Research Center Publications.

Southern Paiute

Sapir, Edward. 1930–1. *The Southern Paiute Language. Proceedings of the American Academy of Arts and Sciences*, vol. 65.

Tagalog

Schachter, Paul and Fe T. Otanes. 1972. *Tagalog Reference Grammar*. Berkeley, Los Angeles, and London: University of California Press.

Tolkapaya Yavapai

Munro, Pamela and Molly Star Fasthorse. In preparation. *Tolkapaya*.

Consider the following sentences from Shakespeare. Segment each one into morphemes, and then identify each morpheme as a prefix, suffix, clitic, or root and as a grammatical or lexical morpheme. Underline each root (independent word) that you would consider a grammatical morpheme. Identify each grammatical prefix or suffix as inflectional or derivational, give another word containing the same morpheme, and do your best to identify the meaning of the morpheme. Discuss each word with an irregular pronunciation and each clitic that you identify. Note any compounds. Tell what (expected) component morphemes you would expect to find in any morphemes you can identify as portmanteau.

EXERCISES

Exercise 2.25

> They have been at a great feast of languages, and stolen the scraps.
>
> (*Love's Labour's Lost*, V, i, 39)

> All the world's a stage, and all the men and women merely players.
>
> (*As You Like It*, II, vii, 139)

> As the old hermit of Prague, that never saw pen and ink, very wittily said to a niece of King Gorboduc, "That that is, is." (*Twelfth Night*, IV, ii, 14)

> How silver-sweet sound lovers' tongues by night, Like softest music to attending ears!
>
> (*Romeo and Juliet*, II, ii, 165)

> I have done a thousand dreadful things, As willingly as one would kill a fly.
>
> (*Titus Andronicus*, V, i, 141)

> Kindness in women, not their beauteous looks, Shall win my love.
>
> (*The Taming of the Shrew*, IV, ii, 41)

> Let's choose executors and talk of wills. (*Richard II*, III, ii, 144)

> Love, first learned in a lady's eyes, Lives not alone immured in the brain.
>
> (*Love's Labour's Lost*, IV, iii, 327)

. . . .

Unlike most of the languages illustrated in this chapter, Spanish grammar identifies every noun phrase as either masculine or feminine.

Exercise 2.26

(a) Segment each word of each Spanish noun phrase below into morphemes, and identify the meaning (or function) of each morpheme by writing a gloss underneath each phrase. (You can regard 'some' as the plural of 'a'/'an'.) Remember that the number of morphemes, hyphens, and spaces in your segmented data and your gloss must match exactly.

el perro negro	'the black (male) dog'
el palo nuevo	'the new stick'
la casa blanca	'the white house'
las mesas negras	'the black tables'
las perras rojas	'the red (female) dogs'
los libros viejos	'the old books'
un libro nuevo	'an old book'
una mesa blanca	'a white table'
una perra vieja	'an old (female) dog'
unas casas rojas	'some red houses'
unos palos negros	'some black sticks'
unos perros blancos	'some white (male) dogs'

(b) The general pattern of masculine versus feminine morphemes is very regular, but there are irregularities. Discuss them.

(c) Notice that the order of adjectives and nouns differs between English and Spanish. Translate the following into Spanish: 'the red sticks', 'an old house', 'some white (female) dogs', 'the white book', 'a red (male) dog'.

Note: Lack of knowledge of Spanish is no disadvantage! If you speak Spanish, you will probably find this exercise easiest if you try to approach it as you would completely new data (perhaps from Swahili or Zapotec).

. . . .

Exercise 2.27 Consider the following examples of Chickasaw verbs with and without 'me', 'you', and 'us' objects, and then answer the questions that follow.

pisa 'see'	*sapisa* 'he sees me'
	chipisa 'he sees you'
	popisa 'he sees us'
ithána 'know'	*sathána* 'he knows me'
	chithána 'he knows you'
	pothána 'he knows us'
lohmi 'hide'	*salohmi* 'he hides me'
	chilohmi 'he hides you'
	polohmi 'he hides us'
afama 'meet'	*asafama* 'he meets me'
	achifama 'he meets you'
	apofama 'he meets us'
chokfiyammi 'tickle'	*sachokfiyammi* 'he tickles me'
	chichokfiyammi 'he tickles you'
isso 'hit'	*chisso* 'he hits you'
	posso 'he hits us'
anokfilli 'think about'	*asanokfilli* 'he thinks about me'
	aponokfilli 'he thinks about us'

(a) Segment each Chickasaw word by putting hyphens between the morphemes. (You may change your mind about some of the segmentations as you work through the problem.)

(b) What are the Chickasaw first-person singular and plural and second-person object affixes?

(c) What is the Chickasaw for 'he tickles us', 'he hits me', and 'he thinks about you'?

(d) *Ipita* means 'feed' in Chickasaw. How would you say 'he feeds me', 'he feeds you', and 'he feeds us'? Give as general an explanation as you can of what happens when the prefixes are attached to these words.

(e) *Apila* means 'help' in Chickasaw. How would you say 'he helps me', 'he helps you', and 'he helps us'? Give as general an explanation as you can of what happens when the prefixes are attached to these words.

(f) Someone proposes that in the formation of a word like *Chisso*, 'He hits you', from *chi-+isso*, the *i* of the *chi* prefix is deleted. This account makes sense for this word, but is not consistent with the rest of the data. Present an argument against it.

(g) Someone proposes that in the formation of a word like *Asafama*, 'He meets me', from *sa-+afama*, the *s* and *a* of the prefix are transposed (undergoing **metathesis**), becoming *as*. This account makes sense for this word, but is not consistent with the rest of the data. Present an argument against it.

. . . .

Consider the following sentences from Ineseño Chumash, a language of the **Exercise 2.28** Chumash family formerly spoken north of Santa Barbara, California. (In the Chumash orthography used here, a consonant followed by ' represents a single consonant sound. *ï* represents a vowel sound that does not occur in English.)

Stelmemen.	'He touches it.'
Noktelmemen.	'I will touch it.'
Nosiytelmemen.	'They will touch it.'
Nokc'imutelew.	'I will bite it.'
Kiyc'imutelew.	'We bite it.'
Sxiliwayan.	'It floats.'
Nokiyxiliwayan.	'We will float.'

(a) Begin by segmenting the morphemes that appear in the data above. Identify the Ineseño lexical and grammatical morphemes used here. How many morphemes can occur in a single Ineseño word? Make a template (as in (20) and Exercise 2.8) to show what order they occur in. Put parentheses around the elements in the template that are not required parts of such Ineseño words.

(b) Translate the following Ineseño sentences into English:

Ktelmemen; Sc'imutelew; Nosiyc'imutelew; Kiyxiliwayan; Nokxiliwayan.

Here are some examples of Ineseño sentences in which reduplication is used:

Nosiyteltelmemen.	'They will grope around for it.'
Kteltelmemen.	'I grope around for it.'
Sc'imc'imutelew.	'He nibbles it.'
Nokxilxiliwayan.	'I will float around.'

(c) What is the semantic effect of reduplication in Ineseño? Is Ineseño reduplication partial or complete? Is it regular or irregular? Describe the Ineseño reduplication process, making reference to the template you developed in (a).

(d) *Kxuniyïw* means 'I look for it'. How would you translate 'They look all over for it'? *Sk'ilitap* means 'He comes in'. How would you translate 'We will push in all over (We will intrude)'?

Now consider these additional sentences:

Salimexkeken.	'He stretches it out.'
Nokalkalimexkeken.	'I will stretch it out all over.'
Seqwel.	'He does it.'
Keqkeqwel.	'I do it all around.'
Nosiysiyeqwel.	'They will do it all around.'

(e) Translate these sentences into Ineseño: 'I do it'; 'He will do it all around'; 'We do it all around'; 'He stretches it out all over'; 'We will stretch it out'; 'We stretch it out all over'.

(f) The new data may require you to modify the description of Ineseño reduplication you developed in (c) above. Explain any changes you need to make.

· ·

Exercise 2.29 Read Sidebar 2.12, and then consider the following additional Egyptian Arabic verbs.

daxal 'he entered'	*sakan* 'he lived in'
badxul 'I enter'	*baskun* 'I live in'
udxul! 'enter!'	*uskun!* 'live in!'
daaxil 'enterer'	*saakin* 'liver in'
madxuul 'entered'	*maskuum* 'lived in'

(a) Verbs like these represent a different class of verbs from the ones illustrated in Sidebar 2.12. Explain how they are different, in terms of specific contrasts in their patterns of grammatical morphemes.

(b) *Na'ash* means 'he carved' (*sh* represents a single consonant sound, like the *sh* of English *she*), and *nashar* means 'he sewed'. These verbs work like the two verbs given earlier in this exercise. Tell how to say 'I carve', 'carve!', 'carver', and 'carved'; 'I sew', 'sew!', 'sewer' ('one who sews'), and 'sewn'.

(c) The normal form of an Arabic verb that is listed in dictionaries and cited by grammarians is the third-person singular masculine perfective (the first verb in each column of verbs above and in Sidebar 2.12). Is this the most basic form, of those listed, from which (given knowledge of possible patterns of grammatical morphemes) all other forms can be predicted? (If you think it is the most basic form, show how the other forms can be predicted from it; if you think that it is not, nominate another form that is more basic.)

(d) *Biyiktib* means 'he writes', *biyudxul* means 'he enters'. Give the equivalent third-person singular masculine imperfective form for each of the six other verbs given here and in Sidebar 2.12.

3

Syntax I: Argument Structure and Phrase Structure

3.0 Introduction

In chapter 2, we saw that words are composed of smaller units, called morphemes, and that languages contain rules of morphology specifying how morphemes may be combined with each other to form grammatical words. In this chapter, we will see how words are combined with each other to form grammatical sentences in a similar rule-governed way.

3.1   Syntactic Data and Syntactic Rules

3.1.1   Grammars and grammaticality

If a sequence of words does not form a grammatical sentence, we indicate this fact by placing a star (*) in front of it, as discussed in chapter 1.

(1)   a.   Desdemona will marry a Moor.
      b.   Macbeth has killed the king.

(2)   a.   *Marry will Moor a Desdemona.
      b.   *Killed the Macbeth has king.

To account for the fact that only certain combinations of words produce acceptable sentences, linguists posit the existence of rules of **syntax** in the unconscious mental grammar, which specify how words may be combined with each other to produce grammatical, well-formed sentences. In this chapter, and in chapters 4 and 5, we will examine these rules, to see what they look like and how they interact with each other.

As discussed in chapter 1, the rules of syntax, together with all the other rules of one's language, constitute the **grammar** of the language. If a sequence of words forming a sentence is consistent with the rules of the grammar, we say that the sentence is **grammatical**; if not, the sequence of words is **ungrammatical**; that is, it does not form a grammatical sentence. The theory of syntax that we will present in this book is made up of **formal rules** – that is, rules that are formulated in a precise way, with clearly defined properties. If rules are not formalized it is difficult if not impossible to test the claims made by the linguist in describing the grammar that constitutes a speaker's linguistic competence. This precision also enables the grammar to define certain sentences as grammatical, and others as ungrammatical. If a grammar defines a sentence as being grammatical, we say that the grammar **generates** that sentence. Linguists refer to grammars of this type as **generative grammars**, and the field of study devoted to discovering their properties is known as the field of **generative grammar**.

The rules of the grammar are not obvious; they are part of speakers' unconscious knowledge of their language. Consequently, we do not know in advance what rules the grammar of a particular speaker consists of. In order to discover what the rules of the grammar are, we construct theories about them, and then evaluate these theories by comparing their predictions with empirical evidence. Thus, linguists test theories by gathering data from native speakers, to determine whether the hypothesized grammar makes correct predictions about the grammaticality of sentences. If the theory's predictions are borne out by some piece of data, then we say that this piece of data confirms the theory; but if it contradicts the predictions of the theory, then we describe it as a **counterexample**, because it provides **counterevidence** to the theory. In general, when we discover counterevidence to a theory, we attempt to revise the theory so that it can account for the new data. The attempt to discover the rules of grammar in this way is not unique to the science of linguistics. Just as the rules of grammar are hidden from view, so are the laws of nature. Physical scientists also construct theories that make predictions, and then test their theories and hypotheses by seeing if data confirm the predictions.

It is beyond the scope of this book to even come close to providing a comprehensive survey of the data that syntacticians attempt to account for, or to provide a complete review of the theories that they have developed; the number of possible sentences in every language is infinite, as discussed in chapter 1, and the number of theories that have been proposed to account for them is very large as well. We will be selective in our choice of data, seeking only to give a representative sample of the facts that syntacticians have discovered, and of the theories that they have posited to explain them. However, we will try to convey a general idea of how syntacticians conduct their research – how they decide what data to pay attention to, how they come up with theories, and how they look for new data to test these theories. At the same time, we will present some of the results of modern syntactic theory.

3.1.2   The nature of syntactic data

How do we know whether an example sentence is grammatical, that is, whether it conforms to the rules of the mental grammar? We rely on the observed behavior of native speakers. As noted above, speakers do not consciously know whether a sentence is grammatical, in the technical sense in which we use this word, because they do not consciously know what the rules of their grammar are. However, native speakers must know these rules unconsciously, because they behave in ways that can only be explained scientifically if we assume that these rules are represented in their minds in some form. By examining speakers' behavior, we can draw inferences about the nature of the rules that unconsciously direct or influence this behavior.

There are at least three types of behavior that native speakers exhibit that provide evidence about grammaticality. First, speakers produce utterances, in conversations with other speakers, or in other situations. Second, speakers understand utterances that other speakers produce, and they can usually explain what these utterances mean by paraphrasing them (using different combinations of words to convey the same ideas). Third, speakers can make intuitive judgments about whether an utterance sounds acceptable, or natural, to them. As a general rule of thumb, if a native speaker is observed to utter a sentence, or to understand a sentence that someone else produces, then it can usually be assumed that the sentence in question is grammatical. Such evidence is not absolutely definitive, however, because of the difference between linguistic knowledge (competence) and linguistic behavior (performance) discussed in chapter 1. We often speak in non-sentences, deviating from the intended grammatical sentence that we wish to produce; in such situations, other speakers can often figure out what we intended to say, even though the sentence was not fully grammatical. This is why speakers' judgments may be even more important than the actual utterances they produce; if a speaker reports that a sentence sounds natural and acceptable, then it is very likely that it is grammatical. On the other hand, if native speakers report that a sentence sounds unnatural or unacceptable, then we usually assume that the sentence is ungrammatical. Furthermore, when speakers produce ungrammatical sentences, which are often referred to as 'slips of the tongue' or speech errors, they may correct these utterances, revealing that they know what is grammatical and ungrammatical.

Syntacticians, like all linguists, rely on the two different types of scientific data discussed in chapter 1: **naturalistic** (naturally occurring) data, and **experimental** data (elicited in controlled experiments). The most common way of gathering experimental data from native speakers of a language is to present them with example sentences, and to study their reactions to these sentences. The linguist may ask these speakers to say whether a sentence sounds acceptable (natural) to them, or to compare two or more similar sentences and to rank them relative to each other in terms of acceptability. Alternatively, the linguist may ask the speakers to explain what they think an example sentence means, or to say whether it sounds more natural or appropriate in the context of a particular preceding conversation, as opposed to some other context. Finally, the linguist may present speakers with a sentence in a language such as English, and ask them to translate it into their native language. In eliciting data from native speakers in this way, the linguist is conducting a scientific experiment, since the linguist is not simply observing the speakers' behavior; rather, the linguist is presenting the native speaker with a stimulus, and then studying the speaker's response to this stimulus. Often, syntacticians who are studying their own native language rely in part on their own intuitions about acceptability, using themselves as a source of experimental data. It is of course advisable for such linguists to double-check their findings, by consulting other native speakers' judgments as well.

In general, when we identify an example sentence as ungrammatical, by placing a star (*) in front of it, we are stating that native speakers report that they judge this sequence of words not to be an acceptable sentence, and that we believe that their judgment is a result of the fact that the example sentence does not conform to the rules of their grammar.

Some linguists distrust the use of elicited data in the form of acceptability judgment tasks. These critics of elicited data state that many of the

Absolute versus comparative judgments

In judgment elicitation experiments, where subjects are asked to determine whether a string of words is acceptable as a sentence or not, subjects sometimes find it easy to respond with an **absolute judgment**. Thus, native speakers of English have no trouble in deciding the status of examples like (1) and (2) above. But in other cases, the task of judging whether a given sentence is 'good' or 'bad' is more difficult. For example, (a) has a questionable status; it is not a sentence that one is likely to hear, but most speakers, when asked, report that they do not find it *completely* unnatural or unacceptable:

(a) ?Which book was Oberon read to out of, without being enchanted by?

With complicated examples of this type, it is often easier for subjects to provide **comparative judgments**, indicating that one sentence, though not entirely natural, still sounds better than certain other sentences. Thus, most speakers will say that they find (a) to be more natural, or acceptable, than (b), but somewhat less natural, or acceptable, than (c):

(b) *Which book did Oberon read to out of, without enchanting by?

(c) Which book was Oberon reading out of, without being enchanted by it?

The question mark (?) preceding (a) is the conventional typographic means of representing a level of acceptability intermediate between the full acceptability of (c) and the complete unacceptability of (b). In general, fully acceptable examples are not preceded by any typographic mark of acceptability, though occasionally a check-mark (√) is used to indicate that a sentence is acceptable or grammatical.

Speakers are capable of drawing distinctions between many levels of grammaticality. For example, when presented with a list of five or six sentences, a speaker may be able to rank each of them on a scale relative to the others. Syntacticians often use combinations of stars and question marks to indicate these subtle distinctions in acceptability, such as ** (very unacceptable; even worse than an example marked with just one star), *? (almost unacceptable; worse than ? but better than *), ?? (marginal; worse than ?, but slightly better than *?), etc. These marks should be understood in comparative, rather than absolute, terms. Even speakers who report firm intuitions about comparative rankings in this way are often unable to provide such fine-grained judgments when a single sentence is given in isolation, and a sentence that they rank near the bottom of the scale in comparison with one set of sentences may get ranked closer to the top of the scale in comparison with another set of sentences. As a result of this, an example of marginal acceptability, such as (a), may be marked inconsistently in different contexts; when it is being compared with a fully ungrammatical sentence, it may be marked ?; but when it is being compared with a less marginal sentence, it may be marked ?? or ?*. These apparently inconsistent markings are not really contradictory; they simply reflect the fact that the marginal sentence is being compared with different examples in each case.

example sentences that syntacticians use as stimuli are seldom, if ever, observed in natural speech situations; they suggest that "only a syntactician would dream up data like these." Such linguists believe that syntactic theory should be based entirely on the observation of naturally occurring data, arguing that elicited judgments about artificially created example sentences should not count as evidence for or against specific hypotheses about the grammar of a language. They also raise objections when investigators make use of their own intuitions as a primary source of data, believing that this could create experimental bias; that is, syntacticians who use themselves as experimental subjects might consciously or unconsciously report intuitions that support the predictions of their own theories.

Syntacticians who defend the use of elicited judgment data point out that elicited judgments are sometimes the only way to get reliable negative evidence that a particular type of sentence is unacceptable (and therefore likely to be ungrammatical), since we cannot infer that a sentence-type is unacceptable just because we have not observed it being uttered. Defenders of elicited judgment data also point out that they are interested in speakers' reactions to certain types of marginal example sentences, even if such sentences seldom occur in natural speech. Insofar as one is constructing a theory about how knowledge of sentence structure is represented in the mind, evidence about how speakers react to complicated sentences is potentially relevant to a theory about the unconscious system of syntactic knowledge that underlies our use of simple sentences in naturalistic speech. Most syntacticians also defend the practice of using their own intuitions as a source of data, pointing out that linguists are often more reliable experimental subjects than 'naive' native speakers, who may sometimes confuse the notion of acceptability with the notion of what their grammar teachers have taught them is 'correct'. Naive speakers may also have other biases, such as the desire to impress or please the linguist. In other words, no experimental situation is totally immune from hidden biases, and a conscientious scientist must always attempt to avoid them, regardless of whose intuitions are being studied. Experimental bias is no more a problem to be guarded against in Linguistics than in any other experimental science. Despite the potential problems associated with the use of experimental data, they have proved to be invaluable in the discovery of syntactic rules and principles, and in testing particular syntactic theories.

3.2 Constituent Order, Case Marking, and Thematic Roles

3.2.1 Lexical categories and the lexicon

We are now ready to look at some syntactic data, drawn from both English and a variety of other languages. In this section, we will discuss these data in relatively traditional descriptive terms; for the most part, we will not propose explicit formal rules to account for them. Rather, we will try to convey an intuitive understanding of certain general syntactic processes, which we will use as a basis for developing a formal theory of syntax in subsequent sections of this chapter and in the following chapters. All of the example sentences cited in this chapter have been constructed by us to illustrate the point under discussion. In every case, the example sentences have been tested with native speakers, to determine whether these speakers found them acceptable or not. All negative evidence (example sentences that native speakers judge to be unacceptable, and which we believe to be ungrammatical) will be marked with a preceding star (*).

In chapter 2, we saw that the words in the English lexicon are subdivided into several lexical classes, or categories. The lexical categories that we discussed include the following:

(3) a. **Verb (V)**   (*attack, appear, burglarize, carry, fall, hit, kill, kiss, love, marry, quit*)

    b. **Adjective (A)**   (*careful, fair, happy, idiotic, lucky, old, red*)

    c. **Adverb (Adv)**   (*again, carefully, fairly, luckily, never, very*)

    d. **Noun (N)**   (*broth, friend, girl, happiness, king, lover, Moor, sword, witch*)

    e. **Proper noun (Name)** (*Bianca, Duncan, Desdemona, Hamlet, Kate, Macbeth, Ophelia*)

    f. **Determiner (D)**   (*a, an, that, the, this*)

    g. **Preposition (P)**   (*about, for, from, in, of, to, under*)

    h. **Pronoun (Prn)**   (*I, me, we, us, you, he, him, she, her, it, they, them*)

    i. **Auxiliary (Aux)**   (*can, must, should, will, did, is, were, have, had*)

As noted in chapter 2, some of these (3a–e) are open-class categories, which speakers regularly add new members to, while others (3f–i) are closed-class categories. Within the open-class categories, some words (such as *fair, girl, Kate, quit,* and *very*) are composed exclusively of root morphemes, while others (such as *burglarize, idiotic, lover,* and *luckily*) are morphologically derived by attaching an affix to a morpheme of some other category.

Most lexical categories are associated with characteristic semantic properties. For example, adjectives typically refer to qualities or properties that speakers attribute to people or things (*careful, lucky, old, red*). Verbs typically refer to actions, events, or states (*carry, attack, quit, marry*). Proper nouns are used as names for particular entities: for people and animals (*Bianca, Kate, Fido*), geographical entities such as cities or countries (*London,*

France), and other things that people give names to, such as restaurants, stores, and commercial products (*Pepsi, Viagra*). On the other hand, words that refer to general kinds of entities are usually common nouns (*dog, elephant, woman, witch, king, tree, house, sword*). We will refer to proper nouns as **names**, reserving the term *noun* for common nouns.

Many semantic notions can be expressed in terms of more than one lexical category, and many lexical categories are used to express several different semantic notions. For example, we can use nouns like *marriage* or *destruction* to refer to actions and events (instead of using the verbs *marry* and *destroy*) and we can use nouns like *honor* and *beauty* to refer to abstract qualities or properties (instead of using the adjectives *honorable* and *beautiful*). Moreover, though many prepositions are usually used to express a relation between two entities involving location (*in, on, under, at, beside*) or direction (*to, from*), some prepositions (such as *of, by, about,* and *with*) can be used in ways that seem to have nothing to do with these notions. Thus, while there is clearly a connection between the lexical category of a word and its meaning, this relationship is more complex and difficult to pin down in simple terms than a superficial examination of a few examples might suggest. For this reason, we will assume that the lexical category of a given word cannot always be predicted solely on the basis of its meaning. Therefore, in determining the lexical category of a given word, we will rely primarily on an examination of its morphological and syntactic properties, which are more reliable diagnostic indicators in many cases.

In chapter 2, our attention was directed mainly at the morphological properties of these lexical categories; in this chapter, we will be concerned mainly with their syntactic properties, and with the rules of the mental grammar that determine where they may occur in sentences. We observed some effects of these rules in chapter 2, in our discussion of diagnostic syntactic frames, involving particular positions within certain **phrases** (groups of words) where only members of a particular lexical category may occur. For example, we saw that only singular nouns may occur within the frame [. . . *a* ___ VERB . . .], and that only adjectives may occur within the frame [. . . *the* ___ NOUN . . .]. So far, however, we have not discussed the logic behind these diagnostic frames; that is, we have not shown how they relate to the rules of English syntax or to the structure of English sentences. We will discuss these issues below.

However, our brief discussion of syntactic frames does illustrate a clear fact about the arrangement of words in sentences, namely that there are specific positions within the structure of phrases and sentences reserved for words belonging to specific lexical categories. (If this were not the case, then these frames would not be reliable diagnostics for membership in these categories.) The same point can be made by reconsidering the example sentences in (1) and (2) above:

(1) a. Desdemona will marry a Moor.
    b. Macbeth has killed the king.

(2) a. *Marry will Moor a Desdemona.
    b. *Killed the Macbeth has king.

All of the words in these sentences belong to the lexical categories in (3). Note that the words *will* and *has* belong to the category of **auxiliary verbs** or **auxiliaries**. This is a closed lexical class, which includes a subgroup of **modal auxiliaries** or **modals**, including words like *can, could, may, might, must, shall, should, will,* and *would*. (Non-modal auxiliaries include *be, do,* and *have*.) The ungrammatical status of the example sentences in (2) shows that each lexical category is only allowed to occur in certain positions in the sentence; the words cannot be randomly placed in any position without regard to their lexical category. The grammatical sentences in (1) conform to the arrangement of lexical categories in (4a); the ungrammatical examples in (2) arrange the lexical categories as in (4b) and (4c), which is not allowed by the rules of English grammar:

(4) a. Name – Auxiliary – Verb – Determiner – Noun
    b. *Verb – Auxiliary – Noun – Determiner – Name
    c. *Verb – Determiner – Name – Auxiliary – Noun

On the other hand, each word in the sentences in (1) can be replaced by another word belonging to the same lexical category, as the examples in (5) illustrate:

(5) a. Macbeth will marry a Moor.
    b. Desdemona may kiss the Moor.
    c. Macbeth must marry that witch.
    d. Duncan has carried this sword.

This is what we should expect, if the composition of sentences is sensitive to the lexical categories of the words that it contains. In effect, the template in (4a) serves as a kind of recipe for constructing a certain type of sentence – namely, sentences like those in (1) and (5).

You might think that it should be possible to construct a list of templates similar to (4a), defining all the orders in which the lexical categories of English words may be arranged to form grammatical English sentences. However, this would be an impossible task. We have already mentioned that the number of grammatical sentences in English (and any other human language) is infinite; moreover, the number of templates for grammatical sentences in English is also infinite; thus, there can be no complete list of such templates. The same problem would arise if we attempted to construct a list of all the templates for ungrammatical sentences; the list would be infinite. For this reason, sentence templates such as these cannot be the basis of our knowledge of sentence structure. Nevertheless, the theory of syntax must be able to account for the facts summarized in these templates (and others like them). Since our brains are finite, there must be some finite system of rules forming the basis of the knowledge that these templates represent. We will discuss such a system in part 3.

Although the number of grammatical English sentences is infinite, the number of English morphemes (and words) is not, as discussed in chapter 2. To be sure, the set of all the different morphemes that each speaker knows is extremely large, numbering in the tens of thousands, but it is still finite. This implies that all the words and morphemes of English may be listed in the mental lexicon. As far as morphemes are concerned, this is generally accepted as a fact; a speaker's mental lexicon contains a **lexical entry** for every morpheme that the speaker knows, including a specification of its pronunciation, its meaning, and its lexical category. As noted in chapter 2, it is less clear that every word is explicitly listed in the lexicon, since most words are derived from morphemes by regular productive rules; if the grammar of English contains a list of all the morphemes and also contains the productive rules for combining these morphemes to form words, then presumably the words formed by these rules do not need to be explicitly listed in the lexicon. This is particularly clear for languages with complex and productive systems of morphological affixation, such as San Lucas Quiaviní (SLQ) Zapotec, where each verb root may occur in well over 2000 different words. Just as some abridged dictionaries save space by omitting many words formed by fully productive morphological rules, it may be that our mental lexicons work in the same way.

On the other hand, some words are morphologically irregular, or idiosyncratic; for example, the past tense form of the verb *go* is *went*, rather than *goed*. Such words must presumably be listed in the lexicon, since their existence cannot be accounted for by the regular rules alone. Many words have a morphological structure that is regular, but derived by morphological rules that are not fully productive; for example, nouns can be formed from verbs by a variety of different nonproductive suffixation rules, as shown by the diversity of suffixes in words such as *pressure, appearance, appendage, government*, etc., which contrast with non-words such as **pressance, *governure, *appearage*, etc. Words of the former type must also be listed in the lexicon.

How do we discover what kind of information is included in a lexical entry? We examine the syntactic distribution of each word, using various kinds of experimental evidence, including grammaticality judgments based on the intuitions of native speakers. Each speaker knows the pronunciation of each morpheme in his or her idiolect – the particular form of the language the speaker uses. This is necessary in order for people to be able to utter sentences, and in order to recognize morphemes in sentences that other speakers produce. Of course, the idiolects of any two speakers of English may differ in terms of the inventory of morphemes in their lexicons, or in terms of how certain morphemes are pronounced; for example, dialects of English differ in terms of how the morphemes *either*, *tomato*, and *Caribbean* are pronounced, and most speakers have idiosyncratic ways of pronouncing certain words (for example, words that they have learned through reading rather than by hearing them in conversation). Nevertheless, within the mental lexicon of any single speaker, there is a pronunciation associated with each morpheme, regardless of whether this happens to be the same as the pronunciation that other speakers have in their mental lexicons.

The lexical entry of a morpheme must also contain a specification of its meaning; this is required in order for speakers to be able to produce coherent sentences and to understand what other speakers are saying. In a few cases, a speaker may hear (or read) an unfamiliar word or morpheme, without knowing what it means; in this case, the speaker might (unconsciously) construct a lexical entry for this morpheme, but this lexical entry would not be complete until the speaker has established a meaning for it. The precise nature of how the meanings of morphemes are represented in the mind is a very complicated issue, and many aspects of it are still poorly understood. Nevertheless, some aspects of the meaning of lexical items affect the rules of syntax in a limited way, as we shall see in section 2.3.

In addition, the lexical entry of a morpheme must contain a specification of its lexical category (*verb*, *noun*, *adjective*, etc.). This is shown both by the fact that speakers unconsciously know rules of morphology that are sensitive to the lexical categories of morphemes, discussed in chapter 2, and by the fact that their ability to create grammatical sentences is also dependent on their knowledge of the lexical categories of words, discussed in this section. Even uneducated speakers who have never studied any grammar know the syntactic categories of the words that they use. Such speakers may not know the meanings of grammatical terms such as *verb* and *adjective*, but they know how to use verbs and adjectives in just the same way that educated speakers do, as long as they speak the same dialect; in other words, they have an unconscious knowledge of the syntactic categories of the words they use. Terms like *verb* and *adjective* are just convenient labels for these notions; all speakers of a language have an instinctive understanding of the grammatical properties that these terms represent. Other grammatical information about lexical entries will be discussed below.

Normal dictionaries contain information about individual words, such as their correct spellings and, sometimes, information about their historical sources. However, this kind of information is not an essential part of the lexical entries of a speaker's mental lexicon, since one can speak a language fluently without knowing how to read or write, and without knowing anything about the history of the language. It is an interesting

SIDEBAR
3.2

Morphology and the lexicon

As noted in the text, it is possible that the lexicon does not contain lexical entries for words formed by productive morphological rules such as *kills* and *killed*; on the other hand, irregular verb forms such as *grew* and *went* must be listed in the lexicon, because they are irregular past tense forms (of the verbs *grow* and *go*, respectively). In fact, these irregular past tense forms cannot even be segmented into sequences of discrete morphemes; as noted in chapter 2, such words are traditionally called **portmanteau** morphemes.

Despite this fact, the rules of English syntax do not treat these irregular portmanteau past tense forms any differently from regular past tense forms produced by the productive morphological rule for suffixing *-ed* to a verb stem. For example, modal verbs (such as *can* or *may*) must be followed by a bare root form of the verb, and may not be followed by a form with the past tense suffix; thus, *Macbeth may kill Duncan* is grammatical, whereas **Macbeth may killed Duncan* is not. Irregular portmanteau past tense forms behave just like irregular past tense forms in this respect: *Henry may go to France* is grammatical, but **Henry may went to France* is not.

Why should the rules of syntax treat all past tense forms identically, regardless of whether they can be segmented into sequences of two distinct morphemes? One possibility is that portmanteau past tense forms like *went* and *grew* actually do contain a sequence of two morphemes: an irregular form of the stem morpheme followed by a zero past tense morpheme. (Recall the discussion of zero-morphemes in chapter 2.) Another possibility is that all past tense forms of verbs have the abstract feature [+PAST] discussed in chapter 2, regardless of whether this feature is associated with a discrete morpheme within the word.

Some linguists have proposed that the lexicon actually contains all the rules of morphology, in addition to the list of all the lexical entries for morphemes and irregular words. According to this theory, these two components of the English lexicon generate all the words of English, either by listing them in lexical entries, or by producing them from other lexical entries by means of productive morphological rules. Other linguists believe that the rules of syntax and morphology are more closely connected to each other; in fact, it has been proposed that rules of syntax actually play a role in word formation, by moving morphemes from one position in a sentence to another position, attaching them to other morphemes in the process. According to this approach, rules of syntax play a role in the creation of past tense forms, by moving (tenseless) verbal roots to a position in the sentence where the past tense morpheme is located. These issues are discussed in chapter 5.

question whether (and to what extent) the mental lexicon of a literate speaker differs from that of an illiterate one; there is much evidence from psycholinguistic experiments and from language deficits (aphasia) following brain damage, that each lexical entry also includes an orthographic representation (spelling). For example, some aphasic patients retain the ability to read and write but lose the ability to speak and vice versa. In discussing the rules of syntax, we do not have to be concerned with the differences between spelling and pronunciation, so we will keep things simple by using traditional spellings for English words to represent their sounds, instead of the system of **phonetic transcription** discussed in chapter 11.

EXERCISE 3.1

(a) Construct five additional sentences conforming to the template in (4a). Select the words for these sentences from the list of words belonging to each lexical category in (3). Are these sentences grammatical? If you are a native speaker of English, use your own intuitions to decide this. If not, try to consult a native speaker of English; if no native speaker is available, make a guess based on your knowledge of English as a second language.

(b) The templates in (4) give three possible arrangements of the five lexical categories *Auxiliary*, *Determiner*, *Name*, *Noun*, and *Verb* within a sentence; one of these is grammatical, while the other two are ungrammatical. However, there are actually 120 possible arrangements of these five lexical categories. Construct five additional templates by rearranging these lexical categories in various ways. Use each template as the basis for forming an actual sentence by choosing words from the list in (3). Try to find at least one additional template for grammatical sentences in this way.

(c) Translate sentences (1a) and (1b) into a language other than English; we will refer to this language as X. (If you are a native speaker of a language other than English, use it as Language X; if not, consult a friend who is a native speaker of another language, or use a language that you have studied.) Do these sentences in Language X contain the same number of words as (1a) and (1b)? If not, explain why. For each sentence, construct a template similar to those in (4). Are these two templates the same? If not, explain why. Construct two additional sentences in Language X that conform to the same template(s), using different words. (If you are unsure which lexical categories these words belong to, just make a guess.)

3.2.2 Thematic roles and English constituent order

Another aspect of syntax discussed briefly in chapter 2 concerns a typological classification of languages in terms of **basic constituent order**, that is, the typical way in which words are arranged in simple sentences such as the following:

(6)   a.   Macbeth murdered Duncan.
      b.   Duncan murdered Macbeth.

(7)   a.   Othello liked Desdemona.
    b.   Desdemona liked Othello.

(8)   a.   Othello pleased Desdemona.
    b.   Desdemona pleased Othello.

The sentences in each pair of examples contain the same three words (two names and a verb), but they convey very different meanings, as a result of their different word orders. Thus, in (6a), Macbeth is the murderer, whereas in (6b), he is the victim; similarly, (7a) and (8b) describe Othello's opinion of Desdemona, whereas (7b) and (8a) describe her opinion of him.

The traditional way of explaining this kind of relationship between word order and meaning involves the interaction between the syntactic rules governing the structure of sentences and the semantic rules of **reference** and **thematic role assignment**. As we have already observed, names like *Macbeth* and *Othello* are typically used as names that refer to people, either real or imaginary; the person that a name refers to is called the **referent** of the name. On the other hand, verbs refer to particular kinds of events or situations, each of which involves one or more participants that play a characteristic role in it. For example, a murder must involve at least two participants: an **agent** who performs the action (the murderer) and a **patient** who the action is performed on (the victim). Similarly, an attitude of liking or pleasing must involve both an **experiencer** whose psychological state is described, and a **theme** that the attitude is about. Terms such as agent, patient, experiencer, and theme, which identify the semantic roles of the participants in the event or situation described by the sentence, are known as **thematic roles**, or **θ-roles** (pronounced 'theta-roles'). The participants that these θ-roles are associated with are known as the **arguments** of the verb. The representation of the meaning of each verb in the mental lexicon specifies the number of arguments that it has, and the θ-roles associated with them.

Each θ-role is assigned to a particular syntactic position in the sentence; for example, in (6), the agent role is assigned to the **subject** position (the position occupied by the name preceding the verb), while the patient role is assigned to the **object** position (the position occupied by the name following the verb). When a θ-role is assigned to a syntactic position in this way, the referent of the name occurring in this position is understood as the participant associated with this θ-role in the event or situation that the verb refers to. In (6a), the name *Macbeth* occupies the subject position, so the referent of this noun (namely, the fictional character in Shakespeare's play) is understood as the agent participant in the event (that is, as the murderer); the name *Duncan* occupies the object position, so its referent is understood as the patient participant in the event (that is, as the victim).

These θ-roles are reversed in (6b) because the names *Macbeth* and *Duncan* have exchanged places. The assignment of the agent θ-role to the subject position and the patient θ-role to the object position is typical of verbs referring to actions that involve these two thematic roles, as the following examples illustrate:

(9) a. Henry kissed Katherine.
    b. Othello suffocated Desdemona.
    c. Shylock sued Antonio.

The regularity of this pattern suggests that these processes of **thematic role assignment** are general rules of grammar; that is, they are not idiosyncratic properties of individual verbs, and therefore do not need to be stated explicitly in the lexical entries of these verbs. As long as the lexical entries of verbs such as *murder* and *kiss* state that these verbs refer to events that involve both an agent and a patient, these θ-roles will be assigned to the subject and object positions, respectively, by the productive general rules of θ-role assignment.

On the other hand, the thematic roles associated with verbs describing psychological states appear to be assigned in a less predictable way. Some verbs (such as *like*, *hate*, and *admire*) associate the experiencer role with the subject position, and the theme role with the object position, as in (7), whereas other verbs (such as *please*, *disgust*, and *impress*) do the opposite, as in (8). This contrast between the two classes of verbs describing psychological states suggests that the lexical entries of at least some verbs must include not only a specification of the thematic roles associated with the situations they describe, but also an explicit statement of which positions in the sentence are associated with each thematic role. Some linguists disagree with this view, and maintain that all θ-roles are assigned by general rules, even with these two classes of verbs denoting psychological states.

In all the example sentences discussed thus far, the subject and object positions are occupied by names. However, pronouns may also occupy these positions, as shown by examples like (10):

(10) a. *He* kissed *her*.
     b. *You* broke *it*.

These positions may also be occupied by **determiner phrases (DPs)**, as in (11):

(11) a. *The king* kissed *the princess*.
     b. *Three witches* prepared *a vile broth*.

A DP typically includes at least a determiner (an article such as *the* or *a* or a numeral such as *three*) and a noun (such as *king, princess, friend,* or *wine*); sometimes one or more adjectives (such as *vile*) occur in between them. DPs may contain other types of categories as well, as we shall see further below. Pronouns and DPs, like names, are used to refer to people or things; thus, when a pronoun or DP occurs in the subject or object position, its referent is understood as the participant associated with the θ-role assigned to that position.

In general, names, pronouns, and DPs all have the same external syntactic distribution; that is, in any position in the sentence where a name may occur, a pronoun or DP may occur instead. In other words, the data in (10) and (11) are representative of a more general pattern. In Part 3, we will suggest an explanation for this fact: names and pronouns are just special types of DPs, even though they do not contain a determiner. (Actually, in some languages, such as French, definite determiners can also be used as pronouns, and in other languages, such as German and Portuguese, names can sometimes be preceded by determiners.) In our subsequent discussion, we will use the term DP to refer to any of these categories.

Verbs such as *have* and *own* refer to situations involving a relation of possession, with two participants: a **possessor** (often, though not always, a person) and a theme (the possessed thing). The possessor θ-role is assigned to the subject position, and the theme θ-role is assigned to the object position:

(12)   a.   Lear has a daughter.
       b.   The Dauphin owns some tennis balls.

In some sentences, a DP is interpreted as a possessor, even though the sentence does not contain a verb like *have*. (Bear in mind that we are now using the term DP to include names and pronouns as well as DPs containing a determiner):

(13)   a.   *Lear's* daughter loved him.
       b.   Henry disliked *the Dauphin's* tennis balls.
       c.   The daughter *of Lear* loved him.
       d.   Henry disliked the tennis balls *of the Dauphin*.

In these sentences, the possessor θ-role is assigned either to the **nominal specifier** position preceding the noun, as in (13a–b), or to a position following the preposition *of*, which occurs after the noun of the DP referring to the possessed theme, as in (13c–d). (The nominal specifier position has the clitic *-'s* attached to its right edge, as discussed in chapter 2.) When a DP immediately follows a preposition, we call it the object of that preposition, analogous to the object of a verb, and the sequence of the preposition and its object is called a **prepositional phrase** or **PP**. Thus the possessor position in (13c–d) is the object of the preposition *of*. Note that the nominal specifier position in (13a) and the position occupied by the PP containing *of* in (13c) are apparently located within the DP that refers to the possessed theme, since *Lear's daughter* and *the daughter of Lear* both occur in the subject position preceding the verb.

Another type of thematic role that is assigned in a regular way to a particular syntactic position in English is the **goal** θ-role, associated either with the endpoint of an action of motion from one place to another, or with the participant who functions as a recipient in an action involving transfer of possession from one person to another. This goal θ-role is assigned to the **indirect object** position following the preposition *to*, which occurs after the object position in examples such as those in (14):

(14)   a.   Shylock lent money *to Antonio*.
       b.   The Dauphin sent tennis balls *to the king*.
       c.   Harry passed the wine *to Falstaff*.

The object position immediately after the verb is often referred to as the **direct object** position, to distinguish it from the indirect object position. In (14), the agent and patient θ-roles are assigned to the subject and direct object positions, respectively, as in the examples discussed above.

The goal and patient θ-roles can also be assigned in a different way. In the so-called **double object construction**, there are two object positions following the verb; the goal θ-role is assigned to the first object position, and the patient θ-role is assigned to the second object position:

(15)   a.   The Dauphin sent Henry tennis balls.
       b.   Hal passed Falstaff the wine.

Thus, the first object position in (15) is assigned the same θ-role as the indirect object position has in (14), while the second object position in (15) is assigned the same θ-role as the direct object position in (14).

This brief survey of the rules of thematic role assignment in English is far from being complete; there are several types of θ-roles that we have not discussed, and also alternative ways of assigning some of the θ-roles that we have discussed. However, our discussion should give you a general idea of what θ-roles are, how they are related to specific syntactic positions in the structure of English sentences, and how this affects the semantic interpretation of these sentences. The main points are summarized in the chart in (16):

(16)

θ-role	Environment	Position	Location
Agent		Subject	at the front of the sentence, before the verb
Patient		Object	immediately after the verb
Experiencer	(a) *like*-verbs	Subject	see above
	(b) *please*-verbs	Object	see above
Theme	(a) *like*-verbs	Object	see above
	(b) *please*-verbs	Subject	see above
Goal	(a) Prepositional Dative Construction	Indirect Object (object of *to*)	within *to*-PP, after the direct object position
	(b) Double Object Construction	First object DP	immediately after the verb
Possessor	(a) *have*-verbs	Subject	see above
	(b) within DP	Nominal Specifier	before the noun
		or Object of *of*	within *of*-PP, after the noun

EXERCISE 3.2

(a) For each of the following example sentences, make a list of every name and DP occurring in the sentence. Remember that some DPs contain other DPs or names within them, in the nominal specifier position. Beside each name or DP in your list, indicate the name of the θ-role assigned to it, based on the list of θ-roles given in (16).

(i) Henry's wife hated Falstaff.
(ii) Iago attacked Othello.
(iii) Falstaff drank the wine.
(iv) Caesar's power frightened Brutus.
(v) Bassanio handed the ring to Portia.
(vi) Claudius gave Hamlet's father some poison.

(b) For each name and DP on your list, indicate the name of the syntactic position that it occupies (subject, object, indirect object, or nominal specifier position).

3.2.3   Constituent order in other languages

We have seen that, in ordinary English sentences, the subject precedes the verb, and the verb precedes the object. For this reason, English is often described as a Subject–Verb–Object (SVO) language. (Note that some English sentences exhibit different word orders; these involve cases where one or more constituents of the sentence move from one position to another; see (22) below.) As we observed in chapter 2, the situation is different in many other languages. For example, simple sentences in languages such as Chickasaw and Turkish typically display SOV constituent order, with the object occurring before the verb (and after the subject), whereas simple sentences in languages such as SLQ Zapotec, Modern Standard Arabic, and Modern Irish typically display VSO order, with the subject occurring after the verb (and before the object). Since we originally defined the subject and object positions in terms of English word order, you may be wondering why we use the same terms to describe different positions in the sentence in these other languages. For example, why do we describe the position immediately after the verb as an object position in English and as a subject position in Standard Arabic? The answer lies in the way θ-roles are assigned to these positions; we use the term 'subject' to refer to the position where the agent θ-role is normally assigned, and the term 'object' to refer to the position where the patient θ-role is normally assigned. (Bear in mind, however, that in some cases, different θ-roles are assigned to these positions, such as the experiencer and theme θ-roles with verbs describing psychological states.) Similarly, we use the term 'indirect object' to refer to the position where the goal θ-role is normally assigned. Thus, the pattern of θ-role assignment provides the basis for identifying these positions in different languages, despite the apparent cross-linguistic variation in where they are located within the structure of the sentence.

Actually, most languages exhibit more than one type of constituent order pattern. For example, in Standard Arabic, VSO is the most commonly attested order, but often the subject precedes the verb, with SVO order, just as in English:

(17) a. qatala   'uTayl Dasdamuuna.   (V–S–O) (Standard Arabic)
          killed+3MSg Othello Desdemona
          'Othello killed Desdemona.'
      b. 'uTayl qatala   Dasdamuuna.
          Othello killed+3MSg Desdemona   (S–V–O)
          'Othello killed Desdemona.'

In (17), grammatical features on affixes and pronouns are glossed as follows. Person features are glossed as 1, 2, and 3 (first, second, and third person); Number is glossed as Sg (Singular), and Pl (Plural); Gender is glossed as M (Masculine) and F (Feminine); Case is glossed as Nom (Nominative),

Acc (Accusative), Dat (Dative), and Gen (Genitive). Tense and aspect are marked as Past, Pres (Present), Perf (Perfect), and Prog (Progressive).

In a similar vein, Modern Irish is often described as a VSO language, but SVO order is also attested in certain types of constructions. For example, either SOV or SVO order is found in certain types of **participial clauses**, depending on the dialect, as noted by McCloskey (1983). (A participial clause is a particular kind of subordinate clause – that is, a smaller sentence embedded within the main sentence; a participial clause contains a verb with a participle suffix attached to it, but without any tense suffix. An example of a participle suffix in English is *-ed*, sometimes called *-en*, which occurs in passive sentences such as *Duncan was murdered*, and in perfect constructions such as *Macbeth has murdered Duncan* and *Portia had given her word*.)

It thus appears either that there are two subject positions in Standard Arabic and Modern Irish (one before the position of the verb, and another one after it) or, alternatively, that there are two positions for the verb in these languages (one before the subject position, and one after it). This may sound like two different ways of saying the same thing, but we shall see below that these are really two different theories about sentence structure in these languages.

German and Dutch are often described as SOV languages, even though they often exhibit other orders, such as SVO. SOV order occurs in clauses that contain an auxiliary verb in addition to the main verb, as in (18a); in this case, the order is actually S–AUX–O–V, with the auxiliary occurring in the second position. SOV order also occurs in certain types of subordinate clauses (sentences contained within the main sentence), as in (18b). However, in main clauses and simple sentences containing just one verb (and no auxiliary), the verb occurs in the second position, often resulting in SVO order, as in (18c) and in the main clause in (18b):

(18) a. Romeo hat Juliet geküsst.   (S–AUX–O–V)   (German)
          Romeo has Juliet kissed
          'Romeo kissed Juliet.'
      b. Ich glaube, dass [Romeo Juliet küsste].   (. . . [S–O–V])
          I   believe that   Romeo Juliet was kissing
          'I believe that Romeo was kissing Juliet.'
      c. Romeo küsste   Juliet.   (S–V–O)
          Romeo was kissing Juliet
          'Romeo was kissing Juliet.'

In (18c), the verb occupies the same position in the sentence that the auxiliary verb occupies in (18a); the same is true of the verb *glaube* 'believe' in the main clause in (18b). This suggests that there are two verb positions in German: one at the end of the sentence, after the object, and another in the second position, before the object.

Turkish typically has SOV order, as in (19a), but orders such as SVO, VSO, and even OVS are also possible, as shown by (19b–d):

(19) a. Hamlet Ophelia-yı   öp-tü.   (S–O–V)   (Turkish)
          Hamlet Ophelia+Acc kiss+Past
          'Hamlet kissed Ophelia.'
      b. Hamlet öp-tü   Ophelia-yı.   (S–V–O)
          Hamlet kiss+Past Ophelia+Acc
          'Hamlet kissed Ophelia.'
      c. öp-tü   Hamlet Ophelia-yı.   (V–S–O)
          kiss+Past Hamlet Ophelia+Acc
          'Hamlet kissed Ophelia.'
      d. Ophelia-yı   öp-tü   Hamlet.   (O–V–S)
          Ophelia+Acc kiss+Past Hamlet
          'Hamlet kissed Ophelia.'

As in the case of the Standard Arabic and German, it seems that Turkish has more than one position reserved for the subject, verb, and object.

Italian is usually categorized as an SVO language, and this is certainly the normal order in clauses containing both a subject and an object. However, it is quite common for the subject to occur after the verb, rather than before it, if there is no object following the verb, as in (20b):

(20) a. Gianni ha telefonato.   (S–AUX–V)   (Italian)
          Gianni has telephoned
          'Gianni (has) telephoned.'
      b. Ha telefonato Gianni.   (AUX–V–S)
          has telephoned Gianni
          'Gianni (has) telephoned.'

Thus, it seems that Italian has more than one subject position. Moreover, French, Italian, Portuguese, and Spanish, all of which are usually classified as SVO languages, actually exhibit SOV order if the object of the verb is an unstressed pronoun:

(21) a. Lear les   aime.   (S–O–V)   (French)
          Lear them loves
          'Lear loves them.'
      b. Portia lo   vió.   (S–O–V)   (Spanish)
          Portia him saw
          'Portia saw him.'

The unstressed pronouns preceding the verbs in these examples are called **pronominal clitics**. Thus, it seems that these languages have two object positions (one after the verb, and the other before the verb), though the latter position can only be occupied by unstressed pronominal clitics.

Even English sometimes displays constituent orders other than SVO under certain conditions – for example, in sentences such as those in (22):

(22) a. Bianca, I admire.   (OSV)
      b. Have you any ducats?   (VSO)
      c. 'I love you,' said Romeo.   (OVS)

Example (22a) is an example of a **Topicalization** construction, where the object of the verb occurs in the Topic position, before the subject; (22b) is a **question**, where the verb *have* occurs in a position before the subject; and (22c) is an example of a **sentence-lifting** construction, where the sentence enclosed in quotation marks, which functions as the object of the main verb *say*, occurs at the front of the sentence, and the verb precedes the subject.

In section 2.2, we saw that the indirect object position in English follows the direct object position; thus, the constituent order of sentences containing indirect objects is S–V–O–IO. On the other hand, the goal θ-role normally assigned to this position can also be assigned to the first object position in a double object construction. In SOV and VSO languages, the indirect object position is also usually located next to the direct object position; in some languages, it precedes the direct object, while in others, it follows it, and many languages allow both options. In SLQ Zapotec, the indirect object position follows the direct object position, resulting in V–S–O–IO order:

(23) B-dèèi'dy Gyeeihlly bx:àady   Li'eb   (V–S–O–IO)
      Perf-give Mike   grasshopper Felipe
      'Mike gave the grasshoppers to Felipe.'

On the other hand, in Modern Arabic (24), Turkish (25), and Chickasaw (26), the indirect object may either precede or follow the object position:

(24) a. ?rasala   'uTayl khiTaab-an   li Dasdamuuna.   (V–S–O–IO)
        sent+3MSg Othello message+Acc to Desdemona
        'Othello send a message to Desdemona.'
     b. ?arsal   'uTayl li Dasdamuuna khiTaab-an.   (V–S–IO–O)
        sent+3MSg Othello to Desdemona   message+Acc
        'Othello sent a message to Desdemona.'

(25) a. Kralbir yabancı-ya   eldiven ver-di   (S–IO–O–V)
        king   a stranger+Dat glove   give+Past
        'The king gave a glove to a stranger.'
     b. Kraleldiven-i-ni   yabancı-ya   ver-di   (S–O–IO–V)
        king glove+his+Acc stranger+Dat give+Past
        'The king gave his glove to the stranger.'

(26) a. Bianca-at   Katharina-A   holisso im-a-tok   (S–IO–O–V)
        Bianca-Nom Katharina+Acc book   dat+give+Past
        'Bianca gave Katharina a book.'

   b. Bianca-at   holisso-A Katharina im-a-tok.   (S–O–IO–V)
      Bianca-Nom book+Acc Katharina dat-give-past
      'Bianca gave Katharina a book.'

These examples of variation in constituent order within a single language are actually quite representative of the world's languages. We could easily cite hundreds of such cases, particularly if we shifted our attention to other types of syntactic positions, such as the positions of adjectives, adverbs, prepositions, negative particles, etc.; some of these are discussed in chapters 4 and 5. Thus, the traditional practice of classifying languages in terms of a typology of dominant word-order patterns is potentially misleading, since it obscures the fact that within each language, there are often two or more verb positions, subject positions, object positions, and so on.

This still leaves open the question of how this variation should be accounted for in terms of the theory of syntax. So far, we have not discussed the rules that define the structure of sentences; we have simply given a brief description of where various positions are located in simple sentences in a small sample of languages. Many linguists believe the basic structure of sentences is the same in all human languages, even though this structure is considerably more complex than it appears to be. Based in part on the observation that subjects, verbs, and objects often occur in a variety of different positions even within the same language, it is suggested that there is a universal template of sentence structure for all languages, containing several distinct positions for each type of constituent; in this view, word-order variation (both within a given language and across languages) arises from the fact that individual constituents have more than one possible position in which they can, in principle, occur. For example, suppose (for the sake of discussion) that all languages have three verb positions, as in the template in (27):

(27)   [Verb]$_1$ – Subject – [Verb$_2$]– Object – [Verb$_3$]

If the verb occurs in the first verb position, VSO order results; if it occurs in the second verb position, SVO order results; finally, if it occurs in the third position, SOV order results. (Of course, this template only accounts for a small part of sentence structure; among other things, it ignores the positions of auxiliaries, indirect objects, and adverbs.) Alternatively, we might assume a different universal template such as that in (28), with just one verb position, but two subject positions and two object positions:

(28)   [Subject]$_1$ – [Object] – Verb – [Subject]$_2$ – [Object]$_2$

If the subject and object both occur in the positions before the verb, SOV order results; if they both occur in the positions after the verb, VSO order results; if the first subject position and the second object position are used,

SVO order results. The facts that we have discussed thus far do not provide the basis for an informed choice between (27) and (28); some linguists believe that both approaches are partly correct.

EXERCISE 3.3

Examine the following sentences in Tibetan. In three of these sentences, the verb is followed by a perfective 'evidential' particle, glossed simply as 'Perf'. You can ignore the differences between these evidential particles in your answer; you should simply assume that each of them functions like an auxiliary verb in English.

(i)   ngas dkaryol chags - song.
      I-Erg cup   break + Perf
      'I broke the cup.'

(ii)   khos   nga-la dep   sprad - byung.
       he-Erg I-Dat   book give + perf
       'He gave me a book.'

(iii)   khos   cookie bzas - duk.
        he-Erg cookie eat + perf
        'He has eaten the cookies.'

(iv)   tengsang   kho khyang-pa rgyab - gi - red.
       these days he   house   build + Habitual
       'These days, he builds houses.'

(a) Make an organized list of all the words occurring in these sentences, and indicate the English translation for each word. Group together words belonging to the same lexical category (verb, adverb, noun, etc.)

(b) Based on these data, determine the basic constituent order for Tibetan sentences. You should state this in terms of a single formula, analogous to the English formula *Subject–(Auxiliary Verb)–Verb–(Object)–(Indirect Object)*, where parentheses are placed around constituents that occur in some sentences but not in others. Be sure to indicate the positions of the verb, the (evidential) auxiliary, the subject, the object, the indirect object, and the time adverbs.

3.2.4   Case marking and constituent order

It is often claimed that in some languages, the notions of subject, object, and indirect object are not related to particular positions in the sentence, but rather are associated with particular affixes, called **case** affixes, or **case markers**, attached to the nouns (or pronouns) that occur in the sentence. We have already seen that in Turkish and Chickasaw, the object of the verb is marked with accusative case, and that the indirect object is marked with dative case instead of being preceded by a preposition like English *to*;

likewise, the subject in Chickasaw is marked with nominative case. In these languages, the subject, object, and indirect object can usually be identified unambiguously on the basis of the case marking alone. Likewise, in Russian, the indirect object is marked with dative case, and the nominal specifier is marked with a genitive case affix:

(29) a. Gamlet otdal čerep Goraciju.   (S–V–O–IO)   (Russian)
         Hamlet gave skull Horatio-Dat
         'Hamlet gave a/the skull to Horatio.'
    b. Gamlet otdal čerep mertvogo advokata   Goraciju.
         Hamlet gave skull dead-Gen lawyer-Gen Horatio-Dat
         'Hamlet gave the skull of the dead lawyer to Horatio.'

Since subjects, objects, and indirect objects are identified by means of case affixes in these languages, speakers do not need to rely exclusively on the order of constituents within the sentence in order to distinguish between them. It is a traditional belief of many scholars of European languages that this factor is responsible for the fact that constituent order is relatively free in these case-marking languages, as illustrated by the Russian examples in (30), and, conversely, that the lack of case marking on subjects and objects in languages such as English and Chinese is responsible for the fact that subjects and objects in these languages are relatively immobile.

(30) a. Gamlet otdal Goraciju   čerep.   (S–V–IO–O)
         Hamlet gave Horatio-Dat skull
         'Hamlet gave Horatio a/the skull.'
    b. Goraciju   Gamlet otdal čerep.   (IO–S–V–O)
         Horatio-Dat Hamlet gave skull
         'Hamlet gave a/the skull to Horatio.';
         'It was to Horatio that Hamlet gave the skull.'
    c. Goraciju   otdal čerep Gamlet.   (IO–V–O–S)
         Horatio-Dat gave skull Hamlet
         'Hamlet gave a/the skull to Horatio.';
         'It was to Horatio that *Hamlet* gave the skull.'
    d. Goraciju   Gamlet čerep otdal.   (IO–S–O–V)
         Horatio-Dat Hamlet skull gave
         'Hamlet gave a/the skull to Horatio.';
         'It was to Horatio that Hamlet *gave* the skull.'

Languages with relatively free constituent order are often referred to as **non-configurational** languages, as opposed to **configurational** languages such as English, with relatively fixed constituent order. In recent years, some linguists have proposed that there is a fundamental difference between case-marking languages and configurational languages, in that only the latter type of languages have an explicit set of **phrase structure rules** defining fixed positions within the structure of the sentence for various types of constituents.

Other linguists are skeptical of this traditional view that case marking is directly related to free constituent order, and have argued that the two types of languages are more similar than they appear at first glance. These linguists point out that even in languages with supposedly free constituent order, there is usually an unmarked (neutral) order that is used more commonly than all others; they also note that changes in the order of constituents in these languages may affect the meanings of sentences in various ways. For example, the Russian sentences in (30b–d), though very similar in meaning to (29a) and (30a), are not precisely synonymous with them; as the secondary glosses for (30b–d) indicate, there are subtle differences in terms of what is being presupposed as old information (the topic of each sentence) and what is being emphasized as new information (the focus). These observations suggest that variations in constituent order in so-called non-configurational languages arise as a result of constituents moving to positions in the sentence that are associated with specific semantic properties involving factors other than thematic roles (such as topic and focus).

It has also been observed that languages such as English display some of the properties commonly associated with non-configurational case-marking languages. For example, the sentences in (22) above illustrate that English also shows variation in word order under certain conditions. English also makes limited use of case marking, though this does not appear to have any direct effect on freedom of constituent order. For example, we have already seen that nominal specifiers are unambiguously identified by the clitic -'s attached to them, and that indirect objects are identified by the preposition *to* preceding them; in fact, -'s and *to* are sometimes analyzed as genitive and dative case markers, respectively. Despite this, these elements must occur in the specific positions in the sentence reserved for them, just like subjects and objects, as (31) shows:

(31)   a.   *Henry disliked tennis balls *the Dauphin's*.   (compare with 13b)
       b.   *Shylock *to Antonio* lent money.   (compare with 14a)

A similar situation obtains with English pronouns, which merge nominative, accusative, or genitive case affixes with pronoun roots into portmanteau morphemes, as noted in chapter 2. As we noted there, cases that are merged with the root morpheme in this way are referred to as **features** of the pronoun, rather than as affixes attached to it. The pronouns *I, we, you, he, she*, and *they* include the nominative case feature, while the pronouns *me, us, you, her, him*, and *them* include the accusative case feature. The pronouns *my, our, your, his, her, its*, and *their* include the genitive case feature, and occur in the nominal specifier position, without the clitic -'s:

(32)   a.   *They* kissed *her*.
       b.   *She* kissed *them*.
       c.   You drank *my* wine.
       d.   *His* daughters betrayed *him*.

Nominative pronouns may only occur in the subject position, while accusative and genitive pronouns may only occur in the object and nominal specifier positions, respectively, as (33) shows:

(33)   a.   **Them* kissed her.
       b.   *She kissed *they*.
       c.   *You drank *him* wine.
       d.   *His daughters betrayed *my*.

Actually, accusative pronouns also occur in the indirect object position, that is, as objects of the preposition *to*:

(34)   a.   The Dauphin sent tennis balls to *him*.
       b.   Shylock lent money to *them*.

Thus, even though most English pronouns are readily identifiable as subjects, objects, or nominal specifiers by virtue of their case features, this does not result in any greater freedom of word order. This supports the view that case marking and free constituent order are not directly related, despite the initial plausibility of this idea.

Examine the following sentences in Japanese. Many of the words in these sentences have case suffixes on them, which we have glossed simply as 'CM' (for case marking).

EXERCISE 3.4

(i)   gakusei-ga   sake-o   nonda.
      student-CM   sake-CM   drank
      'The student drank sake.'

(ii) Taro-ga   sensei-no   hon-o   suteta.
      Taro-CM   teacher-CM   book   threw-away
      'Taro threw away the teacher's book.'

(iii) Sensei-ga   Mari-ni   gakusei-no   hon-o   watasita.
      teacher-CM   Mari-CM   student-CM   book-CM   passed
      'The teacher passed the student's book to Mari.'

(iv) gakusei-ga   sensei-ni   hanasi-ta.
      student-CM   sensei-CM   talked
      'The student talked to the teacher.'

(a)   Make an organized list of the Japanese words occurring in these sentences, and give the English translation of each word. Ignore the case-marking suffixes in answering this question.
(b)   Based on these sentences, state the basic constituent order of Japanese sentences, mentioning the position of the verb, the subject, the object, and the indirect object.
(c)   Now make a list of the different case suffixes. Based on our discussion of case marking in languages such as Russian, identify each of the case suffixes in these sentences, including Nominative, Accusative, Genitive, and Dative.

3.2.5   Predicates and argument structure

Recall that the lexical entry of each verb in the mental lexicon specifies the number of arguments that the verb has – that is, the number of participants in the kind of event or situation that it refers to – as well as the θ-roles associated with each of these arguments. (See section 2.2 above.) This aspect of a verb's meaning is called its **argument structure**. Verbs are often classified according to how many arguments they have in their argument structures. Most of the verbs that we have seen so far have either two arguments (for example, an agent and a patient, or an experiencer and a theme) or three arguments (for example, an agent, a patient, and a goal or recipient). All of these verbs occur in sentences that contain an object position (more specifically, a direct object position); such verbs are called **transitive** verbs. (In a case-marking language, a transitive verb is defined as a verb that has an argument marked with accusative case.) In addition, three-argument verbs occur with an indirect object (or a second object, in the double object construction; such verbs are sometimes called **ditransitive** verbs). However, many verbs in English and other languages have just one argument; since these verbs typically have no direct object after them, they are called **intransitive** verbs. The θ-role associated with this argument is usually assigned to the subject position, as in (35):

(35)   a.   Falstaff laughed (loudly).
       b.   Romeo arrived (late).

It is quite common for intransitive verbs to be followed by an adverb describing the manner or time of the action, as in (35). Many intransitive verbs are followed by a PP (prepositional phrase), which refers either to the location of the event or situation that the verb refers to, as in (36a), or to some other participant in the event or situation, such as a goal in (36b) or a theme in (36c):

(36)   a.   Timon lived *in Athens*.
       b.   The king went *to the witches*.
       c.   The king laughed *at the jester's joke*.

Although these verbs all have two arguments, they are still intransitive verbs, because they are followed by a PP rather than a direct object.

Some intransitive verbs, including *arrive, come* and *occur*, allow their DP argument, if is indefinite, to occur after the verb, apparently in the direct object position, rather than in the subject position, where it normally occurs.

(37)   a.   There has occurred a disaster.
        b.   A disaster has occurred.
        c.   There arrived three wise men from the east.
        d.   They arrived from the east.

Many linguists believe that the θ-role assigned to this DP (the theme θ-role) is always assigned to the direct object position, and that the DP always originates there, even when it surfaces in the subject position. No θ-role is assigned to the subject position, so no DP is allowed to originate there. The object DP may then undergo movement to the empty subject position, as in (37b) and (37d). The moved DP is assigned nominative, rather than accusative, case, as shown by (37d). It has been suggested that this movement is possible only because the verb fails to assign accusative case to its object DP; verbs that behave this way are called **unaccusative verbs**. An indefinite DP may remain in the object position, as in (37a) and (37c); an **expletive pronoun** (*there*) is inserted into the empty subject position, and the object DP is assigned case in a different way.

In fact, verbs are not the only categories that can have argument structures; the same is true of adjectives, prepositions, and nouns. Categories that have argument structures, and which assign θ-roles to their arguments, are called **predicates**. The idea that adjectives may function as predicates should come as no surprise, since adjectives refer to properties that are attributed to persons or things; thus, the adjective indirectly refers to the situation of the person or thing in question having this property. Most adjectives have just one argument; this argument is usually interpreted as a theme participant in the situation described by the adjective.

Adjectives often occur inside a DP, immediately before the noun, as in the DPs *the foolish king, a vile broth, and two Venetian merchants*. In this case, the adjective's theme θ-role is assigned to the DP that the adjective modifies. Sometimes an adjective functions as the main predicate of the sentence in which it occurs, in which case it is usually preceded by the verb *be* in English, as in (38):

(38)   a.   Desdemona was *beautiful*.
        b.   Duncan is *dead*.
        c.   These witches are *strange*.

Here, the verb *be* has no argument structure associated with it, and assigns no θ-roles; instead, it functions like an auxiliary verb, and the subject of the sentence is interpreted as an argument of the adjective. In many languages, such as Russian and Haitian Creole, the translations of sentences such as these have no verb at all:

(39) a. Masha   umnaja.   (Russian)
          Masha+Nom smart+Nom
          'Masha is intelligent.'
      b. Vèdye gwo.   (Haitian Creole)
          Vedve big
          'Vedye is big.'

Even in English, sentences with the verb *be* omitted are perfectly understandable, and in fact are fully grammatical in some dialects (including some varieties of vernacular African-American English).

(40) You crazy.   (African-American English)
      'You are crazy.'

Finally, adjectives sometimes occur as **adjuncts**, displaced from the DPs that they modify, as in (41), where the adjective's theme θ-role is assigned to the subject of the sentence:

(41) a. Falstaff walked home *drunk*.
      b. Caesar fell to the floor *dead*.

   Some adjectives have two arguments. For example, adjectives referring to psychological states, such as *angry* and *suspicious*, have an experiencer argument and a theme argument, just like verbs such as *like*, *hate*, and *suspect*:

(42) a. Katherine was *angry* at Petruccio.
      b. Portia was *suspicious* of Shylock.
      c. Katherine hates him.
      d. Portia suspected Shylock.

Recall that verbs such as *like* or *hate* assign their experiencer θ-role to the subject position, and their theme θ-role to the object position, as in (42c–d). The adjectives *angry* and *suspicious* behave similarly: they assign their experiencer θ-role to the subject position, and their theme θ-role to the DP in the PP following them.
   Although PPs containing *at* are usually used to refer to a location (as in *Falstaff is at a bar*), the *at*-PP in (42a) is not used in this way; rather, the preposition *at* functions like a case affix in a case-marking language: it identifies its object as the theme participant in the situation described by the adjective. The same is true of the preposition *of* in (42b). Thus, these PPs are analogous to the objects of verbs such as *hate* and *suspect* in (42c–d); in fact, we might even describe these PPs as the objects of these adjectives.

Such PPs are usually referred to as **complements** of the adjective rather than as objects. The term *complement* refers to any constituent other than the subject that functions as an argument of a predicate. Thus, the object and indirect object of a verb are also complements – they are complements of the verb that assigns a θ-role to them; in the same way, the object of a preposition is a complement of the preposition.

When a PP is used to locate something (in time or space), it refers indirectly to a situation in which a person, thing, event, or situation, is in this location. In this case, the preposition functions as a predicate specifying a spatial or temporal relation between two arguments; we may refer to the θ-roles associated with these arguments as **Theme** and **Location**, or **Figure** and **Ground**. Like the adjectives in (38) and (42), prepositions sometimes function as the main predicate of the sentence, following the auxiliary verb *be*, as in (43):

(43) a. The magician was *on the island*.
　　　b. Harfleur is *in France*.

Here, the subject of the sentence is interpreted as the theme, or figure, and the object of the preposition is interpreted as the location, or ground. In other cases, when a PP occurs inside a DP, as in (44), the preposition's theme or figure θ-role is assigned to the DP containing the PP:

(44) a. *The magician on the island* had a daughter.
　　　b. Henry besieged *a city in France*.

Thus, prepositions, like adjectives, share with verbs the property of assigning θ-roles to their arguments.

Finally, we have seen that some nouns (such as *marriage, murder,* and *anger*) refer to events or situations. These nouns all have two arguments, and assign θ-roles to them. Like adjectives, nouns are never followed by direct objects; their complements are usually PPs, as in (45):

(45) a. *Katherine's anger at Petruccio* was no surprise.
　　　b. *Macbeth's murder of Duncan* shocked Malcolm.

In (45a), the noun *anger* (like the related adjective *angry*) refers to a situation involving an experiencer and a theme; in (45b), the noun *murder* (like the related verb *murder*) refers to an event involving an agent and a patient. Whereas the experiencer and agent θ-roles of the adjective *angry* and the verb *murder* are assigned to the subject position of the sentence, the experiencer θ-role of the noun *anger* and the agent θ-role of the noun *murder* are assigned to the nominal specifier position; in a sense, this position functions like a subject position within the DP. In each case, the noun's other θ-role is assigned to the PP complement of the noun; thus, like the prepositions in (42a–b), and unlike the prepositions in (43) and (44), the prepositions in (45) function like case affixes.

Even nouns that do not refer to events and situations function as predicates. For example, nouns like *king*, *witch*, and *friend*, which we described in section 3.2.1 as referring to certain types of people, animals, or things, actually refer to properties attributed to the DPs that contain them; thus, when we use a DP such as *the foolish king* to refer to King Lear, it is the entire DP that refers to Lear; the noun within this DP, like the adjective preceding it, is interpreted as a property attributed to this individual.

Unlike adjectives and prepositions, nouns generally may not occur immediately after the verb *be* and function as the main predicate of the sentence, at least in English:

(46)   a.   *Puck is sprite.
       b.   *Banquo was ghost.

Interestingly, sentences similar to this are perfectly grammatical in languages that do not require the use of definite and indefinite articles, such as Russian. (Recall that Russian also omits the verb *be*.)

(47)   a.   Kolja   durak.   (Russian)
            Kolja+Nom fool+Nom
            'Kolja is a fool.'
       b.   Vorona ptica.
            crow   bird
            'A crow is a bird.'

In English, such nouns must generally be preceded by a determiner; in other words, the entire DP functions as a predicate:

(48)   a.   Lear was *the father of Goneril*.
       b.   Puck was *a sprite*.
       c.   Banquo was *a ghost*.

In these so-called **predicate nominal** constructions, the DP occurring as the object of the verb *be* is not interpreted as referring to some new referent, as in the previous sentences containing DPs; instead, it is interpreted as a property attributed to the referent of the subject of the sentence; in other words, it has a **predicative** interpretation, parallel to that of the adjectives in (38). In fact, these DP predicates are structurally parallel to the adjectival predicates in (38) as well; they are both complements of the verb *be*, and they both assign their theme θ-role to the subject position.

In our discussion thus far, we have used the term *Determiner Phrase* (DP) to refer to the sequence of a determiner and the noun that follows it (including any adjective(s) intervening between them), such as *the king* or *the foolish king*. We have also used the term *Prepositional Phrase* (PP) to refer to the sequence of a preposition and its DP object, such as *in the forest*. In the same way, we refer to the sequence of an adjective and its complement as an **Adjective Phrase** (**AP**); thus, *angry at Petruccio* in (42a) is an AP. Likewise, the sequence of a verb and its complement (or complements, if there are more than one) is called a **Verb Phrase** (**VP**); thus, *sent tennis balls to the king* in sentence (14b) *(The dauphin sent tennis balls to the king)* is a VP. Finally, the sequence of a noun and its complement is a **Noun Phrase** (**NP**); thus, the sequence *father of Goneril* within the DP *the father of Goneril* in (48a) is an NP, as is the sequence *murder of Duncan* in (45b). If a word such as a verb, adjective, or noun has no complement after it, the word may function as a complete phrase all by itself. For example, in a sentence such as *Henry laughed*, the word *laughed* is not only a verb; it also functions as a complete VP. Likewise, in (41a), *Falstaff walked home drunk*, the adjective *drunk* functions as a complete AP.

These sequences of words, or phrases, such as DP, PP, AP, VP, and NP, are named after one of the lexical categories that they contain, typically the first lexical category occurring in the phrase, at least in the English data discussed thus far. Thus, the DP *the foolish king* contains the (D)eterminer *the*; the AP *angry at Petruccio* contains the (A)djective *angry*, and so on. These words (D in DP, A in AP, V in VP, etc.) are called the **heads** of the phrases that contain them. If a category X is the head of a phrase XP, we say that XP is headed by X. Thus, a head combines (or merges) with its complement (or complements) to form a phrase with the same lexical-category name as the original head. In section 3.3, we will examine this issue of phrase structure in more detail.

(a) In the following example sentences, indicate whether the verb is transitive, intransitive, or ditransitive. Note that some verbs can be used either as transitive or as intransitive verbs; you should state how each verb is being used in the sentence you are discussing.

   (i)   Romeo sang to Juliet.
   (ii)   Henry's invasion of France terrified the Dauphin.
   (iii) Petruccio resided in Italy.
   (iv)   The soothsayer gave Caesar a warning.
   (v)   Othello was distrustful of his wife.

(b) Make a list of the predicates occurring in the sentences above, and for each predicate, indicate how many arguments it has, identify the arguments, and indicate the θ-role assigned to each argument.

EXERCISE 3.5

(c)   For each verb, noun, preposition, and adjective occurring in these sentences, indicate whether it is followed by a complement, and identify the complement.

3.2.6   Selection, implicit arguments, null pronouns, and the theta-Criterion

The lexical specification of the argument structure of a verb is sometimes referred to as an instance of **selection**; thus, if a verb's lexical entry specifies that it refers to an event involving an agent and a patient, we say that the verb **selects** an agent argument and a patient argument. The notion of selection implies that if a predicate (such as a verb or adjective) selects an argument with a particular θ-role, then any sentence in which this predicate occurs must also contain a DP that this θ-role is assigned to. For example, if a verb selects an agent, a patient, and a goal, or an experiencer and a theme, then each of these θ-roles must be assigned to a DP in any sentence in which this verb occurs. Thus, the ungrammaticality of the examples in (49) can be attributed to the fact that one or another of the verb's θ-roles cannot be assigned, because the sentence does not contain a DP in the position where this θ-role is supposed to be assigned:

(49)   a.   *Harry gave to Falstaff.   (Patient θ-role is not assigned)
       b.   *Harry gave Falstaff.   (Patient θ-role is not assigned)
       c.   *Gave the wine to Falstaff.   (Agent θ-role is not assigned)
       d.   *Loves Desdemona.   (Experiencer θ-role is not assigned)
       e.   *Harry admires.   (Theme θ-role is not assigned)
       f.   *The king besieged.   (Patient θ-role is not assigned)

The idea that every θ-role selected by a verb must be assigned to an argument in any sentence where the verb occurs is one facet of a general principle known as the θ-**Criterion**; we will discuss this below.

On the other hand, there are many cases where the occurrence of certain arguments of some verbs appears to be optional; for example, consider the examples in (50):

(50)   a.   The king attacked (the city).   (compare with 49f)
       b.   Portia gave money (to a charity).   (compare with 49b)
       c.   Soldiers kill (their enemies).
       d.   Romeo arrived (at Juliet's house).
       e.   Harry laughed (at Falstaff).

When an optional argument is omitted, the event or situation that the verb refers to is often understood to include a participant corresponding to the missing argument. For example, if the direct object is omitted from (50a), we still understand the sentence to mean that the king attacked something (or someone); likewise, if the PP is omitted from (50d), we still understand the sentence to mean that Romeo arrived somewhere. The same is true of the optional arguments in (50b) and (50c): they are syntactically optional, but semantically obligatory; they are called **implicit arguments**. On the other hand, (50e) does not necessarily imply that Harry's laugh was directed at anything or anyone. Thus, the object argument in (50e) is not just syntactically optional; it is semantically optional too, because no implicit argument is required here.

It is clear that we must revise the conclusion that we drew based on (49): that all θ-roles of a verb must be assigned in every sentence where the verb occurs. One way of doing this is to assume that each argument in a verb's argument structure may be specified in the lexicon as being either optional or obligatory; the relevant principle of the θ-Criterion would then require only that obligatory θ-roles must be assigned. On the other hand, the contrast between (50a–d) and (50e) shows that there is a difference between syntactic obligatoriness and semantic obligatoriness: some arguments are semantically obligatory even though they need not be syntactically overt. The conditions determining whether a given argument is optional or obligatory are complicated and poorly understood, and we will not discuss them in detail here.

Although individual verbs appear to vary in mysterious ways in terms of the obligatoriness of their arguments, there is an important generalization that is worth noting: English NEVER allows the subject argument to be omitted, at least in complete sentences; it is always obligatory. (The style of writing in diaries is an exception to this, where the first person pronoun *I* is often omitted.) On the other hand, in many languages, such as Italian and Spanish, the subject can ALWAYS be omitted, as in (51):

(51) a. Ha   visto Petruccio.   (Italian)
          has (have+3Sg) seen Petruccio
          'He (or she) has seen Petruccio.'
      b. Vimos   la casa   de Otelo.   (Spanish)
          saw+3Pl the house of Othello
          'We saw Othello's house.'

As in the case of the implicit object arguments in the English sentences in (50a–d), however, the missing subjects in these Spanish and Italian sentences are semantically obligatory. However, the missing subjects in (51) are not interpreted in the same way as the English implicit object arguments in (50a–d); instead, they are understood as though they were definite pronouns (such as *he, we, they,* or *you*). In these languages, the verb usually has a **subject agreement** suffix on it, indicating the person and number (though

SIDEBAR 3.3

Null objects

Although Italian and Spanish allow null pronouns only in the subject position, some languages allow them in other positions as well, including the object position. This is true of Chickasaw, which has agreement affixes for both subjects and objects, though only for first- and second-person pronouns:

(a) Lhiyohli-li.
chase+1SgI
'I chase it' ('I am chasing it')

(b) Ofi'-at sa-lhiyohli.
dog-Nom   1SgII+chase
'The dog is chasing me'

(c) Chi-lhiyohli-li.
2SgII+chase+1SgI
'I am chasing you'

The missing objects in these examples are interpreted as definite pronouns, like the missing subjects in (51), and unlike the indefinite implicit arguments in (50). Thus, it is natural to assume that these languages allow definite null pronouns to occur in both subject and object positions.

Chinese also appears to allow null pronouns in both subject position and object position. For example, the (overt) third-person singular pronoun *ta* is optional, either in the subject position (d) or in the object position (e):

(d) Zhangsan shuo (ta) bu renshi Lisi.
Zhangsan say   (he) not know Lisi
'Zhangsan said that he does not know Lisi'

(e) Zhangsan shuo Lisi bu renshi (ta).
Zhangsan say   Lisi not know (him)
'Zhangsan said that Lisi does not know him'

Note that Chinese has no agreement affixes on the verb, unlike Chickasaw.

There is an interesting difference in interpretation between null subject pronouns and null object pronouns in Chinese. If the pronoun *ta* is overt in (d) and (e), it can refer either to the referent of the subject of the main clause (Zhangsan) or to some other individual, just like the pronouns *he* and *him* in the English translations. This is also true when the subject of the embedded clause is null (that is, when *ta* is omitted) in (d), but when the object pronoun is null in (e), it may only be understood to refer to some other individual. This has led some linguists to reject the view that Chinese allows null pronouns in object position, suggesting instead that a different kind of null argument occurs in the object position in these examples.

not the gender) of the subject; this agreement suffix occurs regardless of whether the subject itself occurs overtly. The verbs in (51) behave as though they are agreeing with invisible, or silent pronouns in the subject position, analogous to so-called zero affixes in morphology, discussed in chapter 2. These silent pronouns are called **null pronouns**. The existence of null subjects in examples like (51) may appear to be counterexamples to the principle that every obligatory θ-role must be assigned. However, these are not really counterexamples if it is assumed that the sentences really contain these silent pronouns, since these sentences are interpreted as if the verb's subject θ-role is assigned to the silent subject pronoun in each of these examples.

Languages differ both in terms of whether they allow null definite pronouns, and in terms of the positions in the sentence where these null pronouns are permitted. In many cases, null pronouns can be identified by agreement affixes on the verb, as in Italian and Spanish. Some traditional grammarians have suggested that these languages allow null subject pronouns because they have subject agreement affixes, and that languages like English disallow null pronouns because of the relative poverty of subject agreement morphology in English, which only marks agreement for third-person singular subjects, and even then only in the present tense. However, a survey of the world's languages reveals that this kind of explanation does not really hold up to close scrutiny. Some languages (such as German) have extensive subject agreement affixes but do not allow null subject pronouns, whereas other languages (such as Chinese) allow null subject pronouns, even though they have no agreement affixes. Despite the fact that this often leads to ambiguity, it is clear that speakers of languages like Chinese can tolerate this kind of ambiguity; if a speaker wishes to be more explicit, it is still possible to use an overt subject pronoun. Thus, the possibility of null pronouns in subject position is a **parameter** of cross-linguistic variation in the grammars of human languages. This parameter has two values, and children in the course of acquisition learn to assign the value of the parameter for the language being acquired as discussed in chapter 6. This **null subject parameter** has been the focus of much research in recent years; syntacticians have compared null subject languages (like Italian) with other languages, to see if other properties of grammar correlate with the possibility of a null subject.

If every obligatory θ-role in a verb's argument structure is assigned to some element in the sentence in which the verb occurs, we should expect to find at least as many DPs co-occurring with the verb as it has arguments; as we have seen in (49), this expectation is fulfilled. The reverse is also the case: in general, each DP in a sentence must be assigned a θ-role; this is another facet of the so-called θ-Criterion mentioned above. Consider, for example, the sentences in (14) above, which contain a subject, object, and indirect object, repeated here as (14'):

(14′)   a.   Shylock *lent* money to Antonio.
      b.   The Dauphin *sent* tennis balls to the king.
      c.   Harry *passed* the wine to Falstaff.

As we have seen, the agent θ-role is assigned to the subject position, the patient θ-role is assigned to the object position, and the goal θ-role is assigned to the indirect object position. Thus, each of these positions is assigned a θ-role that is specified in the argument structure of the verb. Verbs that select fewer than three arguments cannot occur in sentences of this type:

(52)   a.   *Macbeth *murdered* Duncan *to Banquo*.   (compare with 6a)
      b.   *Othello *liked* Desdemona *to Iago*.   (compare with 7a)
      c.   *Othello *pleased* Desdemona *to Cassio*.   (compare with 8a)
      d.   *Henry *kissed* Katherine *to the Dauphin*. (compare with 9a)
      e.   *Three witches *prepared* a vile broth *to*
         Macbeth.   (compare with 11b)

The verbs in (52) refer to events or situations that only involve two participants: either an agent and a patient (*murder*, *kiss*, and *prepare*) or an experiencer and a theme (*like* and *please*). This is why these verbs do not allow an indirect object: an indirect object must be assigned a goal θ-role, and the kinds of events that these verbs refer to do not involve participants with this thematic role. Consequently, there is no way to coherently interpret the sentences in (52), because the indirect object cannot be assigned an appropriate θ-role.

   Similar considerations explain why verbs selecting just one argument generally do not allow a direct object to occur in the sentence; the events that these verbs refer to have no appropriate θ-role (such as a patient participant) to assign to a DP occurring in this position:

(53)   a.   *Harry laughed Falstaff.
      b.   *Romeo died Juliet.

Surprisingly, however, many of these verbs do allow a DP to occur in the direct object position if the DP refers to the event itself, as (54) shows:

(54)   a.   Falstaff laughed *a hearty laugh*.
      b.   Romeo died *a painful death*.

These DPs are called **cognate objects**, because they are often morphologically related to the verb itself; these cognate objects usually include an adjective describing some property of the event. Not all intransitive verbs allow cognate objects in this way; specifically, unaccusative verbs such as *occur* and *arrive* do not:

(55) a.   *A disaster occurred a quick occurrence.
     b.   *Romeo arrived a welcome arrival.

It has been proposed that the reason unaccusative verbs do not allow cognate objects is that they lack the ability to assign accusative case as shown by (37). According to this theory, all referring expressions (pronouns, names, and DPs) must be assigned a case feature such as nominative, accusative, or dative case, even if this case feature is not marked overtly by a morphological affix; this condition is known as the **case filter**. Thus, the ungrammaticality of the sentences in (55) can be attributed to the case filter: there is no way to assign case to these DPs.

The two central principles of the θ-Criterion are given in (56):

(56) **θ-Criterion**
     a.   Each (obligatory) θ-role selected by a predicate must be assigned to a referential expression (such as a DP).
     b.   Each referential expression must be assigned a θ-role.

Some theories of syntax assume a stricter version of the θ-Criterion, imposing a one-to-one correspondence between θ-roles and referential expressions: each θ-role may only be assigned to one argument, and each argument may be assigned only one θ-role; other theories assume that in some cases, individual referential expressions may be assigned two or more θ-roles. We will not go into this issue here.

EXERCISE 3.6

Each of the following pairs of examples contains one grammatical sentence and one ungrammatical sentence. In each case, the ungrammatical example involves a violation of the θ-Criterion, either because an obligatory θ-role cannot be assigned to a referential expression or because a referential expression cannot be assigned a θ-role. For each grammatical sentence, identify the θ-role assigned to each argument by the verb. For each ungrammatical sentence, identify the θ-role or argument that leads to the ungrammaticality of the example, comparing it with the grammatical sentence preceding it.

(i)   (a) Shylock handed the money to Antonio.
       (b) *Shylock handed to Antonio.
(ii)   (a) The king's troops entered the city.
       (b) *The king's troops entered the city to Shylock.
(iii) (a) Henry laughed at Falstaff.
       (b) *Henry laughed the book at Falstaff.
(iv) (a) Juliet died a sad death.
       (b) *Died a sad death.

3.2.7 Semantic selection, categorial selection, and embedded sentences

We have seen that verbs select arguments with particular θ-roles; they also select certain intrinsic semantic properties of these arguments. For example, the verb *murder* requires both its agent and its patient arguments to be human, while the verb *drink* requires its agent argument to be animate and its patient argument to be liquid. Requirements of this type are called **selectional restrictions**. The sentences in (57) violate these selectional restrictions: the DPs occurring in the subject and object positions in these sentences refer to entities that lack the properties that the verb requires of the arguments associated with the θ-roles that are assigned to these positions. (The exclamation marks (!) preceding these examples indicate that they are semantically anomalous.)

(57) a. !The rock murdered the tree.
      b. !The wine drank the king.

For example, in (57b), the DP occupying the object position is assigned the patient θ-role, but the lexical entry of the verb *drink* specifies that this θ-role is associated with an argument that has a selectional restriction imposed on it, requiring that it be liquid. When speaking metaphorically, we can sometimes appear to violate selectional restrictions; for example, an environmentalist might accuse a logger of murdering a tree, and a gardener might say that a particular plant is thirsty and wants to drink some water. In such usages, speakers are metaphorically attributing properties of humanity or animacy to the tree or garden plant in question; the force of the metaphor arises from the existence of the selectional restriction, which leads us to attribute the property of humanity or animacy to these arguments.

Virtually every verb in English imposes selectional restrictions of one kind or another on its arguments. In many cases, these restrictions arise from the type of θ-role assigned to the argument. For example, experiencers must usually be animate, since inanimate objects, abstract qualities, and events are incapable of having psychological attitudes. As a consequence, virtually all verbs selecting an experiencer argument (*like, hate, resent, worry,* etc.) require that the referential expression receiving this θ-role be animate. On the other hand, some verbs that select an agent allow for non-animate subjects, if the action that the verb refers to can be initiated by something inanimate; for example, the verb *kill*, unlike the verb *murder*, allows either animate or non-animate agents:

(58) a. Brutus killed Caesar.
      b. Madness killed Lear.

Inanimate agents are often called **causes**. These should not be confused with **instruments**, which can also occur as subjects of verbs that select agents. Consider (58c):

(58)   c.   A dagger killed Caesar.

This non-animate subject is an instrument rather than a cause, because it is not the initiator of the action. Instruments, unlike causes, can co-occur with an agent as the object of the preposition *with*:

(58)   d.   Brutus killed Caesar with a dagger.

In addition to imposing selectional restrictions on the intrinsic semantic properties of their arguments, predicates may also impose restrictions on the lexical category of their arguments. This kind of selectional requirement is known as **categorial selection**, or **c-selection**, as opposed to semantic selection, or **s-selection**. Most of the verbs in the data cited above select either DPs, PPs, or APs as their complements, or some combination of DPs and PPs. For example, the verb *murder* selects a DP complement (*Macbeth murdered the king*); the verb *live* selects a PP complement (*Timon lived in Athens*); the verbs *give, lend*, and *pass* select either DP and PP (headed by to), or DP and DP (*Shylock lent the money to Antonio; Shylock lent Antonio the money*); and verbs like *be, seem*, and *become* select an AP complement, among other possibilities (*Othello became jealous*).

In general, the lexical categories of these complements are not free; thus, the patient argument of a verb like *murder* must be a DP rather than an AP, and the location argument of a verb like *live* must be a PP rather than a DP, as (59) shows:

(59)   a.   *Macbeth murdered angry at Duncan.   (compare with 6a)
     b.   *Timon lived Athens.   (compare with 36a).

The question arises whether such facts need to be stipulated in the lexical entries of these verbs, or whether they are predictable on independent grounds. At first glance, it seems reasonable to assume that properties of c-selection are entirely predictable. For example, we have already seen that the verb *murder* imposes a selectional restriction on its patient argument, namely that it refer to a human. But only DPs (including names, pronouns, or DPs headed by determiners) may refer to humans; APs such as *angry at Duncan* refer to properties. Therefore, the fact that the complement of murder in (59a) must be a DP is surely predictable, given the semantic selectional restriction that this verb imposes. Similarly, the fact that the location argument of the verb *live* must be a PP, rather than a name or DP as in (59b), can plausibly be explained by assuming that only PPs may refer to locations.

On the other hand, a consideration of related data suggests that the picture is less clear. First, consider the proposal that only PPs may refer to locations, which we introduced to explain (59b). Quite apart from the fact that the name *Athens* arguably does refer to a location, the contrast between (59b) and (60a) shows that sometimes verbs with very similar meanings, selecting arguments with similar or identical θ-roles, may select different categories for those arguments; a similar contrast between another pair of nearly synonymous verbs is illustrated in (60b–e):

(60) a. The Greeks inhabited Athens (. . . long before the age of Pericles).
     b. Romeo arrived *at Juliet's house.*   (=50d)
     c. *Romeo arrived *Juliet's house.*
     d. Romeo reached *Juliet's house.*
     e. *Romeo reached *at Juliet's house.*

These data indicate that the lexical category of a complement is sometimes unpredictable; it is an idiosyncratic property of the verb selecting the argument, and must therefore be specified in the lexical entry of the verb.

So far, we have only looked at a small sample of the types of complements verbs may select; the actual range of categorial selection is much more diverse. To get a more complete picture, we must take a detour from the main line of our discussion and examine the syntax of clausal complementation – the process that allows complex sentences to be formed, by **embedding** a smaller sentence within a larger one. Verbs that refer to speech events (*say, tell, announce, proclaim, inform, promise,* etc.), or to situations involving thought processes (*believe, think, know, forget, remember, doubt,* etc.) typically select complements containing an entire sentence referring to the content of what is reported to be said, believed, known, etc. These embedded sentences are often preceded by a so-called **complementizer** word such as *that*, and the sequence of the complementizer and the embedded sentence that follows it is called a **Complementizer Phrase**, or **CP**. Some verbs, such as *think* and *know*, select just a CP complement, as in (61a); other verbs, such as *tell* and *inform*, select a DP complement followed by a CP complement, as in (61b); other verbs, such as *say* and *mention*, select an optional PP complement followed by a CP complement, as in (61c). CPs may also occur in the subject position, if they are semantically compatible with the θ-role that the verb assigns there, as in (61d):

(61) a. Hamlet knew *that his father had been murdered.*
     b. Antonio told Bassanio *that his ship was lost.*
     c. Antony said (to Cleopatra) *that he loved her.*
     d. *That Lysander had fallen in love with Helena* astonished Hermia.

In traditional grammars, embedded sentences are called **subordinate clauses**, and the complementizers that precede them are often called **subordinating conjunctions**; the latter term is seldom used nowadays in Linguistics, but the term *subordinate clause* is still widely used. In citing complex example sentences such as those in (61), linguists often enclose the subordinate clause CP in square brackets, in order to clearly mark the boundary between it and the **main clause** (or **matrix clause**) within which it is contained, as in (62):

(62)   Portia said [that the quality of mercy is not strained].

Although embedded sentences like those in (61) and (62) are described as CPs, the complementizer is not always obligatory; just as some DPs do not actually contain an overt determiner, likewise some CPs do not contain an overt complementizer; thus, the complementizer *that* can be omitted in (61a), (61b), and (62), though not in (61d) (or in (61c), if there is a PP as well as a CP.) Nevertheless we will refer to all of these embedded sentences as CPs.

The sentences in (61–62) are examples of **indirect discourse**; the embedded sentence conveys the meaning of the reported thought or utterance, but does not necessarily use exactly the same words as the original; in indirect discourse, the subordinate clause may be a paraphrase of what was said or thought, often substituting different tenses and pronouns; for example, the subordinate clauses in (61) all contain third-person pronouns, instead of the first- or second-person pronouns used by the characters in Shakespeare's plays whose speech or thought is being reported by the speaker. When a speaker wishes to repeat the exact words of an original utterance, the complementizer *that* is omitted, and a distinctive intonation or melody is used; in writing, this is conventionally marked by quotation marks; it is called **direct discourse**.

Another way that indirect discourse may differ from direct discourse is in the use of infinitival clauses, as in (63). The embedded sentences or subordinate clauses in (61) and (62) are all finite clauses; apart from the fact that they begin with a complementizer, they could stand alone as complete English sentences. On the other hand, the subordinate clauses enclosed in square brackets in (63) could not stand alone as complete sentences in their own right, as (64) shows; they may only function as embedded sentences, conveying indirect discourse:

(63)   a.   Antonio is hoping [for his ship to come in].
      b.   [For Shylock to shed a drop of blood] would violate the law.
      c.   Petruccio expects [to marry Katherine].
      d.   [To marry Katherine] would please Petruccio.
      e.   Lady Macbeth told her husband [to kill the king].
      f.   Goneril believed [him to be a fool].

(64)   a.   *For Shylock to shed a drop of blood.
  b.   *To marry Katherine.
  c.   *Him to be a fool.

Infinitival clauses in English contain a VP headed by a bare root form of a verb, preceded by the prepositional particle *to*; sometimes, though not always, the infinitive begins with the infinitival complementizer *for*. If the first element of the infinitival clause is the complementizer *for*, as in (63a) and (63b), the infinitive is called a *for-infinitive*. Like finite embedded sentences introduced by the complementizer *that*, these *for*-infinitives are CPs; however, although their structure is similar to that of finite CPs, the two types of clauses are not identical, as we shall see. Therefore, we will use the feature [±FIN(ITE)] (pronounced 'plus or minus finite') to distinguish between them; finite CPs, like their finite complementizer heads, are [+FIN], while infinitival CPs and their infinitival complementizer heads are [–FIN].

If the infinitival clause does not contain the complementizer *for*, but rather begins with an overt subject DP, as in (63f), it is called an **Exceptional Case Marking (ECM)** infinitive. This terminology reflects the fact that the DP in the subject position of the infinitive appears to be assigned accusative case by the verb in the main clause – that is, by the verb *believe* in (63f) – as though it were the object of that verb, even though it is interpreted semantically as the subject of the lower clause. Some linguists believe that ECM infinitives, like *for*-infinitives, are CPs; other linguists believe they should be classified as **TPs (Tense Phrases)**, headed by the infinitival preverbal particle *to*. We will discuss TPs in section 3.3, and in chapter 5.

Many infinitival clauses contain no overt DP preceding the sequence of *to + Verb*, as in (63c) and (63d). In this case, the missing subject is interpreted in a way similar to the null subject pronoun in a null subject language: it is interpreted as a pronoun referring to the same referent as a noun phrase occurring elsewhere in the sentence. For example, in (63c), the missing subject is interpreted as though it were the pronoun *he*, referring to the same individual as the subject of the main sentence (Petruccio); thus, if (63c) were paraphrased using a finite clause instead of the infinitive, we would use a pronoun to replace the missing subject: *Petruccio expects that he will marry Kate*. Thus, English infinitives, unlike regular English finite clauses, resemble finite clauses in languages such as Spanish, Italian, and Chinese, in allowing null pronouns to occur in their subject position. Syntacticians use the abbreviation PRO to represent this implicit silent (null) pronoun in the subject position of an infinitive, as in (65):

(65)   Petruccio$_i$ expects [PRO$_i$ to marry Kate].

The subscript index 'i' in (65) indicates that the silent pronoun (PRO) must be interpreted as referring to the same referent as the subject of the main sentence, *Petruccio*. This relationship between the silent pronoun and the subject of the main sentence is called **co-reference**. Co-reference is optional with overt pronouns in sentences like *Petruccio expects he will marry Kate*. When a silent PRO in the subject position of an embedded infinitival clause must be understood as being **co-referential** with a DP in the main clause, as in (65), we say that the PRO is **controlled** by the DP in the main clause; constructions like those in (65) are described as **subject control** constructions, because the PRO is controlled by the subject of the main clause. As in the case of the Exceptional Case Marking infinitives discussed above, some linguists believe that these control infinitives are CPs, despite the fact that they contain no overt complementizer, at least in standard English. (In some regional dialects of English, control infinitives do contain an overt complementizer, allowing for sentences such as *I am hoping for to see my true love*. Likewise, control infinitives in languages such as French and Italian begin with prepositional particles that have been analyzed as complementizers.)

Another kind of subordinate clause used in English grammar is the so-called **small clause**. Small clauses, as their name implies, are smaller than finite clauses and infinitives in a number of ways; they do not contain complementizers, auxiliary verbs, tense markers, or elements similar to the particle *to* preceding the verb in an infinitive. In fact, many small clauses do not even contain a verb; they just contain a subject DP followed by a predicate, such as an AP or DP, as in (66):

(66)   a.   Goneril considers [her father *foolish*].
       b.   The suitors made [Kate *angry*].
       c.   Goneril considers [her father *a fool*].
       d.   The lords made [Macbeth *their king*].

Verbs of perception (such as *see, hear,* and *feel*) and certain verbs of causation (such as *make* and *let*) typically select small clauses consisting of just a subject DP and a **bare VP**, that is, a VP headed by a bare root form of the verb, as in (67a–c):

(67)   a.   Macbeth saw [the forest *move towards the castle*].
       b.   Juliet heard [Romeo *call out her name*].
       c.   Lear let [his daughters *take over the realm*].

Bare VPs also occur by themselves as complements of modal verbs (*can, should, must, may, will,* etc.) in English, as in (68a–b):

(68) a. Caesar should [follow the soothsayer's advice].
    b. Kate must [choose a husband].

In some languages, such as French, bare VPs are indistinguishable from infinitival complements such as (63f), since the infinitival form of the verb is used instead of a bare root form; even for English, some linguists describe the VPs in (67–68) as infinitives rather than as small clauses.

Since small clauses do not contain any complementizers, auxiliary verbs, or tense markers, they are usually not classified as CPs or TPs; in fact, there is no overt element (other than the subject DP and the predicate phrase) that can be assumed to be the head of the small clause. What kind of phrase, then, is a small clause – if, indeed, it is a phrase? One suggestion is that the head of a small clause is the same element as the head of its predicate phrase; thus, in (66a), the head of the small clause is the adjective, and the entire small clause (including its subject DP) is actually a kind of AP, while in (67a), the small clause is a kind of VP headed by the verb *move*. Others have suggested that small clauses are headed by silent (null) tense markers, and that small clauses are special kinds of TPs. Still other linguists believe that small clauses are not really clauses at all, and that verbs like *consider* in (66a) actually select two independent complements (a DP followed by an AP). We will not discuss the evidence supporting each of these theories about small clauses here; we will simply refer to them as small clauses (SCs), setting aside these issues.

Let us now return to the issue of categorial selection. In the preceding pages, we have examined a wide variety of patterns of clausal complementation; the crucial point to observe is that individual verbs differ from each other in terms of the kinds of pattern that they allow. Some verbs select [+FIN] CP complements; some verbs select [–FIN] CP complements; some verbs select SC complements of one kind or another; and some verbs allow for more than one option. Moreover, among those verbs that select [–FIN] CP complements, some select *for*-infinitives, some select Exceptional Case Marking infinitives, and some select control infinitives. Finally, some verbs select a DP or PP complement in addition to their CP complement, as we have seen. Altogether, this adds up to almost 20 different possible combinations. As the examples in (69) show, verbs may not occur with the wrong type of clausal complement:

(69) a. *Caesar thought Brutus to stab him.
    b. *Petruccio wanted that he married Kate.
    c. *The soothsayer told to Caesar that he should beware the ides of March.
    d. *Portia told for Antonio to repay Shylock.

Moreover, if we look at languages other than English, the situation becomes even more complicated. For example, in languages such as Spanish and Italian, finite CP complements may contain verbs bearing affixes for either **indicative** or **subjunctive** mood; in these languages, verbs selecting CP complements may differ from each other according to whether their CP complements are indicative (that is, contain verbs with indicative mood affixes) or subjunctive. Even in standard American English, some verbs, such as *demand*, *insist* and *require*, select subjunctive CP complements, identifiable by the lack of a subject agreement suffix on the verb, as in (70):

(70)   a.   Antony demands [that the conspirators *be* punished].
        b.   *Antony demands [(that) the conspirators *are* punished].

The data in (61–70) indicate not only that it is necessary to distinguish among various kinds of clausal complements, but also that the lexical entries of the verbs selecting these complements must be able to select specific types of clausal complements.

In some cases, however, the lexical category of an argument selected by a verb is predictable, in whole or in part, either from the θ-role that the verb assigns to that argument, or from the semantic selectional restrictions that the verb imposes on it. We have already discussed one such example, namely the fact that the category of the patient argument of the verb *murder* must be a DP, which we attributed to the selectional requirement that this verb imposes. A more general tendency concerns arguments that are assigned the experiencer θ-role: these must refer to animate referents, as we have seen. Such arguments must always be DPs, rather than members of some other lexical category such as APs or VPs, as (71) shows:

(71)   a.   *Henry* likes Falstaff.
        b.   Shylock annoyed *the judge*.
        c.   **Angry* likes Falstaff.
        d.   *Shylock annoyed *kill*.

This restriction does not need to be stated explicitly in the lexical entries of the verbs *like* and *annoy*, because it is a side-effect of the experiencer θ-role that these verbs assign to their subject and object positions, respectively. The experiencer θ-role can only be assigned to a constituent that refers to an animate being, and only DPs (including names or pronouns, as well as DPs with overt determiners) can refer to such entities; verbs and adjectives cannot.

SIDEBAR 3.4

Questions

The verbs in (61a–c) all select CPs beginning with the complementizer *that*, which is often optional. On the other hand, verbs like *ask* and *wonder* are generally not followed by embedded sentences of this type; instead, they are usually followed by embedded sentences beginning with a **wh-word** such as *who*, *what*, *where*, *why*, etc. CPs of this type are called [+WH] CPs.

(a)   Henry wondered [who Williams served under].
(b)   Guildenstern asked Hamlet [what they should say].
(c)   *Henry wondered [(that) Williams served under Captain Gower].
(d)   *Guildenstern asked Hamlet [(that) they should say something].

This is usually explained in terms of the selectional restrictions that these verbs impose on their theme arguments. Verbs like *ask* and *wonder* refer to events or situations in which someone utters or ponders a question; thus, the lexical entries of these verbs stipulate that their theme argument must refer to a question. In English, sentences beginning with wh-words are usually interpreted as questions, as in (e) and (f):

(e)   Who do you serve under?
(f)   What should they say?

On the other hand, the CP complements in (61) cannot be interpreted as questions; they must be interpreted as declarative statements or beliefs. Thus, the fact that the CP complements of *ask* and *wonder* must begin with a wh-word, as in (a) and (b), rather than with the declarative complementizer *that*, as in (c) and (d), can be explained in terms of the fact that these verbs specifically select theme arguments that can be interpreted as questions. Verbs like *think* and *doubt* have the opposite property: they select theme arguments that are interpreted as declarative statements or beliefs, accounting for the data in (g–i):

(g)   Henry thinks/doubts [that Williams serves under Captain Gower].
(h)   *Henry thinks/doubts [who Williams serves under].
(i)   *Hamlet thought/doubted [what Guildenstern should say].

Many verbs, including *tell*, *know*, and *forget*, allow both types of complements. In general, when a [+WH] CP occurs with one of these verbs, it is understood to refer to the answer to a question, rather than to the question itself.

   Although the **embedded questions** (also called **indirect questions**) in (a–b) resemble simple **direct questions** like (e–f) in terms of the occurrence of a wh-word at the beginning of the sentence, they differ in terms of the word order: in simple (direct) questions, the wh-word is immediately followed by an auxiliary verb, which is displaced from its normal position following the subject position. This movement of the auxiliary verb to a position preceding the subject is known as **Subject–Auxiliary Inversion**; it and other facts about the syntax of direct and indirect questions is discussed in greater detail in chapter 5.

Similarly, although we have seen that individual verbs selecting clausal complements differ from each other in apparently unpredictable ways in terms of the kind of clausal complement that they select, the fact that embedded sentences of one sort or another occur as complements of these verbs, as opposed to verbs like *eat, kiss, murder*, etc., is certainly predictable from the kinds of events or situations that the two groups of verbs describe. Since embedded clauses typically denote propositions (that is, statements or ideas, more or less), rather than material objects such as food or people for example, it follows that they can only occur as complements of predicates that refer to events or situations that involve propositions as participants, thus explaining the unacceptable status of the data in (72):

(72) a.   *Portia ate [that the quality of mercy is not strained].
      b.   *Lysander kissed [that he loved Helena].

These sentences are anomalous because one cannot eat or kiss an idea; the fact that these verbs cannot take CPs as their complements is predictable from their meaning. To sum up, c-selection is *partly* predictable on the basis of other aspects of a verb's argument structure, but not entirely so.

Each of the following sentences is ungrammatical (or semantically anomalous) because it violates one or more selectional properties of the verb. In each case, state the relevant semantic selectional restriction(s) or categorial selectional property that the sentence violates, and provide a grammatical and semantically natural sentence using the same verb.

(i)   *The witches stirred the tree.
(ii)   *Shylock died Bassanio.
(iii) *Portia ate that mercy is admirable.
(iv)   *Antony informed to Cleopatra that she was beautiful.
(v)   *Kate should angry at Petruccio.
(vi)   *The lords made.

**EXERCISE
3.7**

3.3 Phrases and Constituent Structure

3.3.1 Representing phrase structure: trees and brackets

The idea that the words of a sentence are grouped together to form phrases implies that sentences are not just composed of sequences of words; rather, they are composed of phrases. The particular way in which these phrases are formed results in a specific structure for each sentence; this structure can be represented in the form of **syntactic tree diagrams**, similar to the tree diagrams used in chapter 2 to represent the morphological structure of words. In this section, we will show how to draw tree diagrams for phrases and sentences; we will also introduce several technical terms used to describe the structural relations that these trees represent. The concepts associated with these terms are fairly simple, even though the task of learning them may be a bit tedious. Nevertheless, it is important to learn what these terms mean, since the subsequent discussion of syntactic rules will make use of them, and papers and articles you will read will also use these terms.

In section 3.2, we discussed certain parallels between verbs and other lexical categories (such as adjectives, prepositions, and nouns) in terms of the way that they assign θ-roles to their complements. In the course of our discussion, we stated that these lexical categories combine with their complements to form phrases. For example, the sequence of a preposition and its object forms a Prepositional Phrase (PP); likewise, the sequence of an adjective and its complement forms an Adjective Phrase (AP), and so on. The various kinds of phrases introduced in section 3.2 are exemplified in (73). Each line in (73) includes a sequence of constituents forming a particular type of phrase, followed by a few actual examples of phrases that we have already seen in previous example sentences:

(73) a.　　　P + DP forms a PP: *in Athens, to the king*, etc.

　　　b. i.　　A + PP forms an AP: *angry at Petruccio*, etc.
　　　　　ii.　A also forms an AP by itself: *angry, suspicious*, etc.

　　　c. i.　　N + PP forms an NP: *murder of Duncan, father of Goneril*, etc.
　　　　　ii.　N also forms an NP by itself: *murder, wine, lords*, etc.
　　　　　iii.　A + NP forms an NP: *old king of France, happy lover, red sword*, etc.

　　　d. i.　　D + NP forms a DP: *the murder of Duncan, a daughter*, etc.
　　　　　ii.　A Name or Pronoun forms a DP by itself: *Duncan, she*, etc.

　　　e. i.　　V + DP forms a VP: *suffocated Desdemona, sued Antonio*, etc.
　　　　　ii.　V + PP forms a VP: *lives in Athens, laughed at Falstaff*, etc.
　　　　　iii.　V + DP + PP forms a VP: *passed the wine to Falstaff*, etc.
　　　　　iv.　V + CP forms a VP: *say that Falstaff likes wine*, etc.

> v. V + DP + CP forms a VP: *told Bassanio that his ship was lost*, etc.
> vi. V + VP forms a VP: *should follow his advice*, etc.
> vii. V also forms a VP by itself: *arrived, died*, etc.
>
> f.   DP + VP forms a Sentence: *Timon lives in Athens, Henry laughed at Falstaff*, etc.
>
> g.   C + Sentence forms a CP: *that his father had been murdered*, etc.

Almost every phrase listed in (73) is formed by combining a lexical category with a phrase that follows it, forming a new phrase named after the original lexical category; thus, X + YP forms XP; in other words, every phrase XP contains a lexical category X and some additional category YP. The only exceptions to this generalization are the phrase-types *Sentence* (composed of DP + VP), and *DP*, which sometimes contains just a name or a pronoun, instead of a determiner and a noun. We will reconsider the structure of these phrases in section 3.4 below.

The phrases formed by the rules in (73) can be represented in graphic form by means of tree diagrams, as noted above. For each individual phrase, the structure is relatively simple, as illustrated by the trees in (74), which are based directly on the sequences listed in (73). For example, (73a) states that a PP is formed by a sequence of a P followed by a DP; this is represented graphically in (74a) by means of the lines, or **branches**, connecting the PP to each of its component parts: the P on the left branch, and the DP on the right branch. The same is true of the trees for AP, based on (73bi), DP, based on (73di), and NP, based on (73ci):

(74)   a.   PP   b.   AP   c.   DP   d.   NP

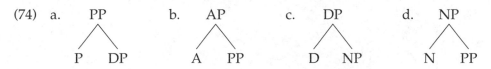

       P   DP   A   PP   D   NP   N   PP

Each tree in (74) has just two branches corresponding to the two parts of the phrase. But some of the verb phrases in (73e) contain three constituent parts, rather than just two; for example, a VP may contain a verb, a DP, and either a PP or CP, as indicated in (73e.iii) and (73e.v). The trees for these phrases therefore contain three branches, as in (75a) and (75b), respectively. On the other hand, some phrases consist of just a single part; for example, a DP may contain just a name, and an NP may contain just a noun; the trees for these phrases have just a single branch, as in (75c) and (75d):

(75)   a.   VP   b.   VP   c.   DP   d.   NP

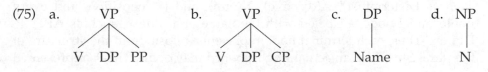

     V   DP   PP   V   DP   CP   Name   N

Tree diagrams such as those in (74–75) consist of a set of labeled **nodes**, connected to one another by vertical or diagonal lines. Each node represents a **constituent**, or component part, of the phrase whose structure it represents. At the bottom of each tree, like leaves at the ends of the branches of real trees, are the **terminal nodes**; all nodes located higher up in the tree are called **nonterminal nodes**. Each tree in (74–75) contains exactly one nonterminal node, and between one and three terminal nodes. These trees represent just one level of structure: they show the component parts of the entire phrase. However, some of these component parts are themselves phrases, and they also have an internal phrase structure. Consider, for example, the tree in (74b) for AP, which is formed by combining an adjective and a PP, as in the AP *angry at the witches*. The PP within this AP also has an internal structure, illustrated in (74a): it contains a P and a DP. Thus, a more complete tree for such an AP would look like (76), combining (74a) and (74b):

(76)

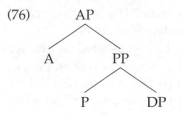

Even this tree is incomplete, since it does not show the internal structure of the DP *the witches*, which contains a determiner followed by an NP, as in (74c); this NP consists of just a noun, as in (75d); thus, a complete phrase structure tree for the AP would correspond to (77):

(77)

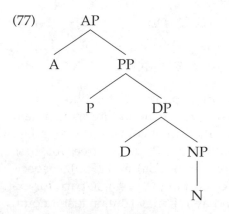

In (77), every terminal node is labeled with the name of a lexical category, such as D(eterminer), A(djective), N(oun), and (P)reposition, and every nonterminal node is labeled with the name of a phrase, such as AP, NP, DP, etc. Thus, each terminal node represents a position in the structure of the phrase in which an actual English word may occur. This is represented on the tree diagram by attaching actual words beneath the lexical category nodes in the tree, as in (78):

(78)

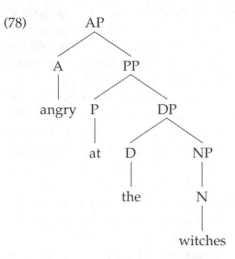

Whenever two nodes are connected to each other by a diagonal line, this indicates that the larger constituent, represented by the higher node, contains the smaller constituent, represented by the lower node. We refer to the smaller constituent as a **subconstituent** of the larger constituent that contains it; thus, in (78), the lexical category node P and the phrase node DP that immediately follows it are both subconstituents of the phrase PP. Linguists often use the term **dominate** instead of *contain*; thus, every constituent dominates all of its subconstituents.

The nodes of the tree are arranged in a linear order, written left-to-right across the page. This left-to-right order represents the temporal order in which the words dominated by these nodes are pronounced, just as in the standard **orthographies** (writing systems) of English and many other languages. Syntacticians usually refer to this ordering in terms of the relation of **precedence**, and use the terms left and right to refer to the temporal order in which the words or pronounced. Thus, the fact that the A-node precedes the PP-node in (78) represents the fact that the word dominated by the A-node (*angry*) is uttered before the words dominated by the PP node (*at the witches*). Although this may seem obvious to you, as a speaker of English, it is important to bear in mind that not all languages use orthographies that employ this left-to-right ordering convention to represent temporal order in spoken language; for example, Arabic and Chinese typically use the opposite order (right-to-left). Nevertheless, in Linguistics, syntactic tree diagrams always employ the left-to-right ordering convention – even in representing the structure of sentences in languages such as Arabic and Chinese.

The relations of precedence (temporal ordering) and dominance (containment) are the fundamental properties of sentence structure that syntactic tree diagrams represent. Both of these relations are **transitive relations**: if A precedes B, and B precedes C, then A also precedes C; likewise, if A dominates B, and B dominates C, then A also dominates C. For example, in (78), the adjective *angry* precedes the preposition *at*, and *at* precedes the determiner *the*; therefore, *angry* also precedes *the*. Similarly, the AP node in (78) dominates the PP node, and the PP node dominates the DP node; therefore the AP node dominates the DP node too. Although precedence and dominance are transitive relations, the relations of **immediate precedence** and **immediate dominance** are not. If a constituent X precedes another constituent Z, then X immediately precedes Z only if there is no other constituent in between them; thus, if X precedes Y and Y precedes Z, then X does not immediately precede Z. For example, in (78), the preposition *at* does not immediately precede the noun *witches*, because the determiner *the* occurs in between them. Likewise, if X dominates Y and Y dominates Z, then X does not immediately dominate Z; for example, the AP node in (78) does not immediately dominate the DP node.

If X immediately dominates Y, then Y is an **immediate constituent** of X; for example, in (78), A and PP are immediate constituents of AP; P and DP are immediate constituents of PP, and so on. When two nodes are immediately dominated by the same node, they are **sisters** of each other; thus, in (78), A and PP are sisters, P and DP are sisters, and D and NP are sisters. Sister constituents are often adjacent to each other, but adjacent constituents are not necessarily sisters. For example, in (78), the preposition *at* is adjacent to the determiner *the*, but these two constituents are not sisters; the determiner is a sister of the NP *witches*, and the preposition is a sister of the entire DP *the witches*. Conversely, sister constituents are not necessarily adjacent to each other; it depends on how many sisters there are. If a node immediately dominates two subconstituents, it is said to be **binary-branching**, since there are two branches beneath it; if it dominates three constituents, it is said to be **ternary branching**, and if it dominates just one node, it is said to be **non-branching**. In a ternary-branching structure, the leftmost sister is not adjacent to the rightmost sister. For example, the tree in (75a), where VP immediately dominates V, DP, and PP (representing the structure of a verb phrase such as *pass the wine to Falstaff* or *murder Duncan with a knife*), the verb is not adjacent to its PP sister. Thus, adjacency and sisterhood are distinct notions.

Now let us consider the phrase structure of an entire sentence, analyzed in terms of the phrases discussed above. We will use (79) as an example:

(79)   The lords will discover that Macbeth murdered Duncan with a knife.

In (79), the nouns *lords* and *knife* each form an NP by themselves; each of these NPs combines with a preceding determiner (*the* or *a*) to form a DP (*the lords* and *a knife*). The words *Macbeth* and *Duncan* are both names, so they each form a DP by themselves; thus, (79) contains a total of four DPs. The final DP (*a knife*) is combined with the preceding preposition *with* to form the PP *with a knife*. This PP is combined with the verb *murdered* and the DP *Duncan* to form the VP *murdered Duncan with a knife*; this VP is combined with the preceding DP *Macbeth* to form the sentence *Macbeth murdered Duncan with a knife*. This sentence is combined with the preceding complementizer *that* to form the CP *that Macbeth murdered Duncan with a knife*; this CP is combined with the preceding verb *discover* to form the VP *discover that Macbeth murdered Duncan with a knife*, which in turn is combined with the preceding modal verb *will* to form the larger VP *will discover that Macbeth murdered Duncan with a knife*. This VP is combined with the preceding DP *the lords* to form the complete sentence (79). We can represent the phrase structure that results from these successive steps of forming phrases by means of the tree diagram in (80):

(80)

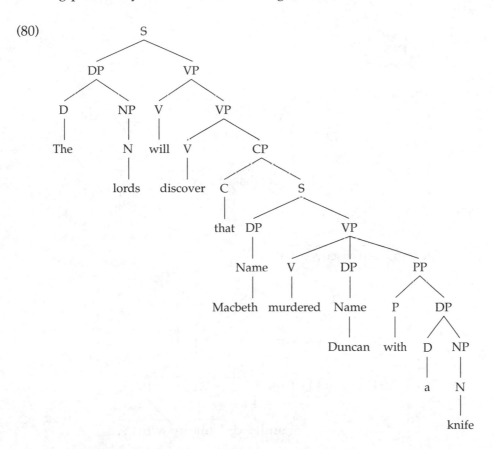

Tree diagrams such as (80) represent every level of the hierarchical phrase structure of the sentence, with a node above each word. However, linguists sometimes use incomplete tree structures, where the internal structure of certain constituents is not shown. Often this is done to save space, especially if the omitted structure would be obvious to other linguists; in other cases, a linguist may choose to omit structure that is irrelevant to the point under discussion, thus simplifying the presentation by highlighting the portion of the structure that is relevant. For example, when a (non-branching) node dominates just one node, either the higher or lower node may be omitted, along with the branch connecting it to the node that remains. When the omitted structure involves one or more branching nodes, a triangle is usually used to represent the portion of the structure that has been omitted from the tree, with the words contained in this part of the tree written under the base of the triangle. Often, some of the words are left out of the tree, or replaced with sequences of dots. The trees in (81) and (82) provide abbreviated and incomplete representations of the structure of sentence (79):

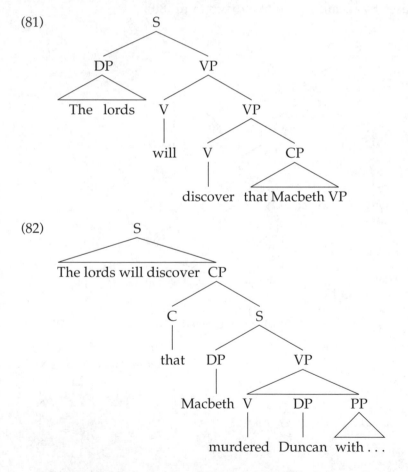

When linguists use tree structures like (80), (81), or (82) to represent the phrase structures of sentences, they are making claims about the structures assigned to these sentences by the mental grammars of native speakers.

However, they are not claiming that these tree diagrams actually pop up in the minds of native speakers whenever they produce or hear these sentences. These tree structures are just a means of representing two important abstract properties of constituent structure: precedence and dominance. It is these abstract properties of constituent structure (or the implicit knowledge of them) that linguists attribute to the mental grammars of native speakers, rather than the actual tree diagrams that represent these properties graphically in visual form. Indeed, linguists sometimes choose a different notation to represent these relations. For example, trees are occasionally drawn upside-down, in a mirror image of the trees we have seen, with subconstituents above the constituents that contain them.

Another method of representing constituent structure involves labeled brackets. Like the tree diagram notation, the labeled bracket notation uses left-to-right order to represent temporal precedence. The main difference between the notations concerns the means of representing dominance (containment): if X dominates Y, then a pair of brackets labeled 'X' surrounds Y; thus, an NP containing only a noun is represented as [$_{NP}$ N], while an NP containing a noun and a PP is represented as [$_{NP}$ N PP]. If X dominates Y and Y dominates Z, then Z is surrounded by a pair of brackets labeled 'Y', and these brackets are surrounded by another pair of brackets labeled 'X'. For example, a DP that immediately dominates both a determiner and an NP composed of a noun and PP is represented as [$_{DP}$ D [$_{NP}$ N PP]]. The information represented by the tree (78) is rendered as in (83):

(83) [$_{AP}$ [$_A$ angry] [$_{PP}$ [$_P$ at] [$_{DP}$ [$_D$ the] [$_{NP}$ [$_N$ witches]]]]]

Like tree diagrams, labeled bracketing representations of a sentence can be abbreviated by failing to represent certain parts of the phrase structure of the sentence; this is achieved by omitting pairs of labeled brackets. For example, the labeled bracketing representation corresponding to the abbreviated tree in (82) is rendered as (84), while the labeled bracketing corresponding to (83) is as in (85):

(84) [[$_{DP}$ The lords] [$_{VP}$ [$_V$ will] [$_{VP}$ [$_V$ discover] [$_{CP}$ that Macbeth VP]]]]

(85) [$_S$ The lords will discover [$_{CP}$ [$_C$ that] [$_S$ [$_{DP}$ Macbeth]
       [$_{VP}$ [$_V$ murdered] [$_{DP}$ Duncan] [$_{PP}$ with . . .]]]]]

Occasionally, labeled boxes are used instead of labeled brackets. In the box notation, the labeled box entirely surrounds its contents; boxes representing subconstituents are enclosed within larger boxes representing the constituents that dominate them. As in the case of labeled brackets, this notation can be abbreviated in various ways, including the omission of boxes.

When alternative notational models represent the same abstract properties of sentences in different ways, as in the cases discussed here, the models are **notational variants**; as linguists, we are primarily interested in the abstract structural properties; the notations that we use to express these properties are just a means to an end.

EXERCISE 3.8

(a) Draw phrase structure trees for each of the following sentences, based on the rules in (73) and the trees given in this section. In sentence (ii), analyze *Law* as a (proper) name.

(i) The Dauphin will give the old balls to the king.
(ii) The Doge believed that Portia was a doctor of Law.
(iii) The soothsayer told Caesar that he should stay in this house.

(b) How many nonterminal nodes are there in the tree for sentence (i)? How many nodes does the VP node dominating the verb *give* in (i) immediately dominate? How many binary-branching nodes occur in the tree for sentence (ii)? How many sisters does the determiner *the* have in sentence (ii)? How many nodes does the CP node in sentence (iii) dominate? What are the immediate constituents of the PP node in sentence (iii)?

(c) Now represent the same constituent structures for sentences (i–iii) in the labeled bracketing notation.

3.3.2 Evidence for phrase structure: distribution, movement, pro-forms, deletion, and coordination

In the previous section, we explained how the constituent structure of phrases can be represented in graphic form, and we highlighted various technical properties of constituent structures. The structures that we assigned to actual phrases and sentences were based on the phrases defined in (73), but thus far we have not provided any evidence that these structures are correct; we have simply assumed this to be the case. In each case, many alternative structures might have been chosen instead; even trained linguists often disagree on what the correct constituent structure is for many constructions.

We can illustrate the problem in a general way with an idealized case. Suppose a phrase P dominates two terminal elements, X and Y, where X precedes Y. There is only one structure possible here: P immediately dominates both X and Y. But suppose P contains three terminal elements (X, Y, and Z), in that order. Hypothetically, three structures are possible:

(86) a.   b.   c.

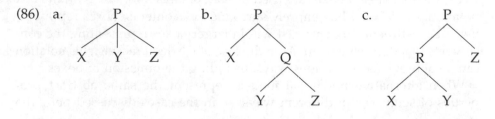

As the number of terminal elements increases, the number of possible structures multiplies even faster. For example, a constituent containing a sequence of four terminal elements would have 11 structures, and a constituent having five terminal elements would have over 40. In actual sentences, where the terminal elements are words, the problem is severe: a sentence of 15 or 20 words has an enormous number of hypothetically possible constituent structures. How can we identify the correct structure? That is the topic of this section.

In trying to decide among alternative possible structures, such as those in (86), linguists identify the constituents that each structure posits, and then seek evidence for or against the existence of these constituents. In (86a), P directly dominates X, Y, and Z, and there are no subconstituents of P other than X, Y, and Z. But in (86b) and (86c), P immediately dominates an additional constituent, which we have labeled 'Q' (in 86b) and 'R' (in 86c). If (86b) is correct, there is a phrase Q containing Y and Z; if (86c) is correct, there is a phrase R containing X and Y; and if (86a) is correct, then neither Q nor R exists. Thus, to discover which of the three candidate structures is correct, we must look for evidence for or against the existence of Q and R.

What kind of evidence would indicate whether a particular sequence of words forms a constituent? Although we can hear each word in a sentence, we cannot hear the constituent structure; it is inaudible, like a silent (null) pronoun. Scientists in other fields of inquiry (such as physics, astronomy, and biology) have argued for the existence of invisible objects such as subatomic particles, black holes, and genes, by showing that the behavior of other, visible, objects can be explained in a natural way only if it is assumed that these invisible objects exist. The same is true of constituent structure in the study of syntax: although we cannot actually see (or hear) the structure of phrases, we can infer that phrase structure must exist, because it plays an important role in explaining patterns in data that we do observe. In choosing among the three structures in (86), we would look for evidence for or against the existence of the subconstituents Q and R posited in (86b) and (86c). Linguists have developed a number of diagnostic tests for determining whether a sequence of words forms a constituent; these are called **constituency tests**. We will now illustrate how these work.

Distributional diagnostic tests

The first kind of evidence that a particular sequence of words forms a constituent involves distribution: within the structure of any sentence, each structural position is reserved for constituents of certain types. Thus, by identifying the boundaries of these positions, we can safely conclude that a given sequence of words forms a constituent if it falls within these boundaries. If the sequence is disallowed in this position, it does not necessarily follow that it does not form a constituent; it might be a constituent of the wrong type, since most positions in the sentence are reserved for constituents of a particular category (DP, VP, PP, etc.). On the other hand, this would still indicate that the sequence does not form a constituent of the type specified for the position in question.

For example, in simple sentences, the subject position is relatively easy to identify, since it occurs at the left edge of the sentence (that is, at the beginning); thus, by identifying its right boundary, we can investigate what sequences of words may occur in it. But how do we identify the right boundary of the subject position? At first, we can do this by trial and error. Since we know that names and pronouns may occur as subjects, we can look at sentences containing one of these elements in the subject position, and then determine which lexical categories may immediately follow it. For example, in a simple declarative sentence, the first verb in the sentence must occur immediately to the right of the subject, as in (87a), unless the sentence also contains an adverb like *obviously*, which may immediately precede a verb, as in (87b–c). No other kind of constituent may intervene between the subject and the auxiliary, as shown by (87d–f):

(87) a. He has visited the witches.
     b. He [$_{ADV}$ obviously] has visited the witches.
     c. He has [$_{ADV}$ obviously] visited the witches.
     d. *He [$_{PP}$ to the forest] has visited the witches.
     e. *He [$_{V}$ walked] has visited the witches.
     f. *He [$_{DP}$ the queen] has visited the witches.

Thus, if a sequence of words may occur to the left of the auxiliary verb in a sentence similar to (87a) or (87c), or the left of the adverb in a sentence like (87b), then this sequence of words must be located in the subject position, and it must therefore form a constituent. It was this kind of reasoning, based on data like (88), that led us in section 2.2 to identify sequences such as *the witches*, *our murderous king*, and *the king of Scotland* as constituents that we called DPs:

(88) a. The witches obviously advised the king.
     b. Our murderous king obviously has visited the witches.
     c. The king of Scotland has obviously visited the witches.
     d. The witches in the forest have advised the king.

It is important to bear in mind that in some types of sentences, the subject is not the first constituent; for example, in questions (discussed in sidebar 3.4) the subject position is preceded by the position of an inverted auxiliary verb, as in (22b), and in Topicalization constructions, such as (22a), it is preceded by the Topic position.

The boundaries of the direct object position are somewhat more difficult to determine, because a wide variety of constituents may follow the object position in the verb phrase; thus, in sentences like (89a), it is not obvious whether the PP *in the forest* is a sister of the DP *the witches* as in (89b), or whether it is actually a subpart of that DP, as in (89c):

(89)   a.   The king met the witches in the forest.
      b.   The king [$_{VP}$ mct [$_{DP}$ the witches] [$_{PP}$ in the forest]]
      c.   The king [$_{VP}$ met [$_{DP}$ the witches [$_{PP}$ in the forest]]]

(Note that the structure of the VP in (89b) resembles the structure of P in (86a), whereas the VP in (89c) resembles P in (86b). If the structure in (89b) is correct, then the verb *meet* selects two complements (the DP direct object and the PP), and the sequence *the witches* forms a complete DP (the object of the verb *meet*). On the other hand, if (89c) is correct, then the verb *meet* selects just one complement (DP), and the sequence *the witches in the forest* is a DP.)

Actually it is likely that (89b) and (89c) are both correct. To be precise, (89a) is structurally ambiguous; it can have either the structure in (89b) or that in (89c). On the basis of (88a), we know that the sequence *the witches* can form a complete DP, as in (89b); on the other hand, on the basis of (88d), we also know that the sequence *the witches in the forest* is also a possible DP, as in (89c). Now consider the examples in (90), with pronouns in the object position. (Recall that a DP may not contain both a pronoun and a PP, as illustrated in (87d).)

(90)   a.   The king met them in the forest.
      b.   The king met them.

Example (90a) shows that the verb *meet* may select two complements (a DP and a PP, as in (89b)), but (90b) shows that it can also select just one complement (a DP, as in (89c)). Thus, the structure in (89b) ought to be possible, since the object DP is identical to the subject DP in (88a), and the VP has the same structure as in (90a); but the structure in (89c) ought to be possible too, since the object DP is identical to the subject DP in (88d), and the VP has the same structure as in (90b). Thus, in all likelihood, (89a) is structurally ambiguous. Moreover, this structural ambiguity is associated with a subtle semantic ambiguity. When a PP is contained within a DP, it modifies the noun in the DP, like a relative clause; thus, in (88d), the witches are described as being in the forest, even though they may not have been there when they advised the king. On the other hand, when a PP is a complement of a verb, as in (90a), it modifies the verb, indicating the location of the action that the verb refers to. Thus, if the structure in (89b) is correct, the sentence should mean that the meeting took place in

**SIDEBAR
3.5**

Other types of DPs

By using the distributional test for DP constituency based on occurrence in the subject position, we can identify additional types of DPs. Thus far, we have seen that a DP may contain (a) a name or pronoun, or (b) a noun, preceded by a determiner or nominal specifier and, optionally, one or more adjectives, as in (a–e):

(a)   *Henry* kissed *Kate*.
(b)   *He* kissed *her*.
(c)   *Henry* kissed *the princess*.
(d)   *The young king* kissed *France's beautiful princess*.
(e)   *The brave young king* kissed *the beautiful princess*.

In other examples, we saw that the noun within a DP may also select a complement of its own, such as PP, as in *The murder of Duncan offended the thanes of Scotland*. Nouns derived from verbs of speech or thought may take CP complements, as illustrated in (f) and (g):

(f)   *The announcement that Caesar was dead* shocked the people of Rome.
(g)   *The belief that the quality of mercy is not strained* inspired Portia.

DPs may also contain relative clauses, which often begin with a wh-word, such as *who* (following a noun referring to a human) or *which* (following a noun referring to a non-human entity):

(h)   *The man who Puck saw in the forest* fell in love with *the first woman who he saw*.
(i)   *The books which Prospero owned* were in his study.

These relative clauses superficially resemble the embedded questions discussed in Sidebar 3.4; unlike embedded questions, however, relative clauses often begin with the complementizer *that* instead of a wh-word; for example, all of the wh-words in (h) and (i) can be replaced by *that*. Many other types of DPs are possible too. For example, if the noun in the DP is plural (*kings*, *forests*, etc.), the determiner can be omitted; the same is true with singular abstract nouns (*beauty*, *integrity*, etc), and mass nouns (*wine*, *sand*, etc.). On the other hand, numerals (*two*, *three*) and some quantifiers (*every*, *all*), which often seem to behave like determiners in DPs like *three witches* and *all fairies*, can also co-occur with some determiners in DPs like *the three witches* and *all those fairies*. Not all determiners can co-occur with other determiners in a DP, however; note that DPs like *many the witches*, *three many witches*, *all many witches* are unacceptable. Thus, DPs may contain zero, one, or two determiners, depending on what kind of noun occurs in the DP, and which determiners are involved.

the forest, whereas if (89c) is correct, then the witches are described as being in the forest (though they might not have been there when the meeting took place). The fact is that (89a) can be interpreted in either way, providing further evidence that both structures are possible.

Another type of distributional argument involves cases where different combinations of elements all share the same external distribution, suggesting that these combinations are all variant forms of the same type of constituent (DP, VP, etc.). In section 2.2, we observed that names and pronouns have the same external syntactic distribution as DPs containing determiners and nouns; in any position in the sentence where a DP may occur, a pronoun or name may occur instead. Based on this observation, we suggested that names and pronouns are DPs too. If pronouns and names did not belong to the same category as other types of DPs, the grammar would have to repeat the same list (pronoun, name, and DP) as possible occupants of the subject position, the direct object position, the nominal specifier position, the object of a preposition, and so on. Moreover, any verb that c-selects a DP complement allows any kind of DP (including a name or pronoun) to occur there. This is expected, if pronouns and names are DPs. On the other hand, if pronouns and names were not DPs, then the verb's lexical entry would have to list all three categories as possible complements, and we would have no way of explaining why the same list (pronoun, name, or DP) is repeated again and again, for one verb after another. In short, the shared distributional properties of pronouns, names, and other types of DPs supports the existence of a unified phrasal category, whatever we choose to call it.

Movement as a constituency test

Another constituency test is based on the rule of **movement**, which is involved in the derivation of the **Topicalization** construction, discussed briefly in section 3.2.3, and exemplified by (22a), repeated here as (91a):

(91)   a.   **Bianca**, I admire.
       b.   I admire Bianca.

This Topicalization construction is identifiable not only by its unusual word order but also by its distinctive intonation, or melody, characterized in part by the higher pitch and volume with which the topicalized word is pronounced. This intonation is indicated in (91a) by bold type and comma punctuation. The direct object of the verb *admire* normally occurs after the verb, as in (91b); in (91a), it occurs instead at the beginning of the sentence, in the Topic position. We can identify the name *Bianca* in (91a) as the direct object, despite its location, by the theme θ-role assigned to it in the semantic interpretation of the sentence, which is identical in (91a) and (91b).

Names are not the only elements that can be topicalized. Pronouns (92a), nouns (92b), adjectives (92c), adverbs (92d), and verbs (92e) may also be displaced to the Topic position at the front of the sentence in the same way:

(92) a. **Her**, I admire; but **him**, I despise.
  b. **Sieges**, I dislike; but **battles**, I can tolerate.
  c. **Reckless**, Falstaff may be; but **criminal**, he is not.
  d. **Slowly**, the witches stirred the cauldron.
  e. Cordelia feared that Lear might die, and **die** he did.

The neutral (non-topicalized) sentences that these examples correspond to are given in (93):

(93) a. I admire **her**; but I despise **him**.
  b. I dislike **sieges**; but I can tolerate **battles**.
  c. Falstaff may be **reckless**; but he is not **criminal**.
  d. The witches stirred the cauldron **slowly**.
  e. Cordelia feared that Lear might die, and he **did die**.

According to the theory of movement, the sentences in (92) have the same underlying structures as their counterparts in (93); the only difference is that the capitalized words in (92) have been moved to the Topic position at the front of the sentence from their original location inside the verb phrase. In fact, it is even possible to displace a word originating in an embedded sentence to the Topic position at the front of the main sentence, as in (94c–d), where the position that the topicalized word originates in is marked by a dash (——):

(94) a. Antony said that he loved Cleopatra.
  b. Juliet heard Romeo call out her name.
  c. **Cleopatra**, Antony said [that he loved——].
  d. **Romeo**, Juliet heard [——call out her name].

The data in (95) show that sequences of two or more words can also undergo movement in Topicalization constructions; the corresponding neutral sentences are given in (96):

(95) a. **The beautiful French princess**, Henry kissed ——.
  b. **The king of England**, I admire ——; but **the Dauphin of France**, I despise ——.
  c. **The unfortunate realm that Lear ruled over**, Cordelia knew [that Goneril and Regan would inherit ——].

(96) a. Henry kissed *the beautiful French princess.*
  b. I admire *the king of England;* but I despise *the Dauphin of France.*
  c. Cordelia knew [that Goneril and Regan would inherit *the unfortunate realm that Lear ruled over*].

On the other hand, some sequences of words may not be moved to the front of the sentence in this way, as the ungrammatical examples in (97) show:

(97) a. **the beautiful French*, I admire ——— princess.
  b. **king of*, I admire ——— England, but **despise the**, I ———
    Dauphin of France.
  c. **would inherit the*, Cordelia knew that Goneril and
    Regan ——— unfortunate realm that Lear ruled over.

In each of the examples in (97), a sequence of consecutive words in the neutral sentences in (96) has been moved from the position marked by the dash to the Topic position at the front of the sentence, just as in (95); but the result in (97) is completely ungrammatical. Why should this be?

The topicalized sequences of words in (95) are composed of the same types of lexical categories as the DPs that we discussed earlier, whereas those in (97) do not correspond to any of the phrase-types that we have seen. Thus, the simplest explanation for the contrast between (95) and (97) is that Topicalization constructions can be formed only by moving a single **constituent** to the Topic position. In (92–94), the moved constituent is composed of just a single word, whereas in (95), the moved constituent is composed of two or more words. However, the movement rule deriving the Topic position is insensitive to this difference: it simply moves a single constituent, regardless of how many words it contains, to the Topic position. Thus, the contrast between (95) and (97) provides evidence that the moved sequences in (95) are constituents, or phrases, whereas those in (97) are not. Since virtually any category can be topicalized, the Topicalization constituency test usually functions as a reliable diagnostic for constituent structure.

If we apply this test to the other categories we have examined, we find the expected result: if a sentence contains a constituent such as PP, AP, CP, or VP, that constituent can usually be moved to the Topic position, creating a new sentence beginning with the topicalized constituent. Sentences containing topicalized predicate phrases, such as AP and VP, often sound much more natural if they are preceded by another sentence containing the same AP or VP. Strikingly, if we try to move a sequence of words that does NOT form a constituent, then the result is ungrammatical, as in (97).

This is illustrated in (98–100). In each sentence in (98), the bracketed sequence of words forms a constituent (PP, AP, CP, and VP, respectively), while the bold type-faced sequence of words does not:

(98)　a.　Harry brought his *army* [to France].　　(PP)
　　　b.　Katherine was [*angry at her* suitor].　　(AP)
　　　c.　Hamlet *knew* [*that his father* had been murdered].　　(CP)
　　　d.　Kate *must* [*choose* a husband].　　(VP)

In (98a), the sequence *army to* is not a constituent, because the word *army* is an incomplete part of the DP *his army*, while the word *to* is not part of this DP; rather, it is an incomplete part of the PP *to France*. Thus, the italicized sequence contains two incomplete parts of different constituents; it is not a constituent itself. In (98b), the sequence *angry at her* would form an AP constituent if the word *her* were a pronoun occurring as the object of the preposition *at*, but in (98b), *her* is part of the DP *her suitor*, and this entire DP is the object of *at*; thus, the italicized sequence does not form a complete constituent; to be complete, it would have to contain the entire DP (including the word *suitor*) rather than just part of that DP. In (98c), the italicized sequence *knew that his father* does not form a constituent, because the sub-sequence *that his father* is an incomplete part of the embedded CP enclosed in square brackets. In (98d), the sequence *must choose* is not a constituent, because the verb *choose* is an incomplete part of the VP *choose a husband*, while the modal verb *must* is not part of this VP.

Now, the contrast between (99) and (100) shows that only the bracketed sequences, which form constituents, may be topicalized:

(99)　a.　**To France**, Harry brought his army ——　　(PP)
　　　b.　Everyone expected her to be angry at Petruccio, and . . .
　　　　　angry at her suitor, Katherine was ——　　(AP)
　　　c.　**That his father had been murdered**, Hamlet knew ——
　　　　　　　　　　　　　　　　　　　　　　　　　　(CP)
　　　d.　Her father ordered her to choose a husband, so . . .
　　　　　choose a husband, Kate must ——　　(VP)

(100)　a.　***army to**, Harry brought his —— France.
　　　b.　Everyone expected her to be angry at Petruccio, and . . .
　　　　　***angry at her**, Katherine was —— suitor.
　　　c.　***knew that his father**, Hamlet —— had been murdered.
　　　d.　Her father ordered her to choose a husband, so . . .
　　　　　***must choose**, Kate —— a husband.

Thus, the Topicalization construction serves as a fairly reliable diagnostic test for constituency, not only for the category DP, but also for the categories PP, AP, CP, and VP.

Pro-forms

We have already observed that pronouns may function as DPs, and that they may be interpreted as being co-referential to a DP preceding them, as in (101):

(101) a. [*Petruccio*]$_i$ expects that *he*$_i$ will marry Kate.
   b. [*The king of France*]$_i$ ordered Henry to pledge allegiance to *him*$_i$.
   c. Cordelia asked [*our foolish king*]$_i$ about *his*$_i$ plans.
   d. Oberon liked [*the forest*]$_i$ for *its*$_i$ climate.

In these examples, the bracketed DPs function as constituents in two respects: they occur in the subject or object position, and they function as the antecedents of the pronouns that they are co-indexed with. In a sense, the pronoun has the same meaning as its antecedent; more precisely, it has the same referent. Note that the pronoun may never have as its antecedent a sequence of words that is not a DP; for example, in (102a), the pronoun *him* may not have the same meaning as the sequence *the king of*, since there is no such constituent that can serve as the antecedent of this pronoun. In (102b), the pronoun *him* may not have the same meaning as the sequence *foolish king*, since this sequence is not a complete DP. (It might be a complete NP, but the antecedent of pronouns such as *him* must be a DP.)

(102) a. *[The king of]$_i$ France ordered Henry to pledge allegiance to him$_i$ England.
   ('*The king of* France ordered Henry to pledge allegiance to *the king of* England')
   b. *Cordelia asked our [foolish king]$_i$ about your him$_i$.
   ('Cordelia asked our *foolish king* about your *foolish king*')

Another category besides DP that can serve as the antecedent of a pronoun is CP, which can serve as the antecedent of the pronoun *it*, as in (103a–b). Only a complete CP can serve as the antecedent of *it*, however, as shown by (103c–d), where it is unnatural to construe the italicized sequences as complete CPs serving as the antecedents of the pronoun *it*. (If this were possible, then (103c) would mean that Shylock believed that Antonio would live in Verona, and (103d) would mean that Hamlet's mother suspected that his father had been killed by indigestion.)

(103)   a.   Portia stated [$_{CP}$ *that Antonio would live in Venice*]$_i$, but Shylock didn't believe it$_i$.
        b.   Hamlet knew [$_{CP}$ *that his father had been killed by poison*]$_i$ because he heard it$_i$ from his father's ghost.
        c.   Portia stated *that Antonio would live* in Venice, but Shylock believed it in Verona.
        d.   Hamlet knew *that his father had been killed* by poison, but his mother suspected it by indigestion.

The contrast between (103a–b) and (103c–d) is particularly striking, because the italicized sequences in (103c–d) sometimes do count as complete CPs, in contexts such as (103e–f):

(103)   e.   Portia stated *that Antonio would live*, but Shylock didn't believe it.
        f.   Hamlet knew *that his father had been killed*, and his mother suspected it.

The reason why it is unnatural to treat these sequences as complete CPs in (103c–d) is that this would require the PPs *in Venice* and *in Verona* (in (103c)) and *by poison* and *by indigestion* (in (103d)) to be located outside these CPs, in the VPs containing them, where they would have to be understood as modifiers of the verbs in these VPs; thus, (103c) would have to mean that Portia made her statement in Venice and that Shylock believed this statement in Verona, while (103d) would have to mean that Hamlet acquired his knowledge by means of poison and that his mother arrived at her suspicion by means of indigestion. Speakers generally find these interpretations implausible, especially in the case of (103d), thus accounting for the oddity of analyzing the italicized sequences as CPs in these contexts.

Predicative categories such as VP and AP may function as antecedents of the pro-form *so*, as illustrated by the data in (104); this pro-form often shows up at the beginning of the sentence in which it occurs, triggering Subject–Auxiliary Inversion (see Sidebar 3.4), as in (104c–d):

(104)   a.   Henry will [pass the wine to Falstaff]$_i$, and Bardolph will do so$_i$ too.
        b.   Kate seems [angry at her father]$_i$, and Bianca seems so$_i$ too.
        c.   Oberon must [face the consequences of his actions]$_i$, and so$_i$ must Puck.
        d.   Kate is [angry at her father]$_i$, and so$_i$ is Bianca.

The pro-form *so* is particularly useful in providing crucial evidence for the constituent structure of VP and AP. For example, we know on the basis of

(105) that the sequence *pass the wine* can function as a VP by itself, and that *angry* can function as an AP by itself:

(105) a. Henry will [pass the wine]$_i$, and Bardolph will do so$_i$ too.
       b. Kate is [angry]$_i$, and so$_i$ is Bianca.

Even though *pass the wine* and *angry* are complete phrases in (105), they aren't in (104a–b); otherwise, it ought to be possible for *so* to refer back to these sequences in (106), which is not the case:

(106) a. ?*Henry will [pass the wine]$_i$ *to Falstaff*, and Bardolph will do so$_i$ *to Pistol*.
       b. ?*Kate is [angry]$_i$ *at her father*, and so$_i$ is Bianca *at her mother*.

The ungrammaticality of the examples in (106) thus provide evidence that *pass the wine* is not a complete VP when it is immediately followed by the PP *to Falstaff*, as in (104a) and (106a), and that the adjective *angry* does not count as a complete AP when it is followed by the PP *at her father*, as in (104b) and (106b). Thus, the structures in (107) cannot be correct:

(107) a. Henry [$_{VP}$ will [$_{VP}$ pass the wine] [$_{PP}$ to Falstaff]]]
       b. Kate [$_{VP}$ is [$_{AP}$ angry] [$_{PP}$ at her father]]

Instead, the PP *to Falstaff* must be included within the smaller VP, and the AP containing *angry* must also contain the PP *at her father*, as indicated by the bracketing in (104). How can we reconcile this with the data in (105)? The most natural way of explaining it is in terms of the interaction between the θ-Criterion and the theory of selection discussed in section 2.6. In order for (104a–b) to receive a coherent interpretation, the PPs *to Falstaff* and *at her father* must be assigned θ-roles, so they must each occur as the complement of a lexical category that has a θ-role available to assign to them. In (104a), the PP *to Falstaff* must be a complement of the verb *pass*, rather than of the modal verb *will* as in (107a), since only *pass* has a goal θ-role to assign to it; in (104b), the PP *at her father* must be a complement of the adjective *angry* for an analogous reason. In section 2.6, we stated that the complement of a lexical category X must occur within the phrase XP that X is the head of; the data in (106) provide evidence supporting this claim.

Another predicative category that can serve as the antecedent of a proform in English is NP, which can serve as the antecedent of the indefinite pronoun *one*. At first glance, the antecedent of *one* appears to be a DP, as in (108):

(108)   a.   Petruccio wanted [a wife]$_i$, and Hortensio wanted one$_i$ too.
        b.   Macbeth stabbed [a king]$_i$ in Scotland, and Claudius poisoned one$_i$ in Denmark.

However, appearances can be deceptive. Unlike other pronouns taking DP antecedents, *one* is not understood to be co-referential with the DPs that it is coindexed with in (108); instead, its referent is another individual of the same kind as the antecedent (a different wife in (108a), and a different king in (108b)). This would make sense if its antecedent were really an NP within a DP, since NPs may be interpreted as predicates, as we observed above in section 2.5. A consideration of more data confirms that *one* is actually an NP, with an NP as its antecedent, rather than an entire DP:

(109)   a.   Petruccio wanted [a vocal wife]$_i$, but Hortensio wanted [a quiet one$_i$].
        b.   Macbeth stabbed [the Scottish king]$_i$, and Claudius poisoned [the Danish one$_i$].

Clearly, the antecedent of *one* in (109a) is the NP *wife*, rather than the DP *a vocal wife*; a similar observation holds for (109b). Moreover, the pronoun *one* is itself an NP, rather than a DP, since otherwise we would not be able to explain why it can be preceded by a determiner and an adjective. Thus, the pro-form *one* forms the basis of a diagnostic test for NP constituency. This test enables us to determine the precise location of PP when it occurs within DP, as in the first clauses in (110):

(110)   a.   ?*Macbeth stabbed the king [of Scotland], and Claudius poisoned the *one* of Denmark.
        b.   ?*Portia's description [of Antonio's obligations] influenced the Duke's *one* of Shylock's sentence.

We can explain the oddness of (110) if we assume two things: first, that *one* is an NP, taking an NP as its antecedent, and second, that the bracketed PPs, which are interpreted semantically as complements of the nouns *king* and *description* respectively, must be immediate constituents of NP rather than of DP. In (110a–b), these two requirements are incompatible; in each case, the final PP must be located inside NP, but the indefinite pronoun *one* fills this position. Thus, (110) provides further support for the hypothesis that the complement of a predicative lexical category X must occur within XP.

Deletion or null pro-forms

Another kind of test for constituency involves a process that is tradition-ally referred to as deletion. The most widely discussed example of this is the process of VP deletion, exemplified in (111), where the position of the deleted VP is marked by a dash:

(111)   a.   Henry has [$_{VP}$ passed the wine to Falstaff], and Bardolph will
—— too.
b.   Petruccio will [$_{VP}$ find a wife], and Hortensio will —— too.

A deleted VP is understood to have the same meaning as the bracketed antecedent VP in the preceding sentence, as the interpretation of the sentences in (111) makes clear; thus, in (111a), the second sentence *Bardolph will too* is understood to be an elliptical way of saying that Bardolph will pass the wine to Falstaff too. According to the theory of deletion, a VP may be deleted when it is preceded by another VP that is identical to it, though the sentence is interpreted as though the deleted VP were still there; one way of accounting for this is to assume that the rules of thematic role assignment apply before the process of VP deletion has occurred.

Another way of analyzing these constructions is in terms of silent (null) VP pro-forms, rather than in terms of a deletion rule. According to this alternative approach, English has a null counterpart to the pro-form *so*, analogous to the null pronouns discussed above; this null pro-form takes a VP as its antecedent, and thus is interpreted identically to it. Regardless of which approach we adopt, VP deletion can be used as a test of constituency, since the antecedent of the null pro-form or deleted VP must be a complete VP according to both theories. For this reason, the following sentences are ungrammatical, because the antecedents are not complete VPs:

(112)   a.   *Henry has *passed the wine to* Falstaff, and Bardolph
has —— Pistol.
b.   *Petruccio will *find* a wife, and Bianca will —— a husband.

VP deletion is only possible when the deleted VP (or null VP pro-form) is preceded by an auxiliary verb; often, the auxiliary verb *do* is used, when no other auxiliary verb is present:

(113)   Petruccio [$_{VP}$ found a wife], and Hortensio did —— too.
('. . . Hortensio did find a wife too.')

Examples such as (113) are particularly interesting, because they suggest that the antecedent VP is actually the bare VP *find a wife*, rather than the tensed VP *found a wife*; if the antecedent were the tensed VP, then the result ought to be ungrammatical, like *Hortensio did found a wife*. In other words, the process of VP deletion seems to indicate, surprisingly, that VP does not contain the tense morpheme; rather, a 'tensed VP' actually consists of two parts – a tense, which functions similarly to the modal verb *will* in (111b), and a tenseless VP that serves as the antecedent of the deleted VP (or null VP pro-form), as in (114):

(114)

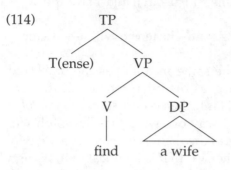

In fact, this conjecture is supported by other tests for VP constituency. For example, the example of VP topicalization that we discussed above involved movement of a bare VP that was preceded by an auxiliary verb; if there is no auxiliary, a tensed VP may not be topicalized, as (115a) shows; instead, a bare VP must be moved, and the auxiliary verb *do* combines with the tense:

(115) a. *Kate's father thought that she loved him, and **loved him**, she————.

      b. Kate's father thought that she loved him, and **love him**, she did————.

The same is true of the VP antecedent of the pro-form *so* in (116): the antecedent of *so* must be a bare VP, rather than a tensed VP, since *so* must itself be understood as tenseless:

(116) a. *Henry [passed the wine to Falstaff]$_i$, and Bardolph so$_i$ too.

      b. Henry [passed the wine to Falstaff]$_i$, and Bardolph did so$_i$ too.

Thus, all three constituency tests lead us to the surprising conclusion that tensed VPs are not actually VPs; if they are constituents at all, they must be constituents of a different type, perhaps a Tense Phrase (TP) as in (114). If the structure in (114) is correct, then we must still explain why the past tense occurs as a suffix on the verb; we will discuss this issue in chapter 5.

Coordination

A final constituency test involves coordination, a class of constructions involving two constituents of the same type, separated by a coordinating particle, or conjunction, such as *and*. Virtually every type of category allows for this, including CP (117a), Sentence (S) (117b), TP (117c), VP (117d), AP

(117e), PP (117f), DP (117g), and NP (117h). In each case, the entire sequence behaves like a single instance of the category in question; thus XP-and-XP behaves like an XP itself:

(117) a   Hamlet knew [$_{CP}$ [$_{CP}$ that his father had been poisoned] and [$_{CP}$ that his stepfather was a murderer]].
       b.   Hamlet knew that [$_S$ [$_S$ his father had been poisoned] and [$_S$ his stepfather was a murderer]].
       c.   Petruccio [$_{TP}$ [$_{TP}$ found a beautiful woman] and [$_{TP}$ married her]].
       d.   Petruccio will [$_{VP}$ [$_{VP}$ find a beautiful woman] and [$_{VP}$ marry her]].
       e.   The [$_{AP}$ [$_{AP}$ strong] and [$_{AP}$ handsome]] king considered the princess [$_{AP}$ [$_{AP}$ beautiful] and [$_{AP}$ intelligent]].
       f.   The king walked [$_{PP}$ [$_{PP}$ across the field] and [$_{PP}$ into the forest]].
       g.   [$_{DP}$ [$_{DP}$ Macbeth] and [$_{DP}$ his wife]] killed [$_{DP}$ [$_{DP}$ him] and [$_{DP}$ his son]].
       h.   The [$_{NP}$ [$_{NP}$ Doge of Venice] and [$_{NP}$ gentlemen of the court]] were impressed by Portia's [$_{NP}$ [$_{DP}$ skill] and [$_{DP}$ intelligence]].

Only constituents may be coordinated; the examples in (118c–d) are ungrammatical because the coordinated sequences are not constituents:

(118) a.   Oberon [$_{TP}$ [$_{TP}$ lived in the forest] and [$_{TP}$ ruled over the forest]].
       b.   [$_S$ [$_S$ The merchant of Venice was broke] and [$_S$ the merchant of Verona was rich]].
       c.   *Oberon *lived in the* and *ruled over the* forest.
       d.   *The merchant of *Venice was broke* and *Verona was rich*.

Furthermore, when the coordinated constituents are not of the same category, coordination is not possible. For example, although it is possible for the verb *write* to take either a DP or PP complement, as in (119a), involving coordinated TPs, it is impossible to coordinate DP and PP in (119b); likewise, though the verb *appear* may be followed either by an infinitival clause beginning with the particle *to* (an infinitival TP), or by a PP such as *outside the castle*, as in (119c), these categories may not be coordinated in (119d):

(119) a.   The scribe wrote a book and the king wrote to his wife.
       b.   *The scribe wrote [[$_{DP}$ a book] and [$_{PP}$ to his wife]].
       c.   The forest appeared [$_{TP}$ to move]. Soon, it appeared [$_{PP}$ outside the castle].
       d.   *The forest appeared [[$_{TP}$ to move] and [$_{PP}$ outside the castle]].

Examples (119b) and (119d) violate the **Law of Coordination of Likes**, which requires that only 'like constituents' (that is, constituents of the same category) may be coordinated. Note that, given this law, the grammaticality of the coordinated DPs in (117f) provides further evidence that pronouns, names, and other types of DPs all belong to the same category.

This concludes our discussion of constituency tests. We have seen that these tests provide empirical support for the constituent structures that we introduced in earlier sections of this chapter. Although our discussion of these tests has been over-simplified somewhat in a few places, ignoring various complicating factors, our presentation has given a fairly accurate idea of how linguists apply these tests to actual data in order to discover the correct constituent structure of sentences in English and other languages.

EXERCISE 3.9

In the following sentence, the adjective *alone* occurs at the end of the sentence:

(i)   Falstaff must drink his beer alone.

This sentence contains two VP nodes: one VP node immediately dominates the verb *must*, and the other VP node immediately dominates the verb *drink*. Since the adjective occurs at the end of the sentence, it is not obvious which VP node immediately dominates it.

(a)   Draw two tree diagrams for this sentence; in one tree, the adjective should be an immediate constituent of the higher VP node, and in the other tree, it should be dominated by the lower VP node.

(b)   The following data provide evidence bearing on the constituent structure of Sentence (i). The data involve movement, VP-deletion, and pro-forms. Use these data to decide which of the tree structures given above is correct. For each example, explain how the constituency test works, and construct an argument for one structure or the other.

(ii)   The king stated that Shylock must drink his beer alone, and drink his beer alone Shylock must.

(iii)   *The king stated that Shylock must drink his beer alone, and drink his beer Shylock must alone.

(iv)   Shylock must drink his beer alone, and Henry must too.
    (This sentence implies that Henry must drink his beer alone.)

(v)   *Shylock must drink his beer alone, and Henry must with Pistol.

(vi)   Shylock must drink his beer alone, and so must Henry.
    (This sentence implies that Henry must drink his beer alone.)

3.3.3 Deriving phrase structure by phrase structure rules: a minigrammar of English

In section 3.2, we introduced a number of basic concepts of syntactic theory and posited the existence of various kinds of phrases. In section 3.3.1, we showed how linguists represent these structures graphically, in terms of tree diagrams and labeled bracketing notation, and in section 3.3.2, we provided some evidence that these structures (as opposed to other possible structures) are correct. In this section, we will discuss how these structures can be derived by means of phrase structure rules. In so doing, we will construct a minigrammar of English, that is, a model of a microcosm of the grammar of English. Although this model is far from complete, it can be expanded and elaborated so as to account for a much broader range of data. In other words, it forms the skeletal core of what a complete grammar of English might look like.

The core of our minigrammar is formed by the phrase structure rules – the rules that define the structure of each type of phrase. We have already given an informal presentation of these rules in (73); in this section we will show how these rules can be formulated using the notation for phrase structure rules traditionally employed by linguists: **context-free rewrite rules**. As a starting point, recall our rule for forming prepositional phrases (73a):

(73) a. P + DP forms a PP: *in Athens, at Falstaff, to the king*, etc.

In the standard phrase structure rule notation, this would be stated as in 120:

(120) PP $\rightarrow$ P   DP

The arrow ($\rightarrow$) in this phrase structure rule means 'contains' (or, to be more precise, 'immediately contains' or 'immediately dominates'). The term occurring to the left of the arrow is the name of the phrase whose structure the rule defines. Finally, the terms listed to the right of the arrow are the names of the immediate constituents of this phrase; they are listed left-to-right in the order that they are pronounced. (As with the phrase structure tree notation, left-to-right ordering is used even to represent the structure of phrases in languages such as Arabic and Japanese, whose traditional orthographies use the opposite right-to-left order.) Thus, (120) states that a PP immediately dominates a P and a DP, and that the P precedes the DP.

Next, consider the rules for forming APs given in (73b):

(73) b. i.   A + PP forms an AP: *angry at Petruccio, suspicious of Shylock*, etc.
          ii. A also forms an AP by itself: *angry, suspicious*, etc.

These rules would be represented as in (121):

(121)   a.   AP → A   PP
       b.   AP → A

Rule (121a) states that an AP immediately dominates A and PP; (121b) states that AP immediately dominates just A by itself. Although these statements may appear to conflict with each other, they actually represent distinct options; in other words, each rule represents a different way of forming a grammatical AP in English. Nevertheless, there is a redundancy in (121); both rules state that an AP immediately dominates A, and that A is the leftmost immediate constituent of AP. Since each rule in (121) states this independently, the theory is missing a generalization. Like theorists in other sciences, linguists always seek to eliminate redundancies in their models; in this case, the redundancy can be eliminated by combining (121a) and (121b) into a single rule, using the abbreviatory convention of parentheses to represent the optionality of the PP following the A in AP:

(122)   AP → A   (PP)

The same abbreviatory convention can be used to represent the content of the informal rules for NP in (73c.i) and (73c.ii), as in (123):

(73)   c.   i.   N + PP forms an NP: *murder of Duncan, father of Goneril,*
                  etc.
            ii.   N also forms an NP by itself: *murder, beauty, wine, lords,*
                  etc.

(123)   NP → N   (PP)

However, the parenthesis notation is unable to represent the three basic options for the internal structure of DP specified in (73d) in terms of a single rule, since the optionality involves a choice among different categories rather than the occurrence (or nonoccurrence) of a single item:

(73)   d.   i.   D + NP forms a DP: *the murder of Duncan, a daughter of
                  Lear,* etc.
            ii.   A Name or a Pronoun forms a DP by itself: *Duncan, he, she,*
                  etc.

To represent this kind of optionality, another abbreviatory convention is needed: the notation of curly brackets, as in (124):

(124)   DP → $\begin{Bmatrix} D & NP \\ Name \\ Pronoun \end{Bmatrix}$

In this notation, each line enclosed in the curly brackets represents an option that can be taken; thus the rule states that a DP may immediately dominate (a) D followed by NP, or (b) Name, or (c) Pronoun. Alternatively, we could have used the curly bracket notation, instead of the parenthesis notation, in (123), by listing Ø (nothing) as alternative to PP, as in (125):

(125)   NP → N $\begin{Bmatrix} PP \\ \varnothing \end{Bmatrix}$

Strictly speaking, (123) and (125) are equivalent.

Another type of optionality that cannot be handled by means of parentheses is exemplified by prenominal adjectives. Recall that NPs may contain any number of adjectives in front of the noun. If we tried to incorporate this into the rule for NP (123) by adding a position for an adjective enclosed in parentheses before the position of the noun, as in (123′), this would not allow for more than one adjective:

(123′)   NP → (A)   N   (PP)

We cannot solve the problem simply by adding more adjective positions in this way, because there is no specific upper limit on the number of adjectives that can occur here. One way of capturing this is to include an additional rule for NP, modeled on (73c.iii), as in (126):

(73)   c.   iii.   A + NP forms an NP

(126)   NP → A   NP

Although (126) only provides one adjective position, it can operate in a **recursive** fashion, reapplying to its own output, adding an additional adjective position each time. For example, suppose that we form the NP *king of England* by means of rule (123). We can then combine this NP with a preceding adjective by rule (126), forming a larger NP such as *old king of England*. We can then combine this larger NP with another preceding adjective by applying rule (126) again, forming an even larger NP such as *stupid old king of England*. Rule (126) can be used recursively (any number of times) to form NPs containing any number of adjectives. Note that this predicts that the prenominal adjectives are not sisters of each other; instead, each adjective is a sister of an NP; this is consistent with the data in (109) above involving the pro-form *one*, which shows that the material following a prenominal adjective within an NP behaves like an NP itself.

We can use a combination of the parenthesis notation and curly bracket notation to represent the various options for the structure of VP listed in (73e):

(73)   e.   i.   V + DP forms a VP: *suffocated Desdemona, sued Antonio,* etc.

   ii.   V + PP forms a VP: *lives in Athens, laughed at Falstaff,* etc.

   iii.   V + DP + PP forms a VP: *passed the wine to Falstaff,* etc.

   iv.   V + CP forms a VP: *say that Falstaff likes wine,* etc.

   v.   V + DP + CP forms a VP: *told Bassanio that his ship was lost,* etc.

   vi.   V + VP forms a VP: *should follow his advice, must choose a husband,* etc.

   vii.   V also forms a VP by itself: *arrived, died,* etc.

In fact, the parenthesis notation alone is sufficient to combine (i), (ii), (iii), and (vii) into a single rule, as in 127:

(127)   VP → V   (DP)   (PP)

This rule states that VP contains a verb, followed optionally by a DP, followed optionally by a PP; thus, it defines exactly the four options in (i), (ii), (iii), and (vii). To incorporate the options in (v) and (vi), the curly bracket notation must be used. Let us begin with (v), which states that a VP may contain V, DP, and CP; in other words, the constituent following DP in VP may be CP instead of PP. One way of representing this would be to list PP and CP as options in curly brackets within the second set of parentheses in (127), as in (128):

(128)   VP → V   (DP)   ($\left\{ \begin{array}{c} \text{PP} \\ \text{CP} \end{array} \right\}$)

As in the case of rule (123), we could eliminate the parentheses around the curly brackets in (128) by adding a third line between the curly brackets, containing Ø (zero, or nothing). By incorporating (73e.v) in this way, rule (128) predicts that CP ought to be able to occur in VP without being preceded by DP, just as PP can, since the preceding DP is optional in (128). Thus, (128) subsumes (73e.iv) as well.

   Finally, to incorporate (73e.vi), which states that a VP may consist of a verb followed by a VP, there are three basic ways of amending (128). First, we could list VP as an alternative to DP, by means of curly brackets, as in (129); this would predict that a VP could contain a verb, followed by another VP, followed by an optional PP or CP.

(129) VP → V $\left(\left\{\begin{array}{l} DP \\ VP \end{array}\right\}\right)$ $\left(\left\{\begin{array}{l} PP \\ CP \end{array}\right\}\right)$

Alternatively, we could list VP as a third alternative to PP and CP between the curly brackets in (127), as in (130); this would predict that a VP containing a verb and another VP could optionally contain a DP between the verb and the VP.

(130) VP → V (DP) $\left(\left\{\begin{array}{l} PP \\ CP \\ VP \end{array}\right\}\right)$

Finally, we could use an additional set of curly brackets to list VP as an alternative to all of the options listed after the verb in (127), as in (131); this would predict that when a VP contains a verb and another VP, no other constituents are possible.

(131) VP → V $\left\{\begin{array}{l} (DP) \quad \left(\left\{\begin{array}{l} PP \\ CP \end{array}\right\}\right) \\ \\ VP \end{array}\right\}$

Rules (129), (130), and (131) represent competing theories about how the structure of VP is defined by the phrase structure rule system of English. In order to determine which theory is correct, we must find out whether a VP immediately dominating a verb and another VP may also contain other constituents; specifically, whether the larger VP may also contain a PP or CP after the smaller VP, as predicted by (129), and whether a DP may occur in between the verb and the smaller VP, as predicted by (130). As it turns out, it is somewhat complicated to test these predictions, since it is not obvious whether the additional constituents are contained within the larger VP, or in the smaller VP, or in some subconstituent of the smaller VP. For example, (129) predicts that a PP or CP may follow the smaller VP; the data in (132c–d) suggest at first glance that this may be possible:

(132) a. Antonio [$_{VP}$ should [$_{VP}$ follow her advice]]
   b. Kate [$_{VP}$ must [$_{VP}$ choose a husband]]
   c. Antonio should follow her advice [$_{CP}$ that he should be silent]
   d. Kate must choose a husband [$_{PP}$ in one month]

However, these data are only relevant if the additional CP in (132c) and PP in (132d) are immediately dominated by the larger VP that immediately dominates the modal verb. This is clearly not the case in (132c), where the CP is interpreted as if it were a complement of the noun *advice*, occurring inside the NP within the DP *the advice that he should be silent*. This is confirmed by the Topicalization and pro-form tests, which treat the CP as part of the DP, and not as an immediate constituent of the higher VP:

(133)   a.   **Her advice that he should be silent**, Antonio should
             follow ———.
        b.   *__Her advice__, Antonio should follow ——— that he should be
             silent.
        c.   Antonio should follow her advice that he should be silent,
             and Bassanio should follow it too.
             (*it = her advice that he should be silent*)
        d.   *Antonio should follow her advice that he should be silent,
             and Bassanio should follow it that he should speak out.
             (*it = her advice*)

If the CP in (132c) were immediately dominated by the higher VP node, as
(129) predicts should be possible, then (133b) and (133d) should be grammatical, and (133a) and (133c) should not. On the other hand, the location
of the PP in (133d) is less clear. If we ignore the unlikely possibility that
this PP is part of the preceding DP, it is still unclear whether it is immediately dominated by the larger VP, as (129) predicts should be possible, or
whether it must be immediately dominated either by the smaller VP or by
the sentence node above the larger VP. Unfortunately, the evidence from
constituency tests is inconclusive on this point. Turning now to the prediction made by rule (130), that a DP may occur in between the verb and
the smaller VP, we have already seen that the complements of perception verbs and causative verbs seem to conform to this pattern, as in the
examples in (67), repeated here as (134):

(134)   a.   Macbeth [$_{VP}$ saw [$_{DP}$ the forest] [$_{VP}$ move towards the castle]]
        b.   Juliet [$_{VP}$ heard [$_{DP}$ Romeo] [$_{VP}$ call out her name]]
        c.   Lear [$_{VP}$ let [$_{DP}$ his daughters] [$_{VP}$ take over the realm]]

If the structures shown in (134) are correct, they provide clear support
for rule (130) over its competitors (129) and (131). However, it is still
not entirely clear that the DP is immediately dominated by the higher
VP node, as (130) predicts should be possible. In our discussion of these
examples under (67), we noted that the DP is interpreted as the subject of
the smaller VP, and we suggested that the DP and smaller VP together
form a constituent, which we called a small clause:

(135)   [$_{VP}$ Verb [$_{SC}$ DP   VP]]   (*SC = Small Clause*)

Actually, our standard constituency tests provide conflicting evidence
on whether the DP is directly dominated by the higher VP, as in (134), or
whether there is a small clause constituent immediately dominating this
DP, as in (135). Namely, the Topicalization test seems to suggest that there
is no small clause constituent formed by the DP and VP, as indicated in
(136a), but the pro-form test seems to suggest that this constituent does
exist with perception verbs, as in (136b), though not with causative verbs,
as in (136c):

(136) a. Juliet hoped that she would hear Romeo call out her name, and
*?[**Romeo call out her name**], she heard ⸺.

 b. Juliet heard *Romeo call out her name*, and her mother heard *it*
too.
(*it* = *Romeo call out her name*)

 c. Lear let *his daughters take over the realm*,
*but Henry VIII didn't let *it*.
(*it* = *his daughters take over the realm*)

Although the evidence is not entirely consistent, let us conclude tentatively that at least some VPs may contain a DP preceding a smaller VP, as (130) predicts. This decides the issue in favor of (130) over the competing theories embodied in rules (129) and (131).

We may now complete our minigrammar of English phrase structure rules by adding two more rules to represent the informal rules given in (73f) and (73g):

(73) f. DP + VP forms a Sentence: *Timon lives in Athens, Henry laughed at Falstaff*, etc.

 g. C + Sentence forms a CP: *that his father had been murdered*, etc.

(137) Sentence → DP   VP

(138) CP → C   Sentence

The complete set of phrase structure rules is given at the end of this section.

It is important to bear in mind that the phrase structure rules that we have introduced here are not intended as a complete list of English phrase structure rules; in fact, they are not capable of accounting for some of the example sentences that we have already discussed in this chapter. For example, DPs containing nominal specifiers or sequences of more than one determiner, are also not accounted for by these rules. A more complete minigrammar of English would contain more complex rules to account for such data.

None of the phrase structure rules mention any actual words; they simply mention lexical categories such as *Name, Verb*, and *Adjective*, and phrasal categories such as PP, DP, AP, etc. Thus, these rules define the phrase structures of sets of sentences, but they do not define the composition of any particular sentence, which of course contains actual words. In order for our minigrammar to account for actual sentences, therefore, it must also include a miniature lexicon of English, that is, a miniature model of the mental dictionary discussed above. Recall that each lexical entry of a predicative category such as a verb or adjective must include a representation of its argument structure, as well as a representation of its selectional properties. The miniature lexicon given in (3) above provides a good basis for this, though it leaves out many words that have played an important role in our discussion; for example, it does not include verbs like *see*, *let*, *say*, *think*, and *tell*, nor does it include nouns such as *murder* and *advice* or complementizers such as *that*. Moreover, the list in (3) does not provide a representation of the argument structures and selectional properties of any of the predicative words that it includes. It would require several pages to list the full lexical entries of all of the words that have appeared in the examples discussed thus far; therefore, we will simply assume that our minigrammar does contain a lexicon, made up of lexical entries with the properties discussed in section 3.2.

Our minigrammar, containing the miniature lexicon and the phrase structure rules introduced in this section, enables us to determine, in a completely mechanical way, whether a given sequence of words is grammatical, at least, according to the rules of this grammar. For example, consider sentence (13c), repeated here:

(13)   c.   The daughter of Lear loved him.

First, we look up each word in the lexicon and determine its lexical category, and place the name of the category for each word in the sequence on the line above it, as in (139):

(139)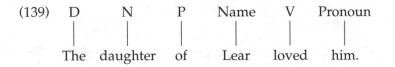

Next, we group these words into phrases in conformance with the phrase structure rules, building up miniature phrase structure trees as we proceed. As a first step, the terms Name and Pronoun must be dominated by a DP node, as in (140), since no rule other than the rule for DP (124) includes pronouns and names:

(140)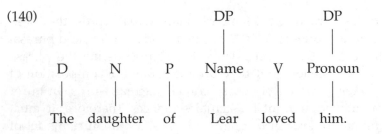

Next, we know that any occurrence of P must be dominated by a PP node, and that there must be a DP following the P within PP, as defined by (120). Moreover, we know that every occurrence of V must be dominated by a VP node; we also know that the DP following the V in (140) may be included within this DP, since this option is allowed by the VP rule (130). Since the lexical entry of the verb *love* states that it selects a DP direct object (to which it assigns the theme θ-role), this requirement can only be satisfied if the DP is in fact a sister of the verb *love* in the VP, as in (141):

(141)

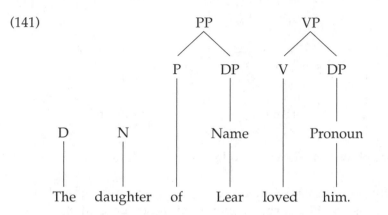

Next, we know that every noun must be dominated by NP, and that the PP following the noun may be included in this NP. Since the PP in (140) is interpreted as an argument of the noun *daughter*, we are safe to assume that this is correct. This NP must be the complement of the determiner (D) that precedes it, since DP is the only rule that introduces the catgegory NP. Combining these steps, we form (142):

(142)

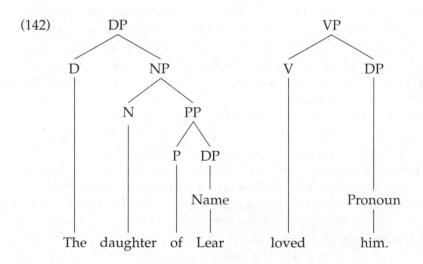

Finally, we know from rule (137) that DP and VP may combine to form a complete sentence, as in (143).

(143)

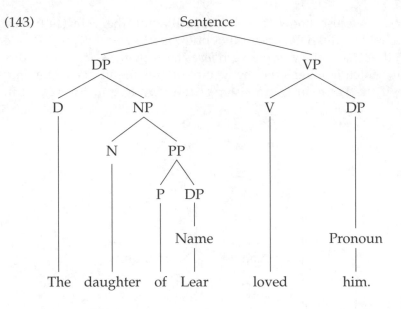

Since we can form a complete Sentence tree in this way, we know that the sequence of words in (13c) forms a grammatical sentence. If it had not been possible to do this, then we would know that the sequence of words does not form a grammatical sentence. For example, if the sequence of words in (13c) had failed to contain a verb, there would be no VP (since V is an obligatory subconstituent of VP) and hence there would be no grammatical Sentence (since VP is an obligatory subconstituent of the category *Sentence*, according to rule (137)). This mechanical application of the minigrammar as a grammaticality-testing device thus serves as a model of the mental computation that a native speaker performs (unconciously) when the speaker is asked by a linguist to provide an acceptability judgment for an example sentence. Note that the same procedure identifies grammatical instances of other categories besides complete sentences; for example, we know that the sequence *daughter of Lear* is a grammatical NP, and that the sequence *loved him* is a grammatical VP.

As we have already seen, the phrase structure rules are not the only rules that a sentence must obey in order to be grammatical. For example, if an example sentence contains a word that does not occur in our lexicon, then our minigrammar will treat it as ungrammatical. Because the lexicon in our minigrammar does not contain any lexical entries for non-words such as *spritchy*, and *becarp*, we cannot replace them with a category-name, such as *verb* or *adjective*. Consequently, we will not be able to produce a sequence of category-names for utterances containing such non-words, such as those in (144), and they will not be defined as well-formed sentences by our grammar:

(144)   a.   *Kate grew spritchy.
        b.   *Portia becarp weary.

Of course, a speaker who hears a sentence such as (144a) might assume that *spritchy* is a word, and guess that it is an adjective with an unknown meaning; in effect, this speaker would be adding this word as a new entry in the lexicon, thus enabling the grammar to recognize it as a grammatical sentence. This provides a very rough model of how children acquire vocabulary during the process of language acquisition, a topic discussed in chapter 6.

In general, our minigrammar predicts that we should be able to freely replace any word in a grammatical sentence with another word belonging to the same lexical category, since the tree structure of the sentence (and the phrase structure rules sanctioning each part of this structure) would be the same. However, it is important to bear in mind that the selectional requirements of predicates must be satisfied. For example, we cannot replace the verb *love* in sentence (13c) with the verb *arrive*, as in (145), because the verb *arrive* does not select a DP complement in addition to its subject; moreover, the verb *arrive* has no additional θ-role to assign to this DP:

(145)   *The daughter of Lear arrived him.

Thus, since the lexicon of our minigrammar contains lexical entries that specify the argument structure and selectional properties of verbs, these conditions must be observed. We can capture this by assuming that selectional properties of lexical items are checked once a structure has been assigned to the sentence. Thus, in (145), the only way of including the pronoun *him* in the structure of the sentence is to include it in the VP headed by the verb *arrive*, but this would violate the selectional property of *arrive* (it selects an optional PP complement, but not a DP), so the sentence is ungrammatical because it violates the selectional property of the verb *arrive*.

We have seen that it is possible to use the model of grammar as a device for testing grammaticality. It is also possible to apply the rules of the grammar in the opposite direction as a model of sentence production, by interpreting the arrow in each phrase structure rule as an instruction to replace the category-name on the left side of the arrow with the sequence of lexical category-names appearing on the right-hand side of the arrow. Thus, to produce a sentence, we apply the Sentence Rule, yielding the sequence *DP – VP*, we then replace each of these category-names with one of the allowable sequences of immediate subconstituents, as defined by the rules for DP and VP. We continue this process until we have created a string of lexical category-names, such as D, N, V, P, etc. At this point, we select an actual word in the lexicon belonging to each lexical category; for instance, we replace *Verb* with a word like *loved*. (This process is called **lexical insertion**.) Once we have replaced every category-name with a lexical item in this way, the resulting structure is checked to ensure that the selectional properties of every lexical item are satisfied; for example, if the verb *murder* is inserted into the verb position, we must check to ensure that the subject and object DPs in the sentence refer to people, in accord with the selectional restrictions on this verb. If the selectional properties of all the words are satisfied, the result should be a grammatical sentence. This step-by-step application of the rules of grammar to derive a grammatical sentence is referred to as the **derivation** of the sentence in question.

Thus, our model of the grammar involves three stages in the derivation of a sentence: first, the application of the phrase structure rules; second, the process of lexical insertion, and third, the process of checking selectional restrictions. There is one additional stage, however, namely the application of **transformational rules** of movement and deletion, which change the structures produced by the first three stages of the derivation, by deleting constituents or moving them to a different position in the sentence from where they are originally derived by the phrase structure rules. For example, we have seen that in Topicalization and Wh-movement constructions, a constituent (such as a DP or PP) may be moved to a position at the front of the sentence, before the subject position. We have also seen that auxiliary verbs may also be moved to a position preceding the subject in main clause questions (as discussed in Sidebar 3.4) and in constructions such as (104c–d) involving preposing of the VP pro-form *so*. It has also been suggested that verb movement is involved in the derivation of sentences with VSO constituent order in languages such as Irish and Arabic, where the verb occurs in a position preceding the subject, outside the verb phrase. Furthermore, we have also seen that a VP may be deleted if it is preceded by an identical VP antecedent, in VP-deletion constructions such as (111) and (113). We will not explain how such transformational rules are formulated at this stage, but it is important to bear in mind that the application of such rules plays a crucial role in the derivation of many sentences.

Although we can apply our minigrammar in this way to produce sentences, it is important to bear in mind that the theory of grammar is not intended as a complete model of what speakers actually do when they produce sentences in natural speech situations. The mental processes involved with actual speech production are doubtlessly much more complex than this, involving many other factors that we have ignored in this over-simplified characterization. Moreover, the grammar is not exclusively oriented toward speech production, since linguistic knowledge is used in other tasks as well – for example, in processing and understanding sentences that we hear other speakers produce. The theory of grammar is a model of the representation of linguistic knowledge; it is not a model of speech production. Nevertheless, it is reasonable to assume that the computational operations that speakers perform in executing these tasks interact with the grammar in a way that is, perhaps, at least partly similar to the procedures we have described.

Complete list of phrase structure rules

(120) PP → P   DP

(122) AP → A   (PP)

(123) NP → N   (PP)

(124) DP → $\begin{Bmatrix} \text{D} \quad \text{NP} \\ \text{Name} \\ \text{Pronoun} \end{Bmatrix}$

(126) NP → A   NP

(130) VP → V   (DP) $\left(\begin{Bmatrix} \text{PP} \\ \text{CP} \\ \text{VP} \end{Bmatrix} \right)$

(137) Sentence → DP   VP

(138) CP → C   Sentence

The phrase structure rules for NP and DP in (123), (124), and (126) do not account for the structure of DPs containing numbers, or nominal specifiers. Based on the following data, propose revisions in either or both of these rules to account for the facts. In answering this question, you will need to decide whether these elements are immediately dominated by NP, DP, or some additional phrase. There is more than one possible answer to this question, so do not be too concerned if you have difficulty in deciding which structure is correct; however, you should explain how your rules account for the data.

EXERCISE 3.10

(i)   Macbeth's unpardonable murder of Duncan shocked the lords.
(ii)   Lear adored his three beautiful daughters.
(iii) The three old witches lived in the dark, mysterious forest.

3.3.4 Deriving phrase structure by constraints

We have seen that sentences have a complex constituent structure that can be represented either in terms of tree diagrams or in terms of the notation of labeled brackets, and that it is possible to determine what the correct structure is for a given sentence-type on the basis of empirical evidence, in the form of various constituency tests. We have also suggested that sentences have these structures (as opposed to other hypothetically possible structures) because the grammar of each language contains a set of phrase structure rules that define the immediate constituent structure of the sentence and of each type of phrase (AP, DP, etc.); every grammatical sentence must have a constituent structure that can be derived by the application of these phrase structure rules – even though the structures produced by these rules may be changed in various ways by the subsequent application of transformational rules of movement and deletion. However, the theory of phrase structure rules is not the only possible way of explaining constituent structure. Phrase structure rules have played an important role in modern linguistic theory, providing a means of deriving the constituent structure of each type of phrase in an explicit formal notation, but many linguists now believe that the grammars of human languages do not actually contain such rules, and they have sought alternative explanations for why certain constituent structures are possible and others are not.

The new approach has been guided in part by the observation that many aspects of traditional phrase structure rules are redundant, given other properties of the grammar, and in part by the discovery of general conditions on phrase structure that account for many aspects of phrase structure in a simpler and more elegant way. According to the new approach, the theory of grammar contains a set of general conditions, or **constraints**, on constituent structures, which every type of phrase must conform to, making it unnecessary to formulate an independent phrase structure rule for each phrase individually. To see how these general constraints on constituent structure allow us to dispense with individual phrase structure rules, let us begin by reconsidering the phrase structure rule for VP in (130), repeated here:

$$(130) \quad VP \rightarrow V \quad (DP) \quad \left(\begin{Bmatrix} PP \\ CP \\ VP \end{Bmatrix} \right)$$

The facts about VP structure that this rule accounts for are enumerated in (146):

(146) a. Every VP contains a position for a verb (V).
       b. The verb is the leftmost subconstituent of VP.
       c. The VP may also contain an (optional) DP.
       d. The VP may also contain an (optional) PP, CP, or VP.
       e. If the VP contains both a DP and another category, the DP occurs before the other category, immediately after the verb.

Let us first consider (146a) and (146b). Although these facts may appear to be specific to VP, very similar facts hold of other types of phrases as well. For example, the AP rule in (122) states that every AP must contain a position for an adjective (A), and that the adjective is the leftmost sub-constituent of AP. Likewise, the rule for NP in (123) states that every NP must contain an N-position, and that the noun is the leftmost subconstituent of NP. This parallelism suggests that there are two general conditions that apply to all types of phrases, given in (147):

(147)   a.   Every phrase XP must contain a position reserved for a lexical category of type X. This position is called the **head** of the phrase.
   b.   Within XP, the X-position (that is, the position reserved for the head of the phrase) is the leftmost subconstituent of XP, preceding the complements selected by the lexical item occupying the head position.

In (147), the term 'X' is a variable ranging over lexical category-types, such as N(oun), V(erb), or A(djective); for example, if X is assigned the value of N, (147a) requires that NP must contain an N-position, and (147b) requires that the N-position must precede any complement(s) of N within NP. If the grammar of English contains the constraints in (147), then the phrase structure rules for VP, AP, and NP do not need to repeat this information independently for each different kind of phrase. In other words, the constraints in (147) not only provide an explanation for the parallel structure of VP, AP, and NP; they also make it possible for us to simplify the grammar by eliminating these redundant aspects of the phrase structure rules for VP, AP, and NP.

Now consider our rule for the structure of PP in (120), which states that every PP must contain a position for a preposition (P), followed by a DP complement of P. Given (147), the only respect in which Rule (120) is not redundant is its statement that the complement of P is a DP, and that this DP is an OBLIGATORY subconstituent of PP. However, if prepositions such as *to*, *on*, and *at* are specified in the lexicon as selecting an obligatory DP complement (just like transitive verbs such as *murder*), then this fact is also accounted for, and the phrase structure rule for PP can be eliminated entirely. Independent support for this approach comes from the fact that certain prepositions, such as *in*, *out*, *over*, and *up*, can occur without a DP complement, as in 148:

(148)   a.   Falstaff ran in (the room).
   b.   Portia walked out (the door).
   c.   Henry sailed over (the channel).
   d.   Othello looked up (the chimney).

The fact that prepositions differ from each other in this respect supports the theory that the obligatoriness of DP complements in PPs containing prepositions such as *to* and *at* is determined by the selectional properties of these prepositions, rather than by the existence of a phrase structure rule for PP such as (120).

The existence of the conditions in (147) also make it possible to eliminate the phrase structure rule for CP in (138), which states that a CP contains a complementizer (C) followed by an embedded sentence. (147a) accounts for the fact that CP must contain a C-position, and (147b) accounts for the fact that C must be the leftmost subconstituent of CP. In order to account for the fact that CP also contains an embedded sentence, all we need to assume is that the Sentence position following the complementizer is a complement position – that is, that complementizers such as *that* select a Sentence as an obligatory complement. This enables us to eliminate the phrase structure rule for CP, further simplifying our theory of the grammar of English.

The theory of general conditions on phrase structure such as those in (147) is known as **X-bar theory**. Condition (147a) is widely accepted as a universal X-bar condition on phrase structure, applicable to all human languages. On the other hand, Condition (147b) may apply only in languages that exhibit consistent **head-initial** phrase structure, such as English, where verbs, adjectives, nouns, prepositions, and complementizers all precede their complements. Many other languages, such as Turkish and Japanese, exhibit consistent **head-final** phrase structure, suggesting that they are subject to a condition that is the mirror-image of (147b), stating that the head position (X) is the rightmost subconstituent of XP, following the complements of the head. In other words, the linear ordering relationship between the head of a phrase and the complements of the head may be another parameter of language-variation; according to this theory, the grammar of each language chooses either the head-initial parameter setting or the head-final parameter setting. This theory predicts that each language should be consistently head-initial or head-final, regardless of the lexical category of the head of the phrase; this seems to be true for most languages, although there are some well-known exceptions. On the other hand, some linguists have argued that Condition (147b) is universal, and that head-final order is derived by transformational rules of movement, analogous to the leftward movement rules involved in Topicalization, Wh-movement, and Subject–Auxiliary Inversion in English. This alternative approach to cross-linguistic variation in head–complement order is known as the theory of **Antisymmetry**.

Returning now to the phrase structure rules for English, we have seen that the adoption of the X-bar conditions in (147) makes it possible to eliminate the phrase structure rules for PP and CP, and to account for at least some of the facts accounted for by the rules for VP, AP, and NP. Let us now consider the other facts listed in (146) that the phrase structure rule for VP in (130) is supposed to account for; (146c) states that VP may optionally contain a position for a DP complement and (146d) states that VP may optionally contain a position for a PP, CP, or VP complement. Recall, however, that it is a bit misleading to describe these complements as optional, since they are obligatory with some verbs and impossible with others. For example, a VP headed by the verb *say* must contain a CP because the lexical entry for *say* states that the verb obligatorily selects this kind of complement, whereas a VP headed by the verb *run* may not contain a CP complement, because the lexical entry for *run* does not include this selectional property. In other words, what really determines whether a given type of complement occurs in VP is not the phrase structure rule for VP, but rather the categorical selection properties of the lexical item occurring in the head position of the VP. The same is true for the categories NP and AP, which may contain a PP complement only if the head noun or adjective selects one. Since these facts are accounted for by the existence of selectional restrictions, there is no need for the grammar to state this information independently in the phrase structure rules for VP, AP, and NP. This suggests that the phrase structure for these categories can also be eliminated, further simplifying our model of the grammar of English.

Suppose that this is correct; there is only one fact about VP-structure that must still be accounted for, namely that if a VP contains both a DP and another complement such as PP, CP, or VP, then the DP must precede the other complement. It has been suggested that this may be a side-effect of a condition on DPs mentioned above, namely the so-called case filter (mentioned in the context of the unaccusative verbs in (55)), which requires that every DP must be assigned case. Specifically, it has been suggested that accusative case can only be assigned to a DP that is adjacent to the verb that assigns accusative case. Actually, this adjacency condition may also apply to case assignment by prepositions, though this is masked by the fact that prepositions never select more than one complement anyway. Given the case filter and the adjacency condition on case assignment, we can account for the fact that an object DP must immediately follow the verb within VP without requiring an explicit phrase structure rule for VP. In recent years, some linguists have suggested alternative theories of accusative case assignment that do not rely on the adjacency condition. These approaches share the underlying assumption that constituent order in VP can be accounted for without resorting to explicit ordering statements in the form of phrase structure rules.

We have seen that it is possible to eliminate the phrase structure rules for VP, AP, PP, and CP, replacing them with more general conditions such as those in (147). This has naturally led to the conjecture that all category-specific phrase structure rules can be eliminated, reducing the theory of phrase structure to general principles of X-bar theory and selection. However, two of our phrase structure rules appear at first glance not to conform to this pattern, namely the rules for the structure of DP and Sentence in (124) and (130), respectively. Turning first to the category DP, (147a) predicts that every DP should contain a D position, but the existence of DPs that contain just a name or a pronoun poses a problem for this approach. Before dealing with this problem, let us consider the structure of DPs that do contain determiners. According to (147b), the determiner should be the leftmost constituent in DP, at least in head-initial languages such as English. In fact, Condition (147b) only applies to categories that select complements, and thus far we have not described determiners in these terms. However, it has been suggested that the NP within DP is actually a complement of the determiner, in which case (147b) derives exactly the correct result; the occurrence of the NP within DP would then follow from the fact that it is an obligatory complement of determiners such as *the* and *a(n)*. Independent support for this approach comes from the behavior of demonstrative determiners such as *this, that, these,* and *those,* where the NP following the determiner is optional, as in (149):

(149)   a.   This (castle of Harfleur) is in France.
        b.   Those (books) belong to Prospero.

It would be difficult to account for optionality of the NP subconstituents within the subject DPs in these examples, given the existence of a phrase structure rule for DP such as (124); on the other hand, if we assume that the occurrence of NP within DP is determined by the selectional properties of the determiner, then we can account for (149) simply by assuming that demonstrative determiners select optional NP complements, in contrast to determiners such as *the* and *a(n),* which select obligatory NP complements.

   Let us now turn to the problem posed by DPs that consist of just a pronoun or a name, which appear to be counterexamples to the general X-bar condition (147a). A consideration of data from other languages suggests that these two cases work slightly differently from each other. As far as pronouns are concerned, it has been proposed that they are actually determiners that fail to select an NP complement. This immediately eliminates the problem of the missing determiner – if pronouns are determiners, then the problem was illusory – and it also explains why the NP is absent; the pronoun simply fails to select it as a complement. Although this solution might seem a bit far-fetched at first glance, there is striking evidence supporting it in languages such as French and Spanish, where definite determiners are homophonous with accusative pronouns, as illustrated by the French examples in (150):

(150)   a.   Jean connaît le   garçon.
             Jean knows the (MascSing) boy
             'Jean knows the boy.'

b. Jean le   connaît
    Jean him knows
    'Jean knows him.'
c. Jean connaît les   garçons
    Jean knows the (MascPlur) boys
    'Jean knows the boys'
d. Jean les   connaît
    Jean them (Masc) knows
    'Jean knows them.'

As for DPs containing names, a consideration of other languages suggests a different kind of solution. In many languages with elaborate systems of case marking on nouns, proper names closely resemble common nouns morphologically, suggesting that names may really be a special kind of noun. Even in English, some nouns often occur without an overt determiner preceding them, as in the case of indefinite plural DPs such as *books* and *soldiers*, and with abstract nouns and mass nouns such as *beauty* and *wine*. It has been suggested that these DPs actually contain null (silent) determiners, analogous to the null pronouns discussed above, in which case the position of the determiner in DP would not really be missing; it would simply be occupied by a silent determiner. This conclusion receives some support from the existence of languages such as German and Portuguese, where proper names can in fact be preceded by definite determiners, although the determiner is optional rather than obligatory. Other linguists have argued that these nouns, including proper names, undergo transformational movement into the empty determiner position, which would account for the missing determiner in a slightly different way. Thus, it may be that all DPs, including those that seem to consist of just a pronoun or proper name, really do conform to the general pattern of phrase structure predicted by X-bar rules in (147), in which case our phrase structure rule for DP can also be eliminated.

If this approach is correct, there is just one phrase structure rule that seems to depart from the pattern defined by the X-bar conditions in (147), namely the Sentence rule (137):

(137) Sentence → DP — VP

This rule seems to be completely unlike the other rules we have considered; neither the subject DP position nor the VP position seems to correspond to the head in the sense defined by (147a). Recall, however, that we suggested in the context of our discussion of VP deletion that sentences might be analyzed as Tense Phrases, or TPs, that is, phrases headed by a lexical category Tense. In sentences containing the future modal *will*, such as (151), we could assume that this modal verb occupies the head T-position within TP, selecting VP as its complement:

(151)   Henry will invade France.

When the sentence contains no modal verb corresponding to *will*, the tense affix on the verb can be assumed to originate in the T-position. In chapter 5, we discuss the issue of how this tense suffix ends up being attached to the main verb.

This still leaves the position of the subject DP unaccounted for, however. To account for the existence of this position in terms of X-bar theory, it has been suggested that there is an additional X-bar condition defining a position for the subject:

(152)   Every phrase XP contains a **Specifier** or **Subject** position
        preceding the head, reserved for another phrase YP.

In (152), Y, like X, is a variable ranging over lexical categories; thus, XP and YP need not belong to the same category. In most cases, Y is D; that is, the subject of a phrase or sentence is normally a DP. This fact is not predicted by X-bar theory, however; it is possible that it can be explained on the basis of the thematic role served by the subject, though we will go into this issue here.

Although it may seem that this condition is unjustified for other types of phrases, we have already discussed a number of constructions in which there is arguably a specifier position occupied by a phrase preceding the head. One such case involves DPs containing nominal specifiers, where a DP bearing genitive case precedes the noun in DP, as in DPs such as *the king's daughters*. It is clear that the genitive DP *the king's* cannot be occupying the D-position in the containing DP, since head positions can only be occupied by words, not by phrases. Thus, if DP also contains a Specifier or Subject position, as predicted by (152), the structure of these DPs could be accounted for. As for categories such as AP, VP, NP, and PP, we observed earlier that these phrases may be preceded by subject DPs in so-called small clause constructions. If small clauses are simply XPs containing overt DP subjects, then we could assume that Condition (152) applies to all of these categories as well. For example, in a sentence like *Juliet heard Romeo call out her name*, the DP *Romeo* would be located in the Specifier position of the VP *Romeo call out her name*. Aside from small clause constructions, VP usually does not contain an overt DP subject; in these cases, X-bar theory predicts that the Specifier position of the VP is empty. It has been suggested, however, that the subject of a sentence actually originates in the Specifier-of-VP position, and undergoes transformational movement to position of the Specifier of TP, at least in languages exhibiting SVO costituent order, such as English; this idea is known as the **VP-Internal Subject Hypothesis**.

Evidence from constituency tests indicates that the Specifier position in XP is not a sister of the head X; rather, it is a sister of a constituent $\bar{X}$, where $\bar{X}$ immediately dominates the head X and the complements of X, as in (153):

(153)

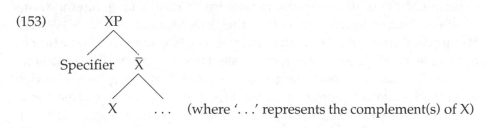

This general template of X-bar structure defines the skeletal structure of all phrases.

3.4 Summary

In this chapter we have covered the basic concepts of syntactic theory. We began with a general discussion of the primary data that theories of syntax are based on: native speakers' acceptability judgments about utterances. Linguists use these data to draw inferences about grammaticality of sentences, which enables them to construct theories about the nature of the rules and constraints concerning the syntactic component of the mental grammar.

We then looked in some detail at properties of lexical categories (classes of words that share important morphological and syntactic properties), and saw that it is possible to draw generalizations about how words may be combined with each other to form grammatical sentences. We saw that some lexical categories are used to refer, while others function as predicates. The lexical entry of each word that functions as a predicate includes a specification of its argument structure (a list of the arguments that it selects) and a statement of the thematic role (θ-role) that it assigns to each argument, such as agent, patient, or goal, indicating the role played by the argument in the situation or event that the predicate refers to. Predicates may also impose restrictions on their arguments, including the syntactic category of the argument (c-selection) and intrinsic semantic properties (selectional restrictions, or s-selection). The assignment of θ-roles is subject to a general constraint called the θ-Criterion, which requires that every obligatory θ-role must be assigned to a referential category, and that every referential category must be assigned a θ-role.

Thematic roles are typically associated with particular syntactic positions in the sentence, such as the subject position, the direct object position, the nominal specifier position, and so on. Individual languages differ from each other in terms of the linear arrangement of these positions in the structure of the sentence, enabling linguists to classify languages in terms of the major constituent orders that they exhibit, such as SVO, SOV, VSO, etc. In configurational languages such as English, the major constituent order is relatively fixed, whereas in so-called non-configurational languages such as Russian, the constituent order is somewhat more free, allowing several different word-order patterns. Free constituent order often correlates with the existence of overt morphemes for case features (Nominative, Accusative, Dative, etc.), though the correlation is not absolute; for example, English pronouns (unlike names and common nouns) have overt case marking, but their syntactic distribution is just as restricted as that of names and common nouns. Although these arguments are usually overt, pronouns are often null (silent), such as the null subject pronouns that occur in certain kinds of infinitival clauses, and in finite clauses in languages such as Spanish and Italian.

Words are grouped together to form constituents, or phrases. Each phrase contains a position for its head (the lexical category that the phrase is named after), such as the noun position in a Noun Phrase (NP), as well as any complements selected by the word occupying the head position. Virtually every type of phrase (NP, DP, AP, VP, CP, etc.) can function as a complement of a lexical head such as a verb; among these, we looked in some detail at different types of clausal complements, including tensed clauses, infinitival clauses, and so-called small clauses. The component parts of each sentence are grouped together in a particular way, giving rise to a particular constituent structure for the sentence that can be represented graphically by means of tree diagrams or labeled bracketing. These constituent structures have formal properties (such as precedence and dominance relations relating the nodes in a tree diagram) that syntactic rules refer to. In many cases, the constituent structures of sentences are not immediately obvious, and linguists must rely on a variety of constituency tests in order to determine the correct constituent structure for each type of syntactic construction; these constituency tests are based on the distributional properties of certain phrases, as well as on the way particular groups of words interact with syntactic processes involving transformational movement rules, deletion rules, coordination of like categories, and the interpretation of pro-forms.

Finally, we examined two types of theories about constituent structures, in terms of the rules and constraints in the grammar that determine which constituent structures are grammatical. The first type of theory was based on context-free rewrite rules, which specify the immediate constituents of each type of phrase (DP, VP, AP, etc.) as well as the order in which these immediate constituents are arranged. These rules apply successively (one after another) to define a skeletal structure for complete sentences, with terminal nodes defining word-positions, labeled with the names of particular lexical categories (noun, verb, determiner, etc.). The process of lexical insertion selects words from the lexicon and places them in the word-positions labeled with the appropriate lexical category-names. The structures formed in this way must then be checked to ensure that lexical selectional properties are satisfied, and also to ensure that general constraints such as the θ-Criterion are observed. Transformational rules of movement and deletion may then apply, as in the case of Question and Topicalization constructions in English. This model of syntactic rule application can form the basis for a model of speech production, or (operating in the opposite direction) for a model of grammaticality checking.

The second type of phrase structure theory assumes that there are general constraints on phrase structure that apply to all types of phrases, such as the principles of X-bar theory, rather than idiosyncratic rules defining the structure of each type of phrase independently. This alternative approach implies that all phrases should have essentially the same hierarchical structure; thus, if a phrase (such as DP or Sentence) has a structure that seems to differ from that of other categories, it must be reanalyzed in a way that eliminates the discrepancy. The advantages of this approach are, first, that it explains why almost all types of phrases have a similar structure (which is impossible to explain if every phrase is defined by a different rule), and, second, that it results in a simpler overall model of grammar, by entirely eliminating complicated phrase structure rules such as those described in section 3.3.3, which were largely redundant in any case.

In the following chapters, we will examine a number of syntactic processes, including those relating to binding and movement, which are based on the structures defined in this chapter.

Acknowledgment

We would like to acknowledge the assistance of the following colleagues for the non-English data discussed in this chapter, including the problems: Tim Beasley (Russian), Edward Garrett (Tibetan), Murat Kural (Turkish), Felicia Lee (SLQ Zapotec), Jamal Ouhalla (Standard Arabic), Matt Pearson (Malagasy), and Maria-Luisa Zubizarreta (Spanish).

Further reading

Cowper, L. 1992. *A Concise Introduction to Syntactic Theory*. Chicago: University of Chicago Press.

Culicover, Peter. 1997. *Principles and Parameters: An Introduction to Syntactic Theory*. Oxford: Oxford University Press.

Haegeman, L. 1994. *Introduction to Government and Binding Theory*. Oxford: Blackwell.

McCawley, J. 1988. *The Syntactic Phenomena of English*. Chicago: University of Chicago Press.

Radford, A. 1988. *Transformational Grammar*. Cambridge: Cambridge University Press.

—— 1997. *Syntax, A Minimalist Introduction*. Cambridge: Cambridge University Press.

Riemsdijk, H. van and E. Williams. 1986. *Introduction to the Theory of Grammar*. Cambridge, MA: MIT Press.

Roberts, I. 1996. *Comparative Syntax*. London/New York: Arnold.

References on languages cited

Chinese:

Huang, C.-T. J. 1984. On the Distribution and Reference of Empty Pronouns, *Linguistic Inquiry*, 15: 531–74.

Haitian Creole:

Déchaine, R. 1993. *Predicates Across Categories*, doctoral dissertation, University of Massachusetts (Amherst); reproduced and distributed by GLSA, Amherst, MA.

Japanese:

Hoji, H., S. Miyagawa, and H. Tada. 1989. NP-Movement in Japanese, in WCCFL VIII, CSLI, Palo Alto, CA.

Kuno, S. 1973. *The Structure of the Japanese Language*. Cambridge, MA: MIT Press.

Russian:

Kondrashova, Natalia. 1996. The Russian Copula: A Unified Approach; in *Annual Workshop on Formal Approaches to Slavic Linguistics: the College Park Meeting 1994* (Jindrich Toman, ed.), 255–85. Ann Arbor: Michigan Slavic Publications.

EXERCISES

Malagasy

Consider the following data from Malagasy, an Austronesian language spoken throughout Madagascar. In these examples, the glosses for some words have been simplified, omitting translations of some morphemes.

Exercise 3.11   (i)   namangy anay ny ankizy
visited   us   the children
'The children visited us.'

(ii)   mihinana ahitra ny omby
eat   grass   the cow
'Cows eat grass.'

(iii)   matory ny mpamboly
sleep   the farmer
'The farmer(s) is/are sleeping.'

(iv) tonga   taorian' ny rahalahi -ko ny mpampianatra antitra
      arrived after   the brother -my the teacher   old
      'The old teacher arrived after my brother.'

(v)   namono ny akoho   tamin' ny antsy ny vehivavy
      killed   the chicken with   the knife the woman
      'The woman killed the chicken(s) with the knife.'

(vi) nandroso vary ny ankizy   tamin' ny lovia vaovao i – Noro
      served   rice the children on   the dish new   Noro
      'Noro served the children rice on the new dishes.'

(vii) nanaseho sari-n'   i-Noro ny lehilahy ny reni-n'   ny zaza
      showed   picture-of Noro the man   the mother-of the child
      'The child's mother showed the man a picture of Noro.'

(a) What is the basic order of major constituents (subject, object, indirect object, verb, PP) in Malagasy?
(b) Construct a lexicon for Malagasy based on the words occurring in these sentences. For each Malagasy verb, state how many arguments it selects, and what θ-roles it assigns to them. Organize your lexicon by grouping together words belonging to the same lexical category.
(c) Construct phrase structure rules for PP, DP, VP, and TP (Sentence) in Malagasy.
(d) Draw tree diagrams for sentences (i), (iv), and (vii) that are consistent with your phrase structure rules.

. . . .

SLQ Zapotec   Exercise 3.12

Consider the following data from SLQ Zapotec, a Zapotecan language spoken in Mexico.

(i)   Y-tàa'az Gyeeihlly Li'eb
       Irr-beat Mike   Felipe
       'Mike will beat Felipe.'

(ii)   B-gu'ty-a'   bzihny
       Perf-kill-1sg mouse
       'I killed the mouse.'

(iii) Y-tòo'oh Gyeeihlly ca'rr
       Irr-sell Mike   car
       'Mike will sell the car.'

(iv)   N-àa-'ng   banguual
       Neut-be-3sg old
       'He is old.' or 'She is old.'

(v)   B-da'uh-zhya' Gyeeihlly bx:àady
        Perf-eat-might Mike   grasshopper
        'Mike might have eaten grasshoppers.'

(vi)   Gw-ùa'il-rëng li'ebr
        Irr-read-3pl   books
        'They will read the books.'

(vii) B-dèèi'dy Gyeeihlly bx:àady   Li'eb
        Perf-give Mike   grasshopper Felipe
        'Mike gave the grasshoppers to Felipe.'

(viii) W-nnàa'az Gyeeihlly bx:àady   cuahnn gyìi'x
        Perf-catch Mike   grasshopper with   net
        'Mike caught grasshoppers with the net.'

(ix)   N-àa   Li'eb banguual
        Neut-be Felipe old
        'Felipe is old.'

(x)   R-càa'z-a'   y-gu'ty-a' bzihny
        Hab-want-1sg Irr-kill-I   mouse
        'I want to kill the mouse.'

(xi)   B-inydyahg Li'eb y-tòo'oh Gyeeihlly ca'rr
        Perf-hear Felipe Irr-sell Mike   car
        'Felipe heard that Mike will sell the car.'

(xii) R-e'ihpy Lia Pa'amm làa'-rëng   gw-ùa'll-rëng li'ebr
        Hab-tell   Ms.   Pam them Irr-read-they book
        'Pam told them to read the books.'

(a)   Construct a lexicon for SLQ Zapotec based on the words occurring in these sentences. For words containing more than one morpheme, try to identify the meaning of each morpheme and add a lexical entry for each of these morphemes. Group together words belonging to the same lexical category.

(b)   What is the basic order of major constituents (subject, verb, object, etc.) in SLQ Zapotec?

(c)   Comment on two differences between English and SLQ Zapotec involving (i) definite articles, and (ii) singular and plural nouns.

(d)   In SLQ Zapotec, the morphemes occurring at the end of the verbs in Sentences (ii), (iv), (vi), and (x) are glossed with features for person and number. There are two possible analyses for these morphemes: they might be pronominal subject clitics, analogous to the pronominal object clitics in French and Spanish in (21), or they might be subject agreement markers, analogous to the subject agreement affixes in Italian and Spanish in (51). Which of these analyses would require us to assume that SLQ Zapotec allows null pronouns to occur in the subject position? Explain your reasoning. Now compare the verbs in sentences (iv) and (ix), and explain why the form of the verb in (ix) supports the pronominal clitic analysis.

(e) In SLQ Zapotec, the order of the subject and verb relative to each other is different from what we find in English. Propose two alternative theories to account for this.

(I) The first theory should account for the word order in the example sentences above using only phrase structure rules. Formulate a set of phrase structure rules to account for all the data above and draw tree diagrams based on these rules to account for sentences (vii) and (xi). Note that SLQ Zapotec does not have an overt complementizer such as English *that*; assume that embedded sentences in this language are simply TPs, without any CP node.

(II) The second theory should assume that the SLQ Zapotec phrase structure rules for VP and TP resemble those of English, with a verb position located inside VP, and the subject DP position located outside of VP (to the left of it). This implies that the word order in the data above must result from the application of a transformational movement rule, similar to the rule that derives Subject–Auxiliary Inversion constructions in English. Formulate phrase structure rules for VP and TP in SLQ Zapotec that are consistent with this assumption, and explain how the transformational movement rule would change the word order produced by these rules. Draw a tree diagram based on these phrase structure rules for sentence (xi), showing the word order before the transformational movement rule has been applied.

. . . .

English Quantifiers

Recall that a finite (tensed) verb in English agrees in person and number features with the DP occurring in the subject position of the sentence in which it occurs, and that this agreement is represented overtly (as the suffix *-s* on the verb) only if the subject DP is third-person singular. Assume that this agreement relation is enforced by a constraint requiring the subject DP and the finite verb to have the same person and number features.

Now consider the data in (i–x) involving the quantifiers *all*, *many*, *some*, *each*, and *every*. These data show that English has another agreement constraint involving quantifiers and nouns (or NPs). In this respect, quantifiers resemble the demonstrative determiners *this*, *that*, *these*, and *those*.

(i)   All lords respect Duncan.
(ii)   Many young lords respect Duncan.
(iii)   Some kings of Scotland admire Macbeth.
(iv)   Each Scottish lord owns a castle.
(v)   Every murder of a king offends his lords.
(vi)   *All/Many (young) lord respect(s) Duncan.
(vii)   *Each/Every Scottish lords own(s) a castle.
(viii) Some lord admires Macbeth.

(ix)   *Some lords admires Macbeth.
(x)   *Each/Every Scottish lord own a castle.

Now answer these questions:

(a) Assume that each quantifier is specified in the lexicon as being either [+Plural], [−Plural] (singular), or ambiguous (allowing either feature value for number). Construct a lexical entry for the quantifiers *all*, *many*, *some*, *each*, and *every*, stating the feature specification for each of them, and propose an agreement constraint that accounts for the data in (i–v) in comparison with the data in (vi–viii). In answering this question, assume that an NP counts as [+Plural] if the noun occupying the head N position in the NP is [+Plural].

(b) Explain why (vi) and (vii) are ungrammatical, with or without the third-person agreement suffix *-s* on the verb. Also explain why (iii) and (viii) are both grammatical.

(c) Explain why (ix) and (x) are ungrammatical.

(d) Assume that quantifiers are determiners. Based on the data in (i–v), what kind of category does each of these quantifiers c-select as its complement?

(e) Draw a tree diagram for sentence (ii), following the constraints of the X-bar theory of phrase structure discussed in section 3.3.4.

(f) Would it be possible to eliminate the agreement constraint that you proposed in your answer to (a) by assuming that the lexical entry of each quantifier can select the number feature of the quantifier's complement? Explain, making explicit reference to how this theory would (or would not) account for the ungrammaticality of (vi) and (vii).

(g) Now consider these additional data:

(xi)   All/Many/Some of the lords respect Duncan.
(xii)   *All/Many/Some of the lords respects Duncan.
(xiii) *All/Many/Some of the lord respect(s) Duncan.
(xiv)   Each of the lords owns a castle.
(xv)   *Each of the lord own(s) a castle.
(xvi)   *Every of the lord(s) own(s) a castle.

Revise your answers to questions (d) and (f) in whatever ways are necessary in order to account for these additional data. Assume that the preposition *of* occurring in these examples is a genitive case particle indicating the genitive case feature of the DP that immediately follows it, rather than a true preposition; thus, the sequence *of the lords* should be analyzed as a [+Genitive] DP, rather than as a PP. Explain why each revision is necessary by making explicit reference to the examples given; note that each example provides a crucial piece of information, so a complete answer will mention every example. Draw a tree for Sentence (xiv).

(h) Now consider these additional data, involving the **Quantifier Float (Q-float)** construction, in which a quantifier occurs after the noun phrase, rather than before it.

(xvii)   The (Scottish) lords all/each own a castle.
(xviii) *The (Scottish) lords many/some own a castle.

(xix)   *The (Scottish) lord(s) every own a castle.
(xx)   *The lords all/each owns a castle.

Before attempting to understand the structure of these sentences, draw some generalizations about the Q-float construction based on these examples. Each sentence provides at least one important clue about Q-float; in each case, state what the example shows. For example, (xvii) shows that the quantifiers *all* and *every* can occur in the Q-float construction, and also that the DP in the subject position of the sentence can be [+Plural], as indicated by the agreement affix on the finite verb.

(i)   Now consider these data:

(xxi)   They all support Duncan.
(xxii)   All of them support Duncan.

Assume that Q-float constructions are formed by a transformational movement rule which moves a DP from a position in which it would normally be assigned Genitive case into the subject position of the sentence, where it is assigned Nominative case. Explain how this analysis would account for the derivation of sentences (xxi) and (xxii). How might the ungrammaticality of (xix) be explained in terms of the ungrammaticality of (xvi)?

(j)   Now consider the constituent structure of the Q-float construction: the quantifier might be contained within the same DP as the determiner and NP preceding it, or it might be part of the VP that follows this DP, or in some other position. Use the following data to answer this question:

(xxiii)   The lords should all respect Duncan.
(xxiv)   The lords may each own a castle.
(xxv)   The lords should all respect Duncan, and all respect Duncan they will!
(xxvi)   *The lords should all respect Duncan, and respect Duncan they will all!
(xxvii)   The lords all should respect Duncan, and respect Duncan they all will!

(k)   Based on your answers to questions (i) and (j), it is possible to propose an analysis of the Q-float construction based on the VP-internal subject hypothesis discussed in section 3.3.4, according to which the subject DP originates in the Specifier position of VP and is moved to the Specifier position of TP by a transformational movement rule. Explain how this analysis would work, using a tree diagram for Sentence (xxii) to illustrate your answer. If possible, also explain why the VP-internal subject hypothesis plays a crucial role in explaining where the quantifier may occur in Q-float constructions, and how it is possible to move the pronoun in (xxi) into a position where Nominative case is assigned. (Hint: assume that Nominative case is assigned only to the subject position, and that it is only possible to move a DP into a position that is not already occupied by another DP.)

. . . .

Exercise 3.14 The Phrase Structure of Language X

This exercise is intended to give you a taste of the experience of working on a language other than English. If this textbook is being used in a class in which there are native speakers of several languages other than English, it may be appropriate for small groups of students to work together on a particular language, with one of the members of the group serving as the native speaker, whose acceptability judgments will serve as the source of data for the group. (Depending on the wishes of the instructor, the assignment may be written up either by the group as a whole, or by individual members of the group working independently after discussing the issues with each other.)

If the textbook is being used in a class where there are very few speakers of a language other than English, it may be appropriate for the instructor to provide judgment data that are distributed to the entire class, so that each student can work independently. Alternatively, it may be appropriate for students to work individually or in groups with a native speaker of a foreign language.

If the textbook is being used in a class in which all or most of the students are native speakers of the same language (for example, if the class is being used in a non-English-speaking country), then it may be appropriate for each student to work independently, relying on his or her own intuitions.

Ask your native speaker to produce some simple sentences, involving translations of the following English sentences (or similar sentences; e.g. feel free to use different names but preserve the gender). Since your native speaker is one of you, you can rely on his/her ability to segment the sentences into words and to supply glosses for each word (and morphemes within the word). For each sentence, give a morpheme-by-morpheme gloss followed by an idiomatic gloss. Feel free to construct additional examples, especially if you have problems with these examples for an unforeseen reason.

(a) Provide translations for the following sentences into Language X. Each example sentence in Language X should have an English gloss listed under each morpheme, in addition to the original English sentence.

1   The king found some books.
2   He read the books to his son.
3   The three soldiers stirred the soup.
4   They stirred it for three hours.
5   The soldier was old and ugly.
6   The castle is on a hill near a lake.
7   Antonio lives in Venice.
8   Duncan arrived at the castle yesterday.
9   Prospero's book will arrive next week.
10 The kind man gave a book to his daughter.
11 She will put the book on a chair.
12 Macbeth may find them in the forest. (Assume that the pronoun *them* refers to people.)

13   Falstaff drank a glass of beer.
14   Falstaff drank because he was thirsty.
15   Miranda knew that Prospero had many books.
16   Hamlet said that his mother was disloyal.
17   Portia told Shylock that he should be kind to Antonio.
18   Macbeth tried to kill the king.
19   Macbeth wanted to meet a witch.
20   Prospero has promised to give her the book.

(b)   Construct a lexicon for Language X, with English translations for each word. Organize the lexicon in terms of lexical categories, as in the previous exercises.

(c)   If you believe that some of the words in your lexicon contain more than one morpheme, try to identify the meaning of each morpheme and formulate morphological rules for combining the morphemes to form words.

(d)   Make a list of the different types of lexical categories (noun, verb, pronoun, preposition, etc.) in Language X. Indicate the lexical category for each word in your lexicon. If in doubt, assume that words in Language X belong to the same category as their English translations unless you have evidence suggesting otherwise.

(e)   Does Language X have pronouns like English *he/she/they/them/his/her*? Can these pronouns be null (silent)? If so, in which syntactic positions (subject, object, indirect object, etc.)? You may need to consult your native speaker to determine whether certain pronouns are optional.

(f)   Does Language X have definite and/or indefinite articles like English *the* and *a(n)*? Illustrate.

(g)   Does Language X allow for tensed sentences to occur as embedded clauses? If so, what changes, if any, do you observe between a main clause and an embedded clause, in terms of complementizers, word order, special suffixes, etc.? Cite examples.

(h)   Does Language X have any auxiliary verbs, or does it just use affixes on the main verb? Illustrate.

(i)   Does Language X have any kind of case marking to indicate which DP is the subject, the object, the indirect object, etc.? Explain, citing examples.

(j)   Does Language X exhibit any kind of subject–verb agreement, of the type we find in English (*the boys are here* vs. *the boy is here*)? Give evidence one way or the other. What about object agreement – does the verb agree with its object? Is there any other kind of agreement, e.g. between a determiner or article and a noun?

(k)   Try to determine the basic constituent order for Language X, identifying the positions for the subject, object, indirect object, verb, etc. If you find that more than one ordering is possible, you may want to consult with your native speaker to find out if Language X allows more than one possible word order for the translations of each of these sentences.

(l)   Try to formulate phrase structure rules for each type of phrase that occurs in these data. Illustrate each rule with an example drawn from your data. Remember that the constituent order within each type of phrase may be different from English. In answering this question, you may come to the conclusion that certain constituents (such as verbs, pronouns, or other categories) may be affected by transformational movement rules; if so, you should feel free to posit the existence of one or more movement rules in addition to your phrase structure rules, but you should explain your reasoning, citing evidence from the data.

(m) Draw tree diagrams for sentences 1, 2, 6, 9, 15, and 20. Make sure that your tree diagrams are consistent with your phrase structure rules.

(n) Identify the c-selection properties of each verb in your lexicon for Language X.

(o) Mention anything else that seems distinctive or interesting about the word order and basic grammar of Language X.

4

Syntax II:
Syntactic Dependencies

CHAPTER CONTENTS

4.0 Introduction

There are two fundamental properties governing the syntactic organization of natural languages. The first one is **constituent structure**, which was introduced in the previous chapter. The second is the existence of **syntactic dependencies**, the fact that the occurrence of a particular word or morpheme in a string of words can depend on the presence of some other word or morpheme in this string of words. This chapter will discuss syntactic dependencies.

4.0.1 Constituent structure

We have seen that strings of words are organized in units called constituents. A sentence, like the following in (1):

(1) The jealous brother betrayed the lord of Florence.

is itself a unit and is composed of other units and subunits as indicated with labeled brackets in (2) or in an equivalent tree notation in (3), as discussed in the previous chapter.

(2) [$_{TP}$ [$_{DP}$ [$_{D}$ The] [$_{NP}$ [$_{A}$ jealous] [$_{N}$ brother]]] [$_{T'}$ [$_{T}$ past] [$_{VP}$ betrayed [$_{DP}$ [$_{D}$ the] [$_{NP}$ [$_{N}$ lord] [$_{PP}$[$_{P}$ of] [$_{DP}$ Florence]]]]]]]]

(3)

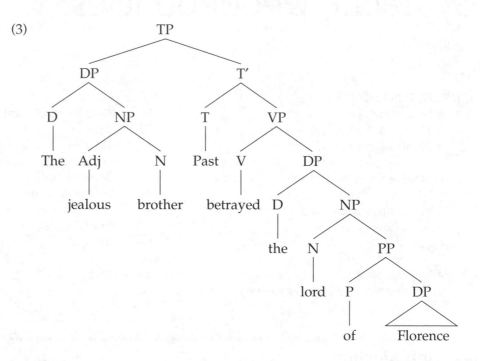

    As also discussed in the previous chapter, this kind of representation illustrates that words cluster together to form larger units (for example the noun *brother* and the adjective *jealous* combine to form an NP), which in turn cluster together to form larger units (for example the DP *The jealous brother* and the VP *betrayed the lord of Florence* combine to form a TP). It is important to remember that one important type of justification for assuming that words form larger and larger units comes from the observation that certain strings of words can be manipulated as groups while others cannot. This is what we observed in the previous chapter with coordination, for example. The strings that can be manipulated as groups are represented as units or constituents. Furthermore, if two groups behave in the same way (e.g. occur in the same positions), they get the same label (for example the NP *jealous brother* and the NP *lord of Florence* can combine with a determiner like *a* or *the* or *this* to form a DP).

4.0.2 C-selection and s-selection: examples of syntactic dependencies

Constituent analysis and constituent labeling, however, do not constitute all our knowledge about the syntactic properties of natural languages. There are dependencies between different positions in a sentence (or in a string of words): that is, whether or not a particular word or expression is allowed to appear in a sentence might depend on the presence or absence of some other word or string of words elsewhere in this sentence.

The examples in (4) further illustrate this. (We again use an asterisk (*) to indicate that the sentence is ungrammatical or unacceptable in some way.)

(4) a. This moat surrounds his castle.
     b. *This moat surrounds
     c. *This moat surrounds from the food
     d. *This moat surrounds two minutes

The deviance of sentences like (4b) led us, in chapter 3, to postulate the existence of **selectional restrictions**. We repeat here briefly what these selectional restrictions refer to. The verb *surround* requires the presence of a direct object, i.e. of a complement of the category DP. We referred to this as **c-selection** or **categorial selection**. This is meant to suggest that the **category** of the complement is selected by the verb *surround*. (4c) illustrates that a PP complement is disallowed. If you try to replace this DP by other categories such as an Adjective Phrase you will see that a DP and only a DP can occur here. Since this c-selection requirement is not satisfied in (4b), this sentence is also judged to be deviant.

The deviance of sentences like (4d) led us in chapter 3 to postulate another kind of selectional restriction, **s-selection** or **semantic selection** because it refers to the **semantic properties** or meanings of the verb and the complements which are selected. This case shows that the verb *surround* requires the presence of a direct object, i.e. a DP complement, of a certain kind: this DP must refer to a concrete object like *castle*, not a measure of time like *minutes*. (4d) is judged to be deviant because this selectional restriction is violated.

Both c-selection and s-selection are examples of syntactic dependencies. In the examples discussed above, they establish a connection between a verb and what, if anything, can occur as complement of this verb.

Another example of dependency is illustrated in (5):

(5) The fairies will not like witchcraft at all.

Using the procedure exemplified in (4), we can make some dependencies more apparent in (5) by trying to replace a word or string of words to see the effect of this substitution. For example, we can substitute the expression *a lot* for *at all* without affecting the well-formedness of this sentence; this substitution produces a well-formed sentence:

(6)   The fairies will not like witchcraft a lot.

This substitution causes the meaning of the sentence to change (not liking at all is not the same as not liking a lot) but both sentences are well-formed. Various substitutions will not affect well-formedness, we can call them good substitutions as in (6). In general, good substitutions are less informative than bad substitutions. Bad substitutions lead to ungrammaticality (ill-formedness) and alert us to an important property of what was replaced which has not been preserved. (7) is one such example:

(7)   *The fairies **does** not like witchcraft at all.

Substituting *does* for *will* leads to ungrammaticality. Unlike the substitution leading from (5) to (6), this last substitution violates a property of grammatical organization. The deviance of (7) is due to the existence of a rule of **subject/verb agreement** in English, a syntactic dependency between the **number** of the subject of the clause and the verb form. The verb *does* can be used only if the subject is singular; since in (7) the subject DP *the fairies* is plural, the sentence is ungrammatical.

We see that a complete account of how words are put together to form larger units in a well-formed way cannot be described solely in terms of constituent structure, that is, in terms of how words are combined to form larger units. The various dependencies that exist between words and larger constituents also play a role.

Whenever there is a dependency, there will be bad substitutions, namely all those substitutions that violate the requirements of this dependency. In trying to discover the dependencies of a language, substitutions (particularly bad ones) are excellent investigative tools since they reveal the existence, the nature, and the limit of these dependencies.

4.1   A Sample Case: Negative Polarity Items

We will now examine a particular case which can exemplify the methods that can be used to discover and investigate syntactic dependencies. We will also see the kind of questions and problems which arise.

4.1.1   Introducing the puzzle

Consider sentence (5) again:

(5)   The fairies will not like witchcraft at all.

Our aim is to find out whether there are any dependencies other than the c- and s-selection dependencies, mentioned above. There is no method that tells us what substitutions we should try in our attempt to answer this question. In the discussion above we saw the result of substituting the auxiliary verb *does* for *will* and in (4) the DP direct object *two minutes* for the DP *his castle*.

Let us now try various substitutions for the word *not*. Replacing *not* with any kind of expression without any constraints will result in an explosion of ill-formed sentences and we might end up not knowing what to do with all these bad substitutions. To see this, let us try a few random substitutions where we replace *not* by any one of the expressions between slashes:

(8)   The fairies will   NOT   like witchcraft at all
           {John / rainfall / proud / ate / with /
           never in a million years / go to school}

As you can see, all of these sentences except *never in a million years* are deviant. These substitutions do not reveal much about what particular role, if any, the word *not* plays. We may be more successful if we limit our search to substitution IN KIND, that is, to words which seem to function in a way similar to *not* in a sentence. The problem is that we do not as yet know what *in kind* means. We probably would know if we knew what *not* means or how it functions in a sentence. But this is in part what we are trying to understand.

This is a common situation in trying to understand a complex system of interacting parts. To understand one part, we need to understand the role it plays in the system. To understand the role it plays, we need to understand the system, which we cannot understand without understanding its parts. To get out of this quandary, we can make an educated guess as to how we should proceed. Whether this guess is a good one will be known only when we have a greater understanding of the relevant factors which can help decide whether this is the proper way to proceed.

To help us make an educated guess, let us look at a simplified case and ask what kind of elements are similar to *not*. That is, what other elements can lawfully occur between an auxiliary verb like *will* and a main verb like *leave* or *like* in a sentence like (9):

(9)   Titania will   not   leave

(10)   a.   {indeed / perhaps / often / probably / never in a million years}
        b.   *{John / rainfall / proud / ate / with / go to school}

The substitutions in (10a) still yield ill-formed results. But all those in (10b) yield well-formed results. This suggests that in order to gain an understanding of the function or influence of the word *not*, we limit substitutions to elements which are similar to *not* in being allowed to occur between the auxiliary verb and the main verb. Many of such items are traditionally classified as preverbal **adverbs**, that is, words that can occur directly in front of the verb, modifying its meaning. This is a vague way of saying that they somehow alter the meaning of the verb. As a first step, then, we will restrict ourselves to substituting other preverbal adverbs for *not*.

Before proceeding, note the following problem: the minigrammar of English introduced in the preceding chapter will not generate a sentence such as (8) or (9) because no rule includes an element like *not* or *at all*. In order to allow such well-formed sentences as (9) that include a *not* or *indeed* or *perhaps* in front of VP, and to allow such well-formed sentences as (8) that include *at all* at the end of VP, we need to add a rule to the inventory of phrase structure rules. If we call such elements or constituents **adverbs** (or **adverbial expressions**), the rule might be stated as:

R1:   VP → Adverb VP Adverb

Given this rule, anything that is specified as an adverb in the lexicon can appear in front of or after a VP. However, since we have seen grammatical, well-formed sentences in which an adverb does not occur, we can reformulate the rule using the parenthesis convention to specify that the enclosed items are optional.

R2:   VP → (Adverb) VP (Adverb)

What we have done so far leads to the conclusion that in using the substitution method of investigation we should not try substitutions that violate the phrase structure of the language: *rainfall* in (10), a noun, is not a candidate for substitution for the simple reason that it is not an adverb (a fact that should be – and can be – confirmed independently).

Substituting other adverbs for *not* in the original sentence (7), gives the following results:

(11)   a.   The fairies will   not / never   like witchcraft at all
        b.   *The fairies will   perhaps / often /   like witchcraft at all
                                  indeed probably / Ø

Only one substitution seems to be a good one: replacing *not* by *never* produces an acceptable result but none of the others do. Note in particular that replacing *not* by the **null string** Ø is not acceptable. We have made two relevant observations (and a guess):

Guess: limiting substitutions to preverbal adverbs (i.e. replacing one preverbal adverb by another) is not going to lead us away from a correct description of the phenomenon we are studying.

First observation: replacing *not* by some preverbal adverbs (as in (11a)) is a good substitution.

Second observation: replacing *not* by other preverbal adverbs is sometimes a good substitution (as in (10a)) but is not always (11b).

Two questions arise from these observations:

First question: what distinguishes cases like (9) from cases like (11)?
Since the substitution of preverbal adverbs in (9) presents less of a problem than in (11) there must be some relevant difference between (9) *Titania will not leave,* and (11) *The fairies will not like witchcraft at all.*

Recall that bad substitutions indicate the violation of some dependency requirement. What element in (11) introduces a dependency that is not present in (9)? Plausibly, there is some sensitive element in (11) which needs a particular kind of preverbal adverb. Since *at all* is present in (11) but not in (9), the expression is a likely candidate. *At all* by itself does not seem to mean anything. Unlike other words describing an extent, such as *a lot*, *at all* cannot be used in isolation. As an answer to the question: *How did you like this movie?* it is possible to answer: *A lot!* but *At all!* is strange and uninterpretable. However, the answer: *Not at all!* is fine. The expression *not at all* does mean something. The expression *at all* makes sense if it is associated with *not* somewhere in the same sentence.

To corroborate the idea that *at all* is the sensitive element, we can remove it from all the sentences in (11). This is a kind of substitution, namely substitution by the null string Ø. If we do this, all the sentences in (11) become acceptable. This result establishes the fact that *at all* is the culprit that makes some of the sentences in (11) ill-formed.

Another way to test this hypothesis is to follow the same procedure we have used earlier, namely substitution by something else. If the element *at all* is the sensitive one, we may be able to replace it by a SIMILAR but DIFFERENT element. To exemplify what is meant by similar we can refer to the case of *not*; we want to replace an element in kind, possibly a constituent of the same category, that occurs in the same place and means the same kind of thing, whatever that may be. By different, we mean replacements that are not sensitive (or not sensitive in the same way). As can be seen in the expression *not at all*, *at all* seems to be a kind of adverbial expression measuring an extent, which we will call a **measure adverb**; let us try to replace it with a variety of measure adverbs or adverbial expressions with a related meaning, for example, *a lot, much, a little bit, more than (something),* . . . We get the following results:

(12) a. Fairies will *not* / *never* like witchcraft *at all* / *a lot* / *much* / *a little bit* / *more than algae.*

  b. Fairies will *indeed* / *perhaps* / *often* / *probably*/ Ø like witchcraft **at all* / *a lot* / **much* / *a little bit* / *more than algae.*

These examples should be read as follows: for each sentence, choose one of the preverbal adverbs and choose one of the measure adverbs. If the result is not acceptable, the adverb in question is starred, if the result is acceptable, the adverb is not starred. We see that with preverbal adverbs such as *not* or *never*, all measure adverbs are acceptable. Without any preverbal adverbs or with preverbal adverbs such as *indeed, perhaps, often* and *probably*, some measure adverbs like *a lot* or *a little bit* are acceptable while others like *at all* or *much* are not.

From these examples, we can draw two conclusions. First, *at all* does seem to be the culprit. If we replace it in a sentence where it is not acceptable with other adverbs or adverb phrases expressing the same kind of idea, such as *a lot, more than (something)* or *a little bit*, the sentence becomes acceptable. This means that the deviance of the bad sentences in (11) is not due to some general property of measure adverbials, but rather, as we had already concluded, due to the particular choice of measure adverb.

Second, we discover that *at all* is not alone among measure adverbs, as *much* seems to function the same way, that is, they are sensitive to what else appears in the sentence in a way that other measure adverbial expressions are not.

In conclusion, the answer to the question: what distinguishes cases like (9) *Titania will not leave,* from cases like (11) *The fairies will not like witchcraft at all*? is the presence or absence of measure adverbials like *at all*.

Second question: what distinguishes cases like (11a) from cases like (11b)? What are these sensitive adverbs sensitive to? On the basis of the examples discussed, adverbs like *at all* are acceptable in the presence of *not* and *never* (or *never in a million years*) but create unacceptable sentences when occurring with *indeed, perhaps, often, probably*. We will call *not* and *never* **licensers**; the elements *not* and *never* license the element *at all*. This terminology reflects the fact that *at all* needs *not* or *never* (or maybe something else, as we will see below) somewhere, but *not* or *never* does not need *at all* (or a similar sensitive element) as is exemplified in (9). The **dependency** between *at all* and its licenser is **directional, asymmetric**.

(13) summarizes what we have discovered so far. It contains two lists, each in a different column, and a rule explaining how to use the items in the two columns.

(13) **Sensitive measure adverbials**   **Licensers**
     at all   not
     much   never (in a million years)

     R3 (first version):   If a sensitive measure adverbial (from the first column) appears in a sentence, this sentence must also contain a preverbal adverb from the licenser column.

This table and rule seem to correctly describe the data. It is important to keep in mind that this rule works for the sentences we have looked at, that is sentences in (12). We do not yet know how it extends to other cases. We will see, however, that it is lacking in many respects. We specified that this is a first approximation, by adding the phrase 'first version'. We will need to revise it several times.

4.1.2 Some problems and how to address them

We now have a preliminary account of our observation. The table in (13) states a generalization about the distribution of the sensitive items in the first column, an observation that was not immediately obvious from the start.

One problem with list (13) is that it refers to specific items, and does not go beyond these items. It makes no prediction as to whether there are any other licensers, and if so whether they function like the two listed. If there is another licenser, we can, of course, simply add it to the second column. This may be the best way to represent a speaker's knowledge of this aspect of the language, but we are not interested in just this set of sentences; rather, we wish to explain or account for how native speakers of English reach the judgments about them that they do. If we conclude that the table in (13) is the best we can do, we are saying that native speakers of English when giving judgments about these sentences, perform some mental computation which taps the information these lists contain.

We still know too little about the mental computations and brain mechanisms involved in making linguistic judgments of this kind; however, we can buttress our conclusions with further linguistic evidence.

Generalizations   **SIDEBAR 4.1**

A major goal in science is to formulate the most general statements compatible with all the available data. Constructing the table in (13) is the analogue to Isaac Newton observing an apple falling to the ground in Oxford, England, and concluding: "Hmm! the ground in Oxford attracts apples to it." Noticing that the same happens to pears, he would conclude: "Ahaa! the ground in Oxford attracts apples and pears to it." Traveling to London and noticing the same events, he would be led to adopt the idea that the grounds of Oxford and London attract apples and pears to them. That would indeed be missing the big picture, which of course he did not miss, but instead formulated the general law of gravitation (bodies attract each other), which pertains to apples and pears and feathers and books and rocks and is applicable everywhere . . . Our big picture appears smaller than Newton's – but the reasoning is the same: generalize as much as possible until you find that you have generalized too much.

To avoid missing the (small) big picture, we will try to modify (13) in such a way that it is as general as is compatible with all the data (that is, with the judgments that speakers have about sentences). There is no general method to decide how much to generalize and in which direction. There is no systematic procedure for finding the laws or rules of language or the laws of nature. Familiarity with the object of study can help. We know from experience, for example, that very broad generalizations – everything licenses everything, or everything licenses sensitive elements – are clearly false. We can ask whether there is some rule that can tell us what belongs in each column, whether there is some generalization pertaining to the members of each column. We should do this for both the column of licensers and the column of sensitive items, but for the purpose of illustrating how one can proceed, we will limit ourselves to examining the licensers.

We first ask what the items in the column of licensers, *not* and *never*, have in common and try to determine whether this common property is what makes them licensers. There is an obvious candidate: both of these words are negative words. We can now formulate an hypothesis generalizing beyond the two words *not* and *never*:

Hypothesis: Licensers required by the sensitive measure adverbials must be negative expressions.

SIDEBAR 4.2

Negative expressions

All of us understand what negative means informally. A negative expression is an expression that has the idea of 'no' or 'not something' in it. Since negative and positive expressions are intuitively the opposite of each other, how can we tell which is which? The way to tell is the same as the way to tell which of the two numbers +1 and −1 is the negative one. The negative number is the only one of the two that changes when multiplied by itself: $+1 \times +1 = +1$ while $-1 \times -1 = +1$. −1 is thus the negative number. Analogically, two negative expressions have a way of canceling each other while positive expressions do not. To give an idea of how this would work, notice that *Oberon will not not trick mortals* means that *Oberon will trick mortals*, that is, the two negative adverbs, *not*, cancel each other out.

Assuming the validity of the hypothesis, we can revise the description and the terminology and refer to licensers as **negative licensers**. We will, in addition, call the sensitive elements in the first column: **Negative polarity items** or **NPI**s. This terminology brings to mind an analogy with electricity or numbers. Imagine that linguistic expressions have different polarities (or different signs), i.e. are positive (affirmative) or negative. A negative element reverses the polarity (or the sign) of the expression it occurs in, making it of negative polarity. A negative polarity item requires an expression with negative polarity.

The revised table and rule is presented in (14):

(14) **Negative polarity measure adverbials**   **Negative licensers**
     at all   not
     much   never (in a million years)

R4 (version 2): If a negative polarity item (from the first column) appears in a sentence, this sentence must also contain a negative expression.

If we compare Rule R3 and Rule R4, we see that the latter drops any reference to the licenser being preverbal or being an adverb. We hypothesize that these two properties are not essential; rather the property of being negative is essential to being a licenser. Unlike (13), (14) generalizes beyond the data we looked at and thus makes predictions about what we expect to find. If these predictions are correct, the advantage of (14) over (13) becomes clear.

Lists and generalizations

SIDEBAR 4.3

Lists of items do not constitute a generalization. One can include any item in a list. That is, lists can be heterogeneous with no common properties. Lists that simply enumerate phenomena have no predictive power. They fail to provide any understanding of why the items are on the list. A list might be a good starting point but should be viewed simply as a starting point. One then needs to look for a property common to all the elements on the list. When such a property is found, a generalization has been discovered and a prediction is possible.

One can proceed by first trying to make the largest generalization possible, and then retreat to less general formulations as problems are encountered. Or, alternatively, one can proceed by trying to generalize more and more by successive approximations. Generally, the first strategy is very powerful: trying to make the description as general as possible and then constructing experimental sentences to test this general rule. The advantage of this is that if new data falsify the rule, the rule's limitations are revealed, which should lead to formulating a less general but more accurate rule. On the down side, there are greater chances that this bold generalization will be wrong.

(14) makes the following prediction: any negative expression should license negative polarity items. Simply by examining the meaning of an expression, we can decide whether it is a negative expression or not, hence conclude whether it is an NPI licenser or not. In particular, such a negative expression need not be an adverb. The property 'being an adverb' was

part of (13) as a consequence of the accidental choice we made to look at sentences like (12). It was included simply to be faithful to the data examined, that is, to describe with precision these particular sentences. If being adverbial is not necessary, any element that is negative should do, even if it is not an adverb.

Elements incorporating the word *no* such as *no one* or *nobody* would appear to be potential NPI licensers. As (15) shows, these words do seem to license negative polarity items, unlike similar words like *someone* or *somebody* without the negative meaning in them:

(15) a. No one will like witchcraft at all / much.
      b. Nobody will like witchcraft at all / much.
      c. *Someone will like witchcraft at all / much.
      d. *Somebody will like witchcraft at all / much.

In (15a–b), the NPI licensers are still preverbal in the sense that they precede the verb (although not immediately). Rule R4 does not require them to be preverbal. Rule R4 predicts that as long as there is a negative element anywhere, negative polarity licensing items can legitimately occur. To check this prediction, we will construct a new experiment, that is new sentences with a negative expression following the verb, as in (16):

(16) a. The fairies will like no one at all / much.
      b. The fairies will like nobody at all / much.

The fact that (15a–b) and (16a–b) are acceptable is consistent with Rule R4, and also shows that Rule R3 was not general enough.

Although Rule R4 is promising and simplifies the description of where licensers must be, strictly speaking it only applies to sentences that are similar to sentences like (12), i.e. that satisfy the following template:

Template T: [DP AUX (ADV) V DP MEASURE-ADV].

Surely we do not want to make it part of our rule that it only applies to such sentences. If we were to include a reference to the kind of sentences (e.g. sentences meeting the template above), it would greatly complicate the statement of the rule: for any acceptable new sentence type containing a negative element and an NPI, we will have to lengthen our list of templates to which our rule applies. Having a list is undesirable, but having a list that becomes longer at every turn is worse.

4.1.3 Structure sensitivity of linguistic rules

Our statement of Rule R4 did not make an explicit reference to the template T, but we implicitly supposed that Rule R4 only applied to sentences like those in (12). Let us again try the generalizing strategy and assume explicitly that Rule R4 applies to all sentences.

R5 (version 3):   If a negative polarity item (from the first column of (14))
appears in a sentence, this sentence must also contain a
negative element.

This represents a considerable simplification and a generalization of the rule. However, as we will see, it is now too simple. Languages simply do not function this way. The conclusion that we are leading to when trying to fix this rule is so important and so general that it is useful to state it in advance:

(17)   Principle: **Linguistic rules are structure sensitive**

As stated, Rule R5 simply requires the presence of a negative licenser whenever a negative polarity item is present, regardless of how these two elements occur in a sentence. Linguistic research has shown that linguistic rules are always sensitive to linguistic structures. In the case of syntactic rules, they are sensitive to constituent structure. A rule will apply only if a certain structural configuration obtains. In other words, we expect the correct rule to be formulated in such a way that it appeals to the tree notions we encountered in the previous chapter such as **sisterhood**, **domination**, and so on. This Principle is sometimes called the **Principle of Structure Dependency of Linguistic Rules**.

To see that Rule R5 is incorrect, we first assume that it is perfectly general and applies to all sentences. Second, we will test it on new experiment sentences to probe various aspects of this new rule. So far we have limited ourselves to sentences with only one clause. Let us construct sentences with two clauses, one embedded (i.e. contained) in the other as below:

(18)   The elves believe that the fairies liked witchcraft.
[The elves [believe [that [the fairies liked witchcraft]]]]

Suppose we add both the word *not* and the measure expression *at all* to this sentence. Since *not* or *at all* can modify either the main verb or the embedded verb, there are four ways of adding these items to (18). Two are given as examples in (19). Rule R5 says that as long as both expressions appear in the same sentence, how they do does not matter. This seems incorrect:

(19)   a.   The elves will NOT believe AT ALL that the fairies liked witchcraft.
b.   *The elves will believe AT ALL that the fairies do NOT like witchcraft.

Rule R5 is respected in both of these sentences: in each, there is a negative polarity item (*at all*) and a negative element (*not*). If the rule is correct, i.e. if it provides an accurate description of the dependency between the negative polarity item and the negative element, we would expect all sentences to be equally acceptable (albeit with different meanings). But this is not the case. Sentence (19a) is acceptable but sentence (19b) is not. Our formulation of the rule is inadequate. Notice that if we do what we did earlier to these cases, i.e. replace the subject of the verb that is negated by a negative element and remove *not*, we get similar results:

(20)   a.   **Nobody** believed **at all** that the fairies liked witchcraft.
      b.   *The elves believed **at all** that **nobody** liked witchcraft.

These examples suggest that it is important where in the structure the licenser or the NPI are found. In all of the good sentences, the negative element is in the **main clause** (i.e. in a clause not contained in any other clause) while in the bad sentences, the negative element is in an **embedded clause** (i.e. a clause part of a larger clause). Let us consider the following addition to the formulation of the rule:

ADDITION #1:   The negative element must be in the main clause.

Let us construct an experiment to see whether this is the correct generalization. Addition #1: a sentence containing a negative polarity item must have a negative element in its main clause. This predicts that no well-formed sentence has a negative polarity item licensed by a negative element in an embedded clause. The experiment will attempt to falsify this conclusion, to show that it is incorrect. The experimental sentence should contain an embedded clause, a polarity item and a negative element in the embedded clause. If some such sentence is acceptable, the generalization Addition #1 will have to be abandoned. If no such sentence is found to be acceptable, Addition #1 can be considered to be (part of) the correct rule.

It is easy to show that Addition #1 is incorrect by observing the following: given a well-formed sentence TP, it is (almost) always possible to turn this TP into an embedded sentence in a larger acceptable sentence. This universal property of all grammars of natural languages mentioned in the previous chapter, called **recursivity**, accounts for the fact that in principle, every language contains an infinite number of well-formed sentences. This property allows us to embed the original sentence into another sentence:

(21)   a.   The fairies did NOT like witchcraft AT ALL.
      b.   The elves believed that the fairies did NOT like witchcraft AT ALL.
      c.   The elves believed that NOBODY liked witchcraft AT ALL.

These two sentences (21b–c) – the first of which turns out to be one combination of *not* and *at all* that we did not give in (19) and (20) – show that Addition #1 is incorrect. Putting the examples in (21b–c) together respectively with those in (19) and (20) points to something more important, as shown in (22).

(22) a. The elves did NOT believe AT ALL that the fairies liked witchcraft.

   b. *The elves believed AT ALL that the fairies did NOT like witchcraft.

   c. The elves believed that the fairies did NOT like witchcraft AT ALL.

   d. NOBODY believed AT ALL that the fairies liked witchcraft.

   e. *The elves believed AT ALL that NOBODY liked witchcraft.

   f. The elves believed that NOBODY liked witchcraft AT ALL.

In both of (22b) and (22c), the negation occurs in the embedded clause with different acceptability judgments. On the other hand, in both (22a) and (22b), the NPI is in the main clause with different acceptability judgments. The same reasoning holds for examples (22d–f). This shows that it is not the absolute position of either the negative element or the negative polarity item that matters but rather, it is their position with respect to each other.

This, it turns out, is a fundamental fact about syntactic dependencies. The possible occurrence of a negative polarity item is contingent on the presence of a negative element; there is a dependency between them. But mere co-occurrence anywhere in a sentence is not sufficient to guarantee that this dependency is fulfilled. Nor is it sufficient for either one of them to occupy some particular position; there are specific requirements as to where these two elements must occur in relation to each other.

What then is the rule governing the relative position of negative polarity items and negative licensers? We will again proceed to look at the earlier examples and try to make an initial guess as to the rule governing the relative position of licenser and licensee. We will then try to construct further experimental sentences to decide whether the guess was correct and how it may be improved.

Let us start with the kind of examples we have already encountered:

(23) a. The fairies did NOT like witchcraft AT ALL / MUCH.

   b. NO ONE will like witchcraft AT ALL / MUCH.

   c. NOBODY will like witchcraft AT ALL / MUCH.

   d. The fairies will like NO ONE AT ALL / MUCH.

   e. The fairies will like NOBODY AT ALL / MUCH.

(24) a.   The elves did NOT believe AT ALL that the fairies liked
          witchcraft.
      b.   *The elves believed AT ALL that the fairies did NOT like
          witchcraft.
      c.   The elves believed that the fairies did NOT like witchcraft
          AT ALL.

(25) a.   NOBODY believed AT ALL that the fairies liked witchcraft.
      b.   *The elves believed AT ALL that NOBODY liked witchcraft.
      c.   The elves believed that NOBODY liked witchcraft AT ALL.

We need to reformulate Rule R5 to separate the good examples from the bad
ones. In order to do this, it may be helpful to take a close look at good and
bad examples that differ minimally from each other. This is to prevent an
unwanted difference sneaking in since that would make it more difficult to
isolate the relevant factor or factors. In other words, it is necessary to vary
only one thing at a time; otherwise one cannot tell which difference is
responsible for the result. In Linguistics we refer to pairs of sentences (or
as we shall see in the chapter on phonology below, pairs of words) as
minimal pairs if they differ in only one aspect.

   For example, the difference between (24b) and (24c) is revealed if we
draw rough tree structures as in (26) and (27), respectively:

(26)

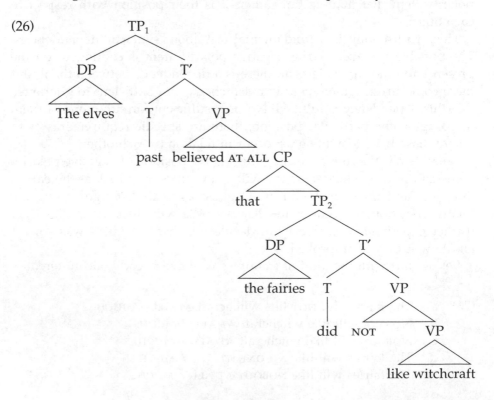

(27)

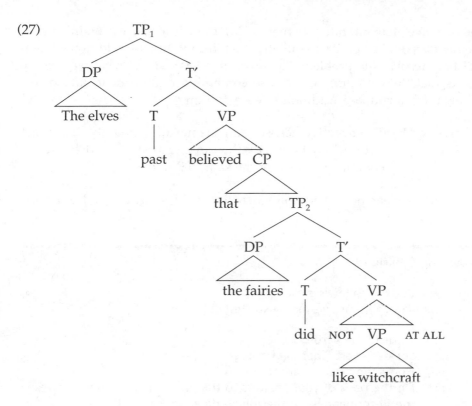

In (26) but not in (27), the negative element and the negative polarity item are in the same clause. We might then hypothesize that the dependency is subject to the Rule R5 amended as follows:

ADDITION #2:   The negative licenser and the NPI must belong to the same clause.

Note that both Addition #1 and Addition #2 are formulated in terms of a **grammatical property**, i.e. a property that is defined in terms of constituent structure and/or category labeling. This type of condition is expected given the Principle of Structure Dependency of Syntactic Rules, discussed above. It is important to notice that we can reach this conclusion only if we know what the constituent structure is for these sentences. This suggests a procedure we should always use when investigating a syntactic phenomenon in specific strings of words: always construct the tree structure for that string.

Now we should make sure that Addition #2 correctly distinguishes the good examples from the bad ones. Unfortunately, Addition #2 does not seem to have the intended effect. To see why this is the case, we need to understand precisely what it means to be in the same clause. In terms of tree representation, two items are in the same clause if there is a node TP – the category label for clauses – that contains both of them. It is true that in (27), node TP_2 contains both elements but in (26) node TP_2 only contains the negative element. But note that in (26), there is a clause containing both elements, namely TP$_1$. Consequently, this formulation of Addition #2 does not help resolve the problem. However, it is easy to fix. What we need to say is that there cannot be a clause containing one element but not the other. We reformulate Addition #2 as Addition #3:

ADDITION #3:   The negative licenser and the negative polarity item must both belong to exactly the same CLAUSES (i.e., they are contained in exactly the same TP nodes).

It should be clear how Addition #3 correctly rules out the bad examples above.

EXERCISE 4.1

Applying Addition #3

(1)   Consider the following example:
      The man John met yesterday stuttered.

      (i)   Identify the verbs.
      (ii)   For each verb, identify its subject.
      (iii)   How many clauses are there?
      (iv)   On the basis of your answers to the preceding questions, explain the ill-formedness of the following example:
              *The man John did not meet yesterday stuttered at all.

(2)   Answer all the same questions for the following examples:

      (a)   *I resent at all that you did not come.
      (b)   *That Mary did not answer my letters bothers me at all.

(3)   Can you construct a well-formed sentence containing *not* and *at all* and violating Addition #3?

Does it also successfully extend to additional data? We will again set up experiments to test the hypothesized Addition #3 which predicts the following:

(28)   Predictions made by Addition #3:
       If a sentence contains both a negative polarity item and a negative element, the sentence will be judged

       (i)   unacceptable if there is some clause containing one but not the other
       (ii)   acceptable if there is no clause containing one but not the other

The first of these two predictions is based on sentences that led us to formulate Addition #3 in the first place, namely the contrast between:

(29)   a.   The elves did NOT believe **at all** that the fairies liked witchcraft.
       b.   *The elves did believe **at all** that the fairies did NOT like witchcraft.

The crucial sentence is the second one, which has the negative polarity item in the main clause and the negation in the embedded clause. The fact that it is only one of the two elements that appears in the main clause should not matter. If the negation were in the main clause and the NPI in the embedded clause, the present rule predicts that this configuration should be ill-formed, i.e. judged unacceptable. To test this, we examine the fourth possible combination of *not* and *at all* not listed in (19):

(30)   The elves did NOT believe that the fairies liked witchcraft **at all**.

Here, we face a difficulty: is the NPI in the main clause or in the embedded clause? In order for the experimental setup to truly test the hypothesis, the NPI must be in the embedded clause. If *at all* is in the main clause, this sentence does not bear on the question at hand. We are asking which is the correct structure for (30): (31) or (32)?

(31)

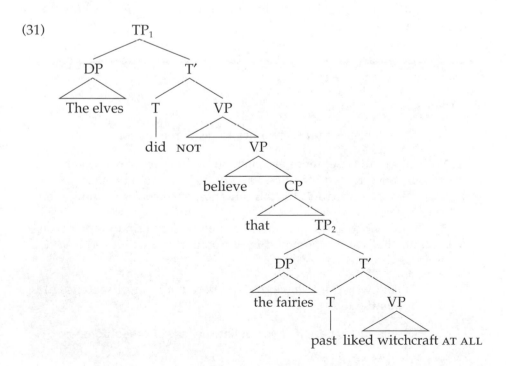

(32)

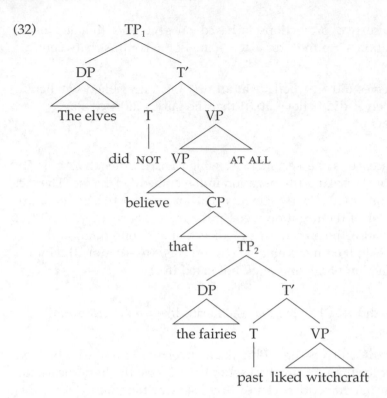

These different structures encode different meanings depending on which verb or VP the measure adverbial modifies. Under (31), the adverbial *at all* says how much the fairies like witchcraft. Under (32), *at all* says how much elves believe.

EXERCISE 4.2

Using a Constituency Test

Consider the following sentence:

(i)   Juliet says that Romeo lies to his parents a lot.

(1)   Note that this sentence is ambiguous as to which verb the measure adverb *a lot* modifies. Paraphrase the two meanings.
(2)   Draw two tree structures for this sentence, each corresponding to one of its meanings.
(3)   Recall that VP-constituency can be established by using VP-**preposing**: A string that can be preposed by VP preposing qualifies as a VP (cf. previous chapter).

(a)   Explain why the following VP-preposed version of sentence (i) is not ambiguous:

(ii)   lie to his parents a lot, Juliet says that Romeo does

> (b) Explain why the following VP-preposed version of sentence (i) is still ambiguous the same way (i) was:
>
> (iii) lie to his parents, Juliet says that Romeo does a lot

It is the second structure hence the second meaning that we are interested in. So we have to formulate the question about (30) as: is sentence (30) acceptable with the adverbial *at all* measuring the amount of witchcraft liking, i.e. with structure (31)? First of all, the answer to the question is positive. This sentence is acceptable with this meaning and this result shows the inadequacy of Addition #3 since TP$_2$ in (31) contains *at all* but not *not*. This conclusion means that we do not yet have the right rule, but it is nevertheless a positive result because we have learned that the rule is incorrect.

Before continuing the search for the correct rule, note that this new knowledge (that Addition #3 is inadequate) came with a price. We are forced to complicate our experiment. We are now not simply asking whether a certain sentence is acceptable but whether it is acceptable with a specific interpretation. This added complexity is not a problem per se, but we aim to keep experiments as simple as possible to make them as transparently interpretable as possible. It would be preferable to find a simpler experiment leading to the same conclusion. So let us examine the origin of this complication. It was introduced due to the fact that these measure adverbs can modify either the main verb or the embedded verb. We might be able to avoid this complication if we instead used an NPI which would unambiguously be part of either the main or the embedded clause.

Because all the NPIs we have seen so far are measure adverbials, we need to look elsewhere. Here are some examples suggesting that expressions such as *anyone, anybody, anything, anywhere, any time, any longer* . . . can count as NPIs.[1] We illustrate here with *anything* or *anyone* but you should try to construct similar examples with the others.

Checking the NPI status of *any longer* and *anytime*

Construct examples showing that *any longer* and *anytime* are NPIs. In order to do this, you will have to produce for each of them a minimal pair of examples: one ill-formed example lacking an NPI licenser and one well-formed example only differing from the ill-formed one by containing an NPI licenser.

EXERCISE 4.3

(33) a. *Portia saw anything / anyone.
     b. Portia did not see anything / anyone.
     c. Nobody saw anything / anyone.
     d. Portia never saw anything / anyone.

The first sentence shows that there are restrictions on where *anything* or *anyone* can appear. The others show that the presence of some negative element allows their presence. The relevant property of *anything* or *anyone* is that it is very easy to tell which clause it belongs to. Let us run the series of experiments on these new NPI items:

(34)　a.　The elves told Hermia that the fairies did **not** like **anything**.
　　　b.　The elves did **not** tell **anyone** that the fairies liked witchcraft.
　　　c.　*The elves told **anyone** that the fairies did **not** like witchcraft.
　　　d.　The elves did **not** tell Hermia that the fairies liked **anything**.
　　　e.　**Nobody** told **anyone** that the fairies liked witchcraft.
　　　f.　*The elves told **anyone** that **nobody** liked witchcraft.
　　　g.　**Nobody** told Hermia that the fairies liked **anything**.

EXERCISE 4.4

Check each sentence in (34) against Rule R5 modified by Addition #3. Do this by drawing a tree structure for each and deciding whether the modified rule is obeyed.

We get the same judgments as before. In particular, the last sentence is well-formed even though there is a clause that the NPI and the negative licenser do not both belong to. This confirms our conclusion that Addition #3 is incorrect, since this addition to the rule says that the negative licenser and the negative polarity item must belong to the same clauses.

But how wrong was Addition #3? Knowing this, might help us find the right rule. Recall that Addition #3 made the two predictions in (28). We have shown that the first one is incorrect. How about the second?

If a sentence contains both a negative polarity item and a negative element, the sentence will be judged acceptable if there is no clause containing one but not the other.

We will test this prediction using the items of the type *anyX* such as *anything, anyone* . . . First note that elements like *anyone* are DPs (as shown, for example, by the fact that they occur in DP positions such as subject). This immediately allows us to expand the kind of sentences we can look at by varying the position within a particular clause in which the NPI occurs. Until now, because we were limited to NPIs that were adverbials, we did not have much choice as to where in a particular clause these elements were allowed to occur. But *anyone*, for example, does not suffer from this limitation. Because it is a DP, it can be a subject, or an object, or the object of a preposition. Thus, parallel to (34) above, we also have:

(35)　a.　Portia thought that the fairies did NOT see ANYBODY.
　　　b.　The elves do NOT think that the fairies liked ANYTHING.
　　　c.　The elves do NOT think that ANYBODY liked the fairies.

All the sentences we have seen so far in which the negation follows the NPI are sentences in which the negation is in an embedded clause and the NPI is in the main clause. Can we put the negation and the NPI in the same clause? Thanks to the expanded list of NPIs which now contain the *anyX* type of NPI, we can. We can have the NPI as subject of a clause that is negated with *not* as in (36):

(36)   *Anyone did not see Portia.

Clearly, this sentence satisfies Addition #3 since it contains only one clause. By necessity, the NPI and the negative item are in the same clauses (which in this case is exactly one). This sentence is unacceptable however. This shows that Addition #3 is still not correct.

If we look at all the good sentences so far, we will notice that the licenser always PRECEDES the NPI and in all the unacceptable sentences, the licenser FOLLOWS the NPI. This suggests that we should forget about Addition #3 and instead amend Rule R5 with the Addition #4:

ADDITION #4:   The negative licenser must precede the negative polarity item.

Addition #4 predicts two different outcomes for a sentence containing both a negative item (call it NEG) and a polarity item (NPI):

(37)   (i)   if NEG precedes NPI, the sentence is acceptable
       (ii)   if NEG follows NPI, the sentence is unacceptable

Reviewing all the sentences we have so far looked at (which the reader should do), Addition #4 appears to be successful at predicting which sentences are ill-formed and which are well-formed. However, we should construct additional experimental sentences to test this new proposal. As usual, the idea is to construct sentences that minimally satisfy the descriptions in (37) but do not behave as expected. If we cannot construct such sentences, it is reasonable to suppose that Addition #4 is correct.

It turns out that Addition #4 is incorrect, and as we will see, it is incorrect precisely for the reason that we mentioned earlier, that is, it does not pay attention to constituent structure. To illustrate this point, consider sentence (38) in which negation does precede the NPI *at all*:

(38)   *The news that Shylock did NOT leave surprised Portia AT ALL.

This sentence is deviant even though *not* precedes *at all*, showing that Addition #4 is inadequate.

4.1.4   Toward a solution

So far, we have tried to formulate the correct rule on the basis of simple observations and simple experiments. It would be misleading to give the impression that by following a simple procedure of this sort systematically, we will always eventually end up with the right solution. There is no guarantee in science that any procedural methods will result in the correct theory. The difficulty comes from the complex nature of what we are observing. There are so many different things to observe that we do not know a priori which observations are the ones that will lead to the correct rule. In fact, as we will see, constituent structure in language plays such an important role that it would be extremely difficult to find the right solution without reference to or manipulating constituent structure.

Thus instead of continuing to slowly build towards the correct rule, we will take a shortcut. The precedence rule Addition #4 works pretty well for a substantial variety of examples. Let us try to understand why it suddenly fails in example (38).

What does negation negate?

Let us think about what the introduction of negation does to a sentence. Consider these few cases:

(39) a.   Macbeth liked witchcraft → Macbeth did not like witchcraft
 b.   Macbeth said that he liked witchcraft → Macbeth said that he did not like witchcraft
 c.   Macbeth said that he liked witchcraft → Macbeth did not say that he liked witchcraft

The first sentence conveys the information that Macbeth liked witchcraft. Its negative counterpart conveys the information that Macbeth did not like witchcraft, or that it is not the case that Macbeth liked witchcraft. Similarly, the negative counterpart of the second sentence intends to convey the information that Macbeth said that it was not the case that he liked witchcraft, and that of the third that it is not the case that Macbeth said that he liked witchcraft. This gives us the following table, where the equal sign ought to be understood as 'is intended to convey the meaning':

(40) a.   Macbeth did not like witchcraft = it is not the case that
       Macbeth liked witchcraft
 b.   Macbeth said that he did not   = Macbeth said it was not the
       like witchcraft   case that he liked witchcraft
 c.   Macbeth did not say that he   = it is not the case that
       liked witchcraft   Macbeth said that he liked
                                         witchcraft

These paraphrases illustrate what is negated when a negative item is introduced. Thus in the first sentence, what is negated is *Macbeth likes witchcraft*. The difference between (39b) and (39c) comes out clearly as (40b) and (40c) respectively illustrate. In (39b), that Macbeth is saying something is not negated. According to this sentence, Macbeth said something. What is negated has to do with what Macbeth's utterance was about. Or to put it differently, the main clause is not negated, only the embedded clause is. Thus it would be contradictory to say: 'Macbeth said that he did not like witchcraft, in fact Macbeth did not say anything at all'. But it would not be contradictory to say: 'Macbeth said that he did not like witchcraft, in fact Macbeth said that he disliked witchcraft' (although it would be a bit odd to say this as it is saying the same thing twice).

In (39c), the main clause is negated and since the embedded clause is part of the main clause, it too is negated. This comes out clearly in (40c): 'it is not the case that Macbeth said that he liked witchcraft' means that what is not the case is that Macbeth said something, specifically that he liked witchcraft.

Thus it would not be contradictory to say: 'Macbeth did not say that he liked witchcraft, in fact Macbeth did not say anything at all.' In fact, because the embedded clause counts as negated as well, neither would it be odd to say: 'Macbeth did not say that he liked witchcraft, in fact Macbeth said that he disliked witchcraft.' This way of translating the meaning of negation extends to the other cases of negation that we have seen, such as *never*, or *nobody*. Thus, we get the following translations:

(41) a. Macbeth said that nobody = Macbeth said it was not the case
          liked witchcraft   that anyone liked witchcraft
      b. Bill never comes to school = it is not the case that Bill ever
                                        comes to school

We can now return to the task of trying to understand why the previous attempts (particularly Addition #4 above) failed in example (38). To do this, we will compare a few good examples (i.e. those that work according to Addition #4) and the unacceptable example (42d):

(42) a. I said that the fairies did **not** see **anyone**.
      b. The elves did **not** say that the fairies saw **anything**.
      c. The elves did **not** say that **anybody** liked the fairies.
      d. *The news that Shylock did **not** leave surprised Portia **at all**.

If we translate the first three well-formed sentences, using the translation procedure above, we get the following where we emphasize what is negated:

(43) a. I said that it was not the case **that the fairies saw anyone**.
      b. It is not the case **that the elves said that the fairies liked anything**.
      c. It is not the case **that the elves said that anybody liked the fairies**.

We see that in all these cases, the NPI is part of the emphasized string. In all these cases, the NPI is part of what is being negated. (Remember that NPI is the abbreviation for Negative Polarity Item.) Suppose we now apply this to the fourth sentence. We get the ill-formed sentence:

(44)   The news that it is not the case **that Shylock left** surprised Portia at all.

Here what counts as negated does not include the NPI. Only part of the subject counts as negated. The rest of the main clause does not. Thus, the sentence says that Portia WAS surprised. It would be contradictory to say: 'The news that Shylock did **not** leave surprised Portia, in fact Portia was not surprised at all.'

These observations lead to the following generalization concerning the rule of licensing polarity items:

ADDITION #5:   A sentence containing an NPI is well-formed if this sentence contains a negative element and the NPI is part of what is negated in the sentence.

We must still make explicit the rule by which we determine what counts as negated. The proper way to do this is to look at a number of sentences (including those we have already seen), translate them as we have done in (40) or (44) and try to come up with the correct generalization. In other words, to restart the procedure we have been following which led to Addition #5, but with a more specific goal.

This method of investigating a problem is extremely important and what precedes was meant to illustrate how it works in a particular case. However, linguists have been working on this problem for quite some time and in the early 1960s proposed a rule that works extremely well. It would be pointless to try to rediscover everything that is already known (although it is useful to do it in a few selected cases to get more familiar with methods of linguistic investigation). The approximate rule as to what counts as negated is the following:

(45)   APPROXIMATE RULE AS TO WHAT COUNTS AS NEGATED:
       If a sentence contains a negative expression which is an XP (i.e. a DP, or an AdvP, etc.), what counts as negated is the smallest constituent containing XP.

Modifying Rule R5 to incorporate Addition #5 understood with the help of (45), we can state:

R6:   A negative polarity item must appear in a constituent that counts as negated.

Let us look at a couple of examples to see how this rule works. Because this rule appeals to constituent structure, in each case we will first need to establish what the constituent structure is before applying Rule R6.

(46) a. Macbeth said that nobody liked witchcraft.
     b. Macbeth did not say that he liked witchcraft.

Their respective constituent structures are given in (47):

(47) a.

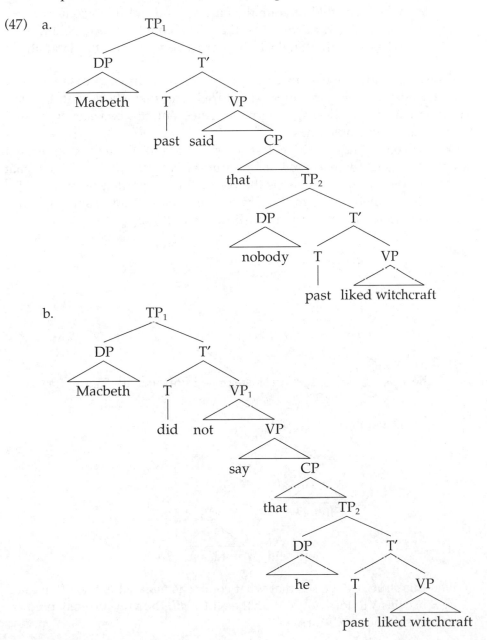

In (46a), the negative expression is the DP *nobody*. The smallest constituent containing it is TP$_2$ [*nobody liked witchcraft*]. It is this TP$_2$ that counts as negated. Similarly in (46b), the first constituent containing the negation *not* is the VP constituent: [*not say that he liked witchcraft*]. Now, we will look at how Rule 6 works:

(48) a. The elves did **not** tell **anyone** that the fairies could like witchcraft.
      b. *The elves told **anyone** the fairies could **not** like witchcraft.
      c. **Nobody** told **anyone** that the fairies could like witchcraft.
      d. *The news that Shylock did **not** leave surprised Portia **at all**.

Because this rule appeals to constituent structure, in each case we need to establish what the constituent structure is and then check that the characterization of NPI licensing correctly rules out the bad sentences and permits the acceptable ones.

We will only go through the last sentence of (48). We may paraphrase it by the (deviant) sentence: *something surprised Portia at all*. This shows that the main verb of this sentence is the verb *surprise*, and that what *something* stands for, namely *the news that Shylock did not leave*, is the subject of this verb. This yields the following constituent structure:

(49)

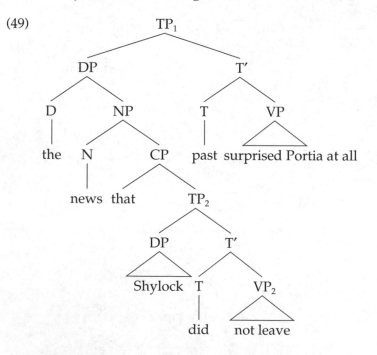

Given this structure we see that what counts as negated is the VP marked VP$_2$. Since this VP does not contain the NPI *at all*, Rule R6 correctly predicts that this sentence is ill-formed.

**EXERCISE
4.5**

For each of the first three sentences of (48)

(i)   Draw its constituent structure tree.
(ii)   Verify and state exactly why it satisfies or fails to satisfy Rule R6.

The notion of c-command

As stated above, in order to determine what is negated in a sentence, we have to look at the smallest constituent containing the negative expression. This notion is important and is useful in all sorts of other contexts having nothing to do with negation.

Given some phrase, e.g. a PP or a DP or a VP or NP, in short an XP where X can be any category, the smallest constituent containing this XP, i.e. the node which is the mother of this XP, is called the **c-command domain** of this XP. The XP is said to **c-command** everything in this c-command domain. The c- in c-command is meant to evoke the idea of constituent. The idea of command is meant to evoke the idea of influence.

(50)   C-COMMAND [Approximate definition]
       **The c-command domain of an XP is the first constituent
       containing this XP. An XP c-commands everything in
       its c-command domain.**

In (47a) for example, the negative expression *nobody* is a DP: the first constituent containing this DP is TP_2. Therefore, this DP has this embedded TP_2 as its c-command domain and the negative element *nobody* c-commands everything within this TP. As a consequence, given the rule, we would expect that a polarity item is allowed anywhere within TP_2. In (47b), the negative expression *not* has the constituent VP_1 as its c-command domain and it c-commands everything within VP_1, and in particular any NPI found in TP_2.

Putting all this together, we can now formulate the rule as given below. This is the final version of the Rule for Polarity Item Licensing that we will discuss here:

(51)   **Negative Polarity Items Licensing Rule**
       A sentence containing an NPI is well formed only if this NPI is in
       the c-command domain of a negative element.

**EXERCISE
4.6**

Consider the example given in (36) repeated below:

(i)   *Anyone did not see Portia

1.   (a)   To determine what counts as negated, use the procedure exempli-
           fied in (40) which replaces negation with *it is not the case that* . . .

> (b)   According to this procedure, is *anyone* part of the negated string?
> (c)   Is sentence (i) grammatical according to Addition #5?
> 2.   (a)   Draw the tree structure for sentence (i).
>   (b)   On the basis of this tree structure, determine what constituent is negated according to rule (51)?
>   (c)   Is sentence (i) grammatical according to rule (51)?
> 3.   Which approach is superior: Rule R5 + Addition #5 or rule (51)?

4.1.5   Important things to remember

There are three important aspects of this section to remember. The first is the method of investigation, and the second and third concern results about the structure of language.

1. The method of investigation – how to tackle a syntax question – involves successive generalizations and approximations.
2. Syntactic dependencies exist and form a necessary part of syntactic descriptions.
3. Linguistic rules are structure dependent, viz. (17) (the Principle of Structure Dependency of Syntactic Rules) and notions such as c-command given in (50) play an important role in the functioning of syntactic dependencies.

4.2   Some Basic Kinds of Syntactic Dependencies

In this section we turn to examples of the kinds of syntactic dependencies that are found in natural languages. A thorough presentation of each example would require an investigation such as we performed in the case of negative polarity items. Here, the intent is to present some of the results of the research that linguists have been conducting in recent decades. We seek to illustrate the kinds of dependencies that exist and the kind of properties of these dependencies.

4.2.1   Selection

In chapter 3, we introduced two important kinds of dependencies that we will now review and discuss: **s-selection** and **c-selection**. We will review them in more detail, particularly as to the role they play in determining constituent structure: a sentence has its particular constituent structure in large part because of the dependencies imposed by s-selection and c-selection.

Predicate/argument dependencies (s-selection)

A simple and basic kind of linguistic property is illustrated by the knowledge we have about the following pairs of examples:

(52) a. Macbeth arrived
      b. Macbeth described Dunsinane Forest

(53) a. *Macbeth described
      b. *Macbeth arrived Banquo

(53a) is derived from (52a) by substituting the verb *describe* for the verb *arrive*, or vice versa in the (b) examples. Since the examples in (53) are deviant they must violate some kind of dependency holding between the verb and its context. Intuitively, the problem is clear: the verb *arrive* attributes a property to some entity (or some set of entities – e.g. if the subject is plural, as in *the children arrived*). If I say *Macbeth arrived*, I am saying that Macbeth has a particular property, namely that of having arrived at some point in the past. With the verb *describe*, the situation is different. The sentence *Macbeth described Dunsinane Forest* establishes a relation between two entities: a 'describer', here Macbeth, and an object that is 'described', here Dunsinane Forest. What is wrong in the sentences in (53) is that the verb *arrive* is used as if it establishes a relation between two entities and this verb cannot do this because of its meaning. The deviance of (53a) is due to the fact that the verb *describe* is used as if it was a verb attributing a property rather than establishing a relation, and this is disallowed.

Knowing the meaning of verbs such as *arrive* or *describe* is, in part, knowing that *arrive* is a property of some entity (or set of entities) and *describe* a relation between two entities (or sets of entities). We possess this knowledge since it forms the basis for the judgment we have about these pairs of sentences. We find an analogy between these properties of verbs and the concept of **valence** in chemistry, which says something about how atoms combine with each other. For example, the atom of oxygen has a valence of 2, which means that it may combine with two elements, each of valence 1 or with one element itself of valence 2. The first option is exemplified by the molecule of water H_2O where hydrogen atoms, each with a valence of 1, combine with an atom of oxygen to form a molecule. The second option is exemplified by O_2 in which two atoms of oxygen combine to form a molecule of oxygen.

The parallel property for a verb like *arrive*, i.e. that of having a valence of 1, is often expressed by stating that *arrive* is a **function of one argument**, or to say it differently, is a **predicate taking one argument** or a **one-place predicate**, or a **monadic predicate**.

We can represent this property of *arrive* as follows:

(54) arrive (x)

in order to express the idea that, to form a complete meaning, the equivalent of a molecule in the chemical analogy discussed above, the verb *arrive* must be combined with some element that we call x here. The resulting meaning is one in which the verb *arrive* will attribute the property of 'arriving' to x. The term **predicate** is another way of talking about words such as verbs which express a property or a relation.

Similarly, to express the idea that *describe* has a valence of two, we say that *describe* is a **function of two arguments** or a **predicate taking two arguments** or a **two-place predicate** or a **dyadic predicate**, and we write:

(55) describe (x, y)

This expresses the idea that to form a complete meaning, the equivalent of a molecule in the chemical analogy above, we need to combine the verb *describe* with two elements, called x and y here. The resulting meaning is one in which the verb *describe* will establish a describing relation between them, one of them a describer and the other the object which is described.

SIDEBAR 4.4

Number of arguments of a predicate

Since there are one-place predicates and two-place predicates, we might ask whether there are three-place predicates (there are: *give* (x, y, z) as in x *gives* y to z) or more (no more than four, apparently, which you get with *trade* (x, y, z, w) as in x *traded* y for z with w). We might also ask whether there are zero-place predicates. Possible examples are atmospheric verbs like *rain* or *snow*, which, though used with a subject (*It rains, It snows*) do not attribute a property to this subject. The subject does not really refer to any kind of entity. These verbs simply describe a state of affairs, namely that raining is taking place.

There is a complication in the case of *describe* that does not arise in the case of *arrive*: the two arguments do not enter into the same kind of relation with the verb *describe*. One of these arguments is understood as referring to the describer, the **agent** of the action. The other is understood as referring to what is described, what undergoes the action, or the **theme**. We modify the notation to encode this further property:

(56) describe (Xagent, Xtheme)

In the case of *arrive*, there is only one argument, and it is understood as undergoing the action. We call it a theme and can write:

(57) arrive (Xtheme)

Although this begins to describe the knowledge we have, it does not exhaust it. In the sentence (52b), we also know that Macbeth is the describer and that what he described, the theme, is Dunsinane Forest. It is important to note that this does not have to do with the fact that it would be odd for Dunsinane Forest to be the describer. Let's reverse the positions of *Macbeth* and *Dunsinane Forest*:

(58)   Dunsinane Forest described Macbeth.

However odd it is, the sentence has a meaning: Dunsinane Forest is the describer and what was described was Macbeth. This tells us that the fact that *describe* is a predicate taking two arguments, one interpreted as an agent and one as a theme, does not suffice to describe what we know. If we draw the tree representation of (52b), we can illustrate the crucial factors:

(59)

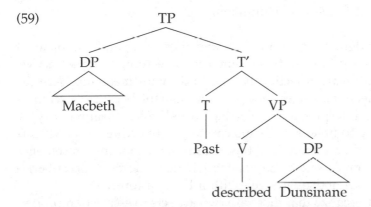

The DP interpreted as the agent is the **subject** of the verb. The DP interpreted as the theme is the **complement** of the verb. This shows that there is a relation between the verb, or, more precisely, the meaning of the verb as we have indicated it in (56), and the constituent structure of a sentence in which this verb appears. Another way of expressing the same idea is to say that there is a dependency between the verb and certain positions in the tree containing this verb.

We can make this dependency explicit in the case of the verb *describe* and briefly discuss the kinds of problems that arise in this connection.

(60)   When the verb [*describe* (Xagent, Xtheme)] appears in a sentence, its subject is understood as its agent argument and its complement is understood as its theme argument.

This kind of dependency between the various arguments that a verb has and the syntactic positions in which they occur turns out to be extremely general. It is usually referred to as the **Linking Property** of the verb. The following sentence illustrates that it is important to require that the agent argument of the verb *describe* must be the subject of the verb *describe*, not any subject:

(61)   Banquo said that Macbeth described Dunsinane.

Can Banquo be understood as the agent argument of *describe*? In other words, is this sentence saying that Banquo described something? Of course not. Banquo is a subject but it occurs in the wrong clause. This shows that the agent argument of *describe* must be the subject of the *describe* clause, i.e. the clause with *describe* as main verb. We modify (60) accordingly:

(62)   **Linking Property** of the Verb *describe*:
       When the verb [*describe* (Xagent, Xtheme)] appears in a sentence, its subject is understood as its agent argument and its complement is understood as its theme argument.

We call the dependency between a verb and its subject and complement described here **s-selection**, short for **semantic selection,** as stated above. Semantic selection means selection having to do with meaning. Here the verb *describe* s-selects its subject and its complement because it requires that its subject be interpreted as referring to its Xagent argument – the describer – and its complement be interpreted as referring to its Xtheme argument – what is described. It is this requirement that makes sentence (58) odd since it forces one to understand Dunsinane as a describer, a proposition that does not square well with it being a forest.

It is important to realize that there are two aspects to s-selection properties of a verb:

(i)   the number and type (agent or theme) of arguments that a verb takes
(ii)   how these arguments link to positions in a tree

In the case of the verb *describe*, we can specify these two aspects as follows:

(63)   describe (Xagent,   Xtheme)
                      | |
                 subject   complement

We interpret this notation as meaning that

(i)   the verb *describe* takes two arguments (an Xagent and an Xtheme).
(ii)   the linking lines going from Xagent and Xtheme to subject and complement mean that the Xagent must be a subject and the Xtheme must be a complement.

SIDEBAR
4.5

Semantic and syntactic properties of arguments

It is important that we carefully distinguish the interpretative properties of arguments, such as being an Agent or a Theme, from their syntactic realization. The very same verb *describe* can appear in structures superficially violating the requirement stated in (63). One such example is given by the **passive** construction exemplified below:

(i)   Dunsinane Forest was described by Macbeth.

Here, the theme argument of *describe* is realized as a subject, while the agent argument is realized as part of the PP headed by the preposition *by*. The interpretative properties of these arguments have not changed but their syntactic realization is completely different. This is why we must distinguish these two notions.

   An investigation of the properties of the passive construction is beyond the scope of this introductory text but it would show that (63) is correct after all!

As we mentioned earlier, the existence of s-selection is not restricted to the verbs *describe* or *arrive* but is general. For all the verbs:

S-selection:
A verb may s-select its subject, its complements (if it has some): the verb may impose that its subject or complement(s) enter into a particular kind of meaning combination with it.

The existence of s-selection is made particularly clear by the existence of certain **idiomatic expressions** or **idioms**, such as the following with their meanings:

(64)   lend assistance = help
       kick the bucket = die
       keep tabs on = put under surveillance

   There are many such expressions in English (and in other languages as well). What makes them special is the fact that the meanings of their parts do not combine according to the 'normal' rules of meaning combination. Thus, *lend assistance* does not mean lend something, namely assistance, the way *lend a book* means lend something, namely a book. The meaning of *lend* in this case is in part determined by its direct object *assistance* whereas one can *lend a book/ten dollars/an apartment* etc. with the meaning of *lend* remaining constant over all these direct objects.

   The idiom case is a strong case of s-selection, of a dependency between a verb and a direct object. Idioms are often used to determine whether a dependency obtains (of the s-selection type for example) between a verb and a DP.

Categorial selection (c-selection)

Another aspect of the dependency between the verb and its complement can be illustrated by the following paradigm:

(65)   a.   Macbeth awaited Banquo   → b.   *Macbeth awaited for Banquo
       c.   Macbeth waited for Banquo → d.   *Macbeth waited Banquo

Exchanging *wait* and *await* causes deviance. Again, the fact that these substitutions yield ill-formed results shows the existence of some dependency. Since the subjects are the same, this dependency must hold between the verb and its complement. What is at stake is not s-selection. S-selection requires that the subjects of the verbs *wait* and *await* be interpreted as the agent, the 'waiter', and the complement as who (or what) is expected. There is no reason, from the point of view of s-selection, why Banquo could not be the theme argument of *wait* in (65d).

The problem lies elsewhere and becomes immediately apparent when we draw the trees of (65a and c):

(66)

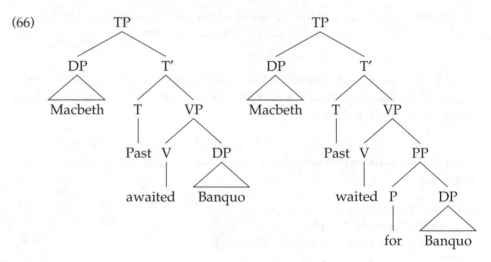

The verb *wait* requires its complement to be of the particular category PP (where, moreover, the P is *for*) while *await* requires its complement to be a DP. Again, this is a general property which has been referred to in the previous chapter and above as **c-selection** (and as stated earlier, sometimes called **subcategorization**). For all the verbs we will see here, we can state:

C-selection:

A verb c-selects its complement(s) by requiring that they be of particular categories.

In order to represent this information about the verbs *wait* and *await*, we can write:

(67) a. wait (Xagent, Xtheme)
                    | |

                subject   complement: [$_{PP}$ for DP]

    b. await (Xagent, Xtheme)
                   | |

                subject   complement: DP

This indicates that the theme argument of *await* must be realized as a DP, while the theme argument of *wait* must be a DP within a *for*-PP.

An example of c-selection and s-selection and how it drives constituent structure

We can illustrate the relation between s-selection, c-selection and constituent structure in the case of a simple clause: *The army could encircle this city.* Knowing the verb *encircle* means knowing the following properties:

(68) *Encircle* takes two arguments, Xagent (the encircler) and Xtheme (what is encircled)
     If *Encircle* has a subject, its agent argument is this subject
     If *Encircle* has a complement, its theme argument is this complement
     The theme argument must be realized as a DP complement

We can express these properties in the following diagram:

(69) encircle (Xagent, Xtheme)
                | |

             subject   complement: DP

Once we combine these requirements with the vocabulary of tree construction that we saw in the previous chapter, we have no choice but to attribute to the sentence the structure which satisfies each property listed in (69):

(70)

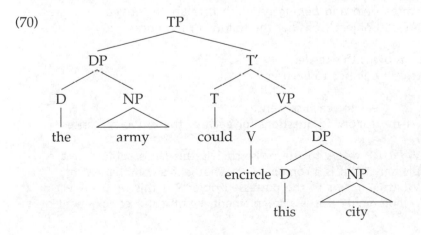

It is important to note that natural languages seem to satisfy the s-selection and c-selection requirements as parsimoniously as possible. For example, in the case of the verb *describe*, because there is only one theme argument – which, by c-selection, must be a DP – there can only be one DP interpreted as theme in a tree containing this verb. There would be nothing wrong from the point of view of interpretation if we could distribute the theme over two DPs as in:

(71)   Macbeth described Arden Forest Dunsinane Forest.

where we would interpret this as meaning that Macbeth described two forests: Arden and Dunsinane. Instead, to get this reading, we must *conjoin* the DPs *Arden Forest* and *Dunsinane Forest* to form one bigger DP:

(72)   Macbeth described [$_{DP}$ Arden Forest and Dunsinane Forest]

C-selection and s-selection are not limited to verbs: nouns, adjectives, prepositions etc. can also have such properties. For example the adjective *fond*, as in *Puck is fond of nectar*, takes two arguments, one of which is realized as the subject of the sentence and the other as a PP introduced by *of*.

EXERCISE 4.7	For each sentence, provide s-selection, c-selection and linking information for the verb it contains and draw its tree.

(i)   Macbeth left.
(ii) The soldiers put their weapons in the tower.
(iii) Petruccio thinks that Bianca left.

EXERCISE 4.8	The verbs *own* and *belong*

The two verbs *own* and *belong* establish a relation between a possessor and a possessed object. Consider the following sentences:

(i)   Bertram owns this castle.
(ii) This castle belongs to Bertram.

1. Draw the trees for each sentence.
2. Answer the following questions for each of these two sentences:

   (a)   What DP refers to the possessor? Is this DP a subject or a complement? If it is a complement, what is it a complement of?
   (b)   What DP refers to the possessed object? Is this DP a subject or a complement? If it is a complement, what is it a complement of?

3. For each of the verbs *own* and *belong*, write a representation of its linking properties as we did in (63) for the verb *describe* or in (67) for the verbs *wait* and *await* (use the labels Xpossessor and Xpossessee to identify the two arguments).
4. What does the answer to the previous question show about the relation between the arguments of a predicate and their syntactic realization?

4.2.2 Morphologically expressed basic dependencies

We now turn to two new dependencies that express relations between positions in a constituent structure tree: **agreement** and **case**. Neither agreement nor case is very prominent in English but they are nevertheless present. Unlike s-selection, both of them can manifest themselves morphologically: when the presence of the relation, of the dependency, is manifested, the words participating in it have particular shapes that depend on each other.

Case

When I use the pronoun *I*, as in the sentence *I saw Macbeth*, I am saying something about myself, the speaker of this sentence. An interesting fact about the English word used to convey this idea of 'I', i.e. of 'reference to the speaker of the sentence presently uttered', is that its shape varies according to where it occurs in a sentence. This first person pronoun, as it is usually called, can assume the shapes *I*, *me*, or *my* as below:

(73) a. I saw Macbeth *Me saw Macbeth *My saw Macbeth
      b. Macbeth saw me *Macbeth saw I *Macbeth saw my
      c. Macbeth saw my *Macbeth saw *Macbeth saw me
          sister I sister sister

Furthermore, there is no choice as to the form that this pronoun can take, as indicated. This kind of behavior is not limited to *I*. It is found throughout the pronominal system of English (*you, you, your; he, him, his; she, her, her; we, us, our; they, them, their*).

The paradigm exemplified in (73) is fully representative of the behavior of pronouns and comprises yet again examples of substitution gone awry; substituting *me* or *my* for *I* in a well-formed sentence yields unacceptable results. This, as usual, indicates the existence of some dependency that these substitutions violate.

Traditionally, stemming originally from Latin grammar, the *I* form is called the nominative form of this pronoun. The *me* form is called the accusative form and the *my* form the genitive form. The pronoun is said to bear different **cases**: nominative case, accusative case, and genitive case

Table 4.1 English pronouns

NOMINATIVE	ACCUSATIVE	GENITIVE
I	me	my
you	you	your
he	him	his
she	her	her
we	us	our
they	them	their

respectively. Thus we get a table as in table 4.1 for English pronouns. As (73) shows, the dependency appears to be between the case that a pronoun must have and the position this pronoun occupies. In such simple sentence, the case dependency or **case assignment rules** can be stated as follows:

(74) **Rules of Case Assignment to Pronouns**
A subject pronoun must bear nominative case
A complement pronoun must bear accusative case
A possessive pronoun must bear genitive case

If we look more closely, we come to realize that the case dependencies must be stated in a slightly more complex form. Compare the emphasized clauses in the examples below:

(75) a. **I will describe Dunsinane Forest**.
b. Ophelia hoped **for me to describe Dunsinane Forest**.

Recall our conclusion that the agent of the verb *describe* is realized as the subject of the verb *describe*. This means that both *I* in the first sentence and *me* in the second are subjects of their clauses. In both cases, the subject is the first-person pronoun, but with nominative case in the first one and accusative in the second. This shows that the rules in (74) are incorrect. What is crucial is whether we are dealing with the subject of a **tensed** clause or of an infinitive clause. Subjects of tensed clauses are indeed nominative but subjects of **tenseless** clauses are accusative. Now recall from the preceding chapter (see also the following chapter) that the tensed or tenseless property of a clause is encoded in the node T. This shows that case assignment of Nominative is really a dependency between subjects and the content of T.

Many languages are relatively impoverished when it comes to expressing case by morphological affixes, for example Arabic, Chinese, English or Swahili. Other languages are more liberal in having a greater variety of cases, such as German, Hungarian or Russian, or in expressing case morphologically on a greater set of nominals, as in Latin or Finnish. (See chapter 2 for other languages.)

German distinguishes Nominative, Accusative, Genitive and Dative cases. Its case rules are somewhat more complicated mostly in that complement pronouns can be Accusative or Dative, depending on what they are complements of. In English, the pronominal complement of a preposition is always marked Accusative (*for him, with them, against me*). In German, a nominal complement of the preposition *mit* or *aus* (which mean 'with' and 'out of') must be in the Dative (*mit mir* 'with me-dative'), while the nominal complement of the preposition *gegen* (which means 'against') is in the Accusative (*gegen mich* 'against me-accusative').

Latin not only distinguishes more cases than German, but marks case morphologically on all nouns. Nouns in Latin come in five basic subsets called declensions. First declension nouns exhibit the behavior as detailed in table 4.2. Both German and Latin illustrate the same point as (75). In both, we see that accusative or dative marking is attributed to the complement of prepositions, depending on the choice of preposition. This means that the case assignment rules express a dependency between P and its DP complement. In other words, for the languages we have discussed, the rules for case assignment should approximately take the form:

(76) **Rules of Case Assignment to DPs**
      A subject of a tensed clause bears nominative case
      A complement of a verb bears accusative case
      A complement of a preposition bears accusative, dative or ablative
      (depending on the language and the choice of preposition)

These rules are not meant by any means to be exhaustive for German, or Latin, but they illustrate the general nature of case dependencies. Case assignment rules for other languages would be similar in general form to these case rules. They establish a relation between the form of DPs and certain categories such as Tense, Verbs, Nouns, Prepositions taking these DPs as subject or complement. The case morphology encodes some element of the DP (such as the noun) onto the grammatical relation that this DP bears with some other category in the sentence.

Agreement
Agreement is a dependency that we have already encountered in examples we repeat below:

(77) a. The fairies do not like witchcraft → *The fairies does *not* like
                                                witchcraft at all
      b. The fairies do not like witchcraft → *The fairy do not like
                                                witchcraft

Table 4.2 Latin case system

GRAMMATICAL FUNCTION OF DP CONTAINING THE NOUN	SUBJECT	ADDRESSEE	COMPLEMENT OF VERB	COMPLEMENT OF NOUN	COMPLEMENT OF CERTAIN PS	COMPLEMENT OF CERTAIN PS
Case name	Nominative	Vocative	Accusative	Genitive	Dative	Ablative
Singular	rosa	rosa	rosam	rosae	rosae	rosa
plural	rosae	rosae	rosas	rosarum	rosis	rosis

Table 4.3 English, German, and French cases

			ENGLISH		GERMAN		FRENCH	
			SING.	PLURAL	SING.	PLURAL	SING.	PLURAL
1ST PERSON			I	we	ich	wir	je	nous
2ND PERSON			you	you	du	ihr	tu	vous
3RD PERSON	HUMAN	MASCULINE	he	they	er	sie	il	ils
		FEMININE	she	they	sie	sie	elle	elles
	NON-HUMAN	MASCULINE					il	ils
		FEMININE					elle	elles
		NEUTER	it	they	es	sie		

Substituting *does* for *do* in (77a) leads to ill-formedness. Similarly, substituting *fairy* for *fairies* in (77b) also leads to ungrammaticality. As we saw earlier, this means that this substitution violates some property of grammatical organization: this property – **agreement** – can be described as follows.

Languages may distinguish between various kinds of DPs on the basis of person, or number, or gender, or other properties (e.g. human, animate, etc.) and these distinctions are very often visible in the pronominal system of the language. Table 4.3 illustrates this for English, French and German in the case of nominative pronouns. The form of a verb is sensitive to the kind of DP it takes as subject. In English, if the subject of a verb is third-person singular, the verb in the present tense must appear with a particular marking – a final *s* – if it can (if it cannot, like, for example, the auxiliary verb *will*, it remains unchanged). In (77) the form *does* of the verb *do* can be used only if the subject is singular (more specifically, third-person singular), the form *do* only if the subject is not third-person singular. We might state the following agreement dependency or rule for English:

(78) **Subject–Verb Agreement Rule**
A verb in the present tense must agree with its subject in English.

Agreement is not limited to subject/verb pairs. Agreement in English is also found between a determiner and a noun. This can be illustrated with the demonstrative determiners *this, that, these, those*. Thus we have the paradigm *this book, *these book, *this books, these books*: a noun and its demonstrative determiner must be both singular or both plural.

English is rather impoverished when it comes to agreement (as for case). Subject/verb agreement is visible only in the third-person singular present tense. Other languages have much more extensive agreement systems.

In French or Spanish, verb and subject agree in all persons, number and tenses. Nouns agree in number with their determiners and also in gender.

Nouns also agree in number and gender with adjectives modifying them. In German, nouns and determiners agree not only in number and gender, but also in case. Some languages have extremely extensive systems of agreement, like many Bantu languages with not just two genders but in many cases between ten and twenty 'genders'. In such Bantu languages, it is typically the case that the verb agrees in gender with its subject in all tenses, and adjectives and determiners agree with the nouns they modify.

Just as in case dependencies discussed above, agreement morphology encodes on a pair of elements (such as subject/verb or noun/adjective) the fact that these two elements are in a particular grammatical relation.

4.2.3   Remote dependencies: movement

We have seen four basic kinds of dependencies: **S-selection**, **C-selection**, **Case** and **Agreement**. We can now use them to probe deeper into grammatical structure. Let us recall the way they function:

(79)   **Basic Dependencies**
  a.   **Basic S-selection**
       A verb s-selects its subject, its complements (if it has any): the verb requires that its subject or complement(s) enter into a particular kind of meaning combination with it.
  b.   **Basic C-selection**
       A verb c-selects its complement(s): it requires that they be of particular categories.
  c.   **Basic Case Rules in English** (Nominative and Accusative)
       A subject of a tensed clause bears nominative case.
       A DP complement of a verb bears accusative case.
  d.   **Basic (subject/verb) Agreement Rule in English**
       A verb in the present tense and its subject must agree.

We will use these basic dependencies to explore some properties of **wh-questions**. Suppose Macbeth described some forest and I want to know what forest he described. I can ask the question:

(80)   What forest did Macbeth describe?

Suppose I think that some child named Calvin eats all the cookies and I want to know which child you think it is. I can ask you the question:

(81)   Which child do you think eats all the cookies?

The existence of such sentences raises challenges for the characterization of the basic dependencies we have just given.

In (80), the problem is that *describe* normally takes a direct object which it s-selects (it is interpreted as its theme argument), or it c-selects (it must be a DP, which, as a DP complement of the verb, gets Accusative Case). However, it seems that in (80), the verb *describe* lacks a direct object.

In (81), we have the same problem with *eat*: it normally takes a subject that it s-selects (it is interpreted as the agent argument, the eater). This subject should get Nominative Case and should agree with the subject. However, in (81), the verb *eat* appears to lack a subject in a normal sense, i.e. in this case a DP immediately preceding it.

While there appears to be no direct object in the normal sense in (80) there is a DP that plays the same role, namely the DP *what forest*. Similarly, while there appears to be no subject in the normal sense in (81) the DP *which child* plays the same role. That *what forest* plays the role of the complement of *describe* (or that *which child* plays the role of subject of *eat*) is corroborated by the observation that the verb *describe* cannot take both a normal complement and this kind of complement:

(82) a. Macbeth described Dunsinane Forest.
      b. What forest did Macbeth describe?
      c. *What forest did Macbeth describe Dunsinane Forest?

This is because *describe* is a two-place predicate and allows only one theme argument. As a consequence, there can only be one DP qualifying as theme. In the sentence (82c), *what forest* and *Dunsinane Forest* both compete to be this theme argument. This leads to unacceptability.

As we will see, the DP *what forest* in (80) behaves as expected in the sense that, if we think of it as the DP complement of *describe*, s-selection, c-selection and case will work according to the way we stated that they do. Similarly, the DP *which child* in (81) also behaves as expected in the sense that, if we think of it as the subject of *eat*, s-selection, agreement and case will work according to the way stated.

To be thorough we would need to show that all four basic dependencies work the way we state in each of these two cases. Instead, we will simply illustrate how this can be established in a couple of cases.

Start with s-selection in (80). According to the s-selection rule, if *what forest* in (80) acts like a complement of the verb *describe*, it should be interpreted as its theme argument, i.e. what is described. The wh-question introduces a complication – the identity of this object is questioned and so we cannot say that what is described is 'what forest'. However, we can paraphrase (80) by the sentence 'Macbeth describe some forest, which one?' where we see that the theme argument refers to a forest, as we would expect, not to the describer or to some third entity. We can support the conclusion that a questioned phrase in sentence-initial position may qualify as a complement by using idioms such as *lend assistance*. Recall that the s-selection is so tight in this case that to get the meaning *help*, we need to use both the verb *lend* and the noun *assistance* as its complement. The following examples illustrate the point we want to make:

(83)   a.   Macbeth lent much assistance to the victims.
       b.   How much assistance did Macbeth lend to the victims?

The fact that the questioned DP has *assistance* as its noun and that we get the meaning *how much did Macbeth **help** the victims* shows that this DP is indeed s-selected by *lend*.

The same reasoning would lead to the same conclusion regarding s-selection of *which child* by *eat* in the case of (81).

We can now illustrate how agreement works for (81). If the NP *which child* is the subject of the verb *eat* in (81), we would expect it to agree with the verb *eat*. According to the (subject/verb) Agreement Rule in English, discussed above, we would expect to see a dependency between the number of the questioned DP and the form of the verb. Observe what happens when we change *which child*, which is a third-person **singular** DP, to *which children*, which is a third-person **plural** DP:

(84)   a.   Which child do you think eats all the cookies?
       b.   *Which children do you think eats all the cookies?
       c.   Which children do you think eat all the cookies?
       d.   *Which child do you think eat all the cookies?

Only the cases in which the verb *eat* and the questioned DP agree are well-formed. We can further illustrate that case marking works as expected by looking at German. As we saw earlier, German has four cases and marks many more items with case than English does. In particular, it marks DP wh-words, i.e. DP question words such as *who*, *what*, etc., with different cases. Table 4.5 gives a sample of this paradigm. The verb *sehen* ('to see') requires its DP complement to be in the accusative case. As indicated, only the form *Ihn* of the masculine pronoun is allowed. As expected, exactly the same property is observed in wh-questions. Even though the wh-word does not appear in the complement position of the verb *sehen*, only the accusative form *wen* of the wh-word is allowed:[2]

(85)   a.   Du hast ihn   / *er / *ihm   gesehen
            You have him-accusative / he / him-dative   seen
       b.   Wen   / *Wer   / *Wem   glaubst du
            Whom-accusative / who-nominative / who-dative think   you
            dass du   gesehen hast?
            that you seen   have
            Who do you think that you have seen?

Table 4.5 German case marking

	NOMINATIVE	ACCUSATIVE	DATIVE	GENITIVE
3rd pers masculine sg pronouns	er (he)	ihn (him)	ihm (him)	sein (his)
3rd pers feminine sg pronouns	sie (she)	sie (her)	sie (her)	ihr (her)
wh-words sg (human)	wer (who)	wen (whom)	wem (whom)	wessen (whose)

In conclusion, these wh-phrases, even though they are not subjects or complements, behave, from the point of view of these basic dependencies, as if they were subjects or complements. We will refer to these elements as **displaced** or **remote** subjects and displaced or remote complements because, although they behave like subjects and complements of particular verbs with respect to the four dependencies, they do not occur in the position of subject or complement of these verbs.

We have established the existence of four new dependencies between verbs and remote subjects and complements:

a. s-selection of remote subjects and complements
b. c-selection of remote complements
c. agreement with remote subjects
d. case assignment to remote subjects and complements

To make explicit the way in which these new dependencies function, we should formulate four new rules modeled on the original ones but everywhere replacing subject by remote subject and complement by remote complement.

(86) **Remote dependencies**
  a. **Remote S-selection**
      A verb s-selects its remote subject and complements (if it has any): the verb requires its remote subject or complement(s) to enter into a particular kind of meaning combination with it.
  b. **Remote C-selection**
      A verb c-selects its remote complement(s); it requires that the complements be of particular categories.
  c. **Remote Case Rules**
      A remote subject of a tensed clause bears nominative case.
      A remote complement of a verb bears accusative case.
  d. **Remote (subject/verb) Agreement Rule**
      A verb in the present tense and its remote subject must agree in English.

We call these rules remote (as opposed to basic) because they deal with displaced (i.e. remote) subjects and complements. Although they define syntactic dependencies between some phrase and a verb in the sentence, they do not require this phrase and the verb to be in the same clause.

The basic rules and the remote rules seem to adequately state the observed facts. However, they raise a problem: they overlap almost completely. This redundancy is made worse by the fact that basic rules and remote rules apply in **complementary** cases; for a particular pair verb/DP, either the basic rule or the remote rule applies but never both. This is because a verb cannot have both a subject and a remote subject, or a direct object and a remote direct object. For example, if the basic subject/verb agreement rule applies to a pair subject/verb, the remote subject/verb agreement rule cannot apply to the same verb since a verb cannot have both a subject and a remote subject. These two observations suggest that we are missing a deeper regularity, namely that there is really only one s-selection (or c-selection, or agreement, or case assignment) dependency but that it may apply either to subjects or to remote subjects.

To solve this problem and find this deeper regularity, notice first that in wh-questions, the remote constituents are all wh-phrases, i.e. they all include a **wh-word** (*who, what, which, where, when, why*, etc.). Suppose that we think of a remote wh-subject or wh-complement as a normal subject or complement that has been made remote by rule and let us describe the process that allows subjects, complements etc. to be realized remotely as **wh-movement.**

(87)   **Wh-movement**
       Wh-movement is the process by which wh-questioned constituents (such as wh-DPs that are subjects and complements of a verb) are realized as remote subjects and complements.

SIDEBAR 4.6	**Wh-movement**

Everything we say about subjects and complements applies equally well to other elements: PP complements, adverbial elements etc. all can be subject to wh-movement as exemplified below:

PP complements: (i)   Othello put it under the bed → Where did Othello put it?

Adverbial adjunct: (i)   Macbeth behaved badly   → How did Macbeth behave?

                    (ii) Banquo left yesterday   → When did Banquo leave?

A subject or a complement realized remotely because of the wh-movement process will be said to be **wh-moved**. For example, the sentence (82b) will be described as involving two steps as indicated below:

(88)   a.   Macbeth described what forest

       b.   Macbeth described | what forest |

       c.   What forest did   Macbeth describe?

In the first step, *what forest*, the complement of the verb *describe*, occurs in the normal position of complement as in (88a). In the second step, the rule of wh-movement applies, displacing this complement to clause-initial position as indicated in (88b), yielding the form in (88c).

Given this rule of wh-movement, we can eliminate the overlap we noted and simplify the system of dependencies by assuming that:

i.   the basic dependencies stated in (79) are correct.
ii.   these basic dependencies only apply to normal subjects and complements **before wh-movement takes place**.

The advantage of this approach is clear – we completely eliminate the redundancy between the basic rules and the remote rules. A remote complement is considered to be a normal complement that has been made remote, i.e. that has been wh-moved after the basic dependencies have been satisfied. This procedure is illustrated below:

(89)   a.   Macbeth describe what forest ← satisfy the basic dependency
                                              requirements on this sentence:
                                              s-selection, c-selection,
                                              agreement, case

            Apply wh-movement (to the wh-phrase *what forest*)

       b.   What forest did Macbeth describe?

The basic dependencies are satisfied in (89a), before wh-movement applies. Note that when wh-movement applies, the auxiliary verb *did* appears in front of the subject. The next chapter will investigates how this takes place. The two sentences in (89a) and (89b) are related by the operation of wh-movement. The structure (i.e. the tree) of (89a) is called the **underlying structure** or **deep structure** of the sentence (89b) and the structure of (89b) is called the **surface structure** of (89a); (89b) is said to be **derived** from

(89a) by the application of the wh-movement operation. The diagram in (89) illustrates a **derivation**.

Wh-questions illustrate an important general property of natural languages: s-selection, c-selection, case marking or agreement (and many other dependencies that we do not talk about here) can be satisfied locally or remotely, i.e. by local subjects and complements or by remote subjects and complements that have been made remote by wh-movement.

The rule of wh-movement that we have introduced is a new kind of dependency. In (89) for example, it is the dependency between the local complement of *describe* and the remote complement of *describe*. Similarly, in (84a), it is the dependency between the local subject of *eat* and the remote subject of *eat*, etc.

Numerous questions can be raised about this new dependency. We already know one property of wh-movement which is illustrated by the fact that a given subject (or complement) is either local or remote. In terms of wh-movement, this means that a subject (or a complement) is either wh-moved or not but cannot be moved and not moved at the same time. Depending on how we formulate wh-movement, it can be seen as a dependency holding between identical categories (e.g. two DPs, or two adverbials or two PPs . . .).

We now briefly address two questions, hinting at their answers.

Question 1: Where does a wh-moved constituent go? Answer: It gets attached to CP – which stands for Complementizer Phrase (the auxiliary verb is also attached under CP – this is discussed in detail in the next chapter, including Subject–Auxiliary Inversion). Thus the structure of (89b) will approximately look like this:

(90)

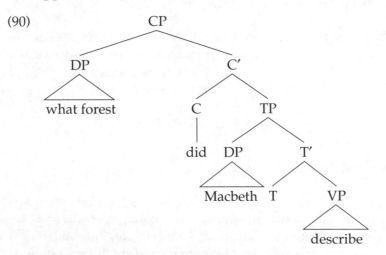

Question 2: How remote can a constituent become? How far can a constituent be wh-moved? The problem is illustrated by the following pairs of sentences:

(91)   a.   What forest did you say that Macbeth believed that Banquo
            had described?
      b.   *What forest did you read a report that Banquo had described?

   The first sentence shows that a complement can become very remote.
Here it has been moved out of two clauses to the front of a third one. The
DP *what forest* is the complement of the verb *describe*. It has been moved
out of the clause *Banquo had described*, and also out of the clause *Macbeth
believes that Banquo had described*. It appears in front of the main clause,
whose main verb is the verb *say*. However, wh-movement is blocked in
certain cases as the second sentence illustrates. Understanding the nature
of and the reason for these blocking effects is a fascinating part of linguistic research.

4.2.4   Some non-movement dependencies

Wh-movement allows a questioned complement to occur at the front of
the sentence instead of after its verb, where it would occur in the absence
of wh-movement. There are other movement dependencies which we will
not discuss here. Furthermore, not all dependencies involve movement.
For example, the basic dependencies we have discussed earlier do not.
There are other dependencies which do not involve movement and we
briefly introduce a few of them below.

Negative polarity items
Certain expressions (some of which were discussed above) are called **negative polarity items** and have a restricted distribution as illustrated above
and by the following examples:

(92)   a.   The fairies did <u>not</u> like witchcraft **at all**
      b.   <u>No one</u> will like witchcraft **at all / much**
      c.   *The fairies will like witchcraft **at all / much**
      d.   *Someone will like witchcraft **at all / much**

   We have already seen that in order to establish what governs this distribution, we need to distinguish between two categories of expressions
(see (14) and also section 4.2 for detailed discussion):

(93)   **Negative Polarity Item (NPI)**   **Negative Elements**
       at all, anyone,   not, no one, nobody
       much, in the least . . .   never . . .

Furthermore, the distribution of NPIs is subject to the following condition:

(94)   **Negative Polarity Items Licensing Rule**
A sentence containing an NPI is well-formed only if this NPI is in the c-command domain of a negative polarity item licenser.

Recall that the **c-command domain** of a particular phrase (XP) is the smallest constituent containing XP. This XP is said to **c-command** everything in its c-command domain.

Reflexives

Another type of dependency not involving movement is exemplified by the rather restricted distribution of English **reflexive pronouns**. These pronouns are formed by suffixing the noun *self* (plural *selves*) to the series of possessive (genitive) personal pronouns, except for third person, where the accusative form is used as base:

my	your	his (him)	her	it	our	your	their (them)
myself	yourself	himself	herself	itself	ourselves	yourselves	themselves

The restricted distribution of reflexive pronouns is shown by substituting each of them for *Banquo* in the following:

(95)   a.   Macbeth cut Banquo.
       b.   Macbeth cut himself.
       c.   *Macbeth cut ourselves.

(96)   a.   We cut Banquo.
       b.   We cut ourselves.
       c.   *We cut himself.

The verb *cut* is a two-place predicate, taking an agent argument as subject and a theme argument complement. Futhermore, the verb *cut* c-selects for a DP complement. The well-formedness of the (b) sentences shows that the reflexive pronouns *yourself* and *himself* qualify as theme arguments, thus meeting the s-selection and the c-selection requirements of *cut*. But the sentences in (c) are ill-formed.

What do the substitutions leading from the (b) sentences to the (c) sentences violate?

The problem of course has to do with the choice of the subject in the presence of the reflexive pronoun complements. Observe that in the well-formed sentences, the subject and the reflexive pronoun agree in person, number, and gender: *Macbeth* and *himself* are both third-person singular masculine and *we* and *ourselves* are both first-person plural (gender is not marked here). But in the deviant sentences, the subject and the reflexive pronoun fail to agree either in person, or in number or in gender.

A reflexive pronoun occurring in a sentence requires the presence of another DP in this sentence with which the reflexive pronoun agrees in person, gender and number. This DP is the **antecedent** of the reflexive. This behavior is reminiscent of what we discovered about polarity items – reflexives cannot occur by themselves in a sentence. Just like negative polarity items, they need a licenser, an antecedent. Reflexives are used to convey a particular kind of meaning. Consider the examples below:

(97) a. Macbeth cut Banquo.
 b. Macbeth cut him.
 c. Macbeth cut himself.
 d. *Macbeth cut ourselves.

The verb *cut* is a two-place predicate taking an agent subject and a theme complement. In *Macbeth cut Banquo,* some individual named *Macbeth* cut some individual named *Banquo*. In *Macbeth cut him*, we cannot say that some individual named *Macbeth* cut some individual named *him*. We understand that there is some person, say Banquo, who we have been talked to about and to whom we refer by using the pronoun *him*, and we are saying that some individual named Macbeth cut him, i.e. some individual named Banquo. We are using the pronoun *him* as a substitute for the name 'Banquo'. Note that in *Macbeth cut him*, *him* cannot refer to Macbeth, but must refer to another individual. (We investigate this observation in Exercise 4.11 below.) If we wish to refer to the fact that Macbeth cut Macbeth, we use the reflexive pronoun *himself* instead, as in *Macbeth cut himself*. This last sentence must be interpreted as meaning that Macbeth cut Macbeth.

What qualifies as an antecedent for a reflexive? What kind of relation must hold between a reflexive and its antecedent? In the well-formed examples above, the reflexive is the direct object of a verb and its antecedent is a subject. However, as the following examples illustrate, none of these properties is necessary:

(98) a. He likes these stories about himself.
 b. She showed him some pictures of himself.

In the (a) sentence, *himself* is the complement of the preposition *about* and the PP *about himself* is itself complement of the noun *stories*. The reflexive pronoun does not have to be a direct object of a verb. In the (b) sentence, the antecedent is not the subject of a verb, it is the complement of a verb.

An approximate characterization of the conditions that the dependency between the reflexive and its antecedent obey is stated in (99) and (100):

(99)   **The Clausemate Requirement**
        The reflexive and its antecedent must be in exactly the same clauses.

(100)   **The C-command Requirement**
        The antecedent DP must c-command the reflexive.

In order to illustrate the (approximate) correctness of this conclusion, we have to show that:

i.   sentences in which both requirements are met are well-formed.
ii.   sentences in which either one of these requirements is violated are ill-formed.

We will first verify that the sentences we have encountered so far do indeed satisfy both requirements. Remember the discussion of polarity items in section 4.2: being in exactly the same clauses means being included in exactly the same TP nodes. These sentences all are on the model of (101):

(101)   a.   Macbeth cut himself.
        b.   He likes these stories about himself.
        c.   She showed him some pictures of himself.

With the following structures:

(102)   a.

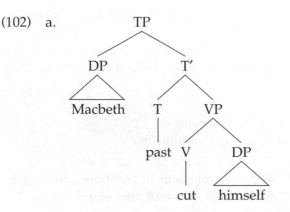

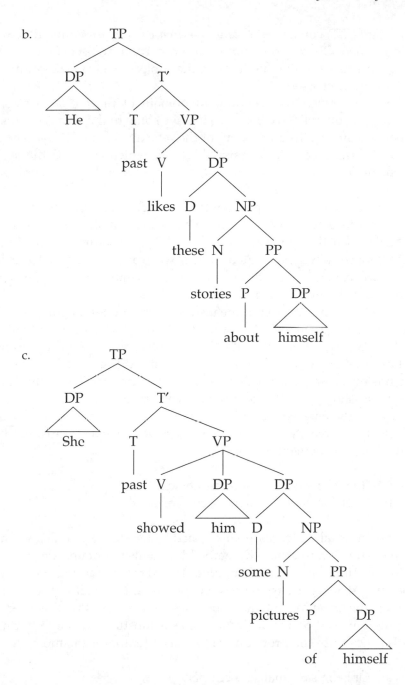

First of all, the **clausemate requirement** is obviously satisfied in all three cases since all three sentences are made up of only one clause each. Let us now verify the c-command requirement.

In the (a) sentence, the c-command domain of the DP *Macbeth* is the smallest constituent strictly containing it: it is the constituent labeled TP. By definition, the DP *Macbeth* c-commands everything in its c-command

domain. Since TP contains the reflexive *himself*, the c-command requirement is satisfied. Observe one important property of subjects here: because
the first constituent containing it is TP, the subject of a clause c-commands
everything in its clause.

In the (b) sentence, the c-command domain of the DP *he* is also TP,
which contains the reflexive *himself*. Thus we come to the same conclusion.

In the (c) sentence, the antecedent of the reflexive is the DP *him*. The first
constituent strictly containing this DP is VP, which contains the second
complement DP *some pictures of himself*, and consequently, also contains the
reflexive.

We can now construct experimental sentences violating either one of
these two requirements. We want to make sure that we only violate one
requirement at a time to make sure that this requirement is indeed required (in other words, as stated above, we want to construct **minimal
pairs**). If we violate both requirements at the same time, we can not be
sure that both requirements are needed.

If the first option is correct, it means that a sentence containing a reflexive and an antecedent which belong to different clauses should be ill-
formed. In the experimental sentence, the antecedent should c-command
the reflexive. We saw from sentence (102a) that the subject of a clause c-
commands everything in its clause. If we make the antecedent the subject
of the main clause it will c-command everything in the sentence. Since
we also want the antecedent and the reflexive to be in different clauses, it
is sufficient to have the antecedent subject of the main clause and the
reflexive in a complement clause:

(103)   a.   *Ophelia said that you cut herself.
        b.   *Ophelia said that herself cut you.

The experimental sentences are ill-formed: antecedent and reflexives must
be in the same clauses but the embedded clause contains the reflexive
without containing its antecedent. Note that there is nothing wrong with
the meaning that we are trying to convey. There is a well-formed way of
conveying the meaning intended by these sentences. But this meaning
cannot be conveyed by using a reflexive as a substitute name for Ophelia.
Instead, we can use the pronoun *she* / *her* as a temporary name.

(104)   a.   Ophelia said that you cut her.
        b.   Ophelia said that she cut you.

To illustrate the necessity of the c-command requirement, we need to
construct a sentence satisfying the clausemate requirement that violates
the c-command requirement. To guarantee that the clausemate requirement is met, we can limit ourselves to sentences having only one clause, as

in the sentences below. By drawing their trees, we can verify that the c-command requirement is violated in all of them with ill-formed results:

(105)   a.   *Herself cut Ophelia.
        b.   *Ophelia's friends love herself.
        c.   *You showed herself some pictures of Ophelia.

We will do this only for the third sentence.

(106)

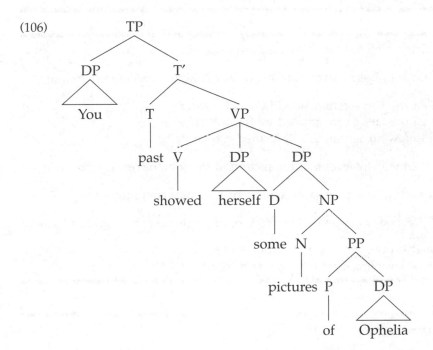

The reflexive *herself* needs an antecedent. This antecedent must be a DP. There are four DPs in this sentence: *You, herself, some pictures of Ophelia,* and *Ophelia*. The first three do not qualify:

- *You* does not qualify because it does not agree with *herself* (wrong person).
- *some pictures of Ophelia* does not qualify because it does not agree with *herself* (wrong number, inanimate instead of animate).
- *herself* does not qualify because the antecedent must be distinct from the reflexive. This is something we had not noted before but that we now need to add to the list of antecedent qualifications.
- *Ophelia* agrees in person, number, gender, and animacy and is distinct from *herself*. However, its c-command domain is the PP that contains it. This PP does not include the reflexive. So it does not qualify either.

EXERCISE 4.9

Practice c-command

1. Draw the trees for each of the sentences (105a and b).
2. For each sentence, list the words c-commanded by the DP *Ophelia*.
3. Explain why these sentences are ill-formed.
4. Explain why the second sentence below is ill-formed:

   (i)   No one cut anyone.
   (ii) *Anyone cut no one.

EXERCISE 4.10

1. Draw the tree for the following sentence:

   (i)   Othello believes that the picture of Desdemona belongs to him.

2. List all the DPs c-commanded by the DP *Desdemona*.
3. List all the DPs c-commanded by the DP *Othello*.
4. The following sentence is ill-formed. Explain why.

   (ii) *Othello believes that the picture of Desdemona belongs to himself.

5. Consider now the well-formedness of the following sentence:

   (ii) *Nobody believes that the picture of Desdemona belongs to anyone.

Verify that it obeys the condition on NPI licensing.
Does NPI licensing obey the clausemate requirement?

4.3   Summary

There are two fundamental properties governing the syntactic organization of natural languages. The first is the existence of **constituent structure**, which was introduced in the previous chapter. The second is the existence of **syntactic dependencies** such as: **selection, case, agreement, movement, negative polarity item licensing** and **antecedent/reflexive relations** (sometimes called **binding relations**). This chapter illustrated the existence of such syntactic dependencies. It also attempted to show how one goes about studying these phenomena.

Notes

1   There is a difficulty here that should not be overlooked: it seems that some anyX expressions such as *anyone* or *anybody* are not always polarity items. So a sentence like *anybody can do it* is well-formed even though there is no negative element. If we did not ignore these possibilities, the discussion would become enormously more complicated because

the use of this type of anyX is sensitive to the presence of all sorts of other things such as modal verbs (*could, can, should, . . .*) as well as the choice of tense (present versus past . . .). To simplify the discussion, all the sentences with *anyone* or *anybody* we will use will be in the simple past or preterit tense without auxiliary verbs of the *could/would/should* type. This makes sure that *anyone* or *anybody* is a well-behaved NPI.

2   Sentence (85b) is allowed only in certain dialects of German.

Further reading

Cowper, L. 1992. *A Concise Introduction to Syntactic Theory.* Chicago: University of Chicago Press.

Culicover, Peter. 1997. *Principles and Parameters: An Introduction to Syntactic Theory.* Oxford: Oxford University Press.

Haegeman, L. 1994. *Introduction to Government and Binding Theory.* Oxford: Blackwell.

McCawley, J. 1988. *The Syntactic Phenomena of English.* Chicago: University of Chicago Press.

Radford, A. 1988. *Transformational Grammar.* Cambridge: Cambridge University Press.

——. 1997. *Syntax, a Minimalist Introduction.* Cambridge: Cambridge University Press.

Roberts, I. 1996. *Comparative Syntax.* London, New York: Arnold.

(An introduction to contemporary Syntactic theory with an emphasis on comparative syntax, i.e. on comparison of syntactic properties across languages.)

van Riemsdijk, H. and E. Williams. 1986. *Introduction to the Theory of Grammar.* Cambridge, MA: MIT Press.

Principle B

EXERCISES

We have seen in the text that the distribution of reflexive pronouns is constrained by the following two principles which we postulated as first approximation:

R1: **The Clausemate Requirement:**   The reflexive and its antecedent must be in exactly the same clauses.

Exercise 4.11

R2: **The C-command Requirement:**   The antecedent DP must c-command the reflexive.

1   Provide two (deviant) sentences containing a reflexive pronoun, each violating only one of these two principles.

2   Remarkably, the distribution of (non-reflexive) pronouns is also constrained. This is illustrated by the following sentence:

*Othello likes him.

Although this sentence is well-formed, it cannot be used to mean that Othello likes himself. In other words, the pronoun *him* cannot be coreferential with the DP *Othello*. In this problem, we investigate this distribution.

2.1   Consider the following sentences (where DPs sharing an index are supposed to be interpreted as referring to the same person):

(a)   *Othello$_j$ saw him$_j$.
(b)   Othello$_j$ said he$_j$ saw Portia$_k$.
(c)   Othello$_j$ said Portia$_k$ saw him$_j$.

(i) Draw the tree for each of these sentences.
(ii) Postulate a principle, let us call it P1, that separates the ill-formed (a) sentence from the well-formed (b) and (c) sentences. (Hint: this principle resembles the clausemate requirement R1: it will state some condition that a pronoun and its antecedent have to meet.)
(iii) If properly formulated, your principle P1 should predict the ill-formedness of:

(d) *Portia_j's description of her_j displeased Othello.

Draw the tree for (d) and verify that your principle handles it correctly. If not, revise it so that it does.

2.2 Consider now the following sentences:

(e) Othello_j's wife met him_j.
(f) Portia's description of Othello_j displeased him_j.

(i) Draw the tree for each of these sentences.
(ii) Postulate a principle, let us call it P2, modeled on the c-command requirement R2, that separates the well-formed (e) and (f) sentences from the ill-formed (a) sentence.

2.3 Comparing P1 and P2 with R1 and R2, can you formulate a general prediction regarding the distribution of pronouns as compared with that of reflexives?

2.4 Consider now the following sentence:

(g) Othello_j trusts his_j wife.

Draw its tree. Do your principles P1 and P2 correctly predict the well-formedness of (g)? If not, amend P1 so that it correctly rules (g) in. (Note: In the syntactic literature, principles R1 and R2 are formulated as one principle called Principle A of the Binding Theory. Principles P1 and P2 are also formulated as one principle called Principle B of the Binding Theory.)

. . . .

Exercise 4.12 Principle C

As the following examples show, a pronoun can have an antecedent preceding it in a different clause (where DPs sharing an index are supposed to be interpreted as referring to the same person):

(a) Othello_j said Portia_k saw him_j.
(b) Othello_j said he_j saw Portia_k.

1 Consider the following sentences:

(c) *He_j said that Othello_j saw Portia.
(d) *He_j said that Portia saw Othello_j.
(e) *He_j said that Portia thinks that Othello_j left.

    (i)   Draw the trees for sentences (a) and (c).

    (ii)   To separate the well-formed examples from the ill-formed ones, formulate a principle C1 stated in terms of the notion **precedence** and regulating the relation between a pronoun and its antecedent. Make sure that your principle correctly distinguishes between the examples (a) and (b) and the examples (c), (d), and (e).

    (iii) To separate the well-formed examples from the ill-formed ones, formulate a different principle – C2 – this time stated in terms of the notion **c-command** and regulating the relation between a pronoun and its antecedent. Make sure that your principle correctly distinguishes between the examples (a) and (b) and the examples (c), (d), and (e).

2 Consider the following two sentences:

    (f)   His$_j$ wife says that Othello left.

    (g)   The rumor that he left pleased Othello$_j$'s wife.

    (i)   Draw the trees for these two sentences (for (g), assume that the CP [*that he left*] is a complement of the Noun *rumor*).

    (ii)   Compare the predictions made by C1 and C2 regarding sentences (f) and (g). What can be concluded?

    (iii) Is this conclusion compatible with the well-formedness of the following example?

    (h)   After he left, Othello fell.

    (you may suppose that the string *he left* forms a TP constituent complement of the preposition *after* and that the PP headed by the P *after* is adjoined to the matrix TP).
    (Note: In the syntactic literature, the principle responsible for accounting for the difference between a and b, and c, d, and e is called Principle C of the Binding Theory.)

· ·

VP Preposing and Reflexive Pronouns   **Exercise 4.13**

1 Construct the tree structure for the following example:

    (a) Ophelia thinks that Othello will survive the war.

2 Consider now the following example:

    (b) Ophelia thinks that survive the war, Othello will.

    Modeling on our treatment of wh-movement, propose a tree structure for (b) deriving it from (a) plus the application of a movement rule – VP preposing – which preposes a VP and adjoins it to TP. Show all the steps of the derivation.

3 The rule of VP preposing preposes a VP and adjoins it to TP. Provide a different sentence that could be derived from (a) by VP preposing and provide its tree structure.

4 State the two principles that the relationship between a reflexive pronoun and its antecedent must satisfy.

5 Draw the tree for the following sentence and verify that its structure satisfies these two principles:

(c) Ophelia expects that Macbeth$_j$ will hurt himself$_j$.

6 Draw the tree for the following sentence and verify that its structure does not satisfy any of these two principles:

(d) Hurt himself$_j$, Ophelia expects that Macbeth$_j$ will.

7 Propose an explanation for the fact that sentence (d) is well-formed despite the fact that its structure does not satisfy the two principles in question. (Hint: reread the section on wh-movement and what was said about how basic dependencies are satisfied in wh-questions.)

. . . .

Exercise 4.14 Indirect wh-questions and wh-islands

1 Draw the tree for the following sentence:

(a) The witches believed that Macbeth's armies would crush his enemies.

2 Describe the s-selection, c-selection and linking properties of the verb *crush*. (Hint: reread section 4.2).

3.1 In the following sentence, assume that the phrase *whose enemies* is the specifier of the embedded CP and draw its tree.

(b) The witches wondered whose enemies Macbeth's armies would crush.

3.2 Underline the phrases selected by the verb *crush*. The structural positions of these phrases should not conform to the linking rules that you established for *crush* on the basis of sentence (a). Propose a syntactic analysis of this discrepancy. (Hint: reread section 4.2.3 on wh-movement.)

4.1 Draw the trees for the following two sentences:

(c) Oberon knew that Othello would kill Desdemona.
(d) Oberon knew when Othello would kill Desdemona.

4.2 What is the determining structural factor explaining why wh-movement fails in (f) but not in (e). (Hint: compare their underlying structures.)

(e) Who did Oberon know that Othello would kill?
(f) *Who did Oberon know when Othello would kill?

(Note: The construction exemplified by the (b) sentence is called an indirect question. The phenomenon exemplified in (f) is called a wh-island.)

5

Syntax III: The Distribution of Verbal Forms: A Case Study

5.0   Introduction

In this chapter, we will study the distribution of verbs and the structure of sentences. We will examine the problem through a case study of the distribution of verbs.

As we learned in the previous chapters, verbs belong to a class of lexical items, which are symbolized as V. A verb appears in several forms since the stem can be combined with different inflectional suffixes as illustrated in the following examples:

(1)   I *love* Mercutio.   Romeo *loves* Juliet.   Juliet *loved* Romeo.
    Romeo promised to *love* Juliet.   Juliet continues *loving* Romeo.
    Romeo has *loved* Juliet.   Juliet was *loved* by Romeo.

Verbs function as the **heads** of Verb Phrases (VPs). (Alternatively we can say that the verb **projects** a VP.) The internal constituent structure of the VP depends on the lexical properties of its head, V. *Laugh*, *kiss*, and *give* occur in different types of VPs (the following representations only show the VP part of the sentence):

(2)

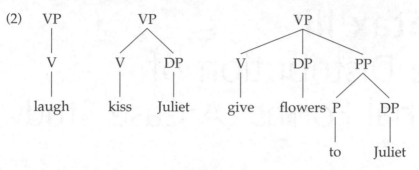

We are concerned in this chapter with the laws or principles which govern the distribution of verbal forms like the ones in (1) in English and in other languages. In this endeavor, we will establish the distribution of different verbal forms in English, extract the relevant generalizations, and construct an analysis that allows an account for these generalizations. The strength of the proposed analysis will lie in how successful it is in accounting for cross-linguistic patterns of variation. To this effect, we will consider some aspects of the distribution of verbal forms in languages other than English (French, Dutch, Norwegian, Irish, Swahili and Korean) as well.

We will conduct a 'syntax lab', equipped with the tools that syntactic theory provides. As a first step we will examine the inventory of environments in which the different verbal forms in (1) occur and extract generalizations. We thus will prepare our slides, put them under our microscope, and make observations. We will then 'zoom in' on these generalizations, first trying to understand them on a case-by-case basis. This means constructing representations that will account for them. We will then step back from the individual cases, and examine these together, broadening the picture. This will allow us to address more general questions, which will yield new generalizations. In the course of our investigation, our basic syntactic 'tools' will change slightly. As we understand the object under investigation better or differently, we will need to adjust or change our lenses, our tools through which we can look at the data. This will allow us to examine objects which were invisible with a less strong lens. As we proceed, we may need to develop new tools, to allow us to take certain objects apart, in order to determine their building blocks and basic design.

We will start on a microscopic level (individual cases in English), zooming in and out, and putting different slides under the microscope. We will then move to a macroscopic level (human languages), examining other languages in the lab.

5.1   English Verbs

5.1.1   Verb forms

As illustrated in (1) and in the discussion of verb morphology in chapter 2, English verbs come in different shapes: the morphologically uninflected form, called the **Infinitive**, and the morphologically complex forms – the stem plus inflectional suffixes illustrated in (3):

---

(3)   Non-finite verb forms

Infinitive		to	*use*	to	*show*
Participles:	past participle		*used*		*shown*
	passive participle		*used*		*shown*
	present participle		*using*		*showing*

Finite verb forms
Past tense   *used*   *showed*
Present tense (third-person singular)   *uses*   *shows*

Verbs inflected for past or present tense and agreement are often referred to as **finite verbs**, and the other verb forms as **non-finite** verbs. The present tense verbs inflect for third-person singular **agreement**.

5.1.2   The syntactic environment

As a first step, we simply list which elements must co-occur.

The perfect auxiliary *have* co-occurs with a **past participle**:

(4)   a.   Many students have *liked* Romeo and Juliet.
     b.   *Many students have *like/likes/liking* Romeo and Juliet.

The passive auxiliary *be* co-occurs with a **passive participle**:

(5)   a.   Juliet was *loved* by Romeo.
     b.   *Juliet was *love/loves/loving* by Romeo.

Although the English past participle and passive participle have identical forms, we distinguish between past participles and passive participles because they occur in different constructions. Past participles occur in active sentences (as in (4)), passive participles in passive sentences (5). In passive sentences, the DP that follows the verb in active sentences shows up in the subject position of the clause, as discussed in the previous chapter.

Progressive *be* co-occurs with a **present participle**:

(6)   Many students are *reading /*read /*reads* Romeo and Juliet.

Infinitives (which in English correspond to the stem form) are found in a number of environments:

As the complement of a **modal** (*will/would/can/could*, etc.):

(7)   Many students could *read* Romeo and Juliet.

As the complement of a causative verb (*make, let*), or of a verb of perception (*see, hear*):

(8)   a.   They let [Romeo and Juliet **die**]
      b.   They saw [Juliet *kiss* Romeo]

In different types of **infinitival** complements:
to-infinitivals

(9)   a.   Many students try [to *read* Romeo and Juliet]
      b.   Many students want [to *read* Romeo and Juliet]

for-to infinitivals

(10)   Many professors want very much [for their students to *read* Romeo and Juliet]

Tensed clauses require **tensed verbs** inflected for past or present tense (and agreement). This is true whether the tensed clause is the **main clause**, or an **embedded clause**:

(11)   *main clause*
       Romeo loved Juliet. *Romeo loving/to love Juliet

(12)   *embedded clause* (headed by the complementizers *that/whether* or *if* etc.)
       a.   I believe *that Romeo loved Juliet.*
       b.   I don't know *if Romeo loved Juliet.*
       c.   No students wondered *whether Romeo and Juliet truly loved each other.*

From this list, we extract the following generalizations:

(13)   a.   particular verbal forms co-occur with particular auxiliaries;
       b.   particular verbal forms co-occur with particular types of clauses (that is infinitival clauses demand infinitive verbs, and tensed clauses require tensed verbs).

These generalizations raise questions as to the exact nature of the co-occurrence restrictions.

Can all cases in (13a) be accounted for in the same way? Can all cases in (13b) be accounted for in the same way? Can the generalizations in (13a) and (13b) be accounted for in a uniform way, or do we need to account for each of them in different ways? We will examine these questions, illustrating the properties of co-occurrence (13a) by looking at the **perfect tense** construction. We will then turn to (13b), moving from individual cases to the bigger picture.

**EXERCISE
5.1**

In the sentences below:

(i)   Romeo seemed to have been kissed.
(ii) Writers try to adapt Romeo and Juliet to the big screen.
(iii) They were told to go buy tomatoes.
(iv) Do you believe that he has the nerves to go on stage?

1. Circle all finite verb forms, underline past participles, double underline passive participles, wavy underline all infinitives.
2. Give five examples of different types of embedded clauses.

5.1.3   The properties of co-occurrence: the perfect construction

The perfect auxiliary *have* co-occurs with the past participle [see Sidebar 5.1].

What are the properties of co-occurrence? Suppose we construe co-occurrence in a broad way as simply requiring that when a particular structure (say a sentence) contains a perfect auxiliary, it must also contain a past participle. (As in chapter 4, rules will be numbered R1, R2 etc.)

R1 (first version)
   A sentence containing the perfect auxiliary *have* must contain a past participle.

If this hypothesis is correct, the following examples should satisfy R1, because *have* and the past participle co-occur.

(14)   a.   *Many students *seen have* Juliet.
       b.   *Seen* many students have Juliet.
       c.   *Many students *have* [$_V$see] Juliet [*died*$_{+\text{past part}}$].

It is clear that these examples are ungrammatical because it is not enough that *have* and the past participle co-occur in a sentence, as R1 requires. It is also necessary that they stand in the correct structural relation. That is, there must be a particular structural relation which holds between *have* and the past participle. (14a) and (14b) show that this relation is such that the

The mapping relation

An hypothesis that students sometimes entertain is that a single semantic concept (like 'perfect tense') maps onto (= corresponds to) a single syntactic building block (a word). The English perfect tense construction shows that this hypothesis, in its crude form, is incorrect. The perfect construction is syntactically complex: it consists of the auxiliary *have* that carries its own inflection and a past participle; it does not consist of a single complex morphological word. The hypothesis may still be correct in some more complex form, however. Suppose, for example, that perfect tense is not a single semantic 'atom', but is composed of smaller semantic building blocks, and that these correspond to the auxiliary *have*, and a past participle verb. Evaluating the correctness of the hypothesis now becomes more complex, since it involves evaluating both the syntactic building blocks and the semantic building blocks.

The basic hypothesis that there is a one-to-one correspondence between semantic notions and words, or maybe smaller units than words like morphemes, takes on many forms and variations, and is often not made explicit.

past participle must follow *have*. (14c) shows that it is not sufficient that the past participle follows *have*: the past participle must also be 'close' to *have*.

What is the precise characterization of 'closeness'? Maybe it is 'being immediately preceded by *have*'. You can see this is incorrect in the following examples, where the past participle is preceded by *all*, *not*, and *carefully* respectively and the sentences are well-formed.

(15) a. The students have *all* studied Juliet.
      b. The students have *not* played Romeo and Juliet.
      c. The students have *carefully* read Hamlet.

The relevant notion of 'closeness' should be defined in terms of structure. To see this, it will be helpful to draw tree diagrams of the grammatical structures (motivated by constituent tests like coordination and displacement (movement) as discussed in the previous chapter). (Assigning structure to examples and making sure the structures are correct is always the first step in syntactic argumentation: all syntactic argumentation is based on structure):

(16)

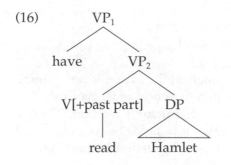

Constituent structure

In the text, the string *have read Hamlet* is assigned the constituent structure in (16). In this exercise you are asked to show that this is indeed the correct structure.

How do you test constituent structure? One of the tests to establish constituent structure is **coordination**, as discussed in chapter 3. Only constituents that are alike can be coordinated by a coordination like *and* or *but*. Coordination forms tree structures like (1), where X stands for V, C, A, P, D, T, etc.:

1.
```
        XP
      /  |  \
   XP  and  XP
```

Now consider the following examples.

(i) (a) Some of the students have read Hamlet and have seen King Lear.
    (b) Some of the students have read Hamlet and seen King Lear.
    (c) Some of the students have read Hamlet and King Lear.

A. Identify the syntactic category (VP, AP, TP, CP, DP, . . .) of the constituent following *and*:
   (a) have seen King Lear is a _____
   (b) seen King Lear   is a _____
   (c) King Lear   is a _____

B. Identify the first part of the coordination:
   (a) _____ is coordinated with *have seen King Lear*
   (b) _____ is coordinated with *seen King Lear*
   (c) _____ is coordinated with *King Lear*

C. Translate your findings in B into tree structures, using the format in (1) above.
   (a) The tree structure for B(a) is:

   (b) The tree structure for B(b) is:

(c)   The tree structure for B(c) is:

D.   State in one or two sentences how the structures in C support the constituent structure in (16). (XP is a constituent because . . . .)

E.   Chapter 3 discusses other constituent tests. List these, and try to apply these to each of the examples in (i) (applying means manipulating the string, and constructing relevant examples).
     Discuss if these constituent tests work for the examples under discussion. If they do, what conclusions can you draw? If not, what conclusions can you draw?

The constituent containing the past participle is a righthand sister of *have*. The past participle is thus contained in the **complement** of the auxiliary *have*. We can now reformulate R1 as R2:

R2 (second version)
     Have requires or demands (= selects) a complement which contains a past participle.

As we saw in chapter 3, complements are **sisters** of a particular head, and follow the head in English. If *have* requires a past participle complement, and if the linguistic system requires this relation to be expressed in the configuration in (17), the basic impossibility of (14a) and (14b) is accounted for because they simply do not fit into the structure.

(17)   English:

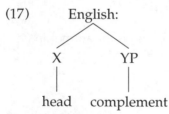

       X   YP

       | |

     head   complement

We are now at the point in our experiment where we have discovered that *have* must combine with a past participle; that this is expressed by a relation such that the past participle is within the complement of *have*. Further questions arise: What is the precise characterization of 'a complement which contains a past participle'? Does it matter how 'far' the past participle is from *have*? In order to answer this type of question, we can compare the structure of the well-formed cases with that of the ill-formed cases like (14c); this provides an important insight.

(18)

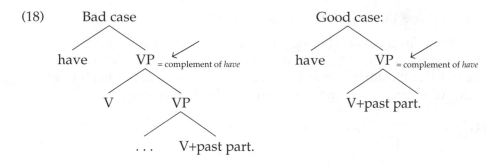

In both the good and the bad case, the participle is in the VP **constituent**. (If you 'lift' the VP node marked with the arrow out of the tree, all branches and nodes that are attached to VP come with it: this is a constituent and it includes the past participle.) What distinguishes the good from the bad case is the location of the past participle. The past participle cannot just be anywhere in the VP complement of *have*. In the bad case, the participle is within the complement of another V. The generalization must therefore be that the past participle occurs in the following stretch of the structure:

(19)

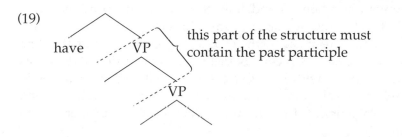

In other words, *have* is quite 'nearsighted'. It demands a past participle where it can see it, in what we can call its **immediate complement**.

R3 (third version)

    Have requires or demands (= selects) a past participle in its 'immediate' complement.

We now need to examine what we mean by *immediate complement*. Ideally we would like to say that *have* requires, or selects, a past participle complement, which translates into the structure in (20):

(20)

    have   VP[past participle]

The next question concerns the relation between the structure that must contain the past participle in (R3), and the label of the constituent. The notion **head** plays a crucial role in understanding this relation.

5.1.4 Projections: heads and phrases

There is a direct relation between the head of a constituent and the label of the constituent it forms, as we saw in chapter 3. A VP is a VP by virtue of the fact that it contains a head V, a PP because it contains a head P, an AP is an AP because its properties are determined by its head, A.

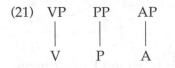

(21)   VP   PP   AP
        | | |
        V   P   A

Thus, heads (i.e. the building blocks of syntactic structures) determine the category of their **projection** (i.e. phrase) in syntax.

Heads in morphology

The notion 'head' not only plays a role in syntax, it also plays an important role in morphology, as was briefly discussed in chapter 2. As we noted in that chapter, morphology deals with how complex words are divided into smaller units (morphemes) and how these units are combined into words. Words function as syntactic heads projecting phrases. We have seen that morphemes are picky with respect to the category of the item they attach to (just as *have* is picky about the fact that it demands a past participle): *-ize* co-occurs with N, *-ment* co-occurs with V, etc. Suffixes in fact **c-select** (select the category of) the morpheme that they attach to, and (can) change the category of the word they attach to. These properties can be stated as in (22).

(22)   -ize   c-selects N   changes N to V   symbol-ize
       -ment   c-selects V   changes V to N   establish-ment

As in syntax, the internal structure of the complex word is structurally expressed (23) (these representations are partial and will be further completed below):

(23)   a.   (first version)   b.   c.

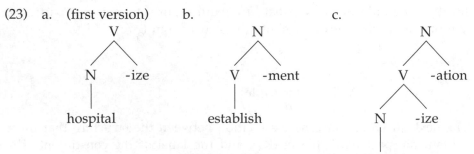

As we see from these examples, the category of the newly formed word is determined by the rightmost suffix (23c). This raises the question as to whether the category of a derived word can be predicted, or whether which affixes do or do not lead to category changes must be specified. English prefixes, in contrast with suffixes, never seem to determine the category of a derived word. For example, if we prefix *re* (a morpheme with a meaning close to that of the adverb *again*), to a verb and form [re+[$_V$ read], the newly formed word is a V, not an adverb. Insight into this question comes from the pattern of English **compounds** (chapter 2):

(24)
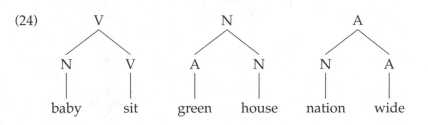

The **category** of the compound is determined by the category of the right-hand member: thus *babysit* is a V, not an N, by virtue of the fact that the righthand member of the compound is V. Compounds have **heads**. In English, compounds are head-final. A morpheme in the head position determines the category of the compound and other features of the compound as well, as discussed in chapter 2.

Is the structural property of having a head specific to compounds, or is it characteristic of the structure of all words? If it is a property of all words, we can understand the prefix/suffix asymmetry discussed earlier. The reason why suffixes can determine the category of the derived word is because they are located in the head position of a word. The reason why prefixes never do so is because they cannot be analyzed as being in the head position. They can therefore never determine the category of the derived word. This presupposes that any morpheme can potentially be a head. It will only realize this potential if it occurs in the right configuration.

If suffixes determine the category of the derived word, suffixes must have the necessary properties to do so. Since *-ize* forms verbs, it must be that *-ize* is treated as a V in the mental grammar. Suffixes are thus like lexical categories, and can be V, A, or N. Thus, *-ize* is a V, *-ment* is a N, *-able* is an A, etc. They differ from regular Ns, Vs and As, in that they are **bound** morphemes (they cannot be pronounced by themselves but need to be attached to a host), not **free** morphemes (which can be pronounced by themselves).

(25) -ize,   V, bound, c-selects N
      -ment, N, bound, c-selects V
      -ation, N, bound, c-selects V
      etc.

This shows that the property of being free or bound is not an inherent property of some class of morphemes, but a discrete property that can be combined with any morpheme. If morphemes can be free or bound, it is not improbable that there should be bound N morphemes, bound V morphemes, next to free N morphemes, and V morphemes.

A more complete representation for the words in (23) is given below:

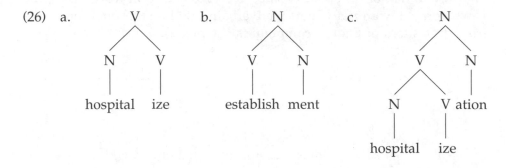

Words are constructed according to specific 'instructions' or rules of the grammar. Heads form a constituent with their complements. In English, heads surface in final position in the morphological structure.

The property that *-ize* possesses which changes the category of the word it attaches to (expressed in (22)) does not need to be stated as an individual property of *-ize*, but follows from the way the structure is put together. What must be stated is that *-ize* is a V (notice that its meaning is verb-like, that is it can be paraphrased by a verb like 'make into'), that it is bound, and that it c-selects for N.

Finding the past participle

The past participle is encoded as a suffix on the verb. VPs can be categorized as a particular kind of VP depending on the inflection that is added:

Table 5.1   Verb Inflections

PARTICIPLES			INFINITIVE	TENSED VERB FORMS	
VP[past part]	VP[pass part]	VP[Pres Part]	VP[Inf]	VP[+pres, +agr]	VP[+past]
|	|	|	|	|	|
V[past part]	V[pass part]	V[Pres Part]	V	V[+pres, +agr]	V[+past]
[V] ed]	[V[ed]]	[V[ing]	[V]	[V]s]	[V]ed]

This allows us to understand exactly what R3 says. The participle must be contained in the immediate complement of *have*, because *have* requires a past participle complement. Since the past participle is the head of the VP complement, the VP projection is marked +past participle, by virtue of the fact that heads determine the properties of the projection as a whole:

(27)

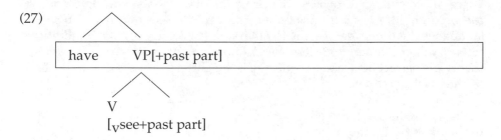

We can now reformulate R3 as R4, which seems to be the minimal statement that must be made:

R4 (final)

Have requires or demands (= selects) a past participle complement.

We now immediately understand what goes wrong in cases like (14c), repeated here as (28):

(28)

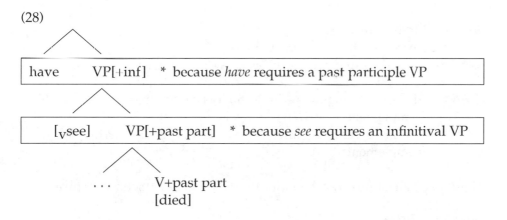

Have requires a past participle complement, not an infinitival complement. Similarly, *see* co-occurs with an infinitival complement (*see Juliet die*), which means *see* requires an infinitival VP complement as sister, not a past participle.

Examples like (14c) are, as far as we know, unattested in human languages. If a verb demands a particular verbal form, this form must be realized on the verb heading the complement of that verb; it cannot appear instead on any other verbal form that does not satisfy that relation. This shows that this type of relationship is encoded in the same way in all human languages.

Building Larger Structures

The co-occurrence of the other auxiliaries with passive and progressive participles has the same properties as *have* and the past participles.

(29)   a.   (Passive) *be* requires (= selects) a [+passive participle] complement
       b.   (Progressive) *be* requires (= selects) a [+present participle] complement

These generalizations translate into the following syntactic structures:

(30)

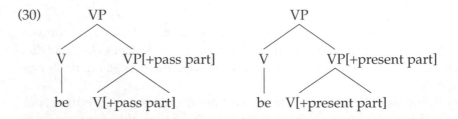

These are little VPs that can be combined into larger structures: they act like pieces of lego or a jigsaw puzzle that can be further assembled:

(31)   a.   This play *is being read* by the students (progressive *be*, passive *be*, main V)

Order	SIDEBAR 5.3

Order

It is interesting that little VPs must combine in a specific order (*perfect auxiliary (have), progressive (be), passive (be),* and *main (V)*). If these VPs are like little pieces of lego or pieces in a jigsaw puzzle, why must they be combined in a particular (hierarchical) order? There is no satisfying answer to this question in current syntactic theories. To find an answer, one can explore several directions. It could be an accidental effect of English grammar; it could be a reflection of a non-derivable part of the language endowment; or it could be an effect of the rules of semantic interpretation. If it were accidental, independent properties of English would conspire to yield the effect. If this were the correct view, the particular ordering would be a somewhat arbitrary property, and one would expect to find languages for which it does not hold. This prediction does not seem correct. In recent work, Guglielmo Cinque (1999) shows that the ordering restrictions hold cross-linguistically. He argues that the hierarchical order is simply given, just as the structure of DNA is given. However, even if the order is universal, it could still be the case that it could be derived, perhaps from the way semantic interpretation operates.

b. This play *has been read* by many students (perfect *have*, passive *be*, main V)

c. Many students *have been reading* this play (perfect *have*, progressive *be*, main V)

d. This play should *have been being read* by the students (perfect *have*, progressive *be*, passive *be*, main V)

The italicized string in (31d) has the following structure:

(32)

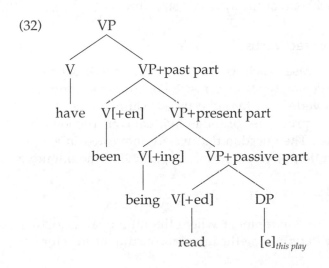

Each of the heads in (32) has the right type of complement VP as its sister. The larger structure is constructed out of small pieces containing a V head projecting a particular type of VP and a particular type of complement. At each point in the structure a particular head can inspect its sister to the right to check that it has the right type of complement.

It is easy to see that the structures formed by the local head complement relation constitute the backbone of the syntactic structure.

EXERCISE 5.3

Constructing trees

Give the tree structures for the italicized strings below:
(Do not forget to represent the internal arguments that V takes. Be careful, DPs may have moved, so that they are pronounced in a different position from where they are interpreted.)

(i)   Dogberry will *be arresting Don John*
(ii) Don John will *have been arrested*
(iii) She will *have eaten*
(iv) I will *be going to the theater*

Summary of relationship between heads and complements
This concludes the lab experiment that deals with the fact that particular verbal forms co-occur with particular auxiliaries (13a). From this experiment, we learned that the mental grammar imposes a very tight condition on the relationship between heads and complements. If a head demands/ selects for a particular type of complement, it must find that complement as its sister. We have seen that heads select and project (i.e. form constituents with their complements, and determine the properties of the projection as a whole). The structures formed by the local head–complement relation constitute the backbone of the syntactic structure.

5.1.5   Infinitives and tensed verbs

We now turn to examine cases such as (13b) – particular verbal forms which co-occur with particular types of clauses. For example, infinitival clauses require infinitival verbs, and tensed clauses require a tensed verb. We will again examine the properties of the individual constructions, before putting them together. The question that we are interested in is how to account for the distribution of verbal forms, in particular, the infinitive and the tensed forms.

Infinitival complements
We will concentrate on the environment where the infinitival V follows *for DP to*, and start out by determining the internal constituent structure of this string.

(33) [For Kate to defy Petruccio] takes courage

The *for DP to VP* string acts as a single **constituent**, as we can establish by applying some of the constituency tests introduced earlier.
  Only constituents can be replaced by a pro-form:

(34) a. [For Kate to defy Petruccio] takes courage
    b. This   takes courage

Given this diagnostic, the *for DP to VP* is a constituent.
  A constituent can be coordinated with another constituent of the same category.

(35) [[For Portia to confront Shylock] and [for Hamlet to confront his step-father]] took courage

We call this constituent a CP. This is because its internal structure is similar to a **tensed CP** such as *that Portia confronted Shylock*. It differs in that it does not contain a tensed verb form but an infinitive. For this reason *for Portia to confront Shylock* is called an **infinitival CP**. The infinitival CP also comprises a further constituent [DP *to* VP], as we can establish by using the coordination test:

(36) [For [Portia to confront Shylock] and [Hamlet to confront his step-father]]

The structure of (36) must be as in (37). The string *Portia to confront Shylock* is a constituent because it can be coordinated with another constituent of the same type.

(37)

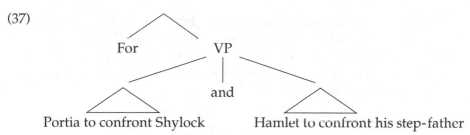

Finally, the *to VP* and the VP behave as constituents as well:

(38) a. for Portia [to confront Shylock] and [to judge the case], . . .
    b. for Portia to [confront Shylock] and [judge the case]

Putting the puzzle pieces together, the structure for the *for DP to VP* constituent must be at least as in (39). Each of the circled nodes can be coordinated with another node of the same type.

(39)

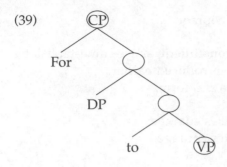

Note that nothing so far requires that the structure be no bigger than (39). It could turn out on the basis of additional evidence that a much larger syntactic structure must be assigned to this string. This is fine, as long as this larger structure contains the constituents in (39), and is independently motivated. Some nodes in (39) are unlabeled. How do we determine what the labels should be? *To* always combines with an infinitival VP to its right. This represents a straightforward case of a head–complement relation: *to* requires a VP complement headed by an infinitival V. It is a property of heads that they select for complements. Therefore, *to* is a head. But what kind of head is *to*? *To* is traditionally treated as a purely grammatical marker of the infinitive, not as a preposition. We treat *to* as a realization of the category T (tense), based on the fact that it has the same distribution as other elements occurring in the T slot. *To* behaves as other heads, and projects a TP. The *to VP* constituent co-occurs with *for*:

(40) a. For Juliet *see/*sees/*seeing/*seen Romeo, . . .
      b. For Juliet to see Romeo, . . .

For therefore selects a complement headed by *to* as its sister. This means that the sister node of *for* should be labeled TP. *For*, like *that* or *if/whether*, is treated as a particular instance of the category C. It is a head that indicates the type of CP that it heads. Since *for* takes a TP complement headed by *to*, the subject DP must be within TP:

(41)

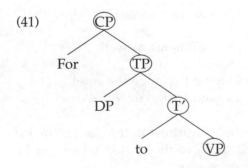

We thus arrive at the conclusion that TP contains two layers of structure, one layer in which the head combines with a complement to its right, forming a constituent labeled T' (T-bar), and a higher layer where T' combines with a specifier (Spec) forming the complete tense phrase (TP). This structure reveals another important property of syntactic phrases (XPs): the TP constituent contains two subparts. The DP forms a constituent with a node (T') containing the *to VP* constituent. The T-bar contains the head and the selected complement.

The DP in Spec, TP entertains relations with both V and with *for*. For its thematic interpretation, the DP depends on V in exactly the same way as the subject of a tensed clause does:

(42) a.   For Juliet to be loved   (Juliet is the theme argument of *love*)
      b.   For Juliet to take poison   (Juliet is the agent argument of *take*)
      c.   For Juliet to be given flowers   (Juliet is the goal argument of *give*)

For its form, however, the DP depends on *for*, as we can see if we replace the DP with a pronoun. The pronoun shows up in its accusative case form (*her/him/them*), which is the form pronouns take when they are complements of a preposition like *for*. Accusative subject pronouns can only appear if *for* is present. Nominative pronouns which occur in tensed clauses are excluded in this environment.

(43) a.   For her/*she to be loved, ... that she/*her should be loved
           (her = accusative case)   (she = nominative)
      b.   (*Her) to be loved is important

The structure we arrive at is constructed out of local head–complement relations (heads select for their sisters). We don't need to say anything special about the selection of infinitives: they are always introduced by some head that requires them.

So far then, the distribution of verbal forms can be successfully and uniformly handled: heads demand certain types of complements. The head–complement relation is always encoded in the same way: the complement is a sister of the head. Not only do lexical categories like V select for particular types of complement but functional categories like D (*that, the*), C (*for*) and T (*to*) do so as well.

Tensed clauses

We next consider the distribution of **finite verbs** or **tensed verbs**. These verb forms occur in tensed clauses, either main or embedded.

(44)   a. *Main clause*:
           Katherina defied (*defy/to defy) Petruccio
       b. *Embedded clause*:
           [That Katherina defied (*defy/to defy) Petruccio] disturbed all
           the men
           Many students concluded that Katherina defied (*defy/to defy)
           Petruccio

As stated above, this is co-occurrence of clause type and verb form: a
tensed clause demands a finite verb. This seems different from the co-
occurrence restrictions discussed so far, which were all relatable to the
head–complement configuration. Can the distribution of finite verbs be
accounted for by local head–complement relations as well? If not, what
does this reveal about the mental grammar? To answer these questions, we
must first decide what the structure of a tensed clause is. We start with
embedded tensed complements (44b). (You might wonder why we don't
start with the apparently simplest case, i.e. main clauses. As we will see
below, their simplicity is deceptive.)

(45)   [That Katherina defied (*defy/to defy) Petruccio] disturbed
       all the men

That Katherina defied Petruccio is a constituent, starting with the C, *that*. Any
clause starting with *that* must contain a finite verb (i.e. a verb inflected for
tense/agreement): *that* and finite verbs therefore co-occur. This indicates
that *that* takes as complement a constituent headed by V carrying a particular type of inflection, call it +T, for tensed V.

(46)   (Structure to be revised)

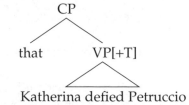

Coordination confirms that *Katherina defied Petruccio* is a constituent, as
expressed in the structure in (46). The coordination test reveals further
presence of increasingly smaller constituents:

(47)   a. [that [Katherina defied Petruccio] and [Portia confronted
           Shyrock]]
       b. that Katherine [[defied Petruccio] and [cursed Bianca]]

We thus need to find room for the subject DP, and a constituent which contains the finite verb and the object (or rather, the rest of the clause). We will call this node V′, by analogy with T′:

(48)   (Structure to be revised)

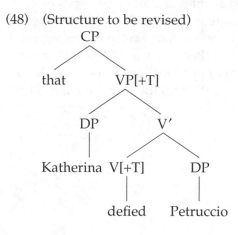

This structure is different from the one presented in chapter 3 (it will be revised below), but is compatible with the assumptions that we have made about morphology and syntax so far. We therefore need arguments, theoretical and empirical, to determine if or why this representation should be rejected.

Tensed main clauses

We have so far assumed that the distribution of different inflected verbal forms can be reduced to head–complement relations, which translate into configurations in which the complement is a sister of the head. Given these assumptions, we arrive at the structure for embedded tensed complements in (48) quite directly. Now we turn to the problem of tensed main clauses. Main clauses in English are not marked by any overt complementizer, yet they require a finite verb form:

(49)   Katherina defied (*defy/to defy) Petruccio.

The form of tensed main clauses would be consistent if they were TPs. But if tensed main clauses are TPs, the presence of a tensed verb would not follow from the presence of a head that requires it, as was true for all the other cases discussed so far, but would have to be stipulated independently:

(50)   Main clauses require tensed verbs.

We might wonder whether this conclusion is warranted. Broadening our perspective, we see that there is in fact an interesting solution to this problem.

The structural asymmetry between tensed main clauses (which look like TP) and embedded declarative clauses (which look like CP) can be made non-existent. Suppose main and embedded clause types are CPs. The difference can be attributed to the fact that they are different types of CPs. This means that they are headed by different C nodes. The C node happens to be silent in main tensed clauses, whereas it happens to be pronounced as *that* in embedded tensed complements. Both Cs would have the formal property of requiring +Tense, and no independent statement is needed to account for the occurrence of finite verbs. We will identify the main clause C as C [+decl, +main], and revise (48) to (51):

(51)

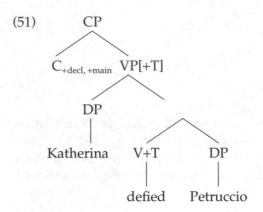

This solution implies the existence of a **silent head** in English, the main clause C, which is endowed with all the properties of heads: it selects for a particular type of complement, in this case a tensed VP, and it determines the properties of the projection as a whole, in this case it identifies a matrix declarative clause. *That* differs from it only in heading an embedded complement:

(52)   C [+decl, +main], c-selects +Tense, C is not pronounced.
       C [+decl, +embedded], c-selects +Tense, C is pronounced as *that*.

From this, we can read off that *that* and the silent complementizer realize the C node that heads declarative clauses. Both Cs c-select for +Tense. They differ in that the silent C node heads main clauses, whereas *that* only heads embedded clauses.

Do such null heads actually exist in the mental grammar? The answer is yes.

We know from morphology that there are silent morphemes ('zero' morphemes (see chapter 2)). Some of these silent morphemes act as heads, as we can conclude from a productive process in English which derives verbs from nouns:

(53)   N   V
       father   (to) father (a child)
       butter   (to) butter (the bread)
       button   (to) button (a shirt)

The category of a word is determined by the head in rightmost position. Since the examples above involve a category change, it must be the case that there is a head responsible for the category change, yet this head is not pronounced, i.e. it is silent. It follows that the word structure for the derived verbs must be like (54):

(54)

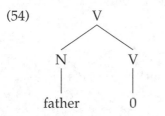

That is, there is a silent suffix in English, which belongs to the category V, selects for N, and has all the properties of a head. Its features determine the features of the newly formed word.

We can therefore conclude that silent heads are part of the mental system. (In addition, psychological experiments on language-processing support the existence of such concepts and elements.) Thus, the postulation of a silent C node is therefore no objection in principle to the solution in (51). Furthermore, if we look at languages other than English, we see that there are languages which have an overt complementizer in all declarative clauses:

(55)   Korean (nom = nominative, dec = declarative)
       romio-ka   culiet-kwa kican-e   ka-ss-ta
       Romeo-nom Juliet-with theater-to go-past-decl (matrix)
       'Romeo went with Juliet to the theater.'

These facts provide quite strong support for the structure shown in (53). This structure allows treating the appearence of a tensed verb form as a function of particular features of C, using the regular head–complement relation. It also allows treating main declarative clauses as identical cross-linguistically, showing the generality of the hypothesis. Thus, clause type can be determined from the structure, by inspecting properties of the C level. We conclude:

(56)   Properties related to clause type are located at the CP level.

Note further that the existence of null heads in syntax is incompatible with the view that words are the building blocks of syntax, since silent heads are clearly not words, yet they are building blocks as well. This suggests that the building blocks of syntax are heads which can be either silent or overt. Heads themselves can be further characterized in terms of features like past tense, plural, person features (first, second, third), case features (nominative, accusative, dative, genitive, etc.), clause type features (like declarative, main etc.).

Comparing infinitives and tensed clauses

We have looked at all the individual cases and can now focus on a glitch in the bigger picture. This glitch becomes visible if we compare the internal structure of *for* DP with VP infinitivals and tensed clauses.

(57)   a.   b.

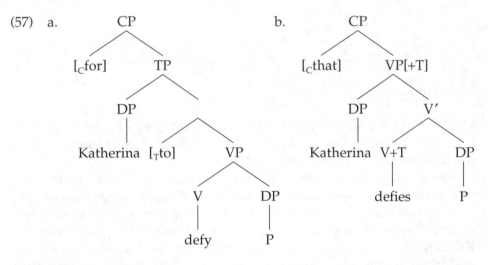

These structures are asymmetric. Infinitival clauses are structurally larger than finite clauses. In finite clauses, TP and VP are 'collapsed', but in infinitives they are not. This is a direct consequence of the way in which T is expressed. Infinitival *to* is a free standing morpheme in T, but finite tense is expressed as a suffix on the verb. This shifts selection of V by T to the morphology (the tense morpheme attaches to V, that is, it selects for V), and leads to the compressed structure in (57). This compression leads to other differences. The subject in the infinitival is located in a different structural position than the subject of a tensed clause. *For* and *that* are both Cs that must combine with (different) values of T. While *for* combines with a TP complement, *that* combines with a tensed VP complement, headed by a tensed V. It might turn out that these representations are correct. However such asymmetries are suspicious because they might arise due to our missing part of the picture. As a general strategy, we look for ways in which to eliminate asymmetries, and see what, if anything, we gain by doing so.

   Some questions arise. Why should different clause types not have symmetrical structures? Why should the DP subject occur in a different configuration in infinitival complements and in tensed clauses? Such questions can only be answered by considering what the system looks like if the internal make-up of infinitives and tensed clauses is identical.

It is unlikely that the structure of infinitival complements can be reduced to that of tensed clauses. To do this, some of the structure in (57a) would have to be deleted; yet each part of this structure has been independently motivated. It is, however, easy to make tensed clauses parallel to infinitivals. This can be achieved by enriching the structure of tensed complements, and assuming that the structure contains a TP level which is separate from VP. In other words, we 'undo' the collapsing of TP and VP. The following structures result:

(58) a.

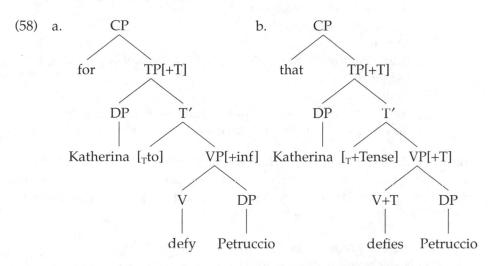

This allows uniform treatment of the subject DP: it is always found in the same syntactic configuration (immediately dominated by TP, and sister to T' in infinitival and tensed clauses alike). We can now say that [$_T$+tense] selects for a tensed VP (just as *to* selects for an infinitival VP): clauses contain a T node that takes VP as its complement. *That*, just like *for*, selects for a TP headed by [T]. Thus different types of heads (*to* or +tense) are able to occupy the T head. This holds for other head positions as well: the C head can be *for*, *that*, *whether* or *if*; the D head of the DP can contain different types of Ds (*that, the, these, a*) etc.

There are numerous empirical arguments in support of the structure in (58b) which will be discussed below. As we will see, the skeleton of this structure is basically correct, although we must add some relation between the [$_T$+tense] and V+tense, which is not indicated in the structure above.

5.1.6   On the structure of tensed clauses

In the following sections, we present empirical support for the structure of tensed clauses in (58b) and introduce another dependency between head positions, called **head movement**.

Auxiliaries, modals and main verbs

For the discussion of the structure of tensed clauses, it is important to distinguish between **auxiliaries** (the verb *have* used in the perfect construction and the verb *be* in all its uses), **modals** (*will/would, can/could, may/might, shall/should, do/did*), and **main verbs** (all verbs that are not listed above).

(59) (1) Auxiliaries:
       a. Juliet *has* gone to the nunnery (perfect auxiliary *have*).
       b. Juliet *is* sad.
       c. Juliet *is* going to the nunnery.
       d. Juliet *was* in the cellar.
       e. Juliet *is* my friend.
    (2) Modals:
    Juliet *will/would/can/could/may/might/shall/should/does/did* go to the garden.
    (3) Main verbs:
    Juliet *left*; Juliet *wrote* to Romeo; Juliet *saw* Romeo; Juliet *has* to leave; Juliet *seems* to be in love, etc.

This distinction is based on the distributional properties of the individual items in question, not on the basis of their interpretation. For example, the auxiliaries and modals can precede the subject in **yes–no questions** in modern English, but main verbs cannot.

(60) a. *Has* she gone to the garden?
     b. *Is* she going to the garden?
     b. *Should* she go to the garden?
     c. *Will* she go to the garden?
     d. **Went* she to the garden?

SIDEBAR 5.4

Verb classes

There are many possible ways to subdivide the verb class. Some of these may be familiar to you from dictionaries. Check any dictionary and look at the introductory pages. Dictionaries typically distinguish between intransitive verbs, that is, verbs that do not combine with a DP complement, like *laugh, arrive* for example, and transitive verbs, i.e. verbs that do combine with a DP complement, like *kiss, hit*. This (crude) distinction reflects the environment in which the verb occurs: i.e. whether it co-occurs with a complement DP or not. It turns out that there are many different environments. The *Advanced Learner Dictionary of Current English* for example lists 25 different verbal patterns, many of which are further divided. Besides distributional criteria, subdivisions can also be made on purely semantic characteristics. None of these distinctions will be relevant in this chapter.

Classify the verbs in the following sentences as main verbs, modals, or auxiliaries. Construct an example for each of the sentences to support your classification.

EXERCISE 5.4

For example:

(i)   They should go to the garden.   Should is a modal verb.

Support: It precedes the subject in yes/no questions: should they go to the garden?

(ii)   John seems to be sick.   seems is a _____
       Support:

(iii) John has a problem.   has is a _____
       Support:

(iv)   Juliet has left.   has is a _____
       Support:

(v)   Frank had his donkey saddled.   had is a _____
       Support:

(vi)   They go see their advisers every week. go is a _____
       Support:

(vii) They want to be left alone.   want is a _____
       Support:

(viii) They are happy.   are is a _____
       Support:

(ix)   They appear happy.   appear is a _____
       Support:

(x)   They need to act.   need is a _____
       Support:

VP ellipsis
Consider the particular sentences in the examples below:

(61) a.   Although Regan has not been a good daughter to Lear,
           Cordelia has.
      b.   Othello will regret his actions, but Iago will not.
      c.   Although Othello couldn't hide the dagger, Cordelia could.

The clauses – *Cordelia has, Iago will not, Cordelia could* – are **elliptical**: part of the sentence is missing, though the sentence is understood in very precise ways.

(62)   a.   Cordelia has [$_{VP}$ *been a good daughter to Lear*] (but not: *read many books/*been a good wife to Lear etc.)

b.   Iago will not [$_{VP}$*regret his actions*] (but not *go to the garden/ *be scared)

c.   Cordelia could [$_{VP}$*hide the dagger*]

That is, no one would interpret these sentences as in the starred examples or in any way other than the unstarred sentences.

This type of elliptical clause minimally consists of a subject, and a (non-reduced) finite auxiliary or modal. A VP constituent is missing, and native speakers interpret the missing VP of the elliptical sentence in very precise ways, i.e. as identical to a VP given in the sentence (or discourse). We refer to this process that allows the VP to be silent as **VP ellipsis**. VP ellipsis can be applied to any type of VP that we have identified in the preceding section, as the following example illustrates:

(63)   Juliet could [$_{VP}$have [$_{VP}$been [$_{VP}$studying . . .]]] and

a.   Romeo *could* [$_{VP}$~~have~~ [$_{VP}$~~been~~ [$_{VP}$~~studying Latin~~]]] *too*

b.   Romeo *could* [$_{VP}$*have* [$_{VP}$~~been~~ [$_{VP}$~~studying Latin~~]]] *too*

c.   Rome *could* [$_{VP}$*have* [$_{VP}$*been* [$_{VP}$~~studying Latin~~]]] *too*

We refer to the pronounced part of the sentence as the **remnant** of VP ellipsis.

By positing that these elliptical sentences are underlyingly full sentences, we can account for their fixed interpretation. VP ellipsis can be conceived of as a process that 'imposes silence' on the phonological material within a particular VP (if the content of the VP can be 'recovered'), but which leaves all other information intact. This we represent as follows:

(64)

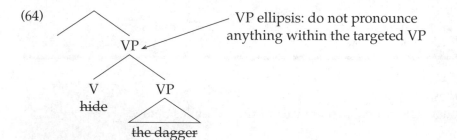

VP ellipsis: do not pronounce anything within the targeted VP

VP ellipsis with tensed main verbs

In the examples above, the remnant contains an auxiliary or a modal, with a silent VP complement. But consider what happens if we apply VP

Main verb *do* and auxiliary *do*

English has two verbs *do* that are homophonous (have the same pronunciation) but have different syntactic distributions. The auxiliary *do* precedes the negative marker *not* or the subject in questions; main verb *do* may neither precede *not*, nor the subject in a question.

(i)   Auxiliary *do*: Othello *did* not believe Desdemona (auxiliary *do* precedes *not*)

Did Desdemona convince Othello?

(ii) Main verb *do* behaves as other main verbs like *kill*: it cannot precede *not*, nor the subject in questions:

(a)   Othello killed Desdemona
(b)   *Othello killed not Desdemona
(c)   *Killed Othello Desdemona
(d)   Othello did something terrible
(e)   *Othello did not something terrible
(f)   *Did Othello something terrible?

ellipsis to a sentence with a finite main verb. (The word *too* appears in the context as well. Ignore *too* for the purpose of the discussion here.)

(65)   a.   *After Othello entered Desdemona's room, Emilia —— too
       b.   After Othello entered Desdemona's room, Emilia did —— too

The verb disappears, but the tense of the verb remains, and shows up on the auxiliary verb *do*.

We can explain the appearance of *do* quite simply, if we assume that the tense morpheme and V come together, not in the morphology, but in the syntax. Treating the tense morpheme and V as separate syntactic entities allows for the possibility that syntactic processes affect one, but not the other. We will see examples of both. VP ellipsis affects VP, but not T; in yes–no questions affects T, but not VP.

Suppose that the tense morpheme is a head (though still a bound head) in T. This yields the following structure:

(66)

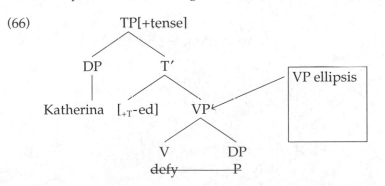

VP ellipsis leaves a remnant *Katherina ed too*. This is an impossible sentence, since *-ed* is a bound morpheme, and must have a verb to its immediate left. VP ellipsis takes away the verbal stem, and leaves *-ed* without an appropriate companion. In comes *do* to rescue the tense morpheme, with *do* +[$_{past}ed$] 'spelled out' (pronounced) as *did*. This process is traditionally referred to as ***do*-support**. This is depicted in the following tree:

(67)   *Do*-support: Insert *do* to 'support' (=save) a stranded suffix in T.

(68)

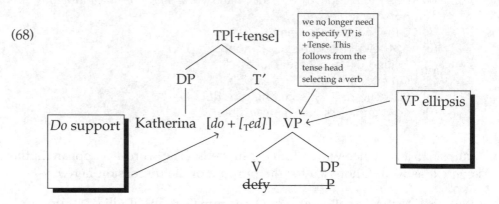

The property of being a verb and the property of being tensed are two separate *syntactic* properties, even though in a simple sentence the inflected verb expresses both properties in a single (though complex) morphological word.

Affix-hopping and head movement

If inflected verbs are not put together in the morphology, we must put them together in the syntax, and the question is how this is achieved. In affirmative, non-negative sentences, the tense suffix attaches to the main verb ([*use+past*] → [*used*]). This is achieved by the syntactic process of **affix-hopping**, which shifts the tense suffix down onto the verbal stem in the following configuration:

(69)   Input: Affix-hopping → Output:

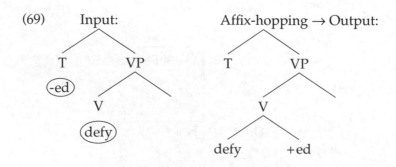

As the trees show, affix-hopping singles out a particular configuration. The affix attaches to the head of the complement. The local head–complement configuration is again encountered as an important syntactic configuration. The output is in fact identical in representation to (51), above. As the output shows, the inflected verb is within VP, not in T. This is an important empirical generalization about English syntax, which will be further supported below:

(70) INFLECTED MAIN VERBS IN ENGLISH ARE WITHIN THE VP.

We can conceive of a different way to combine an affix and a stem, which would use the same configuration as in (69). Instead of hopping the bound morpheme onto the verb, we can imagine the mirror process, with the verb raising to the affix in T. This process is called **head movement**.

(71) Head movement:

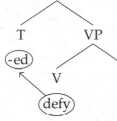

As a result of head movement, the distribution of the finite verb would be identical to the distribution of the T node. As we will see in the next section, this is what finite auxiliaries and modals in English do. In many languages this is what all tensed verbs do. However, finite main Vs in English do not.

(72) IN ENGLISH FINITE AUXILIARIES ARE IN T.

Whenever affix-hopping fails, *do*-support kicks in. *Do*-support is specific to English, and applies in a wide variety of contexts for essentially the same reasons, that is, to save an affix that is stranded in T which is unable to combine with the verbal base in the VP. The following examples list the environments in which auxiliary *do* appears:

(73) a. Yes–no questions: (a question requiring a yes–no answer)
          Did you see Romeo and Juliet?
      b. Negative sentences:
          Juliet didn't see Mercutio.
      c. Tag questions: (little tags, glued on to the end of the sentence)
          Romeo knew Tybalt, didn't he?

    d. Wh-questions: (a question involving a question word)
        Who did Juliet see?
    e. VP preposing: (a sentence involving a 'preposed' VP)
        They wanted him to go to the theater, and go to the theatre he did!

VP ellipsis with tensed auxiliaries

Since inflected main verbs are within VP, we expect this to be true for all finite verbs. If this is correct, tensed auxiliaries should behave as being within the VP as well. We can test this by looking at how VP ellipsis affects clauses with finite auxiliaries: if finite auxiliaries distribute like main verbs, *do*-support should apply.

    A VP complement can be silenced under VP ellipsis, as the following examples illustrate:

(74)   Othello was *listening to Iago*, and Emilia was too.

Structure of the main TP: (disregarding *too*)

(75)

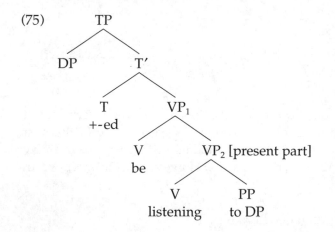

VP ellipsis can target two VPs: the VP containing the auxiliary *be* (VP_1), or its VP complement (VP_2). VP ellipsis of VP_2 does not inform us about the whereabouts of the finite auxiliary, since it results in a remnant that contains VP_1 and T. The finite verb could be either in VP_1 or in T.

(76)   VP ellipsis of VP_2:
      [$_{TP}$ Emilia [[$_{T}$-*s*] [$_{VP1}$be [$_{VP2}$ ~~listening to Iago~~]] too]]

VP ellipsis of VP_1, however, is informative, because it would result in a string with a stranded affix. This should trigger *do*-support to save the stranded tense morpheme. It turns out that *do*-support is in fact impossible:

(77)   VP ellipsis of VP:
[$_{TP}$ Emilia [[$_{T}$-*ed*] [$_{VP1}$be-[$_{VP2}$ ~~listening to Iago~~]] too]]
do-support:
[$_{TP}$ Emilia [$_{T}$[do+ed]] [$_{VP1}$be [$_{VP2}$ ~~listening to Iago~~]] too]]
Output:
*Othello was listening to Iago, and Emilia did too.

The output that would result if auxiliary verbs distribute in the same way as auxiliaries is ill-formed! If VP ellipsis is applied to a sentence with a finite auxiliary, the remnant must contain a finite form of that auxiliary.

This shows that while finite main verbs are in the VP, finite auxiliaries are outside the VP, in T.

We conclude:

(78)   a.   FINITE FORMS OF *HAVE* AND *BE* ARE IN TENSED T.
b.   FINITE FORMS OF MAIN VERBS ARE IN VP.

This allows for a simple and elegant account of the data that we have observed, and finds further empirical support. Whatever VP is deleted (the complement VP (VP$_2$), or VP$_1$ containing the auxiliary), the remnant will contain a finite auxiliary, since the auxiliary has raised to T to combine with the tense morpheme, and is therefore outside of all VPs.

(79)

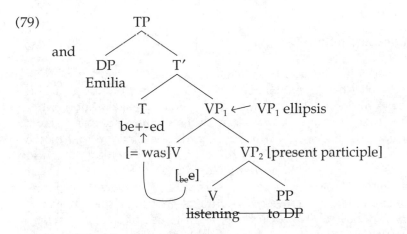

Why do finite *have* and *be* end up outside VP? *Have* and *be* undergo movement from the V position within the VP complement of the tensed T to T. That is, *have* and *be* raise to the head that selects for them. This movement is sometimes referred to as *have* and *be* raising. *Have* and *be* raising is a particular instantiation of V-movement (Verb-movement). V-movement itself is a specific instantiation of a more general process affecting heads, called head movement. Head movement expresses co-occurrence restrictions between head positions. The structure above shows that *was* satisfies

SIDEBAR 5.6

Morphology and syntax

We started with the assumption, familiar from traditional grammar and ingrained in the way we view languages, that words are the building blocks of syntax, and morphemes the building blocks of morphology. Yet we now have strong evidence that at least some morphemes are syntactic building blocks, that some word formation is done in the syntax, and that some syntactic building blocks are silent heads. We have seen that both morphology and syntax use the same building blocks – heads. These can have different phonological properties (they can be free, bound, or even silent). Heads select for the category of their complements. Both words and phrases encode head–complement relations. In morphology the complement precedes the head; in syntax it follows. In both syntax and morphology, the head of the constituent determines the property of the word or phrase as a whole.

   These facts raise questions. How is a language learner to decide if some morpheme is a syntactic head or not? Some linguists assume that inflectional morphemes are part of the syntactic component, while derivational morphemes are part of a morphological component. Other linguists argue that these facts cast doubts on the view that there are two separate components in grammars – syntax and morphology – each with its own rules or principles. The evidence discussed above seems to suggest that both syntax and morphology are part of the same rule system.

SIDEBAR 5.7

On intuition and the notion 'word'

Chapter 2 opened with the question 'What is a word?' It turns out to be surprisingly difficult, maybe even impossible, to give a definition of this seemingly simple notion. It was assumed that native speakers know what words are. However, we don't know what systems native speakers access when they decide such and such a string is a word. One criterion that native speakers use is whether a certain string can be uttered in isolation or not, so they would consider the determiner *that* a word, and *unfair* a word but not the prefix *un*. There are also many cases where speakers simply don't know what to decide. In these cases, spelling conventions – putting a space between individual words – may solve this problem, but the use of spaces between words is arbitrary, as shown in chapter 2 in the discussion of compounds. These spelling conventions may help us in playing a game like Scrabble, where for example *into* would be accepted as a word but *in front of* would not, or *people's* (e.g. *people's minds*) is not an acceptable Scrabble word, yet *its* (*its importance*) is, although both are possessive forms. Speakers seem to access more than one type of system in deciding what a word is, basing their conclusions, not only on the basis of linguistic facts, but on the basis of knowledge of another system, which itself encodes arbitrary criteria such as where spelling conventions place spaces. This means that it is unclear if native speakers' responses reflect the linguistic system in this regard.

We can further illustrate how spelling conventions influence native speakers' conceptions about what a word is, with the help of Swahili and Kalanga, two Bantu languages spoken in Eastern and Southern Africa respectively.

As discussed in chapter 2, Swahili verbs are complex. The same holds for Kalanga. The initial part of the verbal complex in a tensed declarative clause corresponds to the following template: SA = subject agreement, T = tense, OA = object agreement, M* stands for postverbal suffixes that are irrelevant here, FV for a final vowel that partly indicates clause type (indicative versus subjunctive/negative):

(i) (a) (neg) SA (NEG)-T-(OA)-V-M*-FV   (Swahili)
     (b)   SA (NEG) T (OA)-V-M-FV   (Kalanga)

In standard Swahili orthography, this sequence is written as a single word. In Kalanga, SA and T are written as individual words:

(ii) Romeo anampenda Juliet.   (Swahili orthography)
      Romeo a- na-   m- pend-a Juliet
      Romeo SA present-OA-love- FV Juliet
      'Romeo loves Juliet'

(iii) Romeo u no   da   Juliet.   (Kalanga orthography)[1]
       Romeo SA present love+FV Juliet
       'Romeo loves Juliet'

Speakers of Swahili are shocked by the Kalanga convention and typically react with: "These elements are not words, why do you write them as words?" Conversely, speakers of Kalanga are shocked by the Swahili convention, and react: "Why do you want to say that these form one word with the V?" Linguistically speaking, the morphemes which are written as forming a single word with the following verb in Swahili and written as independent words in Kalanga do not seem to behave differently. In people's minds they do, because of the writing system. The notion 'word' is thus not a simple concept, particularly since we seem to be unable to depend on speakers' intuitions as evidence.

two properties: the property of being a V (*be*) and the property of carrying past tense (*was*). These properties are located in different structural positions. Movement is a way to express more than one syntactic property. A given element often has to play one kind of role, defined by the verb in the VP, and simultaneously a separate role, independent of the verb, defined by some other layer in the tree.

5.1.7 The position of main verbs and auxiliaries in the clausal structure

There is additional distributional evidence (internal to English) that supports the different positions that finite auxiliaries and finite main verbs occupy in the syntactic structure. Finite auxiliaries occur in T, finite main verbs in VP.

Not

Finite auxiliaries occur in a different position from main verbs in negative tensed sentences containing *not/n't*. Finite forms of the auxiliaries *have*, *be* and *do* must precede *not* (and *n't*), non-finite forms of the auxiliaries follow *not*:

(80)   a.   She *has not* / *hasn't* climbed the mountain yet   Vf(aux) n't
       b.   You *were not* / *weren't* being followed   Vf(aux) n't
       c.   He *won't have* climbed the mountain yet   n't V$_{inf(aux)}$

This follows if *not* occurs between T and VP. Finite auxiliaries precede *not/ n't* simply because T precedes negation, and finite auxiliaries are in T.

(81)

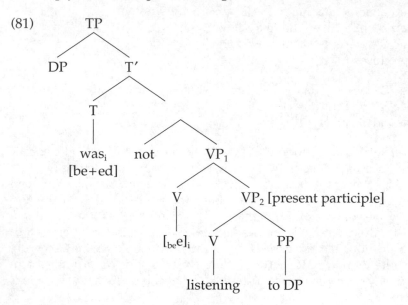

Non-finite auxiliaries follow *not*, for the simple reason that the VP that contains them follows *not*. From this perspective, it is surprising that *not* cannot precede finite main verbs (82a), since these are in VP. Instead the tensed inflection shows up on the auxiliary *do* (82b). Main verbs cannot precede *not* (82c) simply because main Vs are never in T (88):

(82)   a.   *Othello not watched Bianca.
       b.   Othello *didn't*/did not watch Bianca.
       c.   *Othello *watched* n't/not Bianca.

What must be explained, then, is why (82a) yields an ungrammatical English sentence. If the tense suffix and the main verb cannot combine in this

SIDEBAR
5.8

Historical change

English at the time of Shakespeare was different: it did allow main tensed verbs in T (and in the VP as we can see since it also allowed *do*-support). This raises the question as to what changed from Shakespeare's grammar to the grammar of a modern English. It looks as if V to T movement was lost for main verbs. Why was it lost? What changed in the grammar? The intuition that is generally pursued is that this loss is directly related to the erosion of the verbal inflections in the history of English, in particular the loss of person and number marking on the finite verb, that is, the expression of agreement features. English went from a system with person and number (plural) marking (= agreement) on the verb to a system where only third-person singular is expressed, and verbs no longer distinguish between singular and plural forms (with the exception of the verb *be*). Many linguists believe that languages must have 'rich' enough agreement systems to allow finite V in T: earlier stages of English had rich agreement in the relevant sense, modern English has not.

particular configuration, the tense morpheme will be stranded in T, and *do*-support must rescue the stranded tense morpheme. Hence the following generalization:

(83)   The tense suffix and main verb cannot combine over negation
       not/n't.

It is the task of linguistic theory to explain why the tense suffix and the main verb cannot get together in the configuration. Discussion of this issue is beyond the scope of this chapter.

You might also wonder why (82c) – *Othello watched not Bianca* – is impossible in modern English: this pattern was once possible, in Shakespearean times (in Shakespeare, the modern English pattern with *do*-support is also possible):

(84)   a.   *Othello reads not books   (Modern English)
       b.   *I know not how I lost him   (Modern English)
       c.   I know not how I lost him   (Shakespeare, *Othello*, IV, ii, 151)

Distribution of adverbials
Certain adverbials can intervene between T and the main V in English:

(85)   a.   Olivia will probably leave   T Adv V(inf)
            tomorrow.
       b.   You must recently have read   T Adv V(past participle)
            Macbeth.

c. Emilia was carefully slicing   T Adv V(present participle)
    the salmon.
d. The invaders were completely   T Adv V(present participle)
    destroying the fort.
e. Portia was intentionally   T Adv V(present participle)
    confronting Shylock.

When the main verb is inflected, these adverbs precede the main verb:

(86) a. Olivia probably left yesterday.   Adv V+T
      b. You recently read Macbeth.   Adv V+T
      c. Emilia carefully sliced the salmon.   Adv V+T
      d. The invaders completely destroyed the fort. Adv V+T
      e. Portia intentionally confronted Shylock.   Adv V+T

This is exactly what is expected if these adverbs are in pre-VP position, and main inflected verbs are within the VP.

(87)

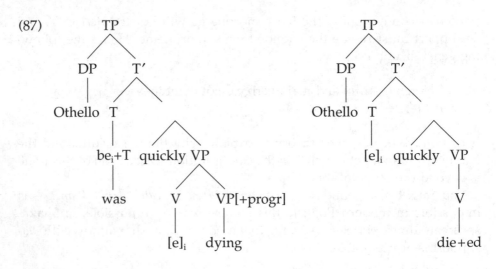

The word order of adverbs with respect to finite auxiliaries and finite main verbs again provides evidence for the different positions these elements fill.

Yes–no questions: Subject–Aux Inversion

English yes–no questions (a type of question that can be answered by yes or no) come in different forms, depending on whether they are matrix yes–no questions or embedded yes–no questions. Matrix yes–no questions start with either a modal, or a finite auxiliary (*have*, *be* or *do*):

(88) a. *Has* Othello died?
      b. *Is* Othello dying?
      c. *Did* Othello die?

Embedded yes–no questions start with a particular C (complementizer), either *if* or *whether*:

(89) a. I wonder *if* Othello died quickly.
      b. I wonder *whether* Othello died quickly.

In matrix yes–no questions T and the subject are inverted, with T preceding the subject DP. This phenomenon is referred to as **Subject–Aux-(iliary) Inversion**. In embedded yes–no questions, the subject precedes T, as in the clause types we have seen so far. Subject–Aux Inversion applies in a number of contexts in English (yes–no questions, wh-questions, environments starting with a negative item (*Never would I say such a sentence!*) and exclamative sentences (*Does Falstaff ever drink a lot!*). We restrict discussion here to yes–no questions.

What, precisely, is Subject–Aux inversion? There are two ways to conceive of Subject–Aux Inversion in structural terms: either the subject moves to a position after T or, alternatively, T moves to a position in front of the subject. It appears that the latter is the right description. We have already seen several times that there is a dependency relation between C and T: C selects values of T. Thus, the C (*that*) selects for a TP headed by +T, and the C (*for*) for a TP headed by *to*. On the one hand, Subject–Aux Inversion cannot apply when there is an overt complementizer present in the C node, as in the examples below:

(90) a. *I wonder *if did* Othello die quickly.
      b. *I wonder *did if* Othello die quickly.
      c. *I wonder *whether did* Othello die quickly.
      d. *I wonder *did whether* Othello die quickly.

On the other hand, Subject–Aux Inversion MUST apply in matrix yes–no questions, when there is no lexical material present in the C node. The lexical complementizer *if/whether* and the inverted T are therefore in **complementary distribution**, that is, as pointed out in the preceding chapter, where one occurs, the other does not. Yes–no questions are headed either by a complementizer, or by a finite auxiliary. Thus, this suggests that the lexical complementizer and the moved T are competing for the same syntactic position: the C position preceding the subject DP. If either of them occupies the C position, you can have one or the other, but not both. We can capture the complementary distribution if T obligatorily moves to the C position in matrix yes–no questions, but does not need to do so in embedded questions, because the C position is already occupied by a lexical item. The tree structures below illustrate this discussion: (91) represents the structure of main clause yes–no questions (91a) and embedded yes–no questions (91b) in sentences with tensed auxiliaries; (91a) also encodes the movement of *have* to T, and of T to C. In (91b) *has* does not move to C position because this position contains *if*.

(91)   Yes–no questions with tensed auxiliaries:

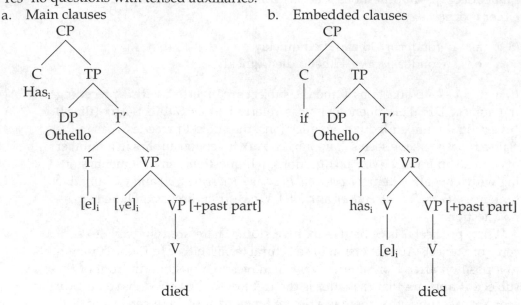

a.   Main clauses
b.   Embedded clauses

The structures in (92) represent main clause yes–no questions (92a) and embedded yes–no questions (92b), in sentences with finite main verbs. (92a) also encodes the movement of the tense morpheme to the C position. *Do*-support applies to the stranded tense morpheme in (92a), affix-hopping to the T morpheme in (92b). T to C movement does not take place in (92b) because the C position already contains *if*.

(92)   Yes–no questions with finite main verbs:

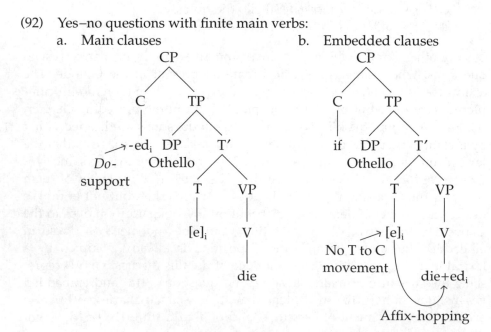

a.   Main clauses
b.   Embedded clauses

The C level: properties of individual complementizers

The property that distinguishes a question from a declarative clause is located in the C position, as the following examples show:

(93) a. Othello thought THAT Desdemona lied.
     b. Othello wondered IF Desdemona lied.

The C node expresses clause type. We can add C[+Q] (Q for question) to the inventory of Cs, which already includes the C[+Decl] (Decl for declarative). A CP with a C+Q head is interpreted as a question, a CP with a +Decl head is interpreted as a declarative. Both C heads have different realizations depending on whether they occur in matrix or embedded contexts:

(94)
	Matrix	Embedded
C[+Q]	0	if, whether
C[+decl]	0	that

The C+Q head and the C+Decl head differ: the C+Q head in English always ends up with some lexical material; either it attracts the content of T in matrix clauses, or it contains a special C in embedded complements. The C+Q head thus seems to have an additional property: it 'detests' silence. It must make itself heard. The declarative C has no such requirement: it can contain overt material or not. In this way, C+Q behaves very similarly to a silent bound morpheme: it needs to be attached to some lexical material. Let us state this as follows:

(95)   C, +Q must contain overt lexical material.

(95) is satisfied in the structures in (96a) and (96b), as indicated by the happy faces, but not in (96c), as indicated by the unhappy face.

(96)   a.   b.

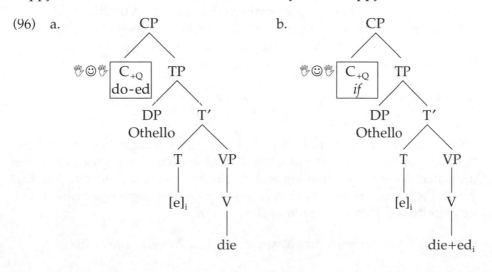

c. *

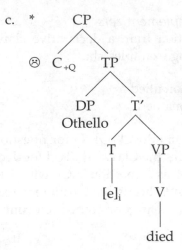

In other words, since main questions do not have an overt complement-izer, the C node must be made lexical in some other way. This is achieved using the lexical items that are already present in the clause, i.e. by attract-ing to C one of the elements which may appear in the head position of the complement position of Q: i.e. a modal (*must, may, might . . .*), a raised tensed auxiliary (*have* or *be*), or a tense suffix.

Why main Vs fail to move to +Q

An interesting question arises: Why cannot the main verb itself appear in C to rescue the suffix? This would result in the ungrammatical modern English sentence, although, as with negation, this was possible in Shake-speare's time:

(97) a. *Comes he tomorrow?   (Modern English)
     b. Talk you of killing?   (Shakespeare, *Othello*, V, ii, 33)

We already saw that English main verbs cannot occur in T (**he comes not*). We now see that main verbs cannot appear in C [+Q] either, although this position may host other verbal elements (*do, have* and *be*, and *modals*). We thus have the descriptive statements below:

(98) a. Main verbs cannot appear in T[+T].
     b. Main verbs cannot appear in C[+Q].

One might question as to whether there is a relation between these two statements, with one following from the other, or whether they are unrelated. When encountering statements such as these in our lab, the general research strategy is always to suppose that there is a relation. Let us hypothesize that (98b) follows from (98a).

(99)   Since a main verb cannot appear in T, it cannot appear in C.

We can explain why (99) holds if V cannot move directly to C, +Q, and if the main V must transit through T on its way to C+Q. Since main V to T is impossible in English, main V to C is impossible as well, because main V to T is a prerequisite for further movement to C. Thus, the question *Died Othello?* is ungrammatical, because the main verb cannot move to T to pick up the tense morpheme, as depicted in the tree in (100):

(100)

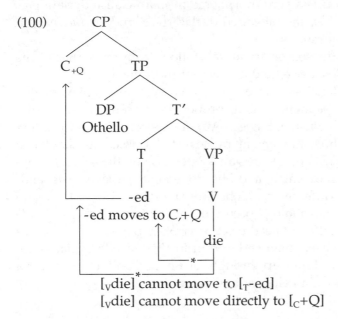

[_Vdie] cannot move to [_T-ed]
[_Vdie] cannot move directly to [_C+Q]

This shows an important property of head movement; movement proceeds by taking only small steps: from a head position in a complement position to the selecting head (V to T to C). Apparent long-distance relations should be undone in small locally defined steps. If you decide to study more syntax, you will see that undoing apparent long-distance dependencies into short steps is a property not just of head movement, but of movement relations in general.

5.1.8 Summary of distribution of English verbs

We now have a detailed fragment of English syntax concerning the distribution of verbs. From this fragment, we learned the following about English syntax, and syntax in general:

- Words, silent morphemes and (at least) some inflectional morphemes (tense/agreement) constitute the input to syntax.
- Words are organized into constituents, according to a specific design which imposes a hierarchical structure on heads and the element they c-select.

- The head–complement relation regulates the distribution of verbal forms (verbal forms are selected by particular heads), and forms the backbone of syntactic representations.
- Different clause types have similar internal make-up.
- The property that identifies particular clause types (declarative clause, main or matrix clause, question, . . .) is located at the C level. Depending on the context, C is a zero morpheme in main clause declaratives and questions; C is *that* in embedded declaratives, and *whether* or *if* in embedded yes-no questions.
- Different TP types (tensed or infinitival) follow from properties of the T head (–T = *to*, +T = tense (and agreement morphemes)).
- There exist dependencies between positions. We have looked at one particular type of dependency and its properties: head movement (affix-hopping, *have* and *be* raising, Subject–Aux Inversion). Head movement is in fact one of three movement processes discussed in chapter 4: wh-movement (movement towards an XP position on the CP level) topicalization and wh-movement, and NP movement (passives). Dependencies between the different positions must be local.
- (Some) inflectional morphology occurs in the syntax.
- Main verbs occupy different head positions from auxiliaries and modals in tensed clauses. Tensed main verbs occur in VP, tensed auxiliaries are in T. This difference shows up throughout English and accounts for a number of differences in behavior and word order.

5.2 Cross-Linguistic Variation: Beyond English

The theory of syntax constrains the grammars of all human languages. Support for a particular theory or hypothesis of the theory will come from how well it accounts for all languages. This is of course a major task, comparable to discovering the major laws in the physical or biological sciences. In this section, we show some results concerning the study of Complementizer, Tense, and Verb, which were discussed in the earlier sections in relation to English. The evidence strongly supports the view that, despite the initial impression that languages are overwhelmingly different, cross-linguistic syntactic variation might in fact be restricted. The analyses of individual languages presented below are not as detailed as the analysis presented for English. They are presented to illustrate specific points, and to reveal these universal characteristics.

5.2.1 The nature of linguistic variation

On the basis of the theory discussed so far, we expect to find the following in all human languages:

Table 5.2   Types of Heads

	+OVERT	−OVERT
+free	[$_N$woman], [$_D$that], [$_P$in], [$_A$big], [$_V$come], [$_T$to], etc.	$C_{,+Decl,+matrix}$
−free	[$_N$ness], [$_A$able], [$_V$ize], [$_T$ed]	$C_{,+Q}$
		V [[$_N$butter[$_V$e]]]

HEADS (= morphemes)

These are the building blocks of syntactic structures. We expect heads representing major lexical categories (N, V, A, P) and heads representing functional categories (T, C, Q, . . .); heads can be pronounced (= associated with overt material) or silent. And, as we saw in chapter 1, morphemes can be free or bound, and thus heads can be free or bound as further illustrated in table 5.2.

STRUCTURE

Structure is the result of projecting heads; structural relations are local head–complement relations, and Spec–head relations.

MOVEMENT

An instance of co-occurrence restrictions between positions. So far, we have seen that DPs and heads may occur in positions where they do not satisfy local head–complement relations. Consider the following example:

(102)   *What$_i$ has*$_T$ Juliet [$_T$e]$_T$[$_V$e]$_t$said [$_{DP}$e]$_i$

The wh-phrase *what* (a so-called question word because of its morphological make-up), simultaneously fulfills the requirement of having a local relation to V within the VP (the who-did-what-to-whom domain) and with the position (Spec, CP) where it is pronounced. It acts as if it were simultaneously occupying two positions. The finite auxiliary encodes two structural properties: it is a V which demands a past participle complement, and it is tensed. In addition it shows up in the C, +Q position, which indicates that the CP is a question. These properties are structurally represented at different levels. The property of being a verb with a particular type of complement is expressed at the VP level, that of being tensed, at the T level. It satisfies a property of the C+Q at the CP level, where it is 'pronounced.'

5.2.2 Language variation and parameters

What follows is a discussion of the extent to which languages can and do vary, exemplified by an examination of heads, structure and movement.

Heads

Languages obviously vary with respect to the spell-out (pronunciation) of their morphemes (e.g. a 'horse' is *horse* in English, *paard* in Dutch, *cheval* in French), and their nature as bound or free forms (*will* (future T) is a free form in English, but a bound form in French: *parler-ai*: '(I) will speak'). Languages also vary with respect to the category they c-select. English *look* c-selects for a PP headed by *at*, French *regarder* ('look, watch') c-selects for a DP. We state this as follows:

(103) LEXICAL VARIATION IS A SOURCE OF LANGUAGE VARIATION
(where lexical variation includes variation in spell-out (form), variation as to the bound or free status of heads, and variation with respect to c-selection).

Structure

It is not easy to determine whether languages vary in their structural make-up. We will restrict the discussion here to word-order variations. In the preceding sections, we have seen that different surface word-order patterns in English (C, T, V) are accounted for by the position in the sentence in which the items are pronounced. Below we provide additional evidence for this view.

   Languages vary in their surface word-order possibilities (as we saw earlier, the majority of languages fall into three language types (SVO, SOV, VSO,) . . .). How should these variations be accounted for? As we have seen, syntactic theory requires heads and complements to be in a local relation. However, there are two ways to satisfy this locality requirement. The head can be ordered before the complement (as in English), or after the complement. These two possibilities immediately yield VO and OV languages, as the structures in (105) illustrate:

(104) E=English, T=Turkish:
       Romeo wanted to kiss Juliet *(E)*
       Romeo Juliet-i   öp-mek iste-di (T)
       Romeo Juliet-acc kiss-inf want-past

We will build up the English and Turkish representations for (104) in (105). These structures have been somewhat simplified. They do not show all Spec positions or all projections, but only those that have some overt material in them. For convenience, heads, complements and Specs are annotated on the tree as subscripts (h, c, spec).

(105)   General schema: (English)   General schema: (Turkish)

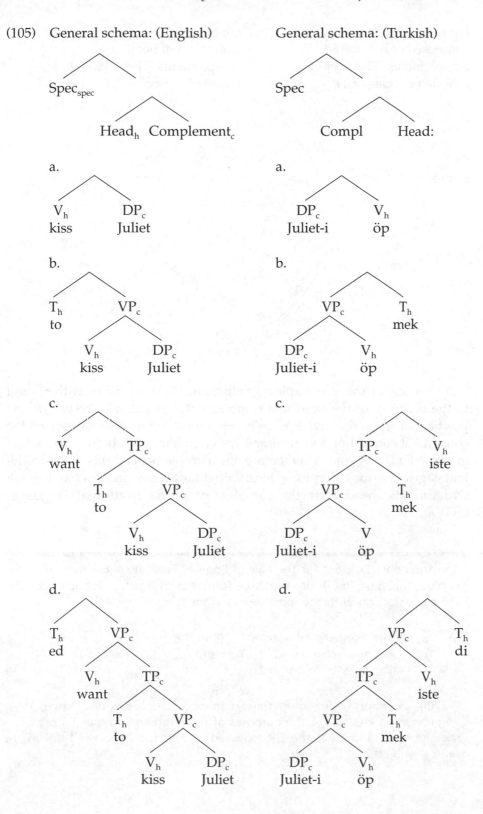

Up to this point, the tree is composed of heads and complements. The subject is added as Spec of TP

Up to this point, the tree is composed of heads and complements. The subject is added as Spec of TP

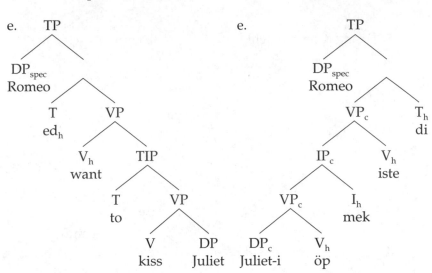

As we see in these examples, English and Turkish differ with respect to the ordering of the head and complement, but not with respect to the position of the structural Spec. The Spec position is ordered before the constituent containing the head and the complement in both types of languages. Ordering the head before the complement yields **head-initial** languages (the major types of head-initial languages are VSO and SVO). Ordering the head after the complement yields **head-final** languages (SOV).

EXERCISE 5.5

Construct parallel trees for the pair of English, Turkish sentences in (i) and English, Japanese in (ii). Use the same format as in figure 5.1, and build up the trees starting with the most deeply embedded constituent.

(i) (a) Juliet went to the theater   (English)
     (b) Juliet tiyatro-ya git-ti   (Turkish)
          Juliet theater-to go-past

For the examples in (ii), treat the Japanese *kiss do* as equivalent to the English *give a kiss to*. For the purposes of this exercise you may ignore the case markers, and treat the DP followed by the topic marker (top) as a regular subject.

> (ii) (a) I think that Juliet gave a kiss to Romeo
>   (b) watashi wa Jurietto ga Romio ni kisu shita to   omo-u
>   I   top Juliet nom Romeo to kiss did   that think-nonpast
>
> Examine your trees. In which ways do the English–Turkish, English–Japanese, and Turkish–English trees differ?

Since head–complement relations are expressed locally in all languages, it seems that this is part of the universal grammar we are all endowed with. Language variation can be described as to which subtree is chosen to express the local relation between a complement and a head: is the head initial or final? Children learning a particular language will have to decide in some way if the language they are learning is head-initial or head-final. Options available to the language learner are called **parameters**. Parameters must be set. That is, the language learner has to decide which value the parameter takes based on the language he hears around him: (head left? head right?). This particular parameter is called the **head-initial/head-final parameter**.

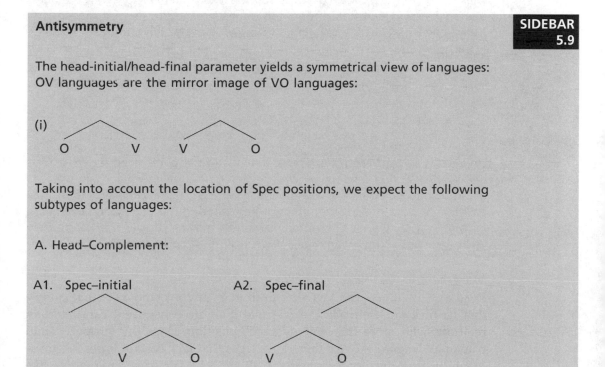

Antisymmetry   SIDEBAR
                                                                    5.9

The head-initial/head-final parameter yields a symmetrical view of languages: OV languages are the mirror image of VO languages:

(i)

        O   V   V   O

Taking into account the location of Spec positions, we expect the following subtypes of languages:

A. Head–Complement:

A1. Spec–initial   A2. Spec–final

            V   O   V   O

B. Complement–Head:

B1.　Spec–initial　　　　　　　　　B2.　Spec–final
　　a.　　　　　　　　　　　　　　　　b.

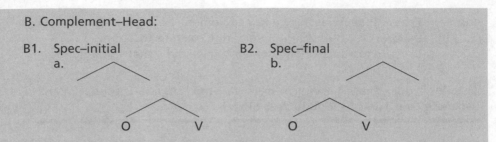

O　　　　　V　　　　　　　　　O　　　　　V

The symmetrical view of syntax leads one to expect languages with Spec positions on the right (type A2 and B2). How can we tell where Spec positions are located? By looking at elements that typically occur in Spec positions. We have seen that subjects are in Spec positions (Spec, TP) and that moved wh-phrases occur in a Spec position (Spec, CP). The distribution of subjects and moved wh-phrases can thus help locate Spec positions. It turns out that subjects and wh-phrases overwhelmingly occur towards the left edge of the clause, pointing to Spec–initial orders. Thus, the predicted language types (A2 and B2) seem to be extremely rare. The symmetrical view of syntax leads one to expect a symmetrical distribution of phenomena across languages. Since this does not seem to be the case, the symmetrical view might simply be incorrect: the grammar does not leave any options other than A1 and B1. In *The Antisymmetry of Syntax*, Richard Kayne (1994) has challenged the symmetrical view and proposes instead that all languages have identical underlying orders (A1, the Spec-head-complement order, is the only one available). Head-final orders are derived through leftward movement from head-initial structures, yielding the two types of languages A1 and B1:

A1.　　　　　　　　　　　　　　　　B1.

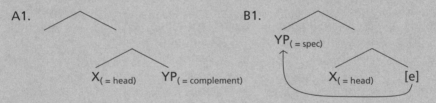

X$_{(= head)}$　　YP$_{(= complement)}$　　　　　　X$_{(= head)}$　　[e]

Under this view, there is no head-initial/head-final parameter; whether the head is final or not depends on whether leftward movement has taken place or not. Syntactic structures are always 'oriented' in the same way, and the problem of word-order variation must be related to the theory of movement in some way (why does the complement in B1 move to a Spec position to the left of the head in B1 languages, but not in A1 languages?).

Movement

We have discussed the fact that grammars involve movement relations, that is, they must encode the fact that a single constituent can entertain relations with more than one syntactic position. Does this property hold true of all languages? Are there languages that lack certain types of movement or that disallow movement altogether? In some languages, like Japanese, wh-phrases occur in the same positions where DPs appear (this is referred to as **wh-in-situ**). In other languages, like English, wh-phrases must appear in a particular structural position (Spec, CP). This is illustrated in the following examples of Japanese and English. The underlining in the gloss and the numbers under the gloss help you read the Japanese example; follow the numbers in ascending order and you will get to the English sentence in (106b) (you can ignore the grammatical markers: top is a topic marker; nom, dat, gen are case markers, past is past tense and Q is a question particle):

(106)   a.   Japanese: wh-in-situ.
            watasi wa Jurietto ga sono gekijoo de nan no   eiga o
            <u>I</u>   top <u>Juliet nom</u> <u>the theater</u>   to <u>what gen movie acc</u>
                 1   4   6   3
            mi-ta   ka kik-ta
            <u>see-past</u> Q <u>ask-past</u>
                 5   2

       b.   English: wh to Spec, CP.
            I asked [what movie Juliet saw [e] in the theater]
            *I asked if Juliet saw what movie

The wh-phrase in Japanese occurs where a Japanese object would: in front of the tensed verb *mitta*, 'saw'. Japanese uses a particular Q complementizer (*ka*) which occurs in the same position as other Japanese Cs (clause finally). In English, the wh-phrase is in Spec, CP, and is in complementary distribution with the Q complementizer, *if*. Presumably the Japanese and English wh-questions have the same semantic interpretations. Apart from basic word order, they differ solely in whether the wh-phrase moves or not. This is stated in the descriptive statement in (107):

(107)   WH-PHRASES IN ENGLISH MOVE TO SPEC, CP.
        WH-PHRASES IN JAPANESE DON'T MOVE TO SPEC, CP.

Does Language X move wh-phrase or not?
It is the task of linguistic theory to explain the Japanese–English difference. What does it tell us about the grammar? Is it restricted to wh-phrases, or does it correlate with other areas of Japanese and English grammar? We can construe it narrowly as a parameter concerning wh-phrases, which must be set when children acquire their language:

(108)   **Wh-phrase parameter:**
        Move wh-phrase to CP: yes/no

Setting the value to 'yes' yields English, setting it to 'no' yields Japanese. Could (108) reflect a broader generalization concerning the presence or absence of movement? (108) would follow if movement itself could be 'parametrized', and thus could be simply completely absent in a particular language, but present in another one. If that were true, English would represent the setting of the parameter of a grammar with movement, Japanese of a grammar without movement. This hypothesis turns out to be incorrect. There are many other constructions in Japanese that involve movement (i.e. one single constituent which has a relation to more than one syntactic position). A substantial body of research in syntax strongly suggests that there are no languages that lack that movement altogether. Movement thus appears to be a fundamental property of the system of human language, just as structure is.

Structure and movement are fundamental properties of the syntax of human languages. Language variation is associated with specific heads (lexical parameters), and parameters associated with word order (head-initial/head-final).

5.2.3   C, T, and V across languages

Since DPs and heads may have co-occurrence restrictions with other positions, we need to apply tests to find out where in the structure specific elements are pronounced. In the previous sections, we equipped our syntax lab with some tests and tools for this purpose, developed on the basis of an examination of English. We now take other languages to our lab, and try to determine the position of different verbal forms. The VP ellipsis test was informative as to the position of main verbs and auxiliaries in English. Examination of English word order provided further insight into the distribution of finite verbs/auxiliaries/non-finite verbs. These have different positions with respect to elements with fixed positions within the sentence (negation and adverbs). We must thus examine the order of the different verbal forms and verbal classes in the language in question. We furthermore saw that we must examine the position of the finite verb/auxiliary with respect to the subject, for example in questions. Again, this means that in the language in question we must do the same. Finally, we must determine if an inflected verb can co-occur with a lexical complementizer.

We can formulate the following research questions which will guide us in investigating the distribution of verbal forms:

- Does the language have VP ellipsis? If it does, do inflected verbs disappear in VP ellipsis contexts? How do finite and non-finite verbs distribute? Is there a difference in the distribution of auxiliaries/modals and main verbs?
- Sentential negation (of the English kind). Where do the different verbal forms occur with respect to negation in different clause types?

- Adverbs. Where do finite verbs/auxiliaries occur with respect to certain adverbials that appear to have rather fixed positions within the clause?
- What position does the finite verb/auxiliary occupy with respect to the DP in subject position in different types of clauses? Does it precede? Does it follow?
- Can an inflected verb co-occur with a lexical complementizer (C) or not?

English (E) and French (F)

We will first examine English and French. Since there is no VP ellipsis in French, we directly turn to word order.

Consider the following English and French sentences illustrating the ordering of pre-VP adverbials and finite verbs. (The English translations are literal translations of the French examples.)

(109) a. Romeo *carefully*   *words*   his letters   (E: *Adv-finite main V*)

      b. *Roméo soigneusement formule ses lettres

(110) a. *Romeo words *carefully*   his letters

      b. Roméo *formule soigneusement* ses lettres   (F: *Finite main V-Adv*)

As these examples illustrate, the respective ordering between the adverbial and a tensed main verb in English is *Adv-finite main V*, but *finite main V+T -Adv* in French. Adverbs occur between T and VP. The finite main verb in English is within the VP, hence the order Adv V+T. The finite verb cannot be within T, and therefore cannot precede the adverb (110a). If French finite main verbs have the same distribution as finite English auxiliaries, the pattern follows:

(111) English: $[_{TP}DP \; [_T e]$ Adv $[_{VP} \; [V+T] \quad]$ (E: *Finite main V in VP*)
        French: $[_{TP}NP \; [_T \; V+T]$ Adv $[_{VP} \; [_V e] \quad]$ (F: *Finite main V in tensed T*)

When the sentence contains a finite auxiliary, English and French show the same order:

(112) a. Romeo *has carefully*   worded his letters.   (E: *Finite-AUX-Adv-Participle*)

      b. Roméo *a   soigneusement* formulé ses lettres.   (F: *Finite-AUX-Adv-Participle*)

(113) a. Romeo *is often*   sick.

      b. Jean   *est souvent* malade.

Thus:

(114)   a.   IN FRENCH, FINITE AUXILIARIES AND MAIN VS ARE IN [+T]
        b.   (i)   IN ENGLISH, FINITE AUXILIARIES ARE IN [+T]
             (ii)   IN ENGLISH, FINITE MAIN VERBS ARE IN [+T]

This is a property of all tensed clauses in French, even clauses that do not contain adverbs. Superficially similar sentences in French and English have the verb in different positions ([$_v$e] indicates the original position of V).

(115)   a.   Roméo [$_T$visite] [[$_v$e] ses voisins]
        b.   Romeo [$_T$ e] [visits   his neighbors]

This analysis is further corroborated by negative sentences. As discussed above, the presence of *not* triggers *do*-support in T with main verbs (116a). *Have* and *be* have no trouble raising over *not* (116b). Verbs in French pattern with English auxiliaries: the V raises to T over negation *pas* (116c).

(116)   a.   Romeo *does not* [visit his neighbors]
        b.   Romeo *has not* [[$_v$e] [visited his parents]]
        c.   Roméo ne *visite pas* [[$_v$e] ses voisins]

We thus see that differences in word-order patterns result from the position finite verbs occupy; they are in +T in French, but in V in English. The clausal structure of French and English with respect to T, negation and V is basically identical. The variation is due to the position particular types are verbs occupy within this structure. Thus:

(117)   The position a particular head occupies is one source of language variation.

We turn to a comparison of English and other Germanic languages.

English and Germanic languages

English differs from other Germanic languages. In English main questions (but not in embedded complement clauses), finite auxiliaries, and modals show up in a specific type of C (C[+Q]). This is due to a property of the C+Q head, which must be attached to overt lexical material. In embedded clauses a lexical C (*whether, if*) satisfies the property of C[+Q], and auxiliaries and modals do not move to C (since there is no need to). Thus, we see that T to C movement is basically restricted to matrix clauses (also called **root clauses**, that is, clauses that are not dominated by any other type of head).

Given the differences between French and English, one would expect to find languages with some properties of French and some of English. For example, one might expect to find a language where all finite Vs raise to T as in French, and which also has some particular C (head) which is silent, and requires overt expression just like English C, +Q.

That is, we might expect the existence of the following surface patterns:

(118)   matrix: [[$_c$V$_f$] [DP . . .
        embedded: [[$_c$C] [DP   Vf

In matrix clauses, all finite verbs would raise to the C position. Embedded clauses always have an overt C, with the finite verb remaining in T. This distribution describes the pattern that is characteristic of Germanic languages. In matrix clauses, the finite verb always follows a constituent in first position (the finite verb therefore is in second position in this clause type; this is called **verb-second**). This is illustrated for Dutch below:

(119)   a.   Morgen *gaat* Juliet met   Romeo naar de film
             Tomorrow goes Juliet with Romeo to   the movies
        b.   Ik geloof niet [$_c$*dat* Juliet morgen met Romeo naar de film *gaat*]
             I believe not that Juliet tomorrow with Romeo to the movies
             goes

If the verb always occurs in second position, and if this position is C, it also implies that the initial position of certain types of root clauses in Dutch (say, Spec, CP) must always be filled with some constituent (otherwise the verb would be first!). We will call this phenomenon, **XP first in matrix clauses**, which holds for verb-second languages.

(120)   XP first in matrix clauses:
        Spec, CP (Matrix) must contain an overt constituent.

This has implications for the analysis of simple declarative clauses that start with the subject. If the finite verb in (121) is in C$_{+matrix}$ the subject cannot be in Spec, TP, because it precedes the finite verb.

(121)   a.   Juliet *gaat* morgen   met Romeo naar de film
             Juliet goes tomorrow with Romeo to   the movies
        b.   Ik denk [[$_c$*dat*] Juliet morgen met Romeo naar de film *gaat*]
             I *think* that Juliet tomorrow with Romeo to the movies goes

We can conclude that (120) forces the subject to undergo an extra step of movement in matrix clauses: i.e. the subject DP occupies a different position in (121a) than it does in (121b).

Thus, depending on properties of individual heads, finite verbs are forced to move or not in root contexts (verb-second). Moreover, certain positions that host phrases can impose a similar requirement: they must contain some constituent (XP first in root contexts).

5.2.4 Other languages

So far, a nice picture arises concerning cross-linguistic variation: languages have a similar (C–I–V) architecture. Differences between the languages depend on which position heads or XPs end up in. These in turn are related to properties of individual heads, or of certain structural positions.

The languages examined so far are closely related (Germanic languages and one Romance language). One could argue that this picture is not representative of the way all languages function, but is rather a characteristic of a particular language family, traceable to a common ancestor.

We now turn to some unrelated languages, to strengthen the view that language variation is not due to structural variation in the basic structure (all languages have the same C-T-V structure), but rather to variation in movement (where in the structure are heads or XPs pronounced).

Vata

In some languages, the effects of V movement are not difficult to detect. We illustrate this for Vata, a West African language spoken in the Ivory Coast, belonging to the Kru family of Niger-Congo languages. In Vata, V movement is quite transparent, because it results in word-order differences. All finite clauses, main or embedded, have the order S V XP* or S Aux XP* V. (Vata is a tone language, ˝ refers to high tone, ´ to a mid high, ¯ to mid, and ` to Low. For the representation of other symbols see chapter 11. Do not be concerned if you do not know how to pronounce these examples; that is not important for the purposes of our discussion here. XP* stands for any number of constituents.)

(122) a. ń ɲɛ̃   yɔ́ɔ   slɛ́é   mlí   sákǎ
           I gave+PERF child+the house+the in rice
           'I gave rice to the child, in the house.'
       b. ń kǎ   yɔ́ɔ   slɛ́é   mlí sákǎ ɲɛ́é
           I Fut+AUX child+the house+the in   rice give(inf)
           'I will give rice to the child, in the house.'

Infinitival complements have the order XP* V, indicating a verb-final VP structure (as in (122b)). The position of the main verb is thus different in finite and non-finite clauses. In finite clauses, either a finite verb or an auxiliary occurs after the subject DP, in non-finite clauses the verb is in the

VP. This distribution can be explained if finite verbs and auxiliaries are in finite T, as in French, and non-finite verbs in the VP. No C nodes in Vata have the property of English C+Q, therefore, no inversion is observed,[2] and matrix and embedded complements have essentially the same word orders.

5.2.5 Languages with no visible change in word order: VP ellipsis

In many other languages, the situation is much less transparent. Often word-order criteria of the English or French type do not show anything. For example, the position of finite or non-finite V with respect to negation never varies, nor are there any elements which intervene between C, T, and V. Because of the strictly head-final nature of the projections (not only complements precede, adverbs do too) in strictly head-final languages, like Japanese or Korean for example, no material can intervene between C, T, and V positions (it is noteworthy that these different projections exist however!).

(123)   [[(Adv)[V$_{VP}$] T $_{TP}$] C $_{CP}$]

How do you determine whether the V in the V–T–C hierarchy is located in the VP in T, or in C?

  As shown earlier for English, we will now show that the behavior of Vs under VP ellipsis is a good diagnostic tool to determine the distribution of Vs. We illustrate this for Irish, a VSO language in which verb movement is easy to detect. We then discuss Swahili (Bantu) (SVO), and Korean (SOV), covering the major word-order types.

Irish
Irish, a Celtic language, shows VSO order in both matrix and embedded tensed sentences:

(124)   Dúirt   sé go dtiocfadh   sé
        say(past) he C come(condit) he
        'He said that he would come.'

VSO order is a characteristic property of finite clauses: non-finite clauses show either SVO order (125) or even SOV order (126):[3]

(125)   Bhreathnaigh mé uirthi agus *í   ag imeacht* uaim
        looked   I   on-her and her leave(prog) from-me
        'I watched her as she was leaving me.'

(126)   Níor mhaith liom iad   *a chéile*   *a phósadh*
        I-would-not-like   them each-other marry(inf)
        'I would not like them to marry each other.'

This suggests that the word order in tensed clauses is derived, with the verb in finite clauses moving out of the VP, to some position higher than the subject. As a result of this movement, the subject intervenes between the finite verb and its object.

Is the finite verb located in C or in T? The finite verb cannot be in C, since it co-occurs with the finite complementizer: VSO order is a property of all tensed clauses, main or embedded. Therefore it is in T.

(127)   THE FINITE VERB IN IRISH IS IN T.

This raises the question as to where the subject is; it immediately follows the finite verb and precedes other constituents.

Support for V being outside VP comes from the process of VP ellipsis in Irish. Irish has no words for *yes*, or *no*. To answer a question positively or negatively, a tensed verb must be used by itself:

(128)   *Question*:
        Ar   chuir   tú   isteach air?
        InterC put[PAST] you in   on-it
        'Did you apply for it?'
        Answers:
        Chuir   Níor chuir
        put[PAST]   NEG put[PAST]
        'Yes'   'No'

These structures are comparable to English, *I do* or *I did not* (although they differ in that the subject in the Irish answer must be absent *Chuir mé, 'put I'*). The part that disappeared is understood in the answer. Elliptical sentences occur in roughly the same range of contexts as English VP ellipsis:

(129)   Dúirt mé go gceannóinn   é agus cheannaigh
        said I   C buy[Condit:S1] it and bought
        'I said that I would buy it and I did.'

(130)   A: Chennaigh siad teach
             buy[PAST]   they house
             'They bought a house.'

B: Níor   cheannaigh
    NEG[PAST] bought
    'They did not.'

They are also used to form Tag questions (question fragments tagged on at the end of the sentence, like 'didn't she' in 'She came, didn't she?' or 'did she' in 'She didn't come, did she?').

(131) Chennaigh siad teach, nár   cheannaigh
       bought   they house NEG INTERR c buy[PAST]
       'They bought a house, didn't they?'

Thus, this looks like VP ellipsis, except for the fact that the remnant contains the finite main V! This situation can arise if the V is outside of the constituent on which silence is imposed. Since the V is not within the VP, but in T, it must be pronounced. Note that subjects in Irish must be silent as well, and in this respect they act as if they are inside the elided constituent:

(132) English: they did!   Irish: bought!

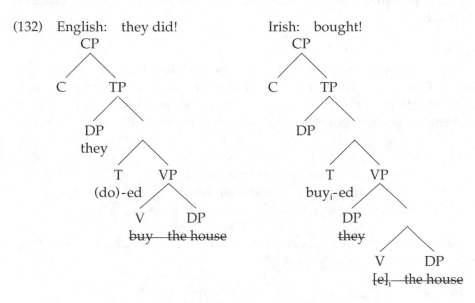

VP ellipsis thus provides an excellent argument for V to T movement in Irish!

English subjects differ from Irish subjects: English subjects are part of the remnant, but Irish subjects are not. Thus, not only verbs can occur in different positions, subject DPs do so as well. This suggests that just as there is more than one structural position for verbs, there is more than one structural position for subjects.

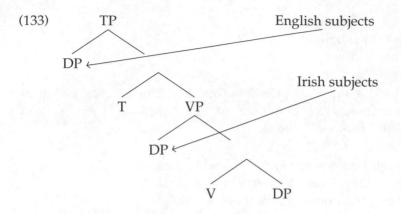

(133)

We can assume that the VP-internal subject position that hosts the subject in Irish is structurally present in English as well. It is not immediately visible upon inspection because English subjects (but not Irish subjects) must be 'pronounced' in Spec TP. There is in fact evidence that this is the correct analysis for English. For example, sometimes a part of the subject DP can be left behind, in which case it shows up in the position where Irish subjects appear (the children have *all* left = all the children have left).

Swahili

We next briefly discuss verb placement in Swahili, a Bantu language, spoken in East Africa. As mentioned in earlier chapters and above, Swahili is an SVO language; the verb occurs in the following position (SA = subject agreement, T = tense marker, OA = object agreement, FV = final vowel):

(134)   SA- T-   OA- V- FV   DP
      a-   na- ya- som-a   (magazeti)
      3s- pres- them-read-a   newspapers
      'He reads the newspapers.'

Where exactly does the V occur in Swahili? Is it within the VP as in English, or is it outside the VP, say in T?

(135)   a. .. $[_T$ na $[_{VP}$ OA+V ...   ]]
      b. .. $[_T$ T +OA+V$_i$+FV] $[_{VP}$ $[_V$e]   ]   ]

Again, this question seems difficult to answer, since the heads always occur in the same order. This is again a configuration in which VP ellipsis can provide an important analytical tool. Swahili turns out to be like English and Irish, in having VP ellipsis. As in English, the subject DP is part of the remnant. As in Irish, the finite verb or infinitival verb is so too (Q = question, numbers represent noun classes, SA = subject agreement, FV is final vowel, INF is infinitival marker):

(136) a. Je, Romeo a- li- tum- a wa-toto soko- ni
        (Q) Romeo 1SA-Past-send-FV 2- child market-Loc
        ku-nunu-a vi-tunguu?
        INF-buy-FV 8-onion
        'Did Romeo send children to the market to buy onions?'
   b. Ndiyo, a -li -tum -a
        Yes, 1SA-Past-send-FV (lit: yes, he send)
        'Yes, he did.'

These data thus establish that the verb is outside VP.[4]

Korean
Korean is an SOV language. The verb occurs in the following environment:

(137) Neg-V-T-C

Like Irish and Swahili, Korean seems to have a process of VP ellipsis. This can be shown by the following examples (SM = subject marker, Decl = declarative marker):

(138) romio-ka culiet-kwa kicaŋ-e ka-ss-ni?
     Romeo SM Juliet-with theater-to go-Past-Q
     'Did Romeo go to the theater with Juliet?'

(139) a. iŋ, ka-ss-ə
        yes, go-Past-Decl (informal) (lit. yes, went)
        'Yes, he did (*go with Juliet to the theater*).'
   b. ani, an ka-ss-ə
        no, Neg go-PAST-Decl (informal) (lit: no, not went)
        'No, he did not (*go with Juliet to the theater*).'

Where in English the main verb disappears under VP ellipsis, and the remaining tense forces *do*-support, the finite verb in Korean is the sole remnant. As in Irish, and in Swahili, this pattern constitutes empirical evidence that V is located outside VP.

Consider the following question and answer pair from Japanese.	**EXERCISE 5.6**

(i) Romio wa tamanegi o kai ni kodomotachi o maaketto ni
   Romeo top onion   acc buy to children   acc market   to
   ik-ase-ta   ka
   go-causative-past Q
   'Did Romeo send (= make go) children to the market to buy onions?'

(ii) Hai, ik-ase-ta
   yes, go-caus-past (lit: yes, send)
   'Yes, he did' (meaning: he sent the children to the market to buy onions)

Discuss in one paragraph what these data show about the position of the verb in Japanese. You may treat *ik-ase* as English *send*.

5.2.6 Further extensions. The noun system: DP

We shall be much less extensive in our discussion of linguistic variation in the noun system. Just like clauses, DPs come in different kinds as well: as definite (or specific) DPs (*the men*, *these women*), quantified DPs (*two men*, *every man*), generic DPs (*people*) etc. We can consider D as being the head of an NP, i.e. as determining what kind of DP we are dealing with. In this section, we simply want to establish that the same patterns of variation discussed in the verb system can be encountered in the noun system as well. Let us start with English and French again, and consider the examples in (140):

(140)   a.   the frequent visits to his parents   (E)
        b.   les visites fréquentes à ses parents   (F)

The order difference here is parallel to the difference we observed in the clausal structures in (109) and (110). In English the noun *visits* is next to its complement ('to his parents'), and the adjective precedes the N. In French, the noun is further to the left. It is separated from its complement *à ses parents* by the adjective. We can analyze this difference in terms of a leftward movement of the noun in French, crossing the adjective to a higher position in the DP structure. Clearly, the position to which movement has taken place here is not the position of D. This is because there is also an overt occurrence of a determiner, *les*, and also because in French a numeral (like two or three) would intervene between the noun and the determiner. This is an indication for the presence of some further functional category, in between D and N. Potentially this position is number. Thus, we have the structure for nominal phrases as in (141) where NumP denotes number. The N moves to Num in French, but not in English:

(141)

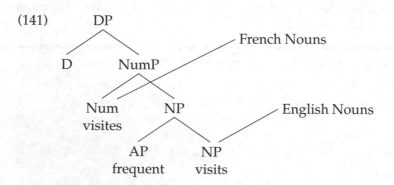

Further movement of the noun to D may also be encountered. Consider the following examples from Hebrew:

(142)   a.   ha-bayit el ha-mora
            the-house of the-teacher
        b.   beit ha-mora
            house the-teacher = the teacher's house

In (142a), the head noun of the construction is preceded by the determiner *ha*, while the possessor relation of *ha-mora* is marked with the preposition *el* 'of'. In (142b), the so-called construct state, we see no overt determiner, and the noun is phonologically reduced. Moreover, the possessor is not marked with *el*. The standard analysis of construct states maintains that the noun moves to D, a situation which is rather similar to V movement to V in Dutch (and Norwegian, German, Swedish) main clauses. In any event, we see in these two examples from French and Hebrew that in the noun system we find a variation in the position of the noun which can be captured by assuming a DP category with DP, NumP and NP dominating the noun, with the noun moving two steps (to D), one step (to Num), or not at all:

(144)

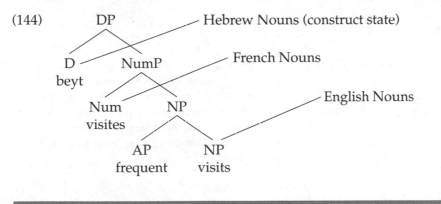

5.3   Summary

In this chapter, we studied the distribution of verbs and the structure of sentences. In the first part, we asked the particular question what the distribution of verbs in English can tell us about necessary properties of the syntactic component.

We learned that the syntactic input consists of words, silent morphemes, and (at least) some inflectional morphemes. Words are organized into constituents, according to a specific design which imposes a hierarchical structure on heads and their dependents. The head-complement relation regulates the distribution of verbal forms (verbal forms are selected by particular heads), and forms the basic backbone of a clause. Different clauses have similar internal structures. The property that distinguishes declarative clauses, questions, etc, is located at the C level. TPs fall into different types depending on properties of the T head ($-T = to$, $+T =$

tense). There exist dependencies between positions: an element can be pronounced in one position, and have a relation to some other position(s). We looked at one particular dependency, head movement, and its properties. In English, tensed main verbs occur in VP, tensed auxiliaries and modals in +T, or, in certain contexts, in C.

In the second part, we explored how these properties can be used to provide insight in the nature of cross-linguistic variation. Languages have quite similar structures, with differences arising from ordering parameters (whether complements precede or follow their heads), and lexical parameters (how a particular head is pronounced and what type of constituent it selects). With respect to the distribution of verbs, we saw that languages have very similar C-T-V architectures. Differences between languages follow from where in the C-T-V structure Vs are pronounced. This in turn seems related to properties of the individual C or T heads.

Notes

1   Thanks to Rose Meleko Letsholo for the Kalanga examples.
2   See Exercise 5.11 on Nawdem imperatives.
3   Examples taken from Chung and McCloskey (1987).
4   Strictly speaking, they do not show that the V is in T. If we were to develop this further, we would see that there is evidence that T and V are in different constituents: the V is outside VP, yet not in T. This means that the architecture of clauses must be more complex than what we have been assuming (i.e. there must be a landing site outside VP, but lower than T).

Further reading

Chomsky, Noam. 1957. *Aspects of the Theory of Syntax*. Cambridge, MA: MIT Press.
Haegeman, Liliane. 1991. *Introduction to Government and Binding Theory*. Oxford: Basil Blackwell. 2nd edn, 1994. Theory.
——. ed. 1998. *Handbook for Syntactic Theory*. Oxford: Basil Blackwell.

Radford, Andrew. 1997. *Syntactic Theory and the Structure of English. A Minimalist Approach*. Cambridge: Cambridge University Press.
Webelhuth, Gert. ed. 1996. *Government and Binding Theory and the Minimalist Program*. Oxford and Cambridge, MA: Blackwell.

Sources

The notion 'head of a word' is introduced by Williams (1981). The placement of verbal forms in English and French is discussed in Emonds (1978) and Pollock (1989). Vata is discussed in Koopman (1984). For discussion on historical change of English, see Roberts (1993). Otani and Whitman (1991) present the basis argument for VP ellipsis for Chinese, Japanese and Korean. VP ellipsis in Irish is argued for at length in McCloskey (1991), VP ellipsis in Swahili by Ngonyani (1996). The Kalanga examples have been provided by Rose Meleko Letsholo, Turkish examples by Murat Kural (personal communication).

The status of *to*

Suppose that you are one of several field linguists working together on English, and that English is a language that has no written tradition. As a field linguist, your task is to determine the status of the infinitival marker *to*. What syntactic category does *to* belong to?

The first problem you encounter is that there are several *tos*, which all sound alike, even though they are spelled differently, (*to, two, too*).

(i) (a) She wants *to* read *two* books.
   (b) These *two* books were fun *to* read.
   (c) He gave it *to* Cordelia.
   (d) He wants *to* read *too*.

A. Basing your answer on the meaning of each of the *tos* in (i), make a list of the different *tos* in English.

B. (1) Which of the *tos* are easy to distinguish? Why?
   (2) Which are difficult to distinguish? Why?

C. In your group of field linguists there is disagreement on how to treat *to* in (ia) and (ic). Some propose to treat *to* in (ia) and (ic) as the same element, i.e. as a preposition (P). Some propose to treat the two *tos* as different elements, the one in (ia) as an 'infinitival marker', of the same category as tense and modals, the one in (ic) as a P. You are asked to argue on the basis of the set of following examples which proposal you want to adopt.
The first set to consider concerns properties of the P *to* (ii):

(ii) (a) she went to the market
   (b) she went to it
   (c) she went right to it
   (d) *she went to not the market

D. Based on the examples in (ii), state what the P *to* co-occurs with. (You may assume that *right* only co-occurs with Ps.)
The second set considers *to* followed by an infinitive:

(iii) (a) She wants to read
   (b) *She wants read
   (c) *She wants to reading
   (d) I wonder what to read
   (e) *I wonder what read
   (f) *I wonder what reading

E. State in one line what infinitival *to* in (iii) co-occurs with.
For the following examples, contrast the set in (iv) with the set in (ii):

(iv) (a) She does not want to not read
   (b) *She wants to it
   (c) *she wants right to read it

F. In what ways does infinitival *to* differ from the P *to* in (ii)?

On the basis of these sets of data, argue if *to* in (iii) is a P or not, and state exactly how you came to this conclusion.

G. Some people argue that *to* is not a P, but basically an element that occupies the T node, just like modals and finite auxiliaries. Construct an argument for this position based on the paradigm in (v):

(v) (a) Will you come here? Yes I will.
(b) Do you want to do this? No, I don't want to.

H. Write one page on the argumentation and present your conclusion.

. . . .

Exercise 5.8 **to: free morpheme or bound morpheme?**

Argue on the basis of the following data if *to* in (i) should be considered a free morpheme (an independent word) or a bound morpheme (part of the infinitive).

(i) (a) Cordelia wants to read.
(b) (Does Cordelia want to read?) No, she does not want to.
(c) He wants me to carefully turn the pages.

. . . .

Exercise 5.9 **Zero heads**

English has two types of compounds. In the first type (called endocentric compounds) the interpretation is determined by the righthand member of the compound: a *tree trunk* is a kind of a trunk, a *girlfriend* is a kind of a friend, etc. In the second type (exocentric compounds) this is not the case: *sabertooth* is not a type of tooth, but a type of tiger. If heads can be silent (zero heads), the second type of compound can be represented as having a silent head (basically meaning tiger), which determines the properties of the compound as a whole.

(a)

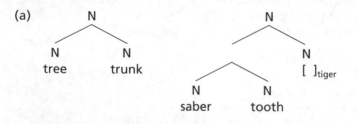

Now consider the following examples of compounds. (Remember that the head of the compound determines the properties of the compound as a whole.)

sabertooth   freeze-dry
beanie baby   poorhouse
tree trunk   pickpocket
redneck   Walkman
in-crowd

A.   Classify each compound as Type 1 (endocentric), or Type 2 (exocentric).

B.   Give structural representations of *pickpocket*, *beanie baby* and *Walkman*.

. . . .

Constructing trees   Exercise 5.10

This is a simple exercise that asks for nothing else than constructing tree representations, and indicating if necessary which movement processes or insertion processes have taken place.

   Give the tree representations for the following examples:

(i)   Cordelia did not insult Shylock.
(ii)   For Portia to confront Shylock, took courage.
(iii)   Mary should not have been playing Cordelia.
(iv)   Can anyone tell me what to do next?
(v)   Did you carefully read this book about linguistics?
(vi)   I did! (vi is an answer to v.)
(vii)   They are constantly wondering if they are constructing a nice set.

. . . .

Imperatives (Nawdem)   Exercise 5.11

While analyzing other languages, always keep the structure of the languages as similar as possible.

   In Nawdem, a Niger-Congo Gur language spoken in Togo, declarative sentences with finite verbs have the following shape, regardless of whether they are matrix or embedded:

(i)   (a)   (. . .) a ʤun   de:te
                 he eat+imperf food
             (. . .) he is eating
      (b)   ne   ʤun   de:te
            you(pl) eat-imperf food
            'you are eating food'

A.   Construct a tree representation for the sentence in (ia). What can you say about the position that the subject pronoun occupies?
     The following set of examples contains (second-)person plural imperatives in Nawdem. (Second-person singular pronouns are zero morphemes in tensed sentences and in imperatives, and thus cannot be used to show anything about order.)

(ii) (a)   de   ne   de:te
            eat+imp you (pl) food
            'Eat food!' (addressed to 2nd person plural)
      (b)   lo   ne   wadga: kan
            put(+imp) you(pl) book-the there
            'Put the book there!'

B.   What do you observe in these imperatives? Propose an analysis for imperative sentences, and state how you came to this analysis.

6

Acquisition of Word and Sentence Structure[1]

6.0 Introduction

Now that we understand something of the morphology and syntax of adult grammars, we are in a position to look more closely at the question of how children acquire these aspects of grammar. As we have seen in the preceding chapters, grammars are very complex. Yet, each of us naturally acquires such a system without any special training and on the basis of unstructured and impoverished data. In this chapter we will examine morphological and syntactic development. We cannot cover all areas of child morphology and child syntax, but we will try to give a sense of what young children know about the structure of their language at various points in their development and how this is the same or different from adult linguistic competence.

6.1   Knowledge of Word Formation

Children begin to produce words sometime towards the end of the first year or beginning of the second year of life and learn words rapidly throughout the preschool years. But what do young children know about words and word formation? Chapter 2 discussed the structure of words and the variety and complexity of word structure. How and when do children acquire this knowledge?

Children appear to know the principles that govern word formation extremely early, suggesting that this kind of grammatical knowledge may be a part of Universal Grammar, the linguistic principles that are present at birth, discussed in Chapter 1. This knowledge about how words are constructed is attested in language development in a number of ways. We will illustrate this by discussing: (1) knowledge of what can be a word and (2) knowledge of morpheme-attachment, focusing on compounds.

Children typically produce novel words, that is, words that are not rote-learned formulas like *patacake* or *peekaboo*, early in the second year of life. The mean age for producing ten words is 15 months, and remarkably, even when these first words emerge, children appear to know the constraints and principles governing the ways morphemes may be combined to form a word. Certain kinds of morphemes may not emerge until much later, and errors of omission and mis-selection of morphemes may persist until the early school years, but violations of the basic constraints of morphological structure are not attested.

6.2   What Can be a Word?

Children's earliest speech consists of one-word utterances. This is often referred to as the **one-word stage**, or the **holophrastic** (which means expressing a complete sentence in one word) stage. From this point on, children appear to know not only what a word is, but what can constitute a word from the standpoint of the morphological structure of their language.

6.2.1   Language-particular constraints

How can we tell from the one-word utterances that very young children produce, that they know and are obeying both universal and language-particular morphological constraints? One kind of evidence is that children learning typologically different kinds of languages from the standpoint of morphology produce morphologically different kinds of words. From the outset of word production, for example, children demonstrate that they know whether a bare root of a major lexical category constitutes a well-formed word in their target language. In one-word speech, children acquiring languages like English or Vietnamese, for example, where bare roots (e.g. *bottle*, *water*, *go*, *want*, *eat*) may be words, produce verbs and nouns without any bound morphology such as tense markers or plural markers attached. In contrast, children acquiring languages like Turkish, Italian, Greenlandic, or Hebrew, where a bare root without bound morphemes rarely, if ever, occurs as a well-formed word, do not produce bare roots, which would be ungrammatical in their language. Children acquiring such languages produce inflected roots – roots with bound affixes attached – even at the earliest stages of language development.

6.2.2 Languages where a bare root is not a well-formed word

Let us examine acquisition in Turkish as an example.

(1) **Turkish** – a highly inflected language in which nouns take the form:

STEM–(PLURAL)–(POSSESSIVE)–CASE

and verbs take the form:

VERB STEM–MODE–TENSE/ASPECT–PERSON/NUMBER

The morphemes in parentheses are present when appropriate; the others are obligatory at all times. This appears to be a complex inflectional system which we might expect to take a long time to acquire. Yet, both noun and verb inflections are present at the one-word stage, and the entire set of inflections is mastered by or before 24 months of age. In fact, with respect to morphological structure, according to Aksu-Koč and Slobin, "... Turkish child speech is almost entirely free of error ... Most of the morphology – nominal and verbal – is used productively at the two-word period, before the age of 2."[2]

(a)–(c) (with the phonology somewhat simplified) are illustrative of early word productions in Turkish.

(The age of the child is represented in years; months. So 2;1 means 2 years, 1 month.)

(a) bit-ti   'allgone'   (1;6)
     finish-past

(b) kalem-i   'the pencil'   (1;10)
     pencil-acc.

(c) sev-mi-eceg-im   onu   daha   'I won't love her anymore'   (2;0)
     love-NEG-fut–1sg. 3sg:acc. more

Note that the verbs and nouns are all inflected stems; in no instance are they bare roots. Other examples of early one-word utterances produced by children learning languages in which a bare root is not a grammatical (content) word are presented in (2)–(4) below, in each case attesting to the same developmental phenomenon: that children produce only words that are morphologically possible words in their language from the earliest stages of acquisition.

(2) **Hebrew** – a highly inflected language with unpronounceable, tri-consonantal (sometimes called triliteral) verb roots which appear as discontinuous morphemes, as discussed in Chapter 2. (Vowels, representing morphemes, are inserted into these roots.) These verb roots are obligatorily inflected for person, number, tense and gender. In the Hebrew examples, the capital letters represent the tri-consonantal roots and pluses (+) are used to show the morphemes contained in these complex roots.

    a. G+a+M+a+R -ti   'I('m) finished'   (1;7)
        finish–past   -1sg.

    b. Ø +o+X+e+L -et   '(I'm) eating'   (1;8)
        eat-pres.-fem.sg.

    c. H+o+L+e+X -et   '(Mommy) is walking'   (1;8)
        walk-pres.   -fem.sg.

(3) **Italian** – a language where verbs are inflected for person + number, and tense/aspect:

    a. pend-o io   'I take'   (1;11)
        take-1sg. I

    b. fai-te fai-te   '(You) do, (you) do'   (1;11)
        do-2sg. do-2sg.

    c. son-o giu   '(I) am downstairs'   (1;11)
        be-1sg. downstairs

(4) **Greenlandic** – a polysynthetic language with 318 inflectional affixes and over 400 derivational bound morphemes. A verb typically consists of a stem followed by derivational affixes, terminating in an obligatory inflectional affix; adjectives and other specifications on the noun are realized as inflections on the noun stem.

    a. nangia-ssa-nngil-anga   'I shan't be scared'
        be scared-fut.-not–1sg.indicative

    b. anar-tar-fi(k)ler-i-su-u-pput   'They are the sewage collectors'
        defecate-habit-place-agentive intran. particip.-be involved
        with-be-3pl.indicative
        sewage   collector   are

c.   tuluar-suaq   'big raven'
     raven-big
d.   una-a-nngit-toq   'It's not that'
     that-be-not–3sg.participial

6.2.3   Languages where a bare root is a well-formed word

Now contrast this acquisition pattern with that in which children are acquiring languages that do allow monomorphemic words, and where monomorphemic words are the basic word type. Such languages include English and Vietnamese. By examining the early words produced by children learning such languages, we find that typical early words include words like *look, see, want, bottle, cookie; water, rice, father, chopsticks, eat, finish, come* – all bare roots, and early two- and three-word utterances are also typically formed with bare-root words, as illustrated in (5)–(6):

(5)   **English**
a.   Want bottle
b.   No sleep
c.   Want more cookie
d.   See Mommy car
e.   Look my shoe

(6)   **Vietnamese**
a.   an   dua   'eat with chopsticks'
     eat chopsticks
b.   ve   nuoc   'finished with the water'
     finish water
c.   bo   den   'father is coming'
     father come
d.   bo   an com   'father is eating rice'
     father eat rice
e.   me   roi   com   'mother is cooking rice'
     mother cook rice

A well-formedness constraint on the structure of content words (Nouns, Verbs and Adjectives in particular) in a given language determines whether a bare root can be a word. A revealing example of how strongly children's language is guided by this constraint in early stages of acquisition can be found in a surprising fact about the acquisition of verb forms in Turkish. In Tukish, the second-person imperative emerges late relative to most other forms of the verb. This is surprising because the second-person imperative (e.g. '(You) Hold me') is typically among the two earliest verb forms to be acquired cross-linguistically, and in Turkish it is just the stem and bears no

affixes. Why would children learning Turkish acquire this morphologically simple verb form, a form they hear very frequently in speech directed
to them, later than more complex forms of verbs? One explanation that
accounts for the patterns of acquisition we have seen is that the early
grammar of the child acquiring Turkish has the constraint that well-formed
verbs may not be bare roots in Turkish, but the second-person imperative
bears no affixes; it is the same as the stem. The second-person imperative,

---

Acquisition of signs   **SIDEBAR 6.1**

The sign languages used by the deaf throughout the world show similar
constraints on word formation similar to those of spoken languages. In sign
languages, morphemes consist of specific gestures or combinations of gestures performed in space. Some sign words consist of only one morpheme,
some signs consist of more than one morpheme. Each sign language has its
own morphemes and its own rules about what can be a well-formed sign/
word. Children learning sign languages use the same word-structure principles in forming their first words as children acquiring spoken languages. This
indicates that children are predisposed to look at the grammar of the language they are learning in just the right way to determine what the basic
word type of their language is – whether it is a sign language or a spoken
language. In American Sign Language (ASL), for example, there is rich verbal
morphology. In Chapter 2, we saw that SLQ Zapotec verbs have separate
forms for six different verb aspects (somewhat like tenses). Similarly, in ASL,
some verb stems have different forms for more than fifteen distinct verb
aspects and also carry subject and object agreement markers on the verb
stem. Therefore, (a) and (b) are signed differently, as are (c)–(g).

(a)   You give to me.
(b)   I give to you.
(c)   Olivia talks (on one occasion).
(d)   Olivia talks all the time.
(e)   Olivia talks over and over again.
(f)   Olivia talks for hours/endlessly.
(g)   Olivia talks over a long period of time.

However, these aspectual and agreement morphemes are obligatory for only
a subset of high-frequency verbs in the language. Children acquiring ASL treat
their target language as a bare root-type language like English because, for
the most part, it is. Thus they produce uninflected roots as their first words,
even for verbs that obligatorily take verbal inflections. Moreover, because
this subset represents a set of exceptions to the basic word-formation pattern of the language and not the rule, children learning ASL begin to use
some of these inflections only between $2\frac{1}{2}$ and 3 years of age; and acquisition
of the full set of inflectional morphemes follows a rather long course of
development.

therefore, violates this constraint, and emerges only later, when the child's grammar is ready to handle such exceptions.

Turkish and English illustrate a linguistic contrast in what can be a morphologically well-formed word; but in each case, children obey the morphological well-formedness constraint on words in their language in their acquisition of word formation rules.

6.3   Morpheme Attachment

We have seen that children know whether bare stems can be words in their language, but when do children know the rules and constraints for putting morphemes together in creating polymorphemic words? Even at the earliest stages of language development children do not seem to make word-internal morpheme attachment errors, even when they are constructing words involving many morphemes, such as verbs in Turkish, Greenlandic, or Quiché. That is, they never use a prefix as an infix or suffix (for example, children acquiring English do not say @*ingplay* instead of *playing*, and children acquiring French do not say @*aisparl* instead of *parlais*); they do not put the morphemes in the wrong order, putting the head of a compound first instead of last (@*brushtooth* instead of *toothbrush*), nor do they attach suffixes in the wrong order, even when there are more than one (@catcheser instead of *catchers*). (Note: @ indicates a form or sentence that is unattested.)

The fact that children always attach morphemes in the grammatically correct order, including the placing of inflectional suffixes after derivational morphemes shows that children from a very early age have an understanding of the hierarchical structure of words and the distribution of different types of morphemes discussed in previous chapters.

6.3.1   Compound formation and Level Ordering

Young children also show their knowledge of the rules for the formation of compounds, such as those discussed in chapter 2. For example, in forming compounds, one needs to be sensitive to the distinctions between nouns that take a regular plural and those that don't. A noun that takes a regular plural, that is, that forms its plural by rule, may not enter a compound in its plural form because the pluralization rule follows the process of compound formation (for example, *rat-infested* but not **rats-infested*), but a noun whose plural form is irregular, that is, whose plural is not formed by rule, may optionally be used in a compound in its plural form (both *mouse-infested* and *mice-infested* are acceptable). Irregular plurals may appear inside compounds because the irregular plural form is stored along with the singular form in the lexical entry for that noun, and so may enter the compound as part of the noun stem. Compare (7), which illustrates the derivation of the word 'rat-infested', where only the singular form of the noun may enter the compound, with (8) and (9), which illustrate the derivations of the words 'mouse-infested' and 'mice-infested', respectively, recalling that either 'mouse' or 'mice' can be used in the compound because the irregular plural form, 'mice', is stored along with the singular form, 'mouse', in the same lexical entry:

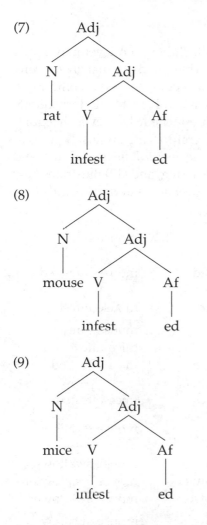

(7)

(8)

(9)

6.3.2 The Level Ordering Model

A model by which irregular inflectional (and idiosyncratic derivational) affixes are attached before regular derivational and inflectional rules apply is referred to as the 'Level Ordering Model,' because the model hypothesizes distinct, sequential levels of operation by which complex morphological forms are constructed, with specific processes occurring at one and only one level, not before, not later. (10) presents a description of the kinds of morphemes which may be attached at each level:

(10)   **Level Ordering Model**
   • Level 1 – unproductive or semantically irregular derivational or inflectional affixes
   • Level 2 – productive and semantically regular derivational affixes
   • Level 3 – regular inflectional affixes

Recall that in this model of morpheme attachment, no level may apply before a preceding level. Thus, Level Ordering predicts that in forming plural compounds, no regular plurals may occur inside the compound, because regular plural markers are attached at level 3, after all derivational and irregular inflectional affixes have been attached. However, irregular plurals may be attached at level 1, and therefore appear inside a compound. (11) illustrates how the compounds *rat-infested*, *mouse-infested*, and *mice-infested* would be formed under Level Ordering, and (12) illustrates how the plural compounds *rat-swallowers*, *mouse-swallowers* and *mice-swallowers* would be formed under Level Ordering.

(11)   (a)   (adult-preferred)   rat infest   mouse infest
              Level 1   ——   ——
              Level 2   rat infest-ed   mouse infest-ed
              Level 3   ——   ——
              Output   rat infested   mouse infested

       (b)   adult dispreferred   rat infest   mouse infest
              Level 1   ——   mice infest
              Level 2   rat infest-ed   mice infest-ed
              Level 3   ——   ——
              Output   rat infested   mice infested

(12)   (a)   (adult-preferred)   rat swallow   mouse swallow
              Level 1   ——   ——
              Level 2   rat swallow-er   mouse swallow-er
              Level 3   rat swallow-er-s   mouse swallow-er-s
              Output   rat swallowers   mouse swallowers

       (b)   adult dispreferred   rat swallow   mouse swallow
              Level 1   ——   mice swallow
              Level 2   rat swallow-er   mice swallow-er
              Level 3   rat swallow-er-s   mice swallow-er-s
              Output   rat swallowers   mice swallowers

We can see, then, that in forming plural compounds, it is never possible to pluralize the first element in a plural compound if it takes a regular plural inflection, because regular plural inflection is carried out at level 3, and therefore may be attached as a suffix only to the entire compound. However, it is possible to pluralize the first element in a compound if it takes an irregular plural, because irregular pluralization occurs at level 1, before any other affixation occurs. Pluralizing the first constituent of the compound in such cases is optional, however, and highly dispreferred among adults. Adults rarely, if ever, use this option to construct plural compounds like *mice-eater* or *teeth-swallower*. Some researchers have hypothesized that Level Ordering is part of UG and thus need not be learned.

6.3.3   An experimental test

How can one test the Level Ordering hypothesis and the hypothesis that Level Ordering is part of UG and so constrains children's word formation, without having to be learned? Peter Gordon (1985) tested these hypotheses by studying whether children obeyed the principles of Level Ordering in forming plural compounds. If children adhered to the constraints of the model, they would never use a noun which takes a regular plural inside a compound, but would optionally allow a noun which has an irregular plural form to appear inside a compound. If, further, the youngest children as well as the older children followed the model, then it would suggest that Level Ordering was not something they had to learn over time, but could be part of UG.

Gordon tested 3- to 5-year-old children's knowledge of how to form plural compounds, such as *dog-catchers*. For the first noun of each compound he used both kinds of nouns: words like *rat, bead*, and *hand*, which take regular plurals (e.g. *rats, beads, hands*), and words that have irregular plural forms (e.g. *tooth, foot, mouse* and *man*). He showed the children objects and using Cookie Monster to ask them questions, elicited a plural form for the object (for example, *'hands'*) and immediately following the production of that plural, elicited a compound using that noun. To elicit the compound, he had Cookie Monster ask, "What do you call someone who eats X" (e.g. hands)? So, for example, Cookie Monster would ask, "What do you call someone who eats hands?" The compound that the child produced with each noun indicated whether or not the child's grammar permitted that noun to occur inside of compounds in its plural form. Recall that adult English speakers strongly prefer to use the singular form of words inside compounds, even when the grammar allows plural forms to occur; thus, children rarely if ever hear plural nouns inside of compounds.

There were three important results in Gordon's experiment. First, by 3 years-of-age the children knew how to form plural compounds, such as *rat-eaters* or *mice-swallowers*. Second, the children consistently followed the

Level Ordering Model. They reduced the regularly pluralized nouns to singular forms inside the compounds, that is, they formed [Noun sg. – Vers] compounds for nouns taking regular plurals (e.g. *rat-catchers*) and created [N pl. – Vers] compounds with nouns forming irregular plurals (e.g. *mice-catchers, teeth-swallowers*). These results indicated that in forming complex words, their grammars already followed level ordering constraints. Children demonstrated this even with their errors, for children who produced incorrect regular plurals such as *mouses* or *tooths*, never produced compounds such as **mouses-eater*. Third, those children who knew the correct irregular plural form of the nouns used in the experiment formed compounds sometimes with the singular (*tooth-swallowers*) and sometimes with the irregular plural, producing forms such as *teeth-swallowers*. Since an examination of speech spoken to children indicates that they rarely if ever hear plural compounds in the input, and probably never hear forms such as *teeth-swallowers* or *mice-catchers*, forms highly dispreferred by adults, their knowledge of how to form plural compounds is an instance of the acquisition of linguistic principles or rules despite the 'poverty of the stimulus' discussed in chapter 1, lending support to the hypothesis that this knowledge is unlearned and part of Universal Grammar. Gordon's work is also an illustration of how acquisition facts can inform or support hypotheses developed solely to account for the adult grammar.

Gordon's results are not unusual. By the time children know how to form and produce compounds, typically by 3 years-of-age, they appear to know almost everything there is to know about forming compounds, such as those discussed in chapter 2. This includes where to place the head constituent and therefore (by and large) how to interpret the compound, what morpheme attachment must precede or follow the formation of the compound (e.g. inflectional morphemes follow derivational morphemes – Level Ordering, again), and how a compound's stress pattern differs from phrasal stress in English. Errors by children in using phrasal versus compound stress appropriately are rare, even when a compound and a phrase consist of the same words as in (13) and (14), where the stressed syllable is in upper case:

(13)   a blueBIRD (a bird that is blue)
(14)   a BLUEbird (a particular species of bird)

6.4   Word-Formation Errors

Children's production of morphologically complex forms is not error-free, but their knowledge of the language's word-formation rules is reflected in the errors they do make. Such errors include creating words using productive word-formation rules of their grammar, words such as *sweeper* or *typer*, for example, which are later replaced by existing words in the language that express the same meanings – *broom* and *typist*, in this case.

Most word-formation errors are rare, but not everything about word formation develops early. Children can take a long time to learn the particulars of word formation which are idiosyncratic and for which there are no general rules or principles that produce them. In English, for example, it is necessary to learn by rote which (non-productive) derivational affixes go with which roots and what they mean. Children make frequent errors of this type along the way, as illustrated by (15) and (16), errors made by RG at the age of 2;6 and 4;2, respectively:

(15)   (Coming in from playing outdoors) (2;6)
       R: I want a yellow bicycle – no, some 'sickle.'
       (Still trying to retrieve the word, R pointed to the freezer, and said)
       Popsicle!

(16)   (R's blanket was in the dryer and R was anxious to have it.) (4;2)
       R: I think it's had enough **dryment*.

In (15) R confused the morphemes *-sicle*, which occurs in words like *fudgesicle* and *icicle*, with *-cycle*, as in *bicycle* and *tricycle*. Both morphemes form nouns, and both are pronounced the same, but they have different meanings and attach to different morphemes. They are homophonous morphemes – same sounds, different meanings, similar to word homophones like *to*, *too*, and *two*. However, in R's lexicon they were still represented as the same morpheme.

In (16), R attached the wrong derivational morpheme to the adjective *dry* to form the noun she wanted. (She should have used *-ing*.) But note that she selected a derivational morpheme which *does* form nouns, but forms them from verbs, not adjectives, as shown in (17a) and (17b):

(17)   a.   b.

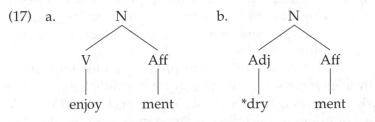

Except for errors in the use of inflectional morphology (which will be discussed below), the word-formation errors children make involve forms which must be memorized, and/or idiosyncratic properties of words which must be listed in the lexicon rather than formed by general principles of morphology. The long period over which these forms are mastered and the many bumps along the way contrasts sharply with the relative rapidity and ease with which the bulk of the grammar is attained, pointing to the difference between what has been viewed as biologically-programmed maturation or unfolding of grammatical knowledge in development, and language *learning*.

6.5   A Note About Function Words

Although early speech of children consists largely of lexical or open class words, some closed class or function words also emerge early, frequently at the onset of two-word speech. Research indicates that children appear sensitive to the function-word/lexical content-word distinction in both comprehension and production, early in development. Before mastering their phonological form, children appear to use simple (often a single vowel), phonetically neutral forms, referred to by some researchers as 'monosyllabic place holders' (MPHs) for function words. These MPHs appear where function words should occur, and knowledge of specific categories of function words is revealed through their appropriate distribution relative to lexical content words – articles (e.g. *a*, *the*) before nouns in English and Italian, for example. Through an examination of the use of such MPH morphemes in combination with content words, then, it has been found that, in some cases, before children have acquired complete knowledge of the syntax or pronunciation of certain morphemes, they appear to know what kinds of morphemes they are (lexical or functional), and the rules governing their distribution relative to other morphemes.

6.6   The Syntax of Child Grammars

In this section we will focus on syntax development. We cannot hope to cover all areas of child syntax, but we will try to give a sense of what young children know about the syntactic structure of their language at various points in their development and how this is the same and yet different from adult linguistic competence.

Sometime around age 2 children begin to produce multi-word utterances. Initially, their utterances are only two or three words long and the form of these early sentences is different in various respects from the adult 'target' language. For example, the following utterances are typical of the 2-year-old English speaking child:

(18)   a.   Make a choo-choo train.
      b.   Mommy throw it away.
      c.   No want this.
      d.   Not making muffins.

    e.   Man sit down.
    f.   See my doggie?
    g.   What cowboy doing?

It is important to note, however, that despite its apparent deviance, the child's language during this early stage (and any other developmental stage) is remarkably regular, and to the extent that it is different from the adult language, these differences are quite systematic. For example, we see in the sentences in (18) that children often omit subjects. However, English-speaking children typically do not leave out objects. We also see that at this age children may omit tense/agreement inflection from the verb, as in (18). Uttered by an adult this sentence would be *Mommy threw it away* or *Mommy throws it away*. On the other hand, progressive *-ing* occurs quite regularly during this stage, as illustrated in (18d, g).

Most of us find child language charming and are amused by the 'errors' that children make. But the child's language is not simply a haphazard approximation to the target. Rather, at each stage of development the child has an internally consistent, rule-governed cognitive system – a grammar, with specific properties that can be studied (just like the grammars of adult speakers). As discussed in chapter 1, the child begins with a universal grammar – UG – template, which specifies the general form of grammar, and then fill in the language-specific details – the gaps in the system – through experience with the particular language in his environment; some gaps are filled in quickly, others take more time, and there may be misformulations along the way, giving rise to acquisition stages. We may think about grammar development as involving the construction of a successive series of grammars. This is schematically shown in (19), where each stage of development is a grammar (G_n), beginning with the principles and structures made available by UG (G_0) and terminating in the adult grammar of a particular language (G_a).

(19) $G_0, G_1, ..., G_n, ..., G_a$

One of the interesting features of language development is the uniformity that we observe across children. Children raised under very different circumstances and who may otherwise differ from one another in all sorts of ways go through very similar stages in their development of language. For example, the **telegraphic stage** typified by utterances such as those in (18), in which certain elements such as articles and auxiliaries are missing, is common to all children (with some variation depending on the particular target). Even children acquiring very different languages, for example signed and spoken languages, show some striking parallels in their language, as discussed above. These commonalities that we find provide further evidence of a rich innate component to language. Otherwise, why would children acquiring different languages come up with similar systems, that is, go through similar stages, especially when the relevant properties are not exemplified in the input? Clearly, sentences such as those in (18) are not modeled by adult speakers. Studying the intermediate grammars that children develop may shed further light on the nature of linguistic knowledge and the mechanisms by which children acquire this knowledge.

6.7 Principles and Parameters

One of the most striking results to come out of recent research into grammar development is that children acquire central aspects of syntax very early in development, almost instantaneously. Even during the early stage illustrated by the examples in (18), children have figured out many of the specific properties of their particular target grammar. For example, as noted above, despite the fact that certain elements are missing from the examples in (18), we can see that the order of major constituents (subject – verb – object – SVO) is correct. The object comes after the verb, as is correct for English, which is a head-initial language. A Japanese-speaking child at this same age shows OV word order, as is correct for a head-final language.

(20) a. hyaku-en choodai
         a hundred-yen give
         'Give a hundred yen.'
     b. Hako tabe-chau wa
         box eat-will have exclamative particle
         'He will have eaten the box!'

More generally, we find that those parts of grammar which have been described as **parameters** are acquired very rapidly, as discussed in chapters 3 and 5. This is what we would expect if grammar acquisition involves **parameter-setting**. Before turning to the acquisition results, however, let us briefly review the theory of parameters and parameter-setting.

Previously, we described UG as a kind of template with gaps that must be filled in by experience. Let us now make this picture more concrete. UG can be viewed as a system of principles and parameters. Principles such as the **structure dependency** of grammatical rules and the **c-command** condition on licensing, discussed in chapter 4, among many others, express those aspects of grammar which are invariant across languages. But as we saw in chapter 5, languages also differ from one another in certain respects and many of these differences can be simply described as parameters. The parameters of UG express the small differences that languages can show with respect to some grammatical property. One example of

> ## Passive knowledge of grammar
>
>
> Children's knowledge of syntax is most apparent at the point at which they are producing multi-word utterances such as those in (20). However, we have reason to believe that children have knowledge of some basic syntactic rules even before this point. Recently, ingenious experiments have been developed which allow researchers to test children's passive knowledge of syntax. These experiments show that children as young as 17 months, who have a productive vocabulary of just a few words and who are not yet able to produce multi-word utterances, are nevertheless sensitive to the differences in meaning signaled by word order. In a technique called the 'preferential looking paradigm' (Hirsh-Pasek and Golinkoff 1996) children are aurally presented with sentences followed by video displays depicting different scenes, one of which corresponds to the sentence they heard. Results show that when children hear a sentence such as *Bert is tickling Ernie*, they will respond more to a video depicting Bert tickling Ernie than to a video depicting Ernie tickling Bert. Results such as these show that children have knowledge of grammar before they use it productively.

parametric variation is the verb–complement relation discussed in chapter 5, and above. Here we have two possibilities, either the object follows the verb, as in English, cf. (21a), or the object precedes the verb, as in Japanese, cf. (21b).

(21) a. Brutus killed Caesar.
      b. Taro-ga gohan-o tabeta.
         Taro   rice   eats
         'Taro eats rice.'

We thus have a 'head-initial/head-final parameter' (as discussed in chapter 5), a point of limited variation among languages.

Another example concerns the subject of the sentence. It is universally true that sentences must have subjects, but, as discussed in chapter 3 (section 3.2.6), languages differ with respect to whether the subject must be lexically realized or not. In many languages, English for example, the subject of a sentence must be pronounced, as in (22a). In other languages, such as Italian, the subject can be 'silent' (though it need not be) and the hearer understands the intended subject through the agreement inflection on the verb and from context. Thus, in the sentence in (22b) the verb is marked for first-person agreement, and hence the unspoken subject is understood as referring to the speaker.

(22) a. Julius Caesar was betrayed.
         (cf. *Was betrayed.)

b.   Fui tradito.
     Was-1st per. betrayed
     '(I) was betrayed.'

This difference that languages show in either licensing a silent subject or not was referred to in chapter 3 as the **Null Subject Parameter (NSP)**. Like the head position parameter, the NSP makes available two options, a null subject is licensed or it is not, in which case the subject must be pronounced.

Further examples of parametric variation involve the position of the finite verb, discussed in chapter 5. As we saw, languages differ in whether the verb appears in V, in T, or in C, the latter known as the verb second phenomenon. These differences can be simply described in terms of parameters of variation. We return to the verb position parameters below.

We noted in the introduction that there is a tight connection between linguistic theory and language acquisition. A particular model of UG is not only a theory about the adult representation of linguistic knowledge and the relation between different adult languages, but also presents a specific picture of the acquisition process. Within the principles-and-parameters model of UG, children approach the acquisition task with a set of (possibly open) parameters and what they must do is 'fix' these parameters at the values which are correct for their target language. They do this on the basis of the linguistic input they receive. Thus, the English-speaking child fixes the NSP to 'pronounce subject,' while the Spanish-speaking child fixes a 'silent subject' option. The Japanese child fixes the head position parameter to 'verb last,' while the English-speaking child fixes it to 'verb initial,' and so on for all the parameters of UG.

The principles-and-parameters model is appealing because it offers a straightforward solution to the logical problem of language acquisition discussed in chapter 1; if much of syntax acquisition can be reduced to the simple fixing of parameters, then these aspects of grammar will be acquired swiftly and efficiently as the child proceeds along a narrow, UG-defined path. The uniformity of the developmental stages may reflect the route of the parameter-setting journey. In addition, on this view the input data serve as 'triggers' for particular parameter settings, rather than as an inductive basis for learning, and thus the fact that the data are impoverished or degenerate in certain respects will not be so important. With this perspective in mind, let us now investigate in more detail the process of parameter-setting by children.

6.7.1   Parameter-setting and early morphosyntactic development

A useful metaphor for parameter-setting is to think of the child flipping a series of switches to either 'on' or 'off' based on linguistic input.

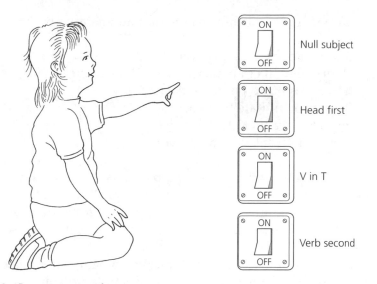

Figure 6.1 Parameter setting

Given the deterministic nature of parameter-setting, we expect that children will quickly acquire these core aspects of grammar. Indeed, much recent research into parameter-setting by children bears out this prediction. Children are extremely sensitive to the particular morphosyntax of the language they are hearing, and hence, many parameters (perhaps all) are set extremely early in development.

Two of the parameters we will discuss, the V in T Parameter and the Verb Second Parameter, involve a distinction between finite and non-finite verbs, so we will begin by talking about the child's use of finite and non-finite verbs.

As discussed in chapter 5, in adult languages, main clauses must contain a finite verb, that is a verb inflected for tense and/or person or other features. Compare the ungrammatical examples in (23) with the examples in parentheses:

(23) a.   *Romeo (to) love Juliet.   (English)
           (cf. Romeo loves Juliet.)
      b.   *Roméo boire du vin.   (French)
           'Romeo drink-inf. some wine'
           (cf. Roméo boit du vin.)
           ('Romeo drink-3rd per. sing. some wine')
      c.   *Romeo Juliet kussen.   (Dutch)
           Romeo Juliet kiss-inf.
           (cf. Romeo kust Juliet.)
           (Romeo kisses Juliet.)

Infinitives appear only as complements to finite main verbs, as in (24):

(24) a. Romeo hopes [to marry Juliet].
      b. Henri veut [aller au palais].   (French)
          'Henry wants to go to the palace.'
      c. Petruccio wil Kate trouwen.   (Dutch)
          Petruccio wants Kate marry-inf.
          'Petruccio wants to marry Kate.'

In many languages the infinitive bears a particular infinitival morphology, for example *-er* in French, *-en* in Dutch. In English the stem form of the verb is used as the infinitive. (The infinitive particle *to* also appears but it is not part of the verb itself, but rather occurs in T.) (This is discussed in chapter 3.)

Children's early sentences do not typically contain subordinate clauses such as those in (24). Rather, they tend to be short and consist of a single verb, and so we might expect not to find infinitival verbs at all at this stage. However, young children (roughly age 2–3) do use infinitives, and in marked contrast to adults, they use them in root (that is, main) clauses. This is best illustrated in languages like Dutch and French, where the infinitive is overtly marked with a suffix. Utterances such as those in (25) and (26) are very common during the third year. Such utterances are referred to as **root infinitives**.

(25) a. Pas manger la poupée.   (French)
          Not eat-inf. the doll
          'The doll doesn't eat.'
      b. Michel dormir.
          Michael sleep-inf.
          'Michael sleeps.'

(26) a. Pappa schoen wassen.   (Dutch)
          Daddy shoes wash-inf.
          'Daddy washes (the) shoes.'
      b. Ik ook lezen
          I also read-inf.
          'I also read.'

This root infinitive 'error' that children make turns out to be quite fortuitous because it allows us to investigate the distribution of finite and non-finite verbs in the early grammar and thus to determine at what point children set verb position parameters. Put slightly differently, we can see at what point children figure out where finite verbs are 'pronounced' in the syntax of their particular language. Let us turn to this directly.

Table 6.1 Finiteness and position of negation in French

	FINITE VERB	NON-FINITE VERB
neg V	9	122
V neg	216	2

Source: Pierce (1992).

V in T parameter

Recall from chapter 5 that in French, the finite verb occurs to the left of negative *pas*, as in (27a), that is, it occur in T. In non-finite clauses, however, as in the embedded clause in (27b), the verb occurs to the right of *pas*.

(27) a. Roméo ne visite pas ses voisins.
          Romeo NEG-visits not his neighbors
          'Romeo isn't visiting his neighbors.'
      b. Roméo a l'habitude de ne pas visiter ses voisins.
          'Romeo has the habit of not visiting his neighbors.'

The different orders arise because in French the finite verb moves across the negative *pas* to T. Several child-language researchers have observed that French children, from their first multi-word utterances, show the correct positioning of finite and non-finite verbs. They place the finite verb to the left of negative *pas*, while placing root infinitives to the right. Contingency table 6.1 shows the distribution of finite and non-finite verbs for three French children (ages 1;8 to 2;6). The table shows that 96 percent (216 of 225 occurrences) of finite verbs used by the children were correctly placed to the left of negation, while 98 percent (122 of 124) non-finite verbs occurred to the right.

While children do make an occasional error in verb placement (under 5 percent), it seems clear that young French children quickly set the verb position parameter such that V occurs in T.

The same is true for English-speaking children. English adopts the opposite setting. The main verb does not move to T, but rather remains within the VP and thus occurs to the right of negation, as in (28a). Recall, however, that *be* does move to T, as in (28b).

(28) a. Othello does not [$_{VP}$ love Desdemona any more].
      b. Iago is not [$_{VP}$——a very nice fellow].

English-speaking children always correctly position the main verb to the right of negation and *be* to the left, showing adult-like knowledge of this aspect of grammar. Thus we do not find children making errors such as (29):

(29)   a.   @Mommy not is going.
       b.   @Mommy likes not cookies.
            (As noted above, @ means 'unattested')

Irish is a very interesting language to look at in connection with verb movement. As noted in chapter 5, finite clauses in Irish show VSO word order, as illustrated by the following examples:

(30)   a.   Chonaic mé spideog ar maidin.
            saw   I   a-robin on morning
            'I saw a robin this morning.'
       b.   Thit mé inne.
            fell I yesterday
            'I fell yesterday.'

In a finite clause, the verb undergoes movement to T, raising above the subject, which in Irish is inside the VP, as illustrated in the structure below.

(31)   [$_{TP}$ thit [$_{VP}$ me ———inne]]
       (The dashes represent the position from which the verb has moved.)

When the main verb is non-finite, as in the progressive construction for example, the verb remains below the subject in the VP and we can see the non-derived SVO word order, as in the following sentence, where *build* follows the subject *Sean*:

(32)   Tá [$_{VP}$ Seán ag tógáil tithe i nDoire.]
       is Sean build (prog.) houses in Derry
       'Sean is building houses in Derry.'

Young Irish-speaking children as young as 14 months adhere strictly to the positional requirements of the verb; finite main verbs occur overwhelmingly in initial position (VSO order), while progressive verbs are always in subject-initial structures, as in (33):

(33)   moncaí ag ithe
       monkey eat (prog.)
       'Monkey (is) eating.'

Like French children, Irish children clearly distinguish finite from non-finite (progressive) verbs and they quickly set the V movement parameter such that finite verbs move to T. In this respect they are fully adult-like. However, the child's progressive construction is not identical to the adult's, as is clear when we compare the adult sentence in (32) with the child sentence in (33). What we notice is that the child drops the auxiliary *be*, and in this respect they have much in common with the young English-speaking child who utters the sentence in (34), in which the auxiliary *be* is also missing (see also example 18d).

(34)   Birdie flying.

Sentences such as (36) are typical of 2-year-old English speakers. We will have more to say below about telegraphic speech and the child's omission of various functional elements. At this point we only wish to point out that copula omission is one example of the kind of uniformity that we see in the development. Children acquiring languages which are typologically quite distinct may nevertheless go through similar grammatical stages.

Verb second
Another parameter which has been extensively studied both in adult languages and also in child language is the verb second or **V to C parameter**. Recall that in certain Germanic languages, notably German and Dutch, finite verbs move to C (second position) as in the Dutch example in (35a), while non-finite verbs (infinitives and participles) occur at the end of the clause, as in (35b):

(35)   a. $[_{CP}$ Romeo$_i$ $[_C$ kust$_j]$ $[_{IP}$ t$_i$ Juliet t$_j]]$
          'Romeo kisses Juliet.'
       b. $[_{CP}$ Hij$_i$ $[_C$ moet$_j]$ $[_{IP}$ t$_i$ Juliet kussen t$_j]]$
          He must Juliet kiss-inf
          'He must kiss Juliet.'

As we said earlier, very young children do not frequently produce complex sentences such as (35b). However, they do use infinitives in root sentences, as illustrated in (25) and (26). If young German and Dutch children have correctly set the V to C parameter, then the distribution of their finite and root infinitive verbs should differ along adult lines; finite verbs should occur in second position, while infinitives should occur in clause-final position. A number of studies confirm that this is indeed the case. Contingency table 6.2, which reports the verb placement results for one German-speaking child, is representative.

Table 6.2 shows that the overwhelming majority of finite verbs occurs in second position, while non-finite verbs most often occur in final position, as predicted. Similar results have been found for children acquiring Dutch, Swedish and other V2 languages. Thus, children acquiring V2 languages correctly set the relevant parameter at a very early age. Indeed, there appears to be no point at which children fail to respect the verb-second requirement.

Table 6.2 The position of finite and non-finite verbs in early German

	FINITE VERB	NON-FINITE VERB
V2 position	197	6
Final position	11	37

Source: Poeppel and Wexler (1993).

Null Subject Parameter

One last parameter we will consider is the Null Subject Parameter. Recall that this parameter determines whether it is grammatical to use a silent subject, as in Italian (36b), or whether the subject must be pronounced, as in English (36a).

(36)   a.   We saw Petruccio . . .
      b.   Abbiamo visto Petruccio . . .
         have-1st per. Plu. Seen Petruccio.
         '(We) have seen Petruccio.'

One of the most salient properties of early language is the apparent optionality of subjects. All children pass through a stage in which they frequently omit subjects. This is true even if the target language is not a null subject language. In (37–39) we provide some examples of subjectless sentences from child English, Dutch and French, all languages which in their adult form do not permit null subjects.

(37)   a.   Want go get it.
      b.   Not making muffins.
      c.   No play matches.

(38)   a.   Ook toren bouwen.   (Dutch)
         also tower build
         '(I) build a tower too.'
      b.   Kann niet slapen op een schaap
         'Cannot sleep on a sheep.'

(39)   a.   Veux pas lolo.   (French)
         want not water
         'I don't want water.'
      b.   Pas manger
         'Not eat.'

Based on data of this sort, it is tempting to suggest that this is a case where a parameter has been mis-set, that is, that English (Dutch, French)-speaking children have the NSP set to the Italian value. Note that there is no reason in principle why this could not be the case. If UG parameters allow a limited range of variation, we might expect this variation to also find expression in the developmental sequence: the child starts out with an Italian-like grammar, and then switches to the English value of the NSP based on exposure to English data. This hypothesis, which we might call the **parameter mis-setting hypothesis**, is appealing because it relates the stages of acquisition directly to the typological variation found in adult languages, and thus explains the developmental stages directly in terms of independently motivated principles and parameters of grammar. As we will see, however, the parameter mis-setting hypothesis cannot be maintained. Rather, the evidence suggests that children set this parameter correctly at a very early age, as they do for the two parameters discussed earlier.

To test the parameter mis-setting hypothesis we can compare early English with early Italian. If English-speaking children initially speak a null subject language, then we would expect their language to look like the language of young Italian children, who are acquiring a real null subject language. However, this is not the case. It has been observed that while Italian children drop subjects at a rate of about 70 percent of the time – about the same rate as Italian adults, English-speaking children drop at a rate of 30 percent to 50 percent (Valian 1991). Although we do not have a good explanation for why children produce forms at the precise frequencies they do, the frequency difference between Italian- and English-speaking children suggests that there are different underlying causes for the subject omissions. A further consideration is that null subjects in early English and early Italian differ in their distribution. Italian children use null subjects essentially the way Italian adult do, in simple finite sentences, as well as in finite embedded clauses, as illustrated in (40).

(40) a. Sono giú.
          am-1st person downstairs
          '(I) am downstairs.'
      b. E mia gonna.
          is-3rd person my skirt
          '(It) is my skirt.'
      c. Mama dice che non è sympatico.
          Mama says that not is nice
          'Mama say that (it) is not nice.'

In early English, in contrast, null subjects are restricted to root clauses. Moreover, as we will discuss further below, they tend to occur predominantly in non-finite clauses. To sum up, Italian children seem to use null subjects with the same frequency and distribution as Italian adults. This leads us to conclude that the children have correctly set the NSP for Italian at a very early age. English-speaking children, on the other hand, use null subjects less frequently and in different contexts and hence do not seem to be speaking a real null subject language. But if this is the case, how can we explain the child's use of null subjects in languages such as English, Dutch and French, which do not license null subjects in their adult form? Interestingly, the answer to this question brings us back to the point at which we began our discussion of parameters – root infinitives.

6.8 Root Infinitives

Recall from the earlier discussion of finiteness in early grammar that children use infinitives in root clauses, as in (25) and (26). A number of important generalizations have emerged from the study of root infinitives in different child languages. One of these concerns the distribution of null subjects in overt subject languages such as Dutch, French, German and Flemish. Whether a subject is null or overt seems to depend on the finiteness of the clause. Thus, root infinitives tend to occur with null subjects, while finite sentences typically contain overt subjects, as shown in table 6.3. (The correlation is not perfect; null subjects do occur with finite clauses and overt subjects with root infinitives, but the percentages are far less than would be expected by chance.)

Table 6.3 Null and overt subjects in finite and non-finite clauses (in percentages)

	FINITE VERB		NON-FINITE VERB	
	OVERT	NULL	OVERT	NULL
Flemish	75	25	11	89
German	80	20	11	89
French	74	26	7	93
Dutch	68	32	15	85

Sources: Flemish and French data from Kraemer (1994); Dutch data from Haegeman (1994); German data from Behrens (1993).

A similar correlation between null subjects and lack of finiteness holds in early English, but for reasons which are beyond the scope of this discussion, it shows up most clearly in wh-questions. Restricting our attention to wh-contexts, then, we find null subjects occurring predominantly in non-finite questions, such as (41a), while finite questions typically have overt subjects, as in (41b). In one study, 49 percent of the non-finite wh-questions had null subjects, while only 5 percent of the finite wh-questions had null subjects (Roeper and Rohrbacher 1994). Thus, sentences such as (43c) are virtually unattested.

(41)   a.   Where _____ go?
      b.   Where dis goes?
      c.   @Where _____ goes?

Notice that we are assuming that the verb in (41a) is non-finite. This is because the intended subject of the sentence (which we infer from context) is third-person, and yet the verb is not marked with either *-s* or *-ed*. Recall from our discussion in chapter 3 that in English the infinitive does not bear a distinctive affix, but is homophonous with the verbal stem, for example, *eat*, *sleep*, *dance*. Thus, the English equivalent of a root infinitive would be a bare verb. Indeed, it has been hypothesized that when the English-speaking child says *Mommy go* or asks a question such as (41a), these are in fact root infinitives, parallel to the French and Dutch examples in (25) and (26). Thus, children acquiring overt subject languages produce null subjects mainly in non-finite clauses. In this regard, it is interesting to note that the subject position of a non-finite clause is in fact the one context in which a null subject is licensed in such languages. In chapter 5 it was pointed out that infinitives and tensed clauses have the same structure. Both have subjects. This is apparent when the subject is overt as in the example in (42a), but there is also a subject in (42b), a silent PRO subject, as discussed in chapter 3.

(42)   a.   It takes courage [for Kate to defy Petruccio].
      b.   It takes courage [PRO to defy Petruccio].

The referent of the PRO subject of (42b) is 'someone', as in 'It takes courage for someone to defy Petruccio.'

The licensing of a null subject by a non-finite verb is in fact a property of UG, and hence, we find this phenomenon in all the languages under consideration. Some examples are given in (43):

(43)   a.   Kate wants   [PRO_____to defy Petruccio]
      b.   Kate wil   [PRO_____ Petruccio uitdagen]   (Dutch)
      c.   Kate veut   [_PRO_____ défier Petruccio]   (French)

Thus, children acquiring overt subject languages are not really making an error in using null subjects in root infinitives. Quite the contrary, they are giving evidence of their knowledge of UG. The null subject facts also provide further evidence that very young children make a grammatical distinction between finite and non-finite clauses. Their use of finiteness is not haphazard, otherwise the distribution of null versus overt subjects would be random. The question of why children use null subjects in root clauses, when adult speakers cannot, now reduces to the question of why they use infinitives in root contexts. If we can answer the latter question, we also have an answer to the former. We have reduced two questions to one.

Now we must provide an explanation for why root infinitives are possible in the language of young children. Another way of asking this question is: Why can children leave the temporal specification of a sentence unmarked when adults cannot? Let us take up this question in the context of a larger issue, namely, why is it that various functional elements, including tense, (subject) pronouns, auxiliaries, and determiners, are often omitted in early language?

6.9　Clause Structure and Functional Categories

As is evident from the various examples provided in this chapter, young children frequently 'drop' functional elements from their utterances. We noted in the previous section that children often omit subject pronouns, resulting in null subject sentences, and they may omit tense inflection, resulting in root infinitives. We also find that determiners and auxiliaries may be missing from positions in which they would be obligatory in the adult language. This early language is sometimes called **telegraphic speech** because of its similarity to the language an adult might use when sending a telegram, in which various function words are omitted:

Stranded in Athens, need money, send immediately.

The adult sending such a telegram might be trying to save money by omitting those words which would be easy to guess from grammatical or non-linguistic context. But why do children drop these elements? Is it for economy reasons as well, and if so, what are they economizing on, grammatical resources or something else? There are various theories concerning the nature of telegraphic speech. We will discuss three different proposals, one which explains telegraphic speech as an effect of the child's grammar, another which says it is a phonological effect, and the last which attributes the phenomenon to the child's pragmatic system.

6.9.1　A prefunctional grammar?

One theory of why children omit tense and other functional elements is that their grammars lack functional categories, DET, INFL, COMP. In this view the early grammar is **prefunctional**, and children's phrase-structure representations consist of lexical projections only, that is, NP, VP, AP, PPs. One instantiation of this idea is the **small clause hypothesis**, according to which children's early sentences are structurally equivalent to adult small clauses, discussed in chapter 3. Small clauses consist of some XP and a subject, but without the functional architecture, as follows:

(44) a. [$_{VP}$* [$_{NP}$ Man] [$_{VP}$ sit down]]
     b. [$_{PP}$* [$_{NP}$ Mommy][$_{PP}$ in house]]
     c. [$_{AP}$* [$_{NP}$ Dolly] [$_{AP}$ happy]]
     d. [$_{NP}$* [$_{NP}$ Mommy] [$_{NP}$ shoe]]

Negative markers and wh-phrases, such as those in (18c, d, g, h), would be adjunctions to the small clause, as in (45), rather than T or C elements, as in the adult grammar.

(45) [No/wh [[$_{NP}$] [$_{VP}$]]]

The small clause hypothesis and related theories provide an account for missing functional elements in a straightforward manner; there is simply no position in the early phrase marker for such elements to be inserted. There can be no tense marking or auxiliaries if there is no TP; determiners and complementizers will be lacking if there is no DP or CP, respectively. This approach may also appeal to an intuition that we have that early language is structurally simpler than adult language. But there is a problem: The prefunctional grammar idea seems to be directly at odds with the various facts discussed earlier. First, functional elements do occur in early language, but they are optional whereas they would be required in the adult grammar. Second, we saw that verb position parameters are set from the earliest multi-word utterances. If finite verbs move in early French and in the V2 languages, as illustrated above, there must be positions to which they raise, presumably I and C. Third, if English-, Dutch-, and French-speaking children omit subjects predominantly with non-finite verbs, they must be able to distinguish finite and non-finite verbs, itself a strong indicator of some functional representation at this early stage. In addition, as pointed out above, children who otherwise omit a fully spelled-out functional element may nevertheless produce a phonological placeholder, indicating that they have the structural position available.

There is also compelling experimental evidence that children have knowledge of functional elements even before they are producing these elements. In one study 2-year-old children were significantly better at identifying pictures in response to grammatical sentences with determiners, such as (46a), than when presented with ungrammatical sentences with the copula *be* in determiner position, such as in (46b) (Gerken and McIntosh 1993).

(46) a. Find *the* bird for me.
     b. Find *was* bird for me.

If children did not have knowledge of the different functional elements, that is, determiner versus *be*, or their positional requirements, then they should perform equally well on the two sentence types, contrary to fact.

The empirical evidence from children's productive language as well as the results of comprehension tasks argues strongly against the hypothesis that children have a prefunctional grammar. Below we will look at children's development of agreement and case systems. These data also point to a grammar with functional structure. But all these data leave us with a puzzle as well: if children have full, adult-like syntactic structures and not just small clauses, what accounts for the telegraphic quality of their utterances?

6.9.2 The metrical hypothesis

A different kind of explanation for the young child's omission of functional elements attributes the phenomenon to a phonological, more specifically metrical, constraint on the child's speech production system. In English, function morphemes usually occur in unstressed syllables. You can recognize a stressed syllable because it tends to be longer and louder than an unstressed syllable. For example, the first syllable in the word *apple – a –* is stressed and the second syllable *ple* is unstressed. In a sentence like *The apple is red*, *the* and *is*, the function words, are unstressed. Various studies have shown that in experimental settings children tend to omit function morphemes most frequently when they occur in an unstressed syllable which is followed by a stressed syllable. (We will represent this type of stress pattern as U–S.) On the other hand, they are less inclined to drop the unstressed function morpheme when it follows a stressed syllable (represented by S–U). For example, in imitation tasks, children are more likely to omit the article in (47a), where it is in a U–S stress pattern, than in (47b), where it occurs in an S–U stress pattern (Gerken 1991). (Unstressed syllables are indicated by lower-case letters and stressed syllables by upper-case letters.)

(47) a. the BEAR + KISSED JANE
      b. PETE + KISSED the + LAMB

Similar results have been obtained for subject versus object pronouns. Because a subject pronoun is in a U–S stress pattern as in (48a), while an object pronoun is most often in an S–U pattern, as in (48b), the subject is more likely to be dropped.

(48) a. he KISSED + JANE
      b. PETE + KISSED her

In this way, the metrical hypothesis also provides an account of early null subjects discussed in the previous section.

According to the metrical analysis there is a kind of phonological filter on the child's ouput which lets pass S–U patterns but not U–S patterns.

Why children have the preference for an S–U structure over a U–S structure in their productions may have to do with the fact that S–U is the predominant stress pattern in English, or it may be that there is an innate preference for S–U stress patterns. We have already seen that infants come prewired with various perceptual biases, and the S–U filter may be another one. Only cross-linguistic research can resolve this issue.

While the metrical hypothesis accounts nicely for the results of the imitation experiments, it fares less well in explaining the various generalizations which emerge from the naturalistic speech data. For example, it does not explain the apparent dependency between null subjects and (non-)finiteness, nor does it explain why children drop (pronominal) subjects even when they are not in a U–S pattern, such as in wh-questions, such as the examples in (41). More generally, the metrical hypothesis provides no basis for understanding the root infinitive phenomenon, which seems to be at the core of 'telegraphic' speech. It does not explain why young English-speaking children produce bare verb forms, as in (18b, e), since tense morphology is either non-syllabic (*does, eats*), or, when syllabic, consitutes a weak syllable in an S–U pattern (*he DANCes*). Nor does it capture the apparent relationship between the English bare verb forms and the root infinitives produced by children acquiring languages with real morphological infinitives, such as Dutch and French (cf. (25), (26). The metrical hypothesis does not lead us to expect that children will add a syllabic inflectional ending to verbs. According to the metrical hypothesis the omission of pronouns and determiners is unrelated to properties of the verb, yet, intuitively, the dropping of tense morphology seems very similar to the omission of determiners and pronouns. These various elements are syntactically similar in that they are heads of functional projections, and as we will discuss shortly, they have a similar pragmatic function.

6.9.3 A pragmatic hypothesis

A rather different account for the optionality of finiteness and the other functional elements is related to the child's knowledge of **pragmatics**. Pragmatics concerns the rules of language use, including how sentences fit into a larger discourse and non-linguistic context. For example, various elements in sentences, such as pronouns (*he*) and definite DPs (*the boy*), require discourse antecedents or their reference will not be clear. And tense is specified relative to discourse time; past tense means prior to the time of discourse and present tense means simultaneous with discourse time. It is well known, however, that children often fail to make explicit information which can be inferred from context, or which constitutes part of their own background knowledge. For example, a child might simply open a discourse by saying *He ate my ice cream*, assuming that the reference of *he* is clear to the interlocutor. The optionality of tense, determiners, and pronouns may have a similar basis; the child does not represent grammatically the temporal reference of the sentence, the (in)definiteness of NPs, and (subject) pronouns because he or she assumes (sometimes wrongly) that this information is available through discourse context or that the background information is shared between speaker and hearer(s). If this view is correct, it means that children's grammatical knowledge is in advance of their knowledge of discourse principles. They know about abstract functional structure but they do not yet know the conditions under which the reference of pronouns – lexical and null – must be grammatically, rather than contextually determined. In contrast to the metrical hypothesis discussed above, the pragmatic hypothesis provides a unified account of the various omissions.

6.9.4   Maturation vs. continuity of grammatical structures and principles

We have considered several hypotheses concerning the nature of telegraphic speech and the grammar of 2-year-olds. While we still have no clear explanation for why children optionally omit functional elements such as determiners, pronouns, and tense marking, the preponderance of evidence argues that children do have functional structure at this early age and that their grammars show the same richness of constituent structure as adult grammars. Children may differ from adults with respect to their productive abilities or in their pragmatic abilities (or both).

Our discussion of functional architecture and adult–child differences raises a more general question about early grammar, namely, do children have all of the principles of UG, or is it possible that certain core properties of grammar mature during the course of development? Behind the small clause hypothesis is the broader hypothesis that certain fundamental aspects of syntax are not present in the early grammar but subject to maturation. This is referred to as the **maturation hypothesis**. The opposite view, referred to as the **continuity hypothesis**, says that all aspects of UG are available throughout development. It is important to note that in either view, UG principles are presumed to be innate – to account for how a child can learn abstract properties. But on the maturational view, principles and/or structures of UG emerge according to a biological timetable, much like secondary sexual characteristics in humans, which are innate but which emerge at puberty.

We know that certain aspects of UG are present as early as we can test for them: basic principles of phrase structure and various movement rules, for example. But whether there are other UG principles which develop later in childhood is still an open question requiring further research. Advances in linguistic theory and the development of more sophisticated experimental techniques allow researchers to test younger and younger children on their knowledge of principles of grammar. What is clear at present is that children are not born speaking an adult language; hence, something must mature to make that possible. The jury is still out on precisely which aspects of the language faculty undergo maturation, whether it is UG itself, the speech production mechanisms, the pragmatic system, the lexicon or some combination of the above.

In the following section we will discuss another fundamental property of grammar – syntactic dependencies. We are interested in learning how and when children acquire basic syntactic dependencies. Of course, syntactic dependencies are defined on phrase structures, so an understanding of children's dependencies also provides us with further information about early constituent structure.

6.10 Syntactic Dependencies

As discussed in chapter 4, syntactic dependencies are one of the fundamental properties of grammar. A syntactic dependency is when a word or a morpheme in a sentence depends on the presence of some other word or morpheme in the sentence. We have already seen one dependency in early grammar – the relation between null subjects and (root) infinitives. In this section we will look at some other syntactic dependencies in early grammar. In particular, we will examine Case and Agreement systems in early language, and children's knowledge of reflexive binding. In this context, we will also examine the role of structure dependency of grammatical rules and c-command, two conditions which regulate syntactic dependencies.

We are interested in determining at what point children show knowledge of these various dependencies and in what ways their grammars might differ from the adult grammar. Are these relations evident at all points or is there a maturational effect?

We will look first at Agreement and Case because this relates closely to our previous discussion of functional structure in early grammar. As in the earlier sections, the results we consider here are based primarily on the spontaneous speech of very young children – around 2 years old. We will then turn our attention to issues concerning structure dependency, c-command, and binding. Most of what we know about these kinds of dependencies comes from experimental studies with somewhat older children, roughly ages 4–6 years.

In chapter 4 we saw that there are certain basic dependencies which are morphologically expressed, such as Agreement and Case. Because these relations are made visible by the morphology, they are fairly easy to investigate in child language. Take, for example, subject–verb agreement. As noted in chapters 2 and 4, in certain languages, such as Italian, each verb

SIDEBAR 6.3

Techniques for investigating child grammars

It is generally the case that studies of very early language are based on naturalistic data, while studies of older children are experimental. This is because children under $2\frac{1}{2}$ are understandably usually not very cooperative in experimental settings. As we noted earlier, however, new techniques are being developed which allow researchers to experimentally probe the syntactic knowledge of very young children – even children who are not yet talking! The most common experimental techniques for studying language development in children over the age of $2\frac{1}{2}$ are act-out/comprehension tasks and modified judgment tasks. In an act-out task the child must act out a particular sentence which is orally presented by the experimenter. This is usually done with the help of dolls and props of various sorts. For example, the child might be asked 'can you show me *the cat jumped over the fence.*' In a modified judgment task (Crain and Mckee 1985), the child is asked to decide whether a particular sentence orally presented by the experimenter matches a particular interpretation, depicted by a video, picture, or scenario acted out by the experimenter. For example, the child may be asked 'Is this a picture of *Ernie is kissing Bert*?' when shown a picture or video of Ernie kissing Bert or a picture of Bert kissing Ernie.

Direct judgments of grammaticality of the sort linguists extract from adults are difficult to elicit from children, though some experimenters have had success with this technique. Children often laugh at ungrammatical sentences, for example, and in some cases are able to 'correct' an ungrammatical sentence spoken by a puppet or toy animal.

Imitation tasks are also sometimes used with very young children, the idea being that the child's grammar acts as a filter on the imitation so that the child will repeat the sentence only as permitted by his or her grammar. Early studies of children in the telegraphic stage, for example, showed that the children would omit function morphemes not only in spontaneous speech but also their repetition of well-formed sentences. For example, presented with *Mommy will eat an ice cream*, the child would repeat *Mommy eat ice cream*. Each of these techniques has its strengths and shortcomings. The choice of technique depends on a variety of factors including the age of the children and the particular aspect of grammar being investigated.

As mentioned in Sidebar 6.2 and Chapter 15, other techniques are used with infants under the age of two.

form is marked to agree in person and number with the subject. The Italian present tense agreement paradigm is given in (49):

(49) *parlare*　'to speak'

	Singular	*Plural*
1st per.	parl<u>o</u>	parl<u>iamo</u>
2nd per.	parl<u>i</u>	parl<u>ate</u>
3rd per.	parl<u>a</u>	parl<u>ono</u>

There have been a number of studies which investigate whether children obey the rules of agreement, particularly subject–verb agreement, and there is a now a wide range of cross-linguistic evidence pointing towards the same conclusion – children acquire agreement rules at a strikingly early age. This is evidenced by the fact that they make agreement errors very infrequently. They typically use the correct verb form corresponding to the subject (e.g. *io parlo*, 'I speak', *lui parla*, 'he speaks' etc.).

The acquisition of agreement has been looked at in a number of different languages, including Spanish, Catalan, Italian, and German. Overall, the results show that in children between the ages of $1\frac{1}{2}$ years and $2\frac{1}{2}$ years, agreement is correct approximately 96 percent of the time. Surely, to perform so well children must know the grammatical requirement that a verb agree with the subject of the sentence. It is important to note, however, that these results do not mean that children have necessarily acquired the entire agreement paradigm by the age of $2\frac{1}{2}$. For example, children this age seldom use plural forms, and depending on the particular language, the second-person singular may emerge in production later than first- or third-person singular. Children acquire inflectional morphemes individually, perhaps in opposition to one another. Just as they do not acquire all the nouns of a language in one fell swoop, neither do they acquire all the inflectional endings in a paradigm. Importantly, however, those forms that they do have, they use correctly. The absence of a full paradigm alongside the correct agreement indicates that initially children are referentially more restricted than adults, not grammatically more restricted. (We return to this point in the discussion of the acquisition of semantic knowledge in chapter 10.)

The agreement results are important for a number of reasons. First, they tell us that the young child's grammatical competence includes knowledge of basic dependencies, and in this respect their grammar is adult-like. Second, they provide further evidence that children have functional structure since agreement is an inflectional category. Finally, these results provide additional insight into the root infinitive phenomenon discussed earlier; children are not using root infinitives simply because they do not know the relevant finite forms.

Another kind of local dependency is realized in the form of case morphology. In many languages the form of a pronoun or NP depends on its grammatical function in the sentence. Thus, as noted in chapter 4, subjects bear nominative case, direct complements bear accusative case, possessors bear genitive case, and so on. The English case system is rather minimal, showing up only on pronouns, for example *he* is the nominative form, *him* the accusative form, and *his* is the genitive form. In other languages, for example, German, Latin, and Russian, non-pronominal DPs may also be marked for case. German distinguishes nominative, accusative, genitive, and dative cases (indirect object complements bear dative case), and Russian has six basic cases.

In looking at the acquisition of case systems, we find that children acquiring languages with a rich case system use case-marking very early, though they may not use all forms in the paradigm with equal accuracy. For example, Russian-speaking children as young as $1\frac{1}{2}$ years old case-mark nominal expressions, and they are extremely accurate. But they do better with some cases than with others. They hardly ever make errors in case assignment to subjects, which always receive nominative case. Direct and indirect objects are also correctly case-marked with accusative and dative case most of the time, but show more errors than subjects. Similar results have been obtained in German. German-speaking children use nominative case with a very high degree of accuracy while accusative and dative cases are used at lower accuracy level, but far above chance. In both languages the most frequent error is for the children to use nominative case where another case is required, as illustrated in (50):

(50)   a.   Du hann   (should be *dich*)
            you-nom. hit
            'I hit you.'
       b.   Meiner au sauber mach ich saube Mama   (should be *meinen*)
            mine also clean make I clean Mama
            'I make mine clean, clean, Mama.'

What is the source of these case errors? One hypothesis we can rule out immediately is that children do not know the relevant case morphology or the rules of case assignment since they in fact use accusative case (and the other cases) correctly most of the time. The reason for using nominative case on objects may be because nominative case is the **default case** in these languages. By default case we mean the case that is used when a DP is not in a structural case-marking position. According to the rules of case assignment to DPs presented in chapter 4, case is assigned in particular structural configurations: a complement to a verb bears accusative case. If the object is outside the case-marking domain of the verb, it cannot receive accusative case. For example, in the sentence in (51) the DP *Der Johan* is outside the VP and hence, even though it is logically the object of the verb *seen*, it bears default nominative case. The pronoun *ihn*, on the other hand, bears accusative case because it is in complement position.

(51)   Der Johan, ich habe ihn gesehen
       the Johan-nom. I have him-accus. seen
       'As for Johan, I have seen him.'

It is therefore possible that children's errors such as those in (50) represent instances in which the complement DP bears the default nominative case instead of the regularly assigned accusative case. Let us call this the **default case hypothesis**. More specifically, the default case hypothesis says that in the early grammar structural case assignment may fail and when it does, the DP takes on default case. This hypothesis will receive some empirical support when we consider some interesting case errors in early English.

As noted earlier, the English case system is rather minimal. We might predict, then, that English-speaking children should make few errors. Indeed, case errors are not frequent in English. But there is one error which is noteworthy, instances in which children use an accusative pronoun in subject position, as in (52):

(52)   a.   Her have a big mouth.
       b.   Him fall down.

Although only about 10 percent of pronominal subjects are accusative, the error is interesting because it contrasts sharply with the results in other languages. We have just seen that in languages such as German and Russian, which have much more complex case systems, children perform best with subject case-marking. In English, in contrast, subject position is the locus of their errors. Why do we find accusative-marked subjects in English? Let us return to our default case hypothesis. In German and Russian the default case is nominative and we hypothesized that the children's errors in these languages involved the use of default (= nominative) case on object complements. In English, in contrast, the children's errors involve accusative case on subjects. Remarkably, in English the default case is accusative. This is easy to see if we take a sentence roughly comparable to the German sentence in (51):

(53)   Him, he left the party early.

The subject of the sentence is *he*, but if we repeat the subject (for emphasis, for example) using a dislocated pronoun, then the pronoun outside the IP is accusative *him*. Thus, in English a pronoun which is not in a position to which structural case is assigned, bears accusative case. The next piece of the puzzle concerns the root infinitive phenomenon, discussed earlier. It turns out that accusative subjects occur ONLY with root infinitives and not with finite verbs, as illustrated in (52) (Schütze 1996). We do not find accusative subjects with verbs which bear present tense morphology, as in @*him does it*. The default case hypothesis can explain this result: the rule of nominative case assignment says that the subject of a tensed clause bears nominative case (as discussed in chapter 2, root infinitives are non-tensed, hence default accusative case may appear).

The fact that young children acquiring case-rich languages such as German and Russian use case morphology at such an early age leads to various

SIDEBAR 6.4

Morphological overgeneralization

One of the best known phenomena in language acquisition is morphological **overgeneralization**. Overgeneralization occurs when the child applies a grammatical rule more broadly than it applies in the adult grammar. Typical examples are forms such as *eated, goed, tooths*, where the child applies the regular rule of past tense or plural affixation to forms which are exceptional or irregular in the adult language, *ate, went, teeth*. Overgeneralization 'errors' are very important because they provide clear evidence that children do not learn language by imitation (they could not have learned *eated* from their parents), but rather that they use the ambient language as a basis for figuring out the rules of the grammar. In fact, the instinct to formulate rules is so strong that children apply the rule even in cases in which it directly contradicts the input, for example *eated* versus *ate*.

Would it make sense to think about the case errors in (52) and (54) as instances of overgeneralization?

conclusions. First, it argues strongly against the idea that the early grammar is prefunctional. Like subject–verb agreement, case relations involve inflectional categories. Second, it illustrates that children know the dependency relations between particular structural positions and particular cases at a very early age. If they did not, then their assignment of the different cases would be random, which is far from the case. The English case errors provide particularly strong evidence that children have knowledge of basic structural dependencies; since RIs are not part of the core adult grammar and hence not in the input the child receives, the fact that there exists a dependency between root infinitives and default accusative case must come from the child's innate knowledge of the principles of case assignment.

6.10.1 Reflexives

Another kind of dependency is shown by anaphors. An **anaphor** is a word that depends on another element in the sentence for its interpretation. Reflexive pronouns are a kind of anaphor. The reflexive pronoun *himself* in sentence (54) is understood as referring to *Macbeth*. The element that provides the reference of an anaphor is called its **antecedent**. In (54) the DP *Macbeth* is the antecedent to *himself*.

(54)   Macbeth cut himself.

As discussed in chapter 4 the reflexive–antecedent relation is governed by two structural principles: the clausemate condition and the c-command condition. The clausemate condition says that a reflexive and its antecedent must be in exactly the same clause. Thus, the sentence in (55) is ungrammatical because it violates the clausemate condition.

(55)   *Macbeth said that you cut himself.

The c-command condition says that the antecedent must c-command the anaphor. Recall that the c-command domain of an XP is the first constituent containing the XP. An XP c-commands everything in its c-command domain.

In (54) the DP *Macbeth*, which is the subject, c-commands *himself*, as shown by the structure in (56):

(56)

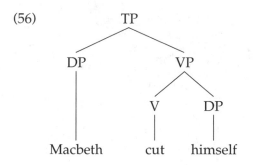

Consider, however, the sentence in (57):

(57)   Macbeth's friend cut himself.

This sentence cannot mean that 'Macbeth cut himself' nor that 'Macbeth cut his friend'. The DP *Macbeth* cannot be the antecedent to the reflexive because the reflexive is not in the c-command domain of *Macbeth*. To see why this is so, we need to draw the tree.

(58)

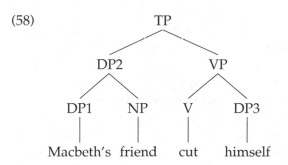

DP1, containing *Macbeth*, does not c-command *himself*. On the other hand, DP2 does and hence *Macbeth's friend* is the only possible antecedent for *himself*.

Do young children have the principles of reflexivization? This question is more properly broken down into three logically independent questions:

Figure 6.2a   Cinderella's sister is touching herself

(1) Do children know that *himself/herself* are anaphors? (2) Do they show evidence of knowing the c-command condition? and (3) Do they show evidence of knowing the clausemate condition? There have been a number of studies which address these questions, some of which make use of the structures of the sort in (56) and (58). In one study (Wexler and Chien 1985) children between the ages of $2\frac{1}{2}$ and $6\frac{1}{2}$ years are given sentences such as in (59) and asked to choose a picture which matches the sentence. In one picture Cinderella's sister is touching herself and in the other Cinderella's sister is touching Cinderella, as shown in figures 6.2a and 6.2b.

(59)   Cinderella's sister is touching herself.

As discussed above, the only grammatical interpretation of this sentence is that Cinderella's sister is touching herself. *Cinderella* cannot be the

Figure 6.2b Cinderella's sister is touching Cinderella

antecedent because it does not c-command the reflexive. Thus, if children know the c-command condition on the reflexive–antecedent dependency, they will choose the picture in which the sister is touching herself, and not the picture in which the sister is touching Cinderella. The results of such experiments show that by about the age of 5 years children are reliably adhering to the c-command requirement on reflexives. Since c-command is defined on hierarchical structure, these results also tell us that the children are imposing adult-like structures onto these sentences.

The youngest children (under age 4) respond at about chance (50 percent correct). Why do the younger children so often choose the incorrect, non-c-commanding antecedent? One possibility is that the c-command condition is not active very early on, but rather is a principle of UG which undergoes maturation – at around age 5. An alternative explanation is that

SIDEBAR
6.5

Structure dependency early grammar

It is sometimes suggested that children adopt a strategy of choosing the closest antecedent for an anaphor pronoun. Notice that such a 'minimal distance strategy' would not be structure-dependent because it would refer to linear order rather than hierarchical structure. In Chapter 4, we saw that linguistic rules must be structure-dependent. Thus, if children did use a minimal distance strategy, they would be violating a basic principle of language structure. In the reflexive experiments we can see that children are clearly not following such a linear strategy since the closest antecedent to the reflexive is *sister*, and the children would choose the picture in which Cinderella's sister touched herself (the correct response but by the wrong means), contrary to fact. The clausemate experiments also show that children do not use a minimal distance strategy since they actually choose the DP which is furthest away. Thus, these experiments argue strongly against the idea that children use structure-independent rules.

the younger children have not yet learned that *himself/herself* are anaphors, and hence subject to the c-command condition. We said earlier that there are three different aspects to understanding reflexive binding, the first of these is to learn that expressions such as *himself/herself* are reflexive. Recall that the words of a language must be learned along with their syntactic properties and this kind of lexical learning might take more experience with the language. One possibility is that children initially misanalyze *himself/herself* as a possessive construction, analogous to 'his/her body'. This receives some support from the fact that young children frequently say 'hisself', rather than 'himself'. If this were the case, then *himself/herself* would first behave more like a special kind of non-reflexive pronoun. We can see in the sentence in (60), where we substitute *her body* for *herself*, that either DP1 or DP2 can serve as antecedent (cf. (58)):

(60)   Cinderella's sister touched her body.
       = Cinderella's sister touched her own body.
       = Cinderella's sister touched Cinderella's body.

Children will continue to allow both antecedents until they recategorize *himself/herself* as reflexives and at that point the relevant constraints become operative. We would maintain, however, that the c-command condition and the clausemate condition themselves, as principles of UG, are always part of the child's linguistic competence, but that they do not show their effect in these cases because the children have made a lexical error.

Children have also been tested on the clausemate condition on reflexives. In these studies the children are given complex sentences of the sort in (61):

(61)   Mulan says that (Sarah) should point to herself.

The child is instructed to act out the sentence. The lower subject (in parentheses) contains the name of the child, in this case *Sarah*, and *Mulan* is a
puppet. The correct adult-like response would be for the child to point to
herself since only the lower subject is a clausemate of *herself*. The incorrect
response would be for the child to point to Mulan since the DP *Mulan* is
not in the same clause as *herself* and hence cannot serve as antecedent.

Results show that by about 5 to $5\frac{1}{2}$ years children reliably choose the
lower subject, that is themselves, as antecedent, thereby demonstrating
their knowledge of the clausemate condition. However, the younger children often choose the antecedent outside the clause, Mulan. In fact, the
very youngest children – $2\frac{1}{2}$ years to 3 years – choose the clausemate as
antecedent only about 20 percent of the time. This is much worse than
their performance on the c-command task, where they were correct for
about 50 percent of the time. Following up on our hypothesis that children
initially treat the reflexive *herself/himself* as a possessive construction, we
can see that it would be possible for a possessive pronoun to take its
antecedent outside of the immediate clause. This is illustrated in (62), where
her can take *Sarah* or *Mulan* as antecedent:

(62)   Mulan says that (Sarah) should point to her body.
       = Sarah should point to Sarah's body.
       = Sarah should point to Mulan's body.

Our hypothesis thus predicts that both the higher and the lower subjects
should be possible antecedents for the children who have not yet learned
that *himself/herself* are reflexives. Why then is there a stronger tendency for
the youngest children to choose the higher subject? To answer this question, we need to return to our discussion of linguistic variation. It turns out
that there are languages in which possessive pronouns behave differently
than they do in English. In English, it is possible for a pronoun inside a
possessive construction to refer to an antecedent inside the same clause, as
illustrated in (62), when *her* can refer to *Sarah*. In other languages, Icelandic
for example, a possessive pronoun inside a possessive construction cannot
take a clausemate as antecedent. In (63) *hann* can only refer to *Pétur*, not
Jón.

(63)   Pétur segir að Jón þvoi bílinn í hverri viku
       Peter says that John washes car-the his in every day
       'Peter says that John washes his (= Peter's) car every day.'

It appears that young English-speaking children are not only treating
himself/herself like a possessive construction, but they are treating it like a

possessive construction of the Icelandic variety. Thus, when presented with a sentence such as (61), they choose the antecedent that is outside the local clause. This 'error' will be corrected when they hear English sentences in which a possessive pronoun clearly refers to a clause-internal antecedent, an example such as *Mulan washed her clothes*. At this point they should allow both the clause-internal and clause-external DPs as antecedents in roughly equal proportions. This appears to happen at around age $4\frac{1}{2}$. Eventually they will also learn that *herself/himself* are reflexives, at which point the clausemate condition will force the local DP to act as antecedent. As we said earlier, this seems to occur at around age $5\frac{1}{2}$. It is important to understand that all these developments happen unconsciously; the child's knowledge of grammar, like the adult's, is tacit knowledge, not accessible to introspection. But we see the effects of the child's grammatical and lexical knowledge in his linguistic performance, which includes speaking and understanding in natural language settings as well as in experimental tasks such as those described here.

The child's development of reflexives illustrates the more general point about acquisition made earlier, which is that idiosyncratic lexical properties of words must be learned. The child must learn the pronunciation and meaning of the words in his language (since these are arbitrary), and he must also learn the syntactic and semantic properties of individual words. These properties include, among other things, whether an element is an anaphor or a pronoun. And to the extent that there are different kinds of pronouns and anaphors the child must figure out which kind his particular language uses.

6.11 Summary

Knowledge of how to build words and sentences is evident throughout language development. In the domain of morphology we see that even at the earliest stages of language development children appear to know the distinctions between types of morphemes – root vs. affix, bound vs. free, inflectional vs. derivational affix, content vs. function word – and the rules governing the ways they may be combined. Moreover, children are sensitive to the fundamental word-structures of their target language; for example, whether roots can stand alone as words. They stick to these patterns even in the face of frequent exceptions until later in development, when their grammars have matured to the point where exceptions can be tolerated. Morphological processes or rules which must be memorized and do not follow from general principles are mastered relatively late in acquisition in contrast with similar phenomena which are the products of grammatical rules or principles.

When we turn to syntax development, we find a similar result; children have knowledge of the particular syntactic properties of the target language at a remarkably early age. This is most clearly evidenced in the early setting of various parameters such as verb position parameters. We also have evidence that very young children have knowledge of general principles of grammar such as principles of phrase structure, including functional structure, and syntactic dependencies such as those expressed by agreement, case, and anaphor–antecedent relations.

We can conclude by returning to the point made in chapter 1 concerning the relation of linguistic theory to language acquisition. Our theory leads us to expect that children will exhibit developmental delays or 'errors' in certain aspects of language development but not others. Children should not have difficulty with those invariant properties which are given by UG, structure dependency and c-command, for example, nor with the setting of UG parameters. We expect, however, that they may 'go astray' at those points where specific lexical properties must be learned, for example whether a word is an anaphor or a pronoun, or what derivational affixes it allows. We can see, then, that an understanding of the properties of different adult grammars is very important to our understanding of development in children. By the same token, an understanding of the stages that children go through and where they show errors and delays can tell us a great deal about the general organization of language in the mind.

Notes

1 Many of the child language examples are taken from the *Child Language Data Exchange System* (MacWhinney and Snow 1985).

2 Aksu-Koč, and Slobin, D. 1985. The acquisition of Turkish. In D. Slobin, ed., *The Crosslinguistic Study of Language Acquisition, Vol. I: The Data*, p. 854. Hillsdale, NJ: Erlbaum.

Further reading

Cairns, H. 1996. *The Acquisition of Language.* Austin, TX: Pro-Ed.

Goodluck, H. 1991. *Language Acquisition: A Linguistic Introduction.* Cambridge: Basil Blackwell.

Hyams, N. 1986. *Language Acquisition and the Theory of Parameters.* Dordrecht: Reidel.

Lightfoot, D. 1992. *Biology of Grammar.* Cambridge, MA: MIT Press.

Radford, A. 1990. *Syntactic Theory and the Acquisition of English Syntax.* Cambridge: Basil Blackwell.

In addition to those cited in the text, the following references were consulted: Radford 1986, Hickey 1990, Wexler 1994, Hoekstra and Hyams 1998, McDaniel, Cairns and Shu 1990.

Part III

Semantics

7

Semantics I:
Compositionality

CHAPTER CONTENTS

7.0 Introduction

Constituent structures like the ones in the previous chapters represent some of the properties of expressions that any competent user of language recognizes, as in the following:

(1)

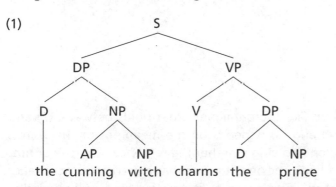

the cunning witch charms the prince

    Understanding this sentence involves determining what the subject DP is, determining what the verb phrase VP is, and determining all the other constituents and relations that are depicted by this tree. To be a competent language user, though, requires something more. A language user needs to know something about what the structures of the language mean.

Semantic theory is the study of the linguistic aspects of the meanings of expressions. It is not always easy to distinguish semantic properties – the linguistic aspects of meaning – from general background knowledge. What is required to understand a sentence like (1), for example, will be a tiny fraction of what most English speakers actually know about witches and princes and charms. The sentence can be understood by people who believe there are witches and by people who do not. That is, understanding this sentence does not require a knowledge of what things, if any, the noun *witch* refers to, or denotes, nor does it require that we know whether it is true or not. Understanding a sentence does, however, require that we recognize some more basic things, such as certain relations between this sentence and others. For example, a speaker cannot be said to understand the sentence:

(2)   Quince is a blond carpenter.

unless the speaker knows that if sentence (2) is true, then so is sentence (3):

(3)   Quince is a carpenter.

When the truth of one sentence guarantees the truth of a second sentence, we say that the first **entails** the second. Therefore, sentence (2) entails sentence (3). This relation between sentences depends on what the sentences mean, and not just on the categories of the words and how they are put together to make phrases; thus it is a **semantic relation**. Notice that sentences (4) and (5) have words with the same categories, put together to make the same kinds of sentence structures, but (4) does not entail (5):

(4)   Quince is a fake lion.

(5)   Quince is a lion.

Recognizing relationships like the entailment that holds between (2) and (3) but not between (4) and (5) depends on the meanings of the words, but it does not depend on knowing whether the sentences are true or not. Rather, the relation is a linguistic one: it is one that any competent speaker knows. A semantic theory aims to account for this kind of knowledge about language.

Semantics in linguistic theory

The need for semantics in a theory of human language is controversial. Noam Chomsky (1995) says, for example, "It is possible that natural language has only syntax and pragmatics; it has a 'semantics' only in the sense of 'the study of how this instrument, whose formal structure and potentialities of expression are the subject of syntactic investigation, is actually put to use in a speech community'." One of Chomsky's ideas here is that natural language is internal to the speaker, and it is not fundamentally for representing things about the world, things that are true or false depending on matters possibly external to the speaker. Chomsky says, "it is not at all clear that the theory of natural language involves relations of 'denotation', 'true of', etc., in anything like the sense of the technical theory of meaning."

It is of course true that linguistic theory should not aim to specify the **denotation** (that is, the **reference**) of a name like *Hamlet* or of a phrase like *the witches*; nor should it aim to say which things a verb phrase like *live in the forest* is actually true of. Those matters are external to the speaker and irrelevant to linguistics. But this observation does not support the conclusion that speakers have no distinctively semantic knowledge. Entailment relations like the one that holds between (1) and (2) apparently hold in virtue of meaning: if (1) is true, then so is (2). These relations can be recognized without knowing which sentences are true in the real world, and without knowing how the sentences are used in discourse. However, this perspective can be challenged in various ways.

Some philosophers have argued that it is impossible to draw a principled distinction between linguistic knowledge and general knowledge about the world, and some linguists have claimed that entailment and other similar relations among sentences can be accounted for syntactically, without any mention of denotations or truth. These foundational questions have had an important influence on how linguists approach the subject. Fortunately, it is possible to say some interesting things about semantic properties without confronting these issues in their full generality, as we will see in this chapter and the next.

7.1 Compositionality

Any account of our ability to recognize semantic relations among sentences has to face the fact that this ability is not limited to just a few sentences, but extends through the unlimited range of sentences that any human language allows. The German logician and philosopher Gottlob Frege (1923) noticed this, and proposed the commonsense idea about how to account for this fact:

> It is astonishing what language can do. With a few syllables it can express an incalculable number of thoughts, so that even a thought grasped by a terrestrial

being for the very first time can be put into a form of words which will be understood by someone to whom the thought is entirely new. This would be impossible, were we not able to distinguish parts in the thought corresponding to the parts of a sentence, so that the structure of the sentence serves as an image of the structure of the thought.

The proposal here is the commonsense one that we understand a sentence by understanding its parts and by assembling those parts according to the structure of the sentence. This allows us to recognize the meaning of familiar parts and the meaning of familiar ways of combining parts even in sentences we have never heard before. Intuitively, the meaning of a sentence has, as parts, the meanings of the parts of the sentence, much as a picture has parts corresponding to parts of the whole scene portrayed. We can understand this as an empirical claim about the meanings of expressions of the language, a claim motivated in part by the psychological hypothesis that people actually determine the meanings of complex expressions in this way:

Semantic compositionality: The meaning of a sentence is determined by the meanings of its parts and by the ways in which those parts are assembled.

In other words, the rules for determining semantic properties are **recursive**, just as syntactic and morphological rules are. People understand sentences by understanding the parts of sentences and by recognizing the semantic implications of how those parts are assembled.

Adopting a compositional approach to semantics, we expect semantic theory to have two aspects: an account of the meanings of the basic elements of the language, and an account of how the meanings of complex expressions are built up from the meanings of their parts.

The relevant parts here are the syntactic constituents; the ways these constituents can be assembled are given by the theory of syntax. As we saw in the previous chapters, syntax assembles words into larger units, and trees like (1) show how this assembly is done. Since the meanings of the most basic elements of language, the morphemes, are not calculated from the meanings of any parts, these basic meanings must be learned. Any speaker of the language will know only finitely many of these basic meanings, but these parts can be assembled in infinitely many different, meaningful ways.

7.2   Entailment

Let's begin with the semantic relation between sentences that was indicated in the introduction, and work back from there to a view about the meanings of the meaningful parts of sentences. We observed that it is beyond the scope of linguistic theory to tell us, for example, what things (if any) are actually witches or forests, but any competent English speaker can recognize that if (2) is true then so is (3). Similarly, any competent English speaker can recognize that if (6) is true, then so is (7):

(6)   Julius Caesar was a famous man.

(7)   Julius Caesar was a man.

Let's define the relation which interests us here as follows:

Sentence S1 entails sentence S2 if, and only if, whenever S1 is true in a situation, S2 is also true in that situation.

It is important to see that this entailment relation involves just the possible circumstances in which the sentences are true, and does not involve any more complicated considerations about whether the two sentences are relevant to each other in any other ways. Defining entailment this way has some surprising consequences, and considering some of these consequences will help us see exactly what relation we are talking about.

Some sentences are true in all possible situations. While sentence (6) happens to be true, it is perfectly possible to imagine a coherent situation in which it would not be true. Caesar might not have been famous. Sentences like (8)–(10), on the other hand, are true in all possible situations:

(8)   Either there are witches in the forest or there aren't.

(9)   People are people.

(10)   The number four is even.

Given what these sentences mean in English, we can see that they are true no matter how things happen to be in the real world. These sentences are true simply in virtue of their meanings. There are no possible situations, situations which are coherent and imaginable, in which these sentences are false. Since these sentences are true in every imaginable situation, it follows that if (4) is true, then so is (8): (4) entails (8). In fact, every sentence entails (8), and every sentence entails (9), and every sentence entails (10). Even if sentence (4) were false it would entail (8) since (8) is true under any circumstances. Similarly, sentence (11) entails (12), but (12) does not entail (11):

(11)   Viola has stockings.

SIDEBAR
7.2

Entailment and possibilities

Understanding our definition of *entailment* requires getting the right sense of *possibility*, and this takes some practice because we commonly refer to many different kinds of possibility. It is an interesting fact that human languages have, in addition to sentences that are true or not depending on the way things are, some sentences that are true simply because of what they mean, so they carry no information about the world. It is impossible, in the sense that it is incoherent, to imagine that one of these sentences is false, given what the sentences mean. These sentences are sometimes said to be true in every logically possible situation, since logics also can have sentences that are always true simply because of what they mean. This notion of possibility differs from physical possibility. For example, it is not physically possible to travel faster than the speed of light, but this is not a linguistic fact. The meaning of the sentence *Nothing travels faster than the speed of light* does not determine that it is always true, and so this sentence is not entailed by (11) for example, the way (12) is. As far as the language is concerned, it is coherent to imagine situations in which this sentence is false, as science fiction authors often do. Obviously, the logical possibility we are interested in is also different from legal or moral possibility, as when we say that the sentence *The king's subjects pay taxes* is necessarily true, necessary in the sense of being legally or morally or practically unavoidable. Whatever necessity this sentence has does not come just from the meanings of the words.

(12)   Brown hedgehogs are hedgehogs.

These facts follow from the definition of entailment and from the fact that these sentences like (8), (9), (10), and (12) are true in every possible situation, unlike (1)–(7) and (11).

One other special convention about entailment is important: a contradiction is said to entail everything. For example, (13) entails (11):

(13)   Some hedgehog is not a hedgehog.

(13) is said to entail (11) because there is no logically possible situation in which (13) is true but (11) is not. The thing that makes this case odd is that (13) is never true, and so the entailment holds vacuously. (13) entails every sentence.

The sort of entailment that holds between (11) and (12) is not quite what common sense might lead you to expect, but it turns out to be a relation that is very basic and easy for linguists and logicians to study. Other sorts of relations that require sentences to be relevant to each other have proven to be much harder to study, and they have revealed less about how language works. A competent speaker's grasp of entailment relations links each sentence into a network of other sentences. When we hear something true, we can infer the truth of all the other sentences that are entailed by that sentence.

Explain why all of the following claims are true:

(i)   The sentence *Viola has yellow stockings* entails the sentence *Viola has stockings*.
(ii) The sentence *Viola has stockings* does not entail the sentence *Viola has yellow stockings*.
(iii) The sentence *Viola has stockings* entails the sentence *Either Viola has stockings or 2 is an even number*.
(iv) The sentence *Viola has stockings* entails the sentence *Either two is an odd number or two is not an odd number*.
(v)   The sentence *Two is an odd number* entails *Viola has stockings*.

EXERCISE 7.1

When someone tells us what a phrase means, or we look something up in a dictionary, we typically learn about entailment relations. For example, when you find out that the verb *cog* means 'cheat', then you know

(14)   The sentence *I will cog* entails *I will cheat*.

Friends, dictionaries, and other sources of information about the language tell us all sorts of different kinds of things when we ask what a word means, but typically at least some important entailment relations are among the things we get in a definition. You may not know whether I cog or not, but now you know something about what it means to cog. In the same way, you may or may not know that Romeo is the name of a fictional character, but as a speaker of English you know that if *Romeo loves Juliet* is true in some scene (or situation or world or model), fictional or otherwise, then *Something or someone loves Juliet* is true in that scene (or situation or world or model).

7.3   Extensional Semantics

7.3.1   Predicates and arguments

Whether a sentence is true or not often seems to depend just on what the subject refers to and on what things have the property represented by the verb phrase. The verb phrase is sometimes called a **predicate**, and the subject denotes the **argument** of the predicate. We could get this picture from simple sentences like the following:

Figure 7.1   Set of laughing people, with Cassandra in it

(15)   Cassandra laughed.

It is natural to assume that sentences like these assert that the thing referred to by the subject *Cassandra* has the property named by the verb phrase *laughed*. Letting ⟦Cassandra⟧ be the person named by the name *Cassandra*, and letting ⟦laughed⟧ be the set of things that laughed, we can say:

(16)   The sentence *Cassandra laughed* is true if, and only if, ⟦Cassandra⟧ is in ⟦laughed⟧.

Notice that knowing (16) does not require knowing who the name Cassandra refers to or who is in the set of people who laughed, or indeed, knowing how laughing differs from crying.
   Claim (16) may seem at first to be just a slightly awkward expression of a very simple fact, but this way of expressing things is really useful, leading us to notice some more general rules about when a sentence is true. One more general claim can be put as follows:

(17)   When DP is a proper name, a sentence of the form [DP VP] is true if, and only if, ⟦DP⟧ is in ⟦VP⟧.

On this approach, the VP is regarded as denoting a **set**, ⟦VP⟧, and the DP denotes or refers to something, ⟦DP⟧, which might or might not be in that set.
   (17), when taken together with basic facts about sets, can tell us about entailment relations. For example, since the set ⟦sits and sings⟧ is a **subset** of ⟦sings⟧ in every possible situation (that is, ⟦sings⟧ is the set of things that sing, and only some of those sit while they sing), (17) tells us that the sentence *Philomela sits and sings* entails *Philomela sings*. This simple relation holds in general, following from (17) and from the fact that everything in a subset of a set S is also in S:

Figure 7.2 Caliban, in a set of drunken singers, which is in a set of singers

(18) When DP is a proper name and we have two verb phrases VP1 and VP2 where ⟦VP1⟧ is always a subset of ⟦VP2⟧, then the sentence [DP VP1] entails the sentence [DP VP2].

Taking another example, since the set ⟦sings drunkenly⟧ is completely included in the set ⟦sings⟧, the sentence *Caliban sings drunkenly* entails *Caliban sings*.

7.3.2 Extensions and intensions

The sets of things with the property named by a noun like *witch* or a verb phrase like *sings* or *loves Juliet* is sometimes called the **extension** of the expression. This approach to semantics, an approach based on reference, extensions and truth, is sometimes called **extensional semantics**. It is rather surprising that extensional semantics has been so illuminating, since it is easy to see that this sort of approach to semantics will not capture everything we might want to know about meaning. For example, there are noun phrases that refer to the same thing but which have different meanings. The phrases *the author of Cymbeline* and *the author of Romeo and Juliet* refer to the same person, and yet they mean different things. How can we be sure that they mean different things? One way to show this is to rely on the intuition that if two expressions mean exactly the same thing, then substituting one for another in any sentence should not change the meaning (and consequently, the possible truth values) of that sentence. Using this substitution test for sameness of meaning, we can show that our two example noun phrases differ in meaning. Sentence (19) can be changed into (20) by substituting one noun phrase for another, where the two noun phrases refer to the same thing. These two sentences do not mean the same thing, as we can see from the fact that it is perfectly possible for (19) to be true when (20) is false:

(19)   Most people know that Shakespeare is the author of Romeo and Juliet.

(20)   Most people know that Shakespeare is the author of Cymbeline.

Clearly, there is an important difference in meaning between *the author of Romeo and Juliet* and *the author of Cymbeline*, even though these two noun phrases refer to the same thing, ⟦the author of Romeo and Juliet⟧ = ⟦the author of Cymbeline⟧. Similarly, the set of things with the property named by the verb phrase *is the author of Romeo and Juliet* is the same as the set of things with the property named by the verb phrase *is the author of Cymbeline*. These two properties correspond to the same set, the set containing just Shakespeare, but the verb phrases clearly mean different things. It is sometimes said that although these expressions have the same **reference**, or the same **extension**, they have different **intensions**. (Notice that intensions are not intentions!) There are theories about intensions, but we will focus on reference and extensions here.

7.3.3   Determiners and nouns

The previous section suggests a first, very simple idea about the relation between meaning and syntactic structure, an idea about how references and extensions are related in simple subject–predicate sentences. The idea is that a subject refers to something, the VP denotes a property, and the sentence asserts that the reference of the subject DP has the property named by the VP. This idea is wrong. We can see that it does not work when we move to even just slightly more complicated sentences. Consider the sentences:

(21)   Every man is odd.

(22)   No man is odd.

(23)   Most men are odd.

(24)   Less than 5 men are odd.

In these sentences, the subjects do not name single objects. The different determiners in these sentences relate the set of men to the set of odd things in different ways, which we can describe as follows:

(25)   [No N VP] is true just in case nothing in ⟦N⟧ is also in ⟦VP⟧.

(26)   [Every N VP] is true just in case ⟦N⟧ is a subset of ⟦VP⟧.

(27) [The N VP] is true just in case there is a particular thing
      (determined according to context) in ⟦N⟧ that is also in ⟦VP⟧.

(28) [Most N VP] is true just in case the set of things in both ⟦N⟧
      and ⟦VP⟧ is larger than the set of things that are in ⟦N⟧ but not
      in ⟦VP⟧.

(29) [Less than five N VP] is true just in case the set of things in both
      ⟦N⟧ and ⟦VP⟧ has less than 5 things in it.

These statements tell us what each of these determiners mean: each one
names a relation between the set denoted by the NP and the set denoted
by the VP. Every competent speaker of English knows these things about
how subjects and predicates are related.

We can state (25)–(29) more concisely with a little notation from set
theory. For any set S, let $|S|$ be the number of things in S. Let $\emptyset$ be the
empty set, the set with nothing in it. For any sets S1, S2, let (S1 $\cap$ S2) be the
set of things in both sets, the intersection of S1 and S2. Now, using A, B for
the sets denoted by N and VP, with this notation we can survey a larger
set of determiners:

every A B = True	if and only if A is a subset of B
no A B = True	if and only if $(A \cap B) = \emptyset$
some A B – True	if and only if $(A \cap B) \neq \emptyset$
most A B = True	if and only if $(2 \times |A \cap B|) > |A|$
at least five A B = True	if and only if $|A \cap B| > 5$
fewer than six A B = True	if and only if $|A \cap B| < 6$
at most seven A B = True	if and only if $|A \cap B| \leq 7$
exactly 2000000 A B = True	if and only if $|A \cap B| = 2000000$
(exactly) five or six A B = True	if and only if $|A \cap B| = 5$ or $|A \cap B| = 6$
infinitely many A B = True	if and only if $|A \cap B|$ is infinite
all but three A B = True	if and only if $|A| - 3 = |A \cap B|$
between 6 and 12 A B = True	if and only if $6 \leq |A \cap B| \leq 12$
two out of three A B = True	if and only if $|A–B| = |A \cap B| \times 2/3$

Looking at this table, it might seem that almost any relation between
two sets could be specified with determiners, just as any object can be
referred to by a name, and any property can be referred to by a predicate.
Suppose figure 7.3 contains all the things in our universe. Area A contains
those that have property A, area B those that have property B. The inhab-
itants of their intersection are those that have both properties, and the area
outside A and B contains those that have neither. We are considering

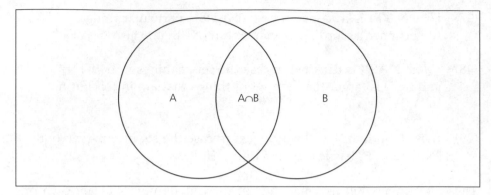

Figure 7.3　The intersection of A and B = A ∩ B

sentences of the form [D NP VP], with D interpreted as some relation Q, NP interpreted as the property A, and VP as the property B. We might expect that in determining whether such sentences are true, various determiners of human language require us to consider all four areas of the above diagram. Surprisingly, this is far from true. The determiners in human languages do not have this kind of flexibility. It turns out that we can always, or almost always, restrict our attention to area A and ignore everything that is outside A. That is, in determining the truth value of [Q A B], we get the same result if we shrink the universe to A and if we keep and consider everything in it. We say that natural language determiners are **restricted** in this sense: the set A serves as their restriction.

This kind of restriction on determiner meanings has received a lot of attention, and different components of the restriction have been identified. The component that is most easily described is called 'conservativity,' a property of determiners noticed by Barwise and Cooper (1981) and Keenan and Stavi (1986):

> **A relation Q named by a determiner is conservative if, and only if, for any properties A and B, relation Q holds between A and B if and only if relation Q holds between A and the things in (A ∩ B).**

For example, the singular determiner *every* is conservative because the sentence *every man is odd* entails, and is entailed by, *every man is a man that is odd* (and similarly for every other sentence of this form with *every*). The subset relation named by *every* holds between the sets ⟦man⟧ and ⟦is odd⟧ if and only if the subset relation holds between the set ⟦man⟧ and the set of things in both ⟦man⟧ and ⟦is odd⟧. Similarly the plural *most* is conservative because the sentence *most men are odd* entails, and is entailed by, *most men are men that are odd*. This property is called **conservativity** because, intuitively, once the subject noun denotation A is given, the determiner Q and the predicate denotation B do not introduce anything new: they serve only to tell us something about the set A.

Notice that being conservative or not is a semantic property. You cannot tell whether a determiner is conservative or not from its phonological or syntactic properties – whether it is conservative or not depends on what it means, and in particular on those aspects of meaning which are treated in extensional semantics.

It is easy to make up a determiner that is not conservative in this sense. Imagine adding the determiner *somenon* to English so that we can say that *somenon nobles are commoners*. We can define *somenon* as follows:

(30)   somenon A B = True if and only if something that is not in A is in B.

With this determiner it is perhaps true to say *somenon nobles are commoners*. And it is certainly true that *somenon kings are not kings* (where A is ⟦is a king⟧ and B is ⟦is not a king⟧).

The important point is that the determiner *somenon* is not conservative. The sentence *somenon kings are not kings* just means that some non-king is not a king. That's obviously true. The sentence *somenon kings are not kings* does not entail *somenon kings are kings that are not kings*. The latter sentence is obviously false. It is obviously not true that some non-king is a king that is not a king. So the special entailment relation that identifies conservative determiners does not hold in the case of this made-up determiner *somenon*. The determiner *somenon* is not conservative.

Other examples are easily constructed. Consider the new determiner *owt*, which can be defined to mean something like the reverse of *two* in the following sense:

(31)   owt A B = True if and only if (at least) two things are in B that are not in A.

So the sentence *owt students speak Quechua* is true, since there are at least two Quechua speakers who are not students. However, the sentence *owt students are students that speak Quechua* is obviously false. There are not at least two students that speak Quechua who are not students. So *owt* is not conservative. Neither are *eerth, rouf, evif, xis*, or any of the other determiners of this kind that we could make up.

The surprising thing is that no human language has determiners that are non-conservative like *somenon* or *owt*. In all human languages, every determiner is conservative. It is easy to check all of the examples listed on pp. 381. There are a couple of apparent counterexamples but the exceptions are very few and seem to be constructions that require special treatment on independent grounds.

Why should all determiners be conservative? It is natural to try to relate this fact to something more basic about the way we understand language. Notice that, with conservative determiners, a sentence of the form [D N

VP] can be regarded as naming a class of things [[N]], and then telling us something about how this class relates to [[VP]]. So when we say *all men are odd*, non-men are not relevant to the truth of this claim, and this sentence can be seen to have a simple sort of **topic–comment** structure. The noun names a topic set, and the determiner relates this set to the property named by the predicate.

When learning any human language, the learner needs to learn which sort of comparison between sets is signaled by which determiner. A learner of English needs to learn the semantic differences between *every, no, three, less than two*, and so on. It is plausible that human learners do not readily consider the possibility that determiners in the language have a meaning like the one we assigned to *somenon*.

7.3.4   Modifiers: recursion and compositionality

In the syntax, the principles of phrase structure allow the construction of infinitely many sentences because they are recursive. In human languages, a phrase of a given category can have other phrases of the same category inside of it; the category can recur any number of times. This idea was introduced in chapter 3, where it was observed that a prepositional phrase inside a DP may contain another DP. The tree shown at the beginning of this chapter provides an example. The DP *the witches by the cauldron* contains the DP *the cauldron*. A DP can contain any number of DPs. The same goes for other sorts of phrases: a PP can contain any number of PPs, a VP can contain any number of VPs, a sentence can contain any number of sentences. How can a speaker have the ability to understand them all? Focusing on entailments, we can ask: how can a speaker recognize the entailment relations for infinitely many different sentences? Frege's answer is that these relations among sentences must be calculated from the meanings of the parts of the sentences. It is not too hard to see how this can be done.

Let's start with simple sentences again. Consider the sentences:

(32)   Every witch laughed.

(33)   Every English witch laughed.

Sentence (32) is true when every member of the set [[witch]] is in the set [[laughed]]. Adding the adjective phrase *cunning* as in (34) serves to make the claim more restrictive, so that (33) just claims that everything that is both in [[witch]] and in [[English]] is also in the set [[laughed]]. This way of putting the matter explains why sentence (32) entails (33), because the set [[witch]] is always a subset of the set of things in both [[witch]] and [[English]]. Adding another adjective makes the claim still more restrictive:

(34)   Every cunning English witch laughed.

Clearly, any number of modifying adjectives can be added in this way, and each one will serve to add a restriction to the set of things denoted by the noun that the adjective modifies. For this recursion in the syntax we have a corresponding recursion in the determination of what sets are being mentioned.

The contribution of [[cunning]] in (34) is restrictive: it adds a restriction to the set it is modifying. This is what one would expect a modifier to do. Adjectives and adverbs can be treated as imposing restrictions of a similar kind. In (33) and (34), the restriction has a particularly simple character. The adjectives there are said to be **intersective**, because they restrict the predication to the **intersection**, the common elements, of two sets:

An adjective is **intersective** if [[every AP NP] VP] is true just in case the set of things that are in both [[N]] and [[AP]] is a subset of [[VP]].

When an intersective adjective or other modifier appears in a noun phrase, we can use this simple principle to figure out when the sentence is true. *An English witch is on the moor* is true if something in both [[witch]] and [[English]] is also in [[is on the moor]]. The set denoted by the NP *brown cow* is the intersection of [[brown]] and [[cow]].

Adverbs sometimes allow a similar treatment. For example, the extensional semantics developed here can be extended to handle the modifiers in a sentence like (35):

(35)   The witches by the cauldron laughed in the forest.

We can regard the PP *in the forest* as providing a restriction on the set [[laughed]] just as we regard *by the cauldron* as providing a restriction on the set [[witch]]. Every language has expressions denoting properties, sets of things, and modifiers that can restrict those sets, in both the nominal and the verbal systems. And given the conservativity of determiners in human languages, we see that the sorts of comparisons made between the sets named in the nominal and verbal systems are of a specific kind.

Many modifiers have more complex semantic properties. In the following sentence, for example, the modifier is not intersective in the sense just defined:

(36)   The oldest witch laughed.

If *oldest* were intersective, the set denoted by the NP *oldest witch* would be the intersection of the set of oldest things and the set of witches, but it makes no sense to talk about a set of oldest things. If King Henry was the only king when he was nine months old, then he was the oldest king, but he was not the oldest boy or oldest person. So was he in the set of oldest things or not? The question has no clear sense, because *oldest* denotes a relative concept. Something can be the oldest member of one set but not the oldest member of another set. Similarly, it makes no sense to talk about a set of big things, since something can be a big member of one set but not a big member of another. A big flea is still a small animal. The biggest thing in our solar system is still a small star. A proper treatment of modifiers like these will have to recognize their relational status.

7.4   Assertion and Presupposition

In the preceding sections we observed that knowing what the entailment relations between sentences are constitutes a core part of linguistic semantic competence. In this section we distinguish between two subspecies of entailment: **assertion** and **presupposition**.

Consider the sentences in (37):

(37)   a.   Desdemona went to the dance with Cassio.
       b.   Desdemona denied going to the dance with Cassio.
       c.   Desdemona regretted going to the dance with Cassio.

(37a) says explicitly that Desdemona went to the dance with Cassio. This kind of saying is called **assertion**. It is canceled by negation. (38a) asserts the exact opposite of what (37a) asserts:

(38)   a.   Desdemona didn't go to the dance with Cassio.

In contrast to (37a), (37b, c) do not assert anything about Desdemona going to the dance with Cassio. The only assertion they make concerns Desdemona's denial or regret. In fact, in (37b) she may or may not have gone to the dance. But in (37c) we still know that she did. Moreover, negation of (37b, c) does not cancel these conclusions:

(38)   b.   Desdemona didn't deny going to the dance with Cassio.
       c.   Desdemona didn't regret going to the dance with Cassio.

(38b) can describe a situation in which Desdemona went to the dance with Cassio and admitted it or, alternatively, a situation in which she either went or did not but neither admitted nor denied that she did. On the other hand, (38c) can only describe a situation in which Desdemona went to the dance with Cassio and did not regret doing so.

What explains this behavior with respect to negation? In addition to asserting that Desdemona did (did not) regret going to the dance with Cassio, (37c) and (38c) are said to presuppose that the complement (*going to the dance with Cassio*) describes a fact. Thus, the content of the complement is a **presupposition** of the whole complex sentence. We can say,

(39)   A sentence S1 presupposes S2 just in case S1 entails S2 and the negation of S1 also entails S2.

So (37c) presupposes (37a), because both it and its negation (38c) entail (37a). On the other hand, (37c) entails that Desdemona regretted something, but its negation (38c) does not, hence this is part of the asserted, not the presupposed, meaning of (37c). Similarly, (40) presupposes (41), and (42) presupposes (43):

(40)   The Prince of Denmark is haunted.

(41)   There is a Prince of Denmark.

(42)   We watched the witches gather.

(43)   The witches gathered.

All (or almost all) declarative sentences assert something, and some but not nearly all have presuppositions in addition.

What does the following sentence assert and what does it presuppose? *The maid who was singing was singing.* What is the peculiarity of this sentence?	**EXERCISE 7.2**

From the point of view of **discourse**, presuppositions serve to both check and build the common ground between speaker and hearer. The hearer is either already aware of everything that the current sentence presupposes, or he accommodates those presuppositions: adds them to the apparent common ground. We can imagine accommodation as the hearer, after hearing the sentence *Desdemona never regretted going to the dance with Cassio*, saying to himself, *Aha, I was supposed to know that Desdemona went to the dance with Cassio. I didn't know, but I have nothing against pretending that I did.* Accommodation is not obligatory. If the hearer has strong objections, he may explicitly protest. But notice that he would not say, *You are lying.* That kind of a protest is reserved for false assertions. He would say, *What are you talking about? How could she regret doing something she never did?*

The presence of a presupposition is usually tied to both a lexical item and some property of the syntactic construction. For example, (44a) presupposes that Emilia gave the handkerchief to Iago, but (44b, c) do not:

(44)　a.　Emilia remembered (did not remember) that she gave the handkerchief to Iago.
　　　b.　Emilia remembered (did not remember) giving the handkerchief to Iago.
　　　c.　Emilia remembered (did not remember) to give the handkerchief to Iago.

Hungarian illustrates another way in which a presupposition may be dependent on the specifics of grammatical form. The language has two verbs that mean 'deny', *tagad* and *letagad*. Formally, the second differs from the first by having a perfective prefix *le*. *Tagad* is like English *deny* in not inducing a presupposition. (Remember that denying an event does not presuppose either that it did or that it did not occur.) *Letagad*, however, differs from the English *deny* in that it does presuppose that what is denied is a fact. If we translate (37b), *Desdemona denied going to the dance with Cassio*, into Hungarian using the verb *letagad*, it means that she went but refused to admit this fact.

We have seen that a sentence with the main verb *deny* does not presuppose the truth of the complement of the main verb, but it does give rise to another kind of presupposition. *Desdemona denied going to the dance with Cassio* presupposes that the question whether she went was raised in some form or another. Suppose, for example, that Othello accuses Desdemona of various things, but he never raises the issue of whether she went to the dance with Cassio. Nonetheless, Desdemona utters the sentence *I didn't go to the dance with Cassio*, out of the blue. Now you can describe this as *Desdemona said she did not go . . .*, but not as *Desdemona denied going . . .*, precisely because the question was never raised.

EXERCISE 7.3

Consider the following verbs and other predicates:

think (that . . .), confirm (that . . .), know (that . . .), be surprised (that . . .), agree (that . . .), suspect (that . . .), accept (that . . .), assume (that . . .).

　Which of them are like *regret* in that the sentence containing them presupposes that the content of the *that*-clause is a fact? Which of them are comparable to *deny* in making some other presupposition about the status of the content of the *that*-clause? Do you find cases that do not fall into either category?

> *Example: Restate (that...)* presupposes that the content of the *that*-clause has previously been stated, because both (a) and its negation (b) entail this.
>
> (a) Emilia restated that she was not guilty.
> (b) Emilia didn't restate that she was not guilty.
>
> On the other hand, both (a) and (b) can be true whether or not Emilia was actually guilty. Thus *restate* belongs to the same category as *deny*.

7.5 Cross-Linguistic Comparisons Involving Word Meanings

In the preceding sections we argued that linguistic semantics is not the study of what sentences are true and what sentences are not: it studies entailment relations between sentences, and truth is but an auxiliary notion in characterizing entailment.

We might ask a somewhat similar question about the meanings of words. Are word meanings (lexical meanings) simple reflections of conceptual distinctions; distinctions that are directly determined by how the world is and how our perceptual and cognitive apparatus works? For instance, it is natural enough to wonder whether we can find that some relations are easily recognized and named by humans, while others are not so easily recognized and will tend not to be named by expressions of human languages. Returning to the consideration of prepositional phrases, an interesting case of this issue presents itself. Prepositions tend to name fairly abstract relationships:

(45)   Some English prepositions:
         on, in, by, of, under, over, near, from, into, onto, through,
         along, towards, above, below, across, around, inside, outside, at,
         about, after, before, with, without, within, behind, past, for,
         until, among, between, as, despite, except, against, amid,
         less, down, up

Some of the relations named by these words seem very basic, and we might expect to find the same relations named by prepositions in other languages. Restricting our attention to spatial relations, consider the English prepositions *on* and *in*:

(46)   The apple is in the bowl.

(47)   The bowl is on the table.

In cognitive terms, the distinction between being in something and being on something is both very clear and very fundamental. At first glance, it seems that (46) entails that the apple is contained in the bowl, while (47) entails that the bowl is on the surface of the table. Considering some other examples, though, shows that the meaning of the prepositions is more abstract. That is, *is in* does not mean quite the same thing as *is contained in*, and *is on* does not mean quite the same thing as *is on the surface of*:

(48)   a.   the runner is in the race ≠ the runner is contained in the race
       b.   the light is in my eyes ≠ the light is contained in my eyes
       c.   the player is in the field ≠ the player is contained in the field
       d.   the work is in a mess ≠ the work is contained in a mess

(49)   a.   the skis are on the wall (in a ski rack) ≠ the skis are on the surface of the wall
       b.   the bruise is on his nose ≠ the bruise is on the surface of his nose
       c.   the break is on the edge (of the glass) ≠ the break is on the surface of the edge
       d.   her work is on the frontier ≠ her work is on the surface of the frontier

Even with such subtleties, it might seem quite natural to assume that the prepositions *in* and *on* are distinguished and mean what they mean simply because language needs to reflect a fundamental cognitive distinction. We might even go further and hypothesize that word meanings in general reflect language-independent cognitive distinctions.

Looking at other languages, this idea is not confirmed. First, we find languages with coarser, and languages with finer, distinctions than English. In Spanish, both of the above sentences may contain the same preposition, *en*. We are using EN as a gloss for both the 'in' and the 'on' senses:

(50)   La manzana está en el   frutero.
       the apple   is   EN the bowl
       'The apple is in the bowl.'

(51)   El frutero está en la   mesa.
       the bowl   is   EN the table
       'The bowl is on the table.'

In German, on the other hand, the basic spatial application of the English preposition *on* is divided among three prepositions: *auf, an* and *um*:

(52)   Die Tasse ist auf   dem Tisch.
       the cup   is AUF the   table
       'The cup is on the table.'

(53)   Das Bild   ist an   der Wand.
       the picture is AN the wall
       'The picture is on the wall.'

(54)   Der Serviettenring ist um die Serviette.
       the napkin ring   is UM the napkin
       'The napkin ring is on/around the napkin.'

German takes into account whether the surface is horizontal (*auf*), vertical (*an*), or is encircled by the object that is on it (*um*).

Since Spanish, English, and German make increasingly finer distinctions, at this point it seems possible to maintain that there is a set of cognitive distinctions that are reflected in different languages with different degrees of precision.

Let us now look at Dutch, a language related to both English and German. Dutch has three prepositions which, as even their forms suggest, are historically related to German *auf*, *an*, and *um*: *op*, *aan*, and *om*, respectively. The Dutch counterparts of the above German examples might suggest that their meanings are the same, too:

(55)   De kop staat   op de tafel.
       the cup stands OP the table
       'The cup is on the table.'

(56)   Het schiderij hangt tegen   de muur aan.
       the picture   hangs against the wall   AAN
       'The picture is on the wall.'

(57)   De servetring   zit om het servet.
       the napkin ring sits OM the napkin
       'The napkin ring is on the napkin.'

But further examples show that this is not the case:

(58)   a.   German: Das Pflaster   ist an   meinem Bein
                     the Band-aid is AN my   leg
                     'The Bandaid is on my leg.'
       b.   Dutch: De pleister   zit op mijn been.
                   the Band-aid sits OP my   leg
                   'The Band-aid is on my leg.'

(59)   a.   German: Die Fliege ist an   der Wand.
              the fly   is AN the wall
              'The fly is on the wall.'
       b.   Dutch: Het vlieg zit op de muur.
              the fly   sits OP the wall
              'The fly is on the wall.'

Bowerman (1989) observes that, "in Dutch, the distinction between *op* and *aan* has less to do with orientation than with method of attachment: if a surface is not horizontal, an object is described as *aan* if it is attached (often hanging or projecting) by one or more fixed points ('picture on wall', 'leaves on twig', 'clothes on line', 'coathook on wall', 'handle on pan'). In contrast, if it is a living creature like a fly (whose means of support are not perceptually obvious) or a flattish object attached over its entire base ('Band-aid on leg', 'sticker on refrigerator', 'pimple on chin'), the relationship is referred to with *op*."

The Dutch data are interesting for a number of reasons. Since they cross-classify the German data, they cast doubt on the assumption that language directly reflects independent cognitive distinctions. It seems more likely that Spanish, English, German, and Dutch each carve up reality in an essentially linguistic manner. Such linguistic distinctions can usually be matched with some sort of cognitive distinctions, or else language would be quite useless as a tool for cognition. But there is no way to predict what the linguistic distinctions will be simply by considering what cognitive distinctions seem to be more fundamental than others.

Pinker (1989) reached a similar conclusion in investigating why verbs like *give* and *throw* have two alternative argument structures and verbs like *donate* and *carry* do not, as shown in (60) and (61):

(60)   a.   Portia gave a ring to Bassanio. [___ DP to DP]
              Portia gave Bassanio a ring. [___ DP DP]
       b.   Nerissa threw a box to Antonio. [___ DP to DP]
              Nerissa threw Antonio a box. [___ DP DP]
       c.   some other verbs like *give* and *throw*:
              lease, lend, pass, pay, rent, sell, serve,
              trade, advance, assign, award, grant, guarantee,
              issue, leave, offer, owe, will, bring, take, ship,
              mail, hand, send, bounce, float, roll, slide,
              address, bring, kick, flip, hit, hurl, wire, ask,
              read, show, teach, tell, e-mail, fax, phone, radio,
              telegraph

(61)   a.   Portia donated a ring to Bassanio. [___ DP to DP]
              *Portia donated Bassanio a ring. [___ DP DP]

b. Nerissa carried a box to Antonio. [___ DP to DP]
*Nerissa carried Antonio a box. [___ DP DP]

c. some other verbs like *donate* and *carry*:
address, administer, broadcast, catapult, convey,
contribute, drag, haul, heave, push, tug, delegate, deliver,
dictate, describe, demonstrate, donate, exhibit,
express, explain, illustrate, introduce, narrate,
portray, recite, recommend, refer, reimburse, restore,
submit, surrender

Interestingly, in another well-known study of verbs that allow these alternative constructions, Levin (1993) classifies *carry* with *give*. That is, there are variations among speakers, and so also among linguists, on these matters. It is striking, though, that all verbs with a [___ DP DP] argument structure seem to signify an action that (at least potentially) brings about some kind of a possession. In (60a), Bassanio will have the ring, in (60b), Antonio will have the box. But not all verbs whose meaning might in principle be understood as signifying an action that brings about possession are actually understood in that way and have a [___ DP DP] argument structure. Both verbs that signify ballistic motion and verbs that signify guided motion caused by continuous force might in principle be understood to cause the recipient to possess the moved object. However, some ballistic motion verbs (like *throw*) have the [___ DP DP] argument structure, while others (like *catapult* in *I catapulted you a rock*) do not, and this varies from one speaker to another. Similarly, while some verbs of motion from continuous force (like *carry*) do not allow the [___ DP DP] construction, others (like *bring* in *I bring you a rock*) do. We must conclude that the distinctions here are arbitrary, part of what the child must learn in learning a language.

7.6 Summary

Competent speakers recognize certain relations among sentences, relations that hold by virtue of what the sentences mean. A true sentence can be said to **assert** the things that it entails, but the sentence can also **presuppose** some things, namely the things that are entailed by both the sentence and its negation. **Entailment** is an especially simple and important relation of this kind. We have assumed that meanings of sentences are determined **compositionally,** and so we expect that entailment relations are recognized compositionally, that is, on the basis of reasoning about the meanings of the parts of the sentences involved.

In simple sentences like *Cassandra laughed*, the subject DP refers to something, the VP names a property which a set of things have, and the sentence asserts that Cassandra is in that set. But it is not always true that the subject of a sentence names something which the VP tells us about! Proper names typically serve to name something, but DPs of the form [D N] are more complicated. Determiners seem to indicate a range of relationships between the set of things with the property named by N, [[N]], and the set of things with the property named by the VP, [[VP]]. The range of relations represented by determiners is limited though: determiners are, almost without exception, conservative. Intersective adjectives A can similarly be regarded as naming properties that sets of things [[A]] have. When an intersective adjective A modifies a noun N, we are talking about the things which are in both of the sets [[A]] and [[N]]. This kind of combination of sets can be repeated any number of times: when two intersective adjectives A1 and A2 modify a noun N (and this is allowed by our syntax), then we are talking about the things which are in all of the sets [[A1]], [[A2]], and [[N]]. This extensional account does not capture everything that we know about meaning, but this kind of account is a beginning that can be systematically developed and related to the structures of the language.

Further reading

Bach, Emmon. 1989. *Informal Lectures on Formal Semantics*. New York: State University of NY Press.

Barwise, Jon and Cooper, Robin. 1981. Generalized quantifiers and natural language. *Linguistics and Philosophy*, 4: 159–219.

Keenan, Edward. 1996. The semantics of determiners. In Shalom Lappin, ed., *The Handbook of Contemporary Semantic Theory*. Oxford: Blackwell.

Keenan, Edward. 1971. Two kinds of presupposition in natural language. In Fillmore, C. and Langendoen, D. T. eds., *Studies in Linguistic Semantics*, pp. 45–54. New York: Holt.

Pinker, Steven. 1989. *Learnability and Cognition: The Acquisition of Argument Structure*. Cambridge, MA: MIT Press.

Talmy, Leonard. 1985. Lexicalization patterns: Semantic structure in lexical forms. In T. Shopen, ed., *Language Typology and Syntactic Description, Volume 3: Grammatical Categories and the Lexicon*. Cambridge: Cambridge University Press.

Stalnaker, Robert. 1978. Assertion. In Peter Cole, ed., *Pragmatics. Syntax and Semantics*, 9, pp. 315–32. New York: Academic Press.

EXERCISES

Exercise 7.4

Are the following claims true or false?

(a) The sentence *Everything is a brown cow* entails *Most things are cows*.

(b) The sentence *All cows are purple* entails *All purple things are cows*.

(c) The sentence *The student ate the cake* entails *The student ate*.

(d) The sentence *The hammer broke the cup* entails *The hammer broke*.

Consider some newly invented determiners: *wurg* and *berf*, so that you can   **Exercise 7.5**
say things like *Wurg daughters of Lear loved him* and *Berf fairies attend Hippolyta*. Let's define these new determiners as follows:

[Wurg N VP] is true just in case there are more things in ⟦VP⟧ than in ⟦N⟧.
[Berf N VP] is true just in case ⟦VP⟧ is a subset of (is completely included in) ⟦N⟧.

With these definitions, answer the following questions:

(i)   Is *wurg* conservative? Defend your answer.
(ii)   Is there an English determiner that means the same thing as *wurg*? That is, how would you say something like *Wurg fairies wait upon the Queen* in English, without using the word *wurg*?
(iii) Is *berf* conservative? Defend your answer.
(iv)   Is there an English determiner that means *berf*?

. . . .

Prepositional phrases are sometimes restrictive and intersective, the way that   **Exercise 7.6**
adjectival modifiers are. For example, *Every witch in the castle smiled* says that every element of ⟦*witch*⟧ ∩ ⟦*in the castle*⟧ is in ⟦*smiled*⟧. We can say:

A prepositional phrase PP is intersective if [every N PP] means that the set of things that are in both ⟦N⟧ and ⟦PP⟧ is a subset of ⟦VP⟧.

Think of some prepositional phrases which are not intersective, and defend your view that they are not intersective.

. . . .

The claim that all determiners are conservative holds up quite well across   **Exercise 7.7**
languages. There are, however, a few apparent exceptions. One of them is the English word *only*, as in *only witches cast spells*.

(a)   Explain why, if *only* is treated as a determiner here, it is not conservative.
(b)   Do the following data support the view that *only* is a determiner? Explain your answer:

the witches cast spells
three witches cast spells
the three witches cast spells
*the the witches cast spells
*the three four witches cast spells
only witches cast spells
only the witches cast spells
only the three witches cast spells
the three witches only cast spells
the three witches cast only spells

. . . .

Exercise 7.8 Most speakers of American English accept the following sentences:

They baked a cake for me
They baked me a cake
They dug a ditch for me
They dug me a ditch
They mixed a drink for me
They mixed me a drink

Some other verbs seem to allow the [___ DP for-DP] but not the [___ DP DP] forms:

A1. a. They opened the door for me
     b. *They opened me the door
A2. a. They arranged the day for me
     b. *They arranged me the day
A3. a. They caught the plane for me
     b. *They caught me the plane

However, these last data are misleading. What is really going on is a little more subtle, and depends on the arguments involved:

A1. c. They opened me a beer
A2. c. They arranged us a wedding
A3. c. They caught me a butterfly

What do you think explains the contrasts between the (b) and (c) examples? (If you are not a native speaker of American English, you may want to consult with a speaker of this language to get a little more data.)

· ·

Exercise 7.9 Compare the following data from English, Hausa, and Hungarian. Where English has a pair of words, Hausa and Hungarian have only one. Discuss how cognitive and linguistic distinctions compare in these languages:

English	Hausa	Hungarian
leather/skin	fata	bőr
meat/flesh	nama	hús
wood/tree	itače	fa

· ·

Exercise 7.10 A motion event can be said to involve at least the following components, the fact of Motion, the Figure that moves, the direction in which the Figure moves, and the Manner in which the Figure moves. (The notion of a Figure goes back to Gestalt-psychology: it is the central element of the event.) Suppose that these are cognitive terms in which motion events can be described. Compare how English and Spanish express these components. Discuss what the results say about the claim that word meanings directly reflect cognitive distinctions.

The bottle   floated   into   the cave.
La   botella entró   a   la   cueva flotando.
the bottle   went+in prep the cave   floating
'The bottle floated into the cave.'

I rolled the keg   into   the storeroom.
Metí   el barril a   la   bodega   rodándolo.
put+in-I the keg   prep the storeroom rolling
'I rolled the keg into the storeroom.'

· ·

Which of the following does the sentence *I regret that I lied to the queen* **Exercise 7.11** presuppose? In deciding, consider the truth conditions of both the above sentence and its negation.

(a)   I regret that I lied to the queen.
(b)   I lied to the queen.
(c)   I am generally an honest person.
(d)   There is a queen.
(e)   A unique queen is identifiable in the context.

· ·

Below is a letter by someone who politely followed the rule that you do not **Exercise 7.12** say anything bad about a person in a letter of recommendation. But he managed to smuggle in some important messages. Exactly what are these and how did he do it?

Mr. X is a great person. He has recently stopped beating his neighbors and kicked his habit of coming to work stone drunk.

· ·

In chapter 4 we talked about the dependency between a wh-phrase and a gap **Exercise 7.13** in the sentence. Such a dependency may span more than one clause, e.g.:

How do you believe (that) I should behave – ?

In such long-distance dependencies the main clause verb is called a **bridge verb**. The above examples show that *believe* is quite a good bridge. Check whether the verbs in exercise 7.3 are good bridges. In checking the acceptability of these wh-dependencies, retain the wh-word *how*, but adjust the tense and the mood of the verbs if necessary. Try to formulate a generalization concerning bridge-hood and presuppositions.

· ·

Exercise 7.14 What do each of the following sentences presuppose? Form their negation by prefixing the sentence by *It is not the case that* . . .

    (a)   Othello, too, wept.
    (b)   Even Othello wept.
    (c)   Only Othello wept.
    (d)   It was Othello who wept.

8

Semantics II:
Scope

8.0 Introduction

The principle of compositionality says that the meaning of an expression is determined by the meaning of its parts. The previous chapter provided a first sketch of how this might work. This chapter will give some attention to the fact that the meaning of an expression can also be influenced by its context, where the relevant context is sometimes the linguistic structure in which the expression occurs. For example, when I say *Henry was King of England*, the name *Henry* refers to someone different than when I say *Henry founded the Ford Motor Company*. These differences in meaning are not determined by the syntactic parts of the sentences but by the pragmatic context in which the sentences are produced. But when we say *Every king admires himself*, the meaning of *himself* is conditioned by its structural context: it refers to each king.

   This chapter will focus on the latter contextual determination of semantic value. In a sense, the reference of *himself* in *Every king admires himself* is being determined not by its parts but by other elements in its structural context. In this kind of case, we say that the subject has the object in its **scope**. This does not negate the basic idea behind compositionality, which was that speakers of the language need to know the meanings of the parts of sentences and recognize how those parts are assembled in order to understand the infinitely many different expressions in their language. The compositionally determined meaning of an expression must allow for the fact that some parts of an expression may have values which are set by the context. To understand what is expressed by a sentence on any particular occasion, a speaker must understand these influences too, appropriately relating constituents like *himself* to their structural contexts. This chapter will explore some of the ways in which the meaning of a constituent can vary systematically with structural context.

8.1   Pronouns and Binding

It should not be surprising that pronouns vary in their interpretation according to the contexts in which they occur. A careful examination reveals that this influence is systematic and sensitive to structure in surprising ways. We got a first glimpse of this in chapter 4, where it was observed that a reflexive pronoun must have an agreeing, c-commanding antecedent in the same clause. To quickly review each of these points, consider the following sentences:

(1)   Cleopatra amuses herself.

(2)   *Antony amuses herself.

(3)   *Cleopatra knows that Antony amuses herself.

(4)   *Antony and Cleopatra amuse herself.

In sentence (1), the reflexive pronoun *herself* has the antecedent *Cleopatra*. The reflexive appears in the same clause as its antecedent, it agrees with the antecedent in number and gender (feminine singular), and it is c-commanded by the antecedent. In (2), the reflexive pronoun has no antecedent. The only possibility is *Antony*, but that name is traditionally masculine and so it does not agree with the pronoun. The problem with (3) is that the antecedent is not in the same clause as the pronoun. And finally, (4) is unacceptable because *Cleopatra* does not c-command *herself*. The only c-commanding phrase is the whole subject, *Antony and Cleopatra*, but that does not agree with the reflexive pronoun. We can say that, in (4), the reflexive is not in the scope of a possible antecedent, meaning that *herself* is not in a position where its meaning can be determined by *Cleopatra*.

These are syntactic facts, since they condition where reflexive pronouns can appear in a syntactic structure, but they are also semantic, since the antecedent determines what the reflexive pronoun refers to. In these cases, we obviously cannot determine the reference of the pronoun by looking at its parts, but must look at the wider context, and furthermore, only certain parts of the wider context are relevant, namely the c-commanding, agreeing phrases in the same clause. Only those c-commanding phrases have the pronoun in their scope. By this, we just mean that only they can serve as antecedents in determining the reference of the reflexive pronouns.

In chapter 4 it was observed that in a sentence like (1), the reflexive pronoun seems to act like a temporary name, standing in a position where we mean to refer to Cleopatra a second time. This description is intuitively right, but it misses an important, special property of pronouns. Pronouns have a property that names lack. They can stand for each of many people named by the antecedent. We see this, for example, in the sentence:

(5)   Every princess amuses herself.

Here, the reflexive pronoun stands in for each of the princesses. A name cannot play this role. Even in a room of princesses or queens, all named Cleopatra, (6) cannot mean the same thing as (5):

(6)   Every princess amuses Cleopatra.

Nor does sentence (5) mean the same thing as (7):

(7)   Every princess amuses every princess.

Reflexive pronouns increase the expressive capability of a language.

The special restrictions on the environments of reflexive pronouns are different from the special restrictions on the environments of non-reflexive pronouns like *he, she, it, him* and *her*. Consider the sentences:

(8)   Every princess knows that Cleopatra will find a prince.

(9)   Every princess knows that she will find a prince.

The name in sentence (8) can refer to different people on different occasions. If the sentence is uttered in a room full of people named *Cleopatra*, the intended referent could be indicated by pointing. The situation is different in sentence (9), where a pronoun occurs instead of a name. Here, we can distinguish two different ways to interpret the pronoun *she*. One possibility is that the pronoun refers to someone mentioned earlier or someone pointed to. This is sometimes called the **referential use** of the pronoun. But the pronoun has an option that the proper name does not have: it can refer to each person that *every princess* picks out. In this case, the sentence means that every princess is such that she will find a prince and she knows it. The sentence is ambiguous between these two readings. We can use the following notation to refer to the latter reading:

(10)   Every princess$_i$ knows that she$_i$ will find a prince.

These **subscripts** indicate that part of the meaning of the sentence (on one reading) is that *she* refers to each of the individuals picked out by *every princess*. In this kind of situation, we say that the pronoun is **bound** by the antecedent *every princess*. This bound use of the pronoun, unlike the referential use, gives us an interpretation of (9) which entails that, if Cleopatra is a princess, then Cleopatra knows that she, Cleopatra, will find a prince. (Note that the fact that Cleopatra in Shakespeare's *Antony and Cleopatra* is a queen is not relevant.) The referential reading gives us a sentence where *she* refers to someone other than every princess, and so we can indicate this reading by giving different subscripts to the noun phrases:

(11)   Every princess$_i$ knows that she$_j$ will find a prince.

In these terms, reflexive pronouns are always bound. Non-reflexive pronouns may be either bound or referential. Names are never bound.

   The contexts in which a non-reflexive pronoun can appear bound are different from those in which a reflexive can appear, as the following contrasts show:

(12)   Every princess$_i$ appreciates herself$_i$.

(13)   *Every princess$_i$ appreciates her$_i$.

(14)   *Every princess$_i$ knows that we appreciate herself$_i$.

(15)   Every princess$_i$ knows that we appreciate her$_i$.

These examples show that while the antecedent of a reflexive must be in the same clause, the antecedent of a non-reflexive pronoun cannot be in the same clause. Can a pronoun have an antecedent in another sentence? We see that it cannot:

(16)   *Every queen$_i$ knows the joke. She$_i$ laughed.

Since non-reflexive pronouns are quite different from reflexives, we can also check to see whether the antecedent of a non-reflexive pronoun must c-command it. This is the reason (4) was not acceptable. Examples like the following suggest that pronouns have this same requirement:

(17) a. [Every queen and every princess]$_i$ knows that we appreciate her$_i$.
   b. *Every queen and [every princess]$_i$ knows that we appreciate her$_i$.

The pronoun in (17a) can refer to each queen and princess, but (17b) is unacceptable; the pronoun cannot refer just to each princess.

   To summarize, it is clear that reflexive pronouns are distinguished from other pronouns in the way their meaning is determined by their context. After just these few examples, we state the following differences:

Binding Principle A:	A reflexive pronoun must be bound to an antecedent in the smallest S (or NP) that contains it.
Binding Principle B:	A pronoun cannot be bound to an antecedent in the smallest S (or NP) that contains it.
Binding Principle C:	Names cannot be bound.

These principles form the beginning of an account of how syntactic structure constrains the meaning of sentences with pronouns and reflexives, in ways that clearly affect the situations in which the sentence is true, and consequently also the entailment relations.

8.2 Negative Polarity Items

The idea that a constituent may be in the scope of expressions that c-command it was applied in chapter 4 not only to reflexive pronouns but also to **negative polarity items** (**NPIs**) like *at all*, and *much*, and *ever*.

(18) He does not like beer at all.

(19) *He likes beer at all.

(20) He doesn't ever drink beer.

(21) *He ever drinks beer.

(22) The princess eats pies and the prince doesn't ever drink beer.

(23) *The princess doesn't eat pies and the prince ever drinks beer.

The proposal in the earlier syntax chapter was stated as:

Negative Polarity Items Licensing Rule
A sentence containing an NPI is well-formed only if this NPI is in the c-command domain of a negative polarity item licenser.

Thus, (19) and (21) are bad because they lack negative elements, and (23) is bad because the negative element does not c-command the NPI. The negative polarity licensing rule constrains the place where NPIs can occur in sentence structures, and this is the sort of thing that we expect syntactic principles to do. But notice that this rule does not say what it is to be a negative element; rather, some examples are listed. This raises the question: Is being a negative element a syntactic property? Let's explore this question a little bit. Consider the following examples, in which we see that NPIs can occur in some contexts that are not obviously negative:

(24)   Less than three knights ever drink beer.

(25)   *More than three knights ever drink beer.

(26)   At most ten knights ever drink.

(27)   *At least ten knights ever drink.

Is there a sense in which *less than three* and *at most ten* are negative but *more than three* and *at least ten* are not? We are now in a position to see that there is. This elaboration is interesting because the characterization of negative elements offered here is semantic, and because the scope of these negative elements is again given in terms of c-command.

We can define a collection of determiners on the basis of their entailment relations as follows:

A determiner D forms a decreasing DP if whenever we have two verb phrases VP1 and VP2 where [[VP1]] is always a subset of [[VP2]], then the sentence [D N VP2] entails the sentence [D N VP1].

Consider for example, a verb phrase like *sings and dances*, which denotes the set [[sings and dances]]. This set will always be a subset of [[sings]], since everything that sings and dances is something that sings. Similarly, the set [[sings beautifully]] is always a subset of [[sings]], since everything that sings beautifully is something that sings.

So let VP1 be *sings beautifully* and let VP2 be *sings*. We can use these verb phrases to test whether the determiner *no* forms a decreasing DP. Let the noun N be *king*, for example. (Any other noun would do just as well.) Clearly sentence (28) entails (29):

Figure 8.1   The people who sing beautifully are a subset of the singers

(28)   No king sings.

(29)   No king sings beautifully.

We conclude that *no* forms a decreasing DP. When we consider the same examples with a different determiner D, like *every*, the results are quite different. (30) does not entail (31):

(30)   Every king sings.

(31)   Every king sings beautifully.

Considering other determiners, we can easily determine whether they are decreasing or not:

(32)   Determiners that form decreasing DPs:
       no, less than 3, at most 30, fewer than 6, no more than 2, . . .

(33)   Determiners that do not form decreasing DPs:
       the, a, every, some, most, exactly 6, at least 5, all but 3, . . .

The claim about negative polarity items then, is this: all decreasing DPs are negative elements, in the sense required by the NPI Licensing Rule. Checking the lists in (32) and (33), we can see that this claim holds up quite well for at least this range of constructions:

(34)   a.   No child ever betrayed her father.
       b.   Less than 3 children ever betrayed their fathers.
       c.   No more than 2 children ever betrayed their fathers.
       d.   *The child ever betrayed her father.
       e.   *Every child ever betrayed her father.
       f.   *Most children ever betrayed their fathers.

This suggests that the semantic property of decreasingness is something that speakers are sensitive to, and it confirms the basic conception of extensional semantics, discussed in the previous chapter, according to which at least some of the basic entailment relations among sentences are part of what every competent language user knows. In effect, the interpretation of a pronoun is influenced by the presence of a c-commanding antecedent, and a negative polarity item requires the presence of a c-commanding decreasing DP. These are both notions of scope: when we have a DP that is decreasing or one that is a possible antecedent, this can have an influence on the structure and interpretation of the c-commanded constituents. Those constituents are in the scope of the DP.

8.3   Relative Scope

In this section, we extend the notion of scope to the relationship of (a) negation and a noun phrase and (b) two noun phrases. We call this **relative scope**.

8.3.1   The relative scope of negation and DPs

Some sentences are ambiguous, at least in their written form. (In spoken language the ambiguity may be resolved by different intonation contours.) Consider the two meanings of (35) and (36):

(35)   Puck didn't solve one problem.
    a.   'There is no problem that Puck solved. Puck didn't solve a single problem.'
    b.   'There is one particular problem that Puck didn't solve (but he might have solved some other problems).'

(36)   Puck didn't trick many of the lovers.
    a.   'There aren't many lovers that Puck tricked; Puck tricked few lovers.'
    b.   'There are many lovers whom Puck didn't trick.'

In (35a), the negation has *one problem* in its scope, and in (36a) the negation has *many of the lovers* in its scope. In effect, the sentences talk about 'not a single problem' and 'not many lovers.' On reading (35b), on the other hand, *one problem* is outside the scope of the negation, and in (36b), *many of the lovers* is outside the scope of the negation. The scope relations which are expressed in the paraphrases (35a–b) are both possible for (35), and the scope relations expressed in (36a–b) are both possible in (36).

Some similar sentences admit only one interpretation. No matter what the intonation, a DP whose determiner is *fewer than five* takes narrower scope than negation when the DP is a direct object, and broader scope than negation when it is a subject:

(37)   Richard III didn't murder fewer than three squires.
    a.   'It is not the case that R. III murdered fewer than three squires; he murdered at least three squires.'
    b.   *'There are fewer than three squires whom R. III didn't murder.'

For example, suppose there are seven available squires. According to (a), (37) means that Richard murdered at least three of them, and that is correct. According to (b), (37) would require that he murdered at least five, and that is too strong.

(38)   Fewer than three squires didn't obey Richard III.
    a.   *'It is not the case that fewer than three squires obeyed R. III; at least three squires obeyed him.'
    b.   'There are fewer than three squires who didn't obey R. III.'

Again, with seven squires, (b) means that at least five obeyed Richard, and that is correct, while (a) would mean that at least three did, which is not strong enough.

The starred paraphrases are in themselves logically possible meanings, in the sense that the thoughts they express are coherent and non-contradictory. Nevertheless, these particular sentences do not, in fact, carry those meanings.

8.3.2   The relative scope of two DPs

Ambiguities
Two DPs may also interact in scope. Sometimes the possible interactions give rise to an ambiguity:

(39)   Two fairies have talked with every Athenian.
    a.   'There are two fairies such that each has talked with every Athenian.'
    b.   'For every Athenian, there are two possibly different fairies who have talked with him/her.'

The situation described by (39a) involves just two fairies. But the one described by (39b) may involve up to twice as many fairies as there are Athenians. (Only 'up to,' because some fairies may have talked with the

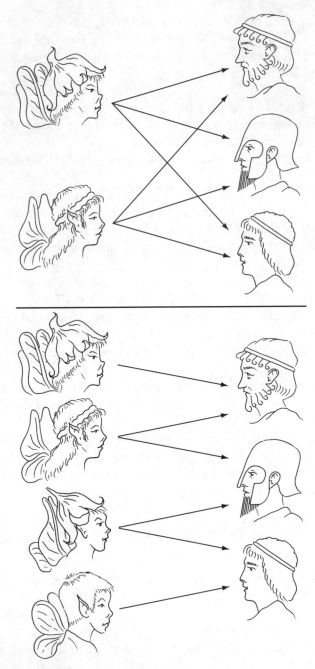

Figure 8.2   Fairies and Athenians

same Athenians.) In (39a), *two fairies* is said to take broader scope than *every Athenian*; in (39b), *every Athenian* is said to take broader scope than *two fairies*. The diagrams in figure 8.2 illustrate possible situations in which these paraphrases are true. Suppose there are just three Athenians.

(39a′) F1   talked with   A1, A2, A3
        F2   talked with   A1, A2, A3

(39b′) F1   talked with   A1
        F2   talked with   A1, A2
        F3   talked with   A2, A3
        F4   talked with   A3

Other examples are not ambiguous: for example, in (40) the direct object *few of the Athenians* cannot be construed as taking broader scope than the subject *every fairy*:

(40)   Every fairy has met few of the Athenians.
       a.   'For every fairy, there are few Athenians he/she has met.'
       b.   *'There are few Athenians whom every fairy met.'

Describe what the subject wide scope and the object wide scope readings of the following sentence are, and specify two situations: one in which the former is true but the latter is not, and one in which the latter is true but the former is not. Draw diagrams of the situations. Exactly two squires greeted three of the earls.	**EXERCISE** **8.1**

How to argue that some reading is or is not there?

Up till now we have merely expressed intuitions about what readings are or are not possible. But intuitions are sometimes not so easy to access directly. There are ways to corroborate that one is correct in thinking that a particular reading is or is not there. These are as important in work on semantics as techniques of establishing constituent structure are in work on syntax. We look for evidence to support our view, methodology common to all science.

   It is usually clear that sentences have a reading on which the subject takes wider scope than the direct object. It may be less clear whether there is a second reading on which the direct object takes wider scope than the subject. This is called **inverse scope**, because it goes against **linear** or c-command relations. Let us look at four examples, two in which we claim that such a reading exists, and two in which we claim that it does not. These examples illustrate different ways of convincing ourselves of the presence or absence of a reading.

   Let us begin with example (41), which we claim has, in addition to the subject wide scope reading (a), an object wide scope reading (b):

(41)   Two fairies have talked with every Athenian.
   a.   'There are two fairies such that each has talked with every Athenian.'
   b.   'For every Athenian, there are two possibly different fairies who have talked with him/her.'

The task is to convince ourselves that (b) exists as a separate reading. We use the 'let the inverse reading shine' method. We modify the example slightly, in such a way that the obvious reading (a) becomes practically implausible. We annotate readings that are excluded on such conceptual grounds with #.

We attempt to make sure that all the relevant syntactic and semantic properties of the sentences are preserved under this modification. Minimally, the determiners and grammatical functions of the relevant noun phrases need to be preserved. Assuming that a glass breaks when it crashes against a mirror and therefore it has no chance to crash more than once, (42) is such a modification:

(42)   Two wine glasses crashed against every mirror.
   a.   #'There is a pair of wine glasses such that each glass has crashed against every mirror.'
   b.   'For every mirror, there is a possibly different pair of wine glasses that has crashed against it.'

Sentence (42) does make sense. We conclude that the object wide scope reading exists as a separate reading for sentences with this pair of quantificational determiners.

The same method can be used to show that an inverse reading does not exist. Give it a chance to shine – if it fails to do so, it is probably not there. Consider (43), which we claim lacks reading (b):

(43)   Every fairy has met few of the Athenians.
   a.   'For every fairy, there are few Athenians he/she has met.'
   b.   *'There are few Athenians whom every fairy met.'

In this case it is difficult to muster a modification that makes reading (a) conceptually implausible; still, a useful modification can be made:

(44)   Everyone who read many of the books read few of the books.

This sentence is obviously false (contradictory) on the easy, subject wide scope reading:

(44)   a.   'For everyone who read many of the books, there are few of
             the books that he/she read.'

On the other hand, the proposition that there are few books that have been
read by all well-read people is most probably true. (Different people read
different books.) The question is whether (44) can be uttered with the
intention of making this very reasonable proposition? Our intuition is that
it cannot. (44) has nothing but a contradictory construal. In other words,
(44b) is not a reading of (44) in English:

(44)   b.   *'There are few of the books that have been read by everyone
             who read many of the books.'

   The 'LET THE INVERSE READING SHINE' method can be invoked when the
difficult, inverse reading (b) can be true without the easy reading (a) also
being true; that is, when (b) does not entail (a).

Show that (41b) does not entail (41a). Follow the procedure outlined for
(43) below.

**EXERCISE
8.2**

**The principle: S1 entails S2 means that if S1 is true, S2 is inescapably
true, too.**

Then, S1 does not entail S2 means that we can construct a situation (**model**)
in which S1 is true but S2 is false.
   We now show that (43b) does not entail (43a). Assume that there are
three fairies and ten Athenians, and consider the following situation:

F1	met	A1, A2, A3, A4, A5, A6, A7, A8, A9
F2	met	A1, A3, A5, A7, A9, A10
F3	met	A1, A2, A4, A6, A8, A10

   In this situation, only one Athenian, A1, was met by each of the three
fairies. Thus, it is true that there are few Athenians whom every fairy met
(= (43b)). On the other hand, every fairy met many Athenians, at least six
of the ten. Thus, it is false that for every fairy, there are few Athenians
he/she has met (= (43a)). This means that (43b) does not entail (43a).

Now compare the following two sentences:

(45)   Every fairy had a taste of two of the pies.

(46)   Every fairy had a taste of two or more pies.

We take it for granted that both sentences have a subject wide scope reading:

(45) a. 'For every fairy, there are two pies that she had a taste of.'

(46) a. 'For every fairy, there are two or more pies that she had a taste of.'

In addition, we claim (45) has an object wide scope reading but (46) does not:

(45) b. 'There are two pies that every fairy had a taste of.'

(46) b. *'There are two or more pies that every fairy had a taste of.'

In other words, if it turns out that every fairy had a taste of the same pies, that is a mere coincidence in the case of (46), the sentence has no reading that guarantees sameness.

We cannot use the 'let the inverse reading shine' method to support these claims about the (b) readings. Recall: this method consists in eliminating the easy (a) reading, so that the difficult (b) reading can shine. But in (45)–(46), reading (b) cannot be true without (a) being also true; (b) entails (a). We must invoke some other method.

EXERCISE 8.3 | Show that (46b) entails (46a).

One way to support the intuition that (46) lacks the object wide scope reading is to use **cross-sentential pronouns** as a test. Consider the following two examples, with *they* referring to pies, not to fairies:

(45′) Every fairy had a taste of two of the pies. They were soon gone.

(46′) Every fairy had a taste of two or more pies. They were soon gone.

What pies does *they* refer to in the two cases? In (45′), *they* can easily refer to those pies, two in number, that every fairy had a taste of. Since (45b) says, precisely, that there are two pies that every fairy had a taste of, the above interpretation of *they* is easily understood if (45b) is an existing reading.

In (46′), however, *they* refers either to all the pies present or to those pies that were tasted by any fairy at all. It does not refer to those pies, two or more in number, that each and every fairy had a taste of. This corroborates the intuition that (46) has no reading according to which there are two or more pies that every fairy had a taste of. In other words, (46b) is not a reading of (46) in English.

Neither the 'let the inverse reading shine' method, nor the cross-sentential pronoun test can spare us the trouble of making intuitive judgments. These methods are useful in that they replace a difficult judgment with one that is easier to make.

8.3.3 Scope interpretation: can non-linguistic knowledge be the source?

Let us return to our main line of thought and ask what accounts for the various scope possibilities. Perhaps grammar leaves scope relations vague and it is the speaker's and hearer's knowledge about a given situation that determines scope interpretation. Recall (35) above, repeated here:

(35) Puck didn't solve one problem.
    a.   'There is no problem that Puck solved; Puck didn't solve a single problem.'
    b.   'There is one particular problem that Puck didn't solve.'

If we know that Puck completely mixed up Oberon's orders and someone says (35), we readily interpret it as (a), i.e. 'Puck did not solve a single problem', with *not* having broader scope than *one problem*. On the other hand, if we know that Puck did a good but not perfect job, we readily interpret it as (b), with *one problem* having broader scope than *not*.

We have also seen that practical (conceptual) implausibility may exclude one reading altogether. As in the previous subsection, we mark the conceptually implausible reading with #:

(42) Two wine glasses crashed against every mirror.
    a.   #'There is a pair of wine glasses such that each glass has crashed against every mirror.'
    b.   'For every mirror, there is a possibly different pair of wine glasses that has crashed against it.'

But situational or conceptual knowledge is not sufficient to account for all scope interpretations. Crucially, we have seen that there are logically possible meanings that are simply never available to particular sentences, such as the readings (37b), (38a), (40b), (44b), and (46b). Knowledge about the world will not salvage these readings. As we have seen, the fact that we contend that there are few books that all well-read people have read does not make *Everyone who read many of the books read few of the books* an acceptable description. This shows that such knowledge cannot possibly be the primary source of scope interpretation.

8.3.4   Syntactic and semantic aspects of relative scope

It turns out that both syntactic and semantic aspects play a role in deter-mining scope options. To highlight the syntactic aspects, notice that in each of (37), (38), and (40), repeated here, the missing reading is the one that goes against c-command relations:

(37)   Richard III didn't murder fewer than three squires.
    a.   'It is not the case that R. III murdered fewer than three squires; he murdered at least three squires.'
    b.   *'There are fewer than three squires whom R. III didn't murder.'

(38)   Fewer than three squires didn't obey Richard III.
    a.   *'It is not the case that fewer than three squires obeyed R. III; at least three squires obeyed him.'
    b.   'There are fewer than three squires who did not obey R. III.'

(40)   Every fairy has met few of the Athenians.
    a.   'For every fairy, there are few Athenians he/she has met.'
    b.   *'There are few Athenians whom every fairy met.'

The tree below illustrates that the subject c-commands negation and the direct object (but not conversely), and negation c-commands the direct object (but not conversely):

(47)

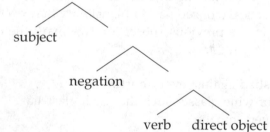

Let the term **operator** cover both negation and DPs with a quantificational determiner. We can now summarize these observations:

(48)   When Operator 1 c-commands Operator 2, the interpretation in which Operator 1 has Operator 2 in its scope is available. The interpretation in which Operator 2 has Operator 1 in its scope (the inverse reading) may or may not be available.

This is interesting, because we found that c-command is also the critical syntactic relation in connection with binding and negative polarity licens-ing. This suggests the following generalization:

(49)   If an expression E1 c-commands expression E2, it is possible for
       E1 to determine some aspect of E2's interpretation.

There is, however, a difference between the various domains. As discussed
above, a DP can only bind a reflexive pronoun if it c-commands that pronoun, and a decreasing operator can only license a negative polarity item
if it c-commands the item. The relative scope of operators is freer. It is
sufficient for Operator 1 to c-command Operator 2 in order for Operator 1
to scope over Operator 2, but it is not always necessary.

   Focusing again on relative scope, what determines whether an inverse
reading is available? This is too complex a question to be thoroughly answered in this textbook. But the tiny sample of data that we have looked at
is suggestive. There are certain operators whose scope behavior is fully
determined by their syntactic position: they only scope over what they
c-command. In the sample of data that we have considered, negation and
DPs whose determiner is *few* or *fewer than n* belong to this class. Interestingly, they are tied together by a semantic property: **decreasingness**.

(50)   An operator OP is decreasing if whenever we have two verb
       phrases VP1 and VP2 where $[\![VP1]\!]$ is always a subset of $[\![VP2]\!]$,
       then [OP VP2] entails [OP VP1].

At most two witches is also a decreasing DP. Check whether this DP in direct object position can take inverse scope over negation or the subject. Model your examples on (37) and (40).	**EXERCISE 8.4**

   Non-decreasing DPs typically have an ability to take inverse scope, at
least with respect to certain other operators.

Every witch, two or more witches, and *two witches* are non-decreasing DPs. Check whether these DPs in direct object position can take inverse scope over (a) negation and (b) the subject. Use the data provided by (39), (45), and (46), and supplement them with your own examples as necessary.	**EXERCISE 8.5**

We can state a preliminary and partial generalization as in (51):

(51)   Different operators have different scope behavior. Some operators
       only scope over what they c-command. Other operators may, to
       various degrees, scope over material that they do not c-command
       (take inverse scope). Semantic properties may be used to predict to
       which class a given operator belongs. One such semantic property
       is decreasingness.

We have not yet explained why each operator exhibits the scope behavior it does, nor have we shown how the correct scope interpretations are obtained compositionally. But we have laid some groundwork. A compositional grammar of quantifier scope is expected to account for (51).

8.4   The Marking of Scope Relations: Morphology and Syntax

Cross-linguistic data can be used to corroborate the claims about scope that have been made on the basis of English. Various languages fix the scopes of operators in their morphology or syntax. We illustrate this with examples from Greenlandic Eskimo and Hungarian.

8.4.1   Greenlandic Eskimo

Greenlandic Eskimo is a **polysynthetic** language. As discussed in chapter 2, this term means that various ingredients of the meaning of the sentence are expressed by bound morpheme affixes attached to the verb; there may or may not be independent constituents in the sentence related to each suffix. Bittner (1995) suggests that (in most cases) an operator suffix in Eskimo includes in its scope everything that it c-commands in the morphological structure of the word containing that suffix. An important background assumption is that Eskimo words have the following structure:

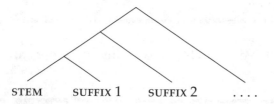

That is, a suffix c-commands those suffixes that precede it in linear order.

The following examples illustrate the correlation of c-command and scope. In (52), the relative scope of the *tariaqa* 'must' and *lir* 'begin' operators is involved. When *lir* follows *tariaqa*, they mean 'begin to have to'. When *tariaqa* follows *lir*, they mean 'have to begin to'. The relevant morphemes and their translations are highlighted. The reader may ignore other details of the examples.

(52)   a.   atuar-TARIAQA-LIR-p-u-q
             study-MUST-BEGIN-indicative-[- transitive]-3sing
             'He began to have to study.'
       b.   atua-LIR-TARIAQAR-p-u-q
             study-BEGIN-MUST-indicative-[- transitive]-3sing
             'He had to begin to study.'

In (53), the relative scope of *nngi* ('not') and an indefinite ('a book') is involved. This relation is encoded by the relation of the negative suffix and the suffix *(s)i* that marks the presence of the phrase 'a book' on the verb. When *nngi* follows *si*, the interpretation is 'not a single book'. When *(s)i* follows *nngi*, the interpretation is 'one book not'. In the glosses, negation is abbreviated as NEG and the morpheme *(s)i* is indicated as SI. Focus on the highlighted morphemes:

(53)   Context: Last year, Jaaku ordered five books. Yesterday, when I talked to her mother,
    a.   suli atuakka-mik   ataatsi-mik
        yet book-instrumental one-instrumental
        tigu-SI-sima-NNGI-nirar-p-a-a
        get-SI-perf-NEG-say-indicative-[+transitive]-3sing
        '. . . she said that he didn't get a single one yet.'
    b.   suli atuakka-mik   ataatsi-mik
        yet book-instrumental one-instrumental
        tassumununnga tigu-sima-NNGI-nira-I-v-u-q
        him-dative get-perf-NEG-say-SI-indicative-[-transitive]-3sing
        '. . . she said that there is one that he didn't get yet.'

One reason why the Eskimo data are important is because Eskimo morphology disambiguates scope, Eskimo speakers have to be systematically clear about the intended scope interpretation of their sentences, in exactly the same way as English speakers need to be systematically clear about the tense (present, past, etc.) of their sentences. This clearly indicates that Universal Grammar is equipped with the means to encode scope distinctions, and scope interpretation is not merely a matter of situational or conceptual knowledge.

8.4.2   Hungarian

Hungarian does not employ verbal affixes to disambiguate scope; it uses constituent order instead. That is, the surface c-command relations of DPs and other free-standing operators determine their scope relations unambiguously:

(54)   a.   Sok   ember   mindenkit   felhívott.
        many man-nom everyone-acc up-called
        'Many men phoned everyone =
        There are many men who each phoned everyone.'
    b.   Mindenkit   sok   ember   felhívott.
        everyone-acc many man-nom up-called
        'Many men phoned everyone =
        For everyone, there are many men who phoned him
        (a potentially different set of callers for each case).'

(55)   a.   Hatnál több ember   hívott fel mindenkit.
           six-than more man-nom called up everyone-acc
           'More than six men phoned everyone =
           There are more than six men who each called everyone.'
       b.   Mindenkit   hatnál több ember   hívott fel.
           everyone-acc six-than more man-nom called up
           'More than six men phoned everyone =
           For everyone, there are more than six men who called him
           (a potentially different set of caller for each case).'

The Hungarian data can be used to make the same point as the Eskimo data: the determination of scope is a matter of grammar. But Hungarian supports a finer point, also.

We observed that the left-to-right order of Hungarian DPs determines their relative scope. But Hungarian DPs are not simply lined up in the desired scopal order. Without going into details of Hungarian syntax (see Szabolcsi 1997a), we can note that the sentences differ in various respects that go beyond placing one of the noun phrases before or after the other. In (54), the DPs meaning 'everyone' and 'many men' are interchangeable in position, and the verbal particle *fel* 'up' precedes the verb stem. In (55), the DP meaning 'more than six men' must immediately precede the verb stem. Neither the other DP, nor the verbal particle can intervene between. (Therefore, in contrast to (54), the DP meaning 'everyone' must occur postverbally in order to take narrower scope.) All this is because each kind of DP occupies some specific position or positions in an articulated syntactic structure. Their linear order, and thus their relative scope, is simply a by-product.

In (51), we observed that different operators have different scope behavior. The syntax of Hungarian suggests that the scopal differences are explained by (derive from) some independent syntactic and semantic properties that govern the general behavior of those operators.

8.5   Summary

In summary, we have seen that certain expressions always depend on others for some aspect of their interpretation. Reflexive pronouns and negative polarity items are some of the examples: a reflexive pronoun needs an antecedent, and a negative polarity item needs a licensor. Certain other expressions may depend on others for some aspect of their interpretation. Personal pronouns and indefinite noun phrases are some of the examples: a quantifier may bind a pronoun, and it may induce referential variation in an indefinite. In all these cases, we said that the dominant member of the relation has the dependent member in its scope, and observed that scope is constrained by the syntactic c-command configuration. Of the four relations mentioned above, the scope interaction between two noun phrases is the most influenced by the linguistic and non-linguistic context. To show that these matters belong within grammar proper, we proposed some methods to corroborate intuitions about particular readings, and observed that there are languages which disambiguate quantifier scope in their overt morphology or syntax.

Further reading

Ladusaw, William. 1979. Polarity Sensitivity as Inherent Scope Relations. Ph.D. dissertation. University of Texas, Austin, Texas.
May, Robert. 1985. *Logical Form: Its Structure and Derivation*. Cambridge, MA: MIT Press.

Szabolcsi, Anna. ed. 1997b. *Ways of Scope Taking*. Dordrecht: Kluwer.
Szabolcsi, Anna. 1999. The syntax of scope. To appear in Mark Baltin and Chris Collins, eds., *The Handbook of Contemporary Syntactic Theory*. Oxford: Blackwell.

EXERCISES

Are the following claims true or false? Defend your answers.

(a) In the sentence, *Every student likes him*, the subject NP *every student* c-commands the object NP *him*.

(b) In the sentence, *Every student likes him*, the subject NP *every student* can bind the object NP *him*.

Exercise 8.6

(c) In the sentence, *Every student likes himself*, the subject NP *every student* c-commands the object NP *himself*.

(d) In the sentence, *Every student likes himself*, the subject NP *every student* can bind the object NP *himself*.

(e) In the sentence, *Every student knows the teacher likes him*, the subject NP *every student* c-commands the NP *him*.

(f) In the sentence, *Every student knows the teacher likes him*, the subject NP *every student* can bind the NP *him*.

(g) In the sentence *I doubt that Brutus ever goes to dramas with no violence*, the NP *no violence* c-commands the NPI *ever*.

· ·

Exercise 8.7

Does the subject wide scope reading of the sentence below entail the object wide scope reading, or the other way around? Justify your claim by drawing diagrams of situations in which the two readings are true.

Two witches overturned every cauldron.

· ·

Exercise 8.8   Paraphrase the following sentences in a way that clearly brings out their meaning difference. Can the difference be seen as one involving relative scope? If yes, which constituents interact in scope?

    (a)   Hermia may marry a fat nobleman.
    (b)   Hermia may marry any fat nobleman.

- -

Exercise 8.9   Compare the sentences in which an indefinite DP contains the determiner 'a(n)' or 'some' with those in which it has no determiner (these are called **bare plurals**). What is the systematic difference in their scope interpretations?

    (a)   Every earl visited some ladies.
          Every earl visited ladies.
    (b)   Hamlet did not like a king.
          Hamlet did not like kings.
    (c)   Hamlet may meet an actor.
          Hamlet may meet actors.

- -

Exercise 8.10   Do the following sentences allow the same relative scope interpretations for *a knight* and *every sword*? Propose a generalization.

    (a)   A knight bought every sword.
    (b)   A knight wanted to buy every sword.
    (c)   A knight thought that I bought every sword.
    (d)   A knight who bought every sword challenged Laertes.

- -

Exercise 8.11   Does scope influence the ability of a DP to license a negative polarity item or to bind a pronoun?
    The following examples are ambiguous with respect to the scope interpretation of *few sons* and *every knight*. Spell out the two readings in both cases.

    (a)   Fathers of few sons have time to sing madrigals.
    (b)   Prayers for every knight were said by this lady.

Now consider the following modifications of the examples:

    (a′)   Fathers of few sons have any time to sing madrigals.
    (b′)   Prayers for every knight were said by his lady.

Do the modified examples retain the same ambiguity? If not, what readings survive? Suggest an explanation, with reference to the conditions for NPI licensing and binding given in the text.

9

Semantics III:
Cross-Categorial Parallelisms

9.0 Introduction

An important insight of semantic theory is that there exist deep parallelisms between the interpretations of expressions that belong to different syntactic categories. This chapter discusses two such cases. The first is the nominal **count/mass** distinction and the verbal (aspectual) **telic/atelic** distinction. We will show that there is a semantic similarity between these. Moreover, they interact in the compositional semantics of the sentence. The second case concerns the observation that certain adverbs in English play a role similar to that played by determiners; moreover, in many languages this role is more typically played by adverbs and other noun-phrase-external elements than by determiners.

9.1 Count/Mass and Telic/Atelic[1]

9.1.1 The count/mass distinction: [+/− quantized]

There is a well-known distinction in English between **count** nouns and **mass** nouns. Count nouns can be pluralized, they co-occur with *many* and are directly modified by numerals; mass nouns do not appear in the plural, they co-occur with *much* and take numerals only with the mediation of **measure expressions**.

(1) count nouns: a chair, ten chairs, many chairs,
       *much chair(s), *ten pounds/pieces of chair

(2) mass nouns: much wine, ten gallons of wine
       *a wine, *ten wines, *many wines,
       much oil, ten drops of oil
       *an oil, *ten oils, *many oils

More precisely, it is not nouns as such that are count or mass. *A wine, an oil*, etc. are unacceptable as meaning 'one minimal (amount of) wine,' or 'one minimal (amount of) oil.' But note that nearly every mass noun has a count counterpart that signifies either a standard serving or a kind. For example:

(3) a. Bring me a wine, a nectar, etc. (acceptable in many but not all dialects)
     b. Cleopatra invented a magical oil.
     c. This cellar produces several famous wines.

Conversely, almost anything count can be turned into a mass, by a regular, or in the majority of cases exceptional, process that destroys its integrity:

(4) a. Here's an apple; but don't put too much apple in the salad.
     b. After the earthquake, there was roof all over the floor.

   Thus, instead of count and mass nouns we should really speak of nouns used in a count or a mass way. The choice signals whether the thing referred to is thought of as being inherently **quantized** or not. Quantized means that the object referred to is articulated into minimal units: it is prepackaged. If it is not, the measure expression (e.g. *piece, pound*) may serve as a **quantizer**. The fact that some nouns are considered count and others mass reflects what the normal behavior of the things referred to is, according to the linguistically canonized belief of the community.

Count/mass across languages

In an overwhelming majority of the cases, the real world predicts whether a noun will be count or mass. But in other cases, the distinction is shown to be linguistic. For example: *chair*, *table*, etc. are count, but *furniture* is mass: **furnitures*, but *a piece of furniture*. *Pebbles* and *gravel* do not differ much as to the size of the individual pieces, but *a pebble* is acceptable whereas **a gravel* is not. You can *make a promise* but not **give an advice*, although one might think that the two do not differ as to quantizedness and, in fact, in French, both *une promesse* 'a promise' and *un avis* 'a piece of advice' are count nouns. Such cross-linguistic examples clearly show that the count/mass distinction is linguistic, that is, determined by the grammar of the language.

9.1.2 Cumulative and distributive reference

The question arises whether the count/mass distinction is one of a kind, or whether it has relatives in other linguistic domains. To help answer this question, we need to explicate the notion of [+/− quantized] such that it can apply to other domains.

Cumulative reference
Consider the following:

Cumulative reference:
Let E be an expression, for example, a noun. We say that E refers cumulatively if whenever we refer to certain things using E, we can also refer to their sum using exactly the same expression E.

The term *cumulative reference* corresponds to the fact that one can accumulate (sum, merge, unite) things that are labeled as, say, *oil* and as a result get something labeled as *oil* again. Two portions of oil united in one container make oil again, and can be referred to as such. That is, the expression *oil* refers cumulatively. On the other hand, the sum of two things each of which is referred to as *(a) chair* is not referred to as *(a) chair*; it is referred to as *chairs*. A chair here and a chair there do not make another chair. So, the expression *(a) chair* does not refer cumulatively.

We may note here that the sum of two things that are referred to as *chairs* is *chairs*. Two stacks of chairs together make chairs again. So determinerless plurals do refer cumulatively. This will become important in section 9.1.4.

We see that mass terms refer cumulatively, but count terms do not. This follows from the notion of quantization. Recall that a count term like *a chair* has quantized reference because its referents come in minimal units. But then each entity that qualifies as *(a) chair* must have exactly one chairful of chair-stuff to it; anything more than what makes up a unit is too much. On the other hand, the fact that mass terms like *oil* lack quantization means that there is no unit size to set an upper limit, so stuff can be merged and merged and still bear the same label.

Distributive reference

Another potentially relevant property is distributive reference, the mirror image of cumulative reference. The term refers to the fact that the label of the whole distributes over the parts:

Distributive reference:
An expression E refers distributively if any part of a thing that is referred to as E is also referred to as E.

Is it the case that any part of something referred to as *a chair* is referred to as *a chair*? That is, does the label *(a) chair* distribute over the parts of a thing that can be labeled as *(a) chair*? Clearly not. If I break a chair, I may be left with a damaged chair plus a leg, but never with a chair plus another chair. So count terms do not refer distributively. This follows from quantization again: nothing less than what makes up a unit is big enough to bear the label.

Do mass terms refer distributively? Suppose you divide a gallon of oxygen into two parts, then divide those parts each into two parts, and so on. This process will leave you with oxygen plus oxygen for a long while. At some point, however, you are down to one molecule, and the process ends: no part of an oxygen molecule is oxygen. There are those who contend that the existence of minimal parts like molecules is a strong argument against distributive reference in mass terms. However, it may be objected that recent scientific knowledge about molecules and submolecular entities is not reflected in language and is therefore irrelevant. Moreover, the referents of abstract mass terms such as *love* and *freedom* are not likely to have minimal parts, even if we find a way, perhaps metaphorical, of dividing those referents into parts. It may be, then, that some mass nouns refer distributively. But is distributive reference a characteristic property of all mass terms? There are convincing counterexamples that involve purely linguistic (and not conceptual) knowledge. For example, it is not the case that any part of furniture is furniture (a leg of a table is not furniture), and it is not the case that any part of chairs is chairs (a stack of chairs can easily be divided into parts at least one of which is an individual chair).

Thus, the conclusion seems to be that a mass term may or may not refer distributively; it depends on the individual case. Unlike cumulative reference, distributive reference is not a defining property of the class.

9.1.3   Extending the distinction to the verbal domain

Telic vs. atelic

Using the notions of cumulative and distributive reference, we can now pose the question again: are there expressions in other linguistic domains for which the quantized versus cumulative distinction is relevant?

We suggest that the domain of events described by verb phrases is such. The issues to be examined belong under the rubric **aspect**, which has to do with the internal structure of events.

Verbal expressions fall into two large categories according to whether one of their basic senses can be modified by *for an hour* or by *within an hour*. The qualification 'in one of their basic senses' is necessary, because the sentence itself may be acceptable on some reading that is presently irrelevant to us. The interpretations appended to the examples will help focus on the intended readings. See the comments that follow the examples. The * in front of a triplet is meant to hold for each member.

(5)   a.   Romeo   wandered   for an hour.
                    hesitated
                    watched Juliet
          'A single event of Romeo wandering lasted for an hour, etc.'
      b.   *Romeo woke   for an hour.
                    recovered
                    glanced at Juliet
          'A single event of Romeo waking (not the resulting state) lasted for an hour, etc.'

(6)   a.   Romeo   woke   within an hour.
                    recovered
                    glanced at Juliet
          'A single event of Romeo waking occurred and terminated within an hour, etc.'
      b.   *Romeo wandered   within an hour.
                    hesitated
                    watched Juliet
          'A single event of Romeo wandering occurred and terminated (not just began) within an hour, etc.'

In (5), *Romeo wandered for an hour* is acceptable as meaning that the wandering lasted for an hour. *Romeo woke for an hour* is unacceptable on the same type of meaning, although it may well mean that the resulting state, Romeo's being awake, lasted for an hour. This latter interpretation does not concern us here, that is why the example is marked as unacceptable.

Similarly irrelevant to us is the iterated reading in (5), on which *Romeo woke for an hour* means that he repeatedly woke and dozed off. This is what the 'single event' qualification intends to exclude. The iterated reading can be isolated by modifying the sentence by *only once*, as below:

(7) a.   Romeo watched Juliet only once, and on that occasion he
          watched her for an hour.
     b.   *Romeo glanced at Juliet only once, and on that occasion he
          glanced at her for an hour.

In (7a), *only once* may mean 'on her birthday' and is perfectly compatible with the watching being rather extended in time. The same addition of *only once* makes (7b) unacceptable, because a single glancing cannot be an hour long, and the possibility of iteration (repetition) is now eliminated. The iterated reading can be more or less readily available, depending on how plausible it is to repeatedly get in and out of a state.

In (6), *Romeo woke within an hour* may be a simple expression of the fact that Romeo's waking was achieved within an hour. *Romeo wandered within an hour* does not have the same type of meaning, although it may mean that something happened that sent Romeo wandering within an hour (that is, it is the start, not the termination, of the wandering that occurred within an hour). Again, this more specialized second interpretation does not concern us.

A comprehensive description of these verbs needs to account for all the readings that we called irrelevant. At present, we are only interested in a particular facet of their meaning, to which we now turn.

The class whose members can be modified by *within an hour* but not by *for an hour* have been called **telic**: this term, deriving from Greek *telos* 'end', means that the event described has an inherent culmination point (end point). Conversely, the class whose members can be modified by *for an hour* but not by *within an hour* have been called **atelic**: the events described have no inherent culmination point (end point). See Sidebar 9.2.

The telic versus atelic distinction is reminiscent of the quantized versus cumulative distinction. Consider, for instance, telic *recover*. *Romeo recovered* means that there was a process, however brief or long, of Romeo recovering, but at one point a qualitative change took place: he was fine again. The recovery event is delimited by this change. Once it has taken place, Romeo needs to fall ill again to recover again; the same event does not continue beyond this point. The existence of an inherent end point means that recovery events come in distinguished minimal units. In contrast, consider atelic *hesitate*. The event described by *Romeo hesitated* does not have such an inherent end point. It may continue indefinitely; or, if it comes to an end because Romeo falls asleep or makes up his mind, this is still not a culmination of his hesitation; the hesitation event simply ceases. (Why?

Classes of atelic and telic predicates	SIDEBAR 9.2

It is common to distinguish two subclasses of atelic predicates: **states** (*know the poem, be tall*) and **activities** (*smile, be polite*), and two subclasses of telic predicates: **accomplishments** (*recover, eat a sandwich*) and **achievements** (*win, die*). These finer distinctions do not play a role in the present discussion.

We understand the culmination of an event to be part of it, e.g. if you recover, the qualitative change that takes place is still part of the recovery event. But falling asleep or making a decision cuts off hesitation without being part of the hesitation event.)

These observations allow us to design tests that check whether a verb phrase refers cumulatively or distributively.

Are the predicates below telic or atelic?	EXERCISE 9.1

(a)   Falstaff sneezed.
(b)   Hamlet sweated.
(c)   Juliet died.
(d)   Romeo grieved.
(e)   The water froze.

Telicity and quantizedness
If Romeo wandered (or hesitated, or watched Juliet) from 9 to 9:30 am and he wandered (or hesitated, or watched Juliet) from 9:30 to 10 am, he can be said to have wandered (or to have hesitated, or to have watched Juliet) from 9 to 10 am. That is to say, the smaller events join smoothly into one big event that bears the same label. Atelic verb phrases, as expected, refer cumulatively.

In contrast, if Romeo woke (or recovered, or glanced at Juliet) within half an hour, and then he did so again, he cannot be said equivalently to have wakened (or to have recovered, or to have glanced at Juliet) within an hour. This would suggest that there was just one waking (or recovery, or glance); but in fact there were two. Thus, telic verb phrases, as expected, cannot refer cumulatively.

The distributive reference test also gives roughly the same results as in the case of count versus mass terms. Telic verb phrases do not refer distributively. An event of waking (or recovery, or glance) cannot be divided into parts that are also waking (or recovery, or glance) events. On the other hand, an event of wandering (or hesitation, or watching Juliet) has many subevents with the same label, although there may be other subevents that do not qualify. For instance, *Romeo watched Juliet from 9 to 9:30 am* is considered true even if Romeo sneezed during the period and his attention was temporarily diverted, that is, the event of watching Juliet may have a subevent which itself is not an event of watching Juliet. So, distributivity is not a defining property of atelic events.

To summarize:

- Mass terms and atelic predicates refer cumulatively.
  Their referents are not quantized.
- Count terms and telic predicates do not refer cumulatively.
  Their referents are quantized.

9.1.4   The interaction of the two domains

The fact that the entities that nominal expressions refer to and the events that verbal expressions describe are structured similarly is interesting. But does it have consequences for compositional semantics, that is, for the question of how the meanings of complex expressions are determined by the meanings of their constituent parts?

We will demonstrate that it does. In the examples above, the lexical verb determined the telicity or atelicity of the verb phrase. But it does not always do so. (Comments on the intended interpretations follow immediately.)

(8) a.   Hamlet's mother consumed a poisoned drink within five
           minutes.
           The vendor sold a pie within five minutes.
     b.   *Hamlet's mother consumed a poisoned drink for five minutes.
           *The vendor sold a pie for five minutes.

(9) a.   *Hamlet's mother consumed ale within five minutes.
           *The vendor sold wine within five minutes.
     b.   Hamlet's mother consumed ale for five minutes.
           The vendor sold wine for five minutes.

(10) a.   *Hamlet's mother consumed poisoned drinks within five
           minutes.
           *The vendor sold pies within five minutes.
     b.   Hamlet's mother consumed poisoned drinks for five minutes.
           The vendor sold pies for five minutes.

Care must be taken in connection with the intended interpretation of the starred *within* examples. As noted in connection with (5) and (6), the starred examples lack one basic reading that is readily available for their unstarred counterpart. The kind of qualifications used in connection with (5) and (6) carry over. In addition, new irrelevant readings may arise in (8)–(9)–(10), or slight modifications of them, due to the presence of the direct object. For example, *Hamlet's mother used to consume drinks in five minutes* is fine if it means that she used to have the ability to consume an individual drink within five minutes.

When *consume* has a direct object whose referent is quantized, the event described by the verb phrase is telic. That is, the noun phrase *a drink* refers in a quantized manner and *consumed a drink* is telic; finishing off the drink is implied. When, however, the same verb has a direct object that refers cumulatively, the event described by the verb phrase is atelic. That is, since the noun phrase *ale* refers cumulatively, *consumed ale* is atelic, and the sentence is uncommitted as to whether there was ale left. Put simply, the events described by these verb phrases inherit their quantized or cumulative character from the referent of the direct object.

This is a fact that compositional semantics can account for. Informally, we may say that the things referred to by the direct object measure out the event: the more ale is consumed, the more ale-drinking has taken place, and the inherent end point is when the given amount of ale is gone. Thus, the verbs under consideration may be said to map the structure of the referent of the direct object to the structure of the event described by the verb phrase.

(a) Determine whether the following examples are telic or atelic: *to work, to work oneself to death, to work on a plan, to work out a plan*

   Use modification by *for five minutes / an hour / a year* (whichever is appropriate) as the primary test. Bear in mind the comments about irrelevant secondary meanings, made in the text.
   Example: *Lorenzo watched the race for an hour*: atelic
   Lorenzo won the race for an hour (unless it means that he was disqualified after that hour): telic

(b) On the basis of your results, suggest what categories should be classified as to telicity. V, VP, something else?

EXERCISE 9.2

A similar phenomenon occurs in these examples (disregarding irrelevant readings, as above):

(11) Romeo walked west(ward) for a minute (*within a minute).

(12) Romeo walked to Juliet's side within a minute (*for a minute).

West(ward) refers to a path cumulatively, whereas *to Juliet's side* is a quantized path delimited by Juliet's whereabouts. *Walk* can be seen to map the structures of these paths to the structures of the events.

Not all verbs have this **structure-preserving mapping** property: verb phrases with verbs like *press on*, *stroke* or *admire* remain atelic no matter what their direct object is. Apparently, the corresponding events cannot be construed as involving any end point.

(13)   a.   Richard stroked a horse/horses for an hour (*within an hour).
       b.   Richard admired a horse/horses for an hour (*within an hour).

Are there verb phrases that are irreparably telic? In most cases, **iteration** (repetition) is possible and yields an atelic interpretation, as was discussed in (7) above. If, however, the kind of event denoted by the verb or verb phrase can take place only once, iteration is excluded, e.g. *She died of a fever for a year*.

In chapter 7 we looked at the fundamentals of model theoretic semantics. The phenomena this section has been concerned with provide further evidence that a theory of semantics for natural language must, and can, be capable of describing and manipulating rather subtle kinds of structures to which linguistic expressions refer.

9.1.5   Do the same distinctions hold in Japanese?[2]

In developing the argument above we relied on that property of English that syntactically distinguishes mass terms and count terms. Do these results carry over to a language like Japanese, where no such distinction needs to be made? For example, *ringo* may mean 'an apple', 'apples', 'some apples', 'the apple', or 'the apples'. In contrast to English, the same verb phrase can be modified both by expressions meaning 'within one minute' and by expressions meaning 'for one minute':

(14)   a.   Watasi-wa ringo-o   ip-pun   de tabe-ru
            I-top   apple-acc one-minute in eat-pr
            'I eat APPLE within one minute.'
       b.   Watasi-wa ringo-o   ip-pun-kan   tabe-ru
            I-top   apple-acc one-minute-for eat-pr
            'I eat APPLE for one minute.'

The (a) sentence means that the apple(s) was/were eaten up, while the (b) sentence only says that apple-eating activity took place for one minute. This parallels what we saw in English. A predicate modified by *ippun de* is telic. When the main verb of a telic predicate is of the 'eat' type, its direct object is interpreted as quantized. And conversely, a predicate modified by *ippunkan* is atelic. When the main verb of an atelic predicate is of the 'eat' type, its direct object is interpreted as referring cumulatively. This indicates that the semantic structures of these Japanese expressions may well be the same as their English counterparts, although surface marking does not make this transparent.

These subtle effects may be made sharper by slightly modifying the above examples. In (15a) the completive morphology is added to the gerund form of the verb to get *tabete-shimau*, meaning 'finish eating' or 'eat up'. (This completive use of *-te-shimau* must be distinguished from another use, meaning something like 'I wound up going and doing . . .'. This other reading has a slightly pejorative or apologetic sense.)

(15)   a.   Watashi-wa ringo-o ip-pun de tabete-shimau.

The completive use of *-te-shimau* does enforce the telic reading of the sentence, but we can make the contrast still clearer. Now add the progressive morphology *-te-iru* to the verb in sentence (15b):

(15)   b.   Watashi-wa ringo-o ip-pun-kan tabete-iru.

(This progressive use of *-te-iru* must be distinguished from another use, which means something habitual like 'Recently I've been doing . . .'.) When the modal senses of these two kinds of verbal morphology are teased away, we have clear completive and progressive aspectual morphology on the verb, requiring telic and atelic interpretations. To see this, try switching *ippun de* and *ippun-kan* around (keeping the aspectual and not the modal senses of the morphology). These sentences degrade:

(16)   a.   *Watashi-wa ringo-o ip-pun de tabete-iru.
      b.   *Watashi-wa ringo-o ip-pun-kan tabete-shimau.

To bring out the reflexes in the noun phrase, add a counter for apples, *ik-ko*, to the sentences. This produces a meaning something like 'I eat one apple . . .':

(17)   a.   Watashi-wa ringo-o ik-ko ip-pun de tabete-shimau.
      b.   Watashi-wa ringo-o ik-ko ip-pun-kan tabete-iru.

The counter *ik-ko* seems to enforce either a quantized or a definite reading of *ringo*. Sentence (17a) is natural, meaning 'I eat up one apple in one minute'. Sentence (17b) is stranger. It can have a forced interpretation in which a particular, definite apple is picked out (and an indefinite quantity of that apple is eaten). Since *ringo* in (17a) or (17b) can equally refer to a piece of an apple, a number of apples, or some quantity of apples, these facts are subtle indeed. The difference is whether a definite or indefinite quantity of apple(s) is(are) completely consumed.

9.2   Determiners and Adverbs[3]

Consider the following sentence:

(18)   Usually, a Shakespearean sonnet contains the word *love*.

What does *usually* mean here? Can it mean that on, say, weekdays Shakespeare's sonnets contain the word *love*, but during the weekend they do not? It clearly cannot. The meaning of this sentence can be roughly paraphrased as:

(19)   Most Shakespearean sonnets contain the word *love*.

(19) shows that determiners and adverbs can play similar roles. In this section we investigate a set of questions related to this phenomenon. First, we examine respects in which determiners and adverbs work similarly in English. Second, we consider some cross-linguistic data pertaining to the division of labor between these two categories.

9.2.1   Determiners and adverbs in English: similarities and differences

Sets of entities and sets of events
In chapter 7 we saw that determiners like *every, some, many, most*, and *few* show us the relation between two sets of individuals:

(20)   Every king is whimsical: kings are a subset of whimsical people

(21)   Few kings are whimsical: the number of whimsical kings is small
OR
the number of whimsical kings is small compared with the number of kings

EXERCISE 9.3	Recall the definition of *most* in chapter 7: [Most N VP] is true just in case the set of things in both [[N]] and [[VP]] is larger than the set of things that are in [[N]] but not in [[VP]]. most A B = True if and only if $(2 \times |A \cap B|) > |A|$ Complete (a) in the manner of (20)–(21): (a) Most kings are whimsical: . . .

Let us now focus on the following question: Are determiners the only category that relate two sets in the way described in chapter 7?

If we look for expressions that might quantify over entities other than individuals in a manner similar to determiners, a certain class of adverbs comes to mind: *always, sometimes, often, usually, seldom*, and so on. These have come to be called **adverbs of quantification**. Granting that their meanings are similar to the meanings of the determiners mentioned above, what might be the sets that they relate?

In at least one type of context this question can be easily answered: they relate two sets of cases, or events, or situations (understood by and large in the everyday sense):

(22) If/when you deal with Puck, you ALWAYS have a good time: cases in which you deal with Puck are a subset of the cases in which you have a good time

(23) If/when you deal with Puck, you USUALLY have a good time: there are more cases in which you deal with Puck and have a good time than cases in which you deal with Puck but don't have a good time

---

Complete the following, modeling the explanation of *seldom* after that of *few* in (21):

(a) If/when you deal with Puck, you seldom have a good time: . . .

EXERCISE 9.4

The adverb's restriction

In addition to supplying definitions of how particular determiners work, we have sampled their purely semantic properties. First of all, we showed that the two sets they relate do not play quite identical roles: the one corresponding to the denotation of NP serves to **restrict** the determiner. For instance, to check whether the sentence *Every king is whimsical* is true, we never need to look beyond the set of kings. This means two things. First, we need not consider entities that are neither kings nor whimsical (e.g. chairs). Second, we need not consider entities that are whimsical but not kings (e.g. queens). This latter fact was expressed by saying that determiners are conservative.

If you now compare (20)–(21) and (22)–(23), you will see that the set of cases described by the *if*-clause plays the same role in (22)–(23) as the set of individuals in the NP's denotation does in the definitions for determiners, in (20)–(21).

Does this similarity extend to the *if*-clause serving as a restrictor for the adverb of quantification?

Check to see whether adverbs of quantification are conservative. Recall the definition from chapter 7:

A relation Q named by a determiner is conservative if, and only if, for any properties A and B, relation Q holds between A and B if and only if relation Q holds between A and the things in (A ∩ B).

Paraphrase (a) in the manner required by the definition and decide whether the paraphrase is equivalent to the original sentence:

(a)   If/when you deal with Puck, you always have a good time: . . .

We can now conclude that the *if*-clause plays the same role for adverbs of quantification as the NP does for determiners: it restricts our attention to the largest set (of events) potentially relevant for the truth of the sentence.

Decreasingness

Other semantic properties that we noted for determiners also carry over to adverbs of quantification. For instance, the determiner *few* was said to be decreasing with respect to the set of individuals denoted by the VP, and we mentioned that negative polarity items are sensitive to this property. We may now add that *seldom* is similarly decreasing with respect to the set of events denoted by the main clause and licenses a negative polarity item there.

Note the fact in (a):

(a)   Relevant set inclusion:
The set of cases in which you have a very good time is a subset of those in which you have a good time.

Now complete (b) and (c). For (b), what is the proposition that *If you deal with Puck, you seldom have a good time* needs to entail in order for *seldom* to be decreasing? Write it down and determine whether the entailment holds. For (c), demonstrate that *seldom* licenses an occurrence of *any* in the dotted part of the sentence:

(b)   Decreasing entailment:
If you deal with Puck, you seldom have a good time
= ? = > . . .

(c)   NPI licensing:
If you deal with Puck, you seldom . . .

To summarize, there are at least two kinds of expressions in natural language that relate two sets in particular ways: determiners and adverbs. The first relate sets of individuals, the second, sets of cases. Syntactically, these two kinds of expressions are different. Thus, their similarity must be semantic. What we have shown, then, is that there are semantic mechanisms and properties that are independent of syntax in that they can be shared by different categories. This squares with the conclusion that we reached in the informal discussion of the count/mass and the telic/atelic distinctions, namely, that nominal and verbal expressions can both have cumulative or non-cumulative reference.

9.2.2 Recovering the adverb's restriction: presuppositions

What happens when the sentence has no *if*-clause? Do these adverbs still relate two sets of cases, and if so, how are those sets determined? There are various possibilities.

First, consider these examples:

(24)   The Fool usually/always/seldom regrets offending Lear.

(25)   The Fool usually/always/seldom denies offending Lear.

(24) is naturally interpreted in the following way ((26a, b) are equivalent ways of expressing the same thing, as we have seen above):

(26)   a.   If/when the Fool offends Lear, he usually/always/seldom
             regrets offending Lear.
       b.   In most/all/few cases when the Fool offends Lear, the Fool
             regrets offending Lear.

How does this interpretation come about? In chapter 7 we observed that *regret* presupposes that its complement describes a fact. In (26), precisely the cases in which this presupposition holds constitute the restriction of the adverb of quantification.

In other words, when the restrictor of the adverb of quantification is not made explicit in the form of an *if*-clause, the presupposition of the sentence may play the role of defining the restriction.

Recalling the discussion of what *deny* presupposes with respect to its clausal or gerundival complement, specify what set of cases constitutes the restriction of the adverbs in (25).	**EXERCISE** **9.7**

9.2.3   Recovering the adverb's restriction: focus

Let us now consider another way in which the adverb's restriction can be recovered. Our examples will have a heavy stress on a particular word. (As discussed below in the chapters on phonology, the stressed syllable of the word on which the primary stress falls is louder, longer in duration, and often higher in pitch than the same word when primary stress does not fall on that word.) In the sentences below, the heavy stress is shown by the word being capitalized.

(27)   Oberon usually/always/seldom talks to PUCK about his problems.

This sentence may be paraphrased as follows (again, (28a, b) are just two ways of saying the same thing):

(28)   a.   If/when Oberon talks to someone about his problems, it is usually/always/seldom Puck.
       b.   In most/all/few cases when Oberon talks to someone about his problems, Oberon talks to Puck about his problems.

How may this interpretation come about? To see this, we need to make a little excursus.

The heavily stressed noun phrase (*Puck*) in (27) is called the **focus** of the sentence. Focus expresses new information or contrast. The rest of the sentence is called the **focus frame**. The following examples (which do not contain an adverb of quantification) illustrate this division:

(29)   a.   PUCK squeezed the magic flower onto Lysander's eyelids.
            focus: Puck
            focus frame: [someone] squeezed the magic flower onto Lysander's eyelids
       b.   Puck squeezed the magic flower onto LYSANDER's eyelids.
            focus: Lysander
            focus frame: Puck squeezed the magic flower onto [someone]'s eyelids
       c.   Puck squeezed the MAGIC FLOWER onto Lysander's eyelids.
            focus: the magic flower
            focus frame: Puck squeezed [something] onto Lysander's eyelids

Returning to (27), we now see that its interpretation in (28) relies on the focus–focus frame division. Specifically, the cases in which the focus frame holds constitute the restriction of the adverb of quantification.

(30)   Oberon talks to PUCK about his problems.
       focus: Puck
       focus frame: Oberon talks to [someone] about his problems

It is an interesting question whether the above two ways of recovering the adverb's restriction can be unified. In other words, may the fact that the focus frame can supply the adverb's restriction be perhaps just a special case of the fact that a presupposition can do so? This question arises because the focus–focus frame division is often equated with a focus–presupposition division. For example, a sentence like (30) is often described as presupposing that Oberon talks to someone about his problems and asserting that he does so to Puck.

In many discourse contexts the focus frame may indeed be presupposed. But it is possible to use a sentence like (30) without such a presupposition:

(31)   Does Oberon talk to anyone about his problems?
       Well, it is unlikely that HE TALKS TO PUCK, and I know that he
       does not talk to anyone else.

This means that it is not generally true that the focus frame is presupposed. Thus, it is not obvious that recovering the adverb's restriction using the focus frame is just a special case of doing so using a presupposition.

9.2.4   Recovering the adverb's restriction: individuals

Each case involves exactly one individual
To see what other factors may be relevant in the definition of the restrictor, recall (18), repeated here as (32):

(32)   Usually, a Shakespearean sonnet contains the word *love*.

Here there are no events in any everyday sense; a sonnet containing a particular word is not an event. So what can be a case? From now on, we begin to extend the everyday sense of the word *case* and turn it into a technical term.

It seems that each sonnet constitutes a case. An alternative paraphrase might make this example more similar to those involving real events:

(33)   If/when something is a Shakespearean sonnet, it usually contains
       the word *love*.

This paraphrase makes it easy to dissolve the mystery of why *Usually, a Shakespearean sonnet contains the word love* means the same as *Most son-*

nets of Shakespeare contain the word **love**. We have just seen that *usually* means 'In most cases, if . . . , then . . .'. Since each sonnet corresponds to a unique case involving that sonnet, cases involving a sonnet can be traded for sonnets. That is, given the one-to-one correspondence, it makes no difference whether we count sonnets or cases involving a sonnet.

Each case involves more than one individual

But do all similar examples involving a determiner and an adverb come out meaning the same? Compare the following sentences, making sure that neither the subject nor the object is focused:

(34)   Most fairies who met a mortal tricked him.

(35)   Usually, if/when a fairy met a mortal, he tricked him.

Imagine the following situation. Five fairies are wandering in the forest. Four of the fairies each meet one or two mortals, and they trick all the mortals they meet. The fifth fairy has a hangover, and although he meets 15 mortals, he does not trick any of them.

(36)

F. 1 meets	M. 1	Does F trick the M(s)?	yes
F. 2	M. 2		yes
F. 3	M. 3		yes
F. 4	M. 4, M. 5		yes
F. 5	M. 6, . . . , M. 20		no

The sentence with *most* seems true here, but the one with *usually* does not. The following paraphrases may help clarify why:

(37)   There are more fairies who met a mortal and tricked him than fairies who met a mortal and did not trick him.

(38)   There are more cases involving a fairy meeting a mortal in which the fairy tricked the mortal than cases in which he did not.

The *most*-sentence wants us to compare the sizes of two sets of fairies. The *usually*-sentence wants us to compare the sizes of two sets of cases of a fairy meeting a mortal. This latter comes down to the same thing as if we were comparing the sizes of two sets of fairy–mortal pairs (providing that each fairy meets each mortal only once). The model we just offered shows that when a minority of the fairies happens to see the majority of the mortals and acts differently from the majority of the fairies, this tips the balance.

In fact, counting pairs is not the worst we can get:

(39)   Most fairies who give a present to a mortal want to take it back from him.

(40)   Usually, if/when a fairy gives a present to a mortal, she wants to take it back from him.

Here the *most*-sentence still wants to compare the sizes of sets of fairies (those who change their minds and those who do not). The *usually*-sentence, however, wants to compare sets of cases involving triplets consisting of a fairy, a present, and a mortal. (Here any fairy dealing with exceedingly many mortals or with exceedingly many presents may tip the balance.) And we might go on to quadruplets, quintuplets, and so on.

It is worth emphasizing that a case will only coincide with an individual or with a pair, triple, etc. of individuals if there is no multiplicity of relevant events that the given individual(s) can be involved in. Compare the following examples:

(41)   Usually, if a knight admires a lady, he sings her praise.

(42)   Usually, if a knight sees a lady, he bows to her.

For each knight and lady, there can be only a single case of him admiring her; *admire* is not an eventive verb, it denotes a more or less permanent property. Therefore, to find out whether (41) is true, it is enough to count knight–lady pairs. On the other hand, each knight and lady can be involved in many events of him seeing her. Each such event constitutes a separate case for *usually* in (42).

Suppose we have 5 knights. Knight 1 sees one lady twenty times a day, and the same for Knight 2. They bow to them dutifully. On the other hand, Knights 3, 4, and 5 see three ladies each, but only once a day. Knights 3, 4, and 5 neglect to bow. First, judge whether (42) is true in this situation. Next, explain what you counted in reaching your conclusion.	**EXERCISE 9.8**

What then determines whether a single individual, or a pair, or a triple, etc. corresponds to a case? In the above examples the singular indefinite DPs do (*a Shakespearean sonnet*, *a fairy* and *a mortal*, etc.). The modified versions of the examples show that determinerless plurals (*sonnets*) work just as well:

(43)   Usually, Shakespearean sonnets contain the word *love*.

(44)   Usually, when fairies meet mortals, they trick them.

(45)   Usually, when fairies give presents to mortals, they want to take them back from them.

We leave open what other expressions may behave in the same way. We also leave open exactly what syntactic mechanisms underlie the interpretation of adverbs of quantification. We note, however, that compositional semantics, which we have committed ourselves to, must answer such questions, and much current research is in fact directed at these tasks.

Adverbs of quantification in generic sentences

As mentioned in chapter 8, in sentences like *Donkeys eat dewberries*, the determinerless plural is called a **bare plural**. Bare plurals in English can have **generic** readings, e.g. the above sentence means: 'Donkeys in general eat dewberries.' It is often assumed in current literature that such generic readings are due to a silent adverb of quantification that operates much like its overt counterparts discussed above. This silent adverb is a **default quantifier**. It is understood to mean, 'In every case in which you have no evidence to the contrary, assume that if . . . , then . . .', e.g. 'Unless you have evidence to the contrary, assume that if something is a donkey, it eats dewberries.' In fact, the actual sentence *If/when something is a donkey, it eats dewberries* has the same generic (default) interpretation.

We may now note that the silent adverb may interact with an overt one in interesting ways. For example, (46) below is ambiguous:

(46)   Donkeys seldom eat dewberries.
    a.   'Few donkeys eat dewberries.'
    b.   'If/when something is a donkey, there are few occasions on which it eats dewberries.'

Reading (a) comes about when the sentence does not contain a default quantifier. Reading (b) comes about when a default quantifier is present and takes broader scope than *seldom*.

To summarize this section, we started out noting that adverbs of quantification operate similarly to determiners. Do these adverbs contribute to the expressive power of English in a significant way? They do, for the following reasons. First, they allow us to quantify over events (e.g. dealing with Puck), which determiners in English do not do directly. Second, they allow us to quantify over cases involving single individuals, pairs, triplets, etc. This liberty is again something that determiners in English do not have. While the sentence *Usually, a Shakespearean sonnet contains the word love* is the truth-conditional equivalent of *Most Shakespearean sonnets contain the word love*, this is only because it is special in having a one-to-one correspondence between sonnets and cases. The sentence *Usually, if a fairy meets a mortal, he tricks him* simply has no equivalent with *most*. The reason is that, as we have seen, *most* (like all determiners) wants us to count single individuals that are in the denotation of its NP, not cases involving arbitrary numbers of individuals.

9.2.5   D-quantification and A-quantification: a cross-linguistic perspective[4]

We have seen that English has at least two kinds of means for expressing quantification: noun-phrase-internal determiners and sentence-level adverbs. Do all languages have both kinds?

Significant current empirical research has been focusing on this question. It turns out that many languages do not have quantificational determiners, but all languages seem to have means like adverbs, adjectives, auxiliaries, or argument structure adjusters for expressing quantification. In contrast to the former, **D-quantification**, this latter group has been termed **A-quantification**. Some other languages do have D-quantification, but their systems of A-quantification are more elaborate than in English.

We first examine Greenlandic Eskimo, which, despite superficial differences, is quite similar to English in this regard, then turn to Salish and Mayali, which are more different.

Greenlandic Eskimo

Greenlandic Eskimo corroborates the cross-linguistic validity of the claim that D-quantifiers count individuals, while A-quantifiers count cases.

Eskimo has both D-quantifiers and A-quantifiers. In (47), *tama-nngaja-*, 'almost all', is associated with the noun *nukappiaqqat* 'boys' (Bittner 1995):

(47)   Nukappiaqqat TAMA-NNGAJA-rmik
       boys.ABS   ALL-ALMOST-ABS
       balloni-si-sima-s-u-t
       balloon-get-perf-PRT-[-transitive]-p.ABS
       minuttit qulit naatinnagit
       minutes ten   within
       quaartuur-p-a-at.
       break-IND-[+transitive]–$3p_1.3s_2$

In (48), *tuaanna-ngajap-*, 'almost always', is a suffix on the verb *qaartuur-*, 'break':

(48)   Nukappiaraq balloni-di-gaannga-mi
          boy.ABS   balloon-get-when.iter-3sPROX
          minuttit qulit naatinnagit
          minutes ten   within
          qaartuur-TUAANNA-NGAJAP-p-a-a.
          break-ALWAYS-ALMOST-IND-[+transitive]-3s.3s

When presented with the scenarios in (49) and (50), Eskimo consultants consistently judged (47), the sentence with D-quantification, true in (49) and false in (50). The judgments were reversed for (48), the sentence with A-quantification: it was judged false in (49) and true in (50). This suggests the following paraphrases:

(47′)   'Almost all the boys who got a balloon burst it within ten
          minutes.'

(48′)   'Almost always, if/when a boy got a balloon, he burst it within
          ten minutes.'

(49)

Boys	Balloons received	Balloons burst within 10 minutes
Jaaku	100	0
Piita	100	1
Jensi	1	1
Tuuma	1	1
David	1	1
Karl	1	1
6	204	5

(50)

Boys	Balloons received	Balloons burst within 10 minutes
Jaaku	100	100
Piita	100	100
Jensi	1	0
Tuuma	1	0
David	1	0
Karl	1	0
6	204	200

To see how this works in detail, notice that in (49), four of the six boys (that is, almost all of them) who got a balloon burst it. (47) counts boys, therefore the fact that Jaaku and Piita got lots of balloons and did not burst them all does not make a difference: (47) is true in (49).

Explain why (47) is false in (50).

**EXERCISE
9.9**

Assume with Bittner that (48) is interested in counting cases, and verify that
(48) is false in (49) and true in (50).

**EXERCISE
9.10**

Eskimo and English share a further similarity in connection with A-quantification. In (48), the suffix meaning 'almost always' appears directly on the verb. There is another way to express the same meaning as (48). In (51), we find a combination of the verbal suffix *-tar* construed with the independent adverbial quantifier, identified by the adverbial quantifier suffix AQ. We turn to the discussion of *-tar* directly.

(51) Nukappiaraq balloni-si-gaannga-mi
        boy.ABS   balloon-get-when.iter–3sPROX
        minuttit qulit naatinnagit TAMA-NGAJA-TIGUT
        minutes ten   within   ALL-ALMOST-AQ
        qaartuur-tar-p-a-a.
        break-TAR-IND-[+ tr]-3s.3s
        'Almost always, if/when a boy got a balloon, he burst it within ten
        minutes (= 48').'

What might be the role of *-tar*? If we remove *-tar* from (51), the sentence becomes ungrammatical, somewhat similarly to the English (52):

(52) *'Almost always, a boy got a balloon, he burst it within ten
        minutes.'

On the other hand, if the adverbial quantifier *tama-ngaja-tigut* is removed from (51), the sentence remains grammatical and takes on a generic meaning, comparable to the English (53):

(53) 'If/when a boy got a balloon, he burst it within ten minutes.' =
        'Generally, if/when a boy got a balloon, he burst it within ten
        minutes.'

These observations suggest that the semantic role of *-tar* is somewhat comparable to that of *if/when*. Both are related to an independent adverbial quantifier, which may be overt or silent; the silent adverbial quantifier is generic in both cases. *-Tar* and *if/when* work differently in that *-tar* apparently marks the scope of the quantifier, while *if/when* marks its restriction.

Salish and Mayali

Straits Salish languages (spoken in British Columbia and Washington state) do not have D-quantification at all. One Straits A-quantifier is the adverbial *mək'ʷ*. It can relate to the predicate ('completely') or to the subject, or to the object. The following sentence is ambiguous (Jelinek 1995):

(54)   mək'ʷ = ł   'əw' ŋa-t-Ø   cə   sčeenəxʷ
       ALL = 1pNOM LINK eat-TR-3ABS DET fish
       'We ate the fish up completely.'   OR
       'We all ate the fish.'   OR
       'We ate all the fish.'

This ambiguity illustrates a typical property of A-quantification that we have already seen in English that sets it apart from D-quantification. Exactly what they quantify over is a design feature of D-quantifiers but not of A-quantifiers. A-quantifiers have also been called **unselective** for this reason.

A-quantifiers may also be selective on independent grounds. Such is *djarrk-* in Mayali, an Australian language belonging to the Gunwinjguan family:

(55)   Garri-djarrk-dulubom   duruk.
       we.plu-together-shootPP dog
       'We all shot the dog(s).'
       '*We shot all the dogs.'

Djarrk- is selective, because it is not simply a universal but carries the extra meaning 'acting together, all doing the same thing at the same time and place'. Thus it requires that the modified participant has control over the event. The dogs that undergo the shooting do not satisfy this requirement; similarly, *djarrk-* cannot be used with verbs like 'die', where the sole participant has no control. The fact that some A-quantifiers are verbal suffixes does not make it necessary for them to develop such extra meanings, but it certainly facilitates this.

9.3   Summary

This chapter discussed two examples of semantic parallelism between syntactically distinct domains.

First, we observed that both the nominal count/mass distinction and the telic/atelic distinction between events can be captured by the opposition between quantized versus cumulative reference. The two domains also interact in determining the compositional semantics of VPs.

Second, we observed that adverbs of quantification relate two sets of cases (events, or more abstract cases) in the same way as determiners relate two sets of individuals. We went into some detail with how the adverb's restriction can be recovered when it is not spelled out as an *if*-clause, and observed the cross-linguistic significance of adverbial quantification.

Both examples show that there exist thoroughgoing semantic similarities between syntactically distinct domains.

Notes

1 The contents of section 9.1 are based primarily on Krifka (1992) and Tenny (1994).

2 We thank Akira Nakamura, Carol Tenny, and Rika Hayami-Allen for giving us this section.

3 The contents of section 9.2 are based primarily on Lewis (1975), Rooth (1996), Portner (1992), and Heim (1990).

4 The contents of this section come from papers in Bach et al. (1995).

Further reading

Tenny, Carol. 1994. *Aspectual Roles and the Syntax/Semantics Interface*. Dordrecht: Kluwer.

Bach, Emmon, et al. eds. 1995. *Quantification in Natural Languages*. Dordrecht: Kluwer.

Chierchia, Gennaro. 1998. Plurality of mass nouns and the notion of 'semantic parameter.' In S. Rothstein, ed., *Events and Grammar*, pp. 53–103. Dordrecht: Kluwer.

de Swart, Henriette. 1993. *Adverbs of Quantification: A Generalized Quantifier Approach*. New York: Garland.

Kiss, Katalin É. 1998. Identificational focus versus information focus. *Language*, 74: 245–73.

Lewis, David. 1973. Adverbs of quantification. In Keenan, ed., *Formal Semantics and Pragmatics for Natural Languages*. Cambridge: Cambridge University Press, pp. 3–15.

Rooth, Mats. 1996. Focus. In Shalom Lappin, ed., *Handbook of Contemporary Semantic Theories*, pp. 271–99. Oxford: Blackwell.

EXERCISES

Collect ten everyday measure expressions (that is, ones of the type *one bar of*, not of the type *one pound of*), together with the mass nouns that they are associated with.

Example: *one bar of soap, chocolate* (but not *bread*).

Exercise 9.11

· ·

Compare the behavior of mass and count terms in English with the other language(s) that you are a native speaker of or know well. Collect at least three cases where the counterpart of an English mass noun is a count noun, or vice versa. (See Sidebar in 9.1)

Exercise 9.12

· ·

Exercise 9.13 Some languages (e.g. Chinese) use measure expressions (called classifiers) even with nouns that are considered count in English.

> E.g. yí   lì   mî   liǎng lì   mî
>   one CL rice   two CL rice
>   'one (grain of) rice'   'two (grains of) rice'
>
>   yí   zhāng zhuōzi   liǎng zhāng zhuōzi
>   one CL   table   two CL   table
>   'one (piece of) table' 'two (pieces of) table'

If you know a language with classifiers, give examples and explain how they work.

· ·

Exercise 9.14 Determine whether the following nouns are basically mass, basically count, or fully ambiguous. Note if the noun is basically mass but has secondary (kind or serving) count uses; similarly, if a count noun has secondary mass uses. Using full sentences will help to isolate the basic and the secondary uses.

Example: *pork*

(i)   I bought pork for dinner.
(ii)   I bought too much pork for dinner.
(iii) I bought four pounds of pork for dinner.
(iv)   *I bought a pork for dinner.
(v)   *I bought four porks for dinner.
(vi)   You need a tender ground pork to stuff the dumplings with.
(vii) ?This butcher offers several tasty porks.

Conclusion: *Pork* is basically a mass noun: see (i–v). It has a kind use, which is count, see (vi), but this is hard to get with the plural, see (vii).

bear, egg, sand, change, rug, lipstick, hair, milk, cement, advertisement, advertising, fabric, metal, crack

· ·

Exercise 9.15 Are the nouns *hose* and *chain* count or mass according to the grammatical tests? Do they refer in a cumulative or a quantized manner? Explain what is peculiar about them.

· ·

Exercise 9.16 The following pairs illustrate important argument structure alternations in English:

to teach Latin to Cleopatra, to teach Cleopatra Latin,
to stuff feathers into the pillow, to stuff the pillow with feathers

The semantic notions introduced in this chapter allow you to recognize a systematic difference between the members of these pairs. What is it?

· ·

Consider the following contrasts in the expression of English nominalizations. **Exercise 9.17** In some, but not all, cases, [the N of DP] can alternatively be phrased as [DP's N], with the same meaning:

the destruction of the city
the city's destruction

the exposure of the corruption
the corruption's exposure

the reenactment of the battle
the battle's reenactment

the performance of the play
the play's performance   but:

the admiration of the art work
*the art work's admiration

the discussion of the future
*the future's discussion

(a)   Collect further examples of both types.
(b)   It has sometimes been suggested that the type that allows both forms involves verbs signifying an action that causes a change in the entity it is directed at. Do the data conform to the generalization? If not, can you suggest another property that distinguishes the two types?

· ·

Underline the focus and the focus frame in each of the following sentences. **Exercise 9.18** The phrase in parentheses will also guide you in how to pronounce the sentence.

(a)   Ophelia threw white flowers into the water (not red flowers).
(b)   Ophelia threw white flowers into the water (not mice).
(c)   Ophelia threw white flowers into the water (not into the fire).
(d)   Ophelia threw white flowers into the water (instead of dropping them).
(e)   Ophelia threw white flowers into the water (instead of dancing a waltz).
(f)   Ophelia threw white flowers into the water (not Gertrude).

· ·

The (a) sentence contains intonational focus and the (b) sentence, a so-called **Exercise 9.19** cleft construction:

(a)   I think that *Oberon talks to PUCK*.
(b)   I think that *it is Puck that Oberon talks to*.

Come up with various contexts in which the two sentences can be used and check whether it is possible to continue them in the following ways:

(c)   ... although perhaps he does not talk to anyone.
(d)   ... although perhaps he also talks to Titania.

Summarize your results concerning whether intonational focus and clefts in English are identical with respect to carrying a presupposition and expressing exhaustive listing.

. . . .

Exercise 9.20 Intonational focus in English is somewhat elusive, but many languages place a contrastively (exhaustively) focused category into a particular syntactic position and/or mark it with a particle, in addition to making it intonationally prominent. The interpretation of such examples is rather similar to that of *it*-clefts in English. The following data from Vata and Hungarian illustrate these two possibilities (Koopman 1984).

Vata focus is marked by linear order and a focus particle (*mó*). The verb 'see' consists of a verb stem and another particle; this is irrelevant to us.

kòfí yê yóò   yé
Kofi see child-the part
'Kofi saw the child.'

yóò   mó kòfí yê yé
child-the focus kofi saw part
'It is the child that Kofi saw.'

In Hungarian, the focused constituent is placed into an immediately preverbal position:

Kati látta a   gyereket.
Kati saw the child-acc
'Kati saw the child.'

Kati a   gyereket látta.
Kati the child-acc saw
'It was the child that Kati saw.'

If you are familiar with a comparable language, describe the syntax and the interpretation of its focus construction.

10

Acquisition of Meaning

10.0 Introduction

The ability to comprehend the meaning of a sentence involves both grammatical and non-grammatical factors. Our knowledge of the meaning of a sentence depends on the lexical component of the grammar, where the meanings of individual words and expressions are represented, and on the syntactic grammatical component, which contains information on the grammatical relations between words in a sentence, the scope of operators, the dependency between anaphors and their antecedents, and so on. It also depends on various contextual or discourse factors, for example, understanding the referent of the pronoun *she* in the sentence *She laughed*, when the pronoun is not related to another element in the sentence. The use of a pronoun requires that the speaker and hearer share a common knowledge of who *she* is. Similarly, the use of a definite DP such as *the boy*, means that there is a specific boy being referred to and that his identity is known to speaker and hearer.

Conceptual knowledge also enters into our understanding of the meaning of a sentence. Children's conceptual knowledge plays a role in the words and other expressions they use or can understand. Thus we see that to understand a sentence or its constituent parts knowledge of language must be integrated with non-linguistic knowledge. However, as children with selective linguistic or cognitive impairments have shown, and as normally developing children make clear, language development does not simply derive from general cognition, or even in lock-step with it. Language is a distinct faculty of mind whose growth unfolds on its own maturational timetable and which is defined and structured by its own (domain-specific) principles of mind. This view of language and other faculties of mind as distinct computational modules of the mind is sometimes referred to as a **modularity** view.

SIDEBAR 10.1

Developmental dissociations and modularity

Developmental dissociations between language and conceptual development provide support for the modularity view, and researchers have found dissociations in both directions in children; namely, where language is selectively intact and where language is selectively impaired. Examples of the former include mentally retarded children who have relatively normal grammars, some verbal autistics, and a linguistic savant who has learned numerous languages, despite being severely mentally retarded. (1)–(8) are examples from different individuals who are retarded, but have remarkably intact grammars, (1)–(6) are in English, (7) and (8) are French examples:

(1)   I don't want Bonnie coming in here.
(2)   You're going to get eaten by one.
(3)   She must've got me up and thrown me out of bed.
(4)   She's the one that walks back and forth to school.
(5)   Isn't she going to come over here and talk with us?
(6)   She does paintings, this really good friend of the kids who I went to school with last year and really loved.
(7)   Il y a encore une maison sur le coin et vous montez un peu plus haut et c'est là que j'habite.
       'There is one more house on the corner and you go up a little further up and it's there that I live.'
(8)   Alors on doit faire attention parcequ'ils sont forts pour entrer dans les maisons.
       'Then one must be cautious because they are clever at breaking into houses.'

The opposite profile is evidenced in children who appear to have selective linguistic deficits – children with so-called **Specific Language Impairment**, or **SLI**. SLI children develop normally but are notoriously late talkers, their acquisition is protracted and belabored, and they show deficits in constructing a grammar. At ages well into the school-age years and beyond, such children may say things like (9)–(11):

(9) Her getting dress.
(10) She swing outside and she broke his elbow.
(11) Me no know why.

Both profiles – good language alongside mental retardation and poor language despite normal non-linguistic cognition – point to the dissociability of language from cognition and are illustrations of modularity.

10.1 Lexical Development

10.1.1 What do words mean? Acquisition of the meaning or extension of words

Understanding the meanings of sentences includes understanding the meanings of words. In chapter 6 we looked at the development of knowledge about the morphological form of words. Now we turn to the mapping of form onto meaning – learning the semantics of words.

Even though children have to memorize or learn by rote the words of their language – which string of sounds corresponds to which meaning – normal children universally understand the inherent power of words to label or represent classes or kinds of referents, to designate states, actions and relationships, to describe (eventually to lie). Thus, when they learn a word, they learn those attributes or characteristic properties which define or represent the extension of that word. To date, there are no fully viable theories of word-learning, but a few principles thought to guide children's word learning have been proposed. One is the **Principle of Reference**, which asserts that words refer – that is, that words refer to objects, actions, states, and attributes in the environment. For this principle to operate, children must attend to the environment and use information from the environment to map onto words representing this information. But the Principle of Reference asserts that children will know to do this, not need to learn to do this.

Another principle proposed to guide early word learning is the **Whole Object Principle**. This principle asserts that upon hearing a novel word in conjunction with an object, the child will assume that the word refers to the whole object, not to just part of it. For example, if a child hears the word *dog* and associates this with the four-legged animal in the environment, they will associate it with the whole animal, not with its tail or legs or ears. This principle accounts for the fact that in children's early vocabulary, we find many words for animals, people and objects, but do not find many words for body parts or parts of objects.

A third principle proposed is the **Principle of Categorial Scope**, which basically asserts that when a word's meaning is **overextended** – that is, generalized to other objects – it will be extended to other members of the same category rather than to items thematically related to it.

Finally, the **Principle of Lexical Contrast** or the **Mutual Exclusivity Assumption** has been proposed, which suggests that children assume that each object has one and only one label. We will see these principles at play as we examine acquisition of the lexicon.

10.2   Bootstrapping

Once children have begun to identify individual words in the stream of speech they hear, how do they make these words – the sound/meaning correspondences – part of their mental lexicon? What do they use to **bootstrap** (from '*lift oneself up by one's bootstraps*') into the lexicon?

Recall that when a child learns a word, they must acquire more than the meaning for that word; they must also acquire the structural information associated with it. One possibility suggested to answer the question regarding how children learn words is that children use a guessing procedure that exploits a fairly systematic association between semantic content or type and syntactic categories. (But as mentioned in chapter 7, this association does not always hold.) The guessing procedure involves or assumes a set of linking or mapping rules which map semantic and syntactic categories onto each other. With this set of rules, if the semantic type is one of a person or thing, such as *Ophelia* or *nunnery*, the guess is that it will be expressed as a *noun*; if the concept is one of an event, like *vouchsafing* or *pooping* (even Richard III, Falstaff and Juliet had to poop), the guess is that it will be expressed in language by a *verb*; and if the concept involves a propositional relation, like *Lear cursing Goneril*, the guess is that it will be expressed as a *sentence*. Note that being armed with this procedure for encoding concepts into language requires three kinds of knowledge: knowledge about the kinds of mental objects that get expressed in language (**semantic** knowledge), knowledge of the categories noun, verb, and sentence (**syntactic** knowledge), and knowledge that there is an association between the two. All of this knowledge is part of adult linguistic knowledge, and to be able to use such knowledge *before* knowing the language to bootstrap into the lexicon and target grammar, entails that the requisite knowledge be available. Within the theoretical framework we are adopting, such knowledge is provided by Universal Grammar, UG.

Notice that this guessing formula can work in both directions. That is, the child can use a word's semantic structure to guess a word's syntax (**semantic bootstrapping**), and a word's syntax to guess its semantics (**syntactic bootstrapping**). This guessing procedure also can be readily expanded to recruit surrounding structure into the guessing, and again can work in both directions: the surrounding semantic structure can be engaged to guess a word's meaning and syntactic category, and the syntactic frame in which a word occurs may be recruited to determine a word's syntactic category and guess a word's semantics. Since children experience language in context, there is good reason to believe that children can and do extensively utilize the non-linguistic context and their conceptual and semantic knowledge to guess a word's meaning and thereby its syntactic category. (Later learners of a foreign language most likely make use of some of the same kinds of information and knowledge to guess a word's meaning and syntactic category from its semantic and discourse context.) However, the linking process can and, in some instances, must work in the other direction; there is evidence that children use syntax (plus context) to guess a word's semantic content. Recall that every verb has associated with it information regarding the syntactic structures in which it can participate (its argument structure). Experiments with young children during the period of rapid verb learning have demonstrated that children use the syntactic frames in which verbs appear to assign meanings to nonsense verbs.

Gleitman and her colleagues have shown that the meanings of many verbs are unlearnable from observable context and semantic information alone; verbs pertaining to the nonobservable – *see* and *look at*, for example – clearly reveal this. Yet blind children demonstrate knowledge of the meanings of such verbs, substituting tactile exploration with the hands for visual exploration with the eyes. Thus, the blind child will distinguish between *look at* which means explore with the hands, and *see* which means 'touch'. In the case of the blind child, experience by visual observation is unavailable for learning the difference in the meaning of these words, so using the syntactic frames (the syntax) to learn the meaning of such verbs is necessary and demonstrates the availability and use of the link in the syntax-to-semantics direction.

Other experimental studies have shown that sighted children also infer the meanings of verbs from the syntactic context, attributing intransitive meanings to nonsense verbs if exposed to them only in intransitive contexts as in (1a):

(1) a. Big Bird and Cookie Monster are gorping.

and attributing transitive meanings to the same verbs if exposed to them in transitive contexts as in (1b):

(1)   b.   Big Bird is gorping Cookie Monster.

Children typically use a combination of semantics and syntactic knowledge to learn new words. We can see this at work in children's early acquisition of the meaning and subclass of lexical items. Children appear able to divide words into grammatical subclasses very early. For example, children considerably younger than two years-of-age can distinguish common and proper nouns, between things that will not have individual names and those that may. This distinction is marked syntactically in many languages. Among other distinctions, common nouns, both concrete and abstract, may occur in phrases such as (2a)–(4a), but proper nouns may not, as illustrated in (2b)–(4b):

(2)   a.   the *sonnet*   b.   *the *Shakespeare*

(3)   a.   a fine *sonnet*   b.   *a fine *Shakespeare*

(4)   a.   a terrible *injustice*   b.   *a terrible *Shakespeare*

(Note that in the b sentences, *Shakespeare* refers to the individual, not to his works or a book of his plays, etc.)

Utilizing nonsense words, Katz, Baker and Macnamara (1974) studied children under 2 years-of-age and examined their ability to discriminate between dolls and blocks on the basis of how the experimenters had referred to the object: using an article, e.g. *a zav*, for the common noun, as opposed to the simple *Zav* for the proper noun.

They found that children as young as 17 months knew the distinction between these two classes of nouns. Children of this age were already sensitive to the presence or absence of an article, a *syntactic* cue, to signal a common or proper noun, in many cases before they produced articles in their own utterances. Recall the discussion on children's early sensitivity to function morphemes in chapter 6.

Children also universally understand the relationship between certain kinds of words and the meanings they can encode. We will see more evidence of this below. But looking at lexical development in isolation from syntax, we can see that children appear to make untaught assumptions about what kinds of words can be used in relation to what kinds of objects. Both blind and sighted children, for example, understand that color is a predictable attribute only of physical objects, not of nonphysical objects. Thus even though blind children cannot see colors, they use color words appropriately; that is, only to describe physical objects. And Katz et al. found that young children do not expect certain objects – blocks, for example – to have proper names.

SIDEBAR
10.2

More about common and proper nouns

There were two other interesting aspects of Katz et al.'s findings. First, the children not only knew that objects such as blocks typically do not carry individual names, but believed that blocks cannot be so individualized and therefore, their labels cannot be proper nouns, even if they are given names and these are used as proper nouns. So the children refused to name blocks and always treated them as common objects, no matter what experimental manipulation the experimenters used. Second, girls were more precocious than boys. The boys showed a sensitivity to the syntactic cues that differentiate between common and proper nouns at a later age than the girls. Gender differences in language development are frequently noted, but as was found in this study, the differences are differences in rate of grammatical maturation, not differences in patterns of acquisition.

There is considerable variability in the onset of vocabulary production, but children typically start producing their first words sometime around the end of the first year. The mean age for producing ten words is 15 months, and children typically have a vocabulary of somewhere around 50 words before they combine words together in their utterances. By the time they enter school, it is estimated that they know 10,000–14,000 words!

Early vocabulary may vary. For some children, greetings (*hi*, *bye-bye*, *night-night*), interjections (*please*, *thank you*), and **deictics** (*this*, *that*, *here*) make up most of their early vocabulary. However, cross-linguistically, regardless of the constituent order in the target language, by the time children have built a vocabulary of 30–50 words, most produce a preponderance of nouns – proper names and labels for common objects.

10.3   Under and Overextensions

Recall the Principle of Reference, which asserts that words refer. This principle allows for a phenomenon which occurs during very early word use; namely that of **underextension** – the mapping of a word onto a very narrow, situation-specific referent. For example, the word *shoe* can be used to refer to a specific pair of shoes, or the word *dog* may refer to only the family dog. The child is clearly mapping information from the environment onto words, but at this very early point in lexical development the Principle of Reference has not fully matured so as to guide the child to apply labels to a whole class rather than to a single member of that class. Note, however, that the Whole Object Principle is already in place. There have been numerous reports of underextension in the literature, but no attested usage of a word to label only part of an object.

Following this early period of underextension, but still during the early period of word acquisition, children often appear to overextend the meanings of words; that is, they use words to refer to larger classes of entities than the words label in their target language. For example, a child may use the word *apple*, to label not only apples, but other round things as well. **Overextensions** may be based on natural kinds (e.g. *kitten* used to refer to all four-legged animals, *Daddy* used for all men), shape (e.g. *cookie* used for moon, the same word used to refer to breast, button on a garment, point of an elbow, an eye in a portrait), color (e.g. *fly* used for specks of dirt), function (e.g. *balloon* for umbrella, *open* used for peeling, opening a box, opening doors, unlacing shoes), material (e.g. *scissors* used for all metal objects, *cat* used for cotton and other soft material), sound (e.g. the same word used for cockerels crowing, music from a piano, violin or accordion, and the sounds of a merry-go-round). The range of parameters on which children overextend the words they use demonstrates their awareness of the many aspects of referents that are part of their designation and thus possession of the concepts for all of these attributes. But again, with overextensions as with underextensions, the Whole Object Principle is at play. Table 10.1 presents more examples of overextensions and some of the parameters along which such overextensions have been reported. An examination of the overextensions in the table, which are typical of the many overextensions reported in the literature, shows the Principle of Categorial Scope in operation – the principle that asserts that overextensions will apply only to members of the same category and not to thematically related items.

The principles suggested to guide word learning do not answer the question as to why children overextend the meanings of words in their vocabulary. Different explanations have been offered to explain semantic overextensions. A widely-held view is that children have very limited vocabularies and simply do not know the words they need at the moment. One theory of lexical representations, the **Semantic Feature Theory**, is consistent with this view. The Semantic Feature Theory suggests that word meanings consist of features, and that as children learn more vocabulary, individual definitions are refined and take on more features. In this way, two things that at one point would be designated by the same word, at a later point would be appropriately labeled by two distinct words, and so on. So, for example, a child's use of *bow wow* to refer to many four-legged animals, not just to dogs, would reflect a semantic representation something like (5):

(5) *bow wow*
     +animal
     +four legs

Table 10.1 Some dimensions organizing semantic overextensions

LEXICAL ITEM	FIRST MEANING	EXTENSIONS	SHARED SEMANTIC PROPERTY
bow wow	dog	dogs, cows, horses, sheep, cat	shape 4-legged
cookie	cookie	doorknob, moon	shape
fly	fly	specks of dirt, dust, all small insects, child's own toes, crumbs of bread	size
bebe	baby	other babies, all small animals, figures in small pictures	size
chemin de fer ('railway')	sound of trains	steaming coffee pot, anything that hissed or made a noise	sound
dany	sound of bell	clock, telephone, doorbells	sound
chocolate	chocolate	sugar, tarts, grapes, figs, peaches	taste
bird	sparrows	any animal moving	movement
ach	sound of train	all moving machines	movement
wauwau	dog	all animals, toy dog, soft slippers, picture of men dressed in furs	texture
kiki	cat	cotton, any soft material	texture
ouvrir ('open')	opening of door	piece of fruit peel	action

but as the child's lexicon develops, this entry would take on more features, differentiating it from other lexical items which would enter the lexicon designating animals, yielding something like the entries in (5') and then (5"):

(5')   *bow wow*   vs.   *kitty*
       +animal   +animal
       +four legs   +four legs
       +barks   +meows
       +lives in people's homes   +lives in people's homes

(5")   *bow wow*   vs.   *kitty*   vs.   *cow*
       +animal   +animal   +animal
       +four legs   +four legs   +four legs
       +barks   +meows   +moos
       +lives in people's   +lives in people's   +lives on
          homes   homes   a farm

A different kind of explanation suggests that children's overextensions may be less the result of not having the relevant lexical items and more the result of the processing mechanisms needed to retrieve words from the lexicon not yet being mature. This explanation is supported by the findings of a number of experiments described in the next section.

10.4   The Comprehension–Production Gap

Even though many children produce overextensions, it is important to note that overextensions only occur in production, never in comprehension. Experimental studies by Hirsh-Pasek and Golinkoff (1996) have shown that children aged 12–14 months who produce *no* words, comprehend many words even before they speak. Determining when first words are actually acquired is, therefore, difficult. Researchers using brain-imaging techniques have found that the brains of young infants respond differently to words they know than to words they don't know, even if that knowledge is only passive; that is, they respond to a word they comprehend but do not yet produce. Thus, there is evidence from a variety of sources indicating that children have knowledge of words before they speak. And whether or not a child speaks early or is a late talker does not seem to affect the number of words comprehended; each will show a comprehension–production gap. Moreover, it is estimated that, especially during early stages of acquisition, comprehension may even exceed production by a factor as large as 100 to one.

SIDEBAR 10.3

Comprehension vs. production

Children continue to show a comprehension–production gap in knowledge of vocabulary for a long time. Like young children, older children and adults also show a comprehension–production gap when learning a second (or third . . .) language. The reason for this may depend on the differences between the two processes. Comprehension requires matching the form one hears onto the phonological and semantic representation of a word in one's mental lexicon, a process sometimes referred to as *recognition*, while production involves in addition, processes psychologists often refer to as *retrieval* – a combination of procedures for locating and retrieving that word from the lexicon and mapping its semantic and phonological representation onto procedures for the motor production, or articulation of the word. Experiments with toddlers have shown that the distinction between what comprehension and production require in terms of mental computation may help to explain the comprehension–production gap and underlie overextensions. It has been shown that what appear to be overextensions may, in part, result from an immature retrieval mechanism – the mental procedure(s) for getting words in the lexicon out for production. It has been demonstrated that as retrieval abilities mature, overextensions disappear. Studies like these show that children comprehend words they may not be able to produce on demand, whether or not they have produced the words on other occasions.

10.5   The Vocabulary 'Burst'

After an initial production vocabulary of about 50 words (approximately 100 words comprehended) there is usually a sudden, large increase in vocabulary. The criterion for defining the beginning of the burst is 10 or more new words acquired in a period of $2\frac{1}{2}$ weeks. Most of the words that comprise this burst in vocabulary are nouns; thus this spurt in vocabulary growth is often referred to as *the naming explosion*.

The vocabulary burst is not related to phonetic growth or articulatory ability. Throughout language development, children tend to be consistent as poor or good articulators. However, there seems to be a birth-order effect, in that first-born children are more likely to show a vocabulary spurt than other children born to the same family.

Experiments conducted by DaPretto in 1994 also indicate that the vocabulary burst is probably related to retrieval abilities. In two experiments devoted to examining the relationship between the vocabulary spurt and word retrieval abilities, thirty 14–24-month-old children who could be divided into three groups – some were 'prespurt', some in the midst of a vocabulary spurt, and some 'postspurt' – were examined. The ability to locate an object by its name (comprehension) was compared with the ability to produce the name (requiring word retrieval). In front of the children, objects all the children had words for were put into boxes. In fact, all of the children in the study could label all of the objects when the objects were in sight.

When asked Where's the _____? children in all stages did well (comprehension). But when asked, What's in the box? the prespurt children did poorly. Picture cues on the box facilitated retrieval of a label, especially for the prespurt children, indicating that the word retrieval processes of these children were not as robust as those of the other children and, therefore, that growth in word retrieval may underlie or at least plays an important part in the burst in vocabulary production. Once again we see that children know more than they say.

10.6   Fast-mapping

By the time children go to school, they have approximately 10,000 words in their productive vocabulary, and 15,000 words in their comprehension vocabulary. This means that children learn from 9–12 words each day – an astonishing feat. If you were to try to duplicate this, chances are low that you would be able to do so, even though you are older, more mature and more cognitively competent, and have many more years of practice at learning things. What is the crucial difference between children and the rest of us? The difference appears to be that preschool children have a remarkable facility to map meanings onto phonetic strings that aren't already in their lexicons. Note that the Principle of Mutual Exclusivity is operative here. Children assume that if they hear a new word, it does not label something for which they already have a word. It has been demonstrated that preschool children may need only a single exposure to a word before it enters their lexicon. While children rely heavily on environmental and linguistic cues to learn words, most of this learning takes place without explicit instruction. Thus, children must rely primarily on positive evidence in word learning, just as they do in their acquisition of syntax. Note that there is insufficient instruction to account for the rapidity and accuracy with which word learning takes place. Children must bring to the task specialized learning mechanisms.

SIDEBAR 10.4

An experiment on word learning

In an experiment on word learning by Bartlett (1977), after it had been established that they had the word *green* in their vocabulary to contrast with *olive*, 3- and 4-year-olds were presented with olive-green items and asked by their teacher, in a naturalistic context, to bring one of them to her, identifying *olive* as *chromium* (e.g. *Bring me the chromium tray; not the red one but the chromium one*). Even with only a single exposure, namely, the teacher's request, the children identified the referent for *chromium*, and when tested, could both comprehend and produce the word *chromium*. When tested six weeks later, most of the children still remembered that *olive-green* bore a label other than *green* or *brown*. Some had given *olive* a name other than *chromium*; but that single exposure was sufficient for them to have mapped *olive* to a label other than *green*.

SIDEBAR 10.5

Continued maturation of lexical representations during the school years

Keil and Batterman (1984) studied how word meanings change in children over the course of development and found that meanings changed from definitions based on expected, characteristic properties, typically based on experience, to definitions based on the properties accepted as those which comprise the adult denotation of a word. They presented children with short, descriptive stories and asked them questions as to whether the descriptions defined a particular word. For example, in asking about the meaning of the word *uncle* they presented children of different ages the following story: *Suppose your Mommy has all sorts of brothers, some very old and some very, very young. One of your Mommy's brothers is so young he's only 2 years-old.* Keil and Batterman then asked, *Could he be an uncle?* A kindergartner's response was as follows:

E (experimenter):   Could he be an uncle?
C (child):   No . . . because he's little and 2 years-old.
E: How old does an uncle have to be?
C: About 24 or 25.
E: If he's 2 years old can he be an uncle?
C: No . . . he can be a cousin.

Contrast a fourth-grader's response:

E: Is he an uncle?
C: Yes . . . because he's still my mother's brother.
E: Can an uncle be any age?
C: Yes.

Thus, Keil and Batterman found a 'characteristic-to-defining' shift in the development of word meaning over the course of the elementary school years.

The mechanism by which children learn a word so rapidly has been termed **fast-mapping**. But fast-mapping a new word into their lexicon does not mean that children learn the full, adult meaning of a word from the onset. The definitions of words in a child's lexicon change over time. Not until the late elementary school years do children's definitions of many words conform to an adult's. Nevertheless, the ability to 'fast-map' word meanings aids the rapid acquisition of so many words each day.

10.7   Semantic Contrast

Children are predisposed to search for contrast in acquiring the sound system (see chapters 11, 12, 13) and morphology of their language, and we will examine its role in phonological development in chapter 15. The Principle of Mutual Exclusivity illustrates that contrast guides vocabulary development as well. Children assume words contrast in meaning. If a child has already assigned a meaning to a word for some entity or class of things (e.g. *cups*, *dogs*, *chairs*, or as we have just seen, *green*) they will assume that a new or different word must have a different meaning. Moreover, there appears to be a hierarchy of concepts used to interpret new words, with labels for classes of things, for example, higher on the hierarchy than labels for the material that things are made of.

Numerous studies indicate that children do make this assumption and use this hierarchy in learning new words. Ellen Markman (1994) for example, studied how young children assign meaning to words by introducing the word *biff* to different groups of preschoolers. When she showed one group a pair of pewter tongs and called them *biff*, the children interpreted *biff* to mean *tongs*. In fact, they interpreted *biff* to refer to tongs in general;

i.e. the class of tongs. Thus, when asked for 'more *biffs*,' they selected a pair of plastic tongs from an array which included other items made of pewter, as well as other tongs not made of pewter. In contrast, when she showed a different group a pewter cup and called it *biff*, the children interpreted *biff* to mean *pewter*, the stuff the cup was made of. They already had a word for *cup*, and so assumed that *biff* must mean something other than 'cup'. This time, when asked for 'more *biffs*,' they picked out other pewter things from the same array.

The assumption that words contrast in meaning is a valuable assumption to make. It is valid for most words of any language and thus true of language generally. Armed with concepts that correspond to the sorts of meanings languages use, the assumption that different words have different meanings can assist infants and young children in their task of learning thousands of words in a short time. Eventually, to acquire a mature and rich lexicon, the Principle of Mutual Exclusivity, which disallows or disfavors synonyms, will have to be abandoned. However, the Mutual Exclusivity assumption also guides a child to assume that their language community will use one particular word to refer to a particular object. This assumption will eventually lead a child to retreat from their idiosyncratic, immature forms for words and adopt the conventional form used by their language community.

10.8 Modularity Revisited: The Development of Spatial Expressions

In chapter 8 we used cross-linguistic facts on spatial prepositions (or adpositions) to examine the relation between spatial concepts and their linguistic expression. There we raised two questions. The first was whether we would find cross-language consistency in the mapping between spatial concepts and the way they are labeled *vis-à-vis* prepositions. The facts led us to conclude that a uniform cross-linguistic mapping does not exist, that even the most basic spatial relations are broken up differently for expression in different languages. This provided evidence for the separability of non-linguistic spatial knowledge from its expression in language. However, the evidence presented was confined to adult language. The second question we raised was whether, given the assumed uniformity of spatial cognition in humans, there would be uniform timing in the emergence of (a) the spatial concepts involved and (b) their linguistic realization *vis à vis* adpositions. If we found evidence in favor of the first but different developmental timing for encoding these concepts into linguistic form cross-linguistically, we would see that in development as in maturity, language is not derivative of nor tied in a simple one-to-one fashion to non-linguistic conceptual knowledge.

There are two kinds of evidence which argue that in development, acquisition of spatial adpositions is not tied to the emergence of the spatial concepts they label. First, in numerous studies, children have been found to exhibit uniform orders of emergence of spatial concepts cross-culturally. These findings provide a 'yes' answer to the question posed in (a) above, whether there would be uniform timing in the emergence of spatial concepts. Second, the set of spatial concepts distinguished linguistically in the target language does not appear to affect the timing or rate with which these distinctions emerge in acquisition. However, language-particular features can affect the rate at which spatial terms emerge. For example, there may be an advantage when a locative is expressed via a postpositional affix (i.e. a suffix) as in Turkish or Serbo-Croatian, as in (6)–(7), as opposed to when it is expressed as a preposition, as in English.

(6) duvar-da   'on the wall'
     wall -on

(7) pol -je   'through the field'
     field -through

Locative terms also emerge earlier when there is a one-to-one mapping of spatial relations onto words as in Turkish and French, e.g. one word for 'behind' in French as opposed to more than one, as in English ('behind' and 'in back of'), illustrated in (8):

(8) derrière   la maison   'behind the house'
     behind   the house   'in back of the house'
     in back of the house

This preference for a one-to-one mapping is another example of the Mutual Exclusivity Principle at work.

Such data provide our answer to (b) above, that there are cross-linguistic differences in the emergence of linguistic expressions for spatial relations. We see, then, a clear developmental separability between the development of spatial concepts and spatial knowledge, and the acquisition of the language-particular ways this knowledge gets encoded in linguistic expressions. We thus find support for modularity with respect to language and spatial cognition.

10.9 Semantic/Thematic Roles and Relations

Even the earliest, one-word speech expresses the basic set of thematic roles used as arguments and predicates, as illustrated in (9)–(14):

(9)   object – *milk* said when reaching for milk.

(10)   patient – *Mommy* said when child giving something to her mother.

(11)   agent – *Mommy* spoken when mother handing something to the child.

(12)   state – *allgone* spoken when the food had been consumed.

(13)   action – *go* spoken when Daddy was going out the door.

(14)   instrument – *knife* spoken when mother cutting meat.

Children also express the basic set of thematic relations between arguments and predicates as well as properties of predication in their first word combinations, as illustrated in (15)–(23):

(15)   agent–action – *Mommy push.*

(16)   action–object – *Bite finger.*

(17)   object–location – *Car garage.*

(18)   action–location – *Sit bed.*

(19)   agent–object – *Mommy sock* (mother is putting the child's sock on her).

(20)   attribution – *Big bed.*

(21)   possession – *Daddy car.*

(22)   existential – *There doggie.*

(23)   negation – *No go.*

The expression of these thematic roles and relations from the beginning of speech indicates that they may be semantic primitives and part of UG.

10.10 Stative vs. Active: Another Semantic Primitive

Another semantic property that emerges early in language acquisition is the distinction between active and stative. In English, this distinction is marked on verbs by whether or not they take the ending /-ing/. Contrast the (a) sentences, which have active or eventive verbs, with the (b) sentences, which have stative verbs.

(24) a. Brutus is betraying Caesar.
     b. *Brutus is weighing 200 pounds.

(25) a. Henry is divorcing Katherine of Aragon.
     b. *Henry is knowing Katherine of Aragon.

(26) a. Rosalind is courting.
     b. *Rosalind is resembling Ganymede.

Children only attach /-ing/ to eventive verbs and never make the mistake of attaching an /-ing/ ending to a stative verb, suggesting that this semantic distinction develops very early in life or need not be learned.

10.11   Interpretation of Pronouns

In chapter 6 we discussed children's development of reflexive pronouns. In the same studies in which children were tested on their understanding of reflexives, they were also tested on their understanding of non-reflexive pronouns such as *him* and *her*. Henceforth, we will refer to non-reflexive pronouns simply as pronouns. Recall that the structural conditions on the pronoun–antecedent relation are complementary to the condition on the reflexive–antecedent relation – where one category of pronouns occurs, the other does not and vice versa. Specifically, whereas a reflexive must be bound by a c-commanding antecedent in its same clause, a pronoun cannot be bound to an antecedent in its same clause, but may take a c-commanding antecedent outside the clause. These conditions are expressed in the Binding Principles A and B given in chapter 8 and repeated below (we will not be concerned with Binding Principle C in this chapter):

Binding Principle A: A reflexive pronoun must be bound to an antecedent in the smallest S (or NP) that contains it.

Binding Principle B: A pronoun cannot be bound to an antecedent in the smallest S (or NP) that contains it.

In the previous chapters we considered only bound pronouns in the scope of quantifiers, such as (27a). But a pronoun may also be bound by a name as in (27b).

(27) a. Every princess$_i$ knows she$_i$ will find a prince.
     b. Cleopatra$_i$ knows she$_i$ will find a prince.

Principle B of the binding principles allows the pronoun *she* to be bound in the sentences in (27) because the antecedent – the quantifier *every princess* in (27a) and *Cleopatra* in (27b) – is in the higher clause. However, Principle B rules out sentences such as (28) where the pronoun is bound by a quantifier or name in its local clause.

(28) a. *Every princess$_1$ appreciates her$_1$.
      b. *Cleopatra$_i$ appreciated her$_i$.

Thus, sentence (28a) is ungrammatical under the interpretation where each princess appreciates herself. And sentence (28b) cannot mean that Cleopatra appreciates herself. Of course, the sentences in (28) are grammatical with the referential use of the pronoun in which *her* refers to some other female, for example, Juliet or Mary. But for the moment we will focus on the bound use of pronouns.

A large number of experimental studies have shown that children are not entirely adult-like in their interpretation of pronouns in simple sentences such as (28b). Presented with a sentence such as (29) children will point to a picture in which Ernie is hitting himself. Or, in judgment tasks in which they hear sentence (29) and see a scene in which Ernie hits himself, children will judge the sentence to be a correct description of the scene (see Sidebar 6.3 in chapter 6). In both cases, they are allowing the pronoun *him* to take a local antecedent, *Ernie*, in apparent violation of Principle B.

(29)   Ernie hit him.

This experimental result has been replicated time and time again by children acquiring many different languages. Children acquiring Dutch, Chinese, Korean, Icelandic and other languages all allow the same ungrammatical interpretation of pronouns, disallowed in the language of their adult grammars. How can we explain this result? Is it the case that children – in contrast to adults – do not have Binding Principle B as part of their linguistic competence? Could this be a case in which a principle of Universal Grammar undergoes a delayed maturation? Let us refer to this hypothesis as the **Late Principle B Hypothesis**. If this hypothesis is correct, then it would argue against the Continuity Hypothesis, the view that children have knowledge of all UG principles right from the beginning.

There is, however, another possible explanation for the children's errors, which has to do with the different interpretation associated with pronouns. Recall that pronouns may receive their interpretation through binding to an antecedent, as in the examples in (27), and they also have a referential use, as in (30a, b) where *her* refers to some female not specified in the sentence (indicated by the use of a different index j).

(30)   a.   Every princess$_i$ knows she$_i$ will find a prince.
       b.   Cleopatra$_i$ knows she$_j$ will find a prince.

In the referential use, a pronoun does not receive its reference from a sentence-internal antecedent, but rather refers directly to some entity mentioned earlier in discourse or present in the non-linguistic context. Principle B regulates pronoun binding only, ruling out the sentences in (28), in which there is a co-indexing relation between the two expressions. But there is a problem: since pronouns have a referential use, there is really nothing to prevent the pronoun *him* in (29) from referring directly to the entity *Ernie*. In this case the DP *Ernie* and the pronoun *him* would happen to refer to the same entity even though there would be no syntactic binding relation. This is referred to as 'accidental' co-reference. We can illustrate this state of affairs graphically in (31). (We represent the entity Ernie as ERNIE and the arrows indicate direct reference.)

(31)   ERNIE

Ernie hit him

Our adult intuitions tell us, however, that co-reference is not possible in this sentence and hence there must be some principle that rules it out. It has been proposed that the principle in question is a pragmatic principle which makes reference to the intentions of the speaker in communicating with an interlocutor. This pragmatic principle – we will call it **Principle P** – is stated (roughly) as in (32):

(32)   **Principle P: If a speaker intends for the hearer to understand that two nominal expressions in a clause have the same reference, then, if possible, he or she should use syntactic binding (either using a reflexive or a bound pronoun).**

Thus, co-reference is ruled out in the sentence in (29/31) because the language provides a way of expressing this same meaning using a reflexive, as in (33):

(33)   Ernie hit himself.

Co-reference is allowed only when syntactic binding is not possible, for example, when the name does not c-command the pronoun, as in (34a). Note that DP is the first branching node dominating *Cleopatra* and does not also dominate *her* so there is no c-command. It is also possible to use co-reference when or if the speaker intends some meaning that cannot be conveyed through binding, as in (34b).

(34) a. All of *Cleopatra's* friends admire *her*.

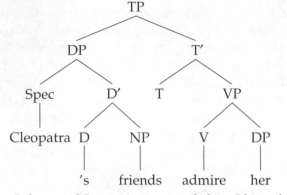

    b. I dreamed I was Antony and then *I* kissed *me*.

The person who utters the sentence in (34b) is not dreaming about kissing herself. Hence this sentence does not really have the meaning that would be expressed by replacing *me* with the anaphor *myself*, as in *I dreamed I was Antony and then I kissed myself*. So we see that there are situations in which co-reference is possible, but crucially not in sentences such as (29). In a sentence such as (29), then, there are two constraints operating; Binding Principle B rules out binding between *Ernie* and *him*, and Principle P rules out co-reference. Hence in the adult system, there is no way for *him* to refer to *Ernie*.

Returning to our experimental results, we begin to see another possible explanation for why children allow a pronoun to take a local antecedent in sentences such as (29). Suppose that children do have Binding Principle B, but they do not have Principle P. Let us call this the Late Principle P Hypothesis. This hypothesis predicts that the child will allow the pronoun in (29) to enter into a co-reference relation with the DP *Ernie*, though like the adult he or she will not allow the pronoun to be syntactically bound to *Ernie*.

A question arises, however. How can we be sure that children are allowing co-reference between *Ernie* and *him* in (29), rather than syntactic binding? After all, we do not see or hear indices and hence we cannot tell directly whether children assign *him* the index i or j. In other words, how do we know that children are missing Principle P rather than Principle B since the meaning is the same in both cases. Fortunately, there is a way to tease apart the binding and co-reference interpretations. As noted in chapter 8, pronouns can be bound to quantifiers, as in the example in (30a), in which case the sentence has the meaning that each princess appreciated herself. However, a quantifier (unlike a name) cannot enter into a co-reference relation because quantifiers do not refer to individuals. Hence,

Principle P does not apply in the quantifier case. Only Principle B applies. Thus, quantifiers provide a way of teasing apart the effects of the binding principles from the effects of the pragmatic principle. With this in mind let us imagine the following experiment. Suppose we give children sentences such as in (35):

(35)   Every princess washes her.

If children lack Principle B, they should allow sentence (35) to mean every princess washes herself (the bound use of the pronoun). On the other hand, this meaning will not be allowed by the children if they have Principle B. We then compare the children's performance on (35) with their performance on (29). If the same child who rejects binding between *every princess* and *her* in (35), still allows *him* to take *Ernie* as an antecedent in (29), then this can only mean that he or she is using co-reference in (29) – an option available when the antecedent is a name but not when the antecedent is a quantifier – since the co-reference possibility arises only if the child lacks Principle P.

Indeed, such experiments have been done and the results provide striking support for the Late Principle P Hypothesis. Children allow *him* to take *Ernie* as antecedent in (29) about 50 percent of the time (using co-reference, by hypothesis), though they reject *every princess* as the antecedent for *her* in sentences like (35) about 84 percent of the time (Chien and Wexler 1990). This result, which has been replicated in studies of children acquiring a number of different languages, shows that the children's 'errors' with respect to pronoun interpretation in sentences have to do with their knowledge of pragmatics, how to use language effectively in context, and not with their knowledge of grammar. It seems that the binding principles, like other aspects of syntax, are available very early, while certain aspects of pragmatic knowledge develop later. In the following section, we will see evidence of other pragmatic difficulties.

10.12 Presupposition: Understanding the Common Ground

Recall from chapter 7 that certain expressions in a language carry presuppositions. Verbs such as *regret*, *know*, *remember* are **factive** verbs; they presuppose that their complement describes a fact and that this fact is known to both speaker and hearer. This is in contrast to non-factive verbs, such as *think*, *guess*, and *believe*, which do not carry such a presupposition. The contrast is illustrated by the pair of sentences in (36). The sentence in (36a) results in a contradiction if we add *but she wasn't*, since the verb *know* carries a factive presupposition, while the sentence in (36b) does not, since the non-factive verb *think* does not pressuppose that *Juliet was dead* is true.

(36) a. Romeo knew that Juliet was dead (??but she wasn't).
      b. Romeo thought Juliet was dead (but she wasn't).

Another kind of presupposition is introduced by the use of the definite determiner. A definite determiner presupposes the existence of the object, as illustrated by the contradiction in (37), and also presupposes that this existence is known to both speaker and hearer, part of the common ground.

(37) The Prince of Denmark is haunted (??but there is no prince of Denmark).

An indefinite determiner is used to refer to a character or entity when it is first introduced, or when the speaker does not wish to refer to a specific character, as in (38):

(38) A prince entered the palace.

Young children have a certain amount of difficulty with both existential and factive presupposition. In experimental studies which test children's knowledge of when to use *a* versus *the*, they tend to use or accept a definite determiner in situations where the indefinite determiner would be more appropriate. For example, in one experiment (Maratsos 1974) children are shown pictures of three dogs, each in a car, and a boy talking to one of them. Then the child is told one of two things, either *Then suddenly the dog drove away* or *Then suddenly a dog drove away*. The child then has to indicate which dog drove away. When the children heard the sentence with the definite article they almost always made the correct choice; they chose the specific dog the boy had been talking to. On the other hand, when they heard the sentence with the indefinite article they chose a dog other than the one that the boy had been talking to – the correct choice – only about 76 percent of the time; the rest of the time they chose the dog that the boy had been talking to – an incorrect, or at least pragmatically odd, choice. These results and many others suggest that young children have some difficulty establishing and checking the common ground between speaker and hearer.

Mental verbs provide another example of how children can fail to understand presupposition. Various studies have shown that prior to age 4 or so, children do not distinguish between factive and non-factive verbs. Presented with statements such as *I know the candy is in the blue box* and *I think the candy is in the red box*, 3 year-olds will pick the red box about as often as the blue box to search for candy. Assuming that children will look for the candy in the most likely location, these results suggest that children fail to understand the presupposition carried by the verb *know* as against *think*.

10.13 Children's Knowledge of the Count/Mass Distinction and Telicity

As discussed in chapter 9, there are semantic properties that extend across different grammatical categories. One example of this was the parallel between the count/mass distinction in nominal expressions and verbal aspect. Atelic verbs (for example, *wander*) are like mass nouns in that they refer cumulatively; if we take a wandering event and add more wandering to it, it is still a wandering event, just as, if we take some water and add more water to it, it is still water. Not so with count nouns and telic verbs, which have an internal structure. The referents of count nouns (e.g. *a dog*) are inherently quantized, that is, prepackaged into minimal units (unlike mass nouns, which need a measure expression to quantize them, e.g. *a glass of water*, *a bottle of wine*, but not *a wine*, *a water*). Similarly, telic events have an inherent endpoint which delimits them. We can see, moreover, that the semantic structure of the direct object can affect the telicity of the verb; *consume ale* is an atelic event since *ale* refers cumulatively, while *consume a beer* describes a telic event since the referent of *a beer* is quantized, as illustrated by the examples in (39):

(39) a. John consumed ale for an hour.
     b. *John consumed a beer for an hour.
     c. John consumed a beer within an hour.
     d. *John consumed ale within an hour.

These examples show that telicity is compositionally determined, which means that it is dependent on linguistic structure and grammatical principles. These cross-categorial effects are rather subtle, clearly not the kind of thing that children are instructed on, or for which they receive much direct evidence. Moreover, the fact that Japanese and other languages are similar to English in these respects suggests that the interaction between verbal aspect and the count/mass distinction reflects something rather fundamental about language, a property of UG. We would thus expect children to have innate knowledge of these semantic properties.

While there has not been much work exploring the semantic parallelism between nominal expressions and verbs in early language, there have been separate studies of children's understanding of telicity and of the count/mass distinction. The evidence suggests that children have knowledge of these semantic distinctions very early on. We know this because they make certain generalizations based on these distinctions which are not in the target adult language. For example, 2-year-old Italian children tend to use the past participle construction only with telic predicates such as *cadere*, 'fall', *rompere* 'break', *arrivare*, 'arrive', etc. but not with atelic predicates such as *volare*, 'fly', and *ballare*, 'dance'. In adult Italian, both telic and atelic verbs occur in participial constructions, as in (40):

(40)   a.   Gianni ha ballato (per un ora).
            'John has danced (for an hour).'
       b.   Gianni è caduto (*per un ora).
            'John fell (*for an hour).'

Thus, Italian children 'undergeneralize' the participle, restricting its occurrence to one kind of verb. They associate certain verbal inflections with particular aspects, even though this strict association is not part of the adult target language. Since they are hearing atelic participles (as in (40a)) in the input, this undergeneralization must be based on their intrinsic knowledge of the telic/atelic distinction.

Similar results have been obtained in other languages. Several studies have shown that English-speaking children use past tense *-ed* predominantly on verbs describing telic events. English-speaking adults, on the other hand, show the opposite tendency, they use *-ed* significantly more often with atelic verbs. Thus, the child's productions cannot be the result of tuning into the frequency of particular forms in the adult input.

How can we explain this strict inflection-aspect mapping that children seem predisposed to make? One proposal is that children first assume that the participle and past tense *-ed* encode only the aspectual property of 'completion' or 'resulting state' and not past tense. This would explain the restriction to telic verbs, since these have an inherent endpoint and a resulting state (compare *danced* with *fell*). In fact, in the respective adult languages, the participle and *-ed* mark both tense and aspect. In *John danced*, *-ed* marks the simple past, while in *John has danced* it marks the perfective (completive) aspect. The aspect-before-tense hypothesis says that temporal relations are cognitively more complex than aspectual ones and hence more difficult for the child to acquire. On this view, children differ from adults in their grammatical representations; tense is not represented in the early grammar. This hypothesis seems too strong, however, since there are languages where children do clearly mark tense distinctions in addition to aspectual ones very early on. For example, Japanese-speaking children mark verbs as being past or non-past before they are 2 years old.

A different interpretation of the above (Olsen and Weinberg 1999) is that children have the capacity to grammatically encode both tense and aspect, but that they assume a strict mapping between inflection and aspect because this provides the most effective learning strategy. Behind the logic of this hypothesis is the observation that there are languages – different from English and Italian – which do show a strict mapping between telicity and particular inflectional elements. In Korean, for example, the perfective auxiliary can only occur with telic intransitive verbs. Since children do not know a priori which language they will be exposed to, they must be ready for any possibility made available by UG. The safest bet would be for them to assume the most restrictive option, which in this case would be a strict mapping between inflection and telicity. This is because a strict mapping can be revised on the basis of positive evidence, that is examples such as (40a), which tell the child that in his or her language (in this case, Italian) participles can be used to describe both telic and atelic events. Similarly, the child born into an English-speaking community will hear plenty of examples of atelic verbs marked with *-ed*, e.g. *Romeo wandered for hours*. He will then learn that his initial mapping is too strict, and can revise accordingly. And if the child is born into a Korean-speaking household, no revision of the grammar will be necessary.

We can see that the child who assumes the strict mapping is in a better position to acquire any adult language. Imagine, on the other hand, that the child first assumes that a particular verbal form encodes both tense and aspect (as does the Italian participle and English *-ed* form). Suppose, moreover, that this child finds himself acquiring Korean. On what basis would he ever learn that the Korean perfective auxiliary encodes *only* aspect and not tense? There would not be any examples in the input that tell him that the auxiliary can *never* encode tense. This would require correction or some other kind of **negative evidence**, that is, explicit information that some form or interpretation (in this case, the tense interpretation) is NOT possible. As we discussed in chapter 1, children do not have systematic access to negative evidence. This fact imposes a certain ordering on the hypotheses that a child can entertain about grammatical structure, whether semantic, syntactic or morphological. Where UG makes available more than one possible analysis, the child must start with the most restrictive option that UG allows. This idea is referred to as the **Subset Principle**.

10.14   Summary

We have seen that knowledge of the kinds of meanings words may express, the thematic roles and relationships they encode, and important distinctions between predicates are all aspects of semantics that develop early or are present from the onset of speech, if not before. Thus even though all children must learn every word of their target language, certain aspects of linguistic semantics may not have to be learned and are good candidates to be part of unlearned properties of the human mind.

The meanings of many linguistic expressions are determined by context: syntactic context and discourse context. For example, pronouns may be bound or referential; in the first case the pronoun must be in a particular syntactic relationship with its antecedent, while in the second case its referential possibilities are governed by a pragmatic rule. Presuppositions check and build the common ground between speaker and hearer, which can be dependent on the discourse context, but presupposition is also tied to properties of the syntactic construction, as illustrated in chapter 7. Even the count/mass distinction and verbal aspect (telicity) are not necessarily inherent properties of nouns and verbs, but are in some measure dependent on context. In the previous sections we briefly considered the child's development of these various semantic properties. Although there is still much work to be done in this area, we begin to see a pattern: those aspects of meaning which are governed by pragmatic rules or closely tied to discourse pose a challenge to the young child. This is in marked contrast to the various morphological and syntactic phenomena which we considered in chapter 6, where development is very rapid.

Further reading

Bowerman, M. 1991. The origins of children's spatial semantic categories: Cognitive vs. linguistic determinants. In J. J. Gumperz and S. C. Levinson, eds., *Rethinking Linguistic Relativity*. Cambridge and New York: Cambridge University Press.

Fodor, J. 1983. *The Modularity of Mind*. Cambridge, MA: MIT Press.

Gleitman, L. and B. Landau eds. 1994. *The Acquisition of the Lexicon*. Cambridge, MA: MIT Press.

Hirsh-Pasek, K. and Golinkoff, R. 1996. *The Origins of Grammar: Evidence from Early Language Comprehension*. Cambridge, MA: MIT Press.

Smith, N. and Tsimpli, I.-M. 1995. *The Mind of a Savant: Language Learning and Modularity*. Oxford: Blackwell.

In addition to those cited in the text, the following references were consulted: Moore et al. 1989; Antinucci and Miller 1976; Clark 1973; Gleitman and Landau 1995, and references therein; Hirsh-Pasek and Golinkoff 1996.

Part IV

Phonetics and Phonology

11

Phonetics:
The Sounds of Language

11.0 Introduction

Linguistic structure is conveyed to a listener by speech. (Although linguistic structure can be conveyed to a viewer by sign or by writing, in this chapter we will consider only oral communication.) **Phonetics** is the study of the physical aspects of speech events, including: **speech production** (how speech is produced by the speaker, an instance of skilled motor performance), **speech acoustics** (the properties of the airwaves that transmit speech from speaker to listener), and **speech perception** (how speech is perceived by the listener). Phonetics is part of linguistics, but it is part of other disciplines as well, such as speech and hearing science, psychology, and engineering. **Linguistic phonetics** is a term sometimes used to describe the aspects of speech articulation, acoustics, and perception that are part of linguistics. It includes the study of the speech sounds of a range of languages, generalizations about sounds that hold across languages, and the study of the relation of phonetics to other areas of linguistics.

In the next section we provide some concepts and terms that let us describe the sounds of speech.

11.1   Tools for Phonetic Description

11.1.1   Segments

A speech utterance can be described, in part, as a sequence of individual **speech sounds**. Speech sounds, also called **segments** or **phones**, are sounds used in languages. As such they exclude various noises humans can make that are not used in languages, including sounds made with the hands, or sounds made by inhaling or sneezing.

Speech sounds are generally divided into two types, consonants (abbreviated C) and vowels (abbreviated V). **Consonants** are sounds in which a significant constriction is made somewhere in the vocal tract – a narrowing that interferes with the flow of air out of the mouth – so that there is at least some reduction in the energy of the sound. **Vowels** are sounds in which no such constriction is made; the air flows out of the mouth relatively freely and the sound is relatively loud and strong.

Consider the word *Macbeth*, which has the shape CVCCVC. Can you feel the constriction for each of the four consonants? (They are: at the lips, at the back of the mouth, at the lips again, on the teeth.) All languages have consonants and vowels. Spoken language must not be confused with writing: even languages which do not use alphabetic writing have consonant and vowel sounds. However, languages do differ in *which* consonants and *which* vowels they have.

The idea that English utterances can be divided into a succession of segments, one consonant or vowel after another, may seem completely obvious to literate speakers of the language – most people feel they hear speech this way. They also think that different instances of a given consonant or vowel are the same – that each 'b' is like every other 'b', for example. But this is not true of the physical sounds in a speech signal, which differ from speakers' psychological idealizations in two ways. First, if we look at actual speech, it is not always obvious that there are separate sounds in succession, because there are not always sharp boundaries between them. Figure 11.1 shows a **spectrogram** of the sentence *Tell me where is fancy bred*.

A spectrogram is a frequency by time display in which the stronger frequency components are highlighted. Abrupt changes in these components

SIDEBAR
11.1

Segmentation and learning to read an alphabet

Alphabets such as the one used for English are based on segmentation of speech into individual sounds. It makes sense, then, that it should be easier for someone who already has psychological representations of words as composed of segments to learn alphabetic reading and writing. Reading experts talk about **phonemic** (or phonological) **awareness** as a prerequisite to reading – when a child can focus on individual sounds in a word, that child is better able to learn the relations between sounds and letters (or **phonics**). Otherwise, the child has to learn whole-word patterns of written and spoken words. Some examples of phonological awareness include the ability to say if two words rhyme or if they begin with the same sound, or (a harder task) to say how many sounds a word contains, or what sound comes after another sound in a word. (You will notice that these skills are relevant in the exercises below.) At the same time, someone who does not already have segmental representations of words is likely to acquire them as a result of learning to read. It seems that phonological awareness and reading ability feed each other as the child learns to read, and success in one predicts success in the other.

show clear visual and auditory boundaries between speech segments. The word *fancy* shows fairly abrupt boundaries between its segments, but the other words do not in every case. The end of *tell* and the beginning of *me* is hard to discern, as is the end of *where* and the beginning of *is*, as well as all the segments in *where*. Most intervals of speech contain information about two or even more speech segments because adjacent sounds overlap. Much of the signal shows changing transitions between segments, where information from both is present. This is particularly true of *where* and *bred*, because of the *r* sounds. That is, while the ordering or sequencing of sounds is usually clearly supported by the speech signal, the feeling that we could make a clean slice between each pair of segments is an idealization from the signal.

Second, if we look at speech signals, we see that it is not true that all 'b's, or all of any other sound, are the same. It is not the case that a language uses a small number of speech sounds over and over, always exactly the same each time. There are many small differences between different instances of what we think of as the 'same' sound, not only across languages and across speakers of the same language, but also within the speech of any one speaker. In Figure 11.1, the two *r* sounds in *where* and *bred*, and the vowels of *tell* and *bred*, for example, look different. These kinds of differences are completely normal and we see similar things across languages. But adults do not hear these small differences, or do so only with training, so that our normal perception is different from what we can measure in the speech signal.

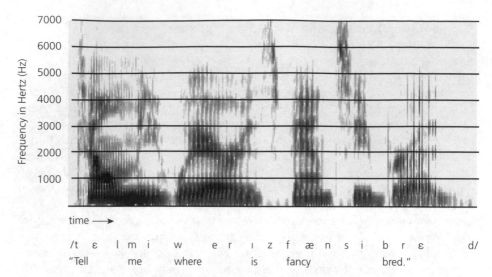

Figure 11.1 Wideband spectrogram, orthograph and broad transcription of *Tell me where is fancy bred* [voice of Margaret Maceachern]

EXERCISE 11.1

For each set of three words, which one begins with a different speech sound? Consider only the *first* sound in each word.

Example: **scale - state - shall** – *shall* begins with a different sound

(1) **countenance - king - cheer**
(2) **sister - she - cease**
(3) **equal - eyes - even**
(4) **again - opponent - all**
(5) **throne - thy - these**
(6) **character - chaste - coldly**
(7) **heart - where - who**
(8) **jelly - giving - gentlemen**
(9) **admiration - against - appears**
(10) **every - each - else**

EXERCISE 11.2

How many speech sounds does each of the following English words contain? For each sound, say whether it is a consonant (C) or a vowel (V).

Example: **still** = 4 sounds, CCVC (there is only one / sound even though there are two letters)

(1) **yet**
(2) **seems**
(3) **boot**

(4)   **have**
(5)   **privy**
(6)   **walks**
(7)   **dumb**
(8)   **theme**
(9)   **health**
(10) **grizzly**

11.1.2   Suprasegmentals

In addition to the individual consonants and vowels (**segments**, or **segmentals**), there are properties of utterances that span more than one segment, usually referred to as **suprasegmentals**, or **prosody**. *Suprasegmental* means 'above the segment.' These properties include variations in loudness, duration and pitch, as well as variation in the degree of energy or effort put into the articulation of each sound. These generally function to make some elements more prominent than others.

For example, vowels are generally more prominent than consonants. A **syllable** is a string of segments in which one of the segments (usually a vowel) is more prominent than the others. Roughly, each vowel is the head of a syllable, and adjacent consonants (if any) belong to the syllable along with the vowel. For example, the word *cat* has one syllable, *adult* has two (which can be indicated as *a.dult*), and *oasis* has three (which can be indicated as *o.a.sis*). If there is no vowel, a consonant may be prominent, as in the second syllable of words like *little, children, button*, and *paper* in many dialects.

Syllables in turn can vary in prominence. Variations in loudness, duration, and effort together produce differences in **stress**: one syllable appears stronger than others in the same word. In some languages such stress differences can distinguish one word from another. For example, in English, the noun *(a) CONvict* is stressed on the first syllable, while the verb *(to) conVICT* is stressed on the second syllable. (Here the stress is indicated by capitalizing.) Here are some words, all with three syllables, but with stress on either the first, second, or third syllable:

(1)   <u>first syllable stress</u>   <u>second syllable stress</u>   <u>third syllable stress</u>

     VANquisher   disCREtion   incorRECT
     FUneral   adVANtage   overWHELM
     IMpotent   reMEMbrance   enterTAIN

Variations in duration, and to some extent loudness, also produce differences in rhythm. Languages sound different one from another in part because of their characteristic rhythms. English rhythm allowed Shakespeare to use a pattern called iambic: weak-strong-weak-strong-weak-strong etc.

Variations in the pitch of the voice give rise to an overall melody for an utterance. In some languages, the pitch of the voice is specified for each vowel in each word; a **tone** is such a pitch specification. In a tone language, a sequence of consonants and vowels will have different meanings depending on the pitch(es) of the voice used to speak that sequence. English is not a tone language, but most languages of Africa and Southeast Asia, and some native American languages, are tone languages. For example, in Kana, a language spoken in Nigeria, *be* (where *e* is pronounced something like the *ay* in *bay*) with a Low tone means 'to fence', *be* with a Mid tone means 'home' or 'compound', and *be* with a High tone means 'fight'.

Finally, in all languages, tone or not, pitch of the voice is also used to convey things about whole utterances, and this is called **intonation**. In English, some kinds of questions are characterized by a rising melody at the end: *Is Hamlet upset?* and *Still here, Laertes?* both usually with a rising melody on the last word, as compared with *What did Polonius say?* and *I shall obey you, madam*, both with a falling melody near the end (e.g. at the end of *Polonius* and *obey*). More generally, however, the amount and kind of variation in the overall prosody of an utterance conveys information about the speaker's attitude towards the utterance. Consider, for example, *To be, or not to be; that is the question*. It can have a flat or an animated intonational melody; some parts can be stretched out or speeded up. Some segments can be more forcefully articulated. All of these suprasegmentals help render an actor's interpretation of this utterance.

EXERCISE 11.3	For each set of three words, one of them has the stress on a different syllable than the other two. Mark that word. If you are not sure where the stress in a word is, look it up in a dictionary. Example: **question - scholar - tonight** – mark 'tonight' (1) **expressed - surprised - triumph** (2) **luxury - malicious - ministers** (3) **porcupine - secrecy - illusion** (4) **possess - answer - gracious** (5) **extravagant - revolution - disposition**
EXERCISE 11.4	Underline the vowel in the stressed syllable in each word. (If two letters spell the vowel sound, underline both of them.) Example: **foolishly** – f<u>oo</u>lishly (1) **extravagant** (2) **intermission**

(3)   encounter
(4)   hospitality
(5)   unworthy
(6)   reputation
(7)   unwillingly
(8)   childishness
(9)   philosophy
(10) messengers

11.2   Phonetic Alphabets

In what follows, we will first consider how to represent what we will call the basic sounds of a language. By basic sounds we mean the minimum number of sounds needed to represent each word in a language differently from all other words, in a way that corresponds to what native speakers think are the same sounds in different words. That requires ignoring differences between two sounds that do not distinguish different words and which native speakers are unaware of. Only after we have established some symbols for transcribing these basic sounds will we go on to consider how finer details, and suprasegmentals, can be transcribed.

11.2.1   Problems with orthography

Phonetic alphabets are sets of symbols used for representing the speech sounds that occur in utterances. The fundamental principle of most phonetic alphabets is that **each symbol should represent only one sound, and each sound should be represented by only one symbol**. Depending on what we mean by 'one sound,' most standard orthographies of the world's languages violate this principle in one or both directions. English is bound to violate it, since it uses only 26 letters to represent some 40 basic sounds (which will be presented below and in the next chapter). Some letters do double-duty in English spelling, like *y* and all of the vowel letters; and combinations of letters are used for single sounds, like *sh*, the first sound in *ship*. Violating the principle in both directions at once, the combination *th* uses two letters to spell two distinct single sounds, the first sounds in *thin* and *this*.

One reason the principle gets violated is that pronunciation may change after an orthography is standardized. For example, there are many pairs or sets of words in English that are spelled differently but pronounced the same, such as *rite/right/write/wright*. These words used to be pronounced differently, in accord with their spelling differences. However, as the language changed they came to be pronounced the same, so that now we have four ways to spell the same sound sequence. For a standard orthography to keep one symbol corresponding to one sound, spellings would have to be updated as the sounds of the language changed. Another reason violations occur is that different speakers of a language have different pronunciations. No standard orthography can keep one symbol for one sound for all speakers of a language; its goal can only be to make the language readable and writable by all its speakers. For example, there are many word pairs/sets in English that are pronounced the same by some speakers, but distinguished by other speakers, as in (2). For these words, the spelling violates the one-symbol/one-sound principle for some speakers but not for others. Read these and decide whether you pronounce them the same or not.

(2)   Some words sometimes pronounced the same:
    a.   witch   which
    b.   horse   hoarse
    c.   morning   mourning
    d.   sot   sought
    e.   bawdy   body
    f.   father   farther
    g.   Mary   merry   marry
    h.   poor   pour   pore

More fundamentally, all orthographies violate the one-sound/one-symbol principle to the extent that orthographies tend to represent only the basic sounds of the language, not the variants that may occur in particular combinations or positions in words. The spelling of a word, by itself, is not enough to tell you how to pronounce that word. You need the native speaker's knowledge of the language to do that. For example, many American speakers pronounce sequences of *tr* (as in *train*), *tw* (as in *twin*), and *t-y* (as in *got you*) as if they contain a sound sequence like *chr*, *chw*, or *ch*, a detail of pronunciation that could not be guessed from the standard spelling. (Though informal spellings like *gotcha* show this.)

In sum, orthographic transcriptions (or written representations) of words do not unambiguously represent every aspect of pronunciation that we might want to represent. Phonetic alphabets are distinct from the orthographic system used for any language. In the best cases, phonetic alphabets are capable of representing different pronunciations for a single word – how a word is usually pronounced, or how some particular speaker pronounced it on some particular occasion. A phonetic transcription can indicate enough about a pronunciation to permit someone who does not know the language being transcribed to nonetheless read the transcription and pronounce it fairly accurately. As mentioned in chapter 2, phonetic symbols will be placed between square brackets to distinguish them from the orthographical symbols of the alphabet.

Pronunciations in dictionaries

Dictionaries, whether intended primarily for native speakers of the language or for learners, almost always give some indication of the pronunciations of words. Many modern dictionaries use the symbols of the International Phonetic Alphabet (IPA – see next section) for this purpose. The major exceptions to this practice are dictionaries of American English, which tend instead to use combinations of letters closer to the spelling, along with keywords that indicate the intended pronunciation for those letters. For example, a dictionary may use *ee* to represent the long e sound as in *see*. Readers are then to use whatever their pronunciation of the vowel of *see* is, for the vowels of *seat, receive,* etc.

Whether the references are external to the language (e.g. IPA symbols) or internal to the language (e.g. keywords), pronunciations in dictionaries always assume some working knowledge of the pronunciation patterns in the language on the part of the reader. Transcriptions of words are usually limited to the basic sounds of the language. It is as if a given sound were pronounced identically in every word in which it occurs. A reader who takes these transcriptions at face value (for example, someone still learning the language) will sound overly careful, even stilted, in their pronunciations, since the natural variations of sounds in connected speech will be lacking.

For a dictionary to provide pronunciations in broad transcription (see next section), a decision must be made about how many distinctions should be recognized for the language. It can be confusing, even annoying, when a dictionary's pronunciations do not match the reader's. Would you prefer to have the dictionary indicate distinctions you do not make (as in (2) above or (5) below), or make as few distinctions as possible for the language as a whole (as in Exercise 11.7 below)?

Each of the following English words contains two instances of the letter *s* or the letter *c*. The letter *s* can spell either the sound [s] or [z]. The letter *c* can spell either the sound [s] or [k]. For each word, decide whether the two letters are spelling the same sound, or two different sounds.

Example: <u>s</u>ea<u>s</u>on the two *s*'s are pronounced differently, as [s] then [z].

(1) Fran<u>c</u>i<u>sc</u>o
(2) pa<u>s</u>tor<u>s</u>
(3) re<u>s</u>olve<u>s</u>
(4) <u>s</u>ometime<u>s</u>
(5) <u>s</u>urpri<u>s</u>ed
(6) di<u>s</u>po<u>s</u>ition
(7) wi<u>s</u>dom<u>s</u>
(8) <u>s</u>e<u>c</u>re<u>c</u>y
(9) <u>s</u>pirit<u>s</u>
(10) <u>s</u>en<u>s</u>ible

EXERCISE 11.6

Each of the following words contains a silent letter. If this letter were removed from the spelling, the spelling would still represent how the word is pronounced. Pronounce each word, decide which letter is not sounded, and circle it.

Example: **answer**: *w* is silent (*anser* would still be a possible spelling for this word).

(1) **guard**
(2) **designed**
(3) **black**
(4) **witch**
(5) **wrung**

11.2.2 The IPA and other phonetic alphabets

Over time and in different countries, many phonetic alphabets have been devised. The one with the most widespread acceptance is the alphabet of the **International Phonetic Association** (or **IPA**). This alphabet is called the **International Phonetic Alphabet** (also abbreviated **IPA**). Unlike most other phonetic alphabets, the IPA attempts to provide a symbol for every sound of every language. Another difference between the IPA and other alphabets is that the IPA was developed by an organization whose members and Council discussed and voted on changes to it. In 1989 an international convention met in Kiel, Germany to update the IPA, resulting in many recent revisions.

The advantage of the IPA is that because it is widely studied and used, transcriptions using it can be interpreted by many readers. Therefore we use the IPA throughout this text. Nonetheless, it must be stressed that other systems are well-suited for other, more limited purposes. Most linguists who work on particular languages have devised their own systems for those languages, systems which may or may not correspond closely to the IPA. American linguists in particular generally use a few phonetic symbols for English which are not part of the IPA, so you are likely to see these in other textbooks. This chapter will present the IPA but your teacher may choose to depart from it.

Finally, it is important to note that even the IPA symbol set does not guarantee complete agreement regarding phonetic transcriptions. Two linguists may disagree about a sound quality they are trying to represent, so that each would chose a different IPA symbol for that sound. Second, the IPA explicitly allows the substitution of simpler symbols for more complex ones in a particular language if no confusion would result. We will take advantage of this provision later, in our choice of symbols for the sounds of English.

11.2.3   Basic IPA symbols for American English

(3) gives a minimum set of symbols sufficient for distinctively representing the consonants and vowels of many speakers of American English. Strictly speaking, #35 [ə] and #37 [ɚ] are not needed for this purpose, but we include them because it is customary and convenient to do so, and because many speakers feel that these are basic sounds of English. Also, #31 [ɔ] is not needed to represent the speech of many speakers of American English, as this vowel is being rapidly lost across the US, but we include it for the benefit of those people who still do have it, and because it is used in all other textbooks and reference books. (It is the vowel in *caught* for those who have different pronunciations for *caught* and *cot*, the latter being pronounced with the [a] vowel.) On the other hand, we do not include vowels of other dialects of English that are not used in America (such as British [ɒ] as in *pot*), and sounds used by relatively few Americans (such as [ʍ] as in *which*).

Among these basic sounds are a few which are written with a sequence of two phonetic symbols: #17, 18, 38, 39, 40. As indicated by the symbols, these sounds consist of a sequence of two different sound qualities. These sequences are included in the table because they function as single sounds in the language.

Many of these symbols and their values are familiar from English orthography, but many are not. Note especially that #19, 25, 30, and 34 do NOT represent their most common English values, although they do correspond to spelling in some words borrowed into English or in proper names.

(3)   **Basic sounds of English using a minimal symbol set**. Unless otherwise indicated by underlining, sound occurs at both beginning and end of word. All of these words appear in Shakespeare's plays.

	Phonetic symbol	Word illustrating it
1	p	pope
2	b	bar<u>b</u>er
3	m	mum
4	f	fife
5	v	vive
6	t	taunt
7	d	deed
8	n	nun
9	r	rare
10	θ	thousandth
11	ð	<u>th</u>is, brea<u>the</u>
12	s	source
13	z	zanies

	Phonetic symbol	Word illustrating it
14	ʃ	shush
15	ʒ	mea<u>s</u>ure
16	l	lull
17	tʃ	church
18	dʒ	ju<u>dg</u>e
19	j	<u>y</u>oke
20	k	cook
21	g	gag
22	ŋ	si<u>ng</u>i<u>ng</u>
23	w	<u>w</u>e
24	h	<u>h</u>e
25	i	easy
26	ɪ	<u>i</u>mitate
27	e	<u>a</u>ble
28	ɛ	<u>e</u>dge
29	æ	b<u>a</u>ttle, att<u>a</u>ck
30	a	f<u>a</u>ther
31	ɔ	f<u>ou</u>ght
32	o	r<u>oa</u>d
33	ʊ	b<u>oo</u>k, sh<u>ou</u>ld
34	u	f<u>oo</u>d
35	ə	aroma
36	ʌ	b<u>u</u>t
37	ɚ (or ɝ or ɹ̩)	b<u>ir</u>d
38	aɪ	r<u>i</u>de
39	aʊ	h<u>ou</u>se
40	ɔɪ (or ɔɪ)	b<u>oy</u>

With just these symbols, some notion of careful pronunciations of many words can be adequately conveyed. However, as noted above, English words can differ in stress. Therefore, to be able to distinguish more pairs of English words – to be able to give words unique transcriptions – we need to transcribe stress as well as consonants and vowels. Although different degrees of stress may be distinguished in some transcriptions, we will note only the most strongly stressed vowel in a word, as in section 11.1.2. above on suprasegmentals. This strongest stress is called the **main stress** or **primary stress**. Following IPA usage, we will mark stress by a raised vertical tick before the stressed vowel (or before any preceding consonants): ['kanvɪkt], the noun form of *CONvict*, but common American practice is to instead use an accent mark on the vowel: [kánvɪkt]. Stress will be shown in transcriptions like those above only where needed to distinguish two words, which is never the case in (3).

A transcription that uses only the minimal set of basic symbols can be said to be a **broad transcription**, or a **phonemic transcription**. (For our purposes we will use these terms interchangeably.) Broad transcriptions are often enclosed in slant brackets, e.g. /a/. When a transcription goes beyond this to indicate details of pronunciation, it can be said to be a **narrow** (or narrower) **transcription**. The difference between a broad and a narrow transcription is one of degree: the more detail included, the narrower the transcription. Therefore, any word can be transcribed in more than one way. As mentioned above, narrow transcriptions are usually enclosed in square brackets, e.g. [a]. However, broader transcriptions are also sometimes enclosed in square brackets, to make clear that a transcription is not maximally broad or phonemic. (See also the next chapter on this point.) Note that a broad transcription is likely to be valid for more speakers on more occasions than a narrow transcription will be, since the broad transcription gives relatively less information about an exact pronunciation.

In a broad transcription, the set of allowed symbols is strictly limited – e.g. those in (3). Words are transcribed by combining these, and only these, symbols. Sometimes, though, certain sound combinations sound different from any allowed symbol combination, so that students (and professional linguists!) may be unsure which symbols to use. For example, vowels before [r] can be quite variable in quality, and speakers may disagree over which basic symbols should be used. Is the vowel in *air* more like the vowel in *able* or in *edge*? Probably for most speakers it is somewhere in between. There are two approaches to such cases. In a broad transcription, some standardized transcription may be adopted, perhaps an arbitrary-seeming one. Thus in this chapter we will use the following vowel+/r/ combinations in broad transcription: /ir, er, ar, or, ur, aɪr, aʊr/.

The second approach is to expand the inventory of symbols from the minimal one, that is, to give a transcription that is somewhat narrower. This can be done both by providing additional symbols, and by supplementing symbols with **diacritics**, marks added to symbols to modify their values. We will provide a few options that go beyond the basic symbols, because there are some sound qualities that most native speakers prefer having separate symbols for.

1   /t/ and /d/ often sound the same and are pronounced in a quick and weak way; they can be transcribed [ɾ]: *city* ['sɪɾi], *ready* ['rɛɾi], *sanity* ['sænɪɾi].

2   For most speakers /m, n, l/ may be pronounced without an accompanying vowel in stressless syllables, as in *bottom, button, bottle*. They are then referred to as **syllabic** consonants and are transcribed with a small vertical line beneath: [m̩ n̩ l̩]. These three syllabic consonants are therefore generally not included among the basic sounds of the

language; instead, such words are broadly transcribed using a [ə] plus the consonant: /əm, ən, əl/. The syllabic symbols [m̩ n̩ l̩] are used only in narrower transcriptions. For example, we would have *bottom* [baɾəm] in broad and ['baɾm̩] in narrow.

In parallel fashion, /r/ may also be considered to occur as a syllabic consonant in words like *butter*. However, we have already defined a basic sound, #37 /ɚ/, to serve that purpose. The reason there is a separate symbol for this sound is that, as in #37 *bird*, but unlike syllabic [m̩ n̩ l̩], /ɚ/ occurs in stressed as well as stressless syllables. However, it would be also possible to transcribe both *bird* and *butter* with [ɹ̩] as will be done in the next chapter.

3   The consonants /p/, /t/, and /k/ are sometimes pronounced with an extra, *h*-like puff of air coming through the vocal cords and out of the mouth when it opens (called **aspiration**). They are then transcribed as [pʰ], [tʰ], [kʰ]. Aspiration will be discussed in greater depth below.

4   The sound at the beginning of a cough or at the beginning and middle of the phrase *uh-oh* is called **glottal stop**, transcribed [ʔ]: ['ʔʌʔo]. This same sound can be made together with the consonants /p/ /t/ or /k/, in which case the consonants are said to be **glottalized** (or **preglottalized**) and can be transcribed [ʔp], [ʔt], and [ʔk].

5   Usually consonants /p t k b d g m n ŋ/ are pronounced so that when the mouth opens up at the end of the consonant, a sound is made. But sometimes that mouth opening is not heard, and the consonant is said to have no audible **release**, or to be **unreleased**, and transcribed [p̚] etc. The consonants /p t k/ may be pronounced as glottalized ([ʔp]), unreleased ([p̚]) or both ([ʔp̚]), in addition to released ([p]) or released and aspirated ([pʰ]).

6   Stressed vowels may sound like sequences of qualities. For example, the vowel /e/ may be transcribed as [eɪ] in narrow transcription.

7   Vowels can be marked with a raised tilde ˜ when they are pronounced with air coming out of the nose (**nasalization**) next to consonants [m], [n], [ŋ].

The list in (4) gives broad and narrower transcriptions of all the words in (3), plus the additional examples given above. In the broad transcriptions, stress is marked only when it is needed to distinguish this word from some other existing word, but in the narrower transcriptions it is marked whenever the word has two or more syllables. It is inevitable that some readers will pronounce some of these words differently from what is given here; the narrow transcriptions in particular are arbitrarily chosen, and purposely have been made to differ across examples. (Compare for example the various final /k/s in *yoke, cook, book,* and *talk* – each of these pronunciations is possible in all of these words.) For some words, the broad and narrow transcriptions given here are the same; there are no special characteristics of any of the sounds to be noted in the narrow transcription. Some of the aspects of the narrow transcriptions shown here will be presented further below.

Providing a narrow transcription of an utterance is an advanced skill that goes well beyond a general introductory course. The particular details included here are intended to give a taste of the kinds of variation that can be observed. In addition, these details will come into later discussions of English and other languages. For example, the pronunciation in some American (and Canadian) dialects of /aɪ/ as [ʌɪ] as in *fife* will be discussed in the next chapter.

(4) **Transcriptions of sample English words**. Broad transcriptions
     use the symbol set in (3). Narrow transcriptions show some uses
     of IPA diacritics, including some not yet discussed, in possible
     pronunciations of these words. Brackets are omitted after
     the first item.

Word (orthography)	Broad transcription	Narrower transcription
pope	/pop/	[pʰoʔp˺]
barber	barbɚ	ˈbarbɚ
mum	mʌm	mʌ̃m˺
fife	faɪf	fʌɪf
vive	viv	viv
taunt	tant	tʰãnt˺
deed	did	did˺
nun	nʌn	nʌ̃n˺
rare	rer	rer
thousandth	θaʊzɪnθ	ˈθaʊzĩntθ
this	ðɪs	ðɪs
breathe	brið	brið
source	sors	sors
zanies	zeniz	ˈzeɪniz
shush	ʃʌʃ	ʃʌʃ
measure	mɛʒɚ	ˈmɛ̃ʒɚ
lull	lʌl	ɫʌɫ
church	tʃɚtʃ	tʃɚtʃ
judge	dʒʌdʒ	dʒʌdʒ
yoke	jok	jokʰ
cook	kʊk	kʰʊk
gag	gæg	gæg˺
singing	sɪŋɪŋ	ˈsɪ̃ŋɪ̃ŋ

Word (orthography)	Broad transcription	Narrower transcription
we	wi	wi
he	hi	hi
easy	izi	ˈizi
imitate	ɪmɪtet	ˈĩmĩtʰeʔt˺
able	ebəl	ˈebl̩
edge	ɛdʒ	ɛdʒ
attack	ətæk	əˈtʰæk
battle	bætəl	ˈbæɾl̩
father	faðɚ	ˈfaðɚ
talk	tak	tʰaʔk
road	rod	rod˺
book	bʊk	bʊk˺
should	ʃʊd	ʃʊd
food	fud	fud˺
aroma	əromə	əˈromə
but	bʌt	bʌʔt˺
ride	raɪd	raɪd˺
house	haʊs	haʊs
boy	bɔɪ	bɔɪ
convict	kanvɪkt	ˈkʰãnvɪʔk˺t
air	er	er
or	or	or
city	sɪti	ˈsɪɾi
ready	rɛdi	ˈrɛɾi
sanity	sænɪti	ˈsænɪɾi
bird	bɚd	bɚd˺
butter	bʌtɚ	ˈbʌɾɚ
bottom	batəm	ˈbaɾm̩

EXERCISE 11.7

For each word, a choice of broad transcriptions is given. Indicate which one is consistent with pronunciation of the word and with the set of IPA symbols for broad transcription used in this chapter and listed in (3).

Example: *cat* (a) /cat/ (b) /kat/ (c) /kæt/ (d) /cæt/   Answer is (c).

(1) **see** (a) /see/ (b) /si/ (c) /cee/ (d) /sy/
(2) **Fuji** (a) /fuji/ (b) /fuge/ (c) /fudʒi/ (d) /fudʒe/
(3) **class** (a) /class/ (b) /klass/ (c) /clæs/ (d) /klæs/
(4) **you** (a) /you/ (b) /ju/ (c) /jou/ (d) /yu/

(5)	spa	(a) /spa/	(b) /spæ/	(c) /spo/	(d) /ʃpa/
(6)	she	(a) /she/	(b) /ʃe/	(c) /shi/	(d) /ʃi/
(7)	sir	(a) /sir/	(b) /sɚ/	(c) /ʃir/	(d) /ser/

Give the regular English orthography for the following words, which are given in a fairly broad transcription but with a few extra symbols. Even if the pronunciation given here is not the same as yours, you should be able to figure it out. If you are not sure of the orthography, look the word up in a dictionary.

EXERCISE 11.8

Example: [mʌtʃ] is *much*

(1) [naɪt]
(2) ['mjuzɪk]
(3) ['bælkəni]
(4) [gost]
(5) ['mɚsi]
(6) ['merɪdʒ]
(7) ['feriz]
(8) ['berli]
(9) ['tʃrædʒəri]
(10) ['kʌntrimɪn]

Give broad transcriptions of the following words, as best you can for your own pronunciation. Or, look the words up in a dictionary and give that pronunciation in IPA symbols. Do not mark stress unless your instructor tells you to.

EXERCISE 11.9

(1) **xerox**
(2) **utopia**
(3) **direct**
(4) **photo**
(5) **triumph**

Even using the limited number of symbols of a broad transcription, many differences between speakers can be indicated. In fact, because the limited symbol set has been chosen to cover just those differences that distinguish words, these differences between speakers will be the ones that listeners hear most readily. Consider some ways in which one of the authors of this text's pronunciations are possibly different from yours even in a broad transcription, as shown in (5). Try comparing the different pronunciations by saying both of them aloud.

(5) **Two pronunciations (in broader transcription) of some English words**

Word		Author's pronunciation	More common pronunciation
1.	forest	farɪst	forɪst
2.	poor	por	pur
3.	merry	mɛri	meri
4.	marry	mæri	meri
	cf. Mary	—meri	—meri
5.	parade	pəred	pɚ·ed
6.	particular	pətɪkjələ˞	pɚ·tɪkjələ˞

EXERCISE 11.10

Compare the pronunciations in (5) with those in a dictionary. First, copy out the pronunciation(s) as given in the dictionary. Then, if necessary, convert these into IPA by referring to the pronunciation key at the beginning of the dictionary. Compare your IPA-pronunciations with the ones in the table to see whether the author's pronunciations are recognized by the dictionary.

We have illustrated the pronunciations of individual words in isolation because that makes it easy to focus on individual sounds. The pronunciations of words in fluent, connected speech, however, can be very different from their pronunciations in isolation. At UCLA we have studied the pronunciation of some words when they occur in recordings of spontaneous telephone conversations. Compared with speech which is read, spontaneous speech shows more weakly pronounced or deleted vowels and consonants.

Today, narrow transcriptions are usually done with a combination of listening and looking. A computer display lets a listener select some portion of a word and listen to it repeatedly, even slowing it down, while seeing its acoustic characteristics. The phonetic transcription is entered into the computer so that it becomes attached to the speech utterance. Figure 11.2 shows the same spectrogram as in figure 11.1, now with its associated narrow transcription. The /t/ in *tell* is aspirated, the vowel in *where* is /ɛ/, the /z/ in *is* is partly voiceless, the vowel in *fancy* is nasalized [ɛ̃], and the final /d/ in *bred* is unreleased.

11.3 The IPA Chart

In trying to understand the sounds of language, one needs to describe specifically the sounds that these transcriptions convey. We need a vocabulary

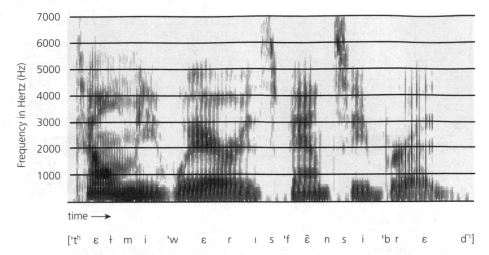

Figure 11.2 Same spectrogram as in figure 11.1, now with narrow transcription [voice of Margaret Maceachern]

for talking about sounds. The terms we use for this purpose make reference to **where** and **how** the sound is produced in the speaker's mouth. Where in the mouth a sound is made is called the **place of articulation**, and how a sound is made is called the **manner of articulation**. The different components of sound production give us descriptions of sounds and also definitions of the phonetic symbols. The terms that we use are given as labels on the **IPA chart**, which organizes symbols with respect to articulation.

Figure 11.3 reproduces the entire most recent (1996) IPA chart. It consists of two consonant charts, a vowel chart, and lists of other symbols. Locate for yourself on this chart the symbols listed in (3) above. Be sure to find the component parts of the symbols that are sequences, such as [tʃ]. You can see that we have used very few of the available symbols! Some of these other symbols, and our use of [r] and [a], will be discussed below.

You can also see that the symbols are organized into a descriptive framework: the individual charts contain descriptive labels as well as just the symbols. For example, the symbol [b] is in a box or cell labeled **Bilabial** and **Plosive**, and the symbol [w] is followed by the phrase *Voiced labial-velar approximant*. The sounds represented by the symbols are defined by how the sounds are articulated. One wants an independent source of information about what the symbols mean, and articulatory definitions attempt to provide this. That is, for each sound a set of properties is given that more or less tells you what that sound is and how it is different from other sounds. Any phonetic transcription can be read in terms of these definitions, even if you do not know the language being transcribed.

Articulatory definitions are not the only possible kind; acoustic or auditory-perceptual definitions, derived from looking at spectrograms,

Consonants (Pulmonic)

	Bilabial	Labiodental	Dental	Alveolar	Postalveolar	Retroflex	Palatal	Velar	Uvular	Pharyngeal	Glottal
Plosive	p b			t d		ʈ ɖ	c ɟ	k ɡ	q ɢ		ʔ
Nasal	m	ɱ		n		ɳ	ɲ	ŋ	N		
Trill	ʙ			r					R		
Tap or flap				ɾ		ɽ					
Fricative	ɸ β	f v	θ ð	s z	ʃ ʒ	ʂ ʐ	ç ʝ	x ɣ	χ ʁ	ħ ʕ	h ɦ
Lateral fricative				ɬ ɮ							
Approximant		ʋ		ɹ		ɻ	j	ɰ			
Lateral approximant				l		ɭ	ʎ	ʟ			

Where symbols appear in pairs, the one to the right represents a voiced consonant. Shaded areas denote articulations judged impossible.

Consonants (Non-Pulmonic)

Clicks	Voiced implosives	Ejectives
ʘ Bilabial	ɓ Bilabial	ʼ Examples:
ǀ Dental	ɗ Dental/alveolar	pʼ Bilabial
ǃ (Post)alveolar	ʄ Palatal	tʼ Dental/alveolar
ǂ Palatoalveolar	ɠ Velar	kʼ Velar
ǁ Alveolar lateral	ʛ Uvular	sʼ Alveolar fricative

Other Symbols

ʍ Voiceless labial-velar fricative
w Voiced labial-velar approximant
ɥ Voiced labial-palatal approximant
ʜ Voiceless epiglottal fricative
ʢ Voiced epiglottal fricative
ʡ Epiglottal plosive

ɕ ʑ Alveolo-palatal fricatives
ɺ Alveolar lateral flap
ɧ Simultaneous ʃ and x

Affricates and double articulations can be represented by two symbols joined by a tie bar if necessary.
k͡p t͡s

Vowels

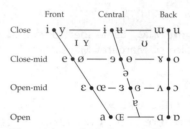

Where symbols appear in pairs, the one to the right represents a rounded vowel.

Diacritics

Diacritics may be placed above a symbol with a descender, e.g. ŋ̊

̥ Voiceless	n̥ d̥	̤ Breathy voiced	b̤ a̤	̪ Dental	t̪ d̪
̬ Voiced	s̬ t̬	̰ Creaky voiced	b̰ a̰	̺ Apical	t̺ d̺
ʰ Aspirated	tʰ dʰ	̼ Linguolabial	t̼ d̼	̻ Laminal	t̻ d̻
̹ More rounded	ɔ̹	ʷ Labialized	tʷ dʷ	̃ Nasalized	ẽ
̜ Less rounded	ɔ̜	ʲ Palatalized	tʲ dʲ	ⁿ Nasal release	dⁿ
̟ Advanced	u̟	ˠ Velarized	tˠ dˠ	ˡ Lateral release	dˡ
̠ Retracted	e̠	ˤ Pharyngealized	tˤ dˤ	̚ No audible release	d̚
̈ Centralized	ë	̴ Velarized or pharyngealized ɫ			
̽ Mid-centralized	e̽	̝ Raised	e̝ (ɹ̝ = voiced alveolar fricative)		
̩ Syllabic	n̩	̞ Lowered	e̞ (β̞ = voiced bilabial approximant)		
̯ Non-syllabic	e̯	̘ Advanced tongue root	e̘		
˞ Rhoticity	ɚ a˞	̙ Retracted tongue root	e̙		

Suprasegmentals

ˈ Primary stress
ˌ Secondary stress   ˌfoʊnəˈtɪʃən
ː Long   eː
ˑ Half-long   eˑ
̆ Extra-short   ĕ
ǀ Minor (foot) group
ǁ Major (intonation) group
. Syllable break   ɹi.ækt
‿ Linking (absence of a break)

Tones and Word Accents

Level		*Contour*	
e̋ or ˥ Extra high		ě or ˩˥ Rising	
é ˦ High		ê ˥˩ Falling	
ē ˧ Mid		e᷄ ˧˥ High rising	
è ˨ Low		e᷅ ˩˧ Low rising	
ȅ ˩ Extra low		e᷈ ˧˩˧ Rising-falling	
↓ Downstep		↗ Global rise	
↑ Upstep		↘ Global fall	

Figure 11.3   The International Phonetic Alphabet, revised to 1996

Phonetic symbols and computers

With the advent of thousands of fonts for computer word-processing, free or inexpensive phonetic fonts have become widely available. Some fonts include a few phonetic characters, while others offer the whole symbol set approved by the IPA in 1989 in Kiel, Germany (the **Kiel IPA**). The home page of the IPA is a good starting point for finding phonetic fonts. With these fonts, every symbol can be assigned to a key or key combination on the keyboard. For example, in one commercially available IPA font, the character [ɔ] (open o) is typed as Shift-o. However, the Kiel symbol set goes beyond just the font characters. It also includes a numerical code for every symbol, so that converting from one font to another is easy and unambiguous. For example, character [ɔ] is number 306. The Kiel conventions also include a system for machine-readable (ASCII-only) equivalents of every symbol. For example, character [ɔ] is ASCII O (upper-case o). This form of the IPA is useful for people doing computer transcription of long speech samples. The **ARPABET** is a different ASCII system developed just for English and used by the American speech technology (recognition and synthesis) community.

---

could be used. When the IPA was set up over a century ago, there really was no choice, as speech articulation was much better understood than either speech acoustics or speech perception. Nowadays you will also see descriptions of sounds in these other domains. For example, vowels are thought to be as well, or better, described in terms of their auditory qualities. (Indeed, IPA vowel descriptions are based in part on a tradition of equal auditory spacings between a subset of the vowel sounds.) One traditional phonetic term, **sibilant** (sometimes **strident**), refers to the particular loud, high-pitched, noisy sound of certain fricatives, more than it refers to a particular articulation. However, we will limit our discussion here to articulation, in accord with the IPA descriptive terms on the chart.

11.3.1   Articulators

The IPA articulatory definitions are provided in part by arranging some of the consonant and vowel symbols into individual charts which are three-dimensional in content but flattened out to two dimensions on paper. One dimension is in the horizontal arrangement, another is in the vertical arrangement, and the third is in the order of symbols that are written in pairs. The main consonant and vowel charts are both three-dimensional in this way, but they use different sets of dimensions. To understand these labels, we need to first consider the speech production mechanism. Figure 11.4a shows what one of the authors' vocal tract looks like along the midline of the head during production of the consonant [s], in a scan taken by Magnetic Resonance Imaging, and Figure 11.4b is a schematic based on

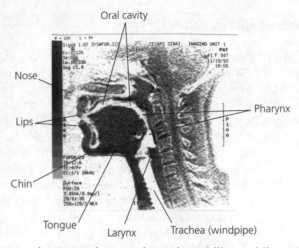

Figure 11.4a   An author's vocal tract, along the midline, while saying /s/

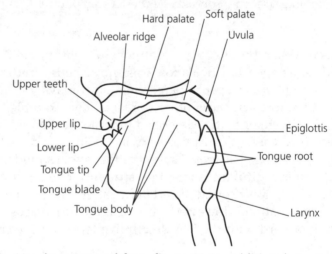

Figure 11.4b   Vocal tract traced from figure 11.4a, additional structures labeled

this figure. The vocal tract is the parts of the body used in producing sounds: the **larynx**, the **pharynx**, the **oral cavity**, and the **nasal cavities**. The pharynx and oral cavity together are sometimes called the **oral tract**. There are several vocal organs that can move independently (**active articulators**), and several anatomical structures that these moving articulators may move towards (**passive articulators**, also called **places of articulation**). The labels on the figure point out several different articulators and structures. They are listed in (6); additional structures not seen in the figure are listed in (7).

For speech to be heard, sound energy must pass out of the vocal tract by means of the movement of air molecules. Therefore you can think of the immediate goal of speaking as setting air molecules into motion. Speech sounds are usually described in terms of acoustic energy sources, and filters that modify the sources. For many speech sounds, the source is **voicing**, which is the regular passage of puffs of air through the larynx as the vibrating vocal cords open and close. Those puffs of air are basically the same for all voiced sounds, but they are then modified as they travel through the air spaces of the pharynx, oral cavity, and/or nasal passages. The various consonants and vowels, with their different configurations of the active articulators creating different patterns of constrictions, each have their own characteristic modifications of the sound.

(6) **Articulator definitions**

ARTICULATOR	DEFINITION
oral cavity	the top, curved-horizontal airspace of the vocal tract.
upper lip	as an active articulator, moves independently to approach the lower lip; as a passive articulator, is approached by the lower lip (or tongue tip).
lower lip	as an active articulator, moves independently, and is also moved by the jaw, to approach the upper lip or the upper teeth; as a passive articulator, is approached by the upper lip.
upper teeth	passive only; can be approached by the lower lip or by the tongue blade/tip.
alveolar ridge	passive only; can be approached by the tongue tip or blade. A short flat stretch just above and behind the upper teeth. At the back edge of the ridge, the palate turns more sharply upward (creating a corner). (Not everyone has a ridge; the author's is more prominent off the midline, so it is not obvious in figures 11.4a, 11.4b. If you have no ridge per se, then the term can be taken to refer to the first half-cm or so behind the upper teeth.)
tongue tip	an active articulator, moved by the tongue blade, of which it is the very end, or frontmost part (also called apex).
tongue blade	an active articulator, moves independently of the rest of the tongue, or is moved by the rest of the tongue. About the first 3 cm of the tongue, behind

ARTICULATOR	DEFINITION
	which there is a point where the tongue can bend and flex. The tongue tip is the very end of the blade.
tongue body	the main part of the tongue; can be divided into a front part and a back part, both of which can be active articulators.
tongue root	active; the bottom part of the tongue, which forms the front wall of the pharynx.
epiglottis	active; the leaf-like appendage to the tongue in the pharynx.
pharynx	the back, vertical airspace of the vocal tract between the uvula and the larynx; usually thought of as the passive articulator approached by the body or root of the tongue, but its walls can also function actively, squeezing the pharynx space.
hard palate	the hard, bony, surface of the roof of the mouth.
soft palate	the soft, non-bony part of the roof of the mouth behind the hard palate, also called the velum, which as an active articulator moves up and down at the top of the pharynx to either block off or open up the air passage to the nose, and as a passive articulator is approached by the tongue body.
uvula	the hanging back tip of the soft palate; as an active articulator it can vibrate in the upper pharynx; as a passive articulator it is approached by the tongue body.
larynx	the cartilage box at the bottom of the pharynx (and at the top of the trachea) housing the vocal cords; the box can move up and down.

(7)   **Some other parts of the body used in producing speech**

lungs	the most common source of airflow for speech (via the trachea).
vocal cords	two bands or folds strung front to back inside the larynx.
glottis	the airspace between the vocal cords.
sides of tongue	Figures 11.4a and 11.4b, taken at the midline of the tongue, show only its center; the two sides of the tongue can curl and roll independently of the center.
the nervous system	controls all motor movements.

Give the term corresponding to the definition given.

Example: **the soft part of the roof of the mouth** = soft palate

(1)   **end of the tongue blade**
(2)   **airspace between uvula and larynx**
(3)   **bottom part of tongue forming front wall of pharynx**
(4)   **cartilage box at bottom of pharynx holding the vocal cords**
(5)   **articulator which is active or passive, and moved by the jaw**

**EXERCISE
11.11**

11.3.2   Consonants

Let us now return to the IPA chart, beginning with the main consonant chart at the top. The main consonant chart contains a subset of the consonants, those made with air flowing out from the lungs (**pulmonic egressive**). Recall that consonants are sounds produced with a significant constriction in the vocal tract. This constriction means that the flow of air through the oral cavity and out of the mouth is affected: either the airstream becomes noisy, or less air is able to flow out than would without the constriction.

Columns: place of articulation
The columns give information about the active and/or passive articulators of a sound: what articulator approaches what along the midline of the vocal tract. Some columns define both active and passive: bilabial, labiodental, glottal. Most columns just define the passive articulator, with the assumption that the normal active articulator is the part of the tongue closest to that passive area. (For some uvular and pharyngeal sounds, the passive, i.e. destination, articulator may also be active.) The retroflex column primarily defines the action of the active articulator, the blade of the tongue raised up, with the assumption that it goes somewhere into the postalveolar region. (The combination of kinds of information given by the columns is often loosely called **place of articulation**, though as stated above, this term more strictly refers to the passive articulator, that is, the place where the articulation is made.) These column headings are listed in (8). Note that there is a single column in figure 11.3, the IPA chart, with dental, alveolar, and postalveolar under it. The base symbol shown in all the rows in this column except for the fricative row is for the alveolar place; the dental place can be indicated by modifying that base symbol with the dental diacritic [ ] under it, and the postalveolar place can be indicated by modifying that base symbol with the 'Retracted' diacritic [ ] under it. There are also special (non-IPA) terms available for the active articulators alone: **labial** means one or both lips are active, and thus includes **bilabial** and **labiodental**; **coronal** means the tongue blade/tip is active, and thus includes **dentals**, **alveolars**, **postalveolars**, **retroflexes**, and sometimes

palatals; **dorsal** means the tongue body is active, and thus includes **velars**, **uvulars**, and sometimes **palatals** and **pharyngeals**; **radical** means the tongue root is active, and thus includes **pharyngeals** and also **epiglottals** (not on the main consonant chart).

(8) **IPA consonant column labels**

	Articulators involved
bilabial	the two lips, each both active and passive.
labiodental	active lower lip to passive upper teeth.
dental	active tongue tip/blade to passive upper teeth.
alveolar	active tongue tip/blade to passive front part of alveolar ridge.
postalveolar	active tongue blade to passive behind alveolar. (When the passive place is specifically the back part or corner of the alveolar ridge, this is also called palatoalveolar or alveopalatal.)
retroflex	active tongue tip raised or curled to passive postalveolar (difference between postalveolar and retroflex: blade vs. tip).
palatal	tongue blade/body to hard palate behind entire alveolar ridge.
velar	active body of tongue to passive soft palate (sometimes to back of hard palate).
uvular	active body of tongue to passive uvula, OR active uvula.
pharyngeal	active body/root of tongue to passive pharynx.
glottal	the two vocal cords, each both active and passive.

Some other places of articulation are not given columns on the chart, symbols for consonants with those places being listed instead under Other Symbols. Two of these places are **labial-velar** (sometimes also called **labiovelar**) and **labial-palatal**, which each combine two separate columns of the main chart by having two primary articulations. Labial-velars combine bilabial and velar articulations. The voiceless fricative [ʍ] is still found in some American dialects in words like *which* and *what* (but not *who*, [hu]). The voiced approximant [w] is a very common sound in the world's languages. The labial-palatal combination is not used in any basic sounds of English. The epiglottal place, also not used in English, refers to the epiglottis as an active articulator in the lower part of the pharynx. The alveolo-palatal place lies between alveolar and palatal; the active articulator is the blade of the tongue. Note that this is different from palatoalveolar or alveopalatal (see above).

SIDEBAR
11.4

Visual knowledge of speech

In this chapter, as in other textbooks, we discuss people's perception and knowledge of speech signals as if the only relevant sensory modality were hearing. Yet this is not correct. Listeners also have extensive experience SEEING speech being spoken. They use this knowledge when they are listening, and may feel at a disadvantage when forced to listen without the visual information. That is, normal listeners generally use both kinds of information when they are available. Hearing-impaired listeners rely correspondingly more on the visual information. **Speech reading** (or lip reading) is the name given to the use of visual information for speech processing by perceivers, especially the hearing-impaired. Speech reading can be explicitly taught, and your library may have teaching materials on this skill from early in the twentieth century.

As you learn in this chapter about how different sounds are articulated, think about which aspects of articulation are likely to be easily recoverable from a visual signal. Some consonant articulations are quite directly observable. For example, in bilabial stops like [b, p, m] the two lips come together. In contrast, most tongue articulations cannot be seen. It turns out that normal-hearing English listeners, in deciding what consonant they have heard, take into account the fact that they expect to see strong visual lip cues for bilabial consonants. The McGurk effect is the name given to the phenomenon in which listeners' percepts are determined by visual as well as auditory information. In now-classic studies, McGurk and MacDonald showed listeners videos of speakers saying certain syllables, but played carefully-synchronized recordings of other syllables. The listeners often reported hearing syllables that were different from both of these, yet they were generally unaware that the visual and auditory signals did not match. When the listeners were played audio [ma] and visual [ta], they reported hearing [na]; when they were played audio [ba] and visual [ga], they reported hearing [da]. That is, listeners seem to require visual confirmation to hear a bilabial consonant, and if they don't get that confirmation, they hear the closest articulation. Interestingly, the effect has subsequently been shown to be larger in some languages compared with others, a finding which remains to be explained.

It should be remembered that normal hearers can understand speech when no visual information is available, at least when the speech is clear. Radio, telephone, and audio recordings show this to be so. However, the intelligibility of such speech is less than when visual information is also present. That is one reason it is easier to understand people in face-to-face conversation.

Rows: manners of articulation

The rows give information about how close the active articulator comes to the passive one, that is, how open the oral air passage is. Five such manners of articulation can be distinguished and are listed in (9).

(9)   **Constriction degrees for consonants**

stop	active and passive articulators touch and hold-to-seal (permitting no flow of air out of the mouth)
trill	active articulator vibrates as air flows around it
tap/flap*	active and passive articulators touch but don't hold (includes quick touch and fast sliding)
fricative	active and passive articulators form a small constriction, creating a narrow gap causing noise as air passes through it
approximant	active and passive articulators form a large constriction, allowing almost free flow of air through oral tract

[*Like the IPA chart, we will not distinguish taps and flaps here, but simply note that the two terms are sometimes used interchangeably, with flap perhaps the more common term in the US.]

Most of these terms appear in the chart. The term *stop* does not; instead, the first two rows of the chart are two kinds of stops, **plosive** and **nasal**. In both of these, there is a complete seal in the oral tract. The two rows distinguish between stops in which the air, once released, flows out of the oral cavity (**oral** flow, a term which does not appear on the chart because it is the typical case) or flows out of the nasal cavity (**nasal** flow). The plosives are **oral stops** and the nasals are **nasal stops**. All other rows of the chart can also be considered to be oral. Other rows of the chart distinguish between sounds in which the airflow is along the center of the oral cavity (**central** passage; *central* does not appear on the chart because it is the typical case) or along one or both sides of the oral cavity (**lateral** passage). The row labels are given in (10). **Affricates** do not have a row on the chart; they combine a stop plus a fricative at the same place of articulation.

(10)   **IPA consonant row labels**

plosive	a pulmonic-egressive, oral stop
nasal	a pulmonic-egressive stop with nasal flow; not a plosive, because not oral
fricative	a sound with fricative constriction degree; implies that the airflow is central
lateral fricative	a fricative in which the airflow is lateral
approximant	a sound with approximant constriction degree; implies that the airflow is central
lateral approximant	an approximant in which the airflow is lateral

You can see that the consonant grid more or less defines an articulatory space within the vocal tract. The columns divide up the places of articulation moving along from the front (the mouth opening) to the back and then down to the bottom of the vocal tract, while the rows characterize the oral air passage from least open to most open. To the extent that this is so, the boxes in the grid cover regions of the available space rather than exact values. For example, *velar* refers to the entire soft palate and even the back of the hard palate. But in any one production of a velar consonant, only some of this region is the passive articulator. Exactly which part varies across productions. In this sense, many subtly different sounds all count as velars.

Another classification that is often made regarding manners of articulation (though not made by the IPA) is that plosives and the two kinds of fricatives (and therefore also affricates) are called **obstruents**, while nasals, trills, taps/flaps, and the two kinds of approximants are called **sonorants**. The obstruents are the sounds in which the airflow is noisy (the air meets an obstruction) while the sonorants are the sounds in which the airflow is smooth. The oral sonorants are often further divided into **glides** (**semivowels**, or vowel-like central approximants) and **liquids** (r and l sounds).

Note that the symbol we are using for the American English r-sound is [r]. This symbol is used on the chart for an alveolar trill, but the American English sound is a postalveolar or retroflex approximant. The IPA system allows substitutions of simpler symbols for unusual ones for a given language – as we are doing with [r] – if no confusion will result. American [r] will be transcribed with this simpler symbol in the next chapter as well.

11.3.3 Voicing

Inside many cells (or boxes) are pairs of consonants with the same row-and-column definition. These pairs differ in **voicing**, that is, in the activity of the vocal cords. Generally, if the vocal cords vibrate for all or part of the sound, it is said to be voiced and appears as the right member of the pair; if the vocal cords do not vibrate at all, the sound is said to be voiceless, and appears as the left member of the pair. Notice that all the unpaired sounds (the nasals, trills, tap/flaps, and approximants) are placed to the right in their cells to show that they are all voiced.

11.3.4 Other consonants

The basic English consonants that are not on this main consonant chart are the affricates and the approximant [w]. For [w], it is not on the chart because it is a combination of two articulations, bilabial and velar. Sometimes on phonetic consonant charts you will see [w] in the bilabial column, sometimes in the velar column, sometimes in both, sometimes in a special column labeled **labial-velar** or **labiovelar**. The IPA now does none of these, instead listing it with other symbols that would otherwise require a new row or column on the main consonant chart. The affricates [tʃ] and [dʒ] do not appear on the chart, but are combinations of sounds that do appear on the chart. An affricate is a stop followed by a fricative made at the same or a similar place, which functions as a single sound. The two affricates of English are postalveolar (commonly called palatoalveolar), voiceless [tʃ] and voiced [dʒ]. (Because in affricates the 'two sounds' combine to function as 'one sound', it has been common practice in the US to use single symbols for affricates: [č] for [tʃ] and [ǰ] for [dʒ].)

To summarize IPA articulatory definitions, then, each sound is described primarily in terms of its oral articulation: which active articulator gets how close to which passive articulator. For example, in [p, b, m], the two lips act as both active and passive articulators, and they touch-and-hold to make a seal. Thus these sounds are all bilabial stops. But in addition, other articulations happen at the same time. The vocal cords are either vibrating ([b, m]) or not ([p]); the velum is either raised ([p, b]), in which case the stop is oral, or it is lowered ([m]), in which case the stop is nasal. When a stop is oral and pulmonic, as with [p, b], it is a plosive. Each symbol, then, is an abbreviation for a combination of properties. To describe a consonant sound, you list these properties, by convention in the order: voiced/voiceless, then place, then manner. Thus [b] is a voiced bilabial plosive; [p] is a voiceless bilabial plosive; and [m] is a voiced bilabial nasal. It is worth noting that these terms are usually used in a kind of shorthand way that presupposes what is typical. Thus plosives and nasals are all stops, but since stops are usually pulmonic and oral the word *stop* is often used by itself to mean plosive; since nasals are usually stops and voiced the word *nasal* is often used by itself to mean voiced nasal stop; since laterals are usually approximants the word *lateral* is often used by itself to mean lateral approximant. For example, then, [m] may be referred to as a bilabial nasal rather than a voiced bilabial nasal, and [l] as an alveolar lateral rather than a voiced alveolar lateral approximant. However, it is never wrong to use all three or four terms, even if some seem redundant.

Sounds can be grouped together according to which of these properties they have in common, and sounds which share several properties are generally more similar than sounds which share few properties.

EXERCISE 11.12

Give the term corresponding to the definition given.

Example: **both lips** = bilabial

(1) **tongue blade to ridge above upper teeth**
(2) **tongue body to soft palate**
(3) **make noise in a gap**
(4) **plosives and fricatives as a group**
(5) **vocal cord vibration**

Provide the IPA symbol whose definition is given. Only IPA terms are used.

Example: **voiced alveolar plosive** = [d]

(1) **voiceless velar plosive**
(2) **bilabial nasal**
(3) **voiced labiodental fricative**
(4) **alveolar lateral approximant**
(5) **glottal plosive**
(6) **alveolar tap or flap**
(7) **voiced postalveolar fricative**
(8) **velar nasal**
(9) **voiceless glottal fricative**
(10) **voiced dental fricative**

11.3.5 Vowels

The vowel chart

Consider the vowel chart in figure 11.5. Like the consonant chart, the vowel chart encodes three dimensions, but the vowel dimensions are different from the consonant ones. The primary active articulator of vowel sounds is always some part of the tongue (almost always the tongue body), the passive articulator is some part of the midline of the outer surface of the vocal tract, but the active articulator never comes very close to the passive. The vowel chart represents a kind of grid of the vocal tract in which the top of the chart is the roof of the mouth, and the left side of the chart is the front of the oral cavity, viewed on the speaker's left side, just as for the main consonant chart. This is shown in figure 11.5. The tongue moves around in this space for different vowel sounds, and the IPA definitions describe its location. That is, the chart's first two dimensions are the height of the tongue (relative to the roof of the mouth) and the backness of the tongue (relative to the front teeth), both usually referring to the highest point on the tongue's surface. Note that although the sides of the tongue touch the sides of the palate for many vowels, the descriptions focus on the midline of the tongue, because that is where the air flows.

The vowel chart is not as clearly divided into rows and columns as the consonant chart is. There are four height categories labeled **close**, **close-mid**, **open-mid**, and **open**. These are often also called **high**, **higher mid**, **lower mid**, and **low**, respectively. There are also three other rows between these that don't appear with labels. The row between **close** and **close-mid** is sometimes called **lower high** or **high lax**. The row between **close-mid** and **open-mid** is usually called simply **mid**. The row between **open-mid** and **open** is sometimes called **higher low**.

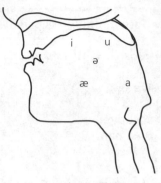

Figure 11.5   Vowel chart superimposed on schematic of vocal tract (from figure 11.4b); [a] is used for the low back vowel.

The third dimension of the chart is the **position of the lips**. **Rounded vowels** usually have the lips constricted (pulled close together) and protruded (pushed out from the face) so that when viewed from the front they make a circle, and when viewed from the side they project out. (Sometimes either the constriction or the protrusion is relatively weak.) For these vowels, then, there is a labial articulation. Unrounded vowels do not have this feature; the lips are either in a neutral posture or they are spread out to press against the face. For the high vowels in particular, these different lip positions can make a large difference in the sound produced with a given tongue position. English uses unrounded front and central vowels; the rounding of the back vowels of English is somewhat variable across dialects. Nonetheless we use the symbols for rounded back vowels in broad transcription. (11) lists all the descriptive terms of the vowel chart.

(11)   **IPA vowel row and column labels**

close	compared with other vowels, overall height of tongue is greatest; tongue is closest to roof of mouth (Also: high)
open	compared with other vowels, overall height of tongue is least; mouth is most open (Also: low)
close-mid, open-mid	intermediate positions (Also: mid/ uppermid/lowermid)
front	compared with other vowels, tongue is overall forward
central	intermediate position
back	compared with other vowels, tongue is overall back (nearer pharynx)
rounded	lips are constricted inward and protruded forward

Locate the vowel symbols we have used for English on the IPA vowel chart. Note that we are substituting simple [a] for the low back vowel of English, often more precisely given as [ɑ]. (In fact American speakers vary so much that it is not obvious which symbol is more precise, especially given that the IPA offers no symbol for a low central vowel.) You will see that most of the English vowels are given as unrounded; only /u ʊ o/ are rounded. Also, except for the central /ə/ and open /a æ/, all of the vowels of English fall into front–back pairs (i-u, ɪ-ʊ, e-o, ɛ-ʌ). (For many speakers, however, the vowel we are representing with [ʌ] is central, i.e. IPA [ɜ].) To describe a vowel sound, these terms are given in the order: row, column, rounding – for example, [i] is a high front unrounded vowel.

The vowel chart can also be viewed not as a row-by-column grid but as more of a continuous representation of the two-dimensional vocal tract space, as seen in figure 11.5 above. When it is used this way, vowel symbols are placed on the chart in a location that is meant to indicate the tongue's position in a speaker's mouth (or the corresponding auditory impression produced by the vowel for a listener). The dots next to the symbols on the IPA chart are used as a reference grid of vowel qualities. So, the [i] in English may be placed somewhat off from the [i] on the chart, to indicate that the English vowel is not as extreme as the reference vowel. When the chart is used in this way, rounding distinctions do not influence the symbol locations.

11.3.6 Diphthongs

Some vowels are represented as sequences of vowel symbols because the tongue and/or lips move from one position to another. Such vowels are called **diphthongs**. We can distinguish *large* diphthongal movements, which cross a large part of the vowel space, from *small* diphthongal movements, which involve only adjacent areas of the chart. The vowel transcriptions provided for English in this chapter represent only large movements: /aɪ, aʊ, oɪ (or ɔɪ)/. Other books give small diphthongs for /e/ and /o/, and sometimes /i/ and /u/ as well. In general, the large diphthongs are diphthongs for most English speakers (though not necessarily between exactly these qualities), while the small diphthongs are diphthongs for fewer speakers, including fewer Californian speakers. Our transcriptions of vowels, like all our broad transcriptions, are thus a compromise, in this case among the different possible pronunciations of English vowels as diphthongs vs. monophthongs (single vowel sounds).

**EXERCISE
11.14**

Give the term corresponding to the definition given.

Example: **made with the tongue overall forward** = front

(1)   **made with the lips pulled together and forward**
(2)   **vowel composed of a sequence of two vowel sounds**
(3)   **made with the tongue maximally low**
(4)   **made with the tongue maximally high**
(5)   **made with the tongue in an intermediate position in the front–back dimension**

**EXERCISE
11.15**

Provide the IPA symbol whose definition is given.

Example: **mid central unrounded vowel** = [ə]

(1)   **high (= close) front unrounded vowel**
(2)   **lower high front unrounded vowel**
(3)   **higher mid (= close-mid) back rounded vowel**
(4)   **low (= open) back unrounded vowel**
(5)   **high back rounded vowel**
(6)   **higher low front unrounded vowel**
(7)   **high front rounded vowel**
(8)   **lower mid front unrounded vowel**
(9)   **high central rounded vowel**
(10) **lower high back rounded vowel**

11.3.7   Different pronunciations mean different symbols

The IPA charts make a big distinction between consonants and vowels, giving them separate charts and descriptive terminology. This puts the glides in an odd position, since they are like both consonants and vowels. Glides are sometimes also called semi-vowels because they are vowel-like. Their position on the consonant chart (as central approximants) obscures their similarity to vowels. The glide [j] is only a bit more constricted than the otherwise-similar vowel [i], and the glide [w] is only a bit more constricted than the otherwise-similar vowel [u]. It may be hard to say in any given case whether a particular glide sound is more like a vowel or a consonant. Similarly, a rhotacized vowel symbol, [ɚ], represents a sound that the IPA also provides a consonant symbol for ([ɻ]). But generally the definitions of the symbols are fixed by the chart; and if you are sure what a given sound is then you pretty much know what symbol to use for it in a narrow transcription. Where there are uncertainties or disagreements, it is about the nature of the sounds themselves. If you pronounce a sound

Articulatory information from the phonetics laboratory

How do we know that these articulatory definitions are accurate, for at least some speakers? Although much useful information about articulation has been acquired through careful introspection, there is also a tradition of laboratory data acquisition from the nineteenth century to the most current technologies. Information about place of articulation can be obtained from ultrasound, Magnetic Resonance Imaging (MRI) and X-rays, palatography, or magnetometry. In dynamic electropalatography a set of contact electrodes on the hard palate records where the tongue touches. In magnetometry an electromagnetic field is established around the head of a speaker and the location of one or more receiver coils is tracked. Information about manner of articulation can be obtained not only from these techniques but also from records of airflow and air pressure. Information about voicing can be obtained from electroglottography, which records contacts between the vocal cords.

differently from how the symbol is defined, then strictly speaking that is the wrong symbol for your pronunciation. For example, if you pronounce [s] as a dental fricative rather than an alveolar, then you will be troubled by the fact that it is in the alveolar column, and you will wonder how a dental should be represented. (The answer is [s̪].) Similarly, if you pronounce [r] as a retroflex rather than a postalveolar approximant. But we can still agree to use the symbols that seem to render the most common pronunciations for our broad transcription, knowing that the IPA does provide the resources for making these distinctions in a narrower transcription.

11.3.8   Other IPA symbols: consonants and vowels

The IPA provides many more symbols than we have used so far. This is in part because other languages use sounds that English does not use. The IPA is meant to provide a symbol for every basic sound of every language. It is beyond the scope of an introductory course to present and discuss all of the symbols of the IPA, but if you understand the conceptual framework you should be able to cope with many of these symbols when you encounter them. In the consonant chart, there are many consonants that English does not use, but which are combinations of phonetic properties which English does use. For example, English has bilabial stops (oral [p, b] and nasal [m]) and labiodental fricatives ([f, v]), but not the reverse combinations, bilabial fricatives ([ɸ, β]) and labiodental stops (nasal [ɱ]) – yet you should be able to figure out what these sounds must be, just from their definitions. Similarly, if you know how to make a particular front unrounded vowel such as [i], you should be able to understand the idea of the corresponding front rounded vowel [y] (keep your tongue in the same position, but round your lips as if for a back rounded vowel); and if you know how to make a back rounded vowel such as [u], you should be able to understand the idea of the corresponding back unrounded vowel [ɯ] (unround your lips, or even smile, while keeping your tongue in the same position). Other sounds are a little harder because they are more different from the basic sounds of English, but some experimentation might yield new phonetic skill. For example, since you can make a palatal approximant (or glide) [j], as in *yonder*, you can try raising the center of your tongue until you make a voiced palatal fricative [ʝ], and then keep raising the tongue until it makes a complete seal for a voiced palatal stop [ɟ]. Nasalize it and you have [ɲ], a sound of Spanish (where it is spelled *ñ*), French (where it is spelled *gn*), and many other languages.

On the other hand, the charts include some dimensions which are not used in any basic sound of English. All of the consonants of English, and most of the sounds on the chart, are pulmonic egressive, meaning that the air comes out of the lungs. Note the separate chart for non-pulmonic consonants: clicks, voiced implosives, and (voiceless) ejectives. These are all sound types in which the airflow is established in some other way. For example, in implosives, there is a downward movement of the larynx during the stop closure. This downward movement gives the voicing during the stop a special strong quality, and at the same time it expands the size of the air cavity in the vocal tract. When the oral stop (e.g. at the lips in the bilabial [ɓ]) is released, air can flow into the vocal tract rather than out of it, making the release strong also.

11.4 Diacritics

We noted before that the cells of the charts cover ranges of articulations. Diacritics serve to narrow down those ranges, and transcriptions using them are often called **narrow**. As stated above, a narrow transcription is used to represent small differences between speakers or languages, to show how a basic sound's exact value can change depending on the surrounding sounds, and to show differences between speech that is more or less careful, etc. However, in many cases diacritics are needed even for the basic sounds of a language. For example, a language that has nasalized (with air coming out the nose) as well as oral vowels will necessarily use the nasalization diacritic. The lower right part of the IPA chart contains a chart of diacritics, of which a few have already been presented. Many of the diacritics in the chart raise subtle definitional issues that go beyond the scope of an introductory text like this one. (12) lists some diacritics that can be used for English and which appear in this chapter or the phonology chapters.

(12) **Some IPA Diacritics**

aspirated	ʰ	noise in the glottis, especially at the end of a consonant ([pʰ])
syllabic	̩	a consonant without a vowel ([r̩])
rhoticity	˞	r-coloring ([ə˞])
dental	̪	upper teeth are passive articulator (used to modify basic symbols in Alveolar column) ([d̪])
nasalized	̃	air flows through nose as well as mouth ([ã])
unreleased	˺	release of consonant as mouth opens is not heard ([d˺])
voiceless	̥	partial or no vocal cord vibration in an otherwise voiced sound ([l̥])
velarized	~	tongue backing during some other primary articulation ([ɫ])

Finally, next to the diacritics chart are some additional diacritics specifically for suprasegmentals. The first is for primary, or main, stress, and has been used already in this chapter. The second is for secondary, or weaker, stress, which we will not cover. The next three convey lengthening and shortening of a consonant or vowel relative to its typical duration. For example, chapter 12 includes a detailed discussion of how English vowels are shortened before voiceless consonants, transcribed with ˘ over the vowel. On the other hand, in some languages consonants or vowels can be roughly doubled in length, transcribed with [ː] after the symbol. The next four diacritics represent breaks or connections between segments; the period to mark syllable divisions has already been used and will be used in later chapters.

The next two columns contain alternative ways of marking tones. Thus the Kana word for *to fence*, with a Low tone, can be transcribed [bè] or [be˨]; the Kana word for *home* or *compound*, with a Mid tone, can be transcribed [bē] or [be˧]; and the Kana word for *fight*, with a High tone, can be transcribed [bé] or [be˦]. We have not considered the tonal phenomena covered by the other tonal diacritics.

Intonational rises and falls of the pitch of the voice can be indicated by rising (↗) and falling (↘) arrows. For example, in 'Is Hamlet upset?', a fall on 'Hamlet' and a rise on 'upset' can be transcribed as in (13), while in 'What did Polonius say?', a rise followed by a final fall can be transcribed as in (14).

(13) Is ↘Hamlet ↗upset?

(14) What did Po↗lo↘nius say?

The following chapters will use a variety of symbols and diacritics from the chart; you can refer back to the chart then to see what kinds of sounds they represent.

EXERCISE 11.16

Give a symbol with a diacritic according to the description provided.

Example: **aspirated voiceless bilabial stop at the beginning of** *pat* = [pʰ]

(1)   **syllabic alveolar nasal at the end of** *sweeten*
(2)   **voiced dental stop in** *breadth*
(3)   **nasalized high front unrounded vowel in** *lean*
(4)   **unreleased final voiced velar stop in** *hag*
(5)   **partially voiceless alveolar fricative in** *buzz*

EXERCISE 11.17

Add in arrows to indicate the intonational rises or falls described.

Example: ***Virtue? A fig!*** **with a rise on the first word and a fall on the last**

↗   ↘
Virtue? A fig!

(1)   *It cannot be.* **with a fall on** *be*
(2)   *Put money in thy purse.* **with a fall on** *purse*
(3)   *Thou art sure of me.* **with a rise and fall on** *sure*
(4)   *Do you hear, Roderigo?* **with rises on** *hear* **and** *Roderigo*
(5)   *How, is this true?* **with a fall on** *how* **and a rise on** *true*

SIDEBAR 11.6

Sound correspondences across languages

When people confront the sound system of a new language, they seem to make correspondences between the sounds of the new language and their native sounds. As much as they can, they equate new sounds with known sounds, as long as the sounds are somewhat similar. Suppose the native language is English, which has a basic sound [ʃ], while the new language has retroflex [ʂ] or alveolo-palatal [ɕ], either of which is similar to [ʃ] but not quite the same. English speakers will think of this as 'the funny [ʃ] in that language'. But then, having identified the new sound as corresponding to a known sound, even though imperfectly, English speakers will tend to use their [ʃ] in speaking that language, and that means they will have an English accent. Worse, the new language might have two of these – 'two different [ʃ]s' – and since both are seen as corresponding to the native [ʃ], they get pronounced the same. On the other hand, sometimes the new sound is so different from any native sound that no correspondence can be made. Suppose an English speaker encounters click sounds. These are patently so unlike any native sound that the speaker realizes they just have to be learned. The speaker may not make them quite right, and so will have an accent, but it will not necessarily be an accent from the native language.

11.5 Summary

Phonetics is concerned with the physical properties of speech. Speech utterances are analyzed as sequences of (partially overlapping) speech segments, plus suprasegmentals. A phonetic transcription represents a speech utterance as a string of phonetic symbols for the segments, accompanied by diacritics for the suprasegmentals.

Languages' orthographies are not always consistent in their letter-to-sound relations. Phonetic alphabets aim to provide one symbol per sound and one sound per symbol. The IPA is an international standard alphabet which aims to provide symbols for the sounds of all the world's languages. Consonant and vowel symbols are defined in terms of speech articulations: consonants in terms of their voicing, place of articulation, and manner of articulation; vowels in terms of their tongue position and lip rounding. These descriptive dimensions also serve to organize the symbols into phonetic charts.

A phonetic transcription can be broad or narrow. This chapter provides a list of 40 symbols for broad transcription of the basic sounds of American English. Narrow transcriptions use additional phonetic symbols and diacritics. Diacritics make symbols more specific. These additional symbols and diacritics are also used for basic sounds of other languages.

Just as native speakers of a language have unconscious knowledge about other aspects of linguistic structure, they have phonetic knowledge. They know the sounds of their language, and exactly how those sounds are pronounced in different combinations. No phonetic transcription conveys every such detail of pronunciation.

Further reading

Adams, Marilyn J. 1990. *Beginning to Read: Thinking and Learning about Print*. Cambridge, MA: MIT Press.

Catford, John C. 1988. *A Practical Introduction to Phonetics*. Oxford: Clarendon Press.

Dodd. B. and R. Campbell. eds. 1987. *Hearing by Eye: The Psychology of Lip Reading*. Hillsdale, NJ: Lawrence Erlbaum Assoc.

Gough, Ehri, and Treiman. eds. 1992. *Reading Acquisition*. Hillsdale, NJ: Lawrence Erlbaum Assoc.

Ladefoged, Peter. 1993. *A Course in Phonetics*, 3rd edn. Fort Worth: Harcourt Brace Jovanovich College Publishers.

—— and Ian Maddieson. 1996. *Sounds of the World's Languages*. Oxford: Blackwell.

Laver, John. 1994. *Principles of Phonetics*. Cambridge: Cambridge University Press.

Pullum, Geoffrey K. and W. A. Ladusaw. 1986. *Phonetic Symbol Guide*. Chicago: University of Chicago Press.

Rogers, Henry. 1991. *Theoretical and Practical Phonetics*. Toronto: Copp Clark Pittman Ltd.

Smalley, William A. 1989. *Manual of Articulatory Phonetics*, rev. edn. Lanham, MD: University Press of America. First edition 1961.

EXERCISES

Give the regular English orthography for the following words, which are given in a broad transcription. The pronunciations given may not be like yours, but the words should be identifiable nonetheless.

Exercise 11.18

(1) bʊk
(2) onli
(3) pepɚ
(4) aʊt
(5) rimaɪnd (or rəmaɪnd)
(6) stap
(7) hɛd
(8) θɪŋk

· ·

Exercise 11.19

Give broad transcriptions for the following pairs of English words. The focus here is on what makes the two words in each pair different. Use a dictionary if you like, but use IPA symbols. (Since each student may transcribe his or her own pronunciations, there can be no single correct answer here.)

(1) **spot - Scot**
(2) **weary - worry**
(3) **cue - few**
(4) **lose - loose**
(5) **man - men**
(6) **woman - women**
(7) **attend - Athens**
(8) **size - seize**
(9) **show - shoe**
(10) **put - putt**

· ·

Exercise 11.20

Give the regular English orthography for the following words, which are given in a narrow transcription. Again, these pronunciations may not be like yours.

(1) [ˈpʰlɛ̃nti]
(2) [bʊk̚]
(3) [tʃrækʰ]
(4) [ˈmorɚ]
(5) [sɛ̃nts] (some speakers will have more than one possible answer for this!)

· ·

Exercise 11.21

Give a broad transcription for the following words, which are given in a narrow transcription.

(1) [ˈwʌ̃ndɚfl̩]
(2) [ˈʔæpl̩]
(3) [pʰʊʔt]
(4) [meɪ]

(5) [wãt˥] (hint: what unpronounced sound would cause the vowel to be
     nasalized?)

. . . .

Compare the sounds in each set below. In each set, all but one are in a single
row or column on the IPA chart. Give the name of that row or column, and
circle the sound which does not belong.

**Exercise
11.22**

(1) m n r ŋ
(2) p t k v d g
(3) p t s l n
(4) f v s z h k
(5) i e u ɛ æ

. . . .

The same as Exercise 11.22, but here all but one sound in each set belong
to a class of sounds that goes beyond a single row or column of the chart
– classes such as *labial, coronal, dorsal, obstruent, sonorant, approximant,
stop, fricative, voiced, voiceless, rounded, unrounded* – or within a single row
or column, such as *voiced stops, labial stops*. Give the name of the class of
sounds, and circle the sound which does not belong.

**Exercise
11.23**

(1) β v ð z ʒ h
(2) i e æ u ʌ
(3) m l r j w
(4) m n k l r j
(5) θ f ð s z ʃ ʒ

. . . .

Here are the basic sounds of Burera, an Australian language. Compare this set
with the basic sounds of English to answer the questions that follow.

**Exercise
11.24**

/p t c k m n ɲ ŋ r l r (as in English) j w i ɛ a ɔ u/

a. Which sounds of Burera are not basic in English (as in (3) in the chapter)?
    You do not need to define these, just indicate them.
b. What labial sound(s) of English are not in Burera?
c. What coronal sound(s) of English are not in Burera?
d. What dorsal sound(s) of English are not in Burera?
e. What glottal sound(s) of English are not in Burera?

12

Phonology I:
Basic Principles and Methods

12.0   Introduction

We have supposed in this text that linguistic knowledge can be factored into a set of relatively independent components (syntactic, semantic, phonetic, etc.). The **phonological component** of a language is the system of rules, representations and principles that govern the patterning of sounds. The phonology of a language is the 'grammar of sound' for that language.

SIDEBAR
12.1

Sign phonology

The main text focuses entirely on the problem of spoken language phonology for reasons of space. But as discussed in earlier chapters, many of the world's languages are sign languages, which employ movements of the hands, arms, and face instead of sound to convey linguistic messages. Research beginning in the 1960s has shown that sign languages have phonologies, too, and a major area of phonological research has been to discover the structural principles of sign phonology, and how they differ from those of spoken language. In this sense, *phonology* refers to the rules of language that pertain to the physical channel of communication.

12.1   What is Phonology?

Phonology differs from other parts of linguistics in that it is not immediately obvious why such a field should exist. We know that languages have words, and that words are made up of speech sounds – why couldn't we specify the string of speech sounds that every word is made up of, and let it go at that? It turns out that the real world of phonological systems is far more complicated. First, the sounds tend to vary with their context, mostly for phonetic reasons. Second, the **distribution** of the sounds is not arbitrary, but follows complex, rule-governed patterns. Third, phonology is interfaced with other components of the grammar, notably morphology and syntax, and there are various ways in which sound patterning reflects these components.

In addition, the phonological rule systems of languages tend towards an elaboration that goes beyond what is needed for speech communication. The phonologies of many languages have a level of complication that make them complex puzzles for the linguist trying to understand them. It can take years of careful research to unlock the sound pattern of a language – even though this pattern is learned quite rapidly, at the intuitive level, by individuals exposed to it in childhood. The natural profusion of form seen in phonologies, going beyond what intuitively seems necessary from a functional point of view, is one of the most intriguing aspects of the field.

This chapter lays out the basics of phonology and phonological analysis. The emphasis is on sounds at work: how they distinguish words in their spoken form, and how a linguist approaches the sound pattern of a novel language and makes sense of it.

12.2   Sounds at Work: Distinctiveness and Contrast

A curious aspect of phonological form is that (aside from a few phenomena covered in Sidebar 12.2) it is intrinsically meaningless. To take an example, the /t/ sound of English has no linguistic interpretation in and of itself. Its only role is to serve as a building block for words. Because English has /t/, then the possibility exists of English having the word *tie* /taɪ/, distinct from the word *die* /daɪ/. In general, the only real duty of a speech sound is to sound different from the other sounds of the language.

To achieve some initial understanding of a language's phonology, we therefore seek to locate all of its basic sounds, which serve as the building blocks for distinguishing words from each other. These basic sounds are called **phonemes**.

(1)   **phoneme** = one of the basic speech sounds of a language

For example, the phonemes of one commonly spoken dialect of English (that of most speakers in the western United States) are arranged phonetically below. Sounds are arranged phonetically when they are in rows and columns as if in an IPA-style chart, such as the one presented in the previous chapter, though not necessarily the exact same rows, columns, or order that the IPA uses. The sound symbols are in slant brackets / / to show that they represent phonemes.

(2)   **Consonants**

		Bilabial	Labio-dental	Dental	Alveolar	Palato-alveolar	Palatal	Velar	Glottal
Stops	voiceless	/p/			/t/	/tʃ/		/k/	
	voiced	/b/			/d/	/dʒ/		/g/	
Fricatives	voiceless		/f/	/θ/	/s/	/ʃ/			/h/
	voiced		/v/	/ð/	/z/	/ʒ/			
Nasals		/m/			/n/			/ŋ/	
Approximant	lateral				/l/				
	central	/w/			/r/		/j/		

(3)   **Vowels and Diphthongs**

	Front Unrounded	Central Unrounded	Back Unrounded	Back Rounded	Diphthongs
Upper high	/i/			/u/	/aɪ/, /aʊ/, /ɔɪ/
Lower high	/ɪ/			/ʊ/	
Upper mid	/e/	/ə/		/o/	Syllabic
Lower mid	/ɛ/		/ʌ/		Consonant
Low	/æ/		/a/		/r̩/

Sound symbolism

On the whole, speech sounds have no inherent meaningful content. But most languages have small corners of their sound systems in which the sounds themselves seem to be meaningful, in a vague way. For example, the high front vowel /i/ often seems to have an inherent meaning of smallness or closeness, in contrast to /a/, which conveys largeness or distance. Thus, in English *teeny* /ˈtini/ conveys a sense of smaller size than *tiny* /ˈtaɪni/; similarly *eensie-weensie* /ˈinsiˈwinsi/ (*spider*). The basis of this may be the acoustics of /i/: the second formant (a special region of greater acoustic intensity) has a higher pitch for /i/ than for any other vowel.

Quite a few languages have a high front vowel for their word for *this* (demonstrative for close things) and a low vowel for their word for *that* (demonstrative for distant things):

Language	'this'	'that'
English	/ðɪs/	/ðæt/
Farsi	/iːn/	/ɑːn/
French	/sœˈsi/	/sœˈla/
Thai	/niː/	/nân/

Another case was mentioned in chapter 2: many words in English which relate to visual aspects begin with /gl/, such as *gleam*, *glow*, or *glossy*. However, the inherent meaningfulness of sounds should not be exaggerated. Typically, only a subset of the vocabulary of a language includes inherently meaningful sounds. Moreover, the meaningfulness of sounds is to some extent arbitrary within a given language: Korean, for example, tends to use low vowels, not high, to designate tininess.

Other dialects differ, having additional phonemes such as /ɔ/, /ʍ/, and so on.

Below, we will discuss methods for establishing the phoneme inventory of a language or dialect. For now, we can say that if any two words of a language are pronounced differently, they must differ in at least one phoneme. Moreover, the phoneme inventory does not contain pointless, redundant members; all of its members are capable of distinguishing words from each other.

Languages vary in the number of phonemes they have. The record low is believed to be held by Rotokas (South Pacific), with 11, and the record high by !Xoo, with 160. English has roughly 37–41, depending on the dialect and the analysis. The average across languages is about 30.

All this is straightforward, but becomes more complex when we add the principles under (4):

(4) **Phonemic Variation**
   a. Phonemes vary by context.
   b. The variation is rule-governed.

Let us consider a simple case, involving the length of vowels. If you listen to a native speaker of English say the following pairs of words (or measure with acoustic equipment), you will find that the vowel phoneme /e/ is quite a bit SHORTER in the second member of each pair. We've indicated this in the transcription with the IPA shortness marker on the shorter vowels:

(5) save   [sev]   safe   [sĕf]
    Abe   [eb]   ape   [ĕp]
    made   [med]   mate   [mĕt]
    maze   [mez]   mace   [mĕs]
    age   [edʒ]   H   [ĕtʃ]
    Haig   [heg]   ache   [ĕk]

All these words have a vowel that speakers are willing, intuitively, to accept as being the 'same vowel' (despite the variable spelling). But phonetically, they are not the same vowel; rather, there are two variants, namely [e] and [ĕ], that we feel to be linguistically the same.

If you look at the data closely, you can see why: [e] and [ĕ] are arranged by English as **predictable variants**. The variant [e] occurs when the next sound in the word is voiced (here: [v, b, d, z, dʒ, g]), and [ĕ] occurs when the next sound in the word is voiceless (here: [f, p, t, s, tʃ, k]). English can then be said to have one 'basic sound' here, with two phonetic variants.

The very fact that the appearance of [e] vs. [ĕ] is predictable is important: it means that the difference between the two cannot be used to distinguish words from each other. In this respect, the difference between [e] vs. [ĕ] is quite different from the difference between (for example) [e] vs. [æ], since the latter pair CAN serve to distinguish words, for example *made* [med] vs. *mad* [mæd].

Thus, in phonological analysis, for any pair of sounds it is necessary to establish their phonological status: either they are separate phonemes, capable of distinguishing words, or mere variants, whose distribution in the language is determined by context.

Why should English arrange the difference between [e] and [ĕ] as it does? It has been suggested that the difference between [e] and [ĕ] may assist the listener in identifying the voicing of the following sound: given [ĕp], the fact that the [ĕ] is short can in principle be used by the listener to help determine that the word being heard is *ape* and not *Abe*. This is important, given that /p/ and /b/ are not always readily discriminable at the end of a word.

Virtually all the phonemes in English show phonetic variation, depending on their context. For example, all of the vowels, and not just /e/, are shorter when a voiceless consonant follows. Similarly, all vowels are nasalized when a nasal consonant follows: compare *ten* [tɛ̃n] with *Ted* [tɛd]. When we look at English in full phonetic detail, taking all the variation into account, it turns out that it has not 39 speech sounds, but thousands.

We can imagine, then, how a phonological system is 'designed'. In every language, the number of sounds that can be uttered is very large. But the phonological system organizes these sounds in a particular way, such that only a small subset of phonetic differences (for example, in English [t] vs. [d], or [e] vs. [æ]) can serve to distinguish words. The remaining phonetic differences are REGULATED BY RULE – for example, the rule that requires vowels in English to be short when a voiceless consonant follows. These differences, the ones that cannot by themselves distinguish words, are also important, because (as just shown for [e] vs. [ĕ]) they can help the listener infer the speaker's intent.

This, then, is a crucial notion in phonology: the particular sound differences in a language that distinguish words one from another. The normal terminology for designating this notion is the following:

(6) The phonetic difference between two sounds is **distinctive** if it can serve as the basis for distinguishing words.

Thus, the difference between [p] and [b] in English is distinctive, since it is the only difference between pairs of words like *pill* [pɪl] and *bill* [bɪl]. The difference between [e] and [ĕ] is non-distinctive, since it is determined automatically by the voicing of the following consonant.

Consider another non-distinctive pair in English: alveolar [n] vs. dental [n̪]. Some words with these sounds are shown below:

(7) | **Words with [n]** | | **Words with [n̪]** | |
|---|---|---|---|
| know | ['no] | tenth | ['tɛn̪θ] |
| annoy | [ə'nɔɪ] | month | ['mʌn̪θ] |
| onion | ['ʌnjən] | panther | ['pæn̪θr̩] |
| nun | ['nʌn] | chrysanthemum | [krə'sæn̪θəməm] |

It is not hard to see that the dental [n̪] occurs in a specific context: before [θ]. Alveolar [n] occurs pretty much everywhere else. The difference between [n] and [n̪] is not distinctive in English.

Again, we can ask why the sounds should be patterned this way. In this case, the most plausible explanation seems to involve the ease with which sequences can be articulated (often referred to as **ease of articulation**): if [n̪] occurs immediately before [θ], then the tongue blade is spared the fairly rapid slide across the alveolar ridge that would be necessary if we said [n] in this context. (Check this by trying actually to say *[tɛnθ] instead of [tɛn̪θ].)

Summing up over the two cases just seen: a language employs a relatively small number of differences between sounds as distinctive; that is, as capable of distinguishing words. The remaining differences are often employed in useful ways: they can serve as extra signals for distinctive differences being made elsewhere in the word (e.g. [e] vs. [ĕ] signals the voicing of the following consonant), or they can be deployed to make the task of articulating speech easier.

12.3   Phonemic Notation and Phonemicization

When one encounters a new language, there is no way of immediately guessing which phonetic differences are distinctive and which are not. Since one cannot make much progress until this is known, linguists have evolved the technique of **phonemicization**, which can be used to determine the basic, distinctive sounds (the phonemes), as well as the system of rules and constraints that govern non-distinctive differences.

A bit of terminology that is commonly used:

(8)   A phonetic variant of a phoneme is an **allophone** of that phoneme.

For example: [e] and [ĕ] are allophones (phonetic variants) of a single phoneme, and so are [n] and [n̪].

It is traditional in linguistics to use ordinary phonetic brackets ([ ]) to designate allophones, and slant brackets (/ /) to designate phonemes. Thus the two allophones we have discussed so far are the longer [e] and the shorter [ĕ], which are allophones of the phoneme /e/; similarly [n] and [n̪] are allophones of /n/.

A phonemic analysis of a language involves two things:

(9)   a.   A set of **phonemes** – the inventory of basic, distinctive sounds in the language;
     b.   A set of **phonological rules**, which specify the arrangement of the non-distinctive differences in the language, by specifying where all the allophones occur.

Some data illustrating allophones of the phoneme /l/ in a number of dialects of English are given in (10). Symbols: [ɫ] is a velarized l, with high back tongue body position. [ɫ̪] is the same as [ɫ], only with a dental instead of alveolar place of articulation. [l̥l] is an l which starts out voiceless and ends voiced.

(10)

Words with [ɫ]	Words with [l̥]		Words with [l̪]	Words with [l]	
file ['faɪɫ]	slight	[sl̥aɪt]	wealth ['wɛl̪θ]	listen	['lɪsən]
fool ['fuɫ]	flight	['fl̥aɪt]	health ['hɛl̪θ]	lose	['luz]
all ['aɫ]	plow	['pl̥aʊ]	filthy ['fɪl̪θi]	allow	[ə'laʊ]
ball ['baɫ]	cling	['kl̥ɪŋ]	tilth ['tɪl̪θ]	aglow	[ə'glo]
fell ['fɛɫ]	discipline	['dɪsəpl̥ɪn]	stealth ['stɛl̪θ]	blend	['blɛnd]
feel ['fiɫ]					

If you inspect the columns, you will see that each phonetic variety of /l/ has its own characteristic environment, as shown in (11):

(11) [ɫ] occurs at the ends of words;
      [l̥] occurs when the preceding consonant is voiceless;
      [l̪] occurs when the next sound is [θ];
      [l] occurs when none of the conditions for any of the other sounds is met.

This description appears to hold for the entire language, not just the sample data given here. Since each type of /l/ is confined to a particular, non-overlapping environment, it is impossible for the difference between any of the various /l/s to be distinctive. Rather, they are allophones of the same phoneme.

Some of the allophones of /l/ appear to be functional, in the senses discussed above. The partially voiceless [l̥] allophone may help make it clear to the listener that the preceding consonant is voiceless and not voiced, since it is only when the preceding consonant is voiceless that [l̥] could have arisen. The dental place of articulation of [l̪] seems clearly motivated by increasing the ease of the articulatory transition between [l] and [θ], much as the case of dental [n̪]. The use of [ɫ] before consonants and at the end of a word is more puzzling. We are familiar with similar uses of [ɫ] in other languages (e.g. Latin, Catalan, Dutch), so there is likely some phonetic reason for it to appear there. Phonetic research may shed light on this question.

When a linguist records words as sequences of phonemes (under an appropriate phonemic analysis), the result is termed a **phonemic transcription**. This is to be distinguished from a **phonetic transcription**, which includes many more details.

(12) This is an orthographic transcription.
      /ðɪs ɪz ə foʊnimɪk trænskrɪpʃən/   (This is a phonemic trancription.)

      ['d̪ðɪs ɪz ə fə'nɛɾi²k s̺ʰɹɛən'skɹɪpʃɪn]   (This is a phonetic transcription.)

12.3.1 Some terminology for phonemicization

There are many ways of talking about contrast in phonology. If two sounds are distinct in a language (i.e. the difference between them can distinguish words), then:

(13)   They belong to separate phonemes.
       They **contrast** (similarly: are **in contrast**)

If two sounds are **nondistinct** (**phonetic variants**):

(14)   They are **allophones** of the same phoneme.
       They do not contrast.

All these terms are roughly equivalent.

12.3.2 Formalization

Where the environments for particular allophones are quite simple, prose usually suffices to make the analysis clear. But often, we find environments that are more complex. In covering such cases, we can increase the level of precision by using a formal notation. Here is basic notation that is widely used in phonology. The **slash**, '/', means 'in the environment.' A **long underline** stands for where the allophone segment occurs relative to its neighbors. Thus:

(15)   / ____ θ

is to be read

(16)   'in the environment "before [θ]"'

or, for short, just 'before [θ]'. If instead we had '/ θ ____', it would be read as 'after [θ]'.

Often, to express the environment of an allophone, we must designate a whole class of sounds. For example, to express the environment for [l̥] we must designate the class of voiceless consonants. To do this, we use square brackets, containing the phonetic properties (called, in the context of phonology, **features**) that designate the relevant class of sounds. Thus, the following formalism can be read 'after any voiceless consonant':

(17)   / $\begin{bmatrix} \text{consonant} \\ \text{voiceless} \end{bmatrix}$ ____

Formalizing further, we use the symbols '+' (plus) and '−' (minus) to mean that a segment either has, or does not have, the phonetic property that a feature designates. Thus, in more standard notation the environment just given would appear as:

(18) / $\begin{bmatrix} +\text{consonant} \\ -\text{voice} \end{bmatrix}$ _____

Where we want to refer to the beginnings and ends of grammatical constituents like words, we can use brackets, much as is done in the study of syntax and morphology. Thus, for example, the notation given below can be read 'at the end of a word.'

(19) / _____]$_{\text{word}}$

'At the beginning of a word' would be / [$_{\text{word}}$ _____.

Finally, in the theory to be adopted here, the **elsewhere** allophone of a phoneme can be characterized as a kind of starting point, the base form or **underlying representation** from which all other allophones are derived.

Putting all this together, we can produce a partially formalized description, using named rules, of the environment for the allophones of /l/ as in (20):

(20) Base form: /l/
Phonological rules:
/l/ Devoicing
/l/ → [l̥] / $\begin{bmatrix} +\text{consonant} \\ -\text{voice} \end{bmatrix}$ _____
/l/ Dentalization
/l/ → [l̪] / _____ θ
/l/ Velarization
/l/ → [ɫ] / _____]$_{\text{word}}$

In this approach, we need not specify that the elsewhere allophone is [l]; that is simply the base form whenever none of the phonological rules happen to alter it.

The system as a whole can be seen clearly if we use the rules to **derive** the phonetic forms (allophones) from the underlying representations, as follows. The notation '—' used in (21) means 'rule is not applicable.'

(21)

	file	*slight*	*wealth*	*listen*	
	/faɪl/	/slaɪt/	/wɛlθ/	/ˈlɪsən/	UNDERLYING FORMS
					RULE APPLICATION:
	—	sl̥aɪt	—	—	/l/ Devoicing
	—	—	wɛl̪θ	—	/l/ Dentalization
	faɫ	—	—	—	/l/ Velarization
	[ˈfaɪɫ]	[ˈsl̥aɪt]	[ˈwɛl̪θ]	[ˈlɪsən]	SURFACE (PHONETIC) FORMS

Phonology and writing

The study of writing systems is an independent field, though closely related to phonology. Apparently every known true writing system is phonological at least to some extent. Even in the writing systems of Chinese, Ancient Egyptian, and Mayan, which are said to be 'ideographic' (one symbol per word or morpheme), the written symbols usually convey some information about the sound of the words that they spell.

A major way in which writing systems differ is in HOW LARGE A PHONOLOGICAL UNIT a symbol represents. The characters of Chinese represent units the size of a single syllable. In a true alphabet, each symbol corresponds roughly to a phoneme, though there are of course complications like *x* (one symbol, two phonemes in sequence) or *th* (two symbols, one phoneme). In addition, there is a widespread kind of writing system in which each symbol conveys a short stretch of sound (often a consonant–vowel sequence) that is larger than a phoneme but smaller than a syllable. Examples include Japanese *kana* and the system for Cherokee invented by Sequoyah in the early nineteenth century. In general, the smaller the phonological unit that a writing system uses, the fewer units it needs. 'Ideographic' systems like Chinese can employ as many as 50,000 characters.

Historically, writing began with systems that symbolized large units (syllables), then gradually evolved towards phoneme-based writing, which was first invented in Ancient Greece. It should not be imagined, however, that phoneme-based writing is necessarily superior, given that other writing types have been steadfastly maintained by their users for centuries.

The majority of the world's languages are unwritten. New writing systems are frequently developed for previously unwritten languages, often by linguists. Such systems can be (and usually are) made far more rational and predictable than systems like English, by assigning one symbol to each phoneme.

12.3.3 Phonemic analysis and writing

The question of phonemicization is in principle independent from the question of writing; that is, there is no necessary connection between LETTERS and PHONEMES. We've seen, for example, that the English phoneme /e/ can be spelled in quite a few ways: *say* /se/, *Abe* /eb/, *main* /men/, *beige* /beʒ/, *reggae* /rɛge/, *H* /etʃ/. There are languages (e.g. Chinese) that are written with symbols that do not correspond to phonemes at all.

Obviously, there is at least a loose connection between alphabetic letters and phonemes: the designers of an alphabet tend to match up the written symbols with the phonemes of a language, insofar as these are understood. Moreover, the conscious intuitions of speakers about sounds tend to be heavily influenced by their knowledge of spelling – after all, most literate speakers receive extensive training in how to spell during childhood, but no training at all in phonology.

Beginners in linguistics often have to work to get over a prejudice our culture holds about writing: writing is prestigious, and our spoken pronunciations are sometimes felt to be imperfect realizations of what is written. In contrast, most linguists feel that spoken language is primary, and that written language is a derived system, which is mostly parasitic off the spoken language and is often rather artificial in character. There are several reasons that support the second view: spoken language is enormously older than writing, it is acquired first (and with greater ease) by children, and it is the common property of our species, rather than of just an educated subset of it. As the subject of scientific study, there seems to be good reason to give priority to spoken language.

12.3.4 Phonemes in other languages

Understanding the notion of phonemes is actually harder if you consider only languages you speak. The problem is that a fluent speaker of a language tends to be more consciously aware of the phonemes than of the allophones, so a phonemicization (at least, an accurate one) will tend to be intuitively obvious. It is only when you take on a new language that phonemicization can become a bit surprising.

The reason is that ONE LANGUAGE'S ALLOPHONE CAN BE ANOTHER LANGUAGE'S PHONEME. The world's languages do not necessarily divide phonetic space in the same way. Thus, a distinction that serves to distinguish words in one language might be predictably distributed in another.

Consider the phonemic system of Spanish. Spanish has many sounds that resemble sounds of English (we will consider only North American dialects of English here). In particular, English has a [t] and a flap [ɾ]. The [d] of Spanish is dental rather than alveolar, and there are also slight differences in the flap, but these are arguably small enough to ignore for our purposes.

In North American English [ɾ] is (to a rough approximation) an allophone of the /t/ phoneme. The environment for [ɾ] is as follows: between two syllabic sounds (vowels or syllabic consonants), of which the second is stressless. Words having /t/ that fit this environment, and which therefore show a flap, are given in the first column below.

(22)	**Phonemic**	**Phonetic**		**Phonemic**	**Phonetic**
data	/ˈdetə/	[ˈdeɾə]	*tan*	/ˈtæn/	[ˈtæn]
latter	/ˈlætr̩/	[ˈlæɾr̩]	*attend*	/əˈtɛnd/	[əˈtɛnd]
eating	/ˈitɪŋ/	[ˈiɾɪŋ]	*guilty*	/ˈgɪlti/	[ˈgɪlti]
Ottoman	/ˈatəmən/	[ˈaɾəmən]	*pat*	/ˈpæt/	[ˈpæt]
rhetoric	/ˈrɛtərɪk/	[ˈrɛɾərɪk]	*active*	/ˈæktɪv/	[ˈæktɪv]
automatic	/atəˈmætɪk/	[aɾəˈmæɾɪk]	*Atkins*	/ˈætkɪnz/	[ˈætkɪnz]

The second column combines other allophones of /t/ which have already been mentioned, without narrowly transcribing their specific properties. In this column, we see where /t/ does NOT appear as the [ɾ] allophone: either because it fails to follow a syllabic sound (*tan, guilty, active*) or because it fails to precede a syllabic sound (*pat, Atkins*), or because the following syllabic sound is stressed (*attend*). But if all the right conditions are met simultaneously, as in the first column, we get the flapped [ɾ].

You can see, then, that the difference between [t] and [ɾ] is not distinctive in English – the flap is a conditioned variant of the /t/ phoneme that shows up in a particular environment. The use of the single letter *t* to spell the two sounds is therefore a sensible employment of the principle that letters should correspond to phonemes.

The Flapping rule can be stated as follows:

(23) *Flapping*
    /t/ → [ɾ] / [+vowel] ___ $\begin{bmatrix} +\text{vowel} \\ -\text{stress} \end{bmatrix}$

That is: the phoneme /t/ is realized as [ɾ] when it is preceded by a vowel or syllabic consonant, and followed by a stressless vowel.

In Spanish, /t/ and /ɾ/ are separate phonemes: there are pairs of words which differ only in that one word contains [t] in the place where the other contains [ɾ]. An example is

(24) ['pita] 'century plant'
    ['piɾa] 'funeral pyre'

Since 'century plant' and 'funeral pyre' are different words, the difference between Spanish [t] and [ɾ] signals a difference in meaning. Therefore [t] and [ɾ] contrast, and are separate phonemes: /t/ vs. /ɾ/. The Spanish spelling system takes account of this fact, and spells [t] as *t*, [ɾ] as *r*. In general, Spanish spelling comes admirably close to the 'one phoneme, one symbol' principle.

Comparing English and Spanish, we see that the [t] vs. [ɾ] difference is allophonic (non-distinctive) for English, but phonemic (distinctive) for Spanish. Thus, in this area, the two languages are phonetically similar but phonologically different.

Here is a similar case. Both English and Spanish have a [d] (the Spanish one is dental, not alveolar, but we will ignore this) and a [ð] (the voiced dental fricative). In English, we know that the two sounds are separate phonemes, because we can find contrasting pairs such as the following:

(25) die   [daɪ]   vs.   thy   [ðaɪ]
    bayed [bed]   vs.   bathe [beð]
    den   [dɛn]   vs.   then   [ðɛn]

But in Spanish, no such pairs exist. Furthermore, by looking at the facts of Spanish pronunciation one can determine that [d] and [ð] are phonetic variants:

(26) [daðo]   'given'
      [deðo]   'finger'
      [usteð]   'you (polite)'
      [donde]   'where'
      [de ðonde] 'from where'

The data indicate that [ð] occurs only after a vowel, while [d] is the elsewhere allophone, occurring after consonants and initially. Thus [ð] and [d] are allophones of the same phoneme.

We can set up the following phonological analysis for the sounds of Spanish discussed so far:

(27)   Phonemes: /t/, /d/, /ɾ/
       Phonological rule: /d/ *Spirantization*
               /d/ → [ð] / [+vowel] ____

That is: the phoneme /d/ is realized as [ð] when it follows a vowel. **Spirantization** means conversion of stops to fricatives, a common phonological process.

A fairly uncontroversial phonemic transcription for all the Spanish words and phrases given so far would be /'pita/, /'piɾa/, /'dado/, /'dedo/, /us'ted/, /'donde/, /de 'donde/. As before, the Spanish spelling system is admirably consistent: it doesn't spell the difference between [d] and [ð] (both are spelled *d*) because they do not contrast.

The differences in phonological organization between English and Spanish reflect a different division of phonetic space. Suppose we construe phonetic space as made up of multiple dimensions. We place [d] at the center of this space, and in different directions show [ð] as differing from [d] minimally in its fricative character; [ɾ] differing from [d] in having short, weak closure; and [t] differing minimally from [d] in voicing:

(28)   [t]

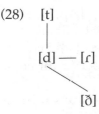

      [d] — [ɾ]

            [ð]

The phones of this phonetic space are grouped into phonemes differently by Spanish and English, as shown below:

(29)   *Spanish*   *English*

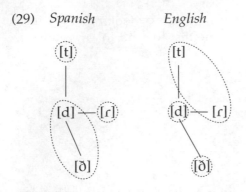

The dotted lines surround groups of sounds that fail to contrast, and thus form single phonemes in the language in question. English has /d/, /ð/, and /t/, with the latter having two allophones [t] and [ɾ]. Spanish has /t/, /ɾ/, and /d/, with the latter having two allophones [d] and [ð]. The chart is intended to show that the sound systems of languages can differ in their **phonological organization**, as well as in the sounds that they contain. In principle, we could imagine two languages that had exactly the same sounds, but a radically different phonological organization. This would happen if the two languages selected different phonetic distinctions to be contrastive vs. non-contrastive. Using the phonemic method, we would analyze two such languages as having the same set of sounds, grouped into phonemes in two different ways.

12.4 Phonemic Analysis

Linguists have developed a number of procedures for conducting phonemic analysis systematically. None of these procedures is infallible, but they are usually fairly helpful.

12.4.1 Minimal pairs

One procedure in phonemic analysis is to look for **minimal pairs**. These are defined as two different words that differ in exactly one sound, in the same place in the word. For example, *sip* [sɪp] and *zip* [zɪp] in English form a minimal pair for the phonemes /s/ and /z/. *Sill* [sɪl] and *zeal* [zil] are not a minimal pair, because their vowels differ. *Seal* [sil] and *eels* [ilz] are not a minimal pair because the /s/ and /z/ occur in different locations.

Two sounds that appear in a minimal pair are almost always distinct phonemes. In the English example just given, [z] could not be an allophone of [s] (or vice versa), because replacing one for the other results in a different word.

Finding a minimal pair serves as a kind of miniature scientific experiment. A common method of scientific experimentation is to arrange two sets of conditions that are identical except in one respect. If the outcomes for the two conditions are consistently different, you can be fairly confident that it was the varying factor that was responsible. Thus, if ['pita] and ['piɾa] are said to be different words by Spanish speakers (and they are), you can be fairly confident that [t] and [ɾ] are the responsible factor, and therefore that they contrast.

Find minimal pairs for the following sounds: [i] vs. [e], [p] vs. [b], [θ] vs. [ð], [v] vs. [u].	**EXERCISE** **12.1**

The **absence** of a minimal pair does not prove much. Often, a language will lack minimal pairs for a pair of relatively rare phonemes simply by accident. (Test this by trying to locate a minimal pair for /ʒ/ vs. /ð/ in English; both are infrequent.)

An obvious generalization of the minimal pair is the minimal triplet, quadruplet, etc. Often, selecting a good 'frame' or phonological context will make it possible to justify quite a bit of the phonemic inventory of a language.

A notation that is commonly used for such frames is to place the environment sounds on either side of an underlined blank, which represents the sound being manipulated in the pair, quadruplet, etc. Thus for American English vowels, the frame /h ____ d/ gets all but /e/ and /ɔɪ/, though admittedly some of the words are a bit forced:

(30)   heed   [hid]   who'd   [hud]
       hid   [hɪd]   hood   [hʊd]
                          hoed   [hod]
       head   [hɛd]   HUD   [hʌd]
       had   [hæd]   hod   [had]

               hide   [haɪd]   how'd   [haʊd]
               heard   [hr̩d]

For the missing sounds /e/ and /ɔɪ/, it is easy to imagine that 'hade' and 'hoyd' COULD be words; their absence from the English lexicon is essentially an accident.

12.4.2 Complementary distribution

Minimal pairs constitute evidence that sounds are phonologically distinct in a language. Consider next how we can show that two sounds are **not** distinct. A fairly reliable method is to show that distribution of the sounds does not overlap. That is, once you know that Sound #1 occurs only in a certain environment, and Sound #2 occurs in a completely different environment, then it would be impossible for the difference between the two ever to be contrastive; that is, to be the sole element distinguishing words from each other. In such cases, the crucial conditioning environments will always be different.

(31)   Two sounds X and Y are said to be in **complementary distribution** if Y never occurs in any of the phonetic environments in which X occurs.

By the reasoning just given, two sounds that are in complementary distribution are likely to be allophones of the same phoneme.

To give an example: alveolar [l] and velarized/dental [ɫ] in English, discussed above under (10–11), (20–21), are in complementary distribution: [ɫ] occurs only before [θ], and alveolar [l] occurs elsewhere (roughly speaking). Thus we can predict for any given environment which version of /l/ we will get, and we conclude that [l] and [ɫ] are allophones of the same phoneme.

Locating minimal pairs and determining complementary distribution are the two most straightforward procedures available for phonemic analysis. Note that they work in opposite directions: minimal pairs help to determine that two sounds form separate phonemes, while complementary distribution helps determine when two sounds are allophones of the same phoneme.

12.4.3   Near-minimal pairs

There are cases in which it is impossible to find minimal pairs for a phoneme. This probably occurs more frequently in languages with long words and large phoneme inventories. But even in English there appear to be cases where, at least for some dialects, a minimal pair cannot be found.

We conducted a computer dictionary search for minimal pairs for English /ð/ and /ʒ/, and found only three plausible candidates:

(32)   bathe   ['beð]   vs.   beige   ['beʒ]
       leather   ['lɛðɾ]   vs.   leisure   ['lɛʒɾ]
       seethe   ['sið]   vs.   siege   ['siʒ]

However, for all three [ʒ] words, the pronunciation varies by dialect: there are many speakers who have ['bedʒ] for *beige*, ['liʒɾ] or ['lɛʒʊr] for *leisure*, and ['sidʒ] for *siege*. In a dialect that employs these latter pronunciations for all three words, there are presumably no minimal pairs for [ð] vs. [ʒ].

Despite this, there is no way that [ð] and [ʒ] could be allophones of the same phoneme, even in these dialects. If they were allophones, we would expect that we could locate the RULES that determine which allophone occurs where. But a moment's reflection will show that there could be no such rules.

This is shown by the existence of NEAR-MINIMAL pairs, which can be defined as pairs which would be minimal except for some quite irrelevant difference. Here are some near-minimal pairs for /ð/ vs. /ʒ/:

(33) tether   ['tɛðr̩]   vs.   pleasure   ['plɛʒr̩]
                             or   measure   ['mɛʒr̩]
      neither   ['niðr̩]   vs.   seizure   ['siʒr̩]
      lather   ['læðr̩]   vs.   azure   ['æʒr̩]
      heathen   ['hiðən]   vs.   adhesion   [æd'hiʒən]
      smoothen ['smuðən]   vs.   illusion   [ɪ'luʒən]
                             or   intrusion   [ɪn'truʒən]
                             or   fusion   ['fjuʒən]

This list shows that the phonetic environment has little to do with whether [ð] or [ʒ] occurs – there is no CONSISTENT factor that could determine which phone appears. Any effort to find the rules that determine the appearance of [ð] vs. [ʒ] would have to make use of a completely arbitrary collection of 'environments' for these phones. If the rules cannot be found, then an analysis that claims that [ð] and [ʒ] are allophones cannot be justified.

It is also easy to imagine that if a new word came into English that created a true minimal pair (say, 'hesion' to go with *heathen*), such a word would readily be accepted. It is logical, then, to assume that /ð/ and /ʒ/ are separate phonemes, and that (for some dialects) no fully minimal pairs happen to be available. The near-minimal pairs suffice to show this.

12.4.4   Establishing complementary distribution from data

Suppose we are given raw phonetic data from a given language, and hope to extract from the data the system of phonemes and their allophonic patterning. In practice, this is a very large job, but for pedagogical purposes we can consider just small parts of a phonology at a time.

Assume, then, that the language under focus is Maasai (Nilotic, spoken in Kenya and Tanzania), and our focus is on the following set of sounds: [p, t, k, b, d, g, β, ð, ɣ]. The last three of these are voiced fricatives: [β] is bilabial, [ð] dental, and [ɣ] velar. Below are 63 words containing these sounds.

(34)   1.   [ailap]   'to hate'
       2.   [aret]   'to help'

3.	[arup]	'to heap up'
4.	[asip]	'to speak truly'
5.	[ɓarːiɣoi]	'reddish brown'
6.	[ɓaða]	'dangerous'
7.	[ɗalut]	'mischievous'
8.	[ɗiɣai]	'elsewhere'
9.	[ɗorːop]	'short'
10.	[emɓiðir]	'female wart hog'
11.	[emaɲaða]	'warriors' village'
12.	[embiʃan]	'bravery'
13.	[emburuo]	'smoke'
14.	[enɗaraða]	'thunder'
15.	[enɗuβai]	'sisal'
16.	[eŋʄirut]	'silent-feminine'
17.	[eŋʄoː]	'small chest'
18.	[enaiβoʃa]	'Naivasha Lake'
19.	[endaːraða]	'fight each other'
20.	[endorop]	'bribe him'
21.	[endulelei]	'sodom apple'
22.	[enduβeiðai]	'Taveta woman'
23.	[eŋgamaniɣi]	'name of age-set'
24.	[eŋgila]	'garment-diminutive'
25.	[eŋgiruðoðo]	'fright'
26.	[eŋgoː]	'advise him'
27.	[eŋoɣi]	'sin'
28.	[ilarak]	'murderers'
29.	[ilkeːk]	'trees'
30.	[ilpaβit]	'hairs'
31.	[iltoːi]	'barrel'
32.	[imɓok]	'you detain'
33.	[imbala]	'papers'
34.	[imbaɣiβak]	'you are restless'
35.	[imbok]	'you clean ceremonially'
36.	[indai]	'you-plural'
37.	[ijːoːk]	'we'
38.	[kaɣe]	'but'
39.	[keɗianje]	'left side'
40.	[keβer]	'heaven'
41.	[kiɓiroðo]	'stunted'
42.	[koɣoː]	'grandmother'
43.	[olɗiret]	'pack saddle'
44.	[olɗuɣa]	'shop'
45.	[olʄilaða]	'room'
46.	[olʃiβet]	'stake'

47.	[olkila]	'garment'
48.	[olkiɣuei]	'thorn'
49.	[olporːor]	'age set'
50.	[olpul]	'slaughtering place'
51.	[olpurɗa]	'meat preserved in fat'
52.	[olpurkel]	'dry steppes'
53.	[oltaː]	'lamp'
54.	[oltulet]	'gourd in its natural state'
55.	[oltuli]	'buttock'
56.	[paɗan]	'skilled in shooting'
57.	[poɣira]	'all'
58.	[pus]	'light colored'
59.	[sarkin]	'intermarriage taboo'
60.	[taruɓini]	'binoculars'
61.	[tasat]	'disabled'
62.	[tisila]	'sift it'
63.	[tiʃila]	'scrutinize it'

The first thing to notice about this problem is that there is an additional series of stops: /ɓ ɗ ʄ ɠ/. These are voiced implosives, made by forming a slight vacuum in the mouth just before release. These form a separate series of phonemes in Maasai, as can be shown by minimal and near-minimal pairs such as the following:

(35) 35. [imbok]   'you clean ceremonially'
vs. 32. [imɓok] 'you detain'

7.   [ɗalut] 'mischievous'
vs. 61. [tasat] 'disabled'

26.   [eŋgoː] 'advise him'
vs. 17. [enʄoː] 'small chest'

41.   [kiɓiroðo] 'stunted'
vs. 40. [keβer]   'heaven'

Having established this, we will ignore the implosives henceforth.

Here is a (rather painstaking) procedure for examining the target sounds in the data. For each sound, we compile all of the contexts in which it appears. Since the conditioning environment for allophones is usually (though not always) found in the immediately preceding and following segments, these should be included in the chart.

Here is one word as it is incorporated into the chart: #5, [ɓarːiɣoi] 'reddish brown' contains the target sound [ɣ]. This sound is preceded by [i] and followed by [o]. Recall that an underscore can be used as a placeholder for a sound of interest in a particular frame or context. We therefore add to our chart the following entry, in a column headed [ɣ]:

(36) [ɣ]
        / i ____ o (5)

This chart entry may be read '[ɣ] occurs where preceded by [u] and followed by [o], in example (5)'.

Sometimes the target sound is the initial or final segment in the word. In that case, the chart should include a bracket of the type]_word to designate this environment:

(37) [k]
        / oː ____]_word (37)

This may be read '[k] occurs where preceded by [oː] and word-final'.

One then continues through the whole set of data in this way. If this is done for the VELAR sounds only, one gets the following:

(38) [k]   [g]   [ɣ]
        / [_word ____ a (38)   / ŋ ____ a (23)   / a ____ e (38)
        / [_word ____ e (39, 40)   / ŋ ____ i (24, 25)   / a ____ i (34)
        / [_word ____ i (41)   / ŋ ____ o (26)   / i ____ a (8)
        / [_word ____ o (42)   / i ____ i (23)
        / l ____ e   (29)   / i ____ o (5)
        / l ____ i   (47)   / i ____ u (48)
        / l ____ i   (48)   / o ____ i (27, 57)
        / r ____ e   (52)   / o ____ i (57)
        / r ____ i   (59)   / o ____ o (42)
        / a ____]_word (28)   / u ____ a (44)
        / a ____]_word (34)
        / e ____]_word (29)
        / o ____]_word (32)
        / o ____]_word (35)
        / oː ____]_word (37)

At this point, one inspects the data in hopes of locating general patterns. For these data, notice that [g] may occur only when the sound [ŋ] immediately precedes it. Further, and crucially, the sounds [k] and [ɣ] are NEVER preceded by [ŋ]. It thus looks likely that [g] is just one allophone of a phoneme, because it has such a highly restricted distribution. The preceding [ŋ] is likely to be the context that requires this allophone.

Inspecting the third column, we see another particular property: all cases of [ɣ] are surrounded by vowels. As before, this is not the case with the other candidate phones. The pattern suggests that [ɣ] is another allophone of the phoneme that includes [g]. In particular, we now know that at least [g] and [ɣ] are in complementary distribution.

Inspection of the [k] column shows no particularly interesting property: [k] may occur initially, after [r] or [l], and in final position. The only really important property here is that these various environments do NOT include the environments for [ɣ] or [g].

We have established then, that [k], [ɣ], and [g] are in complementary distribution: none occurs when any of the others may occur. The environments are shown in (39):

(39) [g]: / ŋ _____
      [ɣ]: / V _____ V   where V stands for any vowel
      [k]: / elsewhere

It is reasonable to suppose that, since [k] occurs in a wide variety of contexts, it is the normal, unperturbed member of the phoneme, which we set up as the underlying representation. The phones [g] and [ɣ] are particular allophones resulting from the action of phonological rules applying in particular environments.

Thus, we can state the phonological analysis of these sounds as follows:

(40) /k/ is a phoneme of Maasai.

     /k/ Spirantization: k → ɣ / [+vowel] _____ [+vowel]
     That is: /k/ is realized as [ɣ] when between vowels.

     Post-Nasal Voicing: k → g / ŋ _____
     That is: /k/ is realized as [g] after [ŋ].

We have just conducted a phonemic analysis in its most explicit (and tedious) form: collecting the environments in which phones occur, establishing complementary distribution, locating environments for the various allophones, and expressing phonological rules that derive various allophones in the appropriate environments. It is possible, for many people and in many cases, to skip steps. If you have a knack for this sort of thing, phoneme problems can be solved by inspection, without the tedious charting of all environments. More important, linguists who have seen many cases of phonemicization have usually seen the very same rules before, or something like them, in other languages. Sounds in all languages respond to the same considerations of articulatory ease and perceptual distinctness, so phonologies often evolve in parallel ways. Languages which realize /k/ as [ɣ] between vowels include Taiwanese, Ewe (Ghana), and Tümpisa Shoshone (Death Valley, California). Languages that realize [k] as [g] after a nasal sound like [ŋ] include Modern Greek, Leurbost Gaelic (Scotland), and Waorani (Amazon basin, Peru).

12.5   Natural Classes

We have not yet considered six of the nine Maasai sounds we set out to analyze, namely [p, b, β] and [t, ð, d]. Before proceeding, it is useful to arrange the relevant sounds into phonetic charts. Ideally, we would do this for all of the sounds of Maasai, but as an example (41) will do:

(41)

	Bilabial	Dental	Velar
voiceless stops	p	t	k
plain voiced stops	b	d	g
voiced implosive stops	ɓ	ɗ	ɠ
voiced fricatives	β	ð	ɣ
voiced nasals	m	n	ŋ

If we sort out the target sounds in the way we did before, we will get the following:

(42)   [p]
/ [word ____ a (56)
/ [word ____ o (57)
/ [word ____ u (58)
/ l ____ a   (30)
/ l ____ o   (49)
/ l ____ u   (50, 51, 52)
/ a ____]word (1)
/ i ____]word (4)
/ o ____]word (9, 20)
/ u ____]word (3)

[b]
/ m ____ a (33, 34)
/ m ____ i (12)
/ m ____ o (35)
/ m ____ u (13)

[β]
/ a ____ i (30)
/ e ____ e (40)
/ i ____ a (34)
/ i ____ e (46)
/ i ____ o (18)
/ u ____ a (15)
/ u ____ e (22)

[t]
/ [word ____ a (60, 61)
/ [word ____ i (62, 63)
/ l ____ a   (53)
/ l ____ o   (31)
/ l ____ u   (54, 55)
/ a ____]word (61)
/ e ____]word (2, 43, 46, 54)
/ i ____]word (30)
/ u ____]word (7, 16)
/ u ____]word (16)
/ u ____]word (16)

[d]
/ n ____ a (19, 36)
/ n ____ o (20)
/ n ____ u (21, 22)

[ð]
/ a ____ a (6, 11, 14, 19, 45)
/ i ____ a (22)
/ i ____ i (10)
/ o ____ o (25, 41)
/ u ____ o (25)

If you consider both the phonetic chart and the list of environments, you can see that the distribution of the bilabial and dental sounds is in complete parallel with the velars: voiced stops appear after nasal consonants, voiced fricatives occur between vowels, and voiceless stops occur elsewhere.

Thus, although we are dealing with three phonemes and nine allophones, we do not need a large number of rules to handle the data. Rather, we can use **phonetic features** to write general rules that cover all three phonemes at once. The specific analysis would be as follows:

(43) **Phonemes**: /p/ /t/ /k/
    Phonological rules:
    Spirantization:

$$\begin{bmatrix} +\text{stop} \\ -\text{voice} \end{bmatrix} \rightarrow \begin{bmatrix} +\text{voice} \\ -\text{stop} \\ +\text{fricative} \end{bmatrix} / [+\text{vowel}] \_\_\_\_ [+\text{vowel}]$$

That is: a voiceless stop is realized as the corresponding voiced fricative when surrounded by vowels.

    Post-Nasal Voicing:
    [+stop] → [+voice] / [+nasal] ____

That is: a voiceless stop is realized as the corresponding voiced stop when it follows a nasal consonant.

Let us make explicit how features are used in rules: if a feature occurs on the right side of the arrow, that feature is changed whenever the rule applies. But ALL OTHER FEATURES REMAIN UNALTERED. Thus, if we are considering a sequence like /mp/, and apply Post-Nasal Voicing, the [−voice] of the /p/ is changed to [+voice], so that /p/ is altered to [b]. But the features [+bilabial] and [+stop] remain unaltered. Likewise, when /nt/ becomes [nd], the voicing of the /t/ is changed from minus to plus, but the features [+alveolar] and [+stop] remain unaltered, so that we get [d]. In this way, we can express rules that alter whole classes of segments (such as all the voiceless stops) in parallel. The features therefore permit a simpler and more general analysis than would be available if all the allophones of each phoneme were derived separately.

To illustrate the analysis, we can (partially) reduce Maasai words to phonemic representations, and derive the actual phonetic forms using the phonological rules. For example, 34, [imbayiβak], 'you are restless' has the phonemic form and phonological derivation given in (44):

(44) /impakipak/ phonemic form
    imbakipak   Post-Nasal Voicing
    imbayiβak   Spirantization
    [imbayiβak]   phonetic form

The fact that the stop phonemes of Maasai vary in parallel fashion is not an accident. The same phenomenon shows up in a great number of languages. Here are some examples we've already covered of how rules apply to classes of sounds:

(45)   **Vowel Shortening in English**: The shortening of /e/ to [ĕ] before voiceless consonants in English is not unique to /e/: in fact, all vowels of English are shortened in this environment. Examples: *coat* [kŏt] vs. *code* [kod], *lap* [lăp] vs. *lab* [læb], etc.
Nasalization in English: In English all vowels are nasalized before nasals, not just /ɛ/ (recall *ten* [tẽn] vs. *Ted* [tɛd] above). Examples: *bin* [bĩn] vs. *bid* [bɪd], *cam* [kæ̃m] vs. *cab* [kæb].
Spirantization in Spanish: Spanish not only has [ð] as a post-vowel allophone of /d/ (section 12.3.4), but also [β] as a post-vowel allophone of /b/ and [ɣ] as a post-vowel allophone of /g/. Examples: /'lobo/ ['loβo] 'wolf', /'lago/ ['laɣo] 'lake'.

The general lesson that we learn from these examples (and countless others) is this: PHONOLOGICAL RULES ARE BASED ON PHONETIC FEATURES. This general principle has three specific subcases.

The SET OF SOUNDS A RULE APPLIES TO is almost always a set of sounds that share a particular phonetic feature or set of features. For example, the Spirantization Rule of Spanish applies to all and only the voiced stops, characterized as [+stop, +voice].

Rules usually change only one or two features of a sound, rather than making massive alterations. For example, the rules we wrote for Maasai alter only voicing and the stop/fricative distinction.

The SOUNDS APPEARING IN THE ENVIRONMENT OF A RULE are almost always a set of sounds that share a particular phonetic feature or features. For example, the rule of English that shortens vowels applies before the complete set of consonants in English that are voiceless, or [−voice].

A **natural class** of sounds is any complete set of sounds in a given language that share the same value for a feature or set of features. For example, /m/, /n/, and /ŋ/ in Maasai and in English form a natural class because they constitute the complete set of sounds that share the feature [nasal]. Likewise, /p/, /t/, and /k/ form a natural class in Maasai and in English because they constitute all the [+stop, −voiced] sounds of the language. However, /m/ and /n/ are NOT a natural class in either Maasai or English, because each language has a third nasal /ŋ/. To form the natural class [nasal] in these languages, one must include all three nasals.

With the notion of natural class, we can make a more specific claim about phonological rules. Rather than saying that 'phonological rules are based on phonetic properties,' we can say that PHONOLOGICAL RULES ARE BASED ON NATURAL CLASSES. That is, in the great majority of instances, the segments that undergo a rule or appear in the environment of a rule form a natural class in the language in question.

12.6 The Psychological Reality of the Phoneme

The material above has covered a fairly mechanical procedure for extracting a phonemic analysis from the data of a language. However, our goal in this book is not simply to contrive useful procedures for arranging linguistic data; rather, we wish to characterize the knowledge of language internalized by speakers. We can ask: is it legitimate to suppose that speakers actually produce and perceive language (at an unconscious level) in terms of phonemes? A fair amount of experimentation has been conducted on this issue, and the practical experience of linguists over many years likewise seems relevant.

We will discuss this issue in three parts. Recall that the most fundamental phenomenon concerns phonetic differences that are **contrastive** vs. **noncontrastive**. Beyond this, there is the analytical effort by linguists to arrange and codify the patterns of contrast in a language into a single system of phonemes. Lastly, there is the system of phonological rules which governs the arrangement of noncontrastive phonetic properties.

12.6.1 Audibility of fine distinctions

There seems to be little doubt that contrastiveness plays a major role in the perceptions of language users. The auditory processing apparatus seems to be specially 'tuned', through experience, to be able to extract precisely those phonetic distinctions that are phonemic in the perceiver's own language.

The practical experience of linguists and other language users attests to this. Suppose we are dealing with two sounds that are phonetically rather close to each other. Suppose further that the two sounds are heard by two different listeners. For listener A, the two sounds are contrastive, serving to distinguish words in her language. The two sounds also occur in Listener B's language, but are allophones, and are not contrastive. What usually happens in such a situation is this: A can hear the difference between the two sounds with perfect ease, but B has tremendous difficulty.

One of the authors of this text can attest to this, having on various occasions played the role of both A and B. Here are some examples.

On one occasion when he was Listener B, A was a speaker of a dialect of Bengali in which dental stops (tongue tip touches upper teeth) contrast with alveolar stops (tongue tip touches alveolar ridge), as in the following minimal and near-minimal pairs:

(46)   [t̪an]   '(vocal) tune'   [tan]   'pull!'
      [sat̪]   'seven'   [sat]   'sixty'
      [d̪an]   'donation'   [dan]   'right (hand)'
      [d̪in]   'day'   [dim]   'egg'

B found that, despite extensive practice, he was unable to learn to hear the Bengali dental/alveolar distinction. This amused A, who as a native speaker found the distinction to be utterly obvious.

An important fact concerning this case is that the native language of B, a variety of American English, **does** include both dental and alveolar consonants. The dentals occur as allophones of an alveolar series, and are derived by a rule that replaces alveolars by dentals before dental fricatives (a generalized version of the rules for /n/ and /l/ dentalization; see (7) and (20)):

(47)   eighth   [eɪt̪θ]   ate the . . .   [eɪt̪ ðə]
      would think   [wʊd̪ θɪŋk]   said this   [sɛd̪ ðɪs]
      tenth   [tɛn̪θ]   in the . . .   [ɪn̪ ðə]

The crucial point is that B's inability to hear the dental/alveolar distinction is not due to a lack of experience with dentals. Rather, it is because B's native language does not include a phonemic distinction between alveolars and dentals.

The same author has also played the role of A, as he is a native speaker of a dialect of English that contrasts /a/ with the lower-mid back rounded vowel /ɔ/. In this dialect, there are minimal pairs such as those in (48):

(48)   caught   [kɔt]   cot   [kat]
      Kaun   [kɔn]   con   [kan]
      paw   [pɔ]   Pa   [pa]
      auto   ['ɔɾo]   Otto   ['aɾo]

This dialect is spoken by perhaps half of the American population, and coexists with a historically innovating dialect in which all occurrences of the old phoneme /ɔ/ have been replaced by /a/. Thus in the new dialect, the words above appear as:

(49)   caught   [kat]   cot   [kat]
      Kaun   [kan]   con   [kan]
      paw   [pa]   Pa   [pa]
      auto   ['aɾo]   Otto   ['aɾo]

Speakers of this newer dialect often claim that hearing this distinction is quite difficult for them. In contrast, speakers of the older dialect, which makes a distinction, feel that it would be very strange NOT to be able to hear it. Just like the dental/alveolar distinction for Bengali speakers, it is completely obvious for them.

Such stories are easily multiplied. Apparently, the contrastiveness of two phonetically similar sounds leads speakers of a language or dialect that has the contrast to develop a refined ability to discriminate the two. Speakers of a language in which the two sounds do not contrast have no such ability, and in general can hear the distinction only with difficulty, if at all.

12.6.2 The notion of 'same sound'

On the whole, linguists have found that speakers usually believe that two allophones of the same phoneme are the 'same sound', despite the phonetic difference between them. Here are some examples.

The words *ten* and *Ted* have phonetically different vowels. In *ten*, the phoneme /ɛ/ occurs before a nasal sound, and is therefore eligible for a phonological rule which we express as follows:

(50) **Vowel Nasalization**
      [+vowel] → [+nasal] / _____ $\begin{bmatrix} \text{+consonant} \\ \text{+nasal} \end{bmatrix}$

That is: a vowel is realized as nasalized when it precedes a nasal consonant. The application of the rule is shown in (51):

(51) *ten*: /tɛn/   *Ted*: /tɛd/   phonemic forms
             ɛ̃   _____   Vowel Nasalization
           [tɛ̃n]   [tɛd]   phonetic forms

Now, in our experience, English speakers are perfectly willing to say that *ten* and *Ted* have 'the same vowel'. Indeed, the difference between the two is felt to be subtle, and observable only with careful attention.

For this phonetic difference, it is useful to compare the behavior of (for example) French speakers. Miminal pairs show that in French, nasal vowels are phonemically distinct from oral vowels:

(52) [mɛ] 'but'   vs.   [mɛ̃] 'hand'
      [tʁɛ] 'very'   vs.   [tʁɛ̃] 'train'

For French speakers, it is quite plain that [ɛ] and [ɛ̃] are different sounds. The crucial difference between a French speaker and an English speaker in this respect is the phonemic structure of the two languages: corresponding nasal and oral vowels in French count as different sounds because they are different phonemes; they count as the same sound in English because they are allophones of the same phoneme.

We can conclude that, to a rough approximation, if two phones are allophones of the same phoneme, a speaker of the language in question will feel that they are the same sound.

But we must supplement this conclusion with certain reservations about conscious awareness of sounds in general. It would appear that it is the natural state of humankind to be completely unaware that languages have sounds at all. That is, the system of phonemes often exists in the mind of the speaker only at a completely unconscious level. What leads speakers to become consciously aware of their phonemes is typically the process of learning to read and write in an alphabetic system, since this focuses the learner's attention on the sounds that correspond to the letters.

We have often encountered students who fluently speak a language for whose phonemes they have no awareness: for instance, a student who grew up speaking one language at home and was educated in another language at school; or a student who speaks a language (such as Chinese) whose writing system is not alphabetic. For such students, studying linguistics is often the first route into bringing phonemes and other structure in their language into conscious awareness.

To revise the original claim, then, we are saying that once speakers have been made aware of the existence of speech sounds in their language, they will naturally tend to consider allophones of the same phoneme as counting as the same sound.

12.6.3   Foreign accents

Another source of evidence bears on the psychological reality, not of the phonemes themselves, but of the system of **phonological rules** that apply to them. This is the behavior of speakers who are attempting to pronounce the sounds of a language new to them. The usual result is a rather poor imitation of the second language. A strong foreign accent can often persist even after years of practice.

If one examines a foreign accent closely, it turns out to be quite systematic: it is the cumulative effect of a large number of specific distortions, applying to particular sounds. These distortions are largely the result of attempting to pronounce a second language using the phonology of one's native language.

One can consider a phonology as specifying, in part, the set of things that are pronounceable in a given language. This set consists of the legal sequences of phonemes, realized as the appropriate allophones for their context. Anything outside this (very large) set will necessarily involve one of three properties:

A sequence can be phonologically illegal in a language because it contains an **illegal phoneme**. For example, any utterance containing the voiced uvular fricative [ʁ], a voiced aspirated stop, or a front rounded vowel is illegal in English, since these sounds do not occur in the language.

A sequence can also be phonologically illegal because it corresponds to an **illegal sequence** of phonemes (even where the phonemes themselves are legal). Thus, [bnɪk] consists of four English phonemes, arranged in an order which English phonology does not permit.

Finally, a sequence can be phonologically illegal in a language because it corresponds to an **impossible distribution of allophones**. For example, [fil], with a non-velarized [l], is illegal in English, because English has an allophonic rule forcing the use of velarized [ɫ] in word-final position, as in the correct pronunciation [fiɫ] 'feel'.

If a word of a foreign language is phonologically illegal in English, for any of these three reasons, it will typically not be pronounced correctly, at least without practice.

Here are some examples. The German proper name *Gödel* is phonetically ['gøːdəl], with a long upper mid front rounded vowel. English has no /øː/ phoneme, so English speakers tend to substitute the acoustically similar English phoneme /ɹ/, and thus pronounce *Gödel* as *girdle*. French *thé* 'tea' is phonetically [t̪e]. Many English speakers speak a dialect in which the monophthong [e] does not occur; the diphthong [eɪ] occurs instead. These speakers must fight the tendency to substitute their own [eɪ] for French [e].

These are cases in which foreign accents arise from substituting native phonemes for phonetically similar foreign ones. We also get cases of substitution of native allophones for phonetically similar foreign sounds. Such substitutions produce an output that is phonologically legal in the native language, by obeying the phonological rules. For example, a typical English mispronunciation of French *thé* is [tʰeɪ], with an aspirated [tʰ], since that is the allophone of /t/ that occurs word-initially in English. Likewise, *Gödel* as pronounced by English speakers tends to receive the velarized [ɫ] allophone of /l/, which further mutilates it to ['gɹdəɫ].

French *huitre* [ɥit̪ʁ] 'oyster' contains three non-English sounds: the high front rounded glide [ɥ], the voiceless dental stop [t̪], and the voiced uvular fricative [ʁ]. This word is likely to trigger the following substitutions: English /w/ is substituted for French /ɥ/; the back rounded glide is apparently the best available approximation for the front rounded glide of French. English alveolar /t/ is the best phonemic approximation to French dental /t̪/; and English alveolar /r/ is the best phonemic approximation to French uvular /ʁ/. Moreover, even with these substitutions, the resulting sequence /witr/ is illegal in English, since words cannot end in /tr/. This is most commonly fixed by adding an unstressed schwa vowel, giving ['witrə].

Thus, to a greater or lesser extent, learners of foreign languages are prisoners of their own phonologies. Lifelong experience leads them strongly to favor the legal phonological sequences of their native language, which may be defined as the sequences of allophones that are derived from legal sequences of native phonemes. The psychological reality of the constraints of the native phonology becomes blatant when one sees them determine the outcome of the native speaker's attempts to pronounce a second language.

Naturally, individuals differ greatly in their ability to overcome these tendencies; in other words, to assimilate a novel phonology. In principle, we believe that explicit knowledge of the phonology of both native and learned language can be of help to foreign language learners in achieving a correct accent.

12.7 The Criterion of Phonetic Similarity

With the introduction of a criterion of psychological reality into phonological analysis, we find that in a number of cases, phonemicization cannot be done in purely mechanical fashion, as was done in the Maasai example above. Here, we will consider some cases in which merely collecting and arranging the non-contrasting phonetic segments is insufficient.

A simple case arises in English, involving the sounds [h] and [ŋ]. [h] occurs at the beginnings of words and before stressed syllabic sounds, as in the examples below:

(53) hill   [hɪl]   ahead   [əˈhɛd]
      high   [haɪ]   prohibit [proˈhɪbɪt]
      how   [haʊ]   behold   [biˈhold]
      Horatio   [həˈreʃio]   rehearse [riˈhr̩s]

The sound [ŋ] occurs at the ends of words, before consonants, and between syllabic sounds of which the second is stressless:

(54) sing   [sɪŋ]   sink   [sɪŋk]   singer   [ˈsɪŋr̩]
      pang   [pæŋ]   anger [ˈæŋgr̩]   Singapore [ˈsɪŋəpor]
      running   [ˈrʌnɪŋ]   hangs [hæŋz]   dinghy   [ˈdɪŋi]
      Langley   [ˈlæŋli]

There are no cases of [h] occurring at ends of words, or before consonants, or between syllabic sounds of which the second is stressless. Likewise, there are no cases of [ŋ] occurring at the beginning of a word, or before a stressed vowel. Therefore, [h] and [ŋ] do not contrast. Given the phonological patterning of English, there is no way that they could distinguish words from each other, because they occur in completely different contexts. Since they do not contrast, should we regard them as allophones of a single phoneme?

The traditional answer of linguists is no, for the following reason. When two sounds are allophones of the same phoneme, they will be felt by native speakers to be the same sound. This is plainly not the case for [ŋ] and [h]. It seems appropriate here to say that /h/ and /ŋ/ are separate phonemes of English, and that for accidental reasons (having to do with where it is legal for them to occur), they are unable to form contrasts. In other words, we reject the idea that phonemes can be established purely on distributional grounds; rather, if we are to posit that two sounds are allophones of a single phoneme, they must be related to each other phonetically in a sensible way.

A similar example makes the same point. By reexamining the distributions of Maasai [p, b, t, d, k, g] given above under (38) and (42), you should convince yourself of the following facts:

[p] and [d] are in complementary distribution.
[t] and [g] are in complementary distribution.
[k] and [b] are in complementary distribution.

This follows, since the voiced stops in Maasai always come after nasals, and the voiceless ones never do. We could imagine, then, a phonemic analysis of Maasai that grouped [p] and [d] together into the same phoneme, and similarly with [t]/[g], [k]/[b]. Such an analysis indeed works on distributional grounds, but would almost certainly fail as a means of capturing the intuitions of the native speaker, who sensibly regards the phonetically similar [t] and [d] as being the same sound, and similarly with [p]/[b], [k]/[g].

12.8   Contextually-Limited Contrast

We have thus far seen a rather simple conception of phonology: a language has a set of phonemes, plus a set of rules that force the appearance of the appropriate allophones of each phoneme in the appropriate context. Thus the division of labor is: distinctive information is the province of the phonemic representations, and non-distinctive information is the province of the rules.

Having gotten this far, we can now complicate matters a bit. Suppose the rules are not limited to manipulating non-distinctive information, but can also manipulate distinctive material. If this is so, what kind of phonology might appear? To see this, we will consider an example from English.

English is slightly unusual among languages in allowing words to end with a sequence of two stops, as in the following examples:

(55)   concept   ['kansɛpt]   contact   ['kɑntækt]
       jumped   [dʒʌmpt]   milked   [mɪlkt]
       rubbed   [rʌbd]   bagged   [bægd]

However, such clusters are strictly limited: the second of the stops must always be alveolar. Thus, there are no words in English like *['kansɛtp], *['kɑntætk], *[mɪlkp], *[bædg], or *[rʌdb]. Speakers of English immediately recognize such hypothetical words as ill-formed, and often regard them as hard to pronounce.

We can attribute these facts to a general phonological principle of English, formalized as follows:

(56)   *Alveolar Place Enforcement*
       [+stop] → [+alveolar] / [+stop] ____]$_{word}$

That is, in word-final position following a stop, all stops must be alveolar.

A property of this rule that is new here is that it has nothing to apply to: all the existing and possible words of English already obey it. Yet the rule is plainly a rule of English, since when we invent hypothetical exceptions they sound ill-formed. Thus, Alveolar Place Enforcement (or something with equivalent effect) is part of English speakers' knowledge of their language.

An important consequence of Alveolar Place Enforcement is that the basic place contrast in English stops (/p/ vs. /t/ vs. /k/, and /b/ vs. /d/ vs. /g/) is SUSPENDED in the relevant environment. Thus while English has many minimal triplets like those in (57):

(57)   pin   [pɪn]   vs.   tin   [tɪn]   vs.   kin   [kɪn]
       sap   [sæp]   vs.   sat   [sæt]   vs.   sack   [sæk]
       bill   [bɪl]   vs.   dill   [dɪl]   vs.   gill   [gɪl]
       bib   [bɪb]   vs.   bid   [bɪd]   vs.   big   [bɪg]

there are no minimal triplets like those in (58):

(58)   *[ækp]   vs.   [ækt]   vs.   *[ækk]
       *[dʒæbb]   vs.   [dʒæbd]   vs.   *[dʒæbg]

To put it differently: English uses a place contrast among stops to distinguish words, but it does not use this contrast in all contexts. This is what is meant by **contextually-limited contrast**.

Limited contrasts are perhaps the rule in phonology, not the exception. Many other contrasts of English, for instance, are contextually limited. Here are a couple of examples.

NASALS

English contrasts three places of articulation in nasals: /m/ vs. /n/ vs. /ŋ/. These can be justified by minimal triplets, such as *hum* [hʌm] vs. *Hun* [hʌn] vs. *hung* [hʌŋ]. However, at the beginning of a word, only /m/ and /n/ are possible: a phonological rule of English (and many other languages) forbids /ŋ/ from appearing word-initially.

OBSTRUENT VOICING

Recall that obstruents consist of the set stops + affricates + fricatives. In English, obstruents contrast for voicing, as is shown by many minimal pairs like:

(59)   pin   /pɪn/   vs.   bin   /bɪn/
      pat   /pæt/   vs.   pad   /pæd/
      chill   /tʃɪl/   vs.   Jill   /dʒɪl/
      bicker /'bɪkr̩/   vs.   bigger /'bɪgr̩/
      mace   /mes/   vs.   maze   /mez/

Consider, though, the words that END IN TWO OBSTRUENTS. In such cases, a phonological rule of English requires that the second obstruent must always agree in voicing with the first.

(60)   **Acceptable**   **Impossible**
      act   [ækt]   'acd'   *[ækd]
      clasp   [klæsp]   'clasb'   *[klæsb]

In other words, there is no voicing contrast in the particular environment 'word-finally, after an obstruent'. In this environment, the voicing of an obstruent is determined entirely by its left neighbor, so no contrast is possible.

In light of the phenomenon of limited contrast, we can reconsider the relation between rules and phonemic forms. Previously, we assumed a relation in which the rules were rather subservient: they simply provided the variants of the phonemes, which stood independent of the rules. Cases like these show a rather different view: the rules DEFINE WHAT IS PRONOUNCEABLE IN THE LANGUAGE. As a result, the phonemic forms must exist in compliance with the rules.

This general scheme of things shows up in two different ways. First, where the rules govern the distribution of noncontrastive information, then the phonetic realization of the phonemes varies, producing what we have called allophones. Second, where the rules govern the distribution of contrastive information, then the distribution of the phonemes will be limited: they may only occur where the rules allow them to, and we will get a contextually limited contrast. We will see a third consequence of this scheme below.

12.9 Variation

A truer picture of phonology results when we recognize that the phonetic forms speakers produce are subject to a great deal of variation. That is, a single phonemic representation can often give rise to quite a few different phonetic forms.

One way to describe such variation is to posit phonological rules that apply OPTIONALLY. An optional phonological rule can be suppressed, with the result that the input form is pronounceable, as one of the available options for speaking. For example, this appears to be true, at least in our speech, of the English rule of Flapping stated above under (23), which derives the flapped [ɾ] allophone of /t/ in words like *outer* ['aʊɾɹ̩], *attic* ['æɾɪk], and *catapult* ['kæɾəpʊlt]. These words, which are phonemically /'aʊtɹ̩/, attic /'ætɪk/, and /'kætəpʊlt/, can therefore be pronounced as ['aʊtɹ̩], ['ætɪk], and ['kætəpʊlt] or as ['aʊɾɹ̩], ['æɾɪk], and ['kæɾəpʊlt], depending on whether one applies the optional Flapping rule or not.

Here is another example of an optional rule, which is found in the dialect of many speakers of English in various northern US cities, such as Detroit and Buffalo. In this dialect, the vowel phoneme /æ/ has a diphthongal allophone we will transcribe as [ɛ̃ə̃]. Some basic data on the distribution of [ɛ̃ə̃] vs. [æ] are as follows:

(61)

	[æ]				[ɛ̃ə̃]	
lap	/læp/	[læp]		*man*	/mæn/	[mɛ̃ə̃n]
pal	/pæl/	[pæl]		*Spanish*	/'spænɪʃ/	['spɛ̃ə̃nɪʃ]
pack	/pæk/	[pæk]		*dance*	/dæns/	[dɛ̃ə̃ns]
lab	/læb/	[læb]				

As can be seen, the diphthongized allophone occurs before /n/, while the lower, monothongal allophone occurs elsewhere. Naturally enough, the diphthongized allophone is nasalized; this is the consequence of the Vowel Nasalization rule that appears above under (50).

Thus we can set up /æ/ as the basic form of the phoneme. Its diphthongal quality before /n/ derives from the following rule:

(62) */æ/ Diphthongization*
  æ → ɛə / _____ n
  That is, the phoneme /æ/ is realized as [ɛə] when it precedes /n/.

The nasality of the allophone is derived by Vowel Nasalization, as shown in (63):

(63) *ban:* /bæn/   phonemic form
           bɛən   /æ/ Diphthongization (62)
           bẽə̃n   Vowel Nasalization (50)
           [bẽə̃n]   phonetic form

However, the pronunciations given above for *man*, *Spanish*, and *dance* are in fact only one option; in the relevant dialect these words can also be pronounced [mæ̃n], [spæ̃nɪʃ], and [dæ̃ns]. Thus the rule of [æ] Diphthongization must be optional. Where it is not applied, the phonemic /æ/ emerges as [æ]. The phonological derivation is given in (64):

(64) *ban:* /bæn/   phonemic form
           NOT APPLIED   /æ/ Diphthongization
           bæ̃n   Vowel Nasalization
           [bæ̃n]   phonetic form

Not all phonological rules are optional. For example, the rule that assimilates basically alveolar /n/ to dental [n̪] before /θ/ is obligatory. To say the word *tenth*, for example, as [tɛnθ], with a true alveolar [n], is difficult and artificial. Vowel Nasalization is likewise obligatory: although [bẽə̃n] and [bæ̃n] are both options for *ban* (in the relevant dialect), *[bɛən] and *[bæn], with oral vowels, are not possible. Some English speakers may find that Flapping and/or /æ/ Diphthongization are obligatory in their speech.

Optional rules and speech style

When a language has an optional rule, it is usually (though not always) the case that the choice of whether to apply the rule or not is determined by the style of speech. In solemn or careful speech, application of optional rules is usually suppressed, while in casual or rapid speech, the rules usually apply. This can be seen clearly if you pick a sequence of words that allows for the application of more than one optional rule. For example, the phrase *tan attic* is phonemically /ˈtæn ˈætɪk/. It can undergo Flapping and [æ] Diphthongization (along with obligatory Vowel Nasalization) to become [ˈtẽə̃n ˈæɾɪk], a clearly casual pronunciation. Alternatively, Flapping and [æ] Diphthongization could be suppressed, yielding [ˈtæ̃n ˈætɪk], a solemn and careful pronunciation. There could also be intermediate variants, in which only one of the optional rules is suppressed.

In general, speakers command a broad range of speaking styles, of which they may only be dimly aware. This variation is amenable to phonological analysis: typically, there are particular optional phonological rules that apply with greater frequency (or derive more dramatically deviating outputs) when the speaker is in a more casual social context. Speakers tune their phonological styles unconsciously, so as to produce appropriate speech

SIDEBAR
12.4

Data collection in phonology

Phonological data is typically collected by fairly informal means: a linguist, armed with pencil and notebook, asks a native-speaker consultant to say various words and utterances, and the result is taken down in phonetic (or, where appropriate phonemic) transcription. This method is of little use in studying optional phonological rules. The problem is that the social context of pronouncing words for a linguist usually is a quite formal one, and speakers will usually give an interviewing linguist only their 'Sunday best'. Simply requesting speakers to speak casually may not help much, since speakers often have little conscious control over their speaking style.

An important approach toward solving this problem has been taken in the subfield of **sociolinguistics**, which studies (among other things) the phonological and grammatical phenomena which respond closely to the social context of speech. Sociolinguists examine phonological variation by observing speech in a variety of social contexts. For example, a sociolinguist might obtain fairly casual colloquial speech by recording on tape a conversation among adolescents who are close friends. After making a careful phonetic transcription of the tape, she might then examine the more formal speech styles of the same speakers by interviewing them one-on-one, by asking them to read certain passages, or (as an extreme) asking them to pronounce minimal pairs.

The great advantage of observing natural speech is that it removes the social context present in elicitation, permitting the full range of speech styles to emerge for observation.

behavior with different conversational partners. Casual speech, then, is not INHERENTLY 'sloppy' or 'incorrect'. Rather, it is usually calibrated to the situation. Choice of the wrong style will produce an impression of either slovenliness or pretentiousness, depending.

12.10   Phonology and its Connection to Morphology

Phonology interacts with morphology in intricate ways. This section assumes that you have read and studied chapter 2 and are therefore familiar with the notion of the morpheme and rules of morphology.

The central phenomenon to be covered here is that of **alternation**, which is defined as follows:

(65)   A morpheme **alternates** when it appears in different forms in different contexts.

Alternation normally results from an interaction of morphological and phonological rules. To show how alternation arises, we will first present some background material on the morphology and phonology of American English.

12.10.1   Alternations of English /t/-final stems

Here are some phonological rules of English, some repeated from earlier sections. The rule of **Preglottalization** derives the preglottalized allophones of /p, t, k/ (transcribed [ʔp, ʔt, ʔk]) when they occur in word-final position:

(66) **Preglottalization**

$$\begin{bmatrix} +\text{stop} \\ -\text{voice} \end{bmatrix} \rightarrow [+\text{preglottalized}] \ / \ \underline{\hspace{2em}}]_{\text{word}}$$

That is, a voiceless stop is realized as preglottalized when in final position.

Examples: cap   /kæp/   [kæʔp]
           hat   /hæt/   [hæʔt]
           hack /hæk/   [hæʔk]

The rule of Flapping realizes the /t/ phoneme as a flap [ɾ] in cases where it occurs between two syllabic sounds of which the second is stressless. We restate the rule here for convenience:

(67) **Flapping**

$$/t/ \rightarrow [ɾ] \ / \ [+\text{vowel}] \ \underline{\hspace{2em}} \begin{bmatrix} +\text{vowel} \\ -\text{stress} \end{bmatrix}$$

The /t/ phoneme is aspirated in a number of contexts. Roughly, the aspiration occurs when a voiceless stop precedes a stressed syllabic sound, but no /s/ precedes it.

(68) **Aspiration**

$$t \rightarrow [+\text{aspirated}] \ / \ X \ \underline{\hspace{2em}} \begin{bmatrix} +\text{vowel} \\ +\text{stressed} \end{bmatrix} \quad \text{condition: } X \neq /s/$$

Examples:

Tom	/tam/	['tʰam]	vs.	Atlas	/ætləs/	['ætləs]
tell	/tɛl/	['tʰɛl]		get	/gɛt/	['gɛt]
obtain	/əbteɪn/	[əb'tʰeɪn]		actor	/'æktɹ̩/	['æktɹ̩]
attest	/ətɛst/	[ə'tʰɛst]		terrific	/tərɪfɪk/	[tə'rɪfɪk]
retain	/riten/	[ri'tʰen]		stun	/stʌn/	['stʌn]

The examples in the left column illustrate a /t/ that precedes a stressed vowel and thus is aspirated. No aspiration occurs in *Atlas*, *get*, *actor*, and *terrific* because the /t/ does not precede stress. *Stun* shows the inhibiting effect of /s/ on aspiration. The Aspiration Rule actually should be stated more generally, to apply to all three of the voiceless stops of English (the full natural class), but only forms with /t/ will be examined here.

Now, the interest of the morphology/phonology interaction is that, on occasion, morphology rearranges the phonological environments of the phonemes. That is, the segments of prefixes and suffixes can themselves be part of the environment of a phonological process. Consider the data in (69):

(69) note   notable   notation
      /not/   /notəbəl/   /noteʃən/
      ['noʔt]   ['noɾəbəl]   [no'tʰeʃən]

      quote   quotable   quotation
      /kwot/   /kwotəbəl/   /kwoteʃən/
      ['kwoʔt]   ['kwoɾəbəl]   [kwo'tʰeʃən]

Observe the particular allophone of /t/ that emerges in these forms. In *note* and *quote* by themselves, the /t/ phoneme is at the end of a word. It is thus eligible for (66) Preglottalization, and emerges as [ʔt]. In *notable* and *quotable*, the suffix /-əbəl/ has added the stressless vowel that is crucial for (67) Flapping, so the /t/ shows up as [ɾ]. Finally, in *notation* and *quotation*, the suffix we've added begins with a stressed syllable (which, in English phonology, has the effect of weakening or eliminating the stress of the base). This puts the /t/ phoneme in pre-stress position, so that (68) Aspiration can apply, and we get [tʰ].

In other words, once the morphology has arranged the appropriate suffixes, the phonological form of words ACCOMMODATES to the new environments that are created. The selection of the proper allophone of /t/ is not established for the stems /not/ and /kwot/ once and for all, but rather is determined on the basis of the environment in which the stem-final /t/ appears.

To illustrate the concept of alternation, we take the forms just given, and strip away the suffixes, giving:

(70)   note: ['noʔt]   ['noɾ]   [notʰ]
       quote: ['kwoʔt]   ['kwoɾ]   [kwotʰ]

Referring back to the definition of alternation given above, we see that the morphemes *note* and *quote* do indeed alternate: depending on the context that the morphology creates for them, they take on different forms.

When a morpheme alternates, the different forms it takes on are called **allomorphs**. Thus ['noʔt], ['noɾ], and [notʰ] are allomorphs of the morpheme /not/.

What we have just seen is a common pattern in languages: alternation results because the phonological rules enforce their demands on the OUTPUT of the morphology. They require selection of the right allophones based on contexts that the morphology creates.

The norm, in fact, is that a morpheme will not have a constant pronunciation. The morphology (also, the syntax) of a language frequently places morphemes in different phonological contexts, and when this happens, the outcome that is demanded by the phonological rules is often different. The differences that result are sometimes subtle, sometimes drastic.

For linguists working on the phonology of a language, the existence of alternations is a great boon, because it gives them much more control over their material. Should a linguist wonder, "What would happen to a /p/ if it occurred before a stressless vowel?", then an easy answer is at hand, provided that there are stems ending in /p/ and suffixes beginning with stressless vowels. In general, the morphology greatly expands the number of sequences that the linguist can examine.

12.10.2   Rhythmic lengthening in Choctaw

The kinds of alternation in the example just discussed are fairly subtle, but this is not always so. We will consider next the phenomenon of Rhythmic Lengthening in Choctaw, a Muskogean language spoken in Mississippi and Oklahoma.

The stem for *see* in Choctaw is /pisa/, and by itself it is pronounced as such. However, if a suffix consisting of a single syllable is added to /pisa/, the stem is pronounced differently, with a lengthened vowel:

(71)   [pisaː + li]   see-I.subject   =   'I see'
       [pisaː + tʃi]   see-causative   =   'cause to see, show'

In other words, *pisa* has (at least) two allomorphs, [pisa] and [pisaː]. Employing a common notation, we have included + signs to make it easier to see the divisions between morphemes; these symbols have no effect on the actual pronunciation. In addition, to keep things clear we have provided both morpheme-by-morpheme translations and translations of the entire words.

Given this much information, we could imagine quite a few hypotheses about what is going on: for example, maybe Choctaw always lengthens vowels before suffixes, or perhaps it lengthens the second to last vowel of all words, so long as it isn't the first vowel. You can probably think of more possibilities.

To make further progress, we need further data. Here is what happens when you put a PREFIX before *pisa*:

(72)   [tʃi + piːsa]   you.object-see   =   '(he) sees you'

The data we've now seen suggest there may be a fairly general phonological principle at work: when a word has two syllables, both are short, but when there are three syllables, then the vowel of the middle syllable is long. It doesn't seem to matter how the word is divided into prefixes and suffixes.

The pattern begins to make further sense if we look at forms of *pisa* with four or five syllables (that is, having two or three affixes):

(73)   [tʃi + piːsa + li]   you.obj-see-I.subj   =   'I see you'
       [tʃi + piːsa + tʃi]   you.obj.-see-causative   =   '(he) causes
                                                                 you to see'
       [pisaː + tʃi + li]   see-causative-I.subj   =   'I cause (him)
                                                                 to see'
       [tʃi + piːsa + tʃiː + li] you.obj-see-causative-   =   'I cause you
                                  I.subj   to see'

The pattern makes sense if we take all the forms we have, and align them vowel for vowel, in a left-justified manner:

(74)   [p   i   s   a]
       [p   i   s   aː   l   i]
       [p   i   s   aː   tʃ   i]
       [tʃ   i   p   iː   s   a]
       [tʃ   i   p   iː   s   a   l   i]
       [tʃ   i   p   iː   s   a   tʃ   i]
       [p   i   s   aː   tʃ   i   l   i]
       [tʃ   i   p   iː   s   a   tʃ   iː   l   i]

Namely: a vowel must be long if it is in an EVEN-NUMBERED SYLLABLE, counting from the beginning of the word, and moreover is NOT IN THE LAST SYLLABLE. Choctaw seems to have a kind of alternating durational rhythm, and for this reason the phenomenon has been called Rhythmic Lengthening by Choctaw scholars.

Let us test out Rhythmic Lengthening with another stem, which in this case means 'to receive as a present'. The basic data, parallel to what we did for *pisa*, are as in (75):

(75)   [habiːna]   receive as.a present
        [habiːna + li]   receive.as.a.present-I.subj
        = 'I receive as a present'
        [habiːna + tʃi]   receive.as.a.present-causative
        = 'cause to receive as a present'
        [tʃi + haːbina]   you.obj-receive.as.a.present
        '(he) receives you as a present'
        [tʃi + haːbinaː + li]   you.obj-receive.as.a.present-I.subj
        = 'I receive you as a present'
        [tʃi + haːbinaː + tʃi]   you.obj-receive.as.a.present-causative
        = '(he) causes you to receive as a present'
        [habiːna + tʃiː + li]   receive.as.a.present-causative-I.subj
        = 'I cause to receive as a present'
        [tʃi + haːbinaː + tʃi + li]   you.obj-receive.as.a.present-
        causative-I.subj
        = 'I cause you to receive as a present'

Examining each form, you should be able to see the alternating pattern of Rhythmic Lengthening, affecting all and only the non-final, even-numbered vowels.

To set up the analysis more explicitly, we suppose that the phonemic forms for the stems for 'see' and 'receive as a present' are /pisa/ and /habina/. The morphological rules of Choctaw may attach to them a variety of prefixes and suffixes. The form that results must comply with the phonological rule of Rhythmic Lengthening, which we state in prose as follows:

(76)   **Rhythmic Lengthening**
      Lengthen the vowels of non-final, even-numbered syllables,
      counting from the beginning of the word.

Thus for the form [tʃipiːsatʃiːli], the phonological derivation is as follows:

(77)   /pisa/   base form for 'see'
       /tʃi+pisa+tʃi+li/   Morphology: addition of prefixes and suffixes
       [tʃipiːsatʃiːli]   Phonology: application of Rhythmic
                             Lengthening

In this view, the phonemic form /pisa/ has no long vowels at all: whenever this stem is pronounced with a long vowel, the rule of Rhythmic Lengthening has created it.

The stem *habina*, 'to give as a present', is more subtle. When this stem is pronounced by itself, it comes out as [habiːna], with a long vowel. But there is good reason to think that this is not a PHONEMIC long vowel, because it appears only when the conditions of Rhythmic Lengthening are met for /i/. When they are not, /i/ appears as short, and other vowels which DO meet the conditions for Rhythmic Lengthening appear as long, as in, for example, [tʃi+haːbina].

This reasoning can be stated more explicitly if we show precisely what is happening when the two forms are constructed by the grammar:

(78)   /habina/   phonemic form for 'receive as a
                                          present'
       _____   /tʃi+habina/   Morphology: addition of prefix (second
                                          column only)
       [habiːna] [tʃihaːbina]   Phonology: Rhythmic Lengthening

This derivation, unlike the earlier ones, includes rules of both morphology and phonology. We add a brief comment on such derivations: the reason for writing derivations is to show explicitly what processes are involved in determining the pronounced form of words. While it may be mentally useful to imagine derivations as having some kind of interpretation in time (as a sort of assembly line for manufacturing phonetic forms), most linguists would probably be agnostic about whether such an assembly line is actually found in the mind/brain. What is truly crucial about derivations is that they show the LOGICAL arrangement of the rules: in particular, the principle of Rhythmic Lengthening holds of FULL WORDS as they are constructed by the morphology, not of single stems. The arrangement of the rules in a derivation is used to describe the logical relationships of the grammar in an explicit way.

12.11   Neutralization

The examples of alternation we've seen so far involve allophones: a particular morpheme varies because its phonemes show up with different allophones when the morphological context is varied. However, there are examples of alternation which go beyond allophony.

12.11.1   Stop nasalization in Korean

In final position of morphemes, Korean contrasts a series of voiceless stops /p, t, k/ with the corresponding nasals /m, n, ŋ/. This is shown by the following minimal pairs.

(79) [otʃiŋətʃət]   'squid pickle'
     [otʃiŋətʃən]   'squid pancake'

    [nuɾinpap]   'scorched rice'
    [nuɾinpam]   'scorched chestnut'

    [tʃakinpak]   'small gourd'
    [tʃakinpaŋ]   'small room'

As it happens, this contrast is not always manifested. The reason is that Korean has a phonological rule which forbids voiceless stops from preceding a nasal, requiring that a nasal appear instead.

(80) ***Korean Stop Nasalization***
$$[\text{+stop}] \rightarrow \begin{bmatrix} \text{+nasal} \\ \text{+voiced} \end{bmatrix} / \underline{\quad} [\text{+nasal}]$$

That is: a stop that immediately precedes a nasal sound must be replaced by the corresponding nasal.

The rule applies to the entire class of stops, which consists of /p/, /t/, and /k/. Since the rule is formulated to change only voicing and nasality, it leaves place of articulation unaltered. Therefore, it changes /p/ to [m], /t/ to [n], and /k/ to [ŋ]. One can see a plausible phonetic purpose for the rule: it eliminates the need for a rapid descending motion of the velum to cover the sharp transition between an oral stop and a nasal.

The significance of Stop Nasalization can be seen when we take pairs like the ones given above, and arrange them in a phrase or sentence such that the next word begins with a nasal sound. Under such circumstances, the word pairs are pronounced exactly the same:

(81) [otʃiŋətʃət]   [otʃiŋətʃən nɛmsɛka]
     'squid pickle'   'squid pickle + smell'   = 'the smell of the
                                                          squid pickle'

    [otʃiŋətʃən]   [otʃiŋətʃən nɛmsɛka]
    'squid   'squid pancake + smell'   = 'the smell of the
    pancake'   squid pancake'

    [nuɾinpap]   [nə nuɾinpam məkəpwanni]
    'scorched   'you + scorched rice +   = 'Have you tried
    rice'   tried-question'   scorched rice?'
    [nuɾinpam]   [nə nuɾinpam məkəpwanni]
    'scorched   'you + scorched chestnut   = 'Have you tried
    chestnut'   + tried-question'   scorched chestnut?'

[tʃakɨnpak]   [tʃakɨnpaŋ nɛmsɛka]
'small gourd'   'small gourd + smell'   = 'the smell of a
                                                  small gourd'

[tʃakɨnpaŋ]   [tʃakɨnpaŋ nɛmsɛka]
'small room'   'small room + smell'   = 'the smell of a
                                                  small room'

This follows from the statement of obstruent nasalization. Below we give phonemic forms and phonological derivations for the second pair of examples:

(82) 'you + scorched rice +   'you + scorched chestnuts
        tried-Q'   + tried-Q'

/nə nuɾɨnpap məkəpwanni/   /nə nuɾɨnpam məkəpwanni/   phonemic forms

             m   ——   Obstruent
                                                       Nasalization (80)

[nə nuɾɨnpam məkəpwanni]   [nə nuɾɨnpam məkəpwanni]   phonetic forms

There is a practical implication of Stop Nasalization: when a Korean speaker hears [nə nuɾɨnpam məkəpwanni], he is not able to determine purely from the phonetic input whether the speaker is talking about rice or chestnuts. One must either make use of the context of the utterance to figure out what is meant, or request clarification.

The Korean example illustrates **neutralization**: the phonemic distinction of /ptk/ vs. /mnŋ/ in Korean is NEUTRALIZED in the context of a following nasal, meaning that the distinction is indeed 'there' in the phonemic forms of the relevant words, but due to a phonological rule is not actually manifested in pronunciation. An explicit definition of neutralization is as follows:

(83) **Neutralization**: the identical phonetic realization of distinct
       phonemic forms

In the example above, the neutralization consists of the realization of distinct phonemic forms like /nuɾɨnpap/ 'scorched rice' and /nuɾɨnpam/ 'scorched chestnut' as the identical phonetic form [nuɾɨnpam]. In this case, we are speaking of the neutralization of two complete phonemic forms. It is also possible to speak of the neutralization of two phonemes: here, /p/ and /m/ are neutralized as [m].

Neutralization is fairly common in languages. We discuss next a case found in some dialects of English.

12.11.2 Post-nasal /t/ deletion in English

There is a **deletion** rule in English which 'erases' a /t/ after /n/, thus wiping out the contrast of /t/ with the absence of /t/. Consider some minimal pairs showing that /t/ in English contrasts with zero: this means you can have words that are identical except for the presence of a /t/ in only one of them.

(84) plant [plænt] vs. plan [plæn]
   stunt [stʌnt] vs. stun [stʌn]
   bent [bɛnt] vs. Ben [bɛn]

For environments other than the end of the word, we can find near-minimal pairs:

(85) Bentley ['bɛntli] vs. Henley ['hɛnli]
   anneal [ə'nil] vs. until [ən'tɪl]

Since in all of the examples, /t/ is preceded by /n/, another way of putting this is to say that /nt/ contrasts with /n/.

Now, let us consider a number of word groups that share the same morphological stem. The pronunciations given are not common to all dialects of English, but are quite common in North America.

(86) plant ['plænt]   planter ['plænɾ̩]
   plan ['plæn]   planner ['plænɾ̩]
   stunt ['stʌnt]   stunting ['stʌnɪŋ]
   stun ['stʌn]   stunning ['stʌnɪŋ]
   punt ['pʌnt]   punting ['pʌnɪŋ]
   pun ['pʌn]   punning ['pʌnɪŋ]

Our assertion is that, at least for some speakers and in some (rather casual) speech styles, *planter* is pronounced identically to *planner*, and similarly for the other pairs.

It would appear, as before in Korean, that phonemic contrasts can be wiped out, in order to satisfy the demands of a phonological rule. The relevant rule forbids the appearance of /t/ after /n/, in a context we will now attempt to specify.

We know that the /t/ is maintained after /n/ when the /t/ is at the end of a word; moreover, in the relatively few cases where an /nt/ sequence is followed by a consonant (others include *entry* ['ɛntri] and *entwined* [ɛn'twaɪnd]), the /t/ survives. Additional data given below indicate that stress also plays a role:

(87)   *plant*   [plænt]   *planting* ['plænɪŋ]   *plantation* [plæn'teʃən]
       mental ['mɛnə']   *mentality* [mɛn'tælɪɾi]
       scientist ['saɪənəst] *scientific* [saɪən'tɪfɪk]

Apparently, /t/ is vulnerable to deletion when it is FOLLOWED BY A STRESSLESS VOWEL. We state the rule as:

(88)   ***Post-Nasal /t/ Deletion***
       $$t \rightarrow \varnothing \;/\; n \underline{\quad\quad} \begin{bmatrix} +\text{vowel} \\ -\text{stress} \end{bmatrix}$$

That is: /t/ is deleted when it occurs between /n/ and a stressless vowel.
   Here are full derivations for some crucial cases. We will assume that phonemically, *plant* is /plænt/ and *plan* is /plæn/. As usual, we let the morphological rules specify the arrangement of morphemes, and then require the result to be modified so as to obey the phonological rules.

(89)   Morphology: affixation of *-ing, -ation*
       plan   *planning*   *plant*   *planting*   *plantation*
       /'plæn/   /'plæn+ɪŋ/   /'plænt/   /'plænt+ɪŋ/   /plæn't+eʃən]

It should be borne in mind that *-ation* is a stressed suffix in English; rules which we will not treat here cause the stress of the suffix to win out over the stress of the stem.
   The rule of Post-Nasal /t/ Deletion asks us to delete any /t/ that follows /n/ and precedes a stressless vowel. As it happens, these conditions are met only in *planting.*

(90)   Phonology: Post-Nasal /t/ Deletion (88)
       ____   ____   ____   /'plæn+ɪŋ/   ____

The output forms that result are as follows:

(91)   Phonetic forms
       ['plæn]   ['plænɪŋ]   ['plænt]   ['plænɪŋ]   [plæn'taʃən]

   As in the Korean example, we can see that sometimes, in order to comply with a phonological rule, forms that we would otherwise expect to be phonemically distinct are merged (neutralized) in their phonetic form. Thus:

(92)   *Word*   *Expected Form without Neutralization*   *Neutralized Form*
       planning   ['plænɪŋ]   ['plænɪŋ]
       planting   ['plæntɪŋ]   ['plænɪŋ]

For this reason, some utterances are ambiguous for phonological reasons, such as: 'They are planning/planting a garden.'

SIDEBAR
12.5

Acquiring Phonemic Form in Cases of Neutralization

In many cases, where this is phonological neutralization, it is not straightforward for the language learner to pick up the right phonemic representation, because neutralization processes may make this information only marginally available. An observation we have made suggests that this is the case for the neutralizing rule of Post-Nasal /t/ Deletion.

A five-year-old of our acquaintance said a number of words that are supposed to have plain /n/ with /nt/ instead: *Panasonic* [pæntə'sanɪk], *monoclonius* (a kind of dinosaur) [mantə'kloniəs]. This child never heard these pronunciations from anyone else, so one wonders where he could have gotten them from. Our conjecture is that (a) he lacks Post-Nasal /t/ Deletion, or else has it only as an option in fast speech; (b) he is tacitly aware that [n] in the appropriate environment can represent either phonemic /n/ or phonemic /nt/, owing to the neutralizing effects of Post-Nasal /t/ Deletion. For these particular words, he has made the wrong guess. Learning the underlying representation of these words is particularly difficult since there is no alternating form (like [pæn] or [man]) that would clearly show an underlying /n/ rather than /nt/.

SIDEBAR
12.6

Near-Neutralization

Many older linguistics textbooks include cases of apparent neutralization in phonology that on closer examination turn out not to be. These are cases in which the phonological rules assign NEARLY identical phonetic forms to two distinct phonological forms, which prove not to be identical when careful measurements are made by machine.

For example, it has been suggested that English has a rule that neutralizes the distinction between /s/ and /ʃ/, whenever another /ʃ/ immediately follows.

/s/ Assimilation
s → ʃ / _____ ʃ (optional)

To see this, imagine a person named 'Russ Schaefer', who is the topic of discussion in the following two sentences:

Let's help Russ Schaefer to the head of the line.
Let's help rush Schaefer to the head of the line.

For many English speakers, these two sentences when spoken fluently will sound almost identical. This is because, under the influence of the following /ʃ/ in *Schaefer*, the /s/ of *Russ* /rʌs/ becomes very close to [ʃ] in its articulation. This would give the following phonological derivation:

Russ Schaefer	*rush Schaefer*	
/rʌs ʃefr̩ /	/rʌʃ ʃefr̩/	phonemic forms
rʌʃ ʃefr̩	_____	/s/ Assimilation
[rʌʃ ʃefr̩]	[rʌʃ ʃefr̩]	output

Phonetic instruments are harder to fool than the ear, however. If we use a sound spectrograph and look closely at spoken versions of *Russ Schaefer*, we find that the phonemic /s/ of *Russ* is NOT realized as [ʃ], but rather as a dynamic sound that starts out like [s] and ends up like [ʃ]: [s͡ʃ]. /s/ Assimilation is thus more properly stated as a NON-NEUTRALIZING rule:

/s/ Assimilation
s → s͡ʃ / ___ ʃ   (optional)

This rule is not neutralizing, but only comes close to being so.

We anticipate that further progress in phonology will take place as linguists gradually abandon the practice of relying entirely on their ears for data, and make use of the more accurate data obtainable by machine. For example, it has recently been verified instrumentally that Korean Obstruent Nasalization is truly and fully neutralizing.

12.12   Phonemic Environments and Rule Ordering

An interesting aspect of phonological systems is that some rules apply in environments defined phonemically, rather than phonetically. Such a rule looks like it is applying in the wrong environment, if one examines only the phonetic data.

Our discussion of this phenomenon will be based on two phonological rules of North American English. One is found in a large number of dialects, especially in the northeastern US and throughout Canada.

(93)   */aɪ/ Raising*

$$aɪ → ʌɪ / \underline{\hspace{2em}} \begin{bmatrix} +\text{consonant} \\ -\text{voice} \end{bmatrix}$$

That is: /aɪ/ is realized as [ʌɪ] when it precedes a voiceless consonant. As a result of this rule, we find the following distribution of data.

(94)

tripe	/traɪp/	[trʌɪp]	tribe	/traɪb/	[traɪb]
right	/raɪt/	[rʌɪt]	ride	/raɪd/	[raɪd]
hiker	/haɪkr̩/	[hʌɪkr̩]	tiger	/taɪgr̩/	[taɪgr̩]
life	/laɪf/	[lʌɪf]	live	/laɪv/	[laɪv]
rifle	/raɪfəl/	[rʌɪfəl]	rival	/raɪvəl/	[raɪvəl]
rice	/raɪs/	[rʌɪs]	rise	/raɪz/	[raɪz]
			rye	/raɪ/	[raɪ]
			ion	/aɪan/	[aɪan]

The other rule is Flapping, formulated above under (67). There, we formulated the rule as applying only to /t/. In fact, Flapping also affects /d/, converting it likewise into a flap. The data in (95) demonstrate this. The left column shows instances of phonemic /d/ that fit the environment for Flapping; namely, they follow a vowel and precede a stressless vowel (again, counting syllabic /r̩/ as a vowel). The right column shows instances of phonemic /d/ in various other environments.

(95)

	Phonemic	Phonetic		Phonemic	Phonetic
Ada	/'edə /	['eɾə]	Dan	/'dæn/	['dæn]
ladder	/'lædr̩ /	['læɾr̩]	adept	/ə'dɛpt/	[ə'dɛpt]
reading	/'ridɪŋ /	['riɾɪŋ]	Camden	/'kæmdən/	['kæmdən]
edify	/'ɛdɪfaɪ /	['ɛɾɪfaɪ]	Hilda	/'hɪldə /	['hɪldə]
sediment	/'sɛdɪmənt/	['sɛɾɪmənt]	pad	/'pæd /	['pæd]
adolescent	/ædə'lɛsənt/	[æɾə'lɛsənt]	Ogden	/'agdən/	['agdən]
			Edgar	/'ɛdgr̩ /	['ɛdgr̩]

This is the same pattern as was seen for /t/, in the data given in (22) above. The generalized version of Flapping can be stated as follows, making use of the natural class of alveolar stops:

(96)   *Flapping* (revised)

$$\begin{bmatrix} \text{+alveolar} \\ \text{+stop} \end{bmatrix} \rightarrow [ɾ] \ / \ [\text{+vowel}] \ \underline{\hspace{1cm}} \ \begin{bmatrix} \text{+vowel} \\ \text{−stress} \end{bmatrix}$$

That is: any alveolar stop is realized as [ɾ] when it is preceded by a vowel or syllabic consonant, and followed by a stressless vowel.

Since Flapping converts both /t/ and /d/ to [ɾ], it is a neutralizing rule, wiping out underlying distinctions. We can tell this with a pair such as *heating* vs. *heeding*. The underlying forms are justified by the stems *heat* [hit] and *heed* [hid]. But when the *-ing* suffix is added, Flapping applies, and neutralizes the underlying /t/ and /d/ as [ɾ]:

(97)   *heat*   *heed*

/'hit/	/'hid/	phonemic forms
'hit+ɪŋ	'hid+ɪŋ	morphology: suffixation of *-ing*/-ɪŋ/
'hiɾɪŋ	'hiɾɪŋ	phonology: Flapping
['hiɾɪŋ]	['hiɾɪŋ]	phonetic form

At least in fluent speech, for most speakers of North American English *heating* and *heeding* do appear to be pronounced identically, so the example constitutes a true neutralization. Similar examples are given below:

(98) bet   betting   bed   bedding
      /'bɛt/   /'bɛt+ɪŋ/   /'bɛd/   /'bɛd+ɪŋ/
      ['bɛt]   ['bɛɾɪŋ]   ['bɛd]   ['bɛɾɪŋ]

      wet   wetting   wed   wedding
      /'wɛt/   /'wɛt+ɪŋ/   /'wɛd/   /'wɛd+ɪŋ/
      ['wɛt]   ['wɛɾɪŋ]   ['wɛd]   ['wɛɾɪŋ]

      butt   butted   bud   budded
      /'bʌt/   /'bʌt+əd/   /'bʌd/   /'bʌd+əd/
      ['bʌt]   ['bʌɾəd]   ['bʌd]   ['bʌɾəd]

With these two rules in hand, we can now see how they might interact. Crucial words that would bear on the question are the following, which for the moment we give in spelled and phonemic form only:

(99) write   writing   ride   riding
      /'raɪt/   /'raɪt+ɪŋ/   /'raɪd/   /'raɪdɪŋ/

      cite   cited   side   sided
      /'saɪt/   /'saɪt+əd/   /'saɪd/   /'saɪd+əd/

      white   whiter   wide   wider
      /'waɪt/   /'waɪt+r̩/   /'waɪd/   /'waɪd+r̩/

The crucial point here is that /aɪ/ Raising ((93)) depends on the voicing of the following consonant. But Flapping ((96)) changes the voicing of a /t/. We can ask whether the allophone of /aɪ/ ([aɪ] vs. [ʌɪ]) that emerges depends on the phonemic form of the following consonant (/t/ vs. /d/), or on the phonetic form ([ɾ]). If /aɪ/ Raising depends on a phonemic environment, then we would expect to get [ʌɪ] in cases where the following consonant is /t/, even though that consonant is actually pronounced as [ɾ]. On the other hand, if /aɪ/ Raising depends on the phonetic form of the following consonant, it will not apply (flaps are voiced, and cannot trigger the rule), so we will get [aɪ] across the board.

It would be nice if we could establish some general principle of phonology that would predict the correct outcome. But this turns out to be impossible: both outcomes can be found, depending on the dialect of English one is examining.

For millions of speakers, found primarily in the northeastern United States and in Canada, /aɪ/ Raising depends on the phonemic voicing of the following consonant. Because of this, the crucial pairs come out distinct, with [ʌɪ] appearing whenever the following sound is a phonemic /t/:

(100)   *write*   *writing*   *ride*   *riding*
       /'raɪt/   /'raɪt+ɪŋ/   /'raɪd/   /'raɪdɪŋ/
       ['rʌɪt]   ['rʌɪɾ+ɪŋ]   ['raɪd]   ['raɪɾɪŋ]

       cite   *cited*   *side*   *sided*
       /'saɪt/   /'saɪt+əd/   /'saɪd/   /'saɪd+əd/
       ['sʌɪt]   ['sʌɪɾ+əd]   ['saɪd]   ['saɪɾ+əd]

       white   *whiter*   *wide*   *wider*
       /'waɪt/   /'waɪt+ɹ̩/   /'waɪd/   /'waɪd+ɹ̩/
       ['wʌɪt]   ['wʌɪɾ+ɹ̩]   ['waɪd]   ['waɪɾ+ɹ̩]

There are also millions of speakers, located mostly in the rest of North America, for whom Flapping depends on the PHONETIC voicing of the following consonant. Since a flap is voiced, this means that whenever Flapping is applicable the outcome in these words is [aɪ]:

(101)   *write*   *writing*   *ride*   *riding*
       /'raɪt/   /'raɪt+ɪŋ/   /'raɪd/   /'raɪdɪŋ/
       ['rʌɪt]   ['raɪɾ+ɪŋ]   ['raɪd]   ['raɪɾɪŋ]

       cite   *cited*   *side*   *sided*
       /'saɪt/   /'saɪt+əd/   /'saɪd/   /'saɪd+əd/
       ['sʌɪt]   ['saɪɾ+əd]   ['saɪd]   ['saɪɾ+əd]

       white   *whiter*   *wide*   *wider*
       /'waɪt/   /'waɪt+ɹ̩/   /'waɪd/   /'waɪd+ɹ̩/
       ['wʌɪt]   ['waɪɾ+ɹ̩]   ['waɪd]   ['waɪɾ+ɹ̩]

Most other dialects of English lack either /aɪ/ Raising or Flapping or both, and therefore do not bear on the question.

A widely employed method of analyzing differences such as the one just shown is to suppose that phonological rules must be **ordered**. We can imagine phonology as a sort of 'assembly line', which takes in phonemic forms, applies phonological rules in a particular order, and outputs phonetic forms. Under such a theory, the difference between the two dialects just described is a difference of rule ordering. In particular, the dialect in which *writing* and *riding* are pronounced distinctly (['rʌɪɾɪŋ] vs. ['raɪɾɪŋ]) orders /aɪ/ Raising before Flapping. The dialect in which *writing* and *riding* are pronounced the same orders Flapping before /aɪ/ Raising.

Here are derivations of pertinent examples, using both orderings:

(102)   **A.   /aɪ/ Raising precedes Flapping**
       writing   *riding*
       'rʌɪtɪŋ   ——————   /aɪ/ Raising (93) (applicable
                                  only to *writing*)
       'rʌɪɾɪŋ   'raɪɾ+ɪŋ   Flapping (96)
       ['rʌɪɾɪŋ]   ['raɪɾɪŋ]   phonetic forms

B. **Flapping precedes /aɪ/ Raising**

writing	*riding*	
/ˈraɪt+ɪŋ/	/ˈraɪd+ɪŋ/	phonemic forms
ˈraɪɾɪŋ	ˈraɪɾ+ɪŋ	Flapping (96)
———	———	/aɪ/ Raising (93) (inapplicable)
[ˈraɪɾɪŋ]	[ˈraɪɾɪŋ]	phonetic forms

Analytically, it is usually fairly easy to determine how two rules must be ordered. You simply try both possibilities, seeing which one outputs the observed phonetic forms. (Often, both will, in which case the ordering doesn't matter.) The only crucial part is to apply the rules quite mechanically, without 'looking ahead' to see if you're going to get the correct answer. If it is not possible to apply the rules in completely mechanical fashion, then they have probably not been stated explicitly enough.

One might wonder why dialects differ in their rule ordering. In the present case (and many parallel ones), we would suggest that the major principle at work in 'Dialect A' is that of maximizing the **distinctness** of phonetic forms. In particular, for Dialect A there is no ambiguity between *writing* and *riding*, which are pronounced [ˈrʌɪɾɪŋ] and [ˈraɪɾɪŋ], respectively, and remain in contrast. Curiously, the contrast is a 'displaced' one: forms which UNDERLYINGLY differ in the voicing of /t/ vs. /d/ differ in their PHONETIC form in the height of the first elements of their diphthongs ([ʌɪ] vs. [aɪ]). This constitutes one kind of case where a minimal pair does not prove a phonemic distinction – because the phonological rule system 'displaces' the phonemic contrast from underlying /t/–/d/ to phonetic [ʌɪ]–[aɪ], the minimal pair is misleading with respect to the actual phonemic forms.

This does not imply that the method of finding minimal pairs is pointless. When a minimal pair is found, the necessary first step is to posit the contrast indicated by the pair. Only subsequently will a view of the whole system – here, the related words like *write* and *ride* – lead to the alternative analysis of a displaced contrast.

We must also consider what general principles guide Dialect B, where *writing* and *riding* come out the same. Here, the phonology seems to be governed more by phonetic principles: whatever phonetic tendency favors [aɪ] before voiced consonants is indeed respected in this dialect, where flap behaves like all the other voiced consonants in taking a preceding [aɪ].

12.13 Summary

This chapter has covered a number of basic notions of phonology and of phonological analysis. To recapitulate briefly, we conceive phonology as embodying a set of contrasting segmental entities, or **phonemes**, which are manifested according to a set of **phonological rules**. Phonological rules lead to a variety of patterns in the observable data. Where they regulate **non-contrastive properties**, the result is **allophonic variation** in the realization of phonemes. Where the rules regulate **contrastive properties**, we get phonological contrasts with limited distribution.

Often, the morphology interacts with the phonological rules in crucial ways, causing morphemes to **alternate**; that is, appear as different **allomorphs**. Alternation can sometimes simply reflect the distribution of allophones in the language, but also can involve **neutralization** of underlying contrasts.

A correct phonological analysis, in our view, is one that characterizes the fluent speaker's internalized knowledge, rather than merely serving as an economical description of the data. As such, it can in principle be corroborated by data going beyond ordinary speech: we expect that the analysis should predict (a) which phonetic distinctions are especially perceptible to speakers of a given language (because they are phonemic in that language); (b) which phonetically distinct sounds should be perceived as being 'the same sound' (because they are phonemically the same), and (c) what sort of errors a speaker will make when attempting to pronounce a new language (because the phonological rule system tends to be carried over to novel contexts).

On the analytic side, we have discussed two methods of delving into a language's phonology. The gathering of **minimal pairs**, with collection of **phonetically similar phones** in **complementary distribution**, can be used to reduce the large set of phonetic sounds in a language to a coherent system of contrasting phonemes, with their allophones distributed by rule. Examining the allomorphs of a large set of morphemes is likewise a useful strategy, since alternation in morphemes often makes clear what are the phonological rules that are CAUSING the alternations, as well as any necessary ordering of those rules.

We add that while both of these methods usually are useful, neither can be regarded as a rigid or infallible recipe. In principle, any sort of reliable observations or sound reasoning about phonological patterning can lead us closer to an adequate account of a sound system.

Further Reading

Gussenhoven, Carlos and Haike Jacobs. 1998. *Understanding Phonology*. London: Arnold.

Kager, René. 1999. *Optimality Theory: A Textbook*. Oxford: Oxford University Press.

Kenyon, John S. and Thomas A. Knott. 1953. *A Pronouncing Dictionary of American English*. Springfield, MA: Merriam.

Labov, William. 1972. *Sociolinguistic Patterns*. Philadelphia: University of Pennsylvania Press.

Maddieson, Ian. 1984. *Patterns of Sounds*. Cambridge: Cambridge University Press.

Wells, John C. 1982. *Accents of English* (in 3 volumes). Cambridge: Cambridge University Press.

English Allophones

In English, [k] and [ḳ] (plain velar and fronted velar stops respectively) are allophones of the same phoneme. Consider the following data:

Exercise 12.2

kitten	['kɪtn]	cop	[kap]	crack	[kræk]
keen	[ḳin]	cool	[kul]	clock	[klak]
cake	[ḳek]	cope	[kop]	quick	[kwɪk]
cat	[ḳæt]	cook	[kvk]	extract	[ɛk'strækt]
lucky	['lʌḳi]	cup	[kʌp]	Exxon	['ɛksan]

(a) What is the environment in which [ḳ] is found? If you don't immediately see the answer, carefully follow the procedure laid out above, collecting and writing down the environments in which [k] and [ḳ] occur. It also may help to examine the English vowel chart under (3) above.

(b) What is the environment in which [k] is found?

(c) Decide on the basis of your answer to the previous question what should be the underlying form of the phoneme. Write a phonological rule, using words, that derives the contextual allophone.

(d) Look at the following data and write an improved version of your rule, using features. [g̟] is a fronted voiced velar stop. You may use [+fronted] as a feature to distinguish [ḳ, g̟] from [k, g].

gill	[g̟ɪl]	got	[gat]	grog	[grag]
geese	[g̟is]	goose	[gus]	glimmer	['glɪmr̩]
game	[g̟em]	go	[go]	Gwendolyn	['gwɛndələn]
gag	[g̟æg]	good	[gvd]	eggs	[ɛg̟z]
soggy	['sag̟i]	Gus	[gʌs]	Muggsy	['mʌgzi]

(e) Provide underlying forms and a phonological derivation for *keen*, *clock*, *soggy*, and *eggs*.

. . . .

Exercise 12.3 Lango

Lango is a Nilotic language spoken in Uganda. Here are phonetic symbols found in the data below that may be unfamiliar:

[á]	High tone (on the vowel [a])
[à]	Low tone
[â]	Falling tone
[ǎ]	Rising tone
[tɕ, dʑ]	voiceless and voiced palatal affricates (Note: these are single sounds, not sequences of sounds.)
[ɾ̥]	voiceless alveolar flap
[Φ]	voiceless bilabial fricative
[ɕ]	voiceless palatal fricative
[x]	voiceless velar fricative
[ɲ]	palatal nasal

Consonants transcribed as double are simply **held longer**; they are not 'rearticulated.' Think of them as single long consonants. [ttɕ] and [ddʑ] are long affricates, held for a long time with an affricated release.

(1)	[pì]	'because of'
(2)	[kètɕ]	'hunger'
(3)	[tɔ́ŋ]	'spear'
(4)	[búttɕó]	'to yell at'
(5)	[tɕɔ̀]	'men'
(6)	[ʔɔ̀t]	'house'
(7)	[dɔ̀ttɔ̀]	'to suck'
(8)	[pàppì]	'fathers'
(9)	[pójó]	'to remember'
(10)	[ljèt]	'hot'
(11)	[bókkó]	'to make red'
(12)	[júttɕú]	'to throw'
(13)	[èŋə̀ɾó]	'lion'
(14)	[ókkɔ́]	'completely'
(15)	[déɸô]	'to collect'
(16)	[dèk]	'stew'
(17)	[tɕùɸâ]	'bottle'
(18)	[gwèk]	'gazelle'
(19)	[kókkó]	'to cry'
(20)	[ɲáɸô]	'laziness'
(21)	[rétɕ]	'fish'
(22)	[bóɾə̀]	'to me'
(23)	[dìppó]	'to smash'
(24)	[dwéɾ̥ê]	'months'
(25)	[kóddó]	'to blow'
(26)	[tɕín]	'intestines'
(27)	[gíɾé]	'really'
(28)	[lòɕə̀]	'man'
(29)	[kwə̀ɕê]	'leopards'
(30)	[kál]	'millet'
(31)	[màɕê]	'fires'
(32)	[àbíɕèl]	'six'
(33)	[dáxô]	'woman'
(34)	[tɕùtɕ]	'pitch black'
(35)	[tójô]	'dew'
(36)	[wókkí]	'a few minutes ago'
(37)	[dìə̀xə̀]	'wet'
(38)	[máxâtɕ]	'scissors'
(39)	[pé]	'snow, hail'
(40)	[kɔ́ppɔ̀]	'cup'
(41)	[pàttɕó]	'to peel'
(42)	[pámâ]	'cotton'
(43)	[mɔ̀ɾ̥ɔ̀xà]	'car'

(44) [bə̀p]   'to deflate'
(45) [lwìttê]   'to sneak'
(46) [ɲàp]   'lazy'
(47) [bwɔ̀ttɔ̀]   'to retort insultingly'
(48) [tèttó]   'to forge'
(49) [tɕám]   'eating'
(50) [tɔ̀p]   'to spoil'
(51) [tɕɔ́k]   'near'
52) [pàɸó]   'father'
(53) [ɲwèttɕó]   'to run from'
(54) [bót]   'to'
(55) [dèppó]   'to collect'
(56) [gɔ̀t]   'mountain'
(57) [jìtɕ]   'belly'
(58) [bìttó]   'to unshell'
(59) [dɔ̀k]   'to go back'
(60) [kɔ̀p]   'matter'
(61) [tîn]   'today'
(62) [kít]   'kind'
(63) [àkká]   'purposely'
(64) [tɕàk]   'milk'
(65) [dʑɔk]   'pagan god'

(a)   Fill in all the consonants found in the problem in the following phonetic chart. You may treat [w] as labial and [j] as palatal. Not all slots in the chart get filled.

			labial	alveolar	palatal	velar
stops and affricates	voiceless	short				
		long				
	voiced	(all short)				
fricatives	(all voiceless)	(all short)				
nasals	(all voiced)	(all short)				
liquids	laterals	(voiced)				
	flaps	voiceless				
		voiced				
glides	(all voiced)	(all short)				

(b)   This problem deals just with the sounds [p, pp, ɸ, t, tt, ɽ (NOT r), tɕ, ttɕ, ɕ, k, kk, x]. For these sounds only, follow the procedure laid out in the text: collect and write down the environments in which each occurs.

(c) Describe in words the environments in which [p, pp, Φ, t, tt, ɾ, tɕ, ttɕ, ɕ, k, kk, x] occur. To the extent that this is possible, state your description in general terms, rather than one sound at a time.

(d) Are [pp, tt, ttɕ, kk] in complementary distribution with [p, t, tɕ, k]? Are [Φ, ɾ, ɕ, x] in complementary distribution with [p, t, tɕ, k]? What is the problem that this gives rise to? Does appealing to phonetic similarity help?

(e) Here are further data that can help solve the problem. These data involve alternations; the same stem appears with or without a suffix. (Do not try to handle the tonal alternations, just consider the final consonants of stems.)

(i)	[dĕp]	'gather-imperative'	[ìdéΦò]	'you gathered'
	[mǎt]	'drink-imperative'	[ìmáɾò]	'you drank'
	[dǎtɕ]	'drop-imperative'	[ìdáɕò]	'you dropped'
	[gĭk]	'stop-imperative'	[ìgíxò]	'you stopped'
(ii)	[jît]	'ear'	[jîɾ̂ê]	'his/her ear'
	[lǎk]	'tooth'	[làxê]	'his/her tooth'
(iii)	[ɲàp]	'lazy'	[ɲáΦô]	'laziness'

What do the alternations tell you about the correct phonemicization of Lango?

(f) State phonological rules that derive the right allophones, using words.

(g) Provide the phonemic forms (underlying representations) for [pə̀ppì] 'fathers', [dĕp] 'gather-imperative', [ìdĕΦò] 'you gathered', and [lòɕə̀] 'man'.

. . . .

Rule Ordering in 'Vancouver'   Exercise 12.4
In a dialect spoken by many English speakers, there is an allophonic rule whereby the phoneme /æ/ gets diphthongized in a particular way before /ŋ/. Individual speakers vary, but this diphthong is often pronounced something like [æi]. The effects of the diphthongizing rule can be seen in pairs such as the following:

pan	/pæn/	[pæn]	pang	/pæŋ/	[pæiŋ]
fan	/fæn/	[fæn]	fang	/fæŋ/	[fæiŋ]
gander	/'gændɾ̩/	['gændɾ̩]	anger	/'æŋgɾ̩/	['æiŋgɾ̩]

Note that in all of these cases, the [æ]'s and [æi]'s are actually nasalized, because of the Vowel Nasalization given earlier under (50). The nasal tildes have been left out for legibility.

The special allophone of /æ/ before /ŋ/ can be derived by a rule that looks like this:

Pre-/ŋ/ Diphthongization: /æ/ → [æi] / ____ ŋ

Most speakers of English also have an optional rule of /n/ Assimilation, which causes /n/ to to shift to the place of articulation of an immediately following consonant:

/n/ Assimilation: /n/ → [same place] / _____ C (in casual speech)

Some examples of this rule are as follows:

input	[ˈɪnpʊt] or [ˈɪmpʊt]
unprepared	[ʌnprəˈperd] or [ʌmprəˈperd]
unbelievable	[ʌnbəˈlivəbəl] or [ʌmbəˈlivəbəl]
I live in Minnesota	[aɪ ˈlɪv ɪn mɪnəˈsorə] or [aɪ ˈlɪv ɪm mɪnəˈsorə]
phone call	[ˈfonkɔl] or [ˈfoŋkɔl]
concourse	[ˈkankors] or [ˈkaŋkors]
con game	[ˈkanˌgem] or [ˈkaŋˌgem]
in college	[ɪn ˈkalɪdʒ] or [ɪŋˈkalɪdʒ]

Note that among other changes, this rule shifts /n/ to [ŋ], when the following consonant is velar.

Determine what the following data tell us about the RELATIVE ORDERING of Pre-/ŋ/ Diphthongization and /n/ Assimilation. To prove an ordering securely, give full derivations for both orders (as in (102) above), and point out which outcome matches the observed facts. Where a rule applies optionally, include both possibilities in your derivations.

Word	Phonemic Form	Pronunciation
pancake	/ˈpænkek/	[ˈpænkeɪk] (careful speech) or [ˈpæŋkeɪk] (casual speech) but not *[ˈpæiŋkeɪk]
Vancouver	/vænˈkuvr/	[vænˈkuvr̩] (careful speech) or [væŋˈkuvr̩] (casual speech) but not *[væiŋˈkuvr̩]
Dan Gurney	/ˈdænˈgrni/	[ˈdænˈgr̩ni] (careful speech) or [ˈdæŋˈgr̩ni] (casual speech) but not [ˈdæiŋˈgr̩ni]
sank	/ˈsæŋk/	[ˈsæiŋk] only
anchor	/ˈæŋkr̩/	[ˈæiŋkr̩] only
Rangoon	/ræŋˈgun/	[ræiŋˈgun] only
pang cake 'cake eaten to assuage pangs of hunger'	/ˈpæŋkeɪk/	[ˈpæiŋkeɪk] only

- -

Exercise 12.5 More on Choctaw

The discussion in section 12.10.2 only scratches the surface of Choctaw phonology. Here, we delve slightly deeper. To do this problem you should carefully re-read the section.

Choctaw is phonologically unusual in having three audible degrees of vowel length. Thus far, we have only included examples with short and long vowels. But there are also OVERLONG vowels. These occur as distinct phonemes. In this

problem, we will transcribe short, long, and overlong vowels like this: [a], [aː],
[aːː].

The overlong vowels have a strong influence on the pattern of Rhythmic
Lengthening. Recall that in words that phonemically have only short vowels,
the EVEN-NUMBERED, NON-FINAL short vowels undergo the rule, and surface as long.

Now consider some inflectional paradigms for stems that include overlong
vowels.

[hopoːːni]	'cook'
[hopoːːni + li]	'cook-I.subj' = 'I cook'
[tʃi + hoːpoːːni]	'you.obj-cook' = '(he) cooks you'
[tʃi + hoːpoːːni + li]	'you.obj-cook-I.subj' = 'I cook you'
[hopoːːni + tʃi]	'cook-causative' = '(he) makes (him) cook'
[tʃi + hoːpoːːni + tʃi]	'you.obj-cook-causative' = '(he) makes you cook'
[hopoːːni + tʃiː + li]	'cook-causative-I.subj' = 'I make (him) cook'
[tʃi + hoːpoːːni + tʃiː + li]	'you.obj-cook-causative-I.subj' = 'I make you cook'

[taloːːwa]	'sing'
[taloːːwa + li]	'sing-I.subj' = 'I sing'
[taloːːwa + tʃi]	'sing-causative' = '(he) makes (him) sing'
[tʃi + taːloːːwa + tʃi]	'you.obj-sing-causative' = '(he) makes you sing'
[taloːːwa + tʃiː + li]	'sing-causative-I.subj' = 'I make (him) sing'

[ʃoːːli]	'hug'
[ʃoːːli + li]	'hug-I.subj' = 'I hug'
[tʃi + ʃoːːli]	'you.obj-hug' = '(he) hugs you'
[tʃi + ʃoːːli + li]	'you.obj-hug-I.subj' = 'I hug you'
[taːːni]	'get out of bed'
[taːːni + li]	'get.out.of.bed-I.subj' = 'I get out of bed'
[taːːni + tʃi]	'get.out.of.bed-causative' = '(he) makes (him) get out of bed'
[tʃi + taːːni + tʃi]	'you.obj-get.out.of.bed-causative' = '(he) makes you get out of bed'
[taːːni + tʃiː + li]	'get.out.of.bed-causative-I.subj' = 'I make (him) get out of bed'
[tʃi + taːːni + tʃiː + li]	'you.obj-get.out.of.bed-causative-I.subj' = 'I make you get out of bed'

[faːːpatʃi]	'push in a swing'
[faːːpatʃiː + li]	'push.in.a.swing-I.subj' = 'I push (him) in a swing'
[tʃi + faːːpatʃi]	'you.obj-push.in.a.swing' = '(he) pushes you in a swing'
[tʃi + faːːpatʃiː + li]	'you.obj-push.in.a.swing-I.subj' = 'I push you in a swing'

You can see that in some of these forms, the pattern of Rhythmic Lengthening is different for words that have overlong vowels. To make this clear, examine the following pairs, focusing on the bold face vowels:

With overlong vowels	Without overlong vowels
[tʃi + hoːpoːːni + tʃiː + li]	[tʃi + haːbinaː + tʃi + li]
'you.obj-cook-causative-I.subj'	'you.obj-receive.as.a.present-causative-I.subj'
= 'I make you cook'	= 'I cause you to receive as a present'
[taːːni + tʃiː + li]	[pisaː + tʃi + li]
'get.out.of.bed-causative-I.subj'	'see-causative-I.subj'
= 'I make (him) get out of bed'	= 'I make (him) see'
[faːːpatʃiː + li]	[habiːna + li]
'push.in.a.swing-I.subj'	'receive.as.a.present-I.subj'
= 'I push (him) in a swing'	= 'I receive as a present'
[ʃoːːli + li]	[pisaː + li]
'hug-I.subj'	'see-I.subj'
= 'I hug (him)'	= 'I see'

(a)   True or false: "Rhythmic Lengthening does not apply to a word if the word contains an overlong vowel." Justify your answer with reference to the data.

(b)   State in words a corrected version of the Rhythmic Lengthening rule that will derive the correct results for all the words given.

(c)   Provide the underlying form and a phonological derivation for [hopoːːni + tʃiː + li] 'cook-causative-I.subj' = 'I make (him) cook'.

(d)   True or false: "The contrast between [aː] and [aːː] is distributionally limited, as it is never found in initial syllables." Explain your answer.

(e)   What would you expect to be the Choctaw form that means 'I make you sing'; that is, 'you.obj-sing-causative-I.subj'? Explain your answer with a full morphological and phonological derivation.

13

Phonology II:
Phonological
Representations

13.0 Introduction

This chapter outlines the elements that comprise phonological representations, the mental images in terms of which knowledge of a sound system is couched. We distinguish features, segments, syllables and metrical grids, which provide representations of stress.

13.1 Features

In chapter 12, we have pointed out that phonological rules act upon phonetic features. This means that most rules alter individual feature values rather than segments in their entirety. This also means that the set of segments affected by a rule are those sharing the feature or feature group being affected: the concept of **natural class**, introduced in chapter 12, refers to such segment groups sharing a feature or feature set. The set functions as a coherent class in virtue of the fact that a phonological process targets the feature shared by all and only its members. Recall the group of sounds /m/, /n/, /ŋ/ in Maasai, which function as a natural class by inducing post-nasal voicing: that's because the feature value [+nasal] shared by these sounds is the conditioning factor of post-nasal voicing. Recall also the earlier statement of Maasai Post-Nasal Voicing, repeated, with minor simplifications, below:

(1)   A voiceless sound is realized as voiced when it follows a nasal sound.

A rule that reflects more directly this belief that phonological rules act upon phonetic features will look like (2):

(2)   The feature [−voice] is replaced by [+voice] when it follows the feature [+nasal].
That is:
[−voice] → [+voice]/[+nasal] ____

The difference between (1) and (2) lies in the phonological representations being assumed by each: the statement in (2), unlike (1), reflects the assumption that segments are decomposed into features, which act as building blocks in the construction of segments and utterances. Individual rules target these sub-segmental building blocks and alter the segments only insofar as they alter their components. In what follows, we outline what distinctive features represent and we illustrate our conception of features as building blocks of the phonological representation.

13.1.1 Feature composition of segments

Segments are combinations of features rather than atomic entities. Any segment can be decomposed into a list of articulatory properties – properties specifying the articulatory movements typically required to produce the utterance – and a list of acoustic features – the properties of the sounds generated by the articulatory movements. Thus the phonetic representation of the word *Tom*, i.e. [tʰãm], can be viewed as consisting, in part, of the articulatory properties **non-continuant**, **coronal**, **voiceless** (all of which characterize [tʰ]), **aspiration** (which is perceived in the transition between [tʰ] and [ã], and **vowel**, **low**, **nasal**, **labial**, **voiced**, which characterize [ã]. An equivalent, more widely used set of terms for the same properties is [−continuant], [+coronal], [−voice], [+spread glottis] (for **aspiration**), [+syllabic, −consonantal] (instead of *vowel*), [+nasal], [+labial], [+voice].

13.1.2   Features and feature values

Some of the properties discussed so far come in natural pairs: [+nasal] is the opposite of [−nasal], and [+continuant] is the opposite of [−continuant]. We distinguish features from feature values: thus [+nasal] and [−nasal] are opposite values of the same feature, which we refer to as [±nasal] or [nasal]. A segment must therefore be either [+nasal] or [−nasal] but not both. But [±nasal] and [±continuant] are distinct features and, in principle, a segment can possess any combination of values from these two features.

A phonological feature is a physical dimension referring to a range of positions or movements of the articulatory organs or to the acoustic quality of speech sounds such movements produce. In the case of the feature [±nasal], the corresponding physical dimension refers to the position of the soft palate (or **velum**): when lowered, the velum permits air to flow through the nose whereas the raised velum blocks the nasal passage. A feature value is some point on the relevant dimension: [−nasal] is the term describing one end of the [nasal] dimension, namely one class of velum positions in which the velum is significantly raised; [+nasal] is the name identifying the other extremity of the same dimension, the class of velum positions in which the velum is significantly lowered. This distinction between feature and feature value is illustrated below.

(3)   The feature [±nasal] represented as an articulatory dimension and two of its values:

velum completely raised - velum completely lowered
sounds articulated here are [−nasal]: [p], [a]   sounds articulated here are [+nasal]: [m], [ã]

A diagram like (3) tells us two distinct facts about nasality: one fact is that this is a continuous dimension and therefore that it could, in principle, have more than two values. We can easily imagine sounds that are articulated with a velum position intermediate between the completely raised and the completely lowered pole. (There are in fact such sounds.) The other fact is that, however many intermediate positions one may define on this continuum of nasality, there are necessarily only two poles: the completely-raised-velum pole and the completely-lowered pole. From this point of view then, features are inherently binary since each dimension allows us to define exactly two poles.

In some cases more than one term is used to specify values on a given dimension. Consider the articulatory dimension corresponding to the degree of elevation of the tongue body (or **height**). The extreme points on this dimension are identified as [+low] and [+high] respectively and correspond to the feature values characterizing low vowels (such as [ɑ], [æ]) and high vowels (such as [i], [u]). Using [±low] and [±high] we can define an intermediate point on the same dimension and label it as [−high, −low]: this corresponds to the mid vowels (e, o, ɛ, ɔ, ʌ).

(4)   The [height] dimension and three of its values:

tongue body raised	-------------------	tongue body lowered
[+high]	[−high, −low]	[+low]
high vowels: [i], [u]	mid vowels: [e], [o]	low vowels: [a], [æ]

Similarly, intermediate points on the articulatory dimensions representing oral airflow and extent of oral stricture can be characterized by using the labels [continuant] and [consonantal], which identify distinct subregions of this dimension. To emphasize that this is a unified physical dimension we can rename it [oral stricture].

(5)   The [oral stricture] dimension and three of its values:

oral airflow completely blocked [−continuant, +consonantal]	__	significant but incomplete obstruction [+continuant, +consonantal]	__	unimpeded oral airflow [+continuant, −consonantal]
stops, affricates, nasals: [t], [d], [tʃ], [n]		fricatives, trills, flaps, laterals: [f], [r], [ɾ], [l]		glides, vowels: [w], [j], [u], [i], [a]

Examples of acoustically based features are [±sonorant] and [±strident]. The feature [±sonorant] refers to the difference between sounds that contain most of their acoustic energy in the lower formants vs. sounds that lack significant acoustic energy in this region of the spectrum. Thus vowels, approximants, liquids and nasals are [+sonorant], meaning that their acoustic energy is predominantly located in the lower formants; in contrast, stops and fricatives are sounds either lacking in acoustic energy throughout all spectral regions for most of their duration (in the case of stops) or possessing acoustic energy only in the higher formants (fricatives). The feature [±strident] distinguishes noisy sounds (such as [s], [ʃ]) from relatively quiet ones (such as [θ], [x], [h]).

Our earlier discussion of how languages organize the phonetic space differently for the purpose of creating an inventory of distinctive sounds can be recast now in feature terms. We can state that the same physical dimensions can be divided in different ways for the purpose of obtaining the set of features that are distinctive in a given language. Many languages, for instance most Eskimo languages, distinguish only two extremes on the height dimension and thus oppose a low vowel /a/ to one or more high vowels (/i/, /u/, /ɨ/). Such languages do not have a contrast between mid and high or mid and low vowels, although they may have mid allophones of the existing phonemes. In other languages (e.g. Spanish) all three points identified in (4) – i.e. the low, mid, and high region – correspond to distinct phonemes (/a/, /e/, /i/). Finally, languages like English and Nzebi generate even finer distinctions of height, such as that between high tense, high lax, mid tense, mid lax, and low vowels (/i/, /[ɪ]/, /e/, /[ɛ]/, /a/).

We have seen that a given speech sound can be characterized in feature terms by identifying the region it occupies on each one of the dimensions corresponding to different features: the sounds /m/ and /a/ can be characterized as follows relative to the dimensions of nasality, oral stricture, and tongue height:

(6) Feature analysis for two sounds:

Feature	Feature values for /m/	Feature values for /a/
[±nasal]	[+nasal]	[−nasal]
[oral stricture]	[−continuant]	[+continuant]
	[+consonantal]	[+consonantal]
[height]		[+low]

Certain features are intrinsically discrete rather than continuous dimensions. For instance, one distinction between the consonants /p/, /t/, and /k/ involves the *active articulator* involved in the production of their oral constriction: the lips for /p/, the tongue blade for /t/ and the tongue body for /k/. The property of being produced with a specific active articulator is a discrete property. There is no such thing as being more or less labial: a segment is either labial, i.e. articulated with the lips, or it is not.

(7) Active articulator features for consonantal sounds:

Sounds	Active articulator	Name of corresponding feature
p, b, m, f	lips	[labial]
t, s, tʃ, ʃ, θ, r, l, n, ɳ, ɲ	tongue blade and tip	[coronal]
k, g, q, ɢ, ɣ	tongue body	[dorsal]

We can now add to the feature analysis of /m/ the specification [+labial]: /m/'s feature values are therefore [+nasal, −continuant, +consonantal, +labial]. These feature values give a good approximation of the nature of /m/'s articulation and they unambiguously identify /m/ in English, since no other English phonemes possess this particular combination of values.

Additional features are required to specify the difference between sounds articulated with the same active articulator: for instance, the difference between the two coronals /n/ and /ɲ/ – which contrast in languages like Spanish or Italian – requires reference to the point in the mouth contacted by the active articulator. This is a more anterior point – closer to the front of the mouth – in the case of /n/ and a more posterior point – closer to the back of the mouth – in the case of /ɲ/. The corresponding feature is [±anterior], the name of the dimension specifying the constriction site along the roof of the mouth: [n] along with /t/, /d/, /s/, /z/, /θ/, /ð/ are [+anterior], while ɲ, along with /ʃ/, /tʃ/, /ʒ/, /dʒ/ are [–anterior]. Equipped with this additional feature, we can say that /n/ is characterized, in part, by the features [+nasal, +coronal, +anterior, +consonantal, –continuant].

EXERCISE 13.1	Give the feature composition of the sounds /e/, /ī/, /s/, /ŋ/, /ʃ/, /w/, /y/ using the features discussed in the preceding section.

13.1.3 Arguments for features

We turn now to the evidence supporting the view that speech sounds are analyzed in this way by untutored native speakers.

Two hypotheses can be compared: the proposal that segments are groups of features and the alternative view that segments are indivisible elements in phonological representations. We will show that the second hypothesis makes it impossible to understand several common phenomena, which find their explanation in feature analysis.

The first phenomenon we discuss is that of natural classes, mentioned earlier in chapter 12. In describing alternation types or allophonic distributions that are common across languages we observe that the rules tend to refer to groups of segments that share in exclusivity some feature value or values. These groups of segments are said to form natural classes. Sounds enclosed in curly brackets, { }, are natural classes.

A typical example involves alternations between the sounds {b, d, dʒ, g, z, ʒ} and the sounds {p, t, tʃ, k, s}. The first group is characterized by the features [+voice, –sonorant], the second by [–voice, –sonorant]. In languages as diverse as Lithuanian, Kolami, Catalan, Hungarian and Polish the [+voice, –sonorant] group of sounds may not occur before other [–voice] sounds: the following Hungarian alternations illustrate the consequences of this restriction (data from Vago 1980):

(8)	a.	*meleg*	'warm'	*melektø:l*	'from the warm'
	b.	*ka:d*	'bathtub'	*ka:tto:l*	'from the bathtub'
	c.	*vi:z*	'water'	*vi:stø:l*	'from the water'

d.	*vɔra:ʒ*	'magic'	*vɔra:ʃto:l*	'from the magic'
e.	*nɔj*	'big'	*nɔc kɔlɔp*	'big hat'
f.	*rɔb*	'prisoner'	*rɔp solgɔ*	'slave'

To account for the alternations in (8), rules such as the following can be formulated, which rely on the feature analysis of the participating segments:

(9)   [–sonorant] → [–voice]/ ____ [–voice]

Notice that the statement in (9) goes beyond the evidence presented, in the sense that it implies that other segments that happen to be voiced obstruents – sounds like [dz], [dʒ], [v], whose behavior we have not illustrated – will also become voiceless under the same circumstances. It also implies that any other voiceless sounds – segments like [p], [ʃ], [f] – will be equally able to condition devoicing. This capacity of feature-based statements to make predictions beyond the immediately observed or observable data will turn out to be an asset rather than a liability.

Suppose however, that the feature analysis in (9) is rejected, if segments are viewed as atomic, non-decomposable entities. Then the Hungarian alternations will have to be analyzed by reference to the specific lists of sounds whose behavior has been observed, as follows:

(10)   {b, d, ɟ, g, z, ʒ} → {p, t, c, k, s, ʃ} respectively/ ____ {t, k, s}.

We believe that this is the wrong rule. The argument against it is that it fails to shed light on the property that gives coherence to these lists of sounds, the property that makes them natural classes. Any segment may be a member of any list, and {ʈ, b, h, ŋ, ã, y, ʃ} is as good a list as {b, d, ɟ, g, z, ʒ}, but only certain groups of sounds can be referred to by a combination of feature values. By opting for (9), we claim that the speakers of Hungarian can generalize beyond the lists in (10) and can identify the defining properties that dictate membership in these lists. These defining properties are the phonological features.

This claim is supported in several ways. First, alternations like (8) between voiced and voiceless obstruents are extremely common and their existence is independent of the actual contents of the phonemic alphabet of a language. This can be seen in the following comparison between the sets of voiced obstruent phonemes in Hungarian, Lithuanian, and Kolami:

(11)   Three inventories of voiced obstruents

Lithuanian voiced obstruents:	b	d			dʒ	g	v	z	ʒ
Kolami voiced obstruents:	b	d	ɖ			g		z	
Hungarian voiced obstruents:	b	d	dz	dʒ	ɟ	g	v	z	ʒ

All three languages in (11) have alternations parallel to (8): therefore a featureless analysis of these alternations along the lines of (10) will have to refer to three different lists. For Lithuanian we must say that {b, d, dʒ, g, v, z, ʒ} undergo the rule, whereas for Kolami we must refer to the distinct set {b, d, ɖ, g, z}. This obscures the fundamental fact that the same phenomenon occurs in all three languages. In contrast, the feature-based analysis in (9) is valid for the voicing alternations encountered in each one of these languages, because it rises above accidental differences in phoneme inventories.

A related argument for the featural analysis in (9) is its ability to project beyond the data speakers have had access to. A Hungarian speaker who happens not to have observed yet alternations involving /v/ and /f/, will nonetheless be able to predict that the combination of morphemes /hiːv/ 'call' and /-tɔ/ (past tense, third-person singular) must be pronounced [hiːftɔ] rather than [hiːvtɔ]. The general point here is that a feature-based analysis of segments may facilitate the process of language acquisition: it gives the learner the means to generate novel segment sequences which conform to the sound pattern of the language.

A final argument in favor of feature analysis is that the vast majority of sets of segments participating in productive alternations like (8) can be shown to be characterized by some combination of feature values that identifies them uniquely. This is why they are natural classes. An absurd list like {ʤ, b, h, ŋ, ã, y, ʃ} is never encountered in the description of productive sound regularities because such a set does not correspond to any conceivable combination of feature values. From this observation a larger point, anticipated earlier, emerges: alternations involve natural classes because they reflect processes affecting features, not lists of segments.

EXERCISE 13.2	The voicing alternations of Hungarian obstruents involve not only voiced {b, d, g . . .} becoming voiceless {p, t, k, . . . } but also voiceless {p, t, k, . . . } becoming voiced {b, d, g . . . }. Consider the following data and formulate a feature analysis – extending the statement of (9) – so that it will characterize all voicing alternations in the language, the ones in (8) as well as those seen below:

ljuk	'hole'	ljugbɔn	'in the hole'
nɔp	'sun'	nɔbbɔn	'in the sun'
sɛrteːʃ	'pig'	sɛrteːʒbɔn	'in the pig'
golf	'golf'	golv bɔjnokʃaːg	'golf championship'

Now consider the additional data below:

list	'flour'	lizdbɛn	'in the flour'
bɔrɔtsk	'apricot'	bɔrɔdzgbɔn	'in the apricot'
tɛkst	'text'	tɛgzdbɔn	'in the text'

Make sure your statement will accurately characterize all alternations. The data is limited and thus compatible with a number of interpretations and analyses: choose the most general one even if your analysis makes predictions that you cannot verify at this point. (Do not consider the *bɔn/bɛn* alternations – they reflect an unrelated phenomenon.)

A feature-based analysis is capable of modelling certain aspects of linguistic knowledge that go beyond the sounds attested in one's native language. With this in mind we asked a Hungarian colleague and co-author of this book how she pronounces in Hungarian the phrase 'in (the city of) Bath'. The suffix -*ban* [bɔn] is used in Hungarian to indicate location (cf. Exercise 13.2). Note that the English place name *Bath* [bɑθ] contains a voiceless interdental fricative [θ] that is unattested in Hungarian. Our colleague had never used the expression *Bath-ban* in Hungarian and had not heard anyone use it either. She uttered [bɑθ] for *Bath* in isolation but [bɑðbɔn] for *Bath-ban*, using [ð], the voiced counterpart [θ]. Explain the significance of this fact for feature-based and segment-based analyses of voicing assimilation. Does your answer to Exercise 13.2 predict the attested [bɑðbɔn] or the form our colleague rejected, namely [bɑθbɔn]?

13.2 Relations Between Features: Constituency and Prominence

We mentioned at the beginning of this chapter that phonological representations consist of features and their relations. We present two of these: constituency and prominence.

The term **constituency** will be familiar from chapters 2 and 4. In phonology it refers to the fact that within the stream of speech certain groups of sounds or groups of features can be identified. A **segment** is a group of features. A **syllable** is a group of segments. A **stress group** is a group of syllables. Like syntactic constituent structure, phonological constituency is hierarchical: smaller groups are contained within larger ones. This section discusses the principles governing the structure of one of these phonological constituents: the syllable.

13.2.1 Syllables

The syllable is a constituent consisting of the segments surrounding a vowel or vowel-like sound. Thus in the word *segment* [sɛgmənt] there are two syllables corresponding to the two vowels – [ɛ] and [ə]: [sɛg] and [mənt]. We use σ to symbolize the syllable node dominating the component segments.

(12)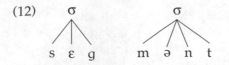

The string of symbols [sɛgmənt] in (12) abbreviates the full-fledged representation using features employed earlier. A graphically simpler representation of syllabic constituency can be obtained by just inserting a period at the boundary between two syllables: [sɛg.mənt]. The notation in (13) is useful in cases where we need to indicate explicitly that a segment belongs to more than one syllable, as in forms such as *happy* [hæpi], in which the medial [p] is considered by some speakers as shared between the first and the second syllable.

(13)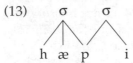

Position within a syllabic constituent may determine the realization of sounds. For instance in English, a nasal followed by a non-coronal stop (*p, b, k, g*) is realized differently depending on whether the two consonants belong to the same syllable or not. The nasal is obligatorily homorganic (articulated at the same place, with the same active articulator) with the stop, when the two are in the same syllable: hence words like *ink* or *thank* contain obligatory [ŋk], never [nk]. When the consonants belong to separate syllables, the nasal in underlying /nk/ may be realized as alveolar: e.g. *congressional* [kəngrɛʃənəl]. A further consequence of the same rule is that the sequence [mk] is a possible cluster in at least some dialects of English (as in *pumpkin* [pʌmkɪn], *Fromkin* [frɑmkɪn]), but does not occur syllable-internally: syllables like *limk* are unthinkable in any variety of English. Thus membership in the same syllabic constituent induces place assimilation in the case of nasal–stop sequences. A parallel observation refers to the English distribution of voicing in sequences of obstruents (stops and fricatives). When such sequences occur in the same syllable (e.g. in *cubs* [kʌbz] vs. *cups* [kʌps]) the entire cluster must have the same voicing value: forms like [kʌpz] or [kʌbs] are not only unattested but sound grossly deviant. When the sequence of obstruents is distributed into separate syllables, as in *absurd* [æb.sɚd], *Hudson* [hʌd.sən], *anecdote* [æ.nək.dot], the voicing values may be distinct.

A distinct effect of syllable division involves the typical difference in realization between syllable-initial and syllable-final consonants. For instance, English voiceless stops may be glottalized (realized with tightly shut glottis) but not aspirated, when they occur in syllable-final position;

whereas syllable-initial stops may be aspirated, depending on their position relative to stress and the beginning of the word, but are never glottalized: thus the /t/s in *tap* [tʰæp] and *between* [bə.tʰwin] are aspirated, while those in *pat* [pʰæʔt] and *atlas* [æʔt.ləs] may be glottalized, as the transcriptions suggest. In many languages, the range of consonant types encountered in syllable-final and syllable-initial position are quite different: almost invariably there are more consonants allowed initially than finally. Thus Thai distinguishes syllable-initial voiced, voiceless unaspirated and voiceless aspirated stops but its syllable-final stops are all realized as voiceless unaspirated and glottalized. Further, in syllable-initial position, Thai allows the affricates ts, tʃ, tsʰ, tʃʰ to contrast with the stops t, tʰ. In syllable-final position only the stops occur.

13.2.2 Syllable-internal structure

Syllables can be divided into further subconstituents. The **nucleus** is the vowel or vowel-like element every syllable contains. The **onset** is the string of consonants that precede the nucleus. The **coda** is the string of consonants that follow the nucleus. The nucleus and the coda are commonly viewed as forming an intermediate subconstituent called the **rime**. The nucleus is the obligatory part of the syllable: there are only as many syllables as there are nuclei. Onsets are frequently optional, but always preferred, members of the syllable. Codas are never obligatory: all languages possess syllables lacking codas (or **open syllables**) in addition to, possibly, syllables with codas (or **closed syllables**). We illustrate some of these points in the following diagram of the English word *imprint* [ɪmprɪnt]. The obligatory constituents appear in bold characters.

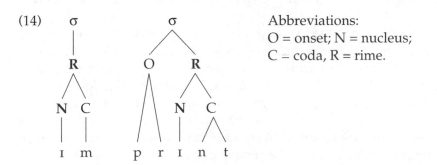

(14) Abbreviations:
O = onset; N = nucleus;
C = coda, R = rime.

Segments occurring in the nucleus of the syllable are said to be syllabic, or [+syllabic]. Thus [m̩] in words like *prism* [prɪzm̩] is syllabic: the word contains two syllables and [m̩] is the nucleus of the second syllable. The same segment occurs as non-syllabic in *prismatic* [prɪz.mæ.tɪk] (where /m/ is an onset) or *broom* (where /m/ is a coda).

13.2.3   Learning syllables, with an excursus on learning phonotactic patterns

Our transcription of syllable divisions (e.g. the period in [sɛg.mənt]) may suggest misleadingly that some unambiguous syllable boundary signals are present in the stream of speech and that speakers' knowledge of syllabification is acquired by listening to these signals. The reality is more complex and more interesting. First, we should make it clear that when we talk about syllable divisions, we refer primarily not to phonetically observable properties of utterances but to speakers' intuitions about how they might break up a longer utterance into one-voweled pieces. Any speaker of English, when invited to break up *segment* into two parts, will most likely come up with [sɛg] plus [mənt], not [sɛgm] plus [ənt] and not [sɛ] plus [gmənt]. The syllable boundaries we postulate are based on such judgments.

It is therefore important to ask how linguistically naive speakers come to know the syllable divisions in their language. This is, to some extent, still a mystery. We know that there is significant agreement among adult speakers with respect to the placement of syllable divisions (Selkirk 1982; Derwing 1992). Therefore, to the extent that they know how to divide words into syllables, these speakers must have inferred this knowledge from some aspect of their phonological system that is readily accessible and learnable. How does the inference proceed? What are the speakers' judgments based on?

In some cases it is clear that these judgments of syllabification reflect speakers' observations about possible words in their language: for instance [sɛgm] and [gmənt] are not possible words in English because [gm] does not occur word-initially or finally. It is therefore probable that rejected syllabic divisions like [sɛgm.ənt] or [sɛ.gmənt] are being rejected on these grounds.

Let us make the reasoning involved here more precise. We are suggesting that speakers are in possession of certain broad generalizations about possible and impossible word-initial and final sequences and that these generalizations play a role in their inferences about syllable structure. These inferences may take two forms. First, the speaker may start from the assumption that a syllable is a sort of small word, a one-voweled word whose edges are identical in structure to the edges of words. From this assumption it follows that [sɛgmənt] must be syllabically divided as [sɛg.mənt] since /gm/ is neither a possible left edge nor a possible right edge for an English word. Alternatively, the speaker may start from the assumption that a word is a string of syllables, a string in which every segment must belong to one or another syllable. Given this assumption, if the speaker observes that words in their language cannot begin with certain segment sequences – e.g. English words cannot begin with /gm/ – they may attribute this observation to the fact that the syllables of the language cannot begin with that sequence. By either of these modes of reasoning, one can infer laws of syllable structure from observations about word structure. The intuitions of syllable division reflect, then, the laws inferred in this way.

Excursus on learning phonotactic patterns

Since we brought up the question of generalizations about possible segment sequences (or **phonotactics**), we should add that speakers draw conclusions not only based on what they have heard, but also based on what they have not: they notice significant gaps in the input data and draw inferences from such gaps. In the case of the sequence /gm/ mentioned earlier, speakers of English can observe a very general law which subsumes the original observation: no consonant–nasal sequence can begin an English word, with the exception of /sm/, /sn/. Thus not only is /gm/ missing as a word-initial sequence, but also /pn/, /bn/, /pm/, /bm/, /fn/, /vn/, /fm/, /vm/, /tn/, /dn/, /tm/, /dm/, /θn/, /θm/, /ðn/, /ðm/, along with all other conceivable C–nasal sequences distinct from /sm/ and /sn/. It is probably the GENERALITY OF THE PATTERN that suggests to the speaker that the /gm/ gap is not accidental. On the issue of generality, we note that English, like many other languages, does not allow sonorant–obstruent sequences at the beginning of the word: /lp/, /rk/, /rp/, /ms/, /nf/ are not attested word beginnings. Speakers appear not only to observe this gap but also to conclude from it that such sequences are not simply accidentally missing from the language: asked to judge the well-formedness of potential words beginning with /lp/, /rk/, /rp/, /ms/, /nf/, several generations of students in the introductory phonology class at UCLA have resolutely rejected such words as utterly impossible. In contrast, sequences like /vl/, /vr/, which are sparsely, if at all, attested in English, did not evoke the same sort of judgment: the probable reason for this is the existence of phonologically parallel sequences /fl/ and /fr/, which are well attested initially. Thus the /vr/, /vl/ initial gap is more likely to be considered accidental, because the unattested sequences are structurally isolated.

We return now to the question of syllable divisions. Corresponding to the fact that sonorant–obstruent sequences are impossible word initially, we observe that sequences of Vowel–Consonant–Consonant–Vowel (VCCV) are systematically divided between the consonants as VC.CV when the sequence involves a sonorant followed by an obstruent. Thus *alpine* and *harpoon* are divided as [æl.paɪn] not [æ.lpaɪn], [har.pun], not [ha.rpun]. In contrast, when the consonant sequence involves a possible word-initial cluster, such as *sk* or *pl*, the VCCV sequence *can* be divided either as V.CCV or as VC.CV: *basket* [bæs.kɪt], *poplar* [pɑp.lər] but also *askew* [ə.skju], *reply* [ri.plaɪ].

The frequently reported intuition that words like *vapid, leper, suburb* divide as [væp.ɪd], [lɛp.ɚ], [sʌb.ɚb] – or with the medial consonant belonging to both syllables at once (Kahn 1976) – is most likely based on the fact that short lax vowels like [æ], [ɛ], [ʌ] do not occur word-finally in English. Note that words like *vapor, viper, sober* are divided as [veɪ.pɚ], [vaɪ.pɚ], [soː.bɚ], and that's because long vowels and diphthongs do occur word-finally. Thus we may wonder whether speakers' intuitions in all such cases are reflecting knowledge of syllables per se rather than some inference that syllables should look like little words.

However, when we look at the data more carefully, it becomes clear that the similarity between possible words and postulated syllables is not the only relevant factor in these judgments. Note first that for many words, more than one potential division exists which results in syllables that pass the possible word test: words such as *Plato* [plei.to] could – in principle – be divided either as [pleit.o] or as [plei.to]. The syllables resulting from either division correspond to possible words in English. But in fact there is a clear preference for dividing such words as [plei.to] with the intervocalic consonant assigned to the position of onset rather than coda. This preference is not based on observations about possible words. Second, in languages like Polish, where words may begin and end in clusters that are highly unusual (by English standards), the preferences for syllable division are nonetheless similar to those of English. Thus words like *filtr* 'filter', *metr* 'meter', *wiatr* 'wind' are monosyllabic in Polish: this shows that Polish words can end in sequences of obstruent plus non-syllabic sonorant. But when such sequences are placed between vowels (as in *wiadro* 'pail', *wiatru* 'wind-Genitive plural', *igratʃ* 'to play') the divisions *wiadr.o*, *wiatr-u*, *igr.atʃ* are unambiguously rejected. In other words, when there is a choice in the matter of assigning consonants to one syllable or another, Polish and English exercise the same choices. This cannot be based on observations about word structure since *wiatr* is a possible word and yet *wiatr.u* is not a possible syllabification. We suggest that in cases where the lexicon of the language does not resolve a parsing ambiguity, syllable divisions are based on universal preferences for certain syllable types and against others.

The preference for dividing VCV strings (V = vowel, C = consonant) as V.CV is very general across languages. And similarly for the preference against dividing VCCV as VCC.V. We can justify the general statements in (15):

(15)   Two universal syllable preference laws:
       All other things being equal, the assignment of segments to
       syllables is such as to create
       (a)   open syllables
       and
       (b)   syllables with onsets.

Backward talk and other tests of syllable divisions

Backward talk is a language game, a way of disguising normal speech by modifying in a systematic way the basic words of the language. Backward talk can be a useful technique for verifying that the syllable divisions postulated by linguists correspond to those internalized by native speakers. One common form of backward talk is that of reversing whole syllables as units: *cat.nip* becomes *nit.cap*, *seg.ment* becomes *ment.seg* etc. This form of the game is common among certain French speakers, who disguise their speech by syllable reversal, a procedure called *Verlan* [veʁ.lã] from the French word *l'envers* [lã.veʁ], meaning 'the reverse'. It is also sporadically encountered in English. By observing the results of backward talk one can infer how segment sequences are divided into syllable units by untutored native speakers. Thus a sequence Vowel–Consonant–Vowel (VCV) is always divided in French as V.CV: *chaton* [ʃatõ] 'kitten', syllabified as [ʃa.tõ] becomes [tõ.ʃa] in Verlan, *pourri* [puʁi] 'rotten' becomes [ʁipu]. A sequence V-C-C-V is differently divided depending on whether the two consonants are an obstruent and a liquid or a different type of cluster. Thus French *secret* [sœkʁe] becomes [kʁesœ] not [ʁesœk]. This confirms that the speakers divide *secret* as [sœ.kʁe]. For other types of clusters the results of backward talk are quite different: French *balcon* [bal.kõ] becomes [kõbal], English *cultures* [kʌl.tʃɚz] becomes [tʃɚz.kʌl] (note that /tʃ/ is considered a single sound, not a cluster of t + ʃ).

The syllable divisions revealed by backward talk correspond closely to those suggested by other facts about French phonology. For instance, the mid vowel /e/ takes on different realizations depending on whether it is followed within the same syllable by a consonant: thus we find only lax [ɛ] in a syllable closed by a consonant, as in *Eskimo* [ɛs.ki.mo], where the initial e is followed by s within its syllable, and therefore laxed. In contrast, in the word *decret* 'decree' [de.kʁe] the two /e/s are final within their syllables and therefore realized as tense [e]. Note that in the case of *decret*, we now have two independent reasons to assume the syllabification [de.kʁe], as against [dek.ʁe]: one reason is the effect of Verlan [kʁe.de.], not [ʁe.dek.]. The other is the absence of laxing in the first syllable: [de.kʁe], not [dɛk.ʁe].

Thus the preference for dividing VCV strings as V.CV rather than as VC.V is based on the fact that the V.CV parse creates an open syllable (V) followed by a syllable with an onset. The rejected parse, VC.V, creates a closed syllable (VC) followed by a syllable lacking an onset (V). In the second class of examples, VCCV is parsed as V.CCV if the relevant complex onset is permitted (as in *de.cree*). VCCV will be parsed as VC.CV if the cluster does not correspond to a permissible complex onset (as in *in.tend*). Finally, VCCV cannot be parsed as VCC.V since this third parse has the double disadvantage of creating a complex coda (VCC) and an onsetless syllable (V), and no compensating virtues.

EXERCISE 13.4	Consider the alternations in vowel length in the Yokuts words seen below. (Yokuts is a California Indian language. Data comes from Newman 1944.) Posit underlying representations for roots and suffixes. Make assumptions about possible Yokuts syllables and about how the Yokuts words below are divided into syllables. State what these assumptions are and use them to explain the distribution of long and short vowels. You will need a rule of the form [+syllabic] → [−long]/ in some context defined in terms of syllable structure. Ignore the alternation between i and zero. The dash (-) indicates morpheme boundaries, which do not necessarily coincide with syllable boundaries:

Nonfuture	Imperative	Dubitative	Future	Gloss
ṣap-hin	ṣap-ka	ṣa:pal	ṣa:p-en	burn
lan-hin	lan-ka	la:nal	la:n-en	hear
ʔa:mil-hin	ʔa:mil-ka	ʔaml-al	ʔaml-en	help
xat-hin	xat-ka	xat-al	xat-en	eat
paʔiṭ-hin	paʔiṭ-ka	paʔṭ-al	paʔṭ-en	fight

Nonfuture	Passive	Gloss
pana:-hin	pana-t	arrive
hoyo:-hin	hoyo-t	name

13.2.4   A case study in syllable constituency effects: Spanish r

We consider now in greater detail the effect of syllable structure on the realization of segments. Our data come from Spanish and have been analyzed by Harris (1983). The sounds we consider are the trill [r] and the flap [ɾ], which contrast in Spanish when they occur between vowels: *perro* [pero] 'dog' vs. *pero* [peɾo] 'but'. Spanish orthography reflects accurately the difference in duration between the two sounds: the trill is considerably longer. In all other positions – word-initial, final, after or before a consonant – the trill and the tap are in complementary distribution. The following data illustrate this:

(16)   After a stop or after f: only [ɾ] occurs.

bravo	*drama*	*otro*	*hombre*	*Africa*
[bɾaβo]	[dɾama]	[otɾo]	[ombɾe]	[afɾika]
'brave'	'drama'	'other'	'man'	

(17)   After other consonants: only [r] occurs.

Israel	*honra*	*alrededor*
[izrael]	[onra]	[alreðeðor]
'Israel'	'honor'	'around'

(18) Before a consonant: only [ɾ] occurs in casual speech, only [r] occurs
in emphatic speech.

martes	*arbol*	*Carlos*
[martes]~[maɾtes]	[arβol]~[aɾβol]	[karlos]~[kaɾlos]
'Tuesday'	'tree'	

(19) Word-initial: only [r] occurs:

rápido	*raro*	*rubor*
[rapiðo]	[raɾo]	[ruβor]
'rapid'	'rare'	'blush'

(20) Word-final: only [ɾ] occurs in casual speech, only [r] in emphatic
speech.

mar	*amor*	*sur*
[mar]~[maɾ]	[amor]~[amoɾ]	[sur]~[suɾ]
'sea'	'love'	'South'

The cases illustrated in (18) and (20) involve both r-like sounds that
occupy the syllable coda position. This is clear in utterances like *mar*. In
cases like *martes* or *Carlos*, this assumption is supported by the intuitions
of Spanish speakers, who divide such sequences as *mar.tes*, *Car.los*, and by
the impossibility of clusters like *rt*, *rl* in word-initial position. We may
therefore reduce these data to the preliminary statements in (21):

(21) a. Syllable-final Spanish r-sounds are normally realized as [ɾ].
  b. Emphatic speech rule: syllable-final r-sound is realized as [r].

The remaining data can also be understood in terms of the r-sound's
proximity to the syllable boundary. Note that the clusters in (16) – a stop
or *f* followed by a r-sound – can be identified as onset clusters: *A.fri.ca*,
o.tro., *hom.bre*. The clusters in (17), on the other hand, straddle a syllable
boundary: *Is.ra.el*, *hon.ra*, *al.re.de.dor*. We know this both by directly consulting the intuitions of Spanish speakers about syllable division, and also
indirectly, by noting that /fr/, /pr/, /kr/, /dr/, /br/, /tr/, /dr/ , /fl/,
/pl/, /bl/, /kl/, /gl/, /sw/, /kw/ are the only sequences of consonants
found at the beginning of native Spanish words; clusters like /rl/, /sp/,
/nt/, /lk/, etc. occur only after a vowel. Since the beginning of every
word is also the beginning of that word's first syllable, this means that
clusters which may not occur word-initially are probably clusters that cannot occur at the beginning of any syllable. This reasoning leads to a second
generalization:

(22) If the r-sound is not in syllable-initial position, then it is realized
  as [ɾ].

We now have to write a statement that will characterize the fact that syllable-initial r-sounds are invariably trills [r] when word-initial or post-consonantal (cases (17) and (19)) but that they can contrast – [r] vs. [ɾ] – after a vowel:

(23)   A syllable-initial r-sound is realized as a trill, unless a vowel precedes.

Note that (23) does not commit us to any particular realization of the rhotic in the case where it is both syllable-initial and postvocalic: this is good, since we do want to allow for the possibility of contrasts like *pero* [pe.ɾo] vs. *perro* [pe.ro] in exactly that position. However, (23) does predict – correctly – the trilled realization of the rhotic in all other instances where it is syllable-initial (cases (17) and (19)).

Although the statements in (21), (22), and (23) represent considerable progress over the original complex data arrangement, we note that a further simplification is possible, since (22) subsumes (21a). The final analysis will therefore take the following form:

(24)   a.   A syllable-initial rhotic is realized as a trill unless a vowel precedes.
       b.   A rhotic that does not occur syllable-initially is realized as a flap.
       c.   In emphatic speech, a syllable-final rhotic is realized as a trill.

The following abbreviatory symbols will be useful as we provide the rule corresponding to (24): reference to constituent edges (syllable-final or syllable-initial position) is made via annotated left and right brackets.

(25)   'syllable-initial' = [$_\sigma$____
       'syllable-final'   = ____$_\sigma$]

To characterize the class of rhotics, the segments targetted in (24), we can use the group of feature values [+sonorant, +consonantal, +continuant, –lateral]. To distinguish trills from taps, we will assume that the feature [±long] differentiates them: the trill being, as noted, the longer sound. Thus one abbreviated expression of (24a) is the following statement:

(26) $\begin{bmatrix} +\text{sonorant} \\ +\text{consonantal} \\ +\text{continuant} \\ -\text{lateral} \end{bmatrix} \rightarrow [+\text{long}]/[_\sigma\underline{\hspace{1cm}}$

The part of this statement that precedes the slash says that a rhotic becomes long. This is the Structural Change of the rule. The second part of the statement – the part that follows the slash – says that this change happens when the target segment is located in syllable-initial position. The dash indicates the position of the target segment relative to the boundary. This second part is a description of the Context or Environment of the rule. The description of the entire string affected by the rule – target and context – is the Structural Description of the rule. We must also explicitly state any negative condition on the rule, such as the fact that it is blocked after a vowel. This can be done as a separate statement describing the context in which the rhotic fails to undergo the rule.

(27) $\begin{bmatrix} \text{+sonorant} \\ \text{+consonantal} \\ \text{+continuant} \\ \text{-lateral} \end{bmatrix} \rightarrow [\text{+long}] / [_\sigma \underline{\qquad}$

Rule blocked in the context: [+syllabic]____

The statement in (24b) refers to a rhotic that is not syllable-initial. This covers both the syllable-final *r* in *mar.tes* and the syllable-medial one in *o.tro*. The position of this class of rhotics can be succinctly described as preceded within the same syllable by some other segment. Both *r*s in *mar.tes* and *o.tro* fit this description. The corresponding rule will be as below:

(28) $\begin{bmatrix} \text{+sonorant} \\ \text{+consonantal} \\ \text{+continuant} \\ \text{-lateral} \end{bmatrix} \rightarrow [\text{-long}] /$

$$\sigma$$

[+segment]   ____

Note that this rule statement provides the minimum information necessary to identify strings to which the rule must apply. For instance, the description of the context in (28) does not mention whether some segment follows the target rhotic within its syllable. It may (as in *o.tro*) or it might not (as in *mar.tes*). Neither does the rule mention whether the segment preceding the target is initial or not within the syllable, since this factor is also irrelevant to the applicability of the rule. It is important to bear in mind that if the statement of the rule does not prohibit explicitly application to some class of contexts, the rule will be expected to apply to them. The statement in (28) is designed so as not to explicitly prohibit its application to any strings other than those where r is initial within its syllable.

13.3 Prominence Relations

In many languages, including English, there are differences of **prominence** or **stress** among the syllables of a word. The most prominent syllable in a word is said to carry its **main**, or **primary stress**. Sometimes several syllables within a word are prominent relative to their neighboring syllables: in such cases we distinguish a primary stress from the **subsidiary stresses** of the word. For instance in *assìmilátion* [əˌsɪməˈleɪʃn̩], there is a main stressed syllable [ˈleɪ] identified by the preposed symbol [ˈ], and a secondary stressed syllable [ˌsɪm], marked by a preposed [ˌ]. The other syllables are completely stressless.

How can different degrees of stress or prominence be identified? Unlike other features, stress cannot be identified with any one acoustic or articulatory feature: it is manifested variously, depending on the language, as the assignment of a particular tone to a syllable, or as the possibility of realizing a variety of tones, or as increased duration and loudness associated with the stressed syllables, or as the possibility of a richer set of contrasts among the segments of the stressed syllables than among those of the unstressed ones. In English, stressed syllables – whether they carry main or subsidiary stress – are chiefly identified through the distinctive vowel qualities they allow: vowels such as [æ], [ɑ], [ɛ], [ɔ], [ʊ], or [u], [i] or [ʌ] are permitted only under stress. The location of main stress is testable in English in part through the observation that a main-stressed syllable attracts **nuclear tones**: these are distinctive pitch values that form the central unit of an intonational melody. For instance the intonational melody marking questions in English contains a low pitch value (**a low tone**) associated with the main stressed syllable of the relevant word. Try saying each one of the words and phrases below as if they represent a question. You will observe that the lowest pitch value in each case is associated with the syllable indicated in bold characters: this is the main stressed syllable. Note that at least in (29c–d), there are other stressed syllables in the expression (judging from the distribution of vowel qualities such as [æ] and [ʊ], which are limited to stressed syllables).

(29)   a.   **nuc**lear [ˈnʊkliɚ]?
       b.   ar**bo**real [ɑˈboriəl]?
       c.   abo**rig**inal [ˌæbəˈrɪdʒənəl]?
       d.   nuclear **plant** location [ˌnʊkliɚ ˈplænt loˌkeʃn]?

Beyond these diverse ways of signalling stress, speakers are nonetheless able to see a unified effect: and this is why we talk about stress or prominence rather than about duration, loudness or pitch accents, as separate and unrelated properties of syllables.

There are multiple ways of representing prominence relations. We present here one of these options, which is based on the observation that there are no clear limits to the number of stress distinctions a language might display. Thus in the word *assìmilátion* there is a three-way distinction between the stressless first, third and fifth syllables, the secondary stressed second syllable, and the main stressed penultimate. When we embed this word in a larger phrase, the number of prominence distinctions multiplies: in the phrase *assimilation between vowels*, the primary stress of the phrase falls on the first syllable of *vowels*, and the stress on [lei] of [ə₁sɪmə'leiʃn̩] is demoted to a secondary stress, while that on [sɪm] becomes an even weaker *tertiary* stress. Further syntactic embedding will add even more degrees-of-stress distinctions. Not all these distinctions are easily perceptible, but it is not the case that one can categorically draw a line and deny the existence of stress distinctions beyond any given fixed point.

To represent the fact that the syllables of an expression may possess indefinitely many degrees of stress we use **grid structures**.

Grids are structures that distinguish discrete but, in principle, infinitely many levels of stress: no stress at all (or 0 stress); primary stress; and any number of stress degrees in between. These degrees of stress are graphically represented as horizontally arrayed layers, with the highest layer representing the greatest degree of stress in a given utterance. Every syllable is associated with a grid position and each grid position carries a column of grid marks denoting the degree of stress of that syllable. The actual height of the grid columns is determined by the following rules:

(30) Grid rules:
    a. If two syllables σ1 and σ2 differ in that σ1 is more prominent than σ2, then the column of grid marks associated with σ1 is higher than that associated with σ2.
    b. Only the minimum necessary of grid marks is used to distinguish stresses.

Note that these rules are not designed to predict which syllables carry what degree of stress: they are rules for representing what is known about the stress degree of a given syllable. Thus, once we know that *assìmilátion* is stressed as it is, with primary stress on the penult and secondary stress on the second syllable, we can construct its grid structure, in accordance with (30). First, each syllable gets a grid mark on the lowest grid layer, to denote the fact that in principle each syllable is a potential stress bearer:

(31)

layer 0	x	x	x	x	x
	σ	σ	σ	σ	σ
	ə	sɪm	ə	lei	ʃn̩

Next, each stressed syllable carries an additional grid mark: this encodes, in our example, the fact that the syllables [sɪm] and [lei] are more prominent than syllables [ə], [ə] and [ʃn̩]. Therefore, in virtue of (30a), the height of the grid column of [sɪm] and [leɪ] must be higher:

(32)

layer 1		x		x	
layer 0	x	x	x	x	x
	σ	σ	σ	σ	σ
	ə	sɪm	ə	leɪ	ʃn

Next we must distinguish [sɪm] and [leɪ]: the second is more strongly stressed than the first and thus must carry a higher grid column:

(33)

layer 2				x	
layer 1		x		x	
layer 0	x	x	x	x	x
	σ	σ	σ	σ	σ
	ə	sɪm	ə	leɪ	ʃn

At this point no further prominence distinction is observed, which means that (33) is the final grid representation for the stress of this utterance. Since the degree of stress of one syllable is measured relative to the degree of stress of the other syllables in the utterance, the height of the grid column on a given syllable varies depending on what syllables it is being compared with, even when the syllable's stress level is felt to be constant. Thus [leɪ] carries a 3-x grid column in (33), but will have to have it augmented to a 4-x column in *màintáin assìmilátion*, as seen below. This is because *assimilation* takes primary stress within this larger utterance, and therefore its most strongly stressed syllable, [leɪ], must be marked as more prominent than the most strongly stressed syllable of *maintain*.

(34)

layer 3						x	
layer 2		x				x	
layer 1	x	x		x		x	
layer 0	x	x	x	x	x	x	
	σ	σ	σ	σ	σ	σ	σ
	meɪn	teɪn	ə	sɪm	ə	leɪ	ʃn

Two types of stress rules act on these representations: some rules will assign line 1 marks (i.e. the [+stressed] status) to certain syllables. Other rules will assign greater degrees of stress to some of the stressed syllables. For instance (35) summarizes the stress rules of Malayalam (a Dravidian language of Kerala, India):

(35) a. Every syllable containing a long vowel is assigned a line 1 grid mark (= i.e. stressed).
      b. If the second syllable is not stressed, the first syllable is stressed.

c.   The primary stress falls on the first stressed syllable of the
word.

We show in (36) how these rules apply to generate the grid structures of
two Malayalam words: *'marjaṇam* and *an'ga:rja,sa:t,mi:karjaṇam*. First we
observe that rule (35a) applies to *an'ga:rja,sa:t,mi:karjaṇam* since this word
has long vowels, but not to *'marjaṇam*, a word that lacks long vowels.

(36)   Every syllable containing a long vowel is assigned a line 1 grid
mark.

layer 1			x		x	x			
layer 0	x	x	x	x	x	x	x	x
	σ	σ	σ	σ	σ	σ	σ	σ
	an	ga:r	ja	sa:t	mi:	kar	ja	ṇam.

Next, we observe that (35b) applies to *'marjaṇam* but not to
an'ga:rja,sa:t,mi:karjaṇam, since the latter already possesses a stress on the
second syllable.

(37)   If the second syllable is not stressed, the first syllable is stressed.

layer 1	x		
layer 0	x	x	x
	σ	σ	σ
	mar	ja	ṇam

Finally, (35c) applies to *an'ga:rjag,sa:t,mi:karjaṇam*, to increase the stress
on the leftmost stressed syllable. The effect of (35c) is already satisfied by
'marjaṇam, since this form possesses a syllable that is more prominent than
all others.

(38)   The primary stress falls on the first stressed syllable of the word.

layer 2			x						
layer 1			x		x	x			
layer 0	x	x	x	x	x	x	x	x
	σ	σ	σ	σ	σ	σ	σ	σ
	an	ga:r	ja	sa:t	mi:	kar	ja	ṇam.

We have observed that our impressions about relative prominence among
syllables can be given a precise representation in the form of grid structures. The grids characterize stressed syllables as positions carrying at least
one mark above layer 0. Further differences among stresses are obtained
by increasing the height of grid columns associated with more prominent

syllables. The primary stress in any given phonological domain (a word, a phrase, an utterance) is identified as the syllable carrying the highest grid column within the domain.

EXERCISE 13.5	Read aloud the following sentences focusing on the noun phrases in bold characters: (a) He is **the editor of a book**. (b) He is **the book's editor**. (c) He is **the book editor**. Mark primary and subsidiary stresses. Provide grid structures for all three noun phrases.

EXERCISE 13.6	Observe the differences in the location of main stress between (a–b) and, on the other hand, (c) in Exercise 13.5. Identify the general class of nominal expressions that are characterized by the stress pattern of (c) as distinct from (a–b).

13.4 Lexical Representations in Phonology

The reader will wonder now what an entry in his or her – or someone else's – mental lexicon looks like. Here we refer to the phonological side of this entry. In addition to it, there will be syntactic information about the form in question (is it a verb? does it subcategorize for a clausal complement?), morphological information (does it form its past tense as a regular verb?), and semantic information (what does it mean?). Here we outline only points pertaining to the phonological side of a lexical entry.

Minimally, a lexical entry will contain information that is sufficient to distinguish its surface realization from that of any other form which, in the judgment of the speaker, is realized distinctly in the same circumstances. Thus the phonological entries of *write* and *rite* will be identical insofar as these forms are always realized identically as [raɪt] in the same circumstances. (*Same circumstances* refers to **speech rate** – faster or slower – and **speech register** – careful, colloquial or casual speech. The point is that, whatever the circumstances may be, when they are identical, these two forms are identically realized.) The entries of *write* and *ride* must be distinct, since they are realized as [raɪt] and [raɪd] respectively under most circumstances. Therefore the voicing values in the final stops of *write* and *ride* will have to be part of the lexical entries, as it is these voicing values that cause the speaker to realize the two forms distinctly.

Here is a possible model of the lexical entry for *ride*: each column of features corresponds to a separate segment. The columns are labeled to facilitate their identification with particular segments. The left-to-right order encodes the speaker's knowledge that some segments precede others in this entry.

(39)

[–syllabic]	[+syllabic]	[+syllabic]	[–syllabic]
[+sonorant]	[+sonorant]	[+sonorant]	[–sonorant]
[+consonantal]	[–consonantal]	[–consonantal]	[+consonantal]
[–lateral]	[–front]	[+front]	[–continuant]
[–nasal]	[+low]	[+high]	[–nasal]
[+voice]	[+voice]	[+voice]	[+voice]
(r)	(a)	(ɪ)	(d)

Now that we have stated the most basic thing about our phonological lexicon – the fact that it must help distinguish distinct utterances – we note that a slew of related questions arise. Should the lexical entry contain information about syllable division? Should it contain stress information even when the location of stress is predictable? Should features that are predictable in context be included in the lexicon or should they be derived by rule? These questions reduce to one: are predictable properties included in the speakers' lexical entries? As there is little consensus among linguists on this point, we will mention only one of the research strategies that may be fruitful in addressing these issues.

Consider a language in which nasalized vowels (e.g. [ã]) occur under two circumstances: some [ã]s occur in contexts where they contrast with oral [a], as in [pak] vs. [pãk]. Others occur predictably, when the following segment is a nasal consonant: [pãn]. In this second context there is no contrast: no oral [a] occurs before nasals, hence no form such as *[pan] is possible. A phonological rule is necessary to characterize this observation:

(40)   Nasalization
       [+syllabic] → [+nasal] / ____[+nasal]

Let us assume further that our language – which we model on Bengali – provides clear evidence for the existence of the rule (40), in the form of alternations between oral [a] – e.g. [pa] – and its nasalized counterpart when the same vowel is followed by a nasal suffix: [pã-na].

Consider now the lexical representations of this language. It is clear that a morpheme like [pãk] must be lexically represented as /pãk/, with underlying /ã/, since the nasality of this [ã] cannot be predicted from any other property of the morpheme. But what about a single morpheme like [pãn]? Although this [ã] is invariably nasalized, rule (40) can derive it from underlying /a/. If so, the lexical entry will be /pan/. The more interesting hypothesis is that the presence of rule (40) in the language allows the speaker to construct lexical entries whose vowels are indeterminate or *unspecified* for nasality: they simply lack a [+nasal] or a [–nasal] specification. They lack it because rule (40) renders such information superfluous in this context. To distinguish the nasality-unspecified vowel from an oral vowel, we will write it as capital A: e.g. /pAn/. The alternative hypothesis is that, although vocalic nasality is predictable in virtue of (40) in morphemes such as [pãn], the [ã] is nonetheless present as such in the lexical entry of such morphemes.

It is possible to test the difference between these hypotheses about the mental lexicon. We know that speakers begin the process of matching an auditory stimulus to a lexical entry as soon as they have heard a small fragment of an incoming word, as small as the first consonant. As more information comes in, speakers progressively narrow down the class of words matching the unfolding stimulus. Eventually, with sufficient information, an unambiguous answer may emerge. As the speaker attempts to identify the incoming word, he or she is comparing it with a stored lexical representation. If this lexical representation is relatively abstract, then a larger number of stimuli will be consistent with it. Thus, if the lexical representation of surface [pãn] abstracts away from the nasality of the vowel then the first CV part of the entry /pAn/ – with a vowel unspecified for nasality – will match both the incoming [pã . . .] of [pãk] or [pãn] and the incoming [pa . . .] of [pak]. On this hypothesis then, we expect that speakers presented with incomplete word-fragments like [pã . . .] will be able to identify them as matching lexical entries like either /pak/ or /pãk/. That is because the speakers possess lexicons in which one class of entries begins as /pA . . . /: there is nothing in the lexical specification of this A to preclude either a nasal [ã] or an oral [a] from matching it. Similarly, incoming [pa . . .] should be identified, on the same hypothesis, either as lexical /pA . . . / (from /pAn/ = [pãn]) or as lexical /pa . . . / (from /pak/). This is schematically represented in figure 13.1:

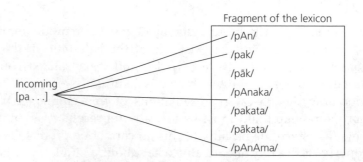

Figure 13.1 Matching an incoming stimulus against specified and partially specified entries of an abstract lexicon

The alternative hypothesis, which postulates relatively concrete lexical entries, predicts that an auditory stimulus like [pa . . .] will be judged by speakers to match only the oral vowel of [pak]: that is because the lexical entry of [pãn] consistent with this second theory contains nasality information about its vowel, even though this information is redundant in context.

There is initial evidence favoring the hypothesis of abstract lexical entries: in one set of experiments (Lahiri and Marslen–Wilson 1992) speakers of Bengali reacted to incoming stimuli of the [pã . . .] and [pa . . .] sort as if they had internalized lexical entries lacking information about vocalic nasality. This interpretation, however, is disputed by other researchers. What is clear, under any interpretation of this type of data, is that hypotheses about speakers' mental lexicons lend themselves to empirical testing.

13.5 Summary

This chapter has outlined the basic elements of phonological representations. The atoms of the representations are the feature values. Features are grouped into segment-sized constituents. The segments themselves are grouped around vowels or vowel-like sounds into syllabic constituents. Syllables relate to each other in terms of relative prominence.

The units and relations we have presented are useful in all explicit grammatical descriptions. But of greatest interest in their scientific study is the question we raised in relation to syllables, in section 13.2.3: How do speakers know that a string of segments in their language is divided into syllables in a certain way? This question can be asked in relation to each aspect of the phonological representations that we have touched on. How do speakers know that the feature of aspiration in a word such as *Tom* [tʰãm] 'belongs to' the segment /t/ rather than representing a segment unto itself? This is a question about the kinds of inferences that result in a particular view of segmentation. How does the speaker come to know that the increased loudness and duration characterizing the second and fourth syllables in *assìmilátion* signal the more abstract property of prominence? We have suggested that such intricate knowledge of phonological representations is based in part on inferences about possible words in the language being studied, inferences drawn from observations about occurring and non-occurring forms, and in part on universal preferences for certain structures.

Further reading

Chomsky, Noam and Morris Halle. 1968 (1991). *Sound Pattern of English*, part iv, chs 7 and 9. Cambridge, MA: MIT Press.

Hayes, Bruce. 1994. *Metrical Stress Theory: Principles and Case Studies*. Chicago: University of Chicago Press.

Kahn, Daniel. 1976. *Syllable-based Generalizations in English Phonology*. MIT Ph.D. dissertation. Garland Press, 1980.

Liberman, Mark and Alan Prince. 1977. On Stress and Linguistic Rhythm. *Linguistic Inquiry*, 8: 249–336.

Selkirk, E. 1982. The Syllable. In Harry van der Hulst and Norval Smith, eds., *The Structure of Phonological Representations, Part 1*. Dordrecht: Foris.

References on languages cited

Cuna

Sherzer, Joel. 1970. Talking backwards in Cuna. *Southwest Journal of Anthropology*, 26: 343–53.

English

Cowan, Nelson and Lewis Leavitt. 1990. Speakers' Access to Phonological Structure of the Syllable in Word Games. In *Proceedings of CLS 26 Parasession on the Syllable*, pp. 45–59.

Derwing, Bruce. 1992. The pause-break task in syllable division. *Language and Speech*, 35: 219–35.

French

Lefkowitz, N. 1991. *Talking Backwards, Looking Forwards: The French Language Game Verlan*. Tübingen: Narr.

Mehler, J., Dommergues, J.Y., Frauenfelder, U., and Ségui, J. 1981. The syllable's role in speech segmentation. *Journal of Verbal Learning and Verbal Behavior*, 20: 298–305.

Hungarian

Nádasdy, A. 1985. Segmental Phonology and Morphology. In Istvan Kenesei, ed., *Approaches to Hungarian*, pp. 225–46, Szeged: JATE.

Vago, Robert. 1980. *The Sound Pattern of Hungarian*. Georgetown: Georgetown University Press.

Polish

Bethin, Christina. 1992. *Polish Syllables: The Role of Prosody in Phonology and Morphology*. Columbus, OH: Slavica Publishers.

Yokuts

Newman, Stanley. 1944. *Yokuts Language of California*. New York: Viking Fund Publications in Anthropology 2.

EXERCISES

Exercise 13.7　The definite article /l/ of Moroccan Arabic is realized in four different ways depending on the structure of the noun it is attached to: [l], [lə] and an allomorph we call C, which consists of substituting for [l] a copy of the first stem consonant (data from Guerssel 1978). Identify in feature terms (a) the class of nouns that requires the C allomorph and (b) the class of nouns that requires the [lə] allomorphs. The form of the noun in isolation is identical to the string that follows the morpheme boundary:

I allomorph	lə allomorph	C allomorph
l-uqid 'the matches'	*lə-ktab* 'the book'	*t-tuma* 'the garlic'
l-kamyu 'the truck'	*lə-brˤa* 'the letter'	*z-zbəl* 'the garbage'
l-biru 'the office'	*lə-qfəl* 'the lock'	*ʃ-ʃəmʃ* 'the sun'
l-firan 'the mice'	*lə-fʒəl* 'the radish'	*ʒ-ʒrad* 'the locust'
	lə-ksˤida 'the accident'	*d-dfal* 'the saliva'
		s-sma 'the sky'

Note: The symbol ˤ indicates that the preceding sound is pharyngealized.

∙ ∙

We present below two rather different looking sets of facts from Sanskrit and Ancient Greek respectively. Your task is to identify, with the help of feature analysis, the common principle that underlies both sets of facts. **Exercise 13.8**

In Sanskrit, the segments {pʰ, tʰ, ʈʰ, kʰ, tʃʰ, bʰ, dʰ, gʰ, dʒʰ} do not occur word-finally or before obstruents. The Sanskrit consonantal phonemes are: {p, t, ʈ, tʃ, k, b, d, ɖ, dʒ, g, pʰ, tʰ, ʈʰ, tʃʰ, kʰ, bʰ, dʰ, gʰ, dʒʰ, s, ʂ, ç, m, n, ɽ, l}.

In Greek, the segments {pʰ, tʰ, kʰ} do not occur word-finally or before obstruents. The Greek consonantal phonemes are: {p, t, k, b, d, dz, g, pʰ, tʰ, kʰ, s, m, n, r, l}.

The answer to this problem must consist of a statement about the distribution of aspirated or unaspirated segments. Use the feature [±aspirated]. The same general statement is valid for the two languages considered, despite the difference of segmental inventories.

∙ ∙

Speakers of Cuna, an Indian language spoken off the coast of Panama, disguise their speech by a form of backwards talk they call *Sorsik Sunmakke* 'talking backwards'. Consider the following data and formulate an explicit rule or rules that transform regular Cuna words into their correspondents in Sorsik Sunmakke. You will need to make explicit assumptions about how Cuna words are divided into syllables. **Exercise 13.9**

Cuna	sorsik sunmakke	gloss
dage	*geda*	come
saban	*bansa*	belly
argan	*ganar*	hand
ina	*nai*	medicine
goe	*ego*	deer
inna	*nain*	chicha (some plant or animal)

∙ ∙

Translate the following statements in the rule notation introduced here and in chapter 12, using annotated brackets or constituent structure trees or reference to # boundaries, where appropriate. Characterize the segment classes mentioned below by some combination of feature values that is minimally sufficient to distinguish them from segments that do not undergo the rule. **Exercise 13.10**

(a)   All nasal consonants become velar when followed by a velar consonant in the same syllable. Thus nk → ŋk, unless they belong to distinct syllables.
(b)   Word-final mid rounded vowels become [+tense].
(c)   A syllable-initial stop is aspirated.

. . . .

Exercise
13.11

Consider the following compound nouns:

(a)   *láw degrèe*
(b)   *láw schòol*
       lánguage requìrements
(c)   *lánguage requìrement chànges*
       (meaning: changes in the language requirements)
       pípe òrgan lèsson
       láw schòol chùm
       (meaning: a friend from law school)
(d)   *làw degrèe lánguage requìrements*
       làbor ùnion fínance còmmittee
       flỳ-ròd tróut fishing

Re-read section 2.7 of chapter 2 and assign constituent structures to all compounds based on what they mean. Now formulate a general rule for assigning main stress in compounds based on the constituent structure.

14

Phonology III: Explanation and Constraints in Phonology

CHAPTER CONTENTS

14.0 Introduction

Rather early in one's career as a linguist, one becomes aware that the same data is consistent with a variety of distinct analyses. How can we decide which of these analyses best represents native speaker competence? This chapter addresses this question. Our aim is to give the reader a sense of how linguists argue that one analysis, out of a large number of conceivable ones, provides the best model of the native speakers' phonological competence.

14.1 Evaluating Competing Analyses

The fact that multiple, very different looking analyses can be given for the same data set is illustrated by the following alternations from English. The past tense and past participle suffixes alternate among the allomorphs *t*, *d*, and [əd].

(1)   Allomorphs of the English past tense and past participle morphemes

	[t] allomorph		[d] allomorph		[əd] allomorph
licked	[lɪkt]	bugged	[bʌgd]	mended	[mɛndəd]
squished	[skwɪʃt]	leaned	[lind]	parted	[partəd]
kept	[kɛpt]	buzzed	[bʌzd]	feasted	[fistəd]
laughed	[læft]	played	[pleɪd]	batted	[bætəd]

We refer to the morphemes that alternate as *t*/*d*/[əd] by the general name T-suffixes. The data in (1) illustrate two points:

(2)   a.   The stop in a T-suffix is voiced [d] after a voiced sound (e.g. [g], [z], [n], [ə]) and voiceless [t] after a voiceless sound (e.g. [p], [ʃ], [k]).

      b.   Schwa [ə] occurs in a T-suffix only between identical consonants (as in *mended* [mɛndəd]) or between consonants that differ only in voicing (as in *feasted* [fistəd]). Moreover, it always occurs in such contexts.

These generalizations can be incorporated into a variety of different analyses. We examine three analyses that at first look equally promising. The comparison between them bears on two analytical points: what is the best rule to describe the voicing alternations ([t] as in [lɪkt] vs. [d] as in [bʌgd]) and what is the best rule to describe the schwa/zero alternations (i.e. schwa, as in [mɛndəd] vs. no schwa, as in [lind]).

The voicing alternations can be analyzed as involving an underlying /d/ that becomes [t] in certain contexts; or an underlying /t/ that becomes [d] in certain other contexts. The schwa/zero alternations can be analyzed by assuming either that schwa is absent from underlying representations, in which case it must be inserted in certain cases; or that it is present underlyingly, in which case it must be deleted in certain contexts. We will see that, whatever assumption is made, appropriate rules can be written to describe the data. But some of these rules are better than others. Our first aim then is to discuss the principles by which a choice can be made between them. A first possibility, Analysis 1, assumes that the underlying representation of the T-suffixes is voiced *d*. In this case, the underlying and surface representations of the first row of forms in (1) will look like this:

(3)   Analysis 1: assuming underlying /d/

Underlying	Surface	Underlying	Surface	Underlying	Surface
/lɪk-d/	[lɪkt]	/bʌg-d/	[bʌgd]	/mɛnd-d/	[mɛndəd]
(licked)		(bugged)		(mended)	

To account for underlying /mɛnd-d/ becoming surface [mɛndəd], we need a rule that inserts [ə] between identical consonants (d-d) or similar ones (t-d). (We will use the term *similar* to mean consonant pairs, like *t-d*, which differ, if at all, only in voicing. Identical consonants are then, necessarily, counted as similar.) To account for underlying /lɪk-d/ becoming surface [lɪkt] we must formulate a rule that devoices word-final /d/ after voiceless segments. The two rules appear below:

(4) The rules of Analysis 1:
    a. **Schwa:** $\emptyset \rightarrow$ [ə] / C_1 ___ C_2, if C_1 and C_2 are similar
                           consonants
                           (similar Cs = which differ, at most, in voicing)
    b. **Devoicing:** [+voice] obstruent $\rightarrow$ [−voice] obstruent/ [−voice]
                           sound___#

We show in (5) how the Schwa and Devoicing rules derive the data in (1). The notation n/a indicates that the rule is inapplicable to a given form. The dashes indicate morpheme divisions: since this is non-phonological information, we omit it from derived representations.

(5) Derivations based on Analysis 1

Underlying representations	/bʌg-d/	/lɪk-d/	/mɛnd-d/
Schwa	*n/a*	*n/a*	mɛndəd
Devoicing	*n/a*	lɪkt	*n/a*
Surface representations	bʌgd	lɪkt	mɛndəd

(*n/a* = not applicable)

The data in (1) are also consistent with Analysis 2, in which the underlying representation of the T-suffixes is /t/.

(6) Analysis 2: assuming underlying /t/

Underlying	Surface	Underlying	Surface	Underlying	Surface
/lɪk-t/	[lɪkt]	/bʌg-t/	[bʌgd]	/mɛnd-t/	[mɛndəd]

What will change, under this new analysis, is the nature of the rule that alters the voicing of the suffix. If we postulate underlying /bʌg-t/ then we need to change it to [bʌgd]; and similarly /lin-t/ to [lind] and [mɛndə-t] (the form derived by the Schwa rule) to [mɛndəd]: a voicing rule, which turns the suffixal /t/ into [d] after a voiced sound, will do this. The Schwa rule remains the same.

(7) The rules of Analysis 2:
    a. **Schwa:** $\emptyset \rightarrow$ [ə] / C_1 ___ C_2, if C_1 and C_2 are similar consonants
                           (similar Cs = which differ, at most, in voicing)

b.   **Voicing**:   [−voice] obstruent → [+voice] obstruent/ [+voice]
sound__   ·
[This rule applies only to the consonants of
T-suffixes.]

The derivations of Analysis 2 are as simple as those of Analysis 1. Note
that schwa is a voiced sound and therefore triggers the Voicing rule.

(8)   Derivations based on Analysis 2

Underlying representations	/bʌg-t/	/lɪk-t/	/mɛnd-t/
Schwa	*n/a*	*n/a*	mɛndət
Voicing	bʌgd	*n/a*	mɛndəd
Surface representations	bʌgd	lɪkt	mɛndəd

There is an important difference between the Analyses 1 and 2 and it
has to do with the generality of the rules they employ. In English there are
occasional sequences of voiceless stop + d (as in *anecdote* [ænəkdoʊt]) but
there are absolutely no such sequences at the end of the word. Words such
as [læpd], [mɪkd] etc. are not just accidentally absent from the English
lexicon: they are impossible as words of English. In fact a much broader
statement can be motivated:

(9)   **The Voice Agreement Principle**:
Obstruent sequences may not differ with respect to [±voice] at the
end of an English word.

The statement in (9) describes the fact that words like [kasb], [mɪfz],
with [−voice]–[+voice] obstruent sequences, are disallowed in English; also
ruled out by (9) are ill-formed [bʊgs], [mæbt], [kɛzp], with word-final
[+voice] [−voice]. Note that the judgment of ill-formedness changes when
the voicing disagreement between the two obstruents is resolved: [kasp],
[mɪfs], [bʊgz] are unattested but not inconceivable.

The significance of (9) for Analysis 1, is that it motivates the Devoicing
rule, (4a). This rule is necessary to create surface forms that comply with
the Voice Agreement Principle. For instance, we understand now why
underlying /lɪkd/ must turn into [lɪkt]: if it didn't, the Voice Agreement
Principle would be violated. Therefore the principle is not just stating a
true fact about English: it is also helpful in explaining why underlying
representations must sometimes differ from their surface forms. Thus an
important property of Analysis 1 is that it views the voicing alternation
between [t] and [d] (e.g. [bʌgd] vs. [lɪkt]) as a necessary consequence of a
general principle of English sound structure. Devoicing (/d/ → [t]) occurs
because English imposes certain standards of well-formedness upon its
surface forms. Principle (9) is one such standard.

Can the Voicing rule of Analysis 2 – (7b) – be justified in a parallel way? Recall that rule (7b) must turn underlying /bʌg-t/ into [bʌgd], /lin-t/ into [lind] and /mɛnd-t/ into [mɛndəd]. The Voice Agreement Principle motivates the change from /bʌg-t/ into [bʌgd], but not the other changes: it does not exclude sequences of a voiced sonorant ([n] or [ə]) followed by a voiceless obstruent. Indeed, such sequences are perfectly well-formed: *secret* [sikrət] *mint* [mɪnt] display [ət] and [nt] respectively. Other words ending in any sequence of a voiced sonorant followed by a voiceless obstruent are *fault, kelp, purse, ark*. For this reason, we cannot motivate a general statement such as (10):

(10) No sequence of [+voice] [–voice] segments may end an English word.

Since (10) is not true in English, the Voicing rule of Analysis 2 is not motivated by any general principle. This is reflected in our formulation of Voicing (7b): we had to state that only T-suffixes undergo this rule. Without this restriction, Voicing would have applied incorrectly to, say, /mɪnt/, deriving *[mɪnd] from it. The Voicing rule had to be stated in this way only because Analysis 2 takes /t/ as the underlying representation of the T-suffix: there was no other reason to suggest that Voicing is a rule of English. We have seen then that Analysis 1 explains why the [t]/[d] alternations exist in the language, whereas Analysis 2 does not. This is a reason to opt for the former. The general basis for this choice is that we prefer analyses in which phenomena observed emerge as consequences of general principles. Analysis 1 has this property.

A further option presents itself now: we could assume for the T-suffixes either an underlying representation in which [ə] is missing – as we have done in Analyses 1 and 2 – or one containing schwa, i.e. /əd/. This is Analysis 3.

(11) Analysis 3: assuming underlying /əd/

Underlying	Surface	Underlying	Surface	Underlying	Surface
/lɪk-əd/	[lɪkt]	/bʌg-əd/	[bʌgd]	/mɛnd-əd/	[mɛndəd]

If the T-suffixes contain an underlying schwa, then schwa will have to be eliminated from /lɪkəd/, /bʌgəd/ and in general everywhere except when it separates similar consonants, i.e. in /dəd/ or /təd/ sequences. We will write then a schwa deletion rule (12a), which will precede the Devoicing rule.

(12) The rules of Analysis 3:

a. **Schwa Deletion**: [ə] → Ø/ C₁ ___ C₂, unless C₁ and C₂ are similar consonants
(similar Cs = which differ, at most, in voicing)

b. **Devoicing**:   [+voice] obstruent → [–voice] obstruent/[–voice] sound__#

The derivations will look as in (13):

(13)   Derivations based on Analysis 3

Underlying representations	/bʌg-əd/	/lɪk-əd/	/mɛnd-əd/
Schwa Deletion	bʌgd	lɪkd	*n/a*
Devoicing	*n/a*	lɪkt	*n/a*
Surface representations	bʌgd	lɪkt	mɛndəd

Once again, we can decide how to choose between Analyses 1 and 3 by considering how general are the principles that drive them. Suppose we opt for Analysis 1: can we then justify the Schwa rule (4a) by appeal to some principle of English sound structure? Yes: the sequences that the Schwa rule separates (*td, dd*) are generally disallowed. Moreover, all other sequences of similar obstruents are disallowed: *kk, kg, gk, gg, pp, pb, bp, bb, ss, sz, zs*, etc. Let us experiment with stating our observation in its most general form, as in (14):

(14) **The Not-Too-Similar Principle**
Sequences of similar obstruents – i.e. obstruents differing at most with respect to voicing – are not permitted in English words.

The insertion of schwa in words like *feasted* is a natural consequence of the Not-Too-Similar Principle in (14): a way that English phonology has devised to make (14) hold not just of some of its representations but of all of its surface representations.

Now suppose we choose Analysis 3. Can the statement of schwa deletion implied by this option – rule (12a) – be justified by reference to some general fact? Is it the case that schwa is always deleted in English, always absent, except between similar Cs? No: there are lots of words, like *Pamela* [pæmələ], *barrack* [bærək], *skeleton* [skɛlətən], containing undeleted schwa between non-similar Cs. There are words like *crooked* [krʊkəd], and *aged* [eɪdʒəd] with undeleted schwa between a final [d] and a non-similar C. Finally, there are also conceivable words containing such a schwa before the T-suffixes: you can turn the word *rhumba* or *fantasia* into verbs, imagining that *to rhumba* means to dance the dance and *to fantasia* someone is to induce them to act like the characters of the Disney movie. The past tense of these novel verbs are surely [rʌmbəd] and [fænteiʒəd] not *[rʌm(b)d] or *[fænteiʒd]:

(15)   He [fænteiʒəd] (*[fænteiʒd]) me into . . .

Schwa should not delete here: but the Schwa Deletion rule in (12a) predicts it will. We can re-write the rule in the appropriately narrow way, as below:

(16)   **Schwa Deletion** (revised):
$$[ə] \rightarrow \emptyset / \; C_1 \underline{\quad} C_2, \quad \text{unless } C_1 \text{ and } C_2 \text{ are similar consonants and}$$
unless [ə] is part of the stem.

This will cover all the data and avoid the incorrect prediction made by the first version of Analysis 3. But even in this revised form Analysis 3 is inferior to Analysis 1: it does not explain why the schwa/zero alternation should occur in the first place. There is no obvious reason why the schwa of T-suffixes should be deleted in contexts where other English schwas seem perfectly stable. In contrast, the necessity of the Schwa Insertion rule (which must be assumed as part of Analysis 1) is made plain by the Not-Too-Similar Principle (14): if we start out with inputs like /mɛnd-d/, that principle explains why such forms must change.

What we have seen so far is that competing analyses can be evaluated in terms of their relative generality. Two analyses may be descriptively equivalent (if the rules generate the same surface forms from the same underlying representations) but may nonetheless differ in their ability to explain the data described and connect it to other known phenomena. The better analysis is the more general one: the one that allows particular phenomena – such as the alternations in a morpheme – to emerge as reflexes of general principles.

14.2   Connecting Rules and Principles

Native speakers know at least two aspects of the sound structure of their language: the morpheme alternations and the principles motivating these. First, speakers know that morphemes alternate and they can make accurate predictions about which alternant will occur in a never-before-encountered word. This can be shown by considering a source of novel verbs: nouns that can be used as verbs. We formed one such verb in (15) from the noun *Fantasia*. Speakers of English will be able to predict whether [t], [d], or [əd] will appear in the past tense forms of such novel verbs. Consider the verbs *to Hamlet*, *to Falstaff* and *to Lear*, whose interpretations are readily supplied by context and knowledge of the plot of the plays they appear in.

(17)   a.   [d]:   He Leared [liərd] his possessions to his older daughters.
   b.   [t]:   He Falstaffed [fɒlstæft] in that pub throughout the war.
   c.   [əd]:   He Hamleted [hæmlətəd] in this way for many months.

The ability to predict which morpheme alternant will occur in a new context is frequently taken to indicate that speakers know the phonological rules that generate and distribute the allomorphs.

Second, quite independently of this, speakers know the principles that motivate the existence of rules and alternations. (This is unconscious knowledge for the most part, as discussed in chapter 1 and elsewhere.) Speakers know the Voice Agreement Principle in (9) and the Not-Too-Similar Principle in (14): they distinguish acceptable forms that satisfy these principles from forms that violate them. Note that the Voice Agreement Principle is more general than the devoicing rule it motivates. The principle rules out any sequence of obstruents with distinct values for the feature [voice] – e.g. both words like *[fæbt] and *[fæpd] – whereas the rule needed to account for the T-suffix alternations is just a devoicing rule: it only needs to turn /d/ into [t]. Therefore knowledge of the Voice Agreement Principle is independent of and extends beyond knowledge of the Devoicing rule (4b).

The same holds of the Not-Too-Similar Principle (14), whose scope is considerably broader than that of the Schwa insertion rule it motivates. Sequences of similar obstruents arising from suffixation are avoided not only via Schwa Insertion but also in other ways: for instance, an adjective ending in [ð] such as *smoo[ð]* cannot undergo suffixation with *-th* (as in *wide–width, broad–breadth, deep–depth*). If it could, the sequence of similar obstruents [ðθ] would be generated. Here the problem posed by the Principle (14) is solved differently from the case of T-suffixes, since the *th*-affixation process is blocked: the abstract noun corresponding to *smooth* is formed in a different way, as *smoothness*. This fact allows us to observe the Principle (14) at work in a case where it is independent from the rule of Schwa Insertion. The diagram in (18) illustrates this point.

(18)   Problems posed by Principle (14) (Not-Too-Similar) and two of their solutions:

Problem: Principle (14) violated in: men $\boxed{d-d}$ smoo $\boxed{ð-θ}$

Solutions: (a)   Insert schwa (rule (4a))
           (b)   Block affixation
               Choose different suffix

Outcome: surface forms satisfy   men[dəd]   smoothness
          Principle (14)

Granting that the suffix *-th* is unproductive in English, there may be more than one reason for the drastic difference in acceptability between *smoothness* and **smooth-th*. But the argument for our point can be reconstructed by comparing two potential *-th* forms: *rough-th* [rʌfθ] and *smooth-th* [smuðð] (or alternatively [smuðθ]). None is perfect – because they employ the unproductive *-th* – but we contend that [smuðð] and [smuðθ] are considerably worse, because they also violate (14).

Consider the following alternations between [t] and [s] in English:

EXERCISE 14.1

(a)

pirate	[paɪrət]	*piracy*	[paɪrəsi]
vacant	[veɪkənt]	*vacancy*	[veɪkənsi]
secret	[sikrət]	*secrecy*	[sikrəsi]
president	[prɛzidənt]	*presidency*	[prɛzidənsi]
accurate	[ækjurət]	*accuracy*	[ækjurəsi]
fluent	[fluənt]	*fluency*	[fluənsi]

Write a phonological rule of the sort you learned in chapters 12–13, to account for this data. Make clear what you consider to be the underlying representation for each pair of alternants. The alternations illustrated above obtain only for certain combinations of stems and suffixes in English: however, for the purpose of this exercise you can ignore this fact and formulate your rules and principles as if the process being analyzed is fully general.

Now consider the forms in (b):

(b)

modest	[madɛst]	*modesty*	[madɛsti]
honest	[anəst]	*honesty*	[anəsti]
pederast	[pɛdəræst]	*pederasty*	[pɛdəræsti]

If the rule that applied in (a) had been able to apply to forms like *modest*, we would observe *[madɛssi], with the second [s] coming from the underlying /t/ of [madɛst]. Based on the discussion of phonological principles provided in this chapter, explain in one sentence why the rule does not apply to forms like (b). The right answer is not to restate the rule so as to exclude /s/ from occurring in its left context but rather to think of possible unwelcome consequences of that rule's application to the sequence /st/.

Consider the following alternations occurring in Afar, a Cushitic language:

EXERCISE 14.2

Accusative	Nominative/Genitive	Gloss
xamíla	*xaml-í*	swampgrass
ʔagára	*ʔagr-í*	scabies
darágu	*dɑrg í*	watered milk

Postulate underlying representations for the three roots. Write a rule that accounts for the root alternations. (There are several possible formulations compatible with this limited data.)

Now consider the following forms, which are representative of a general restriction on the application of the rule you have written. (The sound [dˤ] is a pharyngealized /d/.)

Afar form	Gloss
midˤadˤ-i	fruit-Nominative/Genitive
sababá	reason
xarar-é	he burned

Formulate a principle – akin to one discussed in the text – that explains why your rule did not apply to forms like the above. Make explicit the relation between the rule and the principle by explaining what are the types of representations that must satisfy your principle: underlying representations, intermediate, surface representations or some combination of these?

Since principles are more general than the rules they motivate, we should ask: why do we need the rules at all? Simply knowing that an underlying representation like /mend-d/ violates Principle (14) is perhaps enough to predict that the corresponding surface form [mɛndəd] will contain an inserted schwa. That this cannot be is shown in (18) where we saw that the same problem can be solved in at least two ways, either by altering the phonological make-up of the word (applying a phonological rule) or by selecting a different affix (changing the morphology). In fact, even the phonological solutions applicable to a given problem are multiple. Starting from underlying /lɪk-d/ (*licked*) and /bæt-d/ (*batted*), which violate Voice Agreement and the Not-Too-Similar Principle, we could imagine a variety of corresponding surface forms that satisfy both principles. The Voice Agreement Principle could be satisfied by dropping one consonant (/bæt-d/ → *[bæd]) or by inserting a vowel (/lɪk-d/ → *[lɪkəd]). Thus, simply asserting the truth of Voice Agreement will not give us an analysis. Similarly, an input form like /bæt-d/ could be made to satisfy the Not-Too-Similar Principle in a variety of ways: we could delete one of the two consonants (/bæt-d/ → *[bæd]) or change them so they will become less similar (/bæt-d/ → *[bænd]) or insert between them something other than schwa (/bæt-d/ → *[bæt-ənei-d]). There is nothing wrong with all these starred surface forms – they satisfy all principles of English we can think of – but they're not the proper surface reflexes of the underlying form they are supposedly representing. It appears that we need the rules in order to narrow down the class of possible solutions to the unique solution that's being used in the language.

(19) Alternative solutions to two phonological problems: violations of
Voice Agreement and Not-Too-Similar.

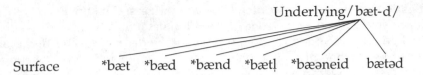

Underlying/bæt-d/

Surface   *bæt   *bæd   *bænd   *bætl̩   *bæəneid   bætəd

Have we concluded from this discussion that rules are needed after all?
Maybe, but it would not be right to conclude from this that the rules
presented in (4) as part of Analysis 1 – the analysis we ended up choosing
– are the right rules. There are two reasons to look for alternatives. One is
that the rules in (4) lack explicit connections to the principles that motivate
them: for instance, nothing in the formulation of the Devoicing rule (4b)
tells us that this is a solution to problems raised by the Voice Agreement
Principle. We conjecture that the Devoicing rule is easy to learn precisely
because it solves a problem: a change of the input that lacked such a
motivation might be harder to learn (see the sidebar below). But then, it
is also natural to think that the Devoicing rule is being learned not just
as an operation that alters the input forms but rather as a solution to a
problem: the problem raised by inputs that violate the Voice Agreement
Principle.

We experiment first with the following way of linking rules and principles, first proposed by Yip (1989). A principle identifies a certain class of
strings as ill-formed: thus the Voice Agreement Principle declares that
words ending in two obstruents with different voice values are ill-formed.
Let us suppose that all underlying forms of a language are inspected for
compliance with such phonological principles. By underlying forms (those
listed in the mental lexicon) we mean both single-morpheme stems (e.g.
dog, yellow, bark) and multi-morpheme combinations (e.g. /yellow-ish/, /un-
presidenti-al/, /bark-d/). Suppose that a violation of some principle is detected
in an underlying form; /bark-d/, for instance, violates the Voice Agreement Principle. For every type of violation detected, a specific modification of the input is prescribed. In this conception, then, the rule's description
(the string that must be modified) coincides with the string that violates
a specific principle. The rule's structural change (the actual modification)
represents a minimal change in the input which succeeds in deriving a
form that satisfies the relevant principle. In (20) we show revised formulations of the Voice Agreement and Schwa Insertion rules seen earlier in (4).
In these formulations, the principles motivating the change dictated by the
rule play a clear role: they identify the string to be modified. (We discuss
the universality or language-specific nature of these principles in the following sections.) The rule itself just prescribes a specific change, identified
by bold characters below:

Knowledge of rules vs. knowledge of principles

Research initiated in the 1950s by the linguist Jean Berko can be interpreted as bearing on one of the questions raised in the text: can knowledge of rules be distinguished from knowledge of the principles motivating the rules? Berko tested adults and young children (preschool, kindergarten, and first grade) on their knowledge of English phonology and word formation. Her subjects were presented with novel, English-sounding words (e.g. *wug*, given as the name of a small bird-like creature; *mot*, a verb denoting a form of physical exercise). The subjects were asked to form plurals, past tenses and comparatives based on these novel words. The adults' performance provided the standard by which the children's words were judged. In some interesting respects the forms supplied by children were systematically different from those of the adults. Thus more than two-thirds of all children failed to insert schwa in the past tenses of the verbs *mot* and *bod* and insisted on using past tenses like *mot* and *bod*, instead of expected *motted*, *bodded*. Similarly, the plurals of novel nouns such as *tas* and *gutch* were given by 30–40 per cent of the children as *tas* and *gutch* respectively, without Schwa Insertion, not the expected *tasses*, *gutches*. In a few cases schwa was inserted in the wrong form, for instance *heafes* [hifəz] was given sometimes as the plural of *heaf* [hif]. The adults, however, produced the expected forms: [hifs], [tæsəz], [gʌtʃəz]. Thus children as old as 7 appear to differ from adults in their understanding of the Schwa Insertion rule.

However, and this is the significant part, the children's performance was consistent with the principles in (9) and (14), Voice Agreement and Not-Too-Similar. Children did not produce obstruents with different voice values, as reflected by the very high percentage of responses labeled correct to novel verbs like *rick*, past tense [rɪkt], not *[rɪkd] and *gling*, past tense [glɪŋd], not *[glɪŋt]. Children also did not produce sequences of similar obstruents ([td], [dd], [sz], [zz]): the erroneous past tense of *to mot* was [mat], not *[matd] or *[matt]; the erroneous plural of *tas* was [tæs], not *[tæsz] or *[tæss]. Thus it appears that principles (9) and (14) are already in place at a stage when at least one of the rules they motivate (Schwa Insertion) is not being reliably applied. This is further evidence that the two forms of linguistic knowledge should be distinguished.

Berko's results were informally confirmed, in a different way, by one of the authors of this book, who asked three boys, aged nine and ten, to form derived words using the novel suffix *-k* 'tiny'. The linguist first told her subjects that a tiny shoe [ʃu] should be called a [ʃuk], a tiny room [rumk], a tiny flower [flawərk], etc. and then asked them to form similar diminutives ('tiny X' forms) based on a large number of other nouns. Among these test cases were included *-k* and *-g* final forms such as *sock*, *rug*, *stick*, *peg*. Some adult subjects, when asked the same question, volunteer [sakək], [rʌgək], etc. with Schwa Insertion; the children, however, began by experimenting with [sakk], [rʌgk], [rʌkk] (each stop distinctly articulated). One of them then decided on using forms [sak], [rʌg] or [rʌk] (with the suffix -k apparently substituting for the stem final -g). During the first session, only these latter forms were volunteered. In this case too, the children and the adults seem to differ, as in Berko's study, in their use of Schwa Insertion, but the children's utterances all end up conforming to the Voice Agreement and Not-Too-Similar principles. On a later session, after hearing [sakək], [rʌgək], and [sakɪk], [rʌgɪk], the children adopted these forms, commenting explicitly that [sakk] and [sak] were not right. What is more interesting is that two children also proposed forms with Schwa Insertion when asked to generate the 'tiny X' form based on *cat, mitt, sip*: thus [kætək], [mɪtək], [sɪpək] were proposed during the second session, along with [sakək], [rʌgək]. In this case, children display awareness of the fact that word-final clusters like [tk], [pk] are impossible in English. Note that no alternations reflect this principle: a child's knowledge must be based on his observation of what does and does not occur in the language. Although these results cannot be considered firmly established since only three children were involved, they further support the view that knowledge of phonological principles is independent of and extends beyond knowledge of the rules and alternations motivated by these principles.

(20) a. **Revised Schwa Rule** (cf. 4a):
   i.   Find every underlying string that violates the Not-Too-Similar Principle.
   ii. In every such string INSERT SCHWA, so that the result satisfies the principle.
   b. **Revised Devoicing Rule** (cf. 4b):
   i.   Find every underlying string that violates the Voice Agreement Principle.
   ii. In every such string CHANGE THE VOICING VALUE OF THE AFFIXAL CONSONANT, so that the result satisfies the principle.

The revised Schwa and Devoicing rules will apply in the same way as their predecessors, rules (4a) and (4b). They will also have to be ordered in the same way as the earlier versions, with the Schwa rule applying before Devoicing. The derivations shown earlier in (5) will remain unchanged under this different conception of what the rules do. The reason to change our formulation of the rules was to explicitly link phonological principles and the rules whose existence they motivate. This was done by identifying the structural description of the rules as the strings which violate one or more phonological principles.

(1) Consider the following alternations in English:

EXERCISE 14.3

A		B	
damn	[dæm]	*damnation*	[dæmneɪʃən]
condemn	[kəndɛm]	*condemnation*	[kandəmneɪʃən]
hymn	[hɪm]	*hymnal*	[hɪmnəl]
solemn	[saləm]	*solemnity*	[səlɛmnɪti]
column	[kaləm]	*columnar*	[kəlʌmnər]

Divide the words in column B into root and suffix and identify the underlying representation of each root. Write a rule in the format of (20), which accounts for the stem alternations. Like the rules in (20), your rule must consist of two parts: a principle, i.e. a generalization about possible surface sequences of consonants in English words; and a procedure by which underlying representations violating this principle yield surface forms that comply with it.

(2) Following the same procedure account for the following alternations. Consider only the changes in the stem consonants and do not attempt to characterize the vowel changes.

A		B	
sign	[saɪn]	*signatory*	[sɪgnətori]
design	[dizaɪn]	*designation*	[dɛsɪgneɪʃən]
malign	[məlaɪn]	*malignity*	[məlɪgnɪti]
assign	[əsaɪn]	*assignation*	[æsɪgneɪʃən]
impugn	[ɪmpjun]	*pugnacious*	[pʌgneɪʃəs]

(*Note*: there are two classes of vowel-initial suffixes in English, only one of which is illustrated above. To simplify your task, you should ignore the behavior of the other class of vowel-initial suffixes, exemplified by the suffixes -*ing* and -*er*.)

EXERCISE 14.4

Consider the alternating shape of the English plural and third singular suffixes, which surface as [z] in forms like *bugs* [bʌgz], *cans* [kænz], as [s] in forms like *packs* [pæks], *laughs* [læfs], *licks* [lɪks] and as [əz] in forms such as *squishes* [skwɪʃəz], *reaches* [ritʃəz], *buses* [bʌsəz]. Gather a fuller set of forms to determine what the generalizations are regarding the distribution of these allomorphs. Then formulate an analysis of these alternations in the format indicated in (20). Determine whether the rules in (20) and the principles they refer to are applicable to this new data set and, if not, how they need to be modified to properly apply to the new data.

14.3 Further Questions

We have suggested so far that phonological rules and alternations exist for a reason: they exist because underlying representations, if left unmodified, will frequently violate general phonological principles. The rules identify such potential violations and avoid them through minimal modifications of the input strings. When this happens, alternations result: a morpheme may be altered in different ways depending on the context, or may be allowed to surface unchanged in one context but altered in the other. The alternations and the changes in underlying structures are the price the grammatical system pays in exchange for obtaining surface forms that comply with the principles deemed important.

The possibility of linking rules and principles as in (20) raises a number of further questions: (a) Should our analysis be allowed to make predictions beyond the data first examined? (b) Are there principles that limit the range of input modifications introduced by phonological rules? and (c) What is the status of phonological principles when examined cross-linguistically? We discuss these below.

14.4 How General?

The first question (Should our analysis be allowed to make predictions beyond the data first examined?) returns to the issue of generality raised at the beginning of the chapter. We stated that the better analysis is the one in which different phenomena emerge as reflexes of general laws. We now have an analysis in which two very general principles (Voice Agreement (9) and Not-Too-Similar (14)) dictate the shape of T-allomorphs in English. With generality come also two other properties. A general analysis is PREDICTIVE; it tells us what to expect regarding facts that were not at first considered or known. This is a good quality. A predictive analysis is also risky: its predictions may turn out to be wrong because they go beyond the data originally examined. We therefore have to address a question of analytical strategy: Is it better to take the safe route and formulate analyses whose predictions are limited to the data already examined, or to formulate general and predictive analyses, albeit at the risk of over-generalizing? (This is a question that concerns the philosophy of science, and the approaches to scientific analysis. It is not limited to the science of linguistics.)

The question can be made concrete by considering the broader predictions of the analysis we have adopted for the T-morphemes. Although our starting point was just two suffixes that alternate as [t], [d] and [əd], our final analysis predicts patterns of sounds that go far beyond this data. The revised Devoicing rule predicts that any word-final C-suffix, if it contains an obstruent, will be modified to agree in voicing with a preceding stem obstruent.

The revised Schwa rule predicts Schwa Insertion between any two similar Cs, regardless of whether they belong to the T-morphemes or to any other affix. Clearly, before adopting the analysis, we must verify that these predictions are correct. If they are, then the strategy of choosing an analysis based on the most general principles has paid off; we will have discovered a significantly broader section of English phonology than we have started out from. But suppose that some predictions are disconfirmed.

Suppose, for instance, that the scope of Schwa Insertion turns out to be narrower than we predict it at present. What then? This possibility, a common occurrence in the work of any linguist, should not deter one from adopting the strategy of experimenting first with the most general analysis; if the analysis is wrong because it is too general this will readily become apparent when its predictions are checked. Revisions can be made to eliminate the wrong predictions. But if we start out with an analysis that is too narrow, this defect is much harder to identify; had we started out with an analysis of T-morphemes consisting of just the narrow rules in (21), nothing would inspire us to look at any fact beyond the behavior of these suffixes.

(21)   Devoicing: The T-suffixes are realized as [t] after a voiceless
                     sound.
       Schwa: A schwa is inserted before a T-suffix when the
                     preceding stem ends in an alveolar stop.

If we fail to look beyond the T-suffixes, we may miss any phenomenon that is parallel or related to the Devoicing and Schwa Insertion occurring with these morphemes. The significant risk then is not that of writing a provably wrong rule – since that defect will be exposed and remedied – but that of forever missing a generalization by writing too narrow a rule.

Some confirmation for the analysis in (20) is provided by the behavior of suffixes which alternate as [s], [z], [əz]. These encode possession, plurality in nouns, and third singular subjects in present tense verbs: the distribution of the three allomorphs is almost entirely parallel to that of the [t], [d], [əd] allomorphs examined earlier. We assume that the underlying form of these suffixes is [z], the form that occurs after sonorants and voiced obstruents. The other alternants are predicted by the rules in (20):

(22)   Allomorphs of three English suffixes: third singular present
       subject; plural; possessive

	[s]-allomorph		[z]-allomorph		[əz]-allomorph
licks	[lɪks]	bugs	[bʌgz]	buzzes	[bʌzəz]
bats	[bæts]	calls	[kɑlz]	buses	[bʌsəz]
Kip's	[kɪps]	Rob's	[rɑbz]	face's	[feisəz]

The classes of suffixes in (22) reveal one point in need of revision: Schwa Insertion also takes place after [ʃ], [tʃ], [ʒ] and [dʒ], though not after [θ], [ð] or any other fricative:

(23) The distribution of the allomorphs of the third singular present
      subject; plural; possessive suffixes after fricatives

	[s]- allomorph		[z]- allomorph		[əz]- allomorph
Keith's	[kiθs]	smooths	[smuðz]	garages	[gəraʒəz]
laughs	[læfs]	bathes	[beiðz]	squishes	[skwɪʃəz]
Bach's	[baxs]	nerves	[nərvz]	badge's	[bædʒəz]

Our present Schwa rule (20a) will insert schwa only after [s] and [z]
since it is only these consonants that fit the definition of *similar* relative to
the suffixal /z/. What is needed then is a modified definition of the notion
similar consonants:

(24) Similar consonants:
      Two consonants are similar if they are identical for all manner
      features ([sonorant], [consonantal], [strident], [lateral], [nasal]) and
      if they employ the same active articulators (cf. (7), chapter 13).

This statement defines pairs of similar consonants in a way that predicts more accurately the location of Schwa Insertion: since [ʃ] and [z], for
instance, are identical for all manner features, and since the active articulator for both consonants is the tongue blade, the revision in (24) identifies them as similar. This predicts correctly Schwa Insertion in forms like
[skwɪʃəz], as against *[skwɪʃz], predicted by the first definition of *similar*.
The consonants [θ] and [s] are not similar because they differ in stridency;
[f] and [s] are not similar because they are articulated with different active
articulators, and thus no Schwa Insertion is expected to separate them,
under (24).

However, a different aspect of our analysis runs into deeper trouble when
tested against a wider set of facts. Although clusters of similar or identical
consonants (e.g. [kg], [pp], [bp], [fv] [ll], [mm] etc.) are indeed impossible
inside morphemes and at the ends of words, as predicted by (14), a subset
of these clusters is attested across certain morpheme boundaries.

(25) Some well-formed clusters of similar consonants

rr	ss	nn	ll	bb	bp
superrich	dissatisfied	unnecessary	vowellike	subbranch	subpolar
[supərrɪtʃ]	[dɪssætɪsfaid]	[ʌnnɛsəseri]	[vawəllaɪk]	[sʌbbræntʃ]	[sʌbpolər]

Rule (20a) makes the wrong prediction that underlying /sub-polar/ will
be pronounced *[sʌbəpolər]. It must therefore be reconsidered. To revise
the analysis, we observe first that the clusters subject to schwa **epenthesis**
occur word-finally, whereas those that surface intact occur word-medially,
especially in intervocalic position (cf. *dissatisfied*) or else between a vowel

and a sonorant (cf. *subbranch*). Our account can recognize this difference by
revising (14) as follows:

(26)   **Not-Too-Similar Principle** (revised)
       Sequences of similar consonants (where similar is defined in (24))
       are not permitted at edges (beginnings and ends) of English words.

With this modification, our principle will no longer predict Schwa Insertion in forms like *dissimilar* or *subpolar*, since the similar sequences /ss/
and /bp/ do not occur in these cases at word edges. With this revision, the
analysis proposed in (20) can be maintained. A further point is the fact that
no similar clusters occur morpheme-internally in English in any contexts:
no morphemes like [æssə], [utdə] occur. In this respect words and single
morphemes differ in the range of sequences they permit and the revision
allows an interesting point to emerge: sequences of similar consonants
are absolutely forbidden word-finally and word-initially, but allowed –
subject to certain morphological limitations – word-medially, especially
between vowels. This same restriction is commonly observed in the distribution of **geminate** consonants. These are distinctively long consonants,
which contrast in duration with consonants of standard duration. Geminate
consonants are transcribed using the length sign, as [tː], [pː], [sː], or by
writing two of them in sequence, as [tt], [pp], [ss]. Italian and Japanese
are among the languages that contrast sequences such as [atta] vs. [ata],
or [ippo] vs. [ipo]. But the geminate consonants are impossible initially
and finally in these languages, and indeed in most languages allowing the
geminate contrast. Thus a principle very similar to (26) characterizes the
distribution of geminate consonants. This is not surprising: clusters of similar
consonants sound essentially like geminates. And, as it turns out, they
are subject to the same restrictions geminates are commonly subject to, in
languages where geminates exist.

The function of this section has been to support the analytical strategy
that leads one to experiment first with the most general hypothesis consistent with known data. It is useful to work with predictive statements.
If the predictions are confirmed, the general statement will have helped
discover a broader pattern of data. If they are disconfirmed, the general
statement will have helped delimit the boundaries of the pattern described.
After experimenting for a while with the general statement in (14), we
came to the conclusion that only a narrower version of it – (26) – is accurate: the lesson of this failed experiment is that now we know with some
confidence exactly where it is permissible to have clusters of similar consonants in English. Had we started with a narrower statement like (14), not
because we understood the pattern but for fear of disconfirmation, the
data in (26) might not have come to light. And this data is itself highly
interesting: for it reveals an unexpected similarity of distribution between

the clusters of similar Cs of English and the geminate consonants of other languages.

Consider the alternations below, which are caused by the addition of the suffixes [jən], [jəl], and [juəl] to stems ending in /s/ and /z/.

(a) Suffix [jən] (as in *rebellion* [rəbɛljən])

confess	[kənfɛs]	*confession*	[kənfɛʃən]
obsess	[absɛs]	*obsession*	[absɛʃən]
fuse	[fjuz]	*fusion*	[fjuʒən]

(b) Suffix [jəl] (as in *serial* [sirjəl])

race	[reɪs]	*racial*	[reɪʃəl]
office	[afɪs]	*official*	[əfɪʃəl]
substance	[sʌbstəns]	*substantial*	[sʌbstænʃəl]

(1) Formulate one or more rules to account for these alternations. The rules should mention only phonological information (features and segments), not morphological information (i.e. not which affixes participate in triggering a given process). State a broad generalization about possible sound sequences in English words which motivates the application of the process above. Formulate this generalization as a constraint, of the same type as the constraints discussed above in (9), (14), and (26). (Hint: try pronouncing *obsession*, as a simple juxtaposition of the verb *obsess* and the suffix [jən], without modifying either the root or the affix.)

(2) State what is the relation between the alternations above and the alternations in (c) below.

(c)

miss	[mɪs]	*miss you*	[mɪʃju]
bless	[blɛs]	*bless you*	[blɛʃju]
lɛt	[lɛt]	*let you*	[lɛtʃju]
cut	[kʌt]	*cut you*	[kʌtʃju]

You will need to assume that some rules apply only word-internally, while others apply both within and across word boundaries. The sequence transcribed [tʃ] – e.g. in [lɛtʃju] – is a palatoalveolar affricate. Palatoalveolars in general (i.e. [ʃ], [ʒ] and [tʃ], [dʒ]) are [+coronal] segments differentiated from alveolars by the feature [±anterior]: alveolars are [+anterior] and palatoalveolars are [–anterior]. In addition, palatoalveolar affricates (i.e. [tʃ], [dʒ]) differ from alveolar stops in that they contain two subparts, an actual stop portion and a palatoalveolar fricative [ʃ]. Therefore they contain the feature sequence [–continuant] [+continuant]. Your rules must reflect the feature composition of the output segments.

(3) Now consider the alternations in (d):

(d) Suffix *-ion* (as in *rebellion*)

digest	[daɪdʒɛst]	*digestion*	[daɪdʒɛstʃən]
exhaust	[ɛgzɔst]	*exhaustion*	[ɛgzɔstʃən]
suggest	[sədʒɛst]	*suggestion*	[sədʒɛstʃən]

Suffix *-ial* (as in *editorial*)

beast	[bist]	*bestial*	[bistʃəl]

Suffix *-ian* (as in *Egyptian* [idʒɪpʃən], *Lilliputian* [lɪləpjuʃən])

Christ	[kraɪst]	*Christian*	[krɪstʃən]

Explain why the rules that apply word-internally to derive [ʃ] from [tj] – as in /lɪləpjut-jən/ → [lɪləpjuʃən] – fail to apply in the forms in (d). Why is it that we say [sədʒɛstʃən], not *[sədʒɛsʃən] and [krɪstʃən], rather than *[krɪsʃən]? And how can the analysis be modified to account for this fact?

14.5 The Cross-Linguistic Validity of Constraints

We have suggested that the limitations observed on the occurrence of similar clusters in English are just a reflex of a more general phenomenon, which encompasses limitations on the occurrence of geminates as well. This brings up a fundamental question, which we address briefly here: are the constraints we discuss limited to the language under analysis? Or are they universal?

Phenomena similar or identical to those covered by Voice Agreement and Not-Too-Similar in English are encountered in many of the languages whose phonologies have been analyzed to date. For instance the solution to Exercise 14.2 – which deals with the phonology of the Cushitic language Afar – must involve reference to a constraint akin to version (14) of the English Not-Too-Similar. A similar type of constraint must be operating in Modern Hebrew where /t/-initial suffixes are systematically separated from stems ending in /t/ or /d/ by an inserted [e]. (A variety of other effects of constraints akin to Not-Too-Similar is documented by McCarthy 1986). You can observe that the sequences subject to /e/ insertion would violate (14) if allowed to surface in their underlying representation.

(27) a. /kiʃat-ti/ → [kiʃateti]   'I decorated'
      b. /jarad-ti/ → [jaradeti]   'I descended'

Similarly, the effects of Voice Agreement have been broadly documented; only a vanishingly small number of languages permit word-initial or final obstruent clusters differentiated by voicing. (A stronger version of Voice

Agreement, requiring agreement in voicing regardless of the cluster's position within the word, is also very frequently encountered.) The productive core of the phonology of practically every language displays the effects of constraints that show up, in one version or another, in most other languages.

Let us consider now the critical qualification 'in one version or another.' Neither Not-Too-Similar nor Voice Agreement have identical effects cross-linguistically. The scope of Not-Too-Similar in other languages can be considerably broader. In many Semitic languages – including Hebrew and Arabic – single morphemes do not contain pairs of consonants that are identical with respect to place-of-articulation features, regardless of whether they are identical for voicing or manner features. Thus, single morphemes tend not to contain the sequences /...b...m.../ or /...p...b.../ regardless of which segments and how many of them separate the two bilabials. The Semitic version of Not-Too-Similar enforces a broader definition of what counts as a similar pair than either (14) or (26) and prohibits such pairs from occurring in a larger class of contexts, i.e. regardless of whether the consonants are adjacent. In Romance languages, such as Romanian, Not-Too-Similar operates to prohibit similar clusters in all contexts, regardless of position relative to the edge of the word or morpheme boundaries: underlying /des-zis/ 'unsaid' /dis-sotʃia/ 'dissociate' will be produced as *dezis* and *disotʃia* respectively. In Polish, native words uphold the strong version of Not-Too-Similar – i.e. (14) – morpheme-internally, but across morpheme boundaries all C sequences surface: this yields forms such as *z-zuvatʃ* 'take off one's shoes' and *bez-zembnʃij* 'toothless'.

The variation we observe in the scope of related constraints has two sources. One of these is the tendency to maintain intact morphemes and words: as a result, languages may differ on whether they enforce a given constraint across morpheme or word boundary as strictly as they do within the bounds of a single morpheme. Sequences that are not tolerated within morphemes – e.g. Polish /zz/ – may nonetheless surface across a boundary, presumably for the sake of allowing recovery of the component morphemes of a word in the canonical form in which they normally surface. This imperative is further discussed in the sections that follow. A second source of cross-linguistic variation is the fact that certain constraints – e.g. Not-Too-Similar – may in principle be construed broadly or narrowly and are differently enforced depending on this. For instance, we have seen that one relevant dimension in the interpretation of Not-Too-Similar is how close the participating segments are to each other. It is suggested that the closer they are, the more strongly enforced the constraint, as noted by Pierrehumbert (1993). Thus sequences of /...s...ʃ.../ are not prohibited when non-adjacent in English, although they give rise to tongue twisters and speech errors (cf. '*she sells sea-shells*...') and may be avoided stylistically; but they are strictly prohibited at close range (cf. (23) and (24) above). We may view this case as one in which two versions of the same constraint coexist cross-linguistically, possessing different degrees of generality. The broad version of (14) refers to any two similar consonants, whether adjacent or not: this version is not systematically enforced in English, although it is enforced in other languages. The narrow version enforced in English involves only adjacent segments.

The reader should consider at this point the possibility that a constraint may exist in a language without being systematically enforced. What would that mean? It would mean that speakers would be aware of the fact that sequences violating the constraint are imperfect, while at the same time being aware that words containing such sequences exist in their language and that the language offers them no recourse against the imperfection. A brief example of this involves long sequences of stressless syllables in English: although words such as *clássificatòry* and *commúnicable* (with three stressless syllables) exist in English, speakers asked to rate for phonological well-formedness the novel forms in (28) showed a clear preference for the lefthand column, i.e. for words that avoided more than two stressless syllables in a row:

(28) | Judged more acceptable | Less acceptable | Least acceptable |
|---|---|---|
| *refréshable* | *vísitable* | *párodiable* |
| *presérvable* | *bórrowable* | *bénefitable* |

The preferences indicated in (28) suggest the existence of an UNENFORCED constraint against three or more stressless syllables, which is in fact enforced in many other languages, as pointed out by Hayes (1995). The more syllables separate the last stress from the end of the word, the less acceptable the form. The grammar of English provides speakers with no means to bring surface sequences into compliance with this constraint, but its effect is nonetheless observed in the relative well-formedness judgments.

Given the possible existence of unenforced constraints, the issue of constraint universality becomes considerably harder to determine empirically: to find whether a given constraint obtains in a given language, it is not simply sufficient to inspect the phonological alternations and the distributional restrictions manifest in the lexicon of the language. By this standard, very few constraints are in fact universal. One must consult speakers' intuitions of relative well-formedness as well, as these may go well beyond what the lexicon and the set of alternations indicate: it is at least conceivable that in this way a much wider set of constraints could be shown to manifest themselves cross-linguistically, in enforced or unenforced form. Thus it is possible to conceive of the possibility that a universal set of phonological constraints exists, and that languages differ only in their mode of enforcement of these constraints.

We have seen so far that a rational way to choose between competing analyses is their comparative generality. The most general analysis we could provide for the data in (1) is the one in (4), which we have now spelled out, in revised form, in (20). From this analysis it emerges, however, that the rules themselves are ways of insuring that surface forms conform to certain general principles. The real driving forces behind the analysis are the principles. The rules take effect because they bring underlying representations into compliance with principles of phonological well-formedness. In what follows, as we are about to introduce a new class of principles, we will refer to the sorts of principles motivated so far as **phonotactic constraints**. (**Phonotactic** means pertaining to permissible sequences of sounds. **Constraint** is a term equivalent to principle or condition: the three are being used interchangeably here.) The ideas presented in what follows draw on the work in **Optimality Theory** by Alan Prince and Paul Smolensky (1993). (Note that phonotactic constraints had been proposed much earlier as auxiliary mechanisms in rule-based phonological analyses.) The question we ask now involves the nature of the modifications introduced by rules. After asking *Why do rules exist?* we ask *Why do these particular rules exist?* as against some conceivable others, which could have achieved the same phonotactic objectives. As we will see, the process of answering this question will lead us to explore a mode of analysis in which the rules themselves play no role.

14.6 Possible Rules and Correspondence Principles

Our current analysis of T-morphemes (the rules in (20) and the principles in (9) and (26)) explain why some underlying representations must be modified. They must be modified to avoid violations of certain principles. It is in fact possible to explain not only why certain underlying strings are subject to modification but also why certain types of modifications are more common than others. The general point is that modifications introduced by rules result in minimal differences between related representations, such as underlying and surface forms or surface alternants of the same morpheme. We will observe that there exist principles which regulate the perceived distance between such related forms. The function of such principles is to insure that related forms maintain, all else being equal, a maximum of phonological similarity.

Consider again underlying forms like /mend-d/ or /bæt-d/, which violate the Not-Too-Similar Principle (26). Recall the diagram in (20) which outlines some of the conceivable ways in which the problem raised by such violations could in principle have been resolved: the English language could have resorted to consonant deletion (e.g. /bæt-d/ becoming [bæt] or [bæd]); consonant modification (i.e. /bæt-d/ becoming [bænd],

SIDEBAR 14.2

Dissimilarity effects

Speakers distinguish more similar from less similar pairs of related forms. Anne Cutler and colleagues have compared speakers' ability to identify a lexical item under two conditions, both of which involved modifications of the original word. In one condition, two-syllable words with the pattern STRESSLESS–STRESSED (e.g. *lagóon* [lə'gun]) were presented to speakers with reversed stress (e.g. *lágoon* ['lægun]). In the other condition, words containing two syllables, both stressed (e.g. *càntéen* [ˌkæn'tin]) but differentiated by degrees of stress, were presented to the subjects with reversed pattern of relative stress (e.g. as *cántèen* ['kænˌtin]). Subjects recognized the target words much faster in the second condition than in the first: thus *cántèen* allowed faster recognition of *càntéen*, than *lágoon* did of *lagóon*. Why this happened is clear. A stressed–stressless pair of syllables – e.g. [lə] vs. ['læ] in *lagóon* vs. *lágoon* – differs drastically in vowel quality, whereas main stressed syllables differ from secondary stressed ones in subtler respects. For this reason, pairs of forms differing in the stressed–stressless category of some syllable are perceived as more dissimilar relative to pairs of forms in which corresponding syllables are differentiated only by the location of primary stress (i.e. by the relative strength of stresses).

More dissimilar	Less dissimilar
lágoon ⟷ lagóon	cántèen ⟷ càntéen

What is more interesting is that this judgment of relative similarity between forms guides speakers in the modifications their own speech introduces in underlying forms. Thus many speakers say *fíftèen mén*, *únmàrked cáse* (instead of the expected *fìftéen mén*, *ùnmárked cáse*), to avoid a sequence of adjacent strongly stressed syllables. When they do, the result is a hardly noticed reversal in the pattern of relative stress between the two syllables of *fìftéen*, *ùnmárked*, which are pronounced unchanged in other contexts (e.g. *She is only fìftéen* or *Unmárked exáms*). But speakers do not change the stress in phrases like *profóund thóught*: they will not say **prófound thóught*, even though this will have the same beneficial effect of lessening the clash of adjacent strong stresses. The reason why stress reversal is impossible in such cases may be precisely the greater perceived dissimilarity between intended *profóund* [prə'faund] and reversed **prófound* ['proˌfaund]. The pair rejected, *profóund/*prófound*, differs both in the location of primary stress and in the stressed–stressless status of the initial syllable; whereas acceptable pairs like *ùnmárked/únmàrked* differ only in the location of primary stress. Thus we may say that modifications in the stress pattern of words are subject to a dissimilarity threshold effect: they are blocked when the resulting pair of related forms exceeds this threshold.

[bæld]); or insertion of a longer string than schwa (e.g. [bæt-ənei-d]). The point of this comparison between what actually happens (Schwa Insertion) and what might have, but didn't happen is to observe that some of these solutions are clearly worse than others. For instance, if we delete the suffix consonant, we lose information about the identity of the suffix morpheme: that is particularly serious if the suffix consists of exactly one consonant. Thus hypothetical [bæt] as the past tense of [bæt] has the disadvantage of looking like a present. (There are of course some exceptional forms, like /hit/, as both the present and the past tense of the verb, but the fact that they are so few illustrates the fact that such forms create problems for interpretation.) Hypothetical forms in which the stem has been modified (e.g. [bæn-d], [bæl-d], [bæ-d]) make it harder to tell that the form is meant as the past tense of [bæt].

Now let us consider the string that has been inserted to separate the two similar consonants in forms like [bætəd]. What is actually being inserted in English is a single segment, the vowel [ə], which happens to be the shortest vowel of the language. Note that the function of the inserted string is to separate the similar segments. All sorts of other strings could have fulfilled this function, so it is reasonable to ask whether there is in fact some principled basis for the choice actually made. We will limit our discussion to two alternative possibilities: /n/ insertion and /ai/ insertion. Many other options reduce to some variant of the ones we will discuss or yield strings that are unacceptable in English. The question we ask is whether some independent consideration can predict the choice of inserted material. Had a consonant like /n/ been inserted to separate the suffix /d/ from a preceding similar consonant, the result would have been forms such as [bætn̩d], which contain a cluster of three consonants. English permits such clusters at the juncture of morphemes but many languages disallow them, both because the clustering of the consonants is cross-linguistically disfavored and because of the fact that a consonant is syllabic, as /n/ would have to be in this context. In contrast, no language disallows a vowel flanked by two consonants, the sort of string that emerges from the actual insertion of schwa. So it appears that the choice of material to be inserted reflects cross-linguistic preferences on the composition of segment sequences: the preference for CVC over CCC and the dispreference for syllabic consonants. Now consider which vowel, out of the large inventory of English vowels, is selected for insertion: the shortest vowel is chosen. By comparison with hypothetical alternatives, the insertion of the very short vowel schwa in [bætəd] looks like a reasonable reaction to the potential violation of Principle (26). It is reasonable because it solves the problem at hand while maintaining a high degree of similarity between underlying and surface structure. This mode of thinking predicts correctly that rules of insertion will in general, not only in English, introduce only the minimal necessary distance between segments that were underlyingly adjacent.

Having observed this, we conjecture that there exist principles that regulate the perceived distance between underlying and surface forms: we
shall call them **faithfulness** or **correspondence** principles. It is also by
appeal to such principles that one can explain why some potential modifications of the input are more likely than others to be successful – i.e.
widely attested – as rules. Consider for instance the following correspondence principle:

(29)   **Recover the Morpheme**
       If a word contains in its underlying representation some morpheme
       μ, then at least one segment of μ must be present in the surface
       representation.

If adopted, principle (29) can explain why the /sz/ sequence in /bʌs-z/
is not realized as [s] (i.e. [bʌs]) but is instead subjected to schwa insertion.
Had /bʌs-z/ been realized as [bʌs], no remnant of the plural morpheme
would be present on the surface. The same principle is useful in explaining
why many languages that delete vowels next to other vowels block or
reverse the direction of this rule when the vowel to be deleted represents
the sole segment of its morpheme (Casali 1997). This situation is summarized, using data from Chichewa, in (30):

(30)   a.   V2 deletes in V1-V2 sequences
            khasu-ili → khasuli   'this hoe'
            hoe-this
            mwana-uɣo → mwanaɣo   'that child'
            child-that
       b.   V1 deletes in V1-V2 sequence when V2 is the only segment in
            its morpheme
            si-u-pita → supita   'you will not go'
            not-you-go
            ti-a-bwela → tabwela   'we have come'
            we-PERFECT-come

A sketch of the Chichewa analysis would involve the principle that
no adjacent vowels are allowed to occur. This motivates the basic deletion process. The principle in (29) can then be invoked to explain why
/si-u-pita/ becomes [supita] as against *[sipita], given that elsewhere in
Chichewa it is the second vowel in the sequence that deletes.
   Consider now the possible principle in (31):

(31)   **Recover Obstruency**
       If an underlying segment is an obstruent, it must surface as an
       obstruent.

Principle (29) can explain why the /td/ sequence in /bæt-d/ does not surface as [nd] or [ld] (yielding [bænd] or [bæld] from /bæt-d/). Principle (31) also explains why violations of the Voice Agreement Principle (10) are never – in English or elsewhere – resolved by turning one of the obstruents into a sonorant: /sɪp-d/ becomes [sɪpt] not *[sɪmd].

We can now pause here to observe the effect of these two correspondence principles on the selection of the surface form of /bæt-d/. We do this by analyzing in the table in (32) some conceivable surface realizations of /bæt-d/. Across the top of the display we list applicable principles: in this example, we limit ourselves to Principle (26) (Not-Too-Similar) and Principles (29) (Recover the Morpheme) and (31) (Recover Obstruency). In the lefthand column we write the underlying representation and various potential ways of realizing it as a surface form. We call such forms **candidates**, which is short for **candidate surface forms**. This sort of table is also referred to as a **tableau**. Every candidate is evaluated for its compliance with the principles named; if a principle is violated in a given candidate, this fact is recorded in the relevant cell as a * mark. You can observe below that if we limit ourselves to four candidates, [bæt-d], [bæn-d], [bæt], and [bæt-əd], then the principles listed are sufficient to exclude all but the actual surface form, namely [bætəd]. That's because this form is the only one that fails to violate any of the principles listed.

(32)

UR = /bæt-d/	Not-Too-Similar	Recover the Morpheme	Recover Obstruency
[bæt-d]	*		
[bæt]		*	
[bæn-d]			*
[bætəd]			

Note now that we have arrived at the surface form [bætəd] as the realization of underlying /bæt-d/ without actually applying a rule. We have simply chosen the optimal surface representation, given the principles considered and the choices offered. What is the significance of this fact? It suggests that perhaps what we refer to as 'rules' are better understood as interactions between phonotactic constraint and correspondence constraints. The structural description of the rule is defined by phonotactic constraints violated in underlying representation (UR) while the structural change is limited by the correspondence constraints that hold between underlying representation and surface representation (SR).

This brings up a question we had not entertained before: are all aspects of a rule predictable in terms of general principles? Many phonologists are now experimenting with the affirmative answer. This means that analyses proposed now consist more frequently in a list of constraints than in a list of rules. In the remainder of this chapter we will examine the issues that arise from this hypothesis. Counting against it may be the fact that not all options were considered in (32): what, for instance, excludes [bætəneid] as a candidate for the realization of UR /bæt-d/? Nothing, as far as the principles enunciated so far go. But we haven't actually considered all plausible correspondence principles either: perhaps some consideration can explain why [bætəd] is better than [bætəneid]. We have to look for it before deciding the force of such examples.

EXERCISE 14.6

Read Exercise 13.3 and item (8) from chapter 13. Reformulate the analysis of Hungarian voicing alternations by writing a principle similar to the English Voice Agreement Principle but appropriate for the Hungarian data and a rule similar to the English (20b). Bear in mind that no sequence of obstruents disagreeing in the feature [±voice] is permissible word-internally in this language. Formulate the corresponding rules using the format in (20).

EXERCISE 14.7

Read again Exercise 14.3 and your solution to it. In your solution, you had formulated a principle stating that certain sequences of consonants are not acceptable in the surface structures of English words. This principle leads to modifications of the underlying representations that would violate it. For instance, underlying *condemn* /kəndɛmn/ surfaces as [kəndɛm] when it is not followed by a vowel-initial suffix like -*ation*. This change of underlying word-final /-mn/ to surface [m] raises an interesting difficulty to the analysis proposed so far in this chapter. Your task in this exercise is to discover this problem. A later section in the chapter will propose a solution. To identify the problem you must consider the faithfulness constraints that have been stated so far in this chapter as well as the constraint you had postulated above.

Form a tableau in which all these constraints are represented and where the following candidates for underlying /kəndɛmn/ are evaluated. Note that only Candidate 1 is the actual surface form that should emerge from a correct analysis.

Underlying	Candidate 1	Candidate 2	Candidate 3	Candidate 4	Candidate 5
kəndɛmn	kəndɛm	kəndɛmd	kəndɛmən	kəndɛmn	kəndɛn

Discuss the problem you have discovered by reference to your tableau.

Read again Exercise 14.5 which discusses the process whereby underlying sequences such as /sj/ become surface [ʃ] in word-internal position: e.g. underlying /kənfɛs-jən/ becomes surface [kənfɛʃən]. Identify at least five candidates, i.e. five distinct potential surface forms corresponding to /kənfɛs-jən/, which avoid in one way or another the forbidden sequence [sj]. If the candidates you list violate principles discussed so far, state what these principles are, in the form of a tableau. Identify candidates distinct from the surface form that do not violate any of the principles stated so far, and propose either phonotactic constraints or faithfulness constraints which are being violated by these candidates.

EXERCISE 14.8

14.7 Constraints Conflict

To clarify the focus of our present discussion, we should state first that our primary concern is not to show that rules are unnecessary. Rules can be useful models of the modifications that underlying representations suffer in order to become lawful surface representations. The reason we explore now rule-free descriptions of the sort sketched in (32) is that we are interested in the principles that differentiate a likely rule from an unlikely or impossible one. We have suggested that a likely rule is a minimal modification of the input that allows lexical information to be recovered. To determine explicitly what counts as 'a minimal modification' we are examining possible correspondence principles that limit the discrepancy between related forms, such as the underlying and surface representations of the same word. The interest of these correspondence principles is the fact that they are likely to be part of the native speakers' linguistic competence.

The suggestion made at the end of the previous section is that a surface form such as [bætəd] is chosen as the representative of underlying /bæt-d/ through a process that sifts through conceivable surface representations and selects the one that satisfies not only phonotactic constraints such as (26) but also correspondence constraints.

The speculation that lists of constraints can replace the use of rules may seem implausible. But if in fact the properties of rules can be derived from principles of the sort examined here then tables like (32) are simply making explicit the principles explaining why a certain underlying structure had to be modified, and why it had to be modified in a certain way. It may of course be the case that not everything can be explained, but, without some experimentation, we cannot discover which aspects of language structure are arbitrary – i.e. resist explanation in general terms – and which ones reduce to more general principles. Therefore it is useful to explore the

The phonology of invented languages

In the nineteenth century two languages, Volapük and Esperanto, were invented with the purpose of fostering harmony and understanding across national and ethnic boundaries. The idea was to allow people to communicate with each other on neutral linguistic terrain, without giving primacy to any existing language. The phonological structure of these invented languages is a window into their inventors' views of what constitutes a useful, easily learnable linguistic system. The lexical stock of Volapük is based on German and Romance; that of Esperanto comes from German, Romance and Polish. It is not surprising then that the segmental composition, syllable shape and stress pattern of the two languages ended up looking like those of German, Romance and Slavic languages. What is interesting however, is the fact that both languages were devised to reduce morpheme alternations to a bare minimum: in this respect neither Volapük nor Esperanto look like any of the languages they were based on. Both Volapük and Esperanto possess suffixes that begin with vowels almost exclusively. This is a design feature that pre-empts most common alternations, which come about from the juxtaposition of consonants to consonants and vowels to vowels: since the vast majority of roots end in consonants and essentially all suffixes begin with vowels, the consonant–consonant and vowel–vowel sequences that would normally generate alternations are successfully avoided. A rare source of Esperanto morpheme alternations is the optional loss of final vowels: *kandélo*, 'candle', can be realized as *kandél*; *kandelíngo*, 'chandelier', as *kandelíng*. However, final vowels representing morphemes whose presence cannot be inferred from the syntactic context do not delete: and this looks like an application of principle (29), Recover the Morpheme. The same property (optional deletion of final vowels, blocked when it leads to unrecoverable morpheme loss) characterizes more recent proposed revisions and improvements based on Esperanto, such as the French-Esperanto language Neo.

idea that all aspects of a phonological rule can be attributed to principles. This is what we are currently doing.

We had noted before that it is only schwa, a very short vowel, that is inserted in underlying /bæt-d/. We now consider possible principles explaining why this is. Consider (33):

(33) a. **Syllabic Equivalence** The underlying representation must contain the same number of syllables as the surface representation.

   b. **Recover Adjacency** Segments that are adjacent in the underlying representation must be adjacent in the surface representation.

More on Recover Adjacency

The principle Recover Adjacency is used in the text to explain why only the shortest possible string is inserted to separate similar segments like /td/. A narrower version of this principle explains a variety of other phenomena. Note that the /t-d/ sequence being separated in words like [bætəd] belongs to separate morphemes: /bæt/ and /d/ do not occur to the lexical entry of the same morpheme. Suppose that the principle Recover Adjacency is more strongly enforced when the adjacent segments belong to the same morpheme. This will have the effect of blocking insertion in the middle of a morpheme more strongly than insertion at morpheme boundaries. This effect has been documented: in Sierra Miwok, an extinct American Indian language of California, the vowel [ɨ] is inserted to break up clusters of consonants. The location of insertion varies with the location of the morpheme boundary. Thus in a form such as /tekm-nt-/, 'to keep on kicking', the inserted vowel appears after the first two consonants of the cluster, before the suffix /nt/: [tekmɨnt-]. Whereas in /hoŋŋoj-ksɨ/, 'his bare knees show', the inserted vowel appears after the first consonant: [hoŋŋojɨksɨ]. The result of varying in this way the location of the inserted vowel insures that adjacent segments belonging to the same morpheme continue to be adjacent on the surface. The same type of variation in the location of insertion has been attested in other languages.

A different effect of Recover Adjacency is the strong preference for locating affixes not inside the stem, as infixes, but rather on its outskirts, as prefixes or suffixes. Note that an infix has the fundamental drawback of inducing necessary violations of Recover Adjacency; its insertion separates segments that were underlyingly adjacent in the stem. Possibly as a consequence of this, most languages lack infixes of any sort. Those languages that allow infixes, limit infixation to morphemes whose syllable structure will be improved when infixed.

These look like reasonable principles. But the first observation we can make about them is that they are in fact not satisfied by the pairs of forms we are interested in: i.e. UR /bæt-d/ vs. SR [bætəd]. There is one syllable in the UR /bæt-d/ vs. two in SR [bætəd]. And the segments /t-d/ are adjacent underlyingly but non-adjacent on the surface: schwa comes between them. Perhaps then we shouldn't adopt these principles.

However, there is a different way to reason about this problem. The principle in (33a) is worth considering because it distinguishes the actual UR–SR pair /bæt-d/–[bætəd] from rejected pairs such as /bæt-d/–[bætəneid]: the actual pair differs by one syllable, the rejected one differs by two and therefore violates (33a) in a more serious way. Similarly, the principle in (33b) seems plausibly useful because it distinguishes the actual UR–SR pair /bæt-d/–[bætəd] from rejected ones like /bæt-d/–[bæt-ən-d].

In this case, the number of syllables differentiating UR from SR is the same but the string separating the underlyingly adjacent /t-d/ is shorter in the actual pair than in the rejected ones: /t-d/ are closer to being adjacent in the [təd] string of [bætəd], even if they are not exactly adjacent. Therefore the degree of surface closeness between underlyingly adjacent segments is not an indifferent matter: this very fact justifies the principle in (32b) to a certain extent. Further justification is presented below.

But now if the principles in (33) are useful and if we adopt them, then we must reconcile this with the fact that the surface representations like [bætəd] violate them. This is a puzzle: we have appealed to the principles in (33) to explain why the rule separating /t/ from /d/ inserts just schwa, nothing more, and yet these very principles are being violated by the actual surface forms they are supposed to explain. The way out of this puzzle is to acknowledge that the complete set of principles motivated so far conflict: it is not possible to always satisfy both Not-Too-Similar (26), and Recover the Morpheme (29), and Recover Adjacency (33b) and Recover Obstruency (31). And if these principles cannot all be satisfied simultaneously, then we must choose which ones among them will be fully satisfied and which one might be violated, so as to satisfy the others. Reasoning from the data examined so far, it appears that it is the principles in (33) that have to pay the price in this case: we can observe this in the table in (34). What is important to note about this table is that every form listed violates some of the principles motivated: no candidate is perfect. But if we assume that Recover Adjacency is less important than the other principles discussed then the optimal candidate is the one that violates only it and satisfies the rest. We record graphically the fact that Recover Adjacency is taken to be the less important principle, by separating its column from those of higher ranked ones with a double line. The priority order we have assumed here is also known as ranking: the first three principles in (34) *outrank* Recover Adjacency.

(34)

UR = bæt-d/	Not-Too-Similar	Recover Obstruency	Recover the Morpheme	Recover Adjacency
(a) [bætd]	*			
(b) [bænd]		*		
(c) [bæt]			*	
(d) **[bætəd]**				*

We can now observe that even the bottom ranked constraint in (34) has an effect in the selection of surface forms. This was anticipated when we noticed that forms such as *[bætəneid] are worse because they impose a greater distance between the underlyingly adjacent segments. This point can now be reflected explicitly in the analysis by assuming that every segment separating two underlyingly adjacent segments is separately penalized by a violation mark. The effect of this convention is that [bætəneid] will be observed to accumulate more violation marks than [bætəd]: one for [ə], one for [n] and one for [ei]. And that is enough to exclude [bætəneid] and all other similar candidates from further consideration.

(35)

UR = /bæt-d/	Not-Too-Similar	Recover Obstruency	Recover the Morpheme	Recover Adjacency
(a) [bætəneɪd]				****
(b) **[bætəd]**				*

Here are in more explicit form the principles that underlie the process of selection illustrated in the tables in (34) and (35):

(36) How to select a winning candidate among a set of candidates based on a ranked set of constraints:

    a. If two candidates in the set, a and b, differ only in that a violates higher ranked constraints than b, then b is optimal with respect to a.
        [e.g. d is better than a, b, or c in table in (34).]
    b. If two candidates in the set, a and b, differ only in that a violates a given constraint more than b does, then b is optimal with respect to a.
        [e.g. b is better than a in the table in (35).]
    c. The winning candidate is optimal relative to all other candidates considered.

These selection principles do not cover the case in which candidates differ both in number of overall violations and in the ranking of the constraints violated. This situation is illustrated abstractly below:

(37)

UR	Constraint 1	Constraint 2
Candidate (a)	*	
Candidate (b)		**

Candidate (b) totals two constraint violations for the lower ranked Constraint 2. Candidate (a) violates the higher ranked Constraint 2, but only once. How should this situation be decided? We have to discover real situations of this sort and observe which candidate surfaces. The bulk of the relevant cases studied so far suggests that (b) should win: the rank of constraints violated carries more weight in the decision than actual numbers of violations. We therefore re-word (36a) as follows:

(38)   For any two candidates, a and b, if the highest ranked constraint violated by a is higher than the highest ranked constraint violated by b then b is optimal with respect to a.

In (37) the highest ranked constraint violated by a is Constraint 1 (C1), and the highest ranked constraint violated by b is Constraint 2 (C2). Since C1 outranks C2, this alone – regardless of violation numbers – decides which candidate is optimal. Our new clause no longer stipulates that a and b differ exclusively in the ranking of the constraints they violate: they may also differ in the number of violations they total.

The same selection procedure can be followed in selecting the surface representation of underlying forms like /sɪp-d/, which violate Voice Agreement. In this case we obtain the correct result by ranking Voice Agreement, as well as all the correspondence principles discussed so far, above the constraint in (39):

(39)   **Recover voicing**: If a segment is voiced underlyingly, it must be voiced on the surface.

The effect of the ranking is illustrated in (40): the double line separating Recover Adjacency and Recover Voicing signals that the latter is lower ranked.

(40)

UR = /sæp-d/	Voice Agreement	Recover the Morpheme	Recover Obstruency	Recover Adjacency	Recover Voicing
(a) [sæpd]	*				
(b) [sæp]		*			
(c) [sæmd]			*		
(d) [sæpəd]				*	
(e) **[sæpt]**					*

The overall ranking of constraints discussed so far is shown in (41): arrows (↘↓↙) indicate that the upper constraints outrank the lower ones.

The symbol >> is used in the same way: C1 >> C2 means that C1 outranks C2.

(41)

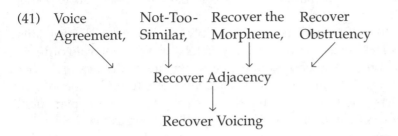

Note that Recover Voicing is not completely idle either, despite its being ranked at bottom: it excludes a candidate such as *[bætət], which nothing so far had disqualified: the table in (42) shows that [bætət] is worse than [bætəd] because it violates not only Recover Adjacency but also, and this time for no good reason, Recover Voicing. Clause (b) in (36) tells us that [bætəd] is still the optimal form: [bætət] and [bætəd] are equivalent in all respects except that the former violates one constraint more (once) than the latter (zero).

(42)

UR = /bæp-d/	Voice Agreement	Recover the Morpheme	Recover Obstruency	Recover Adjacency	Recover Voicing
(a) [bætd]	*				
(b) [bæt]		*			
(c) [bænd]			*		
(d) **[bætəd]**				*	
(e) [bætət]				*	*

A further observation that supports our analysis involves the ordering between the rules of Schwa Insertion and Devoicing (20a and b). In principle, two rules, a and b, can be ordered either so that a precedes b or so that b precedes a. For a given data set, only one order may be correct. If Schwa Insertion precedes Devoicing, underlying /bæt-d/ becomes first [bætəd], after which Devoicing becomes inapplicable (cf. derivations in (5)). This is the right result for our data. If Devoicing precedes Schwa Insertion, then /bæt-d/ becomes [bætt], after which Schwa Insertion applies and yields the incorrect *[bætət]. The mapping between UR /bæt-d/ and SR [bætət] is not just one that happens to be incorrect in English. It is a type of mapping very infrequently attested (if at all) as compared with the straightforward /bæt-d/–[bætəd] mapping: that's because *[bætət] deviates more from the UR than strictly necessary. This is exactly what the table in (43) indicates: *[bætət] violates the same constraint that [bætəd] does, plus an extra one. This extra violation makes it a less optimal candidate and explains why it doesn't surface.

An analysis like (20), which consists of applying two ordered rules, fails to express this fact; no aspect of the analysis tells us why one rule order is better than the other. The observation that some rule orderings are more common and more natural than others has been made for quite some time. And the linguists who first noted this fact have proposed, as its explanation, principles whose intent is close to the idea of UR–SR correspondence principles, of the sort we are discussing now. For example, one can state that when two rule orders (rule a before rule b vs. rule b before a) are such that one order allows a fuller recovery of the underlying form than the opposite one, the former, more transparent order, is preferred. That's essentially the same as stating that it is preferable, all else being equal, to recover intact the underlying representation. Thus, whether they operate only with rules or only with constraints, all analyses must recognize a preference for transparent UR–SR mappings. Where rule-based and constraint-based analyses differ, is that this preference for transparent mappings plays a direct and central role in every constraint-based analysis, in the form of explicitly formulated correspondence constraints which measure the amount of deviation from underlying form.

Another important new point introduced in this section has been that principles may conflict with each other. When they are observed to conflict, this is not necessarily a sign that some of them have to be abandoned: perhaps all can be maintained, but a priority order, a ranking, must be established among them. The ranking tells us which constraints to violate for the sake of satisfying which other ones. This is not to say that all conceivable constraints are in fact part of linguistic competence: like features, syntactic structures or stress representations, individual constraints are hypotheses about the structure of grammatical knowledge. And as hypotheses, constraints can be right or wrong. But the simple fact that they are discovered to conflict is not enough to disqualify them all or indeed any of them.

14.8   Typology, Markedness, and Ranking Variations

The rules for selecting optimal candidates given in the preceding section predict that a different ranking of the constraints considered above will generate a different sound pattern. For instance if we rank Recover Adjacency above Not-Too-Similar, we predict that the winning candidate will be identical to the underlying representation: the table in (43) illustrates this.

(43)

UR = /bæt-d/	Recover Adjacency	Recover the Morpheme	Recover Obstruency	Not-Too-Similar
(a) [bætəd]	*			
(b) [bæt]		*		
(c) [bænd]			*	
(d) **[bætd]**				*

We draw attention to this point for the following reason. The grammar, on the model we have been presenting here, consists of three types of objects: a language-specific lexicon of underlying representations, a set of constraints – many or all of which could be valid across languages – and a language-specific ranking among these constraints. There may be evidence for the existence of the constraints independently of the data we are analyzing, both within one language and by looking at the same phenomena cross-linguistically. The sidebars above presented some such evidence. But the ranking among constraints was proposed solely to derive the data under discussion: it has no justification other than the fact it derives the data. The ranking among constraints may be as arbitrary and as language-specific as the fact that English uses [kæt] and French [ʃa] to designate a cat. If this is so, we should be able to encounter variability in the way different languages rank the same constraints.

And indeed we do. Sequences of similar consonants (e.g. [tt], [dd], [ss]) surface unmodified at the end of the word in Berber dialects; [ss], [zz] sequences surface unmodified at the beginning of the word in Polish. This difference between admissible surface forms in English vs. Polish and Berber can be succinctly characterized as a difference in the ranking of the same principles: Not-Too-Similar >> Recover Adjacency (in English) vs. Recover Adjacency >> Not-Too-Similar (in Polish or Berber).

But now this conclusion only follows if we have some reason to believe that Not-Too-Similar is a constraint that plays some role, any role at all, in the grammars of Polish and Berber. For if it doesn't, then the fact that these languages allow [ss] word-initially and finally is just a consequence of the fact that Not-Too-Similar is missing from their grammars. This is an important and, to an extent, an unsettled issue: how can we tell the difference between linguistic systems in which a constraint is low ranked vs. linguistic systems in which that same constraint is absent?

This is not a question that we have a clear answer for. But we suggest that, whatever the eventual answer will be, the better research strategy is to adopt the more predictive assumption. The most predictive assumption in this case is that the constraints are the same for all languages. Their rankings, however, vary.

Our example is based on observations about syllable structure made in chapter 13. It was noted there that in certain situations syllable divisions are inferred not on the basis of data specific to the language under analysis but on the basis of universal preferences. The two preferences mentioned earlier are repeated below:

(44)   Two universal syllable preference laws:
       All other things being equal, segments are assigned to syllables so
       as to create (a) open syllables and (b) syllables with onsets.

These two preferences can be stated as phonotactic constraints:

(45)   ***Coda**: Syllables cannot have codas.

(46)   **Onset**: Syllables must have onsets.

Since the syllable division preferences in (44) are universal, the corresponding constraints must be universal too. How come then that some languages allow onsetless syllables, others allow closed syllables (i.e. codas) and others – like English – permit both? We can answer this by considering the means by which underlying representations violating (45) or (46) could be made to comply with them. Take the UR /bæg/ in English. This representation violates (45): it has a coda. Why isn't it fixed so as to satisfy (45)? Because any method of fixing the representation would involve a departure from the UR and every such departure is separately penalized by a correspondence constraint. We could eliminate the final C in /bæg/ but a constraint parallel to Recover Voicing and Recover Obstruency will be violated:

(47)   **Recover C**
       An underlying consonant must be present (in identical or possibly
       modified form) on the surface.

(Note that the reason this constraint is violated in English is because it is dominated by other constraints that compel violations of it. The constraint is relevant even to English, where some Cs drop, because they are deleted only under compulsion of some other, more highly ranked well-formedness condition such as avoidance of word-final mn, mb etc.)

If Recover C ranks above *Coda (45), this is sufficient to exclude the deletion method of bringing /bæg/ in compliance with (46). We might also insert some vowel, say [ə], that will allow [g] to syllabify as its onset: /bæg/ → [bæ.gə]. Why isn't this option taken? Perhaps because a different class of correspondence constraints require that no segments occur on the surface if they are not part of the UR.

(48) **No V Insertion**
A surface vowel must be present (in identical or possibly modified form) in the underlying representation.

No V Insertion, when ranked above *Coda, will eliminate the only other route to a codaless realization of this form. The global effect of the rankings postulated so far is that /bæg/ has no choice but to keep its coda, despite the preference against this piece of syllable structure. Recall that this preference must be postulated in any case, simply because it accounts for the syllabification of strings such as *promote* as [pro.mot] rather than as [prom.ot]

(49)	UR = /bæg/	No V Insertion	Recover C	*Coda
	(a) [bægə]	*		
	(b) [bæ]		*	
	(c) [bæg]			*

(Our new constraint No V Insertion is clearly violated in forms such as [mɛndəd], where schwa is inserted. But this observation is compatible with the proposals made, since we only need the ranking Not-Too-Similar >> No V Insertion and this ranking is compatible with No V Insertion >> *Coda, the ranking needed for (49).)

If we vary the ranking between the three constraints in (49) we can derive phonological systems in which potential coda consonants are eliminated through deletion (*Coda >> Recover C) and languages in which codas are avoided through vowel insertion (Recover C, *Coda >> No V Insertion). Thus Maori, a language of New Zealand, possesses only open syllables of the form (C)V on the surface and displays alternations such as [ho.pu] 'catch' vs. [ho.pu.ki.a] 'be caught'. Since we can tell that the passive suffix is -*ia* (not -*kia*) this sort of alternation tells us that the root 'to catch' is /hopuk/: /k/ is deleted when it cannot be syllabified as an onset, by virtue of the ranking No V Insertion, *Coda >> Recover C. The other ranking predicted by the analysis (Recover C, *Coda >> No V Insertion) is also instantiated, for example in Asheninca Campa, a language of South America.

Thus different ranking options among the constraints in (49) yield the three attested ways in which underlying word final Cs are dealt with: they may be kept, as in English, deleted, as in Maori, or made into onsets, through vowel insertion, as in Asheninca. Underlying forms in which some syllables lack onsets give rise to the same type of inter-language variation: an underlying /umi/ will survive intact, if all relevant correspondence constraints outrank Onset (46); or it may lose its onsetless vowel, surfacing as [mi], if Onset >> Recover V; or it may acquire an inserted onset segment, surfacing as, say, [ʔumi], if Onset >> No C Insertion. All three options are in fact attested.

There is a more important benefit provided by the idea that linguistic variation exclusively reflects variation in constraint rankings. Certain conceivable sound patterns cannot be derived by varying the ranking of known constraints. For instance, a language in which every single syllable is closed cannot be characterized by any ranking of the phonotactic and correspondence constraints discussed here. In this hypothetical system, every open syllable that occurs underlyingly is turned into a closed syllable. If this is achieved through systematic vowel deletion (e.g. /aba/ → [ab]) then some constraint must be found to outrank Recover V. If this happens through systematic consonant insertion (e.g. /aba/ → [abaʔ]), that same constraint must outrank No C Insertion. But the high ranked constraint that will have this effect doesn't exist: no preference for codas can be documented in the languages we have studied. And, not surprisingly, no language systematically disallows open syllables. On the question of possible codas, the extent of linguistic variation is limited to the three options considered earlier; will codas be tolerated? And, if not, how will they be avoided?

14.9   Constraint Ranking Effects in Word Formation

We illustrate the utility of ranked constraints by considering now their effects on word-formation processes. Our first observation involves two classes of English affixes. Affixation rules can be classified by their degree of productivity: productive affixes can be added to any stem that fits their syntactic or semantic requirements. Unproductive affixes do not have this ability. For instance, the suffix -*ness* can be added to any adjective denoting a quality and it yields a noun denoting the state of possessing that quality: *sheepishness, greenness, idleness*. The suffix -*er* can be added to any verb denoting an action and yields a noun denoting the agent of this action, especially the habitual agent of such an action: *planter (of trees), recoverer (of lost objects), opener (of doors)*. The suffix -*able* can be added to any transitive verb and yields an adjective referring to the possibility of undergoing the action denoted by the verb: *mesmerizable, induceable, sweepable*. These are all productive affixes: the examples given above are *nonce* words created for the occasion, rather than forms that can be looked up in a dictionary.

In contrast the affix -*al* denoting a verbal action cannot be productively added to all conceivable verbs: there is *arrival* (related to *arrive*) but no *connival* (related to *connive*); there is *perusal* (related to *peruse*) but no *bruisal* (related to *bruise*). The overall number of -*al* forms is thus very limited: and an English speaker who wishes to know whether a given verb has an associated -*al* derivative must resort to looking it up in a dictionary. In the case of productive affixes the looking up is unnecessary; the affixed word, whether it has been used or not before, can always be constructed. Similarly, the adjectival suffixes -*ic* and -*al* (*historic, methodic, geographic; methodical, cerebral, parental, pestilential*), and -*ity*, which creates adjective-based nouns (*curiosity, obesity, serenity, perplexity*) are well-represented in the English lexicon but are not productive in the sense defined above: we can say *methodicalness*, if we need to express this thought, but not *methodicality;* we can confidently say *the quality of an obstruent*, but not (or not confidently) *obstruental quality.*

This difference in productivity is associated, in English, with a phonological characteristic: productive affixes maintain intact the stressed or stressless quality of the syllables in stems they attach to. Unproductive suffixes do not have this systematic quality: many of them induce major phonological changes in the stems they attach to (cf. *insane-insanity; domestic-domesticity, parent-parental; symphony-symphonic*). Now, since native speakers of English can coin on the spot productively suffixed words, the fact that such words maintain intact a constant phonological property of their stems must reflect an aspect of linguistic knowledge. We suggest that this is the correspondence principle in (50):

(50) **Recover Stress**
  If a syllable is stressed in a given word, then that syllable is stressed in any combination consisting of that word plus one or more affixes.
  If a syllable is stressless in a given word, then that syllable is stressless in any combination consisting of that word plus one or more affixes.

Productively affixed words satisfy the correspondence constraints in (50). In so doing, they are forced to violate other principles. For instance all unsuffixed English words – and many suffixed ones – tolerate no more than two stressless syllables at the end of the word. An unsuffixed word may contain its main stress further away from the end of the word (e.g. as in *mélanchòly*) but there will always be some stress – primary or subsidiary – within the last three syllables. Readers can persuade themselves of this by noting that completely stressless syllables have reduced vowels ([ə], [ɨ] or [ɪ] before [ŋ], a syllabic liquid [r̩] or [l̩]); a full vowel such as [æ], [ɛ], [e], [ɔ], [o], [u] is a sign of stress. (Cf. also chapter 13.) In unsuffixed words there aren't more than two syllables containing reduced vowels at the end of the word. And for this reason, a word like ['pæmələnə], which ends in a string of three schwas, will be detected as non-English by native speakers.

(51)   Word-final strings of unstressed syllables in unsuffixed English
        words:
        1 unstressed syllable: *vanílla, devélop, magénta*
        2 unstressed syllables: *mélody, ásterisk, díscipline*
        3 unstressed syllables: ―――――――
        4 unstressed syllables: ―――――――

The preference for locating some stress in the last three syllables of the
word corresponds to the principle in (52), which was alluded to earlier
in our discussion of the data in (28). This is the 'unenforced' constraint
suggested by the preferences in (28):

(52)   The No Lapse Constraint
        There can be no more than two stressless syllables in a row.

No Lapse rules out both unattested forms like ['pæmələnə] – where the
long stressless string is word-final – and hypothetical [ˌtatəmənə'gutʃə],
where three stressless syllables separate the two stressed ones. Indeed
neither type occurs.

But No Lapse is violated in productively suffixed words: forms such
as *dísciplinable* ['dɪsəplənəbl̩], *canónicalness* [kə'nɑnəkəlnəs], *clássificatòry*
['klæsəfəkəˌtori] have precisely the sort of stress contour that is forbidden
in the rest of the English vocabulary. It is not possible to say that such
words are isolated exceptions to the rules of English stress: they represent the productive and regular pattern resulting from adding a suffix to
a stem. Nor is it possible to say that no phonological rules apply to productively suffixed words, for shifts in primary stress occur with many
such suffixes: as in *análỳze* ['ænəˌlaiz] vs. *ànalýzable* [ˌænə'laizəbl̩] where
main stress shifts rightwards upon affixation. The generalization is that
characterized by (50): a stressed syllable remains stressed upon affixation,
a stressless one remains stressless. Our analysis need only rank No Lapse
below Recover Stress to capture this pattern. We illustrate the ranking in
(53):

(53)	base: *canónical* [kə'nɑnəkəl]	Recover Stress	No Lapse
	(a) *canonícalness* [ˌkænə'nɪkəlnəs]	**	
	(b) *canònicálness* [kəˌnɑnə'kælnəs]	*	
	(c) *canónicalness* [kə'nɑnəkəlnəs]		*

The data examined here illustrates the effect on word formation of ranking correspondence constraints (e.g. Recover Stress) above phonotactic

constraints (e.g. No Lapse). Such rankings force morphologically complex forms to violate the phonotactic constraints observed by all morphologically simple forms.

The opposite ranking can be documented as well: word formation may be affected by constraint ranking when some correspondence constraints are outranked by phonotactic constraints. We will use here a schematic example that generalizes over several phenomena encountered in Austronesian languages. The ideas presented come from work by McCarthy and Prince (1995). The Austronesian group (which includes Tagalog, Javanese and Achehnese) permits both closed syllables (C)VC and onsetless syllables V(C). This means that the correspondence constraints mentioned above outrank No Coda and Onset. Nevertheless, these two constraints have an effect on the morphology of Austronesian. The vast majority of Austronesian prefixes are of the form CV(C). Suffixes are rarer and, in languages like Achehnese, non-existent. There are several affixes of the form VC, and these occur as infixes after the first consonant of the root. Thus the Achehnese affix *-um-*, when infixed in forms like *tulak*, will yield *tumulak*. The same affix yields *g-um-leŋ* from underlying *gleŋ*. The syllabification of infixed forms is the expected one: *tu.mu.lak, gum.leŋ*. An analysis of Austronesian infixation must answer two questions. First, why are these morphemes infixed rather than prefixed or suffixed? And why is it the case that all infixes are VC morphemes, rather than CV, the other possible affixal shape? The answer to both questions presupposes the idea of ranked constraints. Suppose that the VC morphemes of Austronesian are basically prefixes: in that capacity they must precede at least some portion of the root, preferably all of it. We postulate the constraint in (54) for this purpose:

(54) **Prefix**
Every segment of the affix precedes every segment of the root.

Now suppose they did precede the entire root, as prefixes normally do? Then the affixation of *um* to *tulak* will yield *um.tu.lak*, a word with two codas and one onsetless syllable. We must admit that the infixed form *tumulak* is phonotactically improved: it lacks the onsetless syllable and it minimizes the occurrence of codas, without resorting to either insertion or deletion of segments. Thus the low ranked constraints Onset and No Coda appear to play a role in the decision to infix VC morphemes. They are low ranked relative to most correspondence constraints but higher ranked than Prefix (54): this explains why *um* is infixed. This ranking also explains why a CV prefix is not infixed: it will yield an onsetless, codaless syllable even if it satisfies Prefix.

(55)

prefix -*um* root *tulak*	Onset	No Coda	Prefix
(a) um.tu.lak	*	**	
(b) tu.mu.lak		*	*

But why is the affix -*um* not placed as a suffix? Note that a form in which -*um* functions as a suffix (e.g. **tulak-um*) is as well formed phonotactically as the attested infixed form (*tumulak*). But in this case the morpheme -*um* precedes NONE of the root segments. Perhaps this is why forms like *tulak-um* are unattested. We assume then the prefix status of a morpheme is not an all-or-none issue: the optimal prefix precedes every root segment, but a morpheme may still be to some extent a prefix if it precedes at least some of the root segments. This is what these infixes do: they are located to precede the largest number of root segments they can, while still avoiding Onset and No Coda violations. We can express this by assuming that violations of the constraint are marked by assigning an asterisk, * for every root segment that precedes a segment of the affix. Under this convention, attested *tumulak* and **tulakum* can be properly differentiated: as (56) shows, the two forms violate the same constraint (Prefix) but one of them violates it more times than the other.

(56)

	Onset	No Coda	Prefix
(a) tu.la.kum			*(t)*(u)*(l)*(a)*(k)
(b) tu.mu.lak			*(t)

We note finally that the constraint Recover Adjacency (cf. (33) and Sidebar 14.4) is violated by the actual form *tumulak* (since -*um*- separates the underlyingly adjacent *t* and *u*) but is satisfied by the unattested **tulakum*. We infer from this that Prefix, although itself quite low ranked, outranks Recover Adjacency in this language.

This section has illustrated the sort of analyses that can be pursued once ranked constraints are adopted. It appears to be the case that none of the generalizations outlined here can be expressed in any direct way without constraints. An infixation rule can be written for Austronesian, but it will not explain why only VC morphemes infix, why they infix rather than prefix or suffix, and why they are located as close to the left edge of the root as permitted by the phonotactics. Also noteworthy is the fact that the analyses discussed here consist only of constraints and their ranking, without assistance from rule statements.

14.10 Summary

Our goal in this chapter was to answer a fundamental question in phonology: why are there rules that modify underlying forms? We first proposed an answer for one half of this question: why can't underlying forms always surface intact? The answer is that phonotactic constraints would be frequently violated if this were so. Then we tackled the other half of the question: given that they have to be modified, why is it that underlying forms must be modified in the specific ways that rules encode? The answer here was more complex. First we noted that some modifications represent more serious departures from the underlying form. It stands to reason that only a minimal departure should be adopted. In the course of making this point precise, we came to the conclusion that a variety of correspondence constraints must be postulated. Next came the discovery that these constraints conflict. The only way to acknowledge their existence, while at the same time characterizing the fact that some are violated in surface forms, is to assume constraint rankings, that is, statements of priority. The last two sections explored the uses of constraint rankings in the analysis of syllabic typology and word-formation processes. We have tried to show that any attempt to answer the fundamental question raised at the outset – Why do rules exist? – will tend to produce answers in which the use of rules as descriptive tools is minimized and perhaps completely eliminated.

Further reading

Archangeli, Diana and Terence, Langendoen. eds. 1997. *Optimality Theory: An Introduction*. Oxford: Blackwell.

Hayes, Bruce. 1995. *Metrical Stress theory: Principles and Case Studies*. Chicago: University of Chicago Press.

McCarthy, John and Alan Prince. 1995. Prosodic Morphology. In John Goldsmith, ed., *Handbook of Phonological Theory*, pp. 318–67, Oxford: Blackwell.

EXERCISES

Yokuts – an almost extinct California American Indian language (Newman 1944) – possesses two types of sonorant consonants in its phonemic inventory: plain voiced sonorants – as in (a) – and glottalized sonorants – as in (b). The glottalized sonorants are produced with vocal folds tense and constricted for part of their length. The feature differentiating the two types of sonorants is [±constricted glottis]: the glottalized series is [+constricted glottis].

Exercise 14.9

(a) Plain voiced sonorants, [–constricted glottis]: m, n, l, w, j
(b) Glottalized sonorants, [+constricted glottis]: m̰, n̰, l̰, w̰, j̰

Part I

The plain sonorants occur within Yokuts words in any position: word-initially, word-finally, between a vowel and a consonant or between a consonant and a vowel. Some examples of voiced sonorants occurring in Yokuts words appear in (c): the relevant sounds are in bold characters.

(c)   word-initial: *me:kit* 'was swallowed', **wow**lal 'may stand up'
       between vowels: *gijit* 'was touched', *?ami**l**ka* 'help!'
       word-final: *xathin* 'ate', *logwol* 'may pulverize'
       between vowel and
       consonant: *?ami**l**ka* 'help!', *logiwka* 'pulverize!'
       between consonant
       and vowel: *?am**l**al* 'may help', *gi**j**mi* 'helping'

However, the glottalized sonorants do not occur word-initially or after a consonant. Relevant examples appear in (d):

(d)   word-initial: _____
       between vowels: *caw̰a:hin* 'shout', *nen̰a:hin* 'make quiet'
       word-final: *xaja:hal̰ij* 'one who is placed'
       between vowel and
       consonant: *jaw̰la:hin* 'follow', *?el̰ka:hin* 'sing'
       between consonant
       and vowel: _____

Formulate a principle of the form *Feature combination x is disallowed in position Y*, which summarizes as succinctly as possible the restriction on the occurrence of glottalized sonorants in Yokuts. Bear in mind that this is not a rule: the data being characterized involves no alternations, but rather just the systematic absence of a sound class from certain positions within the word.

Part II

Now consider the alternation in (e)–(f): some Yokuts suffixes – such as /?in̰aj/ and /?a?/, all of which begin with a glottal stop [?] – cause a sonorant in the preceding root to become glottalized. When this happens, the suffix-initial glottal stop deletes. However, not all sonorants can undergo this process (cf. (g)) and some roots containing sonorants remain unaffected. The sonorants that fail to undergo the process are identifiable by their position: examine the data and state how they can be identified. Explain how the data examined in part 1 sheds light on this fact. Discuss the form *lihm-?in̰aj* and explain why it does not surface as either *lihm̰-in̰aj* or as *l̰ihm-inaj*.

(e)   Underlying form of the suffix /?in̰aj/ appears in:
       dub-?in̰aj   'while leading by the hand'   (root *dub* 'lead by the hand')

(f) Glottal stop of /ʔiṇaj/ realized as sonorant glottalization in:
      c'ow-iṇaj   'while grasping'   (root c'oow 'grasp')
      hiw̱t-iṇaj   'while walking'   (root hiwiit 'walk')
      taṇ-iṇaj   'while going'   (root taan 'go')
      Initial glottal stop of /ʔaʔ/ realized as sonorant glottalization in:
      t'oj̱x-aʔ   'give medicine'   (root t'oj̱x 'medicine')
      ʔaṃl-aʔ   'help, get aid'   (root ʔaml 'help')

(g) Glottal stop of /ʔiṇaj/ is not realized as sonorant glottalization in:
      lihm-ʔiṇaj   'while running'   (root lihm 'run')
      Glottal stop of suffix /ʔaʔ/ is not realized as sonorant glottalization in:
      wis̱-ʔaʔ   'straighten'   (root wis̱ 'straight')
      ʔugn-ʔaʔ   'drink'   (root ʔugn 'drink')
      picw-ʔaʔ   'catch'   (root picw 'catch')

Extra credit: Formulate explicitly the process that turns underlying forms like /t'oj̱x-ʔaʔ/ into surface t'oj̱x-aʔ 'give medicine'.

· ·

Consider again the data of Hungarian voicing alternations presented in chapter 13 (item (8) and Exercises 13.2–13.3). In Exercise 14.6 of this chapter you have formulated a voicing agreement principle that motivates the existence of the voicing alternations. In order to enforce this principle, the voicing value of the stem-final obstruent is modified to agree with the voicing value of the suffix-initial obstruent. Consider now the fact that there are many other ways which could have insured that surface strings comply with the Voicing Agreement Principle. For instance a vowel could have been inserted between the two obstruents that disagree in voice: e.g. underlying /rɔb solgɔ/ 'slave' could have been realized as [rɔbəsolgɔ] with a buffer [ə] separating the two obstruents. This representation satisfies the Voice Agreement Principle through a different modification of the underlying structures from the one actually adopted in Hungarian.

Exercise 14.10

Identify three other procedures through which the language could have insured, but did not, that obstruent sequences agree in surface voice value. Show how underlying representations would be modified if these other means had been adopted to satisfy the Voice Agreement Principle that is active in Hungarian.

· ·

Read Exercise 13.4 from chapter 13. Reformulate the analysis of Yokuts vowel length alternations by writing a principle limiting the occurrence of long vowels to certain contexts. Long vowels do not occur before CC sequences or before word-final Cs. Write the principle – making use of syllable notation – and the rule, using the format in (20).

Exercise 14.11

· ·

Exercise 14.12

Consider the following pairs of underlying and surface representations, discussed earlier:

	Spelling	Underlying	Surface
(a)	*squishes*	[skwɪʃ-z]	[skwɪʃəz]
(b)	*buses*	[bʌs-z]	[bʌsəz]
(c)	*licks*	[lɪk-z]	[lɪks]
(d)	*laps*	[læp-z]	[læps]

For each of the underlying forms above consider the following alternative candidates:

	Candidate class 1	Candidate class 2	Candidate class 3
(a)	[skwɪʃz]	[skwɪʃ]	[skwɪnz]
(b)	[bʌsz]	[bʌs]	[bʌnz]
(c)	[lɪkz]	[lɪk]	[lɪŋz]
(d)	[læpz]	[læp]	[læmz]

Identify the constraint violated by each class of candidates. Write four tables, one for each word considered, in the format of (32), in which you record the constraint violations of each one of the alternative candidates considered and you compare them with the actual surface form of the word.

· ·

Exercise 14.13

Now consider a new class of unsuccessful candidates:

	Underlying	Candidate class 4
(a)	/skwɪʃ-z/	[skwɪz]
(b)	/bʌs-z/	[bʌz]
(c)	/lɪk-z/	[lɪz]
(d)	/læp-z/	[læz]

Formulate a new faithfuless principle that is violated by this class of failed candidates. Write one table for each of the four words: compare the actual surface representation of the word with the corresponding class 4 candidate in terms of your constraint. The result should be that the actual surface form does not violate your proposed principle whereas the class 4 candidate does.

· ·

Exercise 14.14

In Sidebar 14.4 on Recover Adjacency it was pointed out that the adjacency between segments belonging to the same morpheme may be more strictly preserved than that of segments that are concatenated by a morphological operation. Thus the Sierra Miwok vowel insertion rule separates consonants that were adjacent underlyingly but which belonged to separate morphemes; however, it does not separate underlyingly adjacent segments belonging to the same morpheme. In this language, and others, we must distinguish two related versions of Recover Adjacency: a specific one that holds of morpheme-internal position, shown below, and the general version stated earlier in (33b) which does not differentiate morpheme-internal clusters from others.

Recover Adjacency (morpheme-internal) segments that are adjacent in the underlying representation of a single morpheme must be adjacent in the surface representation.

In Sierra Miwok, the constraint written above is undominated (not violated by any surface form), whereas the general constraint in (33b) is in fact violated in cases of vowel insertion. Equipped with this information, propose a solution to the problem identified earlier in Exercise 14.17.

Acquisition of Phonetics and Phonology

15.0 Introduction

In chapters 11–14 we introduced the important theoretical notions of phonetic feature, phoneme, syllable, stress, and prosody. Now we will see that each of these is clearly evidenced in language development, providing further evidence that all human grammars, including child grammars, incorporate these units of representation.

15.1 Infant Speech Perception

A fundamental problem an infant faces in acquiring the phonology of the target language is determining what constitutes a sound in the target language. That is, since sounds may be very similar but not identical phonetically, the infant must determine which of these similar phones comprise the same phonetic category (and later, the same phoneme) in the target language. A necessary first step is perceiving distinctions between sounds, but beyond that, perceiving speech as phonetic categories is crucial for reducing the information in the signal, for programming the production of speech, and for discovering the units used for rules of language.

15.1.1 Experimental paradigms for testing infants

How can researchers determine what an infant, even a newborn infant, is perceiving? Four experimental paradigms have been used extensively to study infant speech perception abilities, each indexing a phenomenon that can be assessed even in a newborn infant: (1) measuring heart rate and (2) measuring sucking rate (referred to as '**High Amplitude Sucking**' or **HAS**). Each of these paradigms operates on the finding that an infant's heart rate or sucking rate increases in conjunction with a novel stimulus, but remains constant or decreases when a stimulus is not discriminably different from the previous stimulus. For example, in the High Amplitude Sucking paradigm, an infant is given a pacifier, and a baseline rate of sucking per minute is established. In one version of this technique, infants control the presentation of a stimulus by sucking on a pacifier. The higher the sucking rate, the more often a stimulus is played. In either version, an infant's baseline sucking rate or heart rate is established, then a set of stimuli are presented. Initially, the heart rate or sucking rate increases with the presentation of new auditory stimuli, but levels off or decreases if the same stimulus (or what is perceived to be the same stimulus) continues to be presented. However, when a novel stimulus is presented, the heart rate or sucking rate jumps, indicating to the experimenter in a measurable manner, that the infant perceives a change in stimuli. In this manner, many different kinds of phonetic (or other) stimuli can be presented to an infant, and the infant can indicate which of these they perceive as distinct from others. Moreover, in the sucking paradigm, the infant has the 'power' to activate the presentation of a stimulus through sucking; thus, some index of conscious choice can be measured.

Two other paradigms have been used with slightly older infants. These procedures involve measuring the time an infant looks at a stimulus (the **Visual Fixation Procedure**), used with infants as young as 2 months, or, for infants 4 months and older, **The Head Turn Preference Procedure**, in which infants are conditioned to turn their heads from the midline position toward a loudspeaker, either in response to an auditory stimulus or to activate speech. In the head turn procedure, 'correct' head turns are reinforced with the illumination of an electrically activated box containing a toy of some kind, and the infants can turn on the toy by turning their heads in the right direction.

15.1.2   Categorical perception in infants

Using these experimental techniques, the abilities of infants to discriminate between sounds, between the sound patterns of different languages, as well as to discriminate between syntactic strings, as mentioned in chapter 6, have been studied. One speech perception ability that has been studied in very young infants, is the ability to perceive consonants **categorically**; that is, to notice some phonetic distinctions between consonants and to ignore others, to put a set of sounds into a single category. This special way of perceiving consonants is characteristic of the way all humans perceive consonants. For example, among other things, stop consonants are distinguished by **Voice Onset Time** (**VOT**), the point at which the vocal folds begin to vibrate relative to the release of the stop. As discussed in chapter 11, stops are described as

(1)   a.   **prevoiced** – when the vocal folds vibrate as long as 100 msecs before the release.
      b.   **voiced** or **voiceless unaspirated** – when vibration is simultaneous with the release.
      c.   **voiceless (aspirated)** stops – when vibration is delayed until after the release.

As discussed in that chapter, languages differ with respect to how many of these categories they contrast (1, 2, or all 3). English contrasts b and c; French and Hungarian contrast a and c; Thai contrasts a, b and c. Importantly, adults perceive only the contrasts that are phonemic in their language; i.e. those that straddle the phonemic boundaries their language uses contrastively.

When do children perceive consonants categorically? Is this something children have to learn or is it a built-in ability? To answer this question, researchers using the high amplitude sucking paradigm demonstrated that 1–4-month-old infants could discriminate between all three categories, regardless of which were used contrastively in their target language. Thus, this perceptual ability appears to be innate, not learned or conditioned by environment. However, as infants get older, they hone their perception to conform to the target phonology, 'losing' this initial ability and the predisposition to 'hear' contrasts at particular VOT boundaries, becoming sensitive to just those distinctions relevant to the phonology of the target language.

Table 15.1 Phonetic discriminations infants can make between consonants

SOUNDS DISCRIMINATED ON	AGE OF INFANTS	PHONETIC FEATURE INVOLVED	KIND OF PHONETIC CONTRAST
(Czech contrast)			
[ra] & [za]	1–4-month-olds	continuant	manner
[bæ] & [dæ]	infants	coronal	place
[ba] & [ga]	6–9-week-olds	dorsal	place
[da] & [ga]	6–12-week-olds	dorsal	place
[wa] & [ja]	2-month-olds	anterior	place
[va] & [ða]	2-month-olds	coronal	place
[fa] & [θa]	2-month-olds	coronal	place
[ra] & [la]	2–3-month-olds	lateral	manner
[ma] & [na]	2–3-month-olds	labial/coronal	place
[va] & [sa]	2–4-month-olds	coronal/voice	place & voice
[sa] & [ʃa]	2–4-month-olds	anterior	place
[as] & [az]	3-month-olds	voice	glottal stricture
[ba] & [ga]	4–5-month-olds	dorsal	place
[ba] & [wa]	6–8-month-olds	consonantal	manner
[ada] & [aga]	6-month-olds	dorsal	place
[da] vs. [ba] vs. [ga]	6-month-olds	coronal/dorsal	place
[fa] & [θa]	6-month-olds	coronal	place
Hindi retroflex vs. dental stops	6-month-olds	alveolar	manner

15.1.3 Other speech perception abilities of infants

In other infant speech perception research utilizing these experimental methods, infants have been found to discriminate many phonetic distinctions. Table 15.1 above presents a sample of the phonetically similar consonant sounds young infants have been shown to discriminate. Note that these sounds differ in each case by only one phonetic feature, suggesting that from birth, infants are sensitive to the kinds of phonetic distinctions that are defined by phonetic features. Note also, that it is essential that infants be sensitive to such distinctions in order to be able to acquire whatever their target language may be.

Table 15.2 presents some of the vowel distinctions infants have been shown to discriminate. Note again that for the most part the members of these vowel pairs differ by only one phonetic feature.

The last two contrasts in table 15.2 – that between a tense high front rounded vowel and a tense high back rounded vowel, and that between a lax high front rounded vowel and a lax high back rounded vowel – contrasts which are phonemic in German and discriminable by 4–6-month-old English-learning infants, are no longer discriminable by 6–8-month-old English-learning infants. This pattern, where infants as young

Table 15.2 Some vowel distinctions English infants discriminate

VOWELS DISCRIMINATED	AGE OF INFANTS TESTED
[a] vs. [i]	1–4-month-olds
[i] vs. [u]	1–4-month-olds
[i] vs. [ɪ]	2-month-olds
[pa vs. [pã]	1–4-month-olds
[y] vs. [u]	4–6-month-olds
[Y] vs. [ʊ]	4–6-month-olds

SIDEBAR 15.1

More on infant perception abilities

Infant speech perception has become a rich field of study with an ever-increasing number of interesting experiments being carried out. One finding that has been well established is the ability of infants to recognize differences in speakers, when that is the relevant variable, but to know (unconsciously, of course) to ignore speaker differences when it comes to identifying whether a given sound is the same or different from another. For example, infants can readily differentiate between their own mother's voice and other speakers and even show a strong preference to listen to their mother's voice over other voices! But importantly, infants know that which speaker is producing the speech is irrelevant to whether sounds are the 'same' phonetically. So like adults, infants ignore the speaker's voice (and other phonetically unimportant differences) in listening for speech sound differences. In addition, 6-month-old infants were able to discriminate [a] vs. [i] even when the pitch of the speaker's voice was varied within and across three different speakers; infants as young as 2 months old were found able to ignore within- and across-speaker variability in discriminating between the words *bug* and *dug*; and 2–3-month-olds perceptually compensated for changes in speaking rate to distinguish [ba] from [wa]. In other words, infants know right away that who is speaking or how rapidly they are speaking does not matter in deciding what sounds are being produced.

A second ability which has been studied is the ability to discriminate utterances of the infant's native language from those of foreign languages. In one study, for example, French newborn infants, listening to a French–Russian bilingual speaker, had higher sucking rates when they heard French. And in a variation of this experiment, the speech was altered so that all of the segmental material was filtered out, and only the prosodic aspects of the signal were played for the infants. Again, the French newborns had higher sucking rates when they listened to French than when they listened to Russian. This performance suggests that at least initially, infants may be paying particular attention to prosodic aspects of the signal. What is more, newborn infants show strong preference for, and thereby seem to recognize, nursery rhymes and even stories which had been spoken to them in the womb. This may indicate that infants are listening and paying attention to speech before they are born!

as 6 months-of-age fail to discriminate between vowels that younger infants can discriminate, has been found for numerous vowel pairs and indicates that infants lose their sensitivity to phonetic distinctions for vowels which are not phonemic in the ambient language at a younger age, approximately 6 months, than they do for consonants. Many researchers believe that this may be true because vowels are more prominent in the speech stream (they're longer and louder), and they carry prosodic information as well (e.g. tone, stress). These may be reasons that vowels may attract infants' attention more than consonants, and so the information they carry may initially be the most salient information in the input. To wit, experiments have also shown 2-month-olds able to discriminate prosodic distinctions relevant to tone languages, for example, between rising and falling pitch on otherwise identical syllables, and American 2-month-olds able to discriminate between bi-syllabic words on the basis of whether the first or second syllable received primary stress. Further, research has demonstrated that from birth, infants are sensitive to prosodic distinctions. We will discuss more about the importance of prosodic information in children's acquisition of phonology in section 15.3.

15.1.4 Changes in perception over the course of the first year of life

Effects of the target language can clearly be seen by the end of the first year. During the first year children go from being able to distinguish contrasts which are non-phonemic in the target language to being able to distinguish only phonemic distinctions in the target language. Infants begin to lose their perceptual abilities for non-native sounds just as their babbling begins to take on characteristics of the input language. The major shift occurs at 8–10 months-of-age. For example, 9-month-old, but not 6-month-old American infants listen significantly longer to lists adhering to the typical, strong–weak stress pattern of English words. (E.g. the stressed syllable is boldfaced: **Amer**ican **in**fants **lis**ten signific**ant**ly **long**er to **lists fo**llowing the **typ**ical, **strong**–weak **stress pa**ttern of **Eng**lish **words. Let's** get **rea**dy to **fix din**ner. **Daddy's coming home** from the **off**ice.)

In another series of experiments using the Head Turn paradigm, American infants and adults were presented with sounds which were contrastive in Hindi (H), in one case, and in Thompson Salish (TS) (Nthlakampa, a Canadian American Indian language), in another. The sounds in question were Hindi dental vs. retroflex stops [ta] vs. [ḍa] and in Thompson Salish, velar vs. uvular ejectives [k'i] vs. [q'i]. American adults do not discriminate these sounds. Young American infants do. But again, a shift in ability appears to occur at approximately 8–10 months, as illustrated in (2).

(2)   Percentage of H and TS sounds discriminated by age.

100	⎯⎯						
70		⎯⎯					
50			⎯⎯				
			⎯⎯				
20					⎯⎯		
0							⎯⎯
	H TS		H TS		H TS		H TS
	6–8		8–10		10–12		11–12
	months		months		months		years
			American infants				

The ability begins to wane noticeably by 8 months, and by 10 months American infants can no longer discriminate either of these non-native phonetic contrasts.

Interestingly, as we shall see, infants begin to lose perceptual abilities for non-native sounds just as their babbling clearly begins to take on characteristics of the target language. One way of characterizing the changes in speech perception over this first year of life is a shift from a "psychophysical" to a "phonological" basis for responses to speech sounds.

15.2   Production

15.2.1   Babbling

Just as is the case for the adult, the sounds infants can produce are constrained by the anatomy of the vocal tract, but the infant vocal tract is quite different from the adult's. It is mainly configured for vegetative requirements, especially sucking and breathing. It is not very good for producing speech. The larynx is higher than in the adult, there is a shorter pharyngeal cavity, which leaves little room for the back portion of the tongue to maneuver, and the tongue is very large relative to the size of the oral cavity – much larger than in the adult. As a consequence, few speech-like sounds are or can be produced in the first few months of life. The sounds that are produced before two months consist mainly of sounds such as sucking, burping, crying, and sounds expressing discomfort. From 2–4 months-of-age, children begin to coo and laugh. No speech sounds are produced, and those that are produced are mainly in response to physical movements by the child.

When a child is about 4–5 months-of-age, the vocal tract reconfigures and the child has more control over articulatory mechanisms. At this point they begin to babble, making speech-like sounds. At this point, babbling is stimulated by the speech of others, even recorded speech, as well as by social interaction and moving about. However, the babbling at this stage lacks the spectral and temporal characteristics of 'real' speech.

At about 6 or 7 months-of-age, the character of the babbling changes. The period referred to as '**canonical babbling**' begins. Canonical babbling has consonant and vowel sounds that have the phonetic characteristics of 'real' consonants and vowels (e.g. clear formant transitions, an open vocal tract, periodic nucleus), and is typically comprised of syllables, usually CV syllables, often *reduplicated* (repeated) syllables, like *bababa* or *gaga*.

The shaping influence of the target language

Early in babbling, children produce a wide variety of the world's speech sounds, regardless of the language they will be speaking. But even early babbling reflects linguistic constraints – at this point, constraints defined by the frequency of occurrence of certain sounds in human languages. The 12 most frequent consonants of the world's languages comprise 95 percent of all consonants produced in early babbling. But as babbling progresses,

---

Babbling in sign language[1]

SIDEBAR 15.2

Up until the onset of canonical babbling, congenitally deaf children make the same kinds of vocalizations as hearing children. But although children with at least moderate hearing impairments continue to vocalize, they do not progress to other stages of spoken language development without intervention. However, there is an intriguing parallel concerning babbling between spoken and sign language development. Psycholinguists have studied three deaf children of deaf parents; i.e. children exposed to a sign language from birth, and three deaf children of hearing parents, children not exposed to sign language. They found that before the age of 7 months, all of the children made scratching or swatting gestures, acted on objects with their hands, or made communicative but non-linguistic gestures. But after 7 months, the three children exposed to sign began to produce different kinds of gestures – those resembling sign syllables. These gestures embodied all of the constraints and characteristics of real sign syllables and so paralleled canonical babbling. Even though both groups made the same number of gestures, only the deaf children exposed to sign language made language-like gestures with any frequency, so only the children acquiring a sign language produced 'sign-babbling.' The point at which children begin to babble in syllable-like babbling, then, may signal an important departure point differentiating the onset of linguistically informed and constrained gestures from non-linguistic gestures, whether they be vocal gestures or gestures made with the hands. Moreover, babbling in sign language suggests that babbling is biologically triggered and shaped by the environment irrespective of modality.

some of these sounds drop out, and later babbling contains almost exclusively the sounds and some of the phonotactics of the language the child is acquiring. For example, infants learning Luo, a Nilotic African language, have lots of initial [n]s in their babbling, whereas English learners do not, reflecting the frequency with which these vs. other consonants are onsets in their respective languages. Experiments have shown that adults can recognize the native language of 8–10-month-old babblers (French, Cantonese or Arabic). Moreover, even by 6 months, Chinese infants show monosyllabic tonal babbling; i.e. babbling with much tonal variation, in contrast to Russian and American infants who show little pitch variation in their babbling.

The first year of life is taken up, in part, with answering, 'What sounds contrast in my language?' The paring down of the sounds that appear in babbling coincides with a change in speech perception. Whereas the young infant can hear differences between sounds that are not used in their target language, the waning of the ability to hear distinctions not used by the target language begins as young as 6 months; by 10–12 months they can no longer do so. By the end of the first year, then, children have already learned to ignore those distinctions which do not provide contrast in the adult language. They can be said to hear language like an adult speaker of their language. (See Sidebar 15.3.)

15.3   Early Speech Production

15.3.1   Building a system of contrasts

A child has to discover and develop the target phonology. This process begins with the child's discovering which of the phonetic categories they know constitute phonemic contrasts in the target language. Phonemic

SIDEBAR 15.3

Native accents

If young enough, children can 'unfix' the adult way of hearing speech and make the necessary changes to acquire other languages. But if the opportunity to learn another language doesn't come early enough, the particular pattern of hearing only certain distinctions and ignoring others remains fixed. Together with the inability to produce sounds in the patterns of other languages, this set way of hearing and speaking is perhaps the most rigid aspect of knowing a language, as shown by the difficulty one has in learning to speak a foreign language without a 'foreign accent'. It is very rare to find someone who learns a language after the 'critical age' and completely loses any trace of such an accent.

contrasts (and phonotactics) develop as a child learns the lexicon of the language. A child must rely on lexical contrasts to determine phonemic contrasts, and must rely on lexical contrasts to determine 'possible word' – thus, phonotactics, as well. As children establish the phonemic contrasts that play a role in their language, we clearly see the importance of phonetic features.

The role of contrast, and thereby features, can be seen in the development of the phonemic repertoire of children's early speech. At first, children's inventories consist, of only a few contrasts, for example a minimal consonant inventory such as in (3), which has only a two-way place distinction:

(3)

labial	nonlabial
p	t
	k

which then develops into (4), which embodies additional place features:

(4)

labial	coronal	dorsal
p	t	k

followed by an inventory where voicing becomes a contrastive feature, either partially as in (5a) or throughout the stop system as in (5b).

(5) a.

labial	coronal	dorsal
p	t	k
(b)		

 b.

labial	coronal	dorsal
p	t	k
b	d	g

Such a system may then incorporate nasality as in (6):

(6)

labial	coronal	dorsal
p	t	k
b	d	g
m	n	

In contrast, a child may initially have a phonological system that has only [sonorant] constraining contrasts as in (7):

(7)

sonorant	nonsonorant
m, n, l	p, s, d

In this initial stage, we might find the relationship between the adult's and child's pronunciation shown in (8):

(8)

target sound	child's sound
p	p, s, d
n	m, n, l

At the next stage, the features [coronal] and [voice] may enter to signal contrasts in addition to [sonorant], producing a system such as in (9):

(9)

+coronal/-coronal	+voice/-voice	+sonorant/-sonorant
d, t, s, n, l vs. p, m, k	d, m, n, l vs. p, s, t, k	m, n, l vs. p, t, d, s, k

which would allow for the following specific contrasts, presented below in a more familiar phonetic feature matrix in (10):

(10)

sound	sonorant	coronal	voice
p	–	–	–
t	–	+	–
d	–	+	+
k	–	–	–
m	+	–	+
n, l	+	+	+
s	–	+	–

(Note that not until the feature [nasal] enters the system will [n] and [l] be systematically distinguished in production.)

As even just these two examples of phonological development illustrate, there is variation across children as to the order in which the distinctive features of the target language take on a contrastive role in the child's phonological system, but the process of a step-by-step building up of the inventory to include an increasing number of contrasts is characteristic of the manner in which children build up segmental inventories cross-linguistically.

There are two ways that this stepwise build-up of contrasts causes the child's phonology to look different from the adult's. First, because some features are not used contrastively initially, we find a fair degree of free variation between sounds that would be distinct phonemes in the adult grammar, but are not yet used contrastively in the child's system. Second, because we do not yet have the full, adult set of contrasts marked on the surface, we find that the same segment on the surface often represents more than one underlying form. (11) presents an example from a child learning Japanese. In this child's phonological system, one segment [t] represents two phonologically distinct segments: one which is [t] in the adult grammar, the other, [k].

(11) a. [t] for /k/   (A age 3;2)

A's form	target form	gloss
[mitaŋ]	[mikaŋ]	'orange'
[potetto]	[poketto]	'pocket'
[neto]	[neko]	'cat'

b. [t] for /t/

A's form	target form	gloss
[tama]	[tama]	'ball'
[terebi]	[terebi]	'TV'
[tobɯ]	[tobɯ]	'fly'

There are two kinds of evidence that indicate that despite their identical phonetic form, the two phonetically identical [t]s in (11a) and (11b) are underlyingly distinct segments. The first kind of evidence comes from the fact that at the same age that A is producing [t] for /t/ and /k/, A has no difficulty perceiving the distinction between them in comprehension. The second comes from A's adherence to the phonotactic constraints governing [t] and [k] in the adult grammar. In the adult grammar of Japanese, /t/ undergoes affrication when immediately followed by the high vowels [i] and [ɯ] (i.e. *[ti] and *[tɯ]); [t] for /t/ obeys this constraint in A's grammar as well. In such cases one finds only [tʃi] and [tsɯ], as illustrated in (12):

(12)   Affrication of [t] for /t/ preceding high vowels.

A's form	target form	gloss
[matʃi]	[matʃi]	'city'
[tsɯta]	[tsɯta]	'ivy'

In contrast, /k/ does not undergo affrication in the same phonetic environments in the adult grammar, and [t] for /k/ does not do so, either, as illustrated in (13):

(13)   Failure of [t] for /k/ to undergo affrication preceding high vowels.

A's form	target form	gloss
[ati]	[aki]	'fall'
[tuɯma]	[kuɯma]	'bear'

The above examples serve to illustrate that despite the many noticeable differences in actual pronunciation of words (*phonetic* form), children's 'errors' are not random. They reflect an abstract system of representation (*phonological* form), based on the same kinds of structural units and constraints embodied in adult phonology.

15.3.2   Phonological processes

In language, there is a tension between articulatory ease and perceptual distinctiveness. In phonological development, we find numerous examples of the greater importance articulatory ease appears to play in early stages of child phonology.

Syllable structure processes: phonotactics
The importance of the least marked syllable type, CV, is reflected in children's early phonologies. Frequently, we see deletion of syllable-final consonants to adhere to the unmarked syllable, as in (14).

(14)

target word	child's word
bed	[bɛ]
bottle	[ba]
cake	[ke]
dog	[dɔ]
foot	[pu]

Second, in early production we often find **reduplications**, a repeated production of the stressed syllable of bi-syllabic words. Reduplications typically contain CV syllables and thus embody articulatory ease in their duplication of articulatory gestures, deletion of unstressed syllables and deletion of consonantal codas. At the same time, since reduplications reflect the fact that there is more than one syllable in the target word, reduplications may allow the child to be faithful to the number of syllables in the target, even though not able to faithfully pronounce them. Examples of child reduplications are presented in (15):

(15)   **target word**   **child's form**

bottle	[baba]
goodnight ('nightnight')	[nana]
banana	[nænæ]
water	[wawa]

A third way children simplify the structure of the syllable in their surface forms is by reducing consonant clusters. A common cluster reduction is the deletion of the consonant nearest the margin of the word in obstruent–obstruent clusters, as illustrated in (16):

(16)   cluster reductions

target word	child's pronunciation
spoon	[pū]
stop	[tap]
desk	[dɛs]

Notice that in the first two examples, the initial stops are not aspirated, possibly reflecting the knowledge that they are not the initial consonant in the underlying representation of the word.

Another reflex of the development of syllable structure from the least marked syllable (CV) to more marked syllable types in child speech can be found in the similar cross-linguistic progression of syllable types found in children's speech. For example, in studies of child English and Dutch, two languages which allow **complex onsets** and codas, the following order of emergence for syllable types has been reported:

(17)   >> A: CVCC>CCV>VCC>CCVC
     CV>CVC>V>VC   >>CCVCC
                                   >> B: CCV>CCVC>CVCC>VCC

Triconsonantal onsets or codas (CCCVCCC) are late to emerge. The principles governing the development of syllable types reflects cross-linguistic principles governing syllable structure; namely, those in (18), discussed in chapter 14.

(18)   major principles governing syllable structure
   a.   Syllables should have an onset.
   b.   Syllables should not have a coda.
   c.   Syllables should not have complex onsets/codas.

Segment structure processes: substitutions
Reduplication in both children's and adult phonology reflects the importance of ease of production. In child language, we find an additional reflex

of the primacy of ease of articulation, one not found in adult languages; namely, **Consonant harmony** – a phenomenon in which the onset and coda Cs assimilate to each other in their feature content. Some examples of consonant harmony are presented in (19):

(19) English:	child's word	target	French:	child's word	target	gloss
	[pap]	pot		[potɔ̃]	[mutɔ̃]	'sheep'
	[gag]	dog		[baʃo]	[moɹso]	'piece'
	[gʌk]	duck		[balaːd]	[malaːd]	'sick'
	[bʌb]	tub		[baːtoː]	[mãtõ]	'chin'
	[bɛps]	steps		[base]	[maɹʃe]	'to walk'

Cross-linguistically, substitutions tend to favor the optimal syllable, where the onset is a stop. Thus we find:

(20)   a.   [t] for [s]   (Amahl, 2;9)
           [ti] for 'sea'
           [tiŋ] for 'sing'
           [tʰɛi] for 'say'

   b.   [p] for [f]   (French examples)
           [po]   for   [flœʁ]   'flower'
           [tɔ]   for   [ʃo]   'hot'
           [te]   for   [sel]   'salt'

   c.   [b] for [v], [p] for [f] and [t] for [s]. Hungarian:
           [bijaːg]   for   [viraːg]   'flower'
           [paːaik]   for   [faːzik]   'he is cold'
           [taːja]   for   [saija]   'his mouth'

These and other assimilatory processes occur even if the child produces the substituted-for sound in other circumstances. Thus, even if the child produces a particular sound faithfully to correspond to the adult form, in some circumstances, that sound may be altered.

15.3.3   The importance of the stressed syllable in production

Recall that at the outset, children know that there are/will be words, but don't know the structure of words ahead of time. (We saw in chapter 2 that words can have many different structures across languages.) The problem for the infant is that the speech (or signed) linguistic signal is largely continuous, and the infant initially has no lexicon. The infant must apply some algorithm for segmenting the signal into words. One theory that has been proposed regarding what that algorithm or strategy may be is called the **Metrical Segmentation Strategy**. According to this 'strategy,' listeners, in this case infants and young children, exploit whatever rhythmic structure characterizes their language. This kind of segmentation algorithm is what is referred to as **Explicit segmentation** – applying a specific mechanism for positing word boundaries – for guiding the location of word boundaries. In chapter 10 we discussed bootstrapping, as a way into the lexicon. **Prosodic bootstrapping** hypothesizes that the main way into the lexicon (and other levels of structure) is via metrical segmentation. And in English, the metrical or prosodic template that children appear to recognize as the unmarked template is one in which the first syllable of content words is stressed. Thus, stress plays a major role in defining word boundaries for the learner. We will see that this idea can be supported, for the importance of stress and the stressed syllable in defining words both in perception and production is reflected in the ways children pronounce words that contain more than one syllable.

The importance of the stressed syllable can be seen in children's truncation of multi-stressed words. In bi-syllabic words, children often appear to reduce the target to a single syllable; namely, the stressed syllable, illustrated in some common words below. This process is not a simple dropping of the final sound or syllable, however. (21) presents sample productions of children's pronunciation of some common bi-syllabic words in which the second syllable is stressed. As you go through these examples, examine their content, making note of the kinds of substitutions and truncations children commonly make. Notice, in particular, the frequent retention of the first segment of the word rather than the first segment of the stressed syllable. The inclusion of this segment in the child's pronunciation demonstrates that more than the stressed syllable is represented in the lexical entries of these words in the child's grammar.

Setting a segmentation parameter

SIDEBAR 15.4

Rhythmic structure differs across languages, and the infant exposed to syllabic-based rhythm, as in French, or stress-based rhythm, as in English, will focus upon the specific rhythmic regularity characteristic of the ambient language. Moreover, experimental evidence suggests that this process of identifying the characteristic rhythmic pattern of the ambient language and using it to segment the linguistic signal occurs only once; that is, that a language user can command only one rhythmic segmentation procedure, even if one is fully bilingual. This fixing of a language processing procedure may be a parallel to setting a syntactic parameter.

(21)

target	child's pronunciation	target	child's pronunciation
again	[gɛn]	away	[we]
behind	[haiːnd] [haiːn]	belong	[bɔŋ] [ɔŋ]
balloon	[bu] [bun] [bum] [buːn]	garage	[gwaːdz] [gaːdʒ] [gardʒ] [gradʒ]
guitar	[tar] [ga] [gaːr]		

The hypothesis that children have a perceptual bias for stressed syllables is one we've discussed above in section 15.1.3. But it has also been hypothesized that they have a perceptual bias for rightmost syllables in polysyllabic words. Both of these hypotheses are supported by the way children pronounce multi-syllabic words before they produce the adult form. Pronunciation of tri-syllabic words is especially revealing, for in a tri-syllabic word, the final (rightmost) **rime** can be distinguished from the medial rime; and we can see that the rightmost rime is generally preserved in children's pronunciations, as shown in (22) and (23).

(22)   Children's reductions of σ'σσ adult targets

target	child's pronunciation	target	child's pronunciation
remember	[mɛmə] [mɛmbə]	tomorrow	[mowo] [moro]
another	[nʌðɚ] [nʌdɚ] [nʌθɚ] [nʌːɚ]	banana	[nænæ] [mænə] [bænə] [nænə]
delicious	[dɪʃəs]	spaghetti	[skɛti]
pajamas	[daməs] [dʒæməʃ] [daːməs]	umbrella	[bwɛa] [bɛla] [breːwa]

target	child's pronunciation	target	child's pronunciation
potato	[pedo]	tomato	[meno]
	[teto]		[meto]
	[teːto]		[meːdo]

We again can see children's adherence to the stress template of the target representation by looking at their pronunciation of tri-syllabic words which follow a different syllabic template; namely, 'σσσ', as illustrated in (23):

(23) Children's reductions of 'σσσ' adult targets

target	child's pronunciation	target	child's pronunciation
animal	['æmʊ]	elephant	['ɛfɛnt]
	['æmo]		['ɛfʌnt]
	['amuː]		['ɛːfɪnt]
	['nənoː]		['ɛːfʌnt]
dominos	['daːnouz]	medicine	['mɛsɪn]
	['daːmnoːθ]		['mɛːsɪn]
tricycle	[twaik]	buffalo	['bʌfo]

Note again that the final rime of the target word is the child's final rime and that the stressed syllable of the target is always the child's stressed syllable. We see that the idea that the child's grammar has an underlying representation more like the adult form than his own pronunciation might at first suggest, finds support, this time from the appearance of the first consonant of the second syllable instead of the first C of the final syllable, as the examples presented in (24) illustrate

(24)   'broccoli'   'camera'   'dungarees'   'favorite'   'spatula'   'maracas'
       [baki]   [kæmʌ]   [gəŋgiːːz]   [fevət]   [bæːtʃʌ]   [makaːs]

Note also that the child appears to choose the least sonorous onset between the medial and final onset of the word. Why might this be so? Hint: Think of the ideal syllable template.

Linguists are not all in agreement as to why children delete certain phonological material in multi-syllabic words, but one view which we have examined is that there is a perceptual bias on the part of the child for stressed syllables and for rightmost syllables. Support for this view came in part from noting that in children's pronunciations, it was the rightmost rime and the stressed syllable that were preserved. Recall, for example, the items repeated in (25):

(25)   tricycle   ['twaik]   animal   ['amo]
       buffalo   ['bʌfo]   broccoli   ['baki]
       elephant   ['ɛɫfn̩t]

However, this view might suggest that the child's perceptual bias may also lead him or her not to represent the perceptually less salient parts of a word underlyingly. Evidence against this view and for a view which espouses that the child has a more target-like representation of most words is supported by the frequent appearance of the first consonant of the first syllable instead of the first consonant of the second syllable in bi-syllabic trochaic words, as we saw in (21).

Producing the stressed syllable at all cost! The example of child Quiché
One of the most striking examples of the importance of the stressed syllable in children's immature speech can be found in their early productions of verbs in Quiché, a Mayan language spoken in Peru. The verb structure of Quiché is quite complex, requiring multiple affixation, resulting in long, multi-syllabic as well as multimorphemic forms.

Verbs are frequently, although not always, in sentence-final position. When the verb is clause-final, the terminal suffix is stressed. During the telegraphic stage, children frequently reduce verb forms to one or two syllables, and during this stage, stress is so important it leads children acquiring Quiché Mayan to pronounce the stressed final affix instead of the verb root! (Verbs often undergo resyllabification when affixes are attached, so that syllable boundaries in the surface form don't always match morpheme boundaries. Under these circumstances, children always observe *syllable* divisions in their reductions, not morpheme boundaries!)

When the verb is clause-medial, the verb stem is stressed, so producing only the stressed syllable results in production of at least some part of the verb stem, but since the syllables children tend to produce in their truncated forms are the stressed syllables, when the verb is clause-final, they still produce the stressed syllable even when that means the verb stem itself is left out. Note that this means that children acquiring Quiché verbs resyllabify in order to produce a "good" (CV(C)) stressed syllable. (26) and (27) illustrate this phenomenon.

(26)   **Target**   **Child's utterance**

kach'aːw + ik   w+ik
'It's talking + TERM'   last <u>segment</u> of verb + TERM

Note that the reduced forms do not reflect what the child knows about the verb stem's phonological content, as can be seen by examining (27).

(27) (same child one week later producing the verb in clause-medial position)

Target	Child's utterance
kach'aːw taj	chaw taj
'It's talking not'	last <u>syllable</u> of verb in 'It's talking not'

Since the phonological content of the verb and stress assignment varies based on phrasal position, we are able to see from such examples that children's knowledge of the phonological structure of the verb exceeds what they produce at this stage, since they produce only parts of it in any given utterance. Moreover, the child's reduction of a verb's underlying structure varies in principled ways. A child uttering a verb in a context in which it would appear clause-finally will produce the final syllable of the verb, which usually consists of the final consonant of the verb stem and the **terminating suffix**, but the same child uttering the same verb in a context in which it would appear clause-medially will produce the verb stem (or most of it). What remains constant is that the child will produce the stressed syllable of the verb.

This example also illustrates that the drive for communication cannot be what guides or governs such reductions, for providing only the final segment of a verb stem often leaves adults uncertain as to what verb the child has produced. Such truncations are clearly governed and constrained by the child's developing grammar, in which the stressed syllable plays a major role in production.

A final illustration of the importance of the stressed syllable in languages that have stress, is that errors of lexical stress are unattested in child language. That is, while other parts of the word may be deleted or otherwise truncated, the stressed syllable will be represented, and pronounced given stress.

15.3.4 Dummy syllables in production

After the earliest periods in phonological acquisition, children will pronounce both the unstressed as well as the stressed syllables of words. At an early stage of producing the full syllabic template, however, the child may simply produce a 'dummy' syllable, which may become standardized into a uniform **epenthetic syllable** to achieve the full prosodic form of the word, as illustrated in (28) and (29).

(28) (data from Amahl, 3;1; Smith 1973)

target	Amahl's pronunciation	
attack	[ri'tæk]	(earlier ['tæk])
disturb	[ri'stəːːv]	(earlier ['dəːv])
design	[ri'dzain]	(earlier [di'dain])
giraffe	[ri'dʒæf]	(earlier [diræf])
thermometer	[ri'məmət]	(earlier ['məmətə])

(29) (data from Gitanjali, a 2-year-old, Gnanadesikan 1995)

target word	Gitanjali's pronunciation
umbrella	[fi'bɛyã]
container	[fi'tenã]
mosquito	[fi'giɾo]
spaghetti	[fi'gɛɾi]
Rebecca	[fi'bɛkã]

15.3.5 Perception vs. production: what we hear is not necessarily what the child knows or even says

We have already seen evidence indicating that the child's underlying representation of words contains more phonological information than what may appear in its surface form. Some researchers have provided further support for this view by demonstrating that children produce even more of the word than we adults hear (or think we hear) and therefore attribute to the child. In one experiment, for example, spectrographic analysis of the production of what adults hear as ['ɛfṇt] for 'elephant' and ['hɛkatɚ] for 'helicopter' showed clear indications of the lateral from the second, supposed, deleted syllable being present in both words. Moreover, when a made-up creature was labeled an ['ɛfṇt] by the examiner, the child systematically distinguished ['ɛləfṇt] from ['ɛfṇt], rejecting ['ɛfṇt] as a way of pronouncing *elephant*, behaving in an adult-like fashion. There would be no source for the minimally but nonetheless present reflexes of the laterals in the child's productions of these words, and no explanation for the child's systematic rejection of an adult's imitation of his own mispronunciation of *elephant* and *helicopter* alongside her systematic differentiation between an ['ɛfṇt] and an ['ɛləfṇt], if the child's underlying representation of these words were not more target-like than not.

Other, well-known examples of the disparity between what the child can produce and what the child's perception and underlying representation of a word is are given in (30)–(32). (They are conversations between the linguist Neil Smith and his son Amahl.)

(30) NVS: What's a [səːt]?
      A: [immediately points to his shirt]

NVS: What's a [suː]?

A: [immediately points to a shoe]

NVS: What's a [sɪp]?

A: When you drink [imitates]

NVS: What else does [sɪp] mean?

A: [puzzled, then doubtfully suggests *zip*, though pronouncing it quite correctly]

NVS: No; it goes in the water.

A: A boat.

NVS: Say it.

A: No. I can only say [sɪp].

(31) NVS: Say *jump*.

A: [dʌp]

NVS: No, *jump*.

A: [dʌp]

NVS: No, *jummmp*.

A: [udi: dɛdi: gæn de: dʌp] (Only Daddy can say jump)!

(32) (A is known to perceive the difference between the words *mouth* and *mouse*.)

NVS: What does [maʊs] mean?

A: Like a cat.

NVS: Yes; what else?

A: Nothing else.

NVS: It's part of your head.

A: [fascinated]

NVS: [touching A's mouth] What's this?

A: [maʊs]

Only after a few more seconds did it dawn on him that they were the 'same.'

A child's tone game

SIDEBAR 15.5

Phonological language 'games', such as Pig-Latin or the one described in chapter 13, can include games in which tones are played with as well. A child-invented tone game has been described, where one Mandarin-speaking child would change the tones of words for play. The child started this word-play on tones at age 2;0, well after her acquisition of tones. At first her parents thought she had her tones mixed up, but when her parents acted confused and asked her what the word was, she would smile and provide the word with the correct tones. The most common pattern was to put a disyllabic word or phrase into a high–low tone sequence, regardless of the tones these syllables should have carried.

15.4   Summary

In this chapter we have seen that child grammars, in this case child phonologies, embody the same representational structures as adult grammars. We looked specifically at how phonetic features, phonemes, syllable, stress, and prosodic structure more generally play a role in phonological development. Although we have taken only a brief look at child phonology, in our examination we have seen further evidence that all human grammars, including child grammars, incorporate the same basic principles of organization and structure. We have also seen how, even at birth, infants appear to be predisposed to attend to the linguistic signal, spoken or signed, in just the right ways to acquire the structure underlying 'their' or any human language.

Note

1   Petitto, L. and Marentette, P. 1991. Babbling in the manual mode. Evidence for the ontogeny of language. *Science*, 251: 1493–6.

Further reading

Clark, E. 1973. What's in a word? On the child's acquisition of semantics in his first language. In T. E. Moore ed., *Cognitive Development and the Acquisition of Language*. New York: Academic Press.

Eimas, P. 1996. 'The perception and representation of speech by infants.' In J. Morgan and K. Demuth, eds., *Signal to Syntax: Bootstrapping from Speech to Grammar in Early Acquisition*, pp. 25–39. Mahwah, NJ: Lawrence Erlbaum Assocs.

Gleitman, L. and Landau, B. eds. 1995. *The Acquisition of the Lexicon*. Cambridge, MA: MIT Press, and references, therein.

Hirsh-Pasek, K. and Golinkoff, R. 1996. *The Origins of Grammar: Evidence from Early Language 'Comprehension.'* Cambridge, MA: MIT Press.

Jusczyk, P. 1997. *The Discovery of Spoken Language*. Cambridge, MA: MIT Press.

Morgan, J. and Demuth, K. eds. 1996. *Signal to Syntax: Bootstrapping from Speech to Grammar in Early Acquisition*. Mahwah, NJ: Lawrence Erlbaum Assocs.

Oller, D. 1980. The emergence of speech sounds in infancy. In G. Yeni-Komshian, J. Kavanagh, and C. Ferguson, eds., *Child Phonology*. New York: Academic Press.

Werker, J. 1995. Exploring developmental changes in cross-linguistic speech perception. In L. Gleitman and M. Liberman, eds., *An Invitation to Cognitive Science: Language*, vol. 1, pp. 87–106. Cambridge, MA: Bradford Books.

References on languages cited

English

Gnanadesikan, A. 1995. *Markedness and Faithfulness Constraints in Child Phonology*. Cambridge, MA: University of Massachusetts.

Ingram, D. 1979. Phonological rules in young children. *Journal of Child Language*, 1: 49–64.

Menn, L. 1983. Development of articulatory, phonetic, and phonological capabilities. In B. Butterworth, ed., *Language Production*, vol. 2, pp. 3–50. London: Academic Press.

Pater, J. 1997. Minimal violation and phonological development. *Language Acquisition*, 6, no. 3: 201–63.

Smith, N. V. 1973. *The Acquisition of Phonology: A case study*. Cambridge: Cambridge University Press.

Japanese

Ueda, I. 1996. Segmental acquisition and feature specification in Japanese. In J. Gilbert and D. Ingram, eds., *Proceedings of the UBC International Conference on Phonological Acquisition*.

French and Hungarian

Ingram, D. 1979. Phonological rules in young children. *Journal of Child Language*, 1: 49–64.

Quiché

Pye, C. 1980. The acquisition of grammatical morphemes in Quiché Mayan. Unpublished doctoral dissertation. University of Pittsburgh.

Glossary

[±**aspirated**] Feature distinguishing sounds articulated with open glottis (e.g. [tʰu]) from other sounds.

[±**continuant**] Oral stricture feature distinguishing sounds during the articulation of which air escapes from the mouth (e.g. [f], [r], [j], [a]) from sounds articulated with complete obstruction of oral airflow (e.g. [p], [d], [m]).

[±**coronal**] Feature distinguishing sounds whose active articulator is the tongue blade (e.g. [n], [z], [ts], [t], [l]) from other sounds.

[±**dorsal**] Feature distinguishing sounds whose active articulator is the tongue body, such as [k], [g], [x], [ɢ], the vowels and the glides, from other sounds.

[±**high**] Feature distinguishing sounds produced with maximally raised jaw and tongue body (e.g. [i], [e], [ɪ]) from other sounds (e.g. [e], [a], [o], [œ]).

[±**labial**] Feature distinguishing sounds whose active articulators are the lips ([p], [f], [m], [o], [u]) from sounds possessing other active articulators.

[±**long**] Feature distinguishing sounds whose oral articulation is held for a relatively long time (e.g. [aː], [tː], [sː]) from sounds in which the oral articulation is of normal duration [a], [t], [s].

[±**low**] Feature distinguishing sounds produced with maximally lowered jaw and tongue body (e.g. [a], [œ], [a]) from sounds articulated with a raised tongue body (e.g. [e], [i], [o], [u]).

[±**nasal**] Feature distinguishing sounds articulated with airflow through the nose (e.g. [m], [ã]), from those lacking nasal airflow ([a], [j], [p], [b]).

[±**sonorant**] Feature distinguishing sounds that contain most of their acoustic energy in the lower formants (e.g. [a], [r], [j], [l], [m]) from those lacking acoustic energy in that region ([s], [p], [g]).

[±**strident**] Feature distinguishing noisy sounds (with intense acoustic energy in the higher formants) such as [s], [ʃ], [dz] from others.

[±**syllabic**] Feature distinguishing sounds that occupy the syllable nucleus (e.g. [a], [i], [n']) from others (e.g. [h], [j], [n]).

[±**voice**] Feature distinguishing sounds produced with vocal cord vibration (e.g. [b], [r], [m], [o]) from sounds produced without it (e.g. [p], [h], [k]).

ablaut A morphological change from one sound to a related one in a word or morpheme, producing a change in meaning without the addition of any extra morphemes.

absolute judgment An evaluation of the acceptability of a linguistic example on an absolute scale, rather than in comparison with another example or set of examples. *See also **acceptability judgment, comparative judgment**.*

acceptability judgment A speaker's introspective judgment of the acceptability of a linguistic example. *See also **grammatical**.*

accommodation (of a presupposition) When a presupposition of the sentence heard is not part of the hearer's knowledge or assumptions about the situation talked about, the hearer typically adds it to the assumed common ground in order to be able to make sense of it.

accusative case (Acc) The case feature that a transitive verb assigns to a direct object DP, or to the DP subject of the transitive verb's ECM infinitive complement or small clause complement. *See also **case feature, ECM infinitive, intransitive verb, small clause, transitive verb, unaccusative verb**.*

active articulator A speech organ which moves to articulate a speech sound.

active verb A verb which expresses an activity or event (e.g. *eating, running*).

adjective (A) A word that describes a property or quality that is attributed to some referent; the head of an Adjective Phrase (AP). Examples: *tall, old, strong*, etc.

Adjective Phrase (AP) A phrase headed by an adjective, also containing the complement(s) selected by the adjective, and also (according to some theories) any degree specifier (such as *very*) or adverbial qualifier (such as *surprisingly*) preceding the adjective. Examples: *angry at her father, very tall, surprisingly beautiful*, etc. According to some theories of small clause constructions, an AP may also contain a subject position, such as *Falstaff unreliable* in *Henry considers Falstaff unreliable*.

adjoin To attach one constituent, A, to another constituent, B, creating a new constituent with the same category-name as B.

adjunct A constituent that is adjoined to another constituent.

adverb (Adv) A word that refers to a property of an event or situation, for example, designating the manner or time of the event.

adverb of quantification Relates two sets of events in the same manner as determiners relate two sets of individuals, e.g. *Always, usually, seldom*.

adverbial expression A string of words having the same interpretive function as an **adverb**.

Adverbial Phrase (ADVP) A phrase headed by an adverb. Adverbial phrases are often assumed to be adjoined to the categories that they modify. *See also* **adjunct**, **adverb**.

affective Referring to a word or morpheme which does not have lexical meaning, but whose use reveals the speaker's attitude.

affix A prefix, suffix, or infix.

affix-hopping Syntactic process by which the lexical content of two syntactic nodes gets combined under a single syntactic node. (For example, the past tense affix *-ed* hops onto V and yields a past tense verb: $[_T\text{ed}] + [_V\text{use}] \rightarrow [_V\text{use} + \text{ed.}]$ Affix-hopping is a particular instance of *head movement*.

affixation The addition of a prefix, suffix, or infix to a word.

affricate A stop plus a fricative produced at the same place of articulation.

agent The thematic role (θ-role) assigned to the argument of a verb (or other predicate) referring to the participant who performs, or initiates, the action referred to by a verb. *See also* **thematic role**.

agreement A syntactic process whereby one constituent must have the same value for certain grammatical features (such as person, number, and/or gender) as another constituent that it bears a particular grammatical relation to. In the phrase *these books*, the **D** *these* and the **N** *books* agree in *number* since they must both be *plural*.

allomorph One of the alternative forms of a morpheme. In some cases, any allomorph may be used in free variation; in others, certain allomorphs must be used in particular environments, in conditioned variation.

allophone A phonetic variant of a phoneme.

alternation A morpheme alternates when it appears in different forms in different contexts.

alveolar Having the (front part of the) alveolar ridge as the passive articulator.

alveolar ridge The short flat stretch of gum ridge just above and behind the upper teeth, serving as a passive articulator for the tongue tip and blade.

alveolo-palatal Having an articulation between alveolar and palatal; the active articulator is the blade of the tongue.

analogy A type of reasoning in which a type of observed pattern is extended to a new case in which it would not otherwise be expected to apply.

analyzable Able to be analyzed or segmented into morphemes.

analyze To divide a word, sentence, or other linguistic form into its component parts, and explain their meaning and relationship.

anaphor A word which depends on another element in the sentence for its interpretation. For example, *himself* in *Hamlet hates himself.*

antecedent The element that provides the reference of an anaphor; *Hamlet* in *Hamlet hates himself.*

anthropological linguistics The study of languages as part of specific cultures.

antisymmetry A theory of phrase structure according to which linear precedence is a direct reflection of hierarchical structure. Some major consequences of this assumption are that all languages have the same underlying constituent order, and all transformational movement processes displacing constituents to a higher position in the structure must involve leftward movement. As a result, structures that appear to be mirror-images of each other (for example, verb–object order in a head-initial language versus verb-final order in a head-final language) must be antisymmetrical, that is, they must represent different hierarchical structures, with one order derived by leftward movement of at least one constituent to a position higher in the tree than its counterpart in the other order.

approximant A sound made with a large opening (approximant constriction degree), allowing almost free flow of air through the oral tract; if not specified as lateral, often used to mean central approximant.

a-quantification Quantification expressed by adverbs, adjectives, auxiliaries, or argument structure adjusters.

argument A participant in the action or situation referred to by a lexical predicate (such as a verb). A predicate selects (and assigns a thematic role to) each of its arguments. *See also* **argument structure, thematic role**.

argument structure The specification of the number of arguments that a lexical predicate (such as a verb) has, as well as the θ-roles associated with each of these arguments. *See also* **thematic role**.

ARPABET A phonetic alphabet using only ASCII characters, developed for English and used by the American speech technology (recognition and synthesis) community.

article In traditional grammatical terminology, a modifier like *the, a,* or *an* used with a noun. Articles may be definite or indefinite. (Articles are now generally analyzed as determiners.)

articulator Anatomical structure acting as a speech organ. Active articulators can move independently; passive articulators are sites that active articulators move towards.

aspect A characteristic of the internal structure of an event described by a verb (an expression), e.g. whether the event is viewed as ongoing or completed, whether it is iterated, whether it has an inherent culmination point, etc.

aspiration Noise produced in the open glottis, which then results in an extra puff of air coming out of the open mouth.

aspiration *See* **[±aspirated]**

assertion That part of the message conveyed by the sentence that is canceled when the sentence is negated in the form *It is not true/the case that . . .*

asterisk* Used to designate ungrammatical or unacceptable sentences.

atelic An event (or verbal expression referring to one) that does not have an inherent culmination point.

auxiliary A term used to describe items such as the perfect auxiliary *have* and *be* in all its uses. These items resemble modals (*will/would/can/ could/may/might/must/ought*) and differ from other verbs in English in that they invert (*Have you read this book?*) and precede *not/n't* (*you haven't read this book*).

back The back location (nearer pharynx) of the tongue.

bare plurals Plural nouns which are not preceded by a determiner. Also referred to as *Determiner*less plurals, e.g. *donkeys* in *There are donkeys in the barn.*

bare VP A VP headed by a bare root form of the verb; these occur as complements of modal verbs (as in *He will go home*) and in small clause complements of perception and causative verbs (as in *He saw her go home*, and *He made her go home*). *See also* **small clause**.

base form The simplest form of a paradigm or the form from which other elements of the paradigm are derived: often, an uninflected form or root.

basic constituent order The normal order that the major constituents of a sentence occur in, in a given language. Examples: Subject–Verb–Object (SVO) as in English, Subject–Object–Verb (SOV), as in Turkish, and Verb–Subject–Object (VSO), as in Arabic.

bilabial Sounds having the two lips as articulators, each both active and passive.

binary-branching node A node in a tree diagram that immediately dominates two subconstituents, since there are two branches connecting the node to its subconstituents. *See also* **node**.

binding relation A relation between two constituents X and Y such that X determines the semantic and grammatical properties of Y. For example, the relation between the antecedent of a reflexive pronoun and the reflexive pronoun is a binding relation (where the antecedent is said to bind the reflexive).

bootstrapping Procedure by which children use contextual, prosodic, semantic, or syntactic information to infer other information about a word.

bound morpheme A morpheme that cannot stand alone, but must be attached to something else.

bound pronouns A pronoun is said to be bound when its reference is determined by a c-commanding antecedent. *See also* **c-command**.

boundary The point of separation between morphemes (*see* **morpheme boundary**), words (*see* **word boundary**), or other grammatical elements.

bracketing *See labeled bracketing*.

broad transcription A transcription which uses only the minimal, or an otherwise limited, set of basic symbols; often enclosed in slant brackets.

C Represents the category of complementizer (*that*, *for*, *whether*, *if*). More abstractly, it expresses a syntactic head indicating clause type (declarative, interrogative, main, embedded, etc.). The syntactic head C projects a CP (a clause).

canonical babbling Babbling which has consonant and vowel sounds that have the phonetic characteristics of 'real' consonants and vowels (e.g. clear formant transitions, an open vocal tract, periodic nucleus), and is typically comprised of CV syllables.

case The case of an expression is a property of this expression that varies with the position that this expression occupies in a sentence and that is often reflected in the form of this expression. This can be seen with the English first-person pronoun: *Nominative case* I (subject), *Accusative case* ME (object), *Genitive case* MY (possessor).

case affix, or **case marker** A morpheme attached to a noun or DP that encodes a case feature, such as nominative, accusative, etc. *See also case feature*.

case assignment rules Rules determining which **case** an expression should have as a consequence of its position in a sentence.

case feature A grammatical feature assigned to DP arguments on the basis of the position in the sentence where they occur. Examples: nominative, accusative, dative, and genitive. *See also case affix*, *accusative case*, *dative case*, *genitive case*, *nominative case*.

case filter A syntactic constraint requiring all referring expressions (DPs, including names and pronouns) to be assigned a case feature, even if this case feature is not marked overtly by a morphological affix.

categorial selection (c-selection or subcategorization) A constraint on the syntactic occurrence of a lexical category (such as a verb), requiring that it be accompanied by a complement belonging to a particular syntactic category (or to one of a restricted set of syntactic categories). Categorial selection requirements are assumed to be specified in the lexical entry of the category selecting the complement; the selecting category is said to c-select the category of its complement.

categorical perception The sensitivity to only certain phonetic distinctions between consonants, such that consonants are perceived as belonging to either one category or another, with between-category distinctions harder to perceive. (Can also refer to non-linguistic perception of objects which are categorized.)

category A term used to denote a set of expressions that share particular linguistic properties. For example in English, the category *verb* includes all words that can inflect for tense (examples: *sing*, *dance*, which can form *sang*, *danced*); another word for class.

causative verb A verb which has the meaning of 'cause'. *Make, let, have* in the following examples are all causative verbs: *I made John play Romeo, I let John play Romeo, I had John play Romeo.*

cause The thematic role (θ-role) assigned to the argument of a verb that causes or initiates an event or situation, in a manner that does not require conscious volition or action, as in the case of an inanimate cause. Example: *The siege of Harfleur made the French king weep.*

c-command A structural relation between two *constituents*. A constituent X c-commands another one Y if Y is in the *c-command domain* of X.

c-command domain The c-command domain of a *constituent* X is the first constituent containing this X.

central In or along the center of the vocal tract on some dimension. Of vowels, having the tongue in an intermediate position on the front–back dimension. Of consonants, having airflow along the center (not the sides) of the oral cavity.

circumfix An affix that is a discontinuous morpheme, with two parts, one prefixed before the root, one suffixed after it.

class A linguistically relevant group. In syntax and morphology, a word's class typically refers to its identification as a noun, verb, adjective, adverb, or member of another lexical category. In phonology, it refers to the category of sounds, voiced, nasals, Vowels etc.

clause *See relative clause.*

clitic A morpheme with a special status between that of an affix and a word.

cliticization The attachment of clitics.

close The highest category of vowel height in the IPA chart. Compared with other vowels, close vowels have the greatest overall height of the tongue. Non-IPA term is *high*.

closed class A class of words to which no members can be added (for example, the classes of prepositions and determiners are closed in English).

closed syllable Syllable possessing a coda.

close-mid The second-highest category of vowel height in the IPA chart. Non-IPA term is *higher mid*.

coda (of the syllable) Consonant(s) following the nucleus within a syllable.

cognate object A type of direct object DP that refers to the event described by the verb, and which is typically related morphologically to the verb itself. Cognate objects often include an adjective describing some property of the event, as in *Falstaff laughed a hearty laugh.*

cognitive distinctions Concepts and distinctions that humans develop on the basis of their innate or acquired knowledge about the world, independently of the way their native language carves up reality. These include, among others, notions pertaining to time, space, and causality.

common ground The knowledge and assumptions that speaker and hearer share about the situation they talk about.

common noun A noun that refers to one of a group of possible referents (for example, *girl* is a common noun that can refer to any young female human being).

comparative Referring to an adjective or adverb expressing an increased degree (for example, *faster* is the comparative of the English adjective and adverb *fast*).

comparative judgment A native speaker's judgment of the relative intuitive level of acceptability of one example sentence in comparison with the level of acceptability of another example sentence.

comparative method Developed in the nineteenth century to compare and establish families of languages and their roots.

competence (linguistic) Speakers' knowledge of their language.

complement A constituent selected by a lexical category, X, which occurs syntactically as a sister of X, immediately dominated by XP or by X' (= X bar). For example, the object and indirect object of a verb are complements of the verb.

complementary distribution Two sounds X and Y are said to be in complementary distribution if Y never occurs in any of the phonetic environments in which X occurs.

complementizer (C) A function-word used to introduce a subordinate clause, such as *that* (used to introduce subordinate finite clauses) and *for* (used to introduce *for*-infinitives). In traditional grammar, complementizers are called *subordinating conjunctions*.

Complementizer Phrase (CP) A phrase headed by a complementizer; the sequence consisting of a complementizer and the embedded sentence (subordinate clause) that follows it.

complete reduplication A reduplication process in which the whole of the affected word or morpheme is copied or reduplicated.

complex Referring to the structure of a word that contains more than one morpheme (alternative term: polymorphemic).

complex onsets Syllable onsets which consist of more than one consonant.

complex sentence A sentence containing more than one verb.

compositionality The idea that the meanings of complex expressions are determined by the meanings of their parts.

compound Two or more words joined together into a new complex word.

compounding The formation of a compound word.

computational linguistics Branch of linguistics concerned with natural language computer applications.

conceptual knowledge Non-linguistic knowledge about the laws of nature, human society, one's life experience, etc.

conditioned variation Variation dependent on the phonological or morphological environment (the opposite of free variation).

configurational language A language with a relatively fixed (inflexible) basic order of major constituents, such as English. *See also **non-configurational language**.*

conflict (between constraints) The situation in which no surface realization of a given underlying form is such that it satisfies all constraints being considered.

conservativity A determiner A is conservative if and only if Q(A)(B) holds if and only if Q(A)(A ∩ B) holds.

consonant Sound in which a significant constriction is made somewhere in the vocal tract – a narrowing that interferes with the flow of air out of the mouth – so that there is at least some reduction in the energy of the sound.

consonant harmony A phenomenon in which the onset and coda consonants assimilate to each other in their feature content.

constituency test A diagnostic test for determining whether a given sequence of words forms a constituent. Examples: the movement test (if a sequence of words can be moved as a unit, then it probably forms a constituent), the coordination test (if a sequence of words can be coordinated with a similar sequence, then it probably forms a constituent of the same syntactic category as the sequence that it is coordinated with), and the deletion test (if a sequence of words can be deleted, then it probably forms a constituent).

constituent A component part of a linguistic expression (such as a sentence or phrase) that functions as a single unit with respect to the rules of grammar. *See also **constituent structure, immediate dominance, subconstituent**.*

constituent structure The internal structure of a sentence, phrase, or word, indicating the hierarchical and linear arrangement of its component parts, or subconstituents. Constituent structures can be represented by *tree diagrams* or by *labeled bracketing*; synonymous with syntactic structure.

constraint A well-formedness condition applying to a structure. Whereas *rules* are generative devices, specifying ways to create linguistic forms or structures, or specifying ways to convert one structure or form into another, constraints function like filters that exclude or prohibit specific types of linguistic representations that fail to satisfy the requirement imposed by the constraint.

constriction degree The extent to which the active articulator comes near the passive.

content word A word from an open lexical class; a noun, verb, adjective, or adverb. (Sometimes referred to as *lexical content word*.)

context-free rewrite rule A phrase structure rule specifying the immediate subconstituents of a given syntactic category or phrase-type. A rewrite rule consists of three elements: an arrow (indicating the relation of immediate dominance); a category occurring to the left of the arrow (indicating the category whose constituent structure the rule defines); and a string of one or more elements occurring to the right of the arrow (indicating the linearly ordered set of the immediate subconstituents). Such rules are said to be context-free because they are applicable regardless of the syntactic context in which the category occurs. Phrase structure rules were traditionally called rewrite rules because they could be used to generate sentence templates by applying sequentially, for example, in a model of speech production.

contextually limited contrast A phonological contrast that is found only in certain phonological environments.

contraction The shortening of a sequence of words or morphemes. In English, this term refers to the use of shortened forms like *'s* instead of *is* in sentences like *He's going*.

contrast Two sounds contrast if the difference between them can distinguish words. Contrasting sounds are said to be 'in contrast'; an opposition between two or more concepts or grammatical entities.

contrastive A phonetic difference is contrastive if it can be used to distinguish words; phonemic; distinctive.

control The relation of co-reference holding between a null (silent) pronoun in the subject position of an embedded infinitival clause and a DP argument in the matrix clause that serves as its antecedent, whereby the antecedent DP is said to control the null subject pronoun (PRO). Example: *Hamlet promised to avenge his father*, where the subject of the main clause, *Hamlet*, controls the null subject of the infinitive.

coordination Coordination is the process by which two or more expressions are joined together by a coordinating conjunction like *and, but, or*.

co-refer *See co-reference*.

co-reference The property of referring to the same entity or individual (or set of entities or individuals). When two or more referential phrases co-refer, they are said to be co-referential. In linguistics, it is common practice to co-index co-referential expressions by means of using identical subscript indices, as in *Lear_i admitted that he_i was ashamed of himself_i*.

co-referential *See co-reference*.

coronal Having the tongue blade/tip as active articulator, thus including *alveolars, dentals, postalveolars, retroflexes*, and sometimes *palatals*.

correspondence constraints Grammatical principles stating that pairs of related forms (e.g. underlying and surface representations of the same lexical item) must resemble each other in some specific respect.

count noun A noun used in such a way that it can pluralize and take the determiners *many* and *three*. Count nouns have quantized reference.

counterevidence Evidence that contradicts the predictions of a given theory, and which therefore suggests that the theory may be incorrect.

counterexample If a speaker's judgment about a linguistic example contradicts the predictions of a theory, then it constitutes a counterexample to the theory; that is, it provides *counterevidence* to the theory.

creative aspect of language use The ability of speakers to produce and comprehend an infinite set of sentences.

cross-sentential pronouns A pronoun that refers back to a DP in a previous sentence.

c-select, c-selection *See categorial selection*.

cumulative reference An expression E refers cumulatively if any sum of parts that can be labeled as E can also be labeled as E.

dative case (Dat) The case feature assigned to the indirect object of a verb in certain languages, such as German and Latin.

dative shift A rule that transforms a verbal argument frame of the form [__ DP/1 (in/on)to DP/2] into another argument frame of the form [__ DP/2 DP/1]. DP/2 in the resulting frame is called a dative, hence the rule's name.

daughter A node that descends from another node, which is its mother.

declarative A term used to describe clauses that express statements (*She went to the theater*), as opposed to imperative (*Go to the theater*), interrogative (*Did you go to the theater?*) or exclamative (*How nice to go to the theater!*).

decreasing DPs A determiner phrase is said to be decreasing if whenever the set [[VP1]] is a subset of [[VP2]], the sentence [DP VP2] entails the sentence [DP VP1].

decreasingness The property of being a decreasing operator, DP or other.

default case The case used when a DP is not in a structural case-marking position.

default case hypothesis States that in the early grammar, structural case assignment may fail and when it does, the DP takes on default case.

default quantifier A quantifier that says, 'Unless you have evidence to the contrary, assume that if something has the NP property, it also has the VP property.'

deictics Words or expressions that locate an entity or event in space or time (e.g. *this, that, here*).

denotation The reference of an expression, what it refers to. In semantic theory, the idea that a name refers to, or denotes, an object is often extended to other sorts of expressions. We say that a common noun denotes the set of things that it can be truly applied to. And a verb phrase denotes the set of things that it is true of. The sets denoted by nouns and verb phrases are sometimes called extensions.

dental Having the upper teeth as the passive articulator (place of articulation).

dependency A dependency is said to hold between two items in a sentence if the occurrence of one of them depends on the presence of the other.

derivation The step-by-step application of the rules of grammar to derive a grammatical sentence.

derivational morpheme A morpheme that is added to one word to create another word, often a word of a different lexical class.

derivational morphology The creation of new nouns, verbs, adjectives, and adverbs by adding derivational morphemes to existing roots or base forms (*morph+ ology* → *morphology*).

derived form A form that includes derivational affixes.

descriptive linguistics The study of particular languages and language families, from both historical and synchronic points of view.

determiner (D) A closed class of lexical items (including definite and indefinite articles such as *the* and *a*, and demonstratives such as *this* and *that*, among others), which combine with noun phrases (NPs) to form Determiner Phrases (DPs). *See also determiner phrase.*

determiner phrase (DP) A phrase headed by a determiner, typically followed by a noun phrase (NP), such as *the merchant of Venice*.

diacritic Mark added to (phonetic) symbols to modify their values.

dialectology Study of regional, class, and social variation in language.

diphthong Vowel represented as a sequence of vowel symbols because the tongue and/or lips move from one position to another.

direct discourse A speaker's report of the utterance or thought of another person by means of quoting (or purporting to quote) the exact words of that person. In spoken language, direct discourse is associated with a distinctive intonation, in writing, this is conventionally marked by quotation marks around the clause conveying the reported utterance or thought.

direct object The DP complement of a transitive verb, to which the verb assigns accusative case (visible in English only on pronouns).

direct object position The DP position within VP, located immediately after the verb in English and other SVO languages, and located immediately before the verb in VSO languages.

direct question A question directly posed by a speaker; a main clause that functions as a question. Direct questions are contrasted with *indirect questions* (**embedded questions**).

disambiguate To eliminate the ambiguity of a phrase or sentence.

discontinuous morpheme A morpheme with a single meaning or function that occurs in two (or more) parts which may be separated from each other by other elements of a word.

distinctive The phonetic difference between two sounds is distinctive if it can serve as the basis for distinguishing words. *See contrastive.*

distinctive feature A linguistically relevant property that has two or more contrasting possible values. For example, the distinctive feature for grammatical number in English distinguishes between two values (singular and plural), whereas the feature for grammatical gender distinguishes among three values (masculine, feminine, and neuter). Likewise, the phonological feature *[±voice]* distinguises sounds by virtue of presence or absence of vocal cord vibration (e.g. [b] vs [p]).

distributive reference An expression E refers distributively if any part of a thing that can be labeled as E can also be labeled as E.

ditransitive verb A verb occurring in a double object construction; a verb selecting two DP complements. *See also **transitive verb**, **double object construction***.

dominate To be above (usually, immediately above) another node in a linguistic tree structure; if a constituent X contains another constituent Y, then X is said to dominate Y. *See also **immediate domination***.

dorsal Having the tongue body as active articulator, thus including *velars*, *uvulars*, and sometimes *palatals* and *pharyngeals*.

do-**support** A process that refers to the appearance of the auxiliary *do* in sentences which otherwise would contain no auxiliary: *He went to the theater. Did he go to the theater?*

double object construction A construction in which a verb is followed by two DPs that function as its complements.

d-quantification Quantification expressed by determiners.

dyadic predicate A predicate taking two arguments.

edge The right or left (initial or final) boundary of a word.

electroglottography Technique for recording contact between the vocal cords by measuring their effect on an electrical current.

electropalatography Technique for recording contact between the tongue and the hard palate as indicated by completion of an electrical circuit.

elsewhere allophone An allophone that has no particular characterizing environment. It occurs wherever one does not find any other of the remaining allophones of the same phoneme, which do have particular characterizing environments.

embedded clause A clause contained in a larger *constituent*.

embedded question *See indirect question*.

entail/entailment One sentence S1 is said to entail another sentence S2 if, and only if, whenever S1 is true in any possible situation, S2 is also true in that situation.

environment The particular grammatical context in which a sound, morpheme, or word appears.

epenthetic syllable An inserted syllable.

epiglottal Sound in which the epiglottis is an (active) articulator.

epiglottis The leaf-like appendage to the tongue in the lower pharynx.

exception A word or morpheme that does not follow the regular rules of the language.

exceptional case marking (ECM) infinitive An infinitival clause occurring as the complement of verbs such as *consider* and *believe*, which does not contain the complementizer *for*, but which does contain an overt subject DP, marked with accusative case, in addition to the infinitival verb phrase. For example: the bracketed clause in *Hamlet believed [Rosenkrantz to be a scoundrel].*

existential presupposition The presupposition that there exists an appropriate number of individuals with the property described by the NP part of the DP, e.g. in *Two boys are intelligent*, it is presupposed that there exist two boys and asserted that they are intelligent.

experiencer The θ-role assigned to the argument of a predicate corresponding to the participant in the situation referred to by the predicate whose psychological state is described. For example, in the sentences *Henry likes Katherine*, and *Katherine pleased Henry*, the Experiencer θ-role is assigned to the DP *Henry*.

experimental data Data collected through controlled experiments.

explicit segmentation The process of locating word boundaries by applying a specific mechanism, such as a metrical segmentation procedure.

extension *See **denotation***.

extensional semantics The part of semantics that deals with the truth and reference of expressions.

factive presupposition The presupposition that the clausal complement within a complex sentence describes a fact.

fast-mapping The ability of young children to map meanings onto phonetic strings that aren't already in their lexicons, sometimes with only a single exposure to a word.

feature A phonologically relevant articulatory or acoustic property of sounds; an abstract representation of a minimal contrastive linguistic unit. In syntax, this can be a minimal unit of meaning, such as [±past]; in phonology, it can be a minimal difference in articulation, such as [±voice].

fem Feminine grammatical gender.

finite clause A clause containing a *finite verb*.

finite verb A verb marked with tense affixes, in a language that distinguishes between finite (tensed) and infinitival (untensed) verb-forms and clauses; the form of verb used in a finite clause.

first person Refers to the speaker or to a group of individuals that includes the speaker (in the case of first-person plural expressions). First-person pronouns in English include *I/me/my/mine* (singular) and *we/us/our/ours* (plural).

fixed order An order of words or morphemes which does not vary. In most cases, the order of morphemes within a word is fixed.

focus A constituent of the sentence highlighted by heavy stress. It typically conveys new or contrastive information.

focus frame The part of the sentence that is obtained by removing the focus from it. It is typically presupposed that the focus frame holds of someone/something.

for-**infinitive** An infinitival clause introduced by the prepositional complementizer *for*, followed by an overt subject DP bearing objective (accusative) case, as in the bracketed sequence in the sentences *[For him to
arrive now] would be unfortunate* and *I would hate [for him to arrive now]*.
See also **complementizer, infinitive**.

form A word or morpheme: specifically, its pronunciation or particular
sequence of sounds in a particular grammatical context; a particular
element of a morphological paradigm: thus, *ran* is the past form of
run; to derive or make a word from its component morphemes.

formal rules Rules that are formulated in a precise way, with clearly defined properties.

formal A style of speaking, or, in San Lucas Quiaviní Zapotec, a form used
to refer to a highly respected individual, such as a parent, priest, or
teacher.

frame A sentence or phrase with a word omitted, used to identify a word's
class (for example, only an adjective can be inserted in the frame *the
____ noun*).

free morpheme A morpheme that can stand alone; a morpheme that is a
complete (monomorphemic) word; an independent morpheme.

free variation Variation that is independent of the phonological or morphological environment (the opposite of conditioned variation).

fricative A sound made with a small opening (fricative constriction degree),
generating noise as air passes through it; if not specified as lateral,
often used to mean central fricative.

front Sound having the tongue in an overall forward location (nearer the
teeth).

fully suppletive Suppletive forms in which no trace of the expected root
or affix is apparent (*be, is, were*).

function word A word from a closed class; e.g. a preposition or determiner.

future A time following the present; in many languages, a verb tense.

geminate A *[+long]* sound.

gender A grammatical opposition between nouns of different categories,
such as masculine vs. feminine, and other similar oppositions. (In
languages like English, these categories are primarily used only for
living creatures, but in some languages every noun in the language
may be specified for category membership. In many languages, there
are other gender categories, such as animate vs. inanimate.)

generate To define as well-formed, or grammatical, used of a grammar or
system of rules. If the rules of a grammar define a certain sequence
of words as a well-formed sentence, then the grammar generates the
sentence in question. In a model of speech production, the term *generate* is sometimes used to mean 'produce'.

generative grammar A grammar that defines certain sentences as being
well-formed, or grammatical, as opposed to other sentences that it

does not define as well-formed, and which it therefore characterizes as ungrammatical. The field of generative grammar assumes that a native speaker's unconscious knowledge of his or her language can be characterized in the form of a generative grammar.

generic reading A reading that expresses a generalization, e.g. the generic sentence *Donkeys bray* means 'Donkeys in general bray.'

genitive Referring to or indicating a possessor.

genitive case (Gen) The case feature assigned to a DP occurring in the nominal specifier position, typically used to identify the DP bearing the *Possessor* θ-role. In English, genitive case is marked by the enclitic particle -'s appended to the right of the Possessor DP, as in *Lear's daughter*, and is incorporated into the portmanteau genitive pronouns *my, our, your, his, her, its,* and *their*.

genitive pronoun The genitive form of a pronoun.

glide Vowel-like central approximant; also called semi-vowel.

gloss A morpheme-by-morpheme translation of linguistic data, in which the number of words and morphemes identified matches exactly. In linguistic studies, usually the gloss is printed directly under the cited data.

glottal Sound made in the glottis: having the two vocal cords as articulators, each both active and passive.

glottal(ized) A segment articulated with the closed glottis.

glottal stop A stop with a glottal place of articulation.

glottis The airspace between the vocal cords.

goal The thematic role (θ-role) referring to the participant who functions as a recipient in an action involving transfer of possession from one person to another, or who functions as the endpoint of an action of motion. *See also* ***thematic role***.

grammar The mental representation of linguistic knowledge; the lexicon and system of rules (of phonology, morpology, syntax, and semantics) constituting a native speaker's unconscious knowledge of his or her language.

grammatical Generated by the grammar; consistent with the rules of the grammar; defined as well-formed by the rules of the grammar. *See also* ***acceptability judgment***.

grammatical morpheme A morpheme used to signal the relationship between a word and the context in which it is used.

grammatical role The syntactic role of a noun phrase in a phrase, clause, or sentence.

grammaticality judgment *See* ***acceptability judgment***.

grid Notation for the identification of the relative degree of stress of different syllables.

hard palate The hard, bony surface of the roof of the mouth.

head The lexical category that determines the syntactic type of the phrase in which it occurs, such as the determiner in DP, the verb in VP, the adjective in AP, etc.; in terms of X-bar theory, the element occupying the position X in a phrase XP.

head-final principle The English rule that the head always comes at the end of a compound word.

head-initial vs. head-final phrase structure The property of phrases determining whether the head of the phrase precedes or follows its complements.

head movement Movement of an element in one head position to another head position; V to T movement, T to C movement are examples of head movement.

head turn preference procedure An experimental procedure used with infants aged 4 months and older, in which infants are conditioned to turn their heads toward a loudspeaker, either in response to an auditory stimulus or to activate speech. In the head turn procedure, 'correct' head turns are reinforced.

height *See [±high]*.

hierarchical structure A structure in which certain elements (constituents) are more closely associated than others in the same structure (but with which they in turn may form larger constituents); can be represented with trees or labeled bracketing.

high Non-IPA term for the highest category of vowel height in the IPA chart (IPA *close*). Compared with other vowels, high vowels have the greatest overall height of the tongue.

high amplitude sucking An experimental paradigm used to test the speech perception abilities of newborn and other very young infants. This procedure measures the rate that infants suck on a pacifier, exploiting the fact that sucking rate will increase when the infant perceives a novel stimulus.

higher low Vowel height between lower-mid and low.

higher mid Vowel height between high and mid, closer to mid (same as IPA close-mid); also called mid tense.

historical linguistics The study of language change.

holophrastic Expressing a complete sentence in one word.

homophone A word that sounds like another word, but that has a different, unrelated meaning, e.g. *bear* in the sentence *She can't bear children*.

homophonous Consisting of the same sounds.

idiom A string of words which has an idiosyncratic meaning, i.e. a meaning not resulting from the normal rules of word–meaning combination (e.g. *kick the bucket = die*).

immediate constituent A constituent that is immediately dominated by another constituent; if X immediately dominates Y, then Y is an immediate constituent of X. *See **immediate dominance***.

immediate dominance The asymmetric relation holding between a pair of hierarchically adjacent constituents, whereby the larger (containing) constituent immediately dominates the smaller (contained) constituent. If a constituent X dominates (contains) another constituent Z, then X immediately dominates Z if and only if there is no other constituent Y, such that X dominates Y and Y dominates Z. *See also **immediate constituent, immediate precedence**.*

immediate precedence The asymmetric relation holding between a pair of linearly adjacent constituents, whereby the first (leftmost) constituent immediately precedes the second. If a constituent X precedes another constituent Z, then X immediately precedes Z if and only if there is no other constituent Y, such that X precedes Y and Y precedes Z; that is, no constituent may occur in between X and Z. *See also **immediate dominance, precedence**.*

imperative A command, or a form used to express one.

implicit argument An argument that does not occur overtly in the syntactic structure, but whose participation in the event or situation referred to by the predicate is implied semantically.

in isolation Alone, not as part of a phrase or sentence: when a word is pronounced in isolation, it may sound different from the way it would sound in a complete phrase.

incorporation A special type of compounding in which one sentence element is regularly compounded with another.

independent Not bound, free. An independent word is a word which can stand alone without any added affixes.

indicative The mood of a simple declarative sentence.

indirect discourse The process of reporting the meaning of a reported utterance or thought, without necessarily using precisely the same words as the original, and without using quotation marks (in written form).

indirect object The complement of a verb to which the Goal θ-role is assigned; typically marked with dative case (in languages such as German or Latin) or preceded by a preposition such as English *to*.

indirect question An embedded question; a subordinate clause used in indirect discourse to report an utterance or thought of another person.

infinitive Verbal form identifiable by the infinitival particle *to* in English.

infinitival clause An embedded sentence containing an infinitival verb.

infinitival complement Complement clause that contains an infinitive. (*I expect [Mary to play Romeo]. They want [to play Romeo].*)

infix An affix added within a single morpheme.

inflected form A form with added inflectional affixes.

inflectional morpheme A morpheme whose presence in a word is mandated by the structure of the sentence in which that word appears.

internal structure Rule-governed (or hierarchical) structure of the morphemes of a word.

International Phonetic Alphabet (IPA) The alphabet of the International Phonetic Association.

International Phonetic Association Professional organization of phoneticians which developed and maintains the International Phonetic Alphabet.

intersection The intersection of two sets, A and B, is just the set of things that are in both A and B. That is, the intersection is just the set of things that A and B have in common. The intersection of A and B is written A ∩ B.

intonation Pitch of the voice used to convey information about whole utterances.

intransitive verb (intran) A verb that does not select a (direct) object DP complement, or which can occur without a direct object.

inverse scope When Operator/1 c-commands Operator/2 but Operator/2 takes scope over Operator/1.

inversion (subject–verb inversion) Process that inverts the relative position of two elements, e.g. the subject and a finite auxiliary in English. (*He can come; can he come?*) Subsumed under head movement (movement of the content of T to C).

irregular Not following a rule.

irregular plural A plural not formed by the productive plural rule, one that must be learned by rote memory.

jargon Technical vocabulary.

kiel IPA Most recent version of the IPA, approved in 1989 in Kiel, Germany.

labeled bracketing A representation of linguistic structure in which all the elements dominated by a given node are enclosed within square brackets, which are labeled with the class label of that dominant node; can be used to represent hierarchical structure as an alternative to tree structure.

labial Sound having one or both lips as active articulator, thus includes *bilabial* and *labiodental*.

labial-palatal Sound combining (bi)labial and palatal articulations.

labial-velar (labiovelar) Sound combining (bi)labial and velar articulations.

labiodental Sound having the lower lip as the active articulator and the upper teeth as the passive articulator.

larynx The cartilage box at the bottom of the pharynx (and at the top of the trachea) housing the vocal cords.

late principle B hypothesis Refers to a case in which a principle of Universal Grammar undergoes a delayed maturation.

lateral Along one or both sides of the oral cavity; a sound having lateral airflow; if not specified, often used to mean lateral approximant.

lateral approximant An approximant in which the airflow is lateral, not central.

lateral fricative A fricative in which the airflow is lateral, not central.

law of coordination of likes The grammatical constraint requiring that only 'like constituents' (that is, constituents of the same category) may be coordinated with each other. For example, only a verb can be coordinated with another verb; only an AP can be coordinated with another AP, etc. *See also* **coordination**.

length Duration.

Level Ordering A model hypothesizing distinct, sequential levels of operation by which complex morphological forms are constructed.

lexical category The category of a class of lexical items with identical or very similar syntactic distributional properties, and usually also sharing the same kind of semantic function. Examples: Adjective, Noun, Determiner, Preposition, Complementizer, Verb.

lexical entry A vocabulary item, or the listing of a vocabulary item, in the *lexicon*.

lexical insertion The process of selecting a lexical item from the lexicon and inserting it into a syntactic structure in a particular syntactic position. The process of lexical insertion is associated with a model of sentence generation, either in a model of speech production, or in a more abstract model of passive grammatical knowledge.

lexical item *See lexical entry*.

lexical morpheme A morpheme such as a noun, verb, adjective, or adverb, denoting an item, action, or concept that could be described with words or pictures. *See content word*.

lexicalized meaning A meaning that is not predictable from the component words or morphemes in a phrase or word. The compound *redwood* has an unpredictable or lexicalized meaning: it refers to a specific variety of wood (or tree), not to any red wood, as its literal meaning would suggest. Lexicalized meanings must be specially noted in the lexicon, and memorized individually by the language learner.

lexicon The words and morphemes (vocabulary) in the mental dictionary including a specification of the idiosyncratic properties of each lexical item. Each lexical entry specifies (at least) the phonological form of the lexical item (i.e. how it is pronounced), its syntactic category, its selectional properties, and its meaning.

licensing The process of sanctioning the occurrence of a given constituent.

linear Left-to-right order.

linguist A scientist who investigates human language, its structure, its use, its history, and its place in society.

linguistic phonetics The aspects of speech articulation, acoustics, and perception that are part of linguistics.

linguistics The scientific study of human language.

linking The linking rules are the rules relating the *arguments* of a *predicate* with their grammatical function. For example, the verb *hit* as in *Isaac hit Jacob* has two arguments, an *agent Isaac* and a *theme* or *patient Jacob*. The linking rules for *hit* specify that the agent is realized as a *subject* and the patient as a *complement* of the verb.

liquid r or l type of sound.

literal meaning A meaning derived from the component words or morphemes in a phrase or word. The literal meaning of the compound *redwood* would be 'red wood', 'wood that is red', but *redwood* is a variety of wood (and the tree that it comes from) that need not be red.

locative prepositions Prepositions that signify spatial relations, especially ones signifying the static relation of an object being at a certain location, as opposed to moving to/from there.

logical problem of language acquisition Problem of explaining the ease, rapidity and uniformity of language development in the face of impoverished data.

low Non-IPA term for the lowest category of vowel height in the IPA chart (IPA *open*). Compared with other vowels, low vowels have the greatest overall opening of the mouth.

lower high Vowel height between high and higher mid, closer to high; also called high lax.

lower mid Vowel height between mid and low, closer to mid (same as IPA *open-mid*); also called *mid lax*.

magnetic resonance imaging (MRI)/functional MRI A technique for viewing structures inside the body using differential effects of magnetic fields on different materials.

magnetometry Technique for measuring positions of articulators by tracking the location of receiver coils in an electromagnetic field.

main clause A complete sentence; a sentence that is not a subordinate clause, that is, any sentence that is not embedded within another sentence. This term is usually used to refer to sentences containing one or more subordinate clauses (embedded sentences), and in particular to the portions of these sentences that are not contained within a given subordinate clause. For example, in the sentence *Lear said that he was unhappy*, the subordinate clause is *that he was unhappy*, and the main clause is *Lear said CP*, where 'CP' represents the entire subordinate clause. *See also **matrix clause, subordinate clause**.*

main stress Most prominent syllable in a given word or expression.

manner of articulation How a sound is made, especially in terms of its constriction degree, but also in terms of its voicing and nasality.

marker An indicator of a grammatical concept; a grammatical morpheme.

mass noun A noun used in such a way that it cannot pluralize and takes the determiner *much* or combines with a measure expression. Mass nouns have cumulative (non-quantized) reference (*rice*).

mathematical linguistics Study of the formal and mathematical properties of language.

matrix clause The clause immediately dominating a given subordinate clause (embedded sentence). This term is often used to refer to the main clause, especially in reference to sentences containing just one subordinate clause. The terms 'main clause' and 'matrix clause' are not synonymous, however; for example, if a main clause, CP-1, dominates a subordinate clause, CP-2, and CP-2 dominates another subordinate clause, CP-3, CP-2 is the matrix clause for CP-3, even though it is not a main clause.

measure expression Turns a mass term into a count term, e.g. *A pound of, two pieces of.*

metathesis The transposition or reversal of two sounds or sound sequences, usually adjacent to each other.

metrical segmentation strategy A procedure for defining word boundaries on the basis of the language's characteristic rhythmic structure.

mid The vowel height between (IPA) close-mid and open-mid; non-IPA, the major vowel height category between *high* and *low*.

minimal pair (in phonology) Two different words that differ in exactly one sound, in the same location, e.g. *bat, pat.*

minimal set (in phonology) Two or more words that differ in exactly one sound in the same location, e.g. *bat, pat, mat, gnat, cat, gat, hat, rat, etc.*

modal auxiliary *See auxiliary.*

modal, modal verb (Mod) An auxiliary verb referring to modal necessity (*must, shall, should, will,* or *would*) or possibility (*can, could, may,* and *might*). In English, modal verbs share a distinctive grammatical property: they select bare VP complements, as in *Falstaff can drink a lot, Shylock should spare Antonio.*

model The representation of a situation on phenomenon that singles out certain relevant aspects of it.

modularity The view that the mind is composed of distinct mental faculties, of which language is one, each with its own structural principles and computational machinery for constructing and processing representations.

monadic predicate A predicate taking one argument.

monomorphemic Consisting of a single morpheme.

monosyllabic Consisting of a single syllable.

morpheme The smallest meaningful linguistic unit. Some morphemes are identical with words, but many morphemes are smaller than words.

morpheme boundary A boundary between two morphemes, represented by – or by + (morph-eme, morph + eme).

morphological process A process which operates to change morphology; typically, a process other than affixation, such as *ablaut compounding,* or *reduplication.*

morphology The structure of words; the study of words and how they are formed.

mother node A node that dominates another node, its daughter.

movement The syntactic displacement of a constituent from one position in the structure of a sentence to another, e.g. wh-movement (the displacement of a wh-phrase to the beginning of a question-sentence or relative clause) and topicalization (the movement of a phrase that is being topicalized to the Topic position. Only constituents can be moved.

name A proper noun; a word or phrase that is used as if it has a unique referent. Examples include *Falstaff, Henry, Portia, Noam Chomsky.*

narrow (phonetic transcription) Representing small differences in sounds, especially using diacritics.

nasal Pertaining to the nose; having an opening from the oral cavity to the nose through which air may flow; often used by itself to mean a voiced nasal stop.

nasal cavities Cavities lying above the palate, between the pharynx and the nostrils.

nasal stop A consonant in which a stop is formed in the oral cavity but the nasal passage remains open, so that all airflow must be through the nose.

nasality *See [±nasal].*

nasalization Airflow through the nose.

nasalized Strictly, having airflow through both mouth and nose; often used to mean *nasal*.

nasalized vowel A vowel pronounced with air released through the nose.

natural class Any complete set of sounds in a given language that share the same value for a feature or set of features.

naturalistic data Naturally occurring data; data that are passively (and preferably unobtrusively) observed, rather than being elicited in an experimental situation. *See also* **experimental data**.

near-minimal pair A pair of words that would count as a minimal pair, but for some phonologically irrelevant additional difference, e.g. *bat* [bæt] – *pat* [pʰæt].

neg Negative.

negative evidence Direct information that certain sentences are ungrammatical; such information is not provided to the child. *See* **positive evidence**.

negative polarity item An item that may occur only in the presence of a negative expression (that c-commands it).

neurolinguistics Branch of linguistics concerned with the biological basis of language acquisition and the brain/mind/language interface; study of linguistic aspects of aphasia.

neutralization The identical phonetic realization of distinct phonemic forms.

node A nexus in a tree diagram representing a *constituent*, or component part, of the sentence or phrase that the tree structure diagram represents; an element in a linguistic tree structure, either a class label or a terminal node (an actual word or morpheme).

nominal specifier position A DP position within a larger DP, preceding the noun phrase (NP), and to which the Possessor θ-role is assigned, as in *Lear's daughter, the dauphin's gift to the king*.

nominalizer A morpheme which derives a noun from a verb or adjective.

nominative Form used for subjects.

nominative case (Nom) The case feature assigned to the subject of a finite sentence.

non-branching node A node that immediately dominates just one constituent.

non-configurational language A language in which the basic constituent order is relatively free; that is, any order of major constituents is allowed.

non-finite verbs *See finite verbs*.

non-future The present or past.

non-linear An affix positioned without ordinary regard to linear order (usually, as with infixes or reduplicated elements, not at the right or left edge of a word).

nonterminal node A node in a constituent tree diagram that dominates at least one other node. *See also* **terminal node**.

notational variant A notational model (for example, a model of a theory of grammar) that represents the same set of abstract properties as an alternative notational model, but in a superficially different way, and which makes the same empirical predictions as the alternative model. (The relation of notational variance is symmetrical – that is, if X is a notational variant of Y, then Y is a notational variant of X.)

Noun (N) The head of NP; the name of the lexical category of words that describe classes of referents, such as people, places, objects, events, situations, etc.

Noun Phrase (NP) A phrase headed by a noun; the sequence formed by a noun and its complements, perhaps also containing some or all pre-nominal adjectives.

NPI *See negative polarity item*.

nucleus The vowel element in a syllable.

null pronoun A silent pronoun, such as the non-emphatic form of a subject pronoun in a null-subject language, or the silent subject pronoun of a control infinitive.

null subject parameter The parameter of cross-linguistic variation that determines whether a (non-emphatic) pronoun occurring in the subject position of a finite clause may be null (that is, silent, or unpronounced).

number The property words realize, for example, as *singular* or *plural* marking.

object The DP complement of a (transitive) verb or preposition. So-called ditransitive verbs select two DP complements: the *direct object* and the *indirect object*. Verbs assign accusative case to the direct object, though this is overtly marked in English only on pronouns (including the human wh-pronoun *whom*, in traditional dialects).

obstruent Consonant in which the airflow is noisy (the airflow meets an obstruction), thus including plosives and fricatives (and affricates); a [–sonorant] sound.

one-word stage The stage at which children produce utterances consisting of a single word.

onset (of the syllable) Consonant(s) preceding the nucleus within a syllable.

open class A class of words to which new members may freely be added. The classes of nouns, verbs, adjectives, and adverbs are open classes. *See content word.*

open IPA term for the lowest category of vowel height; compared with other vowels, overall height of tongue is least and mouth is most open. Non-IPA term is *low*.

open-mid The third-highest category of vowel height in the IPA chart; lower than *close-mid* and higher than *open*. Non-IPA term is *lower mid*.

open syllable Syllable without coda.

operator Modal auxiliaries, negation, quantifiers, and particles like *only*.

oral cavity The top airspace of the vocal tract, under the palate.

oral stop Consonant sound in which a complete obstruction is formed in the oral cavity and the nasal cavities are also blocked off. Air, once released, flows out of the oral cavity.

oral stricture Degree to which air flows freely out of the mouth.

oral tract Pharynx and oral cavity together.

orthography A conventionalized writing system for writing a particular language; alphabet.

overextension The use of a word to refer to a larger class of entities than the word labels in the adult lexicon.

overgeneralization When a child applies a rule more broadly than it applies in the adult grammar.

overt Referring to a morpheme or other element that is physically present in a word or sentence (as opposed to being merely hypothesized).

palatal Sound having the hard palate as the passive articulator.

palatography Technique for recording the amount of contact with the palate.

paradigm The set of morphologically related forms derived from a root. Generally these are the forms derived by inflection.

parameter A dimension along which particular languages may vary, by selecting from a limited range of options. According to the 'Principles and Parameters' theory, the theory of Universal Grammar (UG) contains a set of invariant universal principles and a set of parameters (such as the *null subject parameter*), with a fixed set of possible values; in acquiring a language, the language learner must decide which value to choose for each parameter.

paraphrase A restatement of the meaning of a word, phrase, or sentence, using different words or a different arrangement of the same words.

partial reduplication A process in which only part of an affected word is copied or reduplicated.

partially suppletive Referring to suppletive forms in which some relationship to the expected root and affixes is apparent. Partially suppletive forms look related, but the relationship appears irregular.

participial clause A subordinate clause headed by a participle, that is, by a verb bearing a participial affix. *See participle.*

participle A form of the verb bearing a participial affix, and which may function as the head of a participial clause.

passive articulator A speech organ towards which an active articulator moves.

past participle Verbal form appearing after the perfect auxiliary in the perfect tense construction (*played* in *John has played Romeo*).

past A time before the present, or before the time of speaking; a verb tense.

patient The thematic role (θ-role) assigned to the participant in the action referred to by a verb, who the action is performed on. *See also thematic role.*

perfective prefix A prefix that signifies that the verb's action is completed.

performance Linguistic behavior; linguistic processing; speech production and comprehension.

person *See first person, second person, third person.*

pharyngeal Sound having the pharynx as an active or passive articulator.

pharyngeal(ized) A sound articulated with narrowed pharyngeal cavity, e.g. [ʔ], [tˤ].

pharynx The back, vertical airspace of the vocal tract between the uvula and the larynx; usually thought of as the passive articulator approached by the body or root of the tongue, but its walls can also function actively, squeezing the pharynx space.

phone Speech sound.

phoneme One of the basic distinctive speech sounds of a language.

phonemic awareness Knowledge that words can be decomposed into sequences of phonemes.

phonemic transcription A broad transcription that represents words or utterances as sequences of phonemes.

phonemicization An analytical technique for determining the phonemic structure of a language.

phonetic alphabet Set of symbols used for representing speech sounds.

phonetic transcription A transcription that represents words or utterances with greater detail than would be represented in a phonemic transcription.

phonetics The study of the sounds of human language; the study of the physical aspects of speech events.

phonics The relations between sounds and letters in a given language.

phonological component The system of rules, representations and principles in a language that govern the patterning of sounds.

phonological derivation A derivation that includes only the application of phonological rules (as opposed to morphological or other rules).

phonological word A linguistic string pronounced as a single word according to the rules of phonology (for instance, with a single stress), though possibly consisting of more than one element speakers would identify as words.

phonology The sound patterns of language.

phonotactic The constraints on what is a possible word or syllable in a language; conditions characterizing permissible segment sequences in a given language.

phrase A sequence of adjacent words that form a syntactic unit or constituent (a component part) in the structure of a sentence.

phrase structure The constituent structure of a phrase or sentence. *See also constituent, tree diagram.*

phrase structure rule *See context-free rewrite rule.*

place of articulation The passive articulator – where in the mouth a sound is made.

place assimilation A process whereby a segment becomes like a neighboring one with respect to its place-of-articulation features.

plosive Pulmonic-egressive, oral stop.

plural More than one; plural expression receives a particular marking.

polyglot An individual who speaks many languages.

polysynthetic language A language in which complex meanings are expressed in a single word; specifically, a language in which a single verb word may express the meaning of a complete sentence consisting of pronoun subject, verb, pronoun object, and such additions as the negative, modals, and so on.

portmanteau morpheme Morpheme that contains more than one meaningful unit, but that cannot be analyzed into separate elements.

positive evidence Evidence that a particular linguistic example is acceptable to native speakers, from which a linguist may infer that the example is grammatical.

possessive adjective The genitive form of a pronoun in the nominal specifier position before a noun phrase within a DP, as in *my wife, his bloody knife,* etc. Often referred to as a genitive pronoun.

possessor The thematic role (θ-role) associated with the possessor in a relation of possession or ownership, including abstract possession as in kinship relations, or of the whole in a part–whole relation, such as the relation between a person and a body part, or between a table and one of its legs.

postalveolar Sound having as passive articulator some part of the palate at or behind the end of the alveolar ridge.

poverty of the stimulus Lack of information provided to the child language learner, for example, the lack of negative evidence.

pragmatics Language in context and the influence of situation on meaning; the rules of language use, including how sentences fit into a larger discourse and non-linguistic context.

precedence The asymmetric relation holding between two linearly ordered constituents, whereby one constituent precedes (occurs before) the other. *See also* ***immediate precedence***.

predicate Certain words such as *adjectives* or *verbs* are names of properties (e.g. the property *blue*) or relations (e.g. *Marry*). Such words are called predicates. The entities to which the property is assigned (e.g. The sky in *The sky is blue*) or which are related by the predicate (e.g. Toranaga and Keiko in *Toranaga married Keiko*) are called the argument(s) of the predicate.

predicate nominal construction A small clause construction in which a DP or NP functions as the predicate of the small clause, referring to a property that is attributed to another DP.

predicate phrase A phrase functioning as a predicate. *See* ***predicate***.

predictable Referring to a regular change in phonology and morphology which is consistent with the rules of the grammar.

prefix A bound morpheme added before a root, or at the beginning of a word.

preglottalized Sound having glottalization begin before the oral articulation.

preposing Leftward movement (movement of a constituent towards the beginning of the sentence).

preposition (P) The head of PP; a word used to locate one referent (such as an entity, group of entities, event, or situation) in relation to another referent, either in terms of space (*on, in, under, near, between, beside*, etc.) or in terms of time (*after, before, during*, etc.), or to designate the source or trajectory of motion (*from, to, into*, etc.). Sometimes prepositions are used instead of case markers to encode certain thematic roles with particular predicates or semantic classes of predicates (such as *at*, as in *laugh at Falstaff*).

Prepositional Phrase (PP) A phrase headed by a preposition; the sequence formed by a preposition and its DP object.

prescriptive grammars Term referring to rules set up by language 'purists' who consider one variety or dialect of a language better than other varieties.

present The time of speaking; a verb tense.

present participle Verbal form appearing in the progressive construction. *John is playing Romeo.*

presupposition A non-asserted part of the message conveyed by the sentence that is not canceled when the sentence is negated in the form *It is not true/the case that* .... If a situation does not conform to the presupposition(s) of the sentence, the sentence cannot assert anything meaningful about that situation.

primary stress Strongest stress in a word.

principle of categorial scope A principle which asserts that when a word's meaning is overextended, it will be extended to other members of the same category.

principle of lexical contrast or the mutual exclusivity assumption Principles which postulate that children assume that each object has one and only one label.

principle of reference A principle that asserts that words refer to, that is represent, objects, actions, states and attributes in the environment.

principle of structure dependency of linguistic rules The principle that linguistic rules are sensitive to **constituent structure**.

productive morpheme A morpheme which may be added regularly to any root of the appropriate class. English -*s* is the productively plural morpheme in English, for example.

prominence *See stress.*

pronominal clitic An unstressed pronoun that is phonologically dependent on another word or phrase as its host, and which typically occurs in a different syntactic position from that of non-clitic DP arguments.

pronoun (Prn) A closed class of lexical items that are used to refer, but which (unlike DPs containing nouns) do not indicate any property of the referent other than those associated with grammatical features for person, number, and gender (or class features, in languages with noun class systems). Pronouns are normally definite, and are sometimes homophonous with determiners in certain languages (e.g. in the case of accusative pronouns in French, Spanish, and Italian). *See also **first person, second person, third person**.*

proper noun A noun (usually a name) which refers to a specific, clearly identifiable individual (for example, *Ophelia* is a proper noun when used to refer to a specific person (usually known to both speaker and hearer) named *Ophelia*). *See name.*

prosodic structure The rhythmic pattern of stress, accent, or tone in a word or phrase.

prosody Properties of utterances that span more than one segment.

psycholinguistics The branch of linguistics concerned with linguistic performance, including the production and comprehension of speech (or sign) and child language acquisition.

pulmonic egressive sounds Having air pushed out by the lungs.

quantificational determiner A determiner that relates two sets of individuals: the set denoted by the NP that the determiner forms a constituent with and the set denoted by the rest of the sentence, e.g. the VP. For example: *every, few, some, less than five but more than one.*

quantifier A noun phrase with a quantificational determiner, or an adverb that plays a similar role, e.g. *Everyone/always, two men/twice, few men/ seldom.*

quantifies over (E.g. a determiner quantifies over the individuals in the denotation of its NP); unselective if it may quantify over different kinds of entities, depending on its sentential context.

quantized reference Articulated into minimal units: count nouns, telic events.

radical Sounds having the tongue root as active articulator, thus including *pharyngeals* and also *epiglottals*.

ranking Between constraints, grammatical statement that indicates which constraint takes priority over which others in cases of conflict.

reanalysis A change in speakers' perception (or analysis) of the position of a word or morpheme boundary.

recognition A term used in psychology to refer to processes involved in comprehension; i.e. matching the form one hears (sees or reads) onto the phonological and semantic representation of a word in one's mental lexicon.

reduced vowel sound A vowel sound that is shorter and often more like the vowel of English *but* than a vowel sound that is not reduced.

reduplication A process by which all or part of a word is copied or duplicated to indicate a change in the meaning or usage. Reduplication may be complete or partial.

reference The property or process of referring to some entity, situation, event, time, or location.

referent The element that a referential category refers to in a case of reference.

referential category A category that is used to refer. The canonical example of a referential category is DP (including names and pronouns, as well as DPs containing a determiner and NP).

reflexive pronouns In English, a pronoun affixed with the form *self* such as *myself* or *himself*. More generally, a pronoun that has an equivalent interpretative function in other languages.

regular Following a rule.

regularize To change an irregular form so that it works regularly.

relative clause A modifying phrase like *who picked flowers* in the sentence *The girl who picked flowers was Ophelia.*

release (of a consonant) Opening up of an oral constriction, allowing (more) air to flow.

restriction The set of individuals or events that determiners or quantificational adverbs quantify over; the sets denoted by the NP or by the *if*-clause, respectively.

retrieval A term used in psychology to refer to processes involved in production; i.e. a combination of procedures for locating and getting a word from the lexicon and mapping its semantic and phonological representation onto procedures for the motor production, or articulation of the word.

retroflex Having as active articulator the tongue tip raised or curled back to a postalveolar.

rhoticity R-coloring.

rime A constituent of a syllable consisting of the nucleus and coda.

root A lexical morpheme (usually free, in English) which is the base to which grammatical or derivational morphemes are added to form a complex word. Most roots can themselves be used as uninflected base forms, but not all uninflected base forms are roots.

rounded Sounds having the lips constricted inward and protruded forward.

rule A statement of regularity in grammatical structure. A rule can describe the order in which morphemes occur, how words with a certain structure come to be pronounced, the constituent structure of phrases and clauses, and so on.

schwa Vowel [ə] appearing in the stressless syllables of English.

scope That unit or section of the sentence within which another expression may be dependent on the operator for its interpretation. Syntactically, the scope of an operator often coincides with the segment of the sentence that it c-commands.

scope interaction, relative scope The constellation of two operators.

second person A grammatical category of pronominal forms which include the hearer or hearers, but not the speaker (*you* in English; second-person plural may be expressed in English as *you, you guys, you all, you lot*, and so on).

(to) segment To divide a word into morphemes. Segmentation is the first step in analysis.

segment Individual speech sound (consonants and vowels); unit of sound consisting of one or more features that are realized as roughly simultaneous.

segmental Pertaining to segments.

segmental structure The arrangement of sounds in a morpheme, word, or phrase.

selection The property of a lexical item requiring (or allowing) one or more complements with certain intrinsic properties (such as the lexical category of the head of the complement, or some semantic property of the phrase as a whole). *See also **categorial selection, semantic selection**.*

selectional restriction A lexical requirement imposed by a lexical category on one or more of its arguments, involving an intrinsic semantic property of the argument(s). For example, the verb *murder* requires both its agent and its patient arguments to be human, while the verb *drink* requires its agent argument to be animate and its patient argument to be liquid. *See also **semantic selection**.*

semantic bootstrapping Using a word's semantic structure or the surrounding semantic structure to guess a word's syntactic category.

semantic feature theory A theory proposing that word meanings consist of features, and that as children learn more vocabulary, individual definitions are refined and take on more features.

semantic properties Properties dealing with linguistic meaning.

semantic selection (S-selection) A semantic requirement imposed by a predicative lexical category on one or more of its arguments. For example, the verb *elapse* requires that its subject denote a time period as in *[three minutes] elapsed*. S-selection is sometimes used to refer specifically to *selectional restrictions*, but selection of specific thematic roles constitutes another type of semantic selection.

semi-vowel Glide.

sentence As defined by the grammar a sentence is a constituent TP containing at least a subject position (the specifier of TP) and a predicate phrase containing the VP.

sentence-lifting A construction associated with direct discourse, where the embedded sentence enclosed in quotation marks, which functions as the complement of a verb of speech or thought, occurs at the front of the sentence, followed immediately by the verb of speech. Example: *"Beware the ides of March!" warned the soothsayer.*

sibilant A fricative with a loud, high-pitched, noisy sound.

sign languages Languages of the deaf using a gestural/visual modality instead of the sound/aural perceptual modality of speech.

simple sentence A sentence containing only one verb.

simple word A word that contains only one morpheme.

singular A singular expression which receives a particular marking usually interpreted to mean that the expression denotes one entity (for example, *a book* is a singular expression marked with the number suffix -Ø and denoting one book).

sister A constituent that is immediately dominated by the same element as another constituent.

sister nodes Nodes that descend from the same node.

slot An individual category or position in a template or frame.

small clause A type of subordinate clause containing just a subject and a predicate, but none of the inflectional elements (such as tenses or auxiliary verbs) associated with normal sentences; the predicate of the small clause may simply be an AP or PP, as in *Portia considered Shylock vengeful*. Bare VP complements are sometimes analyzed as small clauses. *See also* **predicate nominal construction, bare VP.**

sociolinguistics Study of language and society, including language and social class, ethnicity, and gender.

soft palate The soft, non-bony part of the roof of the mouth behind the hard palate, also called the velum, which, as an active articulator, moves up and down at the top of the pharynx to either block off or open up the air passage to the nose, and as a passive articulator, is approached by the tongue body.

sonorant Sound in which the airflow is smooth, not noisy.

sound symbolism The use of sounds in languages that occurs when the sounds themselves are felt to be inherently meaningful.

spec Phrasal position to the left of the head in English: position where the *subject* in English occurs (*John plays Romeo, John* is in Spec, TP).

specific language impairment (SLI) A disability affecting language development in children who appear to be otherwise normal. Children with SLI are late talkers, their language acquisition is protracted and belabored, and they show deficits in constructing a grammar.

specifier The specifier of an XP is the phrasal constituent YP *daughter* to XP and *sister* to X'.

specifier position The position defined by X-bar theory corresponding to the subject position in a clause or the nominal specifier position in a DP. According to standard X-bar theory, the Specifier position is the leftmost immediate constituent of XP, and a sister of the X constituent that dominates the head X and the complements of X.

spectrogram A frequency-by-time display in which the stronger frequency components are highlighted.

speech acoustics The properties of the airwaves that transmit speech from speaker to listener.

speech perception How speech is perceived by the listener.

speech production How speech is produced by the speaker.

speech reading (or lip reading) Use of visual information for speech processing by perceivers, especially the hearing-impaired.

speech sounds Sounds used in languages.

spirantization A phonological rule that converts stops to fricatives.

S-selection *See semantic selection.*

stative verb or predicate A predicate expressing a state of being or perception (e.g. *weigh, be, resemble, see*).

stop A consonant in which the active articulator forms a complete seal in the oral tract against the passive articulator, stopping the flow of air out of the mouth; often used by itself to mean plosive.

stress Degree of relative prominence characterizing the syllables of a word or other linguistic expression; the stressed syllable appears stronger than others in the same word, due to variations in loudness, duration, and effort.

strident Similar to sibilant, but sometimes applied to more sounds.

structure preserving mapping A mapping M from A to B is structure preserving if the images of the elements of A in B under M (that is, the elements of B that M maps elements of A to) are structured in the same particular way.

subcategorization, subcategorize *See categorial selection.*

subconstituent A constituent dominated by a larger constituent. For example, in the sentence *Lear was the king of England*, the PP *of England* is a subconstituent of the NP *king of England*, which is itself a sub-constituent of the DP *the king of England*.

subject The argument of a predicate that occurs in a Specifier position rather than as a complement of the predicate. Most subjects are DPs, though sometimes CPs function as subjects. The subject of a sentence is the DP that is immediately dominated by the Sentence node.

subject agreement *See agreement.*

subject/verb agreement *Agreement* between the verb and the *subject* of a *clause.*

subjunctive *See indicative.*

subordinate clause A sentence or clause that occurs as a subconstituent of the main sentence. *See also* **main clause, matrix clause**.

subordinating conjunction The traditional term for complementizer. *See* **complementizer**.

sub-regularity A morphological pattern which does not follow the general or expected rule, but for which a general description can nonetheless be given.

subset principle A learning principle which requires that the child choose the more restrictive option where UG makes available more than one possible. The subset principle assures that the child does not have to rely on negative evidence to get to the target grammar.

suffix A bound morpheme added after a root, or at the end of a word.

superlative Form of an adjective or adverb expressing the greatest degree (for example, *fastest* is the superlative of the English adjective and adverb *fast*).

suppletive Refers to elements of a morphological paradigm which are irregular, in that they do not contain the expected roots or affixes, or that they are pronounced unexpectedly. Irregularly related forms may be either fully or partially suppletive.

suprasegmentals Properties of utterances that span more than one segment.

SVO Subject, verb, object constituent order.

syllabic The most prominent sound in a syllable; syllabic consonants are pronounced without an accompanying vowel.

syllable A string of segments in which one of the segments (usually a vowel) is more prominent than the others.

syllable structure processes Phonological rules that affect the structure of the syllable.

syntactic bootstrapping Using a word's syntax or the surrounding structure to guess a word's meaning.

syntax The structure of phrases and sentences; the system of rules in the grammar of a language that determines the ways in which words are combined to form meaningful phrases and sentences.

tap Sound in which the active and passive articulators touch but do not hold.

teaching or **pedagogical grammars** Texts used to teach a second language or a variation (dialect) of one's native language.

telegraphic stage An early stage in child language characterized by the production of content words with function morphemes omitted.

telic An event (or verbal expression referring to one) that has an inherent culmination point.

template A schematic representation similar to a mathematical formula, in which terms or symbols indicate categories which can be filled by specific linguistic elements, such as morphemes or sounds.

tense A syntactic category referring to, or used to locate, an event or situation in time, usually in relation to the time at which the sentence is uttered. In English, present and past tense morphemes occur as suffixes on the verb, while the future tense morpheme occurs as the modal verb *will* or *shall* (in some dialects).

Tense Phrase (TP) A phrase headed by the syntactic category Tense, as defined by X-bar theory; a Sentence, according to the theory that stipulates that Sentences are headed by the category Tense.

tensed A property expressed on a verb or on an auxiliary verb interpreted as placing the action described by the main verb in time. Thus the form *spoke*, past tense of *speak*, indicates that in the sentence *Oberon spoke*, Oberon's speaking took place in the past.

tenseless A word or constituent not carrying tense information.

terminal node A node in a syntactic tree structure that dominates no other node.

terminating suffix An affix which is attached at the end of the word.

ternary branching node A node representing a constituent that immediately dominates three subconstituents. According to some theories of syntax, ternary branching structures are disallowed; only non-branching or binary branching nodes are permitted.

the naming explosion The spurt in vocabulary growth, which typically occurs late in the second year of life, that is predominated by the acquisition of nouns.

thematic role (θ-role) The semantic role played by a participant in an event or situation, such as Agent, Patient, or Goal.

thematic role assignment The process whereby a thematic role is assigned to, or associated with, a referential expression occurring in a sentence.

theme A term used to describe the interpretive function (semantic or thematic role) which a particular type of argument plays in a sentence. Typically, it is associated to a DP denoting an entity undergoing the effect of an action or happenstance (as *Macbeth* in *Shakespeare described Macbeth*). Sometimes the term Patient is used instead.

theta-Criterion (θ-Criterion) A constraint relating to the linguistic expression of argument structure, requiring that each (obligatory) θ-role selected by a predicate must be assigned to a referential expression (such as a DP), and that each referential expression must be assigned a θ-role. The strict version of this constraint requires a bi-unique (one-to-one) correspondence between θ-roles and referential expressions. (As traditionally formulated, this constraint mentions 'arguments' rather than 'referential expressions'.)

theta-role (θ-role) *See* **thematic role**.

third person Referring to an individual who is neither the speaker nor the addressee, or to a group of individuals that includes neither the speaker nor the addressee (in the case of third-person plural expressions). Third-person pronouns in English include *he/him/his* (masculine singular), *she/her/hers* (feminine singular), *it/its* (neuter singular), and *they/them/their/theirs* (plural).

tone A linguistic specification of (relative) pitch.

tongue blade About the first 3 cm of the tongue, behind which there is a point where the tongue can bend and flex; an active articulator, which can move independently of the rest of the tongue, or is moved by the rest of the tongue.

tongue body The main part of the tongue; can be divided into a front part and a back part, both of which can be active articulators.

tongue root The bottom part of the tongue, which forms the front wall of the pharynx; an active articulator which constricts the pharynx.

tongue tip The very end or frontmost part of the tongue blade (also called apex); an active articulator, moved by the tongue blade.

topic A constituent referring to an individual or entity that is already under discussion, and which the sentence is understood to be commenting on.

topic position The syntactic position reserved for the constituent that is interpreted as the Topic of the clause. In English, the Topic position occurs only in finite clauses, immediately preceding the subject position. The Topic position rarely occurs within a subordinate clause, though if it does, it immediately follows the position of the complementizer *that*, as in *Macbeth said that Duncan, he would never be able to kill*.

topicalization construction A syntactic construction in which a particular constituent that is interpreted as the Topic occurs in the Topic position.

transcription Written representation.

transformational rule, or **transformation** A rule that changes a structure produced by the basic rules of phrase structure and lexical insertion, for example, by deleting constituents or moving them to a different position in the sentence from where they are originally derived by the phrase structure rules.

transitive relation A relation holding between two elements, A and B, such that if this same relation holds between B and a third element G, then it also holds between A and G. For example, the relation of precedence is a transitive relation, since if A precedes B, and B precedes G, then A also precedes G.

transitive verb A verb that selects a direct object DP complement, and which assigns accusative case to this complement. *See also **accusative case, ditransitive verb**.*

tree diagram A notation for representing constituent structure, including both linear precedence and hierarchical structure, in the form of an inverted tree consisting of nodes representing constituents, with branches beneath them, connecting them to their subconstituents. *See also **node, binary branching node, non-branching node, terminal node, ternary branching node, labeled bracketing**.*

trill Sound in which the active articulator vibrates as air flows around it.

typology The study of relationships between different linguistic features in unrelated languages. One important concern of typology is the relationship between basic word order and other syntactic and morphological phenomena.

umlaut A type of vowel ablaut used in germanic languages. For instance, English singular/plural pairs like *goose—geese* reflect umlaut.

unaccusative verb A verb that is unable to assign accusative case to a direct object DP complement; according to some theories, unaccusative verbs select DP objects, but these objects must undergo movement to the subject position of the sentence containing the unaccusative verb in order to get case-marked. Examples include *arrive, go*.

underextension The mapping of a word onto a very narrow, situation-specific referent.

underlying representation The form of words and morphemes that is hypothesized to be the input to the set of phonological rules.

ungrammatical Failing to conform to the rules of the grammar; not generated by the grammar; violating some constraint imposed by the grammar. Ungrammatical utterances are written with a preceding asterisk, *.

uninflected form A form without any added inflectional affixes. An uninflected form is often analyzed as the base form or root to which other affixes are added.

union The union of two sets, A and B, is the set of things that are in either A or B. That is, you just put the two sets together. The union of A and B is written A ∩ B.

Universal Grammar (UG) A genetically determined mental system present at birth which permits the acquisition of the complex grammar of any human language.

unmarked Containing no marking for (or marker of) a given morpheme or idea.

unreleased Sound having the mouth open without an audible release.

unrounded Sound produced with the lips either in a neutral posture or spread out to press against the face.

(un)selective A quantifier is selective if it is a design feature of these entities it quantifies over (e.g. a determiner quantifies over the individuals in the denotation of its NP) and unselective if it may quantify over different kinds of entities, depending on its sentential context.

uvula The hanging back tip of the soft palate; as an active articulator it can vibrate in the upper pharynx; as a passive articulator it is approached by the tongue body.

uvular Sound having the uvula as an active or passive articulator.

variation Alternation between two sounds, morphemes, or other grammatical elements. Variation may be conditioned or free.

velar Sound having the soft palate (sometimes the back of the hard palate) as passive articulator.

velarized Sound having tongue backing in addition to a primary articulation.

Verb (V) A word used to describe an event or situation, or a word belonging to a lexical class that includes such words as canonical members; the head of VP. Examples include *run, murder, kiss, have, will*. *See also* ***auxiliary, ditransitive verb, modal verb, intransitive verb, transitive verb, unaccusative verb***.

Verb Phrase (VP) A phrase (XP) headed by a verb; the sequence of a verb and its complement(s), as well as any adverbial phrases adjoined to it. *See also* ***bare VP, small clause***.

visual fixation procedure Experimental procedure used with young infants to assess speech perception abilities. This procedure measures the length of time an infant looks at a screen associated with a particular stimulus.

vocal cords Two bands or folds strung front to back inside the larynx.

voice onset time (VOT) Refers to the point in time at which the vocal folds begin to vibrate relative to the release of the stop.

voiced Sounds produced with vocal cord vibration for part or all of the sound.

voiceless (usual meaning) Having no vocal cord vibration; (alternative meaning) Partial or no vocal cord vibration in an otherwise voiced sound (= devoiced).

voicing Vibration of the vocal cords; regular passage of puffs of air through the larynx as the vibrating vocal cords open and close. *See [±voice]*.

vowel Sound in which no extreme constriction is made; the air flows out of the mouth relatively freely and the sound is relatively loud and strong.

VP-ellipsis Describes the phenomenon/process by which a VP can be left unpronounced though its content is understood, e.g. *Did you go to the theater? Yes, I did* (silent VP = *go to the theater*).

VP-internal subject hypothesis The hypothesis that the subject of a sentence originates within the verb phrase, perhaps in the Specifier of VP position, and undergoes transformational movement to the position of the Specifier of TP, at least in languages exhibiting SVO constituent order, such as English.

wh-movement The process of transformational movement of a wh-word, or of a phrase containing a wh-word, to the front of a sentence, into a position preceding the subject of the sentence.

whole object principle A principle which posits that upon hearing a novel word in conjunction with an object, a child will assume that the word refers to the whole object, not to just part of it.

wh-word A word such as *who, what, when, where, which, why,* and *how,* used in forming questions that seek the identity or type of one or more constituents of the sentence. Although the terms wh-word and *wh-movement* are based on the morphological form of wh-words in English, the same term is used for words in other languages that serve the same syntactic and semantic function.

word A complete linguistic unit that is meaningful on its own and can be freely reordered into new phrases and sentences. A word may be simple (containing only one morpheme) or complex (containing more than one morpheme). *See also phonological word.*

word boundary A boundary between two words. In most orthographies, a word boundary is indicated by the space between words, but this can be confusing.

word order The order of the basic sentence elements (constituents, whether words or phrases), subject, object, and verb. (This is different from the order of morphemes representing these elements in a complex verb.)

X' ($\bar{X}$) The nonmaximal projection of a lexical head X; the constituent that immediately dominates a lexical head X and which is itself immediately dominated by the maximal projection of that head (XP). *See X-bar theory.*

XP The maximal projection of a lexical head X; a phrase headed by a lexical category X. *See X-bar theory.*

X-bar theory The theory that all phrases conform to a uniform structural template. Most versions of X-bar theory assume that every lexical head X is dominated by a phrase XP, where X is a variable ranging over names of lexical categories – A(djective), N(oun), V(erb), etc.; thus, A is dominated by AP, V is dominated by VP, and so on. According to the classical version of X-bar theory, a complete phrase XP (the maximal projection of X) immediately dominates a Specifier position and a nonmaximal projection of X, called X' or $\bar{X}$; this $\bar{X}$ constituent in turn immediately dominates the head X and any complement(s) that the head X selects.

yes–no question A question that can be appropriately answered with *yes* or *no,* e.g. *Did you see Romeo?*

zero allomorph An allomorph of a morpheme that is not pronounced, an allomorph whose form is zero.

Bibliography

Abney, Steven 1987. The English Noun Phrase in Its Sentential Aspect. Doctoral Dissertation, MIT, Cambridge, MA.

Adams, Marilyn J. 1990. *Beginning to Read: Thinking and Learning about Print.* Cambridge, MA: MIT Press.

Aksu-Koč, and Slobin, D. 1985. The acquisition of Turkish. In D. Slobin (ed.), *The Crosslinguistic Study of Language Acquisition*, Hillsdale, NJ: Erlbaum.

Anderson, Stephen R. 1974. *The Organization of Phonology.* Academic Press.

Anderson, Stephen R. 1992. *A-Morphous Morphology.* Cambridge: Cambridge University Press.

Antinucci, F. and Miller, R. 1976. How children talk about what happened. *Journal of Child Language*, 3: 167–89.

Archangeli, Diana and Langendoen, Terence (eds.) 1997. *Optimality Theory: An Introduction.* Oxford: Blackwell.

Aronoff, Mark 1976. *Word Formation in Generative Grammar.* Cambridge, MA: MIT Press.

Aronoff, Mark 1993. *Morphology by Itself: Stems and Inflectional Classes. Linguistic Inquiry Monograph, no. 22.* Cambridge, MA: MIT Press.

Babyonyshev, M. 1993. Acquisition of the Russian case system. In C. Phillips (ed.), *Papers on Case and Agreement, II.* MIT Working Papers in Linguistics, 19, pp. 1–43.

Bach, Emmon 1989. *Informal Lectures on Formal Semantics.* New York: State University of New York Press.

Bach, Emmon et al. (eds.) 1995. *Quantification in Natural Languages.* Dordrecht: Kluwer.

Bartlett, E. 1977. The acquisition of the meaning of colour terms: A study of lexical development. In P. Smith and R. Campbell (eds.), *Proceedings of the Stirling Conference on the Psychology of Language*, New York: Plenum.

Barwise, Jon and Cooper, Robin 1981. Generalized quantifiers and natural language. *Linguistics and Philosophy*, 4: 159–219.

Bauer, Laurie 1983. *English Word-formation.* Cambridge: Cambridge University Press.

Behrens, H. 1993. Temporal reference in German Child Language. Ph.D. dissertation, University of Amsterdam.

Berko, Jean 1958. The child learning of English morphology. *Word*, 14: 150–77.

Berwick, R. 1985. *The Acquisition of Syntactic Knowledge.* Cambridge, MA: MIT Press.

Bethin, Christina 1992. *Polish Syllables: The Role of Prosody in Phonology and Morphology.* Columbus OH: Slavica Publishers.

Bittner, Maria 1995. Quantification in Eskimo: a challenge for compositional semantics. In Bach et al. (eds.), *Quantification in Natural Languages.* Dordrecht: Kluwer, pp. 59–81.

Bloom, L. 1970. *Language Development: Form and Function in Emerging Grammars.* Cambridge, MA: MIT Press.

Bottari, P., Ciprani, P. and Chilosi, A. 1994. Protosyntactic devices in the acquisition of Italian free morphology. *Language Acquisition*, 3 (4): 327–69.

Bowerman, M. 1989. Learning a semantic system: What role do cognitive predispositions play? In M. L. Rice and R. L. Schiefelbusch (eds.),

The Teachability of Language. Baltimore: P. H. Brookes, pp. 133–69.

Bowerman, M. 1973. *Early Syntactic Development: A Cross-linguistic Study with Special Reference to Finnish.* Cambridge: Cambridge University Press.

Bowerman, M. 1991. The origins of children's spatial semantic categories: Cognitive vs. linguistic determinants. In J. J. Gumperz and S. C. Levinson (eds.), *Rethinking Linguistic Relativity*, Cambridge, MA: Cambridge University Press.

Cairns, H. 1996. *The Acquisition of Language.* Austin, TX: Pro-Ed.

Casali, Roderick 1997. Vowel elision in hiatus contexts: Which vowel goes? *Language*, 73: 493–533.

Catford, John C. 1988. *A Practical Introduction to Phonetics.* Oxford: Clarendon Press.

Chien, Y.-C. and Wexler, K. 1990. Children's knowledge of locality conditions in binding as evidence for the modularity of syntax and pragmatics. *Language Acquisition*, 1 (3): 225–95.

Chierchia, Gennaro 1998. Plurality of mass nouns and the notion of 'semantic parameter.' In S. Rothstein (ed.), *Events and Grammar*, Dordrecht: Kluwer, pp. 53–103.

Chomsky, Noam 1955. *The Logical Structure of Linguistic Theory.* Mimeographed. Cambridge, MA: MIT Press.

Chomsky, Noam 1957. *Syntactic Structures.* The Hague: Mouton.

Chomsky, Noam 1968. *Language and Mind.* New York: Harcourt Brace Jovanovich. Extended edition, 1972.

Chomsky, Noam 1965. *Aspects of a Theory of Syntax.* Cambridge, MA: MIT Press.

Chomsky, Noam 1970. Remarks on nominalization. In *Readings in English Transformational Grammar*, ed. Roderick Jacobs and Peter Rosenbaum (1970), Waltham, MA: Ginn, pp. 184–221.

Chomsky, Noam 1973. Conditions on transformations. In Stephen Anderson and Paul Kiparsky, *A Festschrift for Morris Halle*, New York: Holt, Rinehart & Winston, pp. 232–86.

Chomsky, Noam 1981. *Lectures on Government and Binding.* Dordrecht: Foris.

Chomsky, Noam 1981. Principles and parameters in syntactic theory. In Norbert Hornstein and David Lightfoot (eds.), *Explanation in Linguistics*, London: Longman, pp. 32–75.

Chomsky, Noam 1986. *Barriers.* Cambridge, MA: MIT Press.

Chomsky, Noam 1986. *Knowledge of Language: Its Nature, Origin and Use.* New York: Praeger.

Chomsky, Noam 1995a. *The Minimalist Program.* Cambridge, MA: MIT.

Chomsky, Noam 1995b. Language and nature. *Mind*, 104: 1–61.

Chomsky, Noam and Halle, Morris 1968 (1991). *Sound Pattern of English.* Cambridge, MA: MIT Press, part iv, chs 7 and 9.

Chung, Sandra and McCloskey, James 1987. Government, barriers and small clauses in Modern Irish. *Linguistic Inquiry*, 18: 173–237.

Cinque, Guglielmo (1999). *Adverbs and Functional Heads: A Cross-linguistic Perspective.* Oxford: Oxford University Press.

Clark, E. 1973. What's in a word? On the child's acquisition of semantics in his first language. In T. E. Moore (ed.), *Cognitive Development and the Acquisition of Language*, New York: Academic Press.

Clark, E. 1987. The principle of contrast. A constraint on language acquisition. In B. MacWhinney (ed.), *The 20th Annual Carnegie Symposium on Cognition*, Hillsdale, NJ: Erlbaum, pp. 1–33.

Clark, E. 1993. *The Lexicon in Acquisition.* New York: Cambridge University Press.

Cowan, Nelson and Leavitt, Lewis 1990. Speakers' access to phonological structure of the syllable in word games. In *Proceedings of CLS 26 Parasession on the Syllable*, pp. 45–59.

Cowper, L. 1992. *A Concise Introduction to Syntactic Theory.* Chicago: University of Chicago Press.

Crain, S. and McKee, C. 1985. Acquisition of structural restrictions of anaphora. *Proceedings of NELS 16*, Amherst, MA: GLSA, University of Amherst.

Culicover, Peter 1997. *Principles and Parameters: An Introduction to Syntactic Theory.* Oxford: Oxford University Press.

Curtiss, S. 1994. Language as a cognitive system: Its independence and selective vulnerability. In C. Otero (ed.), *Noam Chomsky: Critical Assessments*, 4, London: Routledge.

Cutler, Anne 1979. The psychological reality of word formation and lexical stress rules. In

Proceedings of the 9th International Congress of Phonetic Sciences, Copenhagen.

Cutler, A. 1994. Segmentation problems, rhythmic solutions. *Lingua*, 92: 81–104.

DaPretto, M. 1994. Early lexical development: A new perspective on the naming explosion. Unpublished Ph.D. dissertation, UCLA.

de Swart, Henriette 1993. *Adverbs of Quantification: A Generalized Quantifier Approach*. New York: Garland.

Demuth, K. 1995. The prosodic structure of early words. In J. Morgan and K. Demuth (eds.), *Signal to Syntax: Bootstrapping from Speech to Grammar in Early Acquisition*, Mahwah, NJ: Lawrence Erlbaum, pp. 1–17.

Derwing, Bruce 1992. The pause-break task in syllable division. *Language and Speech*, 35: 219–35.

Di Sciullo, Anne-Marie and Williams, Edwin 1987. *On the Definition of Word*. Cambridge, MA: MIT Press.

Dodd, B. and Campbell, R. (eds.) 1987. *Hearing by Eye: The Psychology of Lip Reading*. Hillsdale, NJ: Lawrence Erlbaum.

Eimas, P. 1975. Speech perception in early infancy. In L. B. Cohen and P. Salapatek (eds.), *Infant Perception: From Sensation to Cognition*, New York: Academic Press.

Eimas, P. 1996. The perception and representation of speech by infants. In J. Morgan and K. Demuth (eds.), *Signal to Syntax: Bootstrapping from Speech to Grammar in Early Acquisition*, Mahwah, NJ: Lawrence Erlbaum, pp. 25–39.

Emonds, Joseph 1978. The verbal complex V'-V in French. *Linguistic Inquiry*, 9: 151–75.

Fernald, A. 1985. Four-month-olds prefer to listen to motherese. *Infant Behavior and Development*, 8: 181–95.

Fisher, C., Hall, G., and Rakowitz, S. 1994. When it is better to receive than to give: Syntactic and conceptual constraints on vocabulary growth. *Lingua*, 92: 333–75.

Fodor, J. 1983. *The Modularity of Mind*. Cambridge, MA: MIT Press.

Fortescu, M. 1984/5. Learning to speak Greenlandic: A case study of a two-year-old's morphology in a polysynthetic language. *First Language*, 5: 101–13.

Frege, Gottlob 1923. *Compound Thoughts*. Reprinted in E. D. Klemke (ed.), *Essays on Frege*, Chicago: University of Illinois Press.

Fromkin, Victoria A. and Rodman, Robert 1998. *An Introduction to Language*. Fort Worth, TX: Harcourt Brace.

Gerken, L.-A. 1991. The Metrical basis for children's subjectless sentences. *Journal of Memory and Language*, 30: 431–51.

Gerken, L.-A. and McIntosh, B. 1993. Interplay of function morphemes and prosody in early language. *Developmental Psychology*, vol. 29, no. 3: 448–57.

Gleitman, L. and Landau, B. (eds.) 1994. *The Acquisition of the Lexicon*. Cambridge, MA: MIT Press.

Gnanadesikan, A. 1995. *Markedness and Faithfulness Constraints in Child Phonology*. Cambridge, MA: University of Massachusetts.

Goldsmith, John 1976. *Autosegmental Phonology*. MIT Ph.D. dissertation, distributed by the Indiana University Linguistic Club.

Goldsmith, John 1993. *The Last Phonological Rule*. Chicago: University of Chicago Press.

Goodluck, H. 1991. *Language Acquisition: A Linguistic Introduction*. Cambridge: Basil Blackwell.

Gordon, P. 1985. Level-ordering in lexical development. *Cognition*, 21, no. 2: 73–93.

Gough, P. B., Ehri, L. C. and Treiman, R. (eds.) 1992. *Reading Acquisition*. Hillsdale, NJ: Lawrence Erlbaum.

Grimshaw, J. 1981. Form, function, and the language acquisition device. In C. Baker and J. McCarthy (eds.), *The Logical Problem of Language Acquisition*, Cambridge, MA: MIT Press, pp. 183–210.

Gruber, J. 1965. *Studies in Lexical Relations*. Doctoral dissertation, Massachusetts Institute of Technology, Cambridge.

Guerssel, Mohammed 1978. A condition on assimilation rules. *Linguistic Analysis*, 4: 225–54.

Gussenhoven, Carlos and Jacobs, Haike 1998. *Understanding Phonology*. London: Arnold.

Haegemann, Liliane. 1994. Root infinitives, tense and truncated structures. *Language Acquisition*, 4 (3): 205–55.

Haegeman, Liliane 1991. *Introduction to Government and Binding Theory*. Oxford: Basil Blackwell. 2nd edn, 1994.

Haegeman, Liliane (ed.) 1998. *Handbook for Syntactic Theory*. Oxford: Basil Blackwell.

Hammond, Michael and Noonan, Michael (eds.) 1988. *Theoretical Morphology: Approaches in Modern Linguistics*. San Diego: Academic Press.

Harris, James 1983. *Syllable Structure and Stress in Spanish: A Non-Linear Analysis.* Cambridge, MA: MIT Press.

Hayes, Bruce 1995. *Metrical Stress Theory: Principles and Case Studies.* Chicago: University of Chicago Press.

Heider, E. R. 1972. Universals in color naming and memory. *Cognitive Psychology,* 3: 337–54.

Heim, I. 1990. E-type pronouns and donkey anaphora. *Linguistics and Philosophy,* 13: 137–77.

Hickey, T. 1990. The acquisition of Irish: A study of word order development. *Journal of Child Language,* 17 (1): pp. 17–43.

Hirsh-Pasek, K. and Golinkoff, R. 1996. *The Origins of Grammar: Evidence from Early Language Comprehension.* Cambridge, MA: MIT Press.

Hoekstra, T. and Hyams, N. 1998. Aspects of root infinitives. *Lingua,* 106: 81–112.

Hyams, N. 1986. *Language Acquisition and the Theory of Parameters.* Dordrecht: Reidel.

Hyams, N. 1994. The underspecification of functional categories in early grammar. In *Generative Perspectives on Language Acquisition,* ed. H. Clahsen, Amsterdam: J. Benjamins.

Ingram, D. 1979. Phonological rules in young children. *Journal of Child Language,* 1: 49–64.

Jackendoff, R. 1972. *Semantic Interpretation in Generative Grammar.* Cambridge, MA: MIT Press.

Jacobson, R. 1968. *Child Language, Aphasia, and Phonological Universals.* The Hague: Mouton.

Jelinek, Aloise 1995. Quantification and scope in Mayali. In Bach et al. (eds.), *Quantification in Natural Languages,* Dordrecht: Kluwer, pp. 207–71.

Jensen, John T. 1990. *Morphology: Word Structure in Generative Grammar.* Amsterdam/Philadelphia: John Benjamins.

Johnston, J. and Slobin, D. 1979. The development of locative expressions in English, Italian, Serbo-Croatian, and Turkish. *Journal of Child Language,* 6: 529–45.

Jusczyk, P. 1997. *The Discovery of Spoken Language.* Cambridge, MA: MIT Press.

Jusczyk, P. and Aslin, R. 1995. Infants' detection of sound patterns of words in fluent speech. *Cognitive Psychology,* 29: 1–23.

Jusczyk, P., Frederici, A., Wessels, J., Svenkerud, V., and Jusczyk, A. 1993. Infants' sensitivity to the sound patterns of native language words. *Journal of Memory and Language,* 32: 402–20.

Jusczyk, P., Hohne, E., Jusczyk, A., and Redanz, N. 1993. Do infants remember voices? *Journal of the Acoustical Society of America,* 93: 2373.

Jusczyk, P., Luce, P., and Charles-Luce, J. 1994. Infants' sensitivity to phonotactic patterns in the native language. *Journal of Memory and Language,* 33: 630–45.

Kager, René 1999. *Optimality Theory: A Textbook.* Oxford: Oxford University Press.

Kahn, Daniel 1976. *Syllable-based Generalizations in English Phonology.* MIT PhD dissertation, Garland Press, 1980.

Katz, N., Baker, E., and Macnamara, J. 1974. What's a name? On the child's acquisition of proper and common nouns. *Child Development,* 45: 469–73.

Kayne, R. 1994. *The Antisymmetry of Syntax.* Cambridge, MA: MIT Press.

Keenan, E. L. 1971. Two kinds of presupposition in natural language. In C. Fillmore and D. T. Langendoen (eds.), *Studies in Linguistic Semantics,* New York: Holt, pp. 45–54.

Keenan, Edward L. and Stavi, Jonathan 1986. A semantic characterization of natural language determiners. *Linguistics and Philosophy,* 9: 253–326.

Keenan, Edward 1996. The semantics of determiners. In Shalom Lappin (ed.), *The Handbook of Contemporary Semantic Theory,* Oxford: Blackwell.

Keil, F. and Batterman, N. 1984. A characterizing-to-defining shift in the development of word meaning. *Journal of Verbal Learning and Verbal Behavior,* 23: 221–36.

Kenyon, John S. and Knott, Thomas A. 1953. *A Pronouncing Dictionary of American English.* Springfield, MA: Merriam.

Kiparsky, P. 1983. From cyclic phonology to lexical phonology. In Van der Hulst and Smith (eds.), *The Structure of Phonological Representations, I,* Dordrecht: Foris.

Kiparsky, P. 1983. Word formation and the lexicon. In F. Ingermann (ed.), *Linguistics in the Morning Calm,* Seoul: Hanshin, pp. 3–91.

Kiss, Katalin É. 1998. Identificational focus versus information focus. *Language,* 74: 245–73.

Klima, Edward S. and Bellugi, Ursula 1979. *The Signs of Language.* Cambridge, MA: Harvard University Press.

Koopman, Hilda 1984. *The Syntax of Verbs: From*

Verb Movement Rules in the Kru Languages to Universal Grammar, Dordrecht: Foris.

Koopman, H. and Sportiche, D. 1991. The Position of Subjects. *Lingua*, 85: 211–58.

Kraemer, I. 1994. *The licensing of subjects in early child language*. MIT Working Papers in Linguistics, 19, pp. 197–212.

Krifka, Manfred 1992. Thematic relations as links between nominal reference and temporal constitution. In I. A. Sag and A. Szabolcsi (eds.), *Lexical Matters*, Stanford: CSLI Publications.

Kuhl, P., Williams, K., Lacerda, F., Stevens, K., and Lindblom, B. 1992. Linguistic experience alters phonetic perception by 6 months of age. *Science*, 255: 606–8.

Labov, William 1972. *Sociolinguistic Patterns*. Philadelphia: University of Pennsylvania Press.

Ladusaw, William 1979. Polarity sensitivity as inherent scope relations. Ph.D. dissertation, University of Texas, Austin, Texas.

Ladefoged, Peter 1993. *A Course in Phonetics*, 3rd edn. Fort Worth: Harcourt Brace Jovanovich College Publishers.

Ladefoged, Peter and Maddieson, Ian 1996. *Sounds of the World's Languages*. Oxford: Blackwell.

Lahiri, Aditi and Marslen Wilson, William 1992. Lexical processing and phonological representation. In Gerard Dougherty and D. Robert Ladd (eds.), *Papers in Laboratory Phonology, I: Gesture, Segment, Prosody*, Cambridge: Cambridge University Press.

Laver, John 1994. *Principles of Phonetics*. Cambridge: Cambridge University Press.

Leben, Will 1974. *Suprasegmental Phonology*. MIT PhD dissertation.

Lefkowitz, N. 1991. *Talking Backwards, Looking Forwards: The French Language Game Verlan*. Tübingen: Narr.

Levin, Beth 1993. *English Verb Classes and Alternations: A Preliminary Investigation*. Chicago: University of Chicago Press.

Levy, Y. 1983. It's frogs all the way down. *Cognition*, 15: 75–93.

Lewis, David 1973. Adverbs of quantification. In E. Keenan (ed.), *Formal Semantics and Pragmatics for Natural Languages*, Cambridge: Cambridge University Press, pp. 3–15.

Liberman, Mark and Prince, Alan 1977. On stress and linguistic rhythm. *Linguistic Inquiry*, 8: 249–336.

Lightfoot, D. 1992. *Biology of Grammar*. Cambridge, MA: MIT Press.

MacDaniel, D., Cairns, H., and Hsu, J. 1990. Binding principles in the grammars of young children. *Language Acquisition*, 1 (4): 121–38.

MacWhinney, B. and Snow, C. 1985. The child language data exchange system. *Journal of Child Language*, 12: 271–96.

Maddieson, Ian 1984. *Patterns of Sounds*. Cambridge: Cambridge University Press.

Maratsos, M. 1974. Preschool children's use of definite and indefinite articles. *Child Development*, 45: 446–55.

Maratsos, M. 1976. *The Use of Definite and Indefinite Reference in Children*. Cambridge: Cambridge University Press.

Marchand, Hans 1969. *The Categories and Types of Present-Day English Word-Formation*, 2nd edn. Munich: C. H. Beck'sche Verlagsbuchhandlung.

Markman, E. 1994. Constraints on word meaning in early language acquisition. In L. Gleitman and B. Landau (eds.), *The Acquisition of the Lexicon*, Cambridge, MA: MIT Press, pp. 199–227.

Matthews, P. H. 1991. *Morphology: An Introduction to the Theory of Word Structure*. Cambridge: Cambridge University Press.

May, Robert 1985. *Logical Form: Its Structure and Derivation*. Cambridge, MA: MIT Press.

McCarthy, John 1986. OCP effects: gemination and anti-gemination. *Linguistic Inquiry*, 17: 187–263.

McCarthy, John 1988. Feature geometry and dependency. *Phonetica*, 43: 84–108.

McCarthy, John and Prince, Alan 1995. Faithfulness and reduplicative correspondence. *University of Massachusetts Occasional Papers in Linguistics*, vol. 15.

McCarthy, John and Prince, Alan 1995. Prosodic morphology. In John Goldsmith (ed.), *Handbook of Phonological Theory*, Oxford: Blackwell, pp. 318–67.

McCawley, J. 1988. *The Syntactic Phenomena of English*. Chicago: University of Chicago Press.

McCloskey, James. 1983. A VP in a VSO Language? In J. Gazdar, E. Klein and G. Pullum (eds.), *Order, Concord, and Constituency*, Dordrecht: Foris Publications, pp. 9–55.

McCloskey, James 1991. Clause structure, ellipsis and proper government in Irish. *Lingua*, 85: 259–302.

McDaniel, D., Cairns, H. S., and Shu, J. R. 1990. Binding principles in the grammars of young children. *Language Acquisition*, 1: 121–38.

Mehler, J., Dommergues, J.-Y., Frauenfelder, U., and Ségui, J. 1981. The syllable's role in speech segmentation. *Journal of Verbal Learning and Verbal Behavior*, 20: 298–305.

Menn, L. 1983. Development of articulatory, phonetic, and phonological capabilities. In B. Butterworth, ed., *Language Production*, vol. 2, pp. 3–50. London: Academic Press.

Mohanan, K. P. 1986. *The Theory of Lexical Phonology*, Drodrecht: Reidel.

Moore, C. and Davidge, J. 1989. The development of mental terms, pragmatics or semantics. *Journal of Child Language*, 16: 633–41.

Moore, C., Bryant, D., and Furrow, D. 1989. Mental verbs and the development of certainty. *Child Development*, 60: 167–71.

Morgan, J. and Demuth, K. (eds.) 1996. *Signal to Syntax: Bootstrapping from Speech to Grammar in Early Acquisition*. Mahwah, NJ: Lawrence Erlbaum.

Munro, Pamela, and Lopez, Felipe, H. et al. 1999. *Di'csyonaary X:tèe'n Dìi'zh Sah Sann Lu'uc (San Lucas Quiaviní Zapotec Dictionary/ Diccionario Zapoteco de San Lucas Quiaviní)*. Los Angeles: UCLA Chicano Studies Research Center Publications.

Nádasdy, A. 1985. Segmental phonology and morphology. In Istvan Kenesei (ed.), *Approaches to Hungarian*, Szeged: JATE, pp. 225–46.

Newman, Stanley 1944. *Yokuts Language of California*. New York: Viking Fund Publications in Anthropology, no. 2.

Newmeyer, Frederick J. 1983. *Grammatical Theory: Its Limits and Its Possibilities*. Chicago and London: University of Chicago Press.

Newport, E. and Meier, R. 1985. The Acquisition of American Sign Language. In Slobin, D. (ed.), *The Crosslinguistic Study of Language Acquisition*, Vol. I: *The Data*. Hillsdale, NJ Erlbaum.

Ngonyani, Deogratis 1996. *The Morphosyntax of Applicatives*. Ph.D. thesis, UCLA.

Oller, D. 1980. The emergence of speech sounds in infancy. In G. Yeni-Komshian, J. Kavanagh, and C. Ferguson (eds.), *Child Phonology*, New York: Academic Press.

Olsen, M. and Weinberg, A. 1999. Innateness and the acquisition of grammatical aspect via lexical aspect. *Proceedings of the 23rd Boston University Child Language Conference*, Somerville, MA: Cascadilla Press.

Olsen, M., Weinberg, A., Lilly, J., and Drury, J. 1997. Mapping innate lexical features to grammatical categories: Acquisition of English -ing and -ed. University of Maryland manuscript.

Otani, Kazuyo and Whitman, John 1991. V-Raising and VP-ellipsis. *Linguistic Inquiry*, 22 (2): 345–58.

Paradis, Carole and La Charité, Darlene (eds.) 1993. *Constraint-based Theories in Non-linear Phonologies*. Special issue of *Revue Canadienne de Linguistique/Canadian Journal of Linguistics*, 38: 127–303.

Pater, J. 1997. Minimal violation and phonological development. *Language Acquisition*, 6, no. 3: 201–63.

Petitto, L. and Marentette, P. 1991. Babbling in the manual mode. Evidence for the ontogeny of language. *Science*, 251: 1493–6.

Pierce, A. 1992. *Language Acquisition and Syntactic Theory: A Comparative Analysis of French and English Child Grammars*. Dordrecht: Kluwer.

Pierrehumbert, Janet 1993. Dissimilarity in the Arabic verbal roots. In *Proceedings of the North-East Linguistic Society*, 23, pp. 367–81.

Pinker, Steven 1989. *Learnability and Cognition: The Acquisition of Argument Structure*. Cambridge, MA: MIT Press.

Pinker, Steven 1994. *The Language Instinct: How the Mind Creates Languages*. New York: William Morrow.

Poeppel, D. and Wexler, K. 1993. The full competence hypothesis of clause structure in early German. *Language*, 69: 1–3.

Pollock, J.-Y. 1989. Verb movement, universal grammar and the structure of IP. *Linguistic Inquiry*, 20: 365–424.

Portner, Paul 1992. *Situation Theory and the Semantics of Propositional Expressions*. Ph.D. dissertation, University of Massachusetts, Amherst, MA.

Prince, Alan and Smolensky, Paul 1993. *Optimality Theory*. Cambridge, MA: MIT Press.

Pullum, Geoffrey K. and Ladusaw, W. A. 1986. *Phonetic Symbol Guide*. Chicago: University of Chicago Press.

Pye, C. 1980. The acquisition of grammatical morphemes in Quiche Mayan. Unpublished doctoral dissertation, University of Pittsburgh.

Radford, A. 1986. Small children's small clauses. *Research Papers in Linguistics*, no. 1. Department of Linguistics, University College of North Wales, Bangor.

Radford, A. 1988. *Transformational Grammar*. Cambridge: Cambridge University Press.

Radford, A. 1990. *Syntactic Theory and the Acquisition of English Syntax*. Cambridge: Basil Blackwell.

Radford, Andrew 1997. *Syntactic Theory and the Structure of English: A Minimalist Approach*. Cambridge: Cambridge University Press.

Reinhart, T. 1983. *Anaphora and Semantic Interpretation*. London: Croom Helm.

Riemsdijk, H. van and Williams, E. 1986. *Introduction to the Theory of Grammar*. Cambridge, MA: MIT Press.

Ritter, Elizabeth 1989. A head movement approach to construct-state noun-phrases. *Linguistics*, 26: 909–29.

Roberts, I. 1993. *Verbs and Diachronic Syntax: A Comparative History of English and French*. Studies in Natural Language and Linguistic Theory. Dordrecht: Kluwer Academic Publishers.

Roberts, I. 1996. *Comparative Syntax*. London/New York: Arnold.

Roeper, T. and Rohrbacher, B. 1994. True pro-drop in child English and the Principle of Economy of Projection. Ms, University of Massachusetts at Amherst.

Rogers, Henry 1991. *Theoretical and Practical Phonetics*. Toronto: Copp Clark Pittman.

Rooth, Mats 1996. Focus. In Shalom Lappin (ed.), *The Handbook of Contemporary Semantic Theory*, Oxford: Blackwell, pp. 271–99.

Scalise, Sergio 1984. *Generative Morphology*. Dordrecht, Holland/Cinnaminson, USA: Foris Publications.

Schutze, C. 1996. INFL in child and adult language: Agreement, case and licensing. PhD dissertation, MIT.

Selkirk, E. 1982. *The Syntax of Words*. Cambridge, MA: MIT Press.

Selkirk, E. 1982. The syllable. In Harry van der Hulst and Norval Smith (eds.), *The Structure of Phonological Representations, Part 1*, Dordrecht: Foris.

Sherzer, Joel 1970. Talking backwards in Cuna. *Southwest Journal of Anthropology*, 26: 343–53.

Slobin, D. (ed.) 1985. *The Crosslinguistic Study of Language Acquisition*, Vol. I: *The Data*. Hillsdale, NJ: Erlbaum.

Smalley, William A. 1989. *Manual of Articulatory Phonetics*, rev. edn. Lanham, MD: University Press of America. First edition 1961.

Smith, N. and Tsimpli, I.-M. 1995. *The Mind of a Savant: Language Learning and Modularity*. Oxford: Blackwell.

Smith, N. V. 1973. *The Acquisition of Phonology: A Case Study*. Cambridge: Cambridge University Press.

Spencer, Andrew 1991. *Morphological Theory*. Oxford and Cambridge, MA: Blackwell.

Stalnaker, R. 1978. Assertion. In Peter Cole (ed.), *Pragmatics, Syntax and Semantics*, 9, New York: Academic Press, pp. 315–32.

Stowell, T. 1981. Origins of phrase structure. Doctoral dissertation, Massachusetts Institute of Technology, Cambridge.

Szabolcsi, Anna. 1997a. Strategies for scope taking. In Szabolcsi (ed.), 1997b, *Ways of Scope Taking*, Dordrecht: Kluwer, pp. 109–10.

Szabolcsi, Anna (ed.) 1997b. *Ways of Scope Taking*. Dordrecht: Kluwer.

Szabolcsi, Anna 1999. The syntax of scope. To appear in Mark Baltin and Chris Collins (eds.), *The Handbook of Contemporary Syntactic Theory*, Oxford: Blackwell.

Talmy, L. 1985. Lexicalization patterns: Semantic structure in lexical forms. In T. Shopen (ed.), *Language Typology and Syntactic Description*, Vol. 3: *Grammatical Categories and the Lexicon*, Cambridge: Cambridge University Press.

Tenny, Carol 1994. *Aspectual Roles and the Syntax/Semantics Interface*. Dordrecht: Kluwer.

Ueda, I. 1996. Segmental acquisition and feature specification in Japanese. In J. Gilbert and D. Ingram, eds., *Proceedings of the UBC International Conference on Phonological Acquisition*.

Vago, Robert 1980. *The Sound Pattern of Hungarian*. Georgetown: Georgetown University Press.

Valian, V. 1991. Syntactic subjects in the early speech of American and Italian children. *Cognition*, 40: 21–81.

van Riemsdijk, H. and Williams, E. 1986. *Introduction to the Theory of Grammar*. Cambridge, MA: MIT Press.

Webelhuth, Gert (ed.) 1996. *Government and Binding Theory and the Minimalist Program*. Oxford, and Cambridge, MA: Blackwell.

Weist, R., Wysocka, H., Witkowska-Stadnik, K., Bucaowska, E., and Koniccana, E. 1984. The Defective Tense Hypothesis: On the emergence of tense and aspect in child Polish. *Journal of Child Language*, 11 (2): 247–373.

Wells, John C. 1982. *Accents of English* (in 3 volumes). Cambridge: Cambridge University Press.

Werker, J. 1995. Exploring developmental changes in cross-linguistic speech perception. In L. Gleitman and M. Liberman (eds.), *An Invitation to Cognitive Science: Language*, Cambridge, MA: Bradford Books, vol. 1, pp. 87–106.

Werker, J. and Tees, R. 1984. Phonemic and phonetic factors in adult cross-language speech perception. *Journal of the Acoustical Society of America*, 75: 1866–78.

Wexler, K. 1994. Optional infinitives, verb movement and the economy of derivation in child grammar. In D. Lightfoot and N. Hornstein (eds.), *Verb Movement*, Cambridge: Cambridge University Press.

Wexler, K. and Chien, Y.-C. 1985. The development of lexical anaphors and pronouns. *Papers and Reports on Child Language Development*, Stanford University, Stanford University Press.

Williams, E. S. 1981. On the notions 'lexically related' and 'head of word'. *Linguistic Inquiry*, 12: 245–74.

Yip, Moira 1989. The OCP and phonological rules: a loss of identity. *Linguistic Inquiry*, 20: 65–100.

Index